Contemporary Physical Distribution and Logistics

3rd Edition

Contemporary Physical Distribution and Logistics

James C. Johnson
St. Cloud State University

Donald F. Wood
San Francisco State University

Macmillan Publishing Company
New York
Collier Macmillan Publishers
London

Macmillan Publishing Company
866 Third Avenue, New York, New York 10022

Collier Macmillan Canada, Inc.

Library of Congress Cataloging in Publication Data

Johnson, James C.,
    Contemporary physical distribution & logistics.

    Includes bibliographies and index.
    1. Physical distribution of goods.   2. Business
logistics.   I. Wood, Donald F.   II. Title.   III. Title:
Contemporary physical distribution and logistics.
HF5415.6.J6 1986   658.7'88   85-21400
ISBN 0-02-360840-4

Printing: 1 2 3 4 5 6 7 8   Year: 6 7 8 9 0 1 2 3

ISBN   0-02-360840-4

Dedication
To Cammy and Doreen

Preface to the
Third Edition

When we wrote the first edition of our book, which was entitled *Contemporary Physical Distribution*, we said that the subject was dynamic and filled with both problems and opportunities for practicing and future managers. This continues to be the case. In preparing this, the third edition of our book, we have tried to take into account the "real-world" happenings of the first half of the 1980s, which have had major impacts on physical distribution and logistics thinking and practice. Some of the most prominent of these are

1. The many changes (some almost chaotic) that have taken place in our domestic freight transportation industry as a result of carrier deregulation.
2. The developing interest in Japanese-based management techniques, especially those dealing with closer controls over inventories of components used in the production process.
3. The prodigious growth in the use of computers, especially small computers and their applications, in almost every aspect of logistics.

In addition to updating our textual materials and cases, we have made some other changes that should improve even further this book's usefulness as a teaching—and learning—tool. We appreciate the helpful comments from our colleagues—in both the United States and Canada—with respect to changes they thought would make the book even better suited to their classroom needs.

Among the changes in the third edition are the inclusion of key terms and learning objectives for the student at the beginning of each chapter. A complete glossary of terms has been added at the end of the text.

In addition, we have prepared an extensive instructor's manual which contains chapter summaries, answers to all the end-of-chapter questions, multiple choice and true/false test questions for each chapter, complete solutions for all cases, and transparency masters. Many of the figures for the transparency masters are not found in the text.

Our list of acknowledgments is long, and includes individuals who helped with at least one of the editions of this book. We would like to thank them for their help. We hold them blameless for whatever errors may remain. These persons are Glen Adams of Standard Oil Company; Fred Altstadt of Four-phase System; Folger Athearn, Jr., of Athearn & Co.; Donald W. Baldra of Schering Corp.; Charles L. Ballard of Hudson Valley Community College; James H. Barnes of the University of Georgia; Warren Blanding of Marketing Publications, Inc.; James F. Briody of Fairchild Camera and Instrument Co.; W. R. Callister of Del Monte Corporation; Neil D. Chaitin of Challenge Equipment Corporation; W. M. Cheatham of Specialty Brands; Bob J. Davis of Western Illinois University; George Derugin of San Francisco State University; John R. Doggett of *Warehousing Review*; W. R. Donham of Cambridge Plan International; A. J. Faria of the University of Windsor; Donald C. Garland of Zellerbach Paper; Mark Haight, University of Wisconsin Center: Barron County; Jay P. Hamerslag of Hamerslag Equipment Co.; Lowell Hedrick of Phillips Petroleum Co.; Weldon G. Helmus of Shaklee Corporation; Lynn Hill of Heublein, Inc.; Stanley J. Hille, University of Missouri, Columbia; Donald Horton of the American Warehousemen's Association; Rufus C. Jefferson; Creed Jenkins of Consolidated Distribution Services; J. M. Johnson of Johnson & Johnson; J. Richard Jones of Memphis State University; Robert E. Jones, F. E. Warren Air Force Base; Henry M. Karel, Shelby State Community College; R. L. Kemmer of GTE Service Corp.; C. John Langley, Jr., University of Tennessee; Art LaPlant of Schlage Lock Co.; Joseph R. Larsen of C.I.B.A. Pharmaceutical Co.; Harry Loomer, University of Wisconsin Center: Barron County; Irving C. MacDonald; Ernest Y. Maitland, British Columbia Institute of Technology; Don Marsh of United Air Lines Maintenance Operations; Frank McDonald; Chinnubbie McIntosh of Warren Petroleum Co.; Edward J. Meyers of Pacific Gas & Electric Co.; Donald D. Mickel of the Sacramento Army Depot; Lowell S. Miller; Joseph F. Moffatt, University of Southwestern Louisiana; Paul R. Neff of Boeing Company; Thomas Paczkowski of Cayuga Community College; Donald Pefaur of Trammell Crow Distribution Corp.; Ray Perin of Perin Co.; Andru M. Peters of Andros Inc.; Lee Plummer of North Carolina State University; Richard L. Rickenbacher of Safeway Stores; Karl Schober; Frank R. Scheer of the University of Tennessee; Skip Sherwood of California State University, Fresno; Charles S. Shuken of Metropolitan Warehouse Co.; Melvin Silvester; F. J. Spellman; Jack M. Starling of North Texas State University, Joseph J. Stefanic of Agrico Chemical Co.; Wendell M. Stewart of Kearney Management Consultants; Stephen Stover of San Francisco State University; T. M. Tipton of USCO Services, Inc.; Teddy N. Toklas of the Oakland Naval Supply Center; Frances Tucker of Syracuse University; Peter F. Walstad; Boyd L. Warnick of Utah Technical College; Terry C. Whiteside of the Montana State Department of Agriculture; Kenneth C. Williamson of James Madison University; and Ronald S. Yaros.

Frank Burinsky, Carolyn Coggins, Joseph Garfall, David Kupferman, Michael McGinnis, Ira Pollack, Doreen Wood, and Mark Zborowski provided material used in several cases, and Rory K. Miller of the California Maritime Academy pretested some of our cases in his classes. Professor Christopher R. Low of San Francisco State University helped develop some of the cases for the third edition.

The co-authors also wish to acknowledge that several meetings held for the benefit of college and university teachers of transportation were also useful to them in terms of achieving a better understanding of how logistics and distribution systems function. Specific meetings of this type were hosted by the American Trucking Associations and the Association of American Railroads, at the University of Minnesota; the Association of Oil Pipe Lines, in Houston; the 1907 Foundation Business Logistics Educators' Workshop, at the Harvard University Graduate School of Business Administration; and the Yellow Freight System's meetings in Kansas City.

This third edition has been developed with some exceptional reviewing help. The authors wish to thank the following people for their insightful suggestions and recommendations: Carl Bankard, York College of Pennsylvania; Hank Bullwinkel, Towson State University; Gary Dicer, University of Tennessee; Stanley Groover, Towson State University; Carl Guelzo, Towson State University; Ron Lennon, Towson State University; Lee Totten, Western New England College; Roy Dale Voorhees, Iowa State University; Mary Margaret Weber, Missouri Western State College; Ken Williamson, James Madison University; and Jean Woodruff, Western New England College.

Last, at Macmillan Publishing Company, we would like to thank our editors, Bill Oldsey and Ron Stefanski, our production supervisor, J. Edward Neve, and our designer Eileen Burke.

James C. Johnson
Donald F. Wood

Brief Contents

Part III   Analyzing, Designing, and Implementing a Physical Distribution/Logistics System   469

Detailed Contents

Part III Analyzing, Designing, and Implementing a Physical Distribution/Logistics System 469

13. Logistics System Controls   509

14. Organization for Managing Physical Distribution/Logistics   547

15. Physical Distribution/Logistics: Future Directions   576

Contemporary Physical Distribution
and Logistics

Overview of Physical Distribution and Logistics

Part I sets the stage for the entire text by introducing the many dimensions of the complex and dynamic subject of physical distribution and logistics. The first three chapters of *Contemporary Physical Distribution and Logistics* are designed to serve as the structural foundation upon which the remainder of the text is built.

Chapter 1 discusses the physical distribution and logistics concepts and examines the reasons for their recent growth in importance in business firms.

Chapter 2 analyzes the interfaces that the physical distribution and logistics department encounters *internally* with an organization's other functional areas—marketing, production, finance, accounting. This chapter clearly reveals the importance of each functional area recognizing the mutual interdependency of each aspect of the firm relative to the others.

Chapter 3 examines the *external* relationships between physical distribution and the firm's ability to successfully meet customer service standards. The importance of the order cycle is emphasized in this chapter.

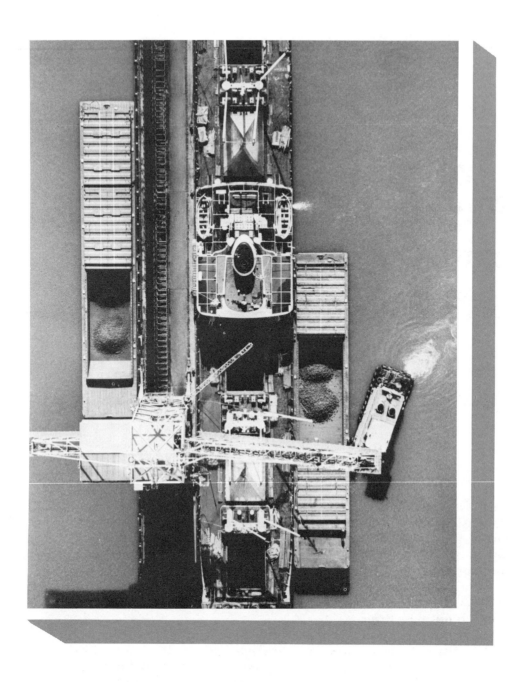

A major concern in logistics and physical distribution is to determine the sites where materials should be transferred from one mode or scale of transportation to another. This overhead view, taken in New Orleans, shows the transfer of coal between an ocean-going ship in the middle, and two barges with partially opened covers, on either side. A small tug is at the right. Up until the mid-1980's most such transfers at New Orleans were of U.S. coal for export. However, the strong U.S. dollar resulted in fewer exports of U.S. coal. Instead, New Orleans now handles some import coal—from Columbia—which is transferred to barges and towed along the Gulf of Mexico to Florida utilities.

(Credit: Port of New Orleans)

The Physical Distribution and Logistics System: Its Concept and Growth

Prior to recent years, American management's philosophy has typically been: "If you're smart enough to make it, aggressive enough to sell it—then any dummy can get it there." And now we're paying for it.

Bernard J. LaLonde
1978

Since the early 1970s, physical distribution has developed into a true profession unto itself. Computers have revolutionized the jobs many of us do. Intermodalism has evolved from a concept to reality. Perhaps the greatest and most beneficial change has been the new relationship between shipper and carrier. As a result of deregulation, shippers and carriers now find themselves communicating much more.

Thomas A. Foster, Publisher
Distribution
January 1985

Certainly, the transition to a less regulated environment has not been without difficult challenges. Rail managements, employees, shippers, shareholders and government have been forced to implement quickly changes that evolved over decades in other businesses and other industries. Some have adapted successfully; others begrudgingly; and some, their dissent seemingly carved in stone, refuse to acknowledge reality.

CSX (A major railroad) Annual Report
February 1985

Key Terms

- Physical distribution
- Materials management
- Logistics
- Systems approach
- Total-cost concept
- Avoidance of suboptimization
- Cost trade-offs

Learning Objectives

- To differentiate between physical distribution, materials management, and logistics
- To examine briefly the history of physical distribution and logistics [PD/L]
- To understand why PD/L has become more important in recent years
- To explain the objective of a PD/L system
- To distinguish between the total-cost approach, the avoidance of suboptimization, and cost trade-offs
- To note the importance of computer utilization for PD/L management
- To examine a number of PD/L systems in action

PD/L: What It Is and Why It Is Important

The world of business, especially since World War II, has been a world of change. New ideas and strategies replacing old "tried and true" approaches have come at an ever-increasing rate. Of all areas of business, marketing has probably been most affected by rapid-fire change. And of all the areas of marketing most characterized by change, physical distribution/logistics (PD/L) has seen the most revolutionary changes and is probably the most fertile ground for dramatic innovation in the years ahead.[1]

Whenever there is rapid change in a field, terms and definitions abound. And PD/L has been no exception. *Business logistics, physical distribution, materials management, distribution engineering, logistics management:* these are only *some* of the terms being used to describe approximately the same subject area—what we will call *physical distribution/logistics.*

In this book we will use three key terms: logistics, materials management, and physical distribution. *Logistics* will describe the entire process of materials and products moving into, through, and out of the firm. *Materials management* will describe the movements of materials and components into the firm. Our use of *physical distribution* is somewhat narrower than the definition used by the National Council of Physical Distribution Management (NCPDM), probably the most authoritative PD/L organization:

---

[1] See James E. Morehouse, "Operating in the New Logistics Era," *Harvard Business Review* (Sept.–Oct. 1983), pp. 18–19; Roy D. Shapiro, "Get Leverage from Logistics," *Harvard Business Review* (May-June 1984), pp. 119–126; and Graham Sharman, "The Rediscovery of Logistics," *Harvard Business Review* (Sept.–Oct. 1984), pp. 71–79.

Physical Distribution is the integration of two or more activities for the purpose of planning, implementing, and controlling the efficient flow of raw materials, in-process inventory, and finished goods from the point of origin to the point of consumption. These activities may include, but are not limited to, customer service, demand forecasting, distribution communications, inventory control, material handling, order processing, parts and service support, plant and warehouse site selection, procurement, packaging, return goods handling, salvage and scrap disposal, traffic and transportation, and warehouse and storage.[2]

All of our terms owe a lot to the NCPDM definition of physical distribution, though we make additional distinctions. Our use of physical distribution is more specialized—it is the concern for the outbound goods (i.e., toward the customer). Our use of these terms is somewhat arbitrary, though all professionals and academics will recognize them and their application. (See Figure 1-1.)

Logistics costs are a major cost item for American business. A. T. Kearney, a well-known management consulting company, estimated that in 1982 logistics costs were equal to 21 per cent of the U.S. Gross National Product (GNP), or $650 billion. Transportation costs were $300 billion; $180 billion was spent on storage and warehousing; inventory carrying costs accounted for $130 billion; and $40 billion was spent on the administration of logistical activities.[3]

Although PD/L was neglected in the past, it has been receiving more and more attention in recent years, and the reasons for this new interest are closely tied to the history of American business. At the beginning of the Industrial Revolution in the early 1800s, the emphasis was on production. A firm stressed its ability to decrease the cost of production of each unit. In the early 1900s production started to catch up with demand, and businesses began to recognize the importance of sales. But physical distribution/logistics, as we know it, was still ignored by the business community until much later.[4]

During World War II military forces made effective use of logistics models and forms of systems analysis to ensure that materials were at the proper place when needed. One indication of the increased use of the term *logistics* at that time could be seen in the frustration of Chief of Naval Operations Admiral Ernest H. King, who reportedly said, "I don't know what the hell this logistics is that [Army Chief of Staff General George C.] Marshall is always talking about, but I want some of it."[5]

Many of the logistical techniques learned during the war were temporarily ignored during the postwar surge in economic activity. Marketing

[2] The National Council of Physical Distribution Management, general information pamphlet, 1977.

[3] "Distribution Managers' Challenge to Boost Productivity Is Renewed," *Traffic World* (Feb. 6, 1984), p. 16.

[4] Bernard J. LaLonde and Leslie M. Dawson, "Early Development of Physical Distribution Thought," in Donald J. Bowersox, Bernard J. LaLonde and Edward W. Smykay (eds.), *Readings in Physical Distribution Management* (New York: Macmillan, 1959), pp. 9–18.

[5] U.S. General Accounting Office, *Welcome to the Logistics & Communications Division* (1974), p. 2.

The Physical Distribution and Logistics System: Its Concept and Growth   5

6

Figure 1-1 Control Over Flow of Inbound and Outbound Movements

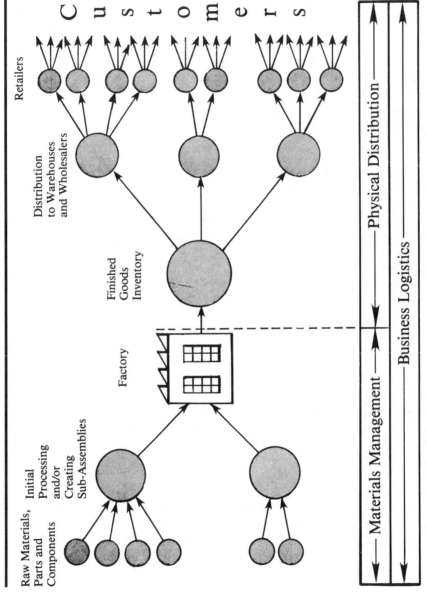

Source: Adapted from Richard A. Lancioni, "The Physical Distribution Concept and Its Implementation," in *Papers, NCPDM Annual Meeting,* 1978 (Chicago): 102; and Alan J. Stenger and Joseph L. Cavinato, "Adapting MRP to the Outbound Side," in *Production and Inventory Management* (Fall 1979):2–4.

managers turned their attention to filling the postwar demand for goods. It was not until the recessions of the 1950s that managers started to examine their physical distribution networks. The 1958 recession and profit squeeze created an environment in which business people began searching for more effective cost control systems. Almost simultaneously, many firms realized that physical distribution and logistics were items whose cost had neither been carefully studied nor coordinated. A number of other trends were becoming apparent, and they made it necessary to focus attention on product distribution. Six trends can be identified.

First, transportation costs rose rapidly. Traditional methods of distribution had become more expensive, and management became aware of the need to control these costs better. In the 1970s these factors became more critical with soaring fuel prices and spot shortages. Transportation could no longer be considered a stable factor in the business planner's equations. Higher-level management had to become involved in transportation-related aspects of logistics at both the operating and policy levels because of the many new decisions that had to be made in order to adapt to the rapid changes in all areas of transport. In addition, and more recently, deregulation of common carrier transportation has changed many of the long-established "rules of the game" that governed shippers' use of transportation. Many operating- and policy-level decisions must be made by the users of transportation in order to take advantage of the new laws and regulations.

Second, production efficiency was reaching a peak. It was becoming very difficult to generate significant additional cost savings because the "fat" had been taken out of production. On the other hand, physical distribution and logistics were still a relatively untouched area.

Third, there was a fundamental change in inventory philosophy. At one time retailers held approximately half of the finished product inventory, and wholesalers and manufacturers held the other half. During the 1950s more sophisticated inventory control techniques, especially in the grocery business, reduced total amounts of inventory and changed the ratio to only 10 per cent held by the retailers and 90 per cent by distributors and manufacturers.[6]

Fourth, product lines proliferated, a direct result of the marketing concept of giving each customer the exact product he or she desires. For example, until the mid-1950s products such as typewriters, light bulbs, appliances, and tissue paper, were largely functional in nature. More recently, differences in the products were no longer limited to real structural dissimilarities. A typewriter dealer could no longer stock the standard black office electric typewriter with pica type. He had to be able to match the typewriter color to the decor of the office with the type face chosen to support the image that the buyer wanted to project. One writer observed:

> Want to . . . get your glasses fixed? American Optical Company stocks some 60,000 line items. Get a tire for your car? Firestone carries some 48,000 line items. Or maybe after your shopping ordeal you feel you need

[6] Donald J. Bowersox, "Physical Distribution in Semi-Maturity," *Air Transportation* (Jan. 1966).

The Physical Distribution and Logistics System: Its Concept and Growth

some beautification—Revlon offers 33,000 items to satisfy your specific needs.[7]

> A *line item* or *SKU* (stock-keeping unit) is each individual type or separate kind of item that one must keep track of.

Fifth was computer technology. Management of the physical distribution/logistics approach involved a tremendous amount of detail and data. The following are examples of the information that must be available: (1) location of each customer; (2) size of each order; (3) location of production facilities, warehouses, and distribution centers; (4) transportation costs from each warehouse or plant to each customer; (5) available carriers and the service levels they offer; (6) location of the suppliers; and (7) inventory levels currently available in each warehouse and distribution center. The sheer magnitude of these data rendered manual analysis virtually impossible. Luckily, just as the physical distribution and logistics concepts were being developed, along came the mathematical beast of burden—the computer—which allowed the concepts to be put into practice. Without the development and use of the computer at this time, logistics and physical distribution concepts would have remained interesting theories with few "real-world" applications.

The sixth factor is also related to the increased use of computers because even if a specific firm did not use computers, its suppliers (vendors) and customers did. It became possible for firms to systematically study the quality of service they received from their suppliers. Based on this kind of analysis, many firms were able to pinpoint suppliers who consistently offered substandard levels of physical distribution. Many firms were rudely awakened and made to realize the need to upgrade their distribution systems. (More recently some manufacturing firms have adopted "just-in-time" materials-delivery requirements, which place very exacting demands upon suppliers.)

The "Total-System" Concept of PD/L

PD/L is a classic example of the systems approach to business problems. From a company's point of view the systems approach indicates that the company's objectives can be realized by recognizing the mutual interdependence of the basic functional areas of the firm (marketing, production, and finance). The same reasoning can be applied to the areas of physical distribution and logistics. The PD/L manager must balance each functional area and see that none is stressed to the point where it becomes detrimental to the others.[8]

[7] Warren Blanding, *The Fernstrom System Feedback* (March–April 1974), p. 1.
[8] See: George G. Mellios, "Logistics Management: What, Why, How," *Journal of Business Logistics*, (Vol. 5, No. 2, 1984) pp. 106–122.

One definition of *systems approach* is: "The systems approach to a problem involves not only a recognition of the individual importance of the various elements of which it is composed, but an acknowledgment of their interrelationship. Whereas the field specialist concentrates restrictively on his own particular bailiwick, the more versatile systems man, in his capacity as generalist, seeks the optimum blend of many of these individual operations in order to fulfill a broader objective."[9]

The Objectives of PD/L

Three important terms used in this book are logistics, physical distribution, and materials management. The objective of a physical distribution system is, with a specified level of service provided to customers, to minimize the costs involved in physically moving and storing the product from its production point to the point where it is purchased. The objective of *materials management,* which is concerned with the inbound flows of materials the firm needs, is the meeting of the firm's need for materials in an orderly, efficient, and low-cost manner.

The objectives of *logistics* encompasses efforts to coordinate physical distribution and materials management in order to save money or improve service. (Figure 1-2 is an advertisement for the Cargill Salt Company. Note that because salt is basically a homogeneous product, Cargill is differentiating its product by stressing a dependable logistical system to serve its food processing customers.) Examples of such coordination would be use of the same truck both to make deliveries and to pick up supplies or the use of a computer program that monitors orders being processed and determines how filling the orders will deplete stocks of goods on hand, require new production runs, and consume raw materials in these new production runs. To achieve these objectives, the logistics manager uses three interrelated concepts of the systems approach: (1) the total-cost approach, (2) the avoidance of suboptimization, and (3) cost trade-offs.

The Total-Cost Approach. The total-cost approach to logistics is built on the premise that *all* relevant functions in physically moving and sorting materials and products should be considered as a whole and *not individually.* The following functions should be included in the total-cost approach to physical distribution and logistics:

1. Transportation.
2. Warehousing.
3. Inventory location and plant location.
4. Inventory control of materials and products.
5. Materials handling.
6. Information flow, including order processing.
7. Packaging.

[9] Colin Barrett, "The Machine and Its Parts," *Transportation and Distribution Management* (April 1971), p. 3.

Figure 1-2 The Utilization of Logistics Service as a Major Selling Point

Source: Reproduced with permission of the Cargill Salt Company.

The key to the total-cost concept is that all cost items are considered simultaneously when attempting to meet specified service levels. When testing alternative approaches, the costs of some functions will increase, some will decrease, and some will stay the same. The objective is to find the alternative with the lowest *total* cost.

Avoidance of Suboptimization. Suboptimization occurs when each member's best efforts fail to produce optimal results. Professor Warren Rose explains suboptimization in terms of a talented football team that has a losing record: the team's members hold and make many individual league records for passing, rushing, and so on, but the team as a group always loses.[10]

The logistics consultant John F. Magee has observed:

> There is in business today, however, a growing tendency to recognize that the *efficiency* of an individual function examined in isolation may be quite different from the *effectiveness* of the function as part of the total logistic process. Compromises must be found among all the functions to obtain a total system operation that achieves a better cost/effectiveness balance. For example, low cost per ton shipped may be a very expensive target for the system as a whole if the traffic function achieves this target by sacrificing speed and particularly reliability of service or if the mode of transportation chosen makes special packaging necessary.[11]

Why does suboptimization happen? It occurs when each separate logistics activity is judged by its abilities to achieve given management objectives, which are often at cross-purposes with each other. For example, a warehouse manager in a firm that owns both warehouses and trucks may decide not to pay warehouse workers overtime to load a company truck. This keeps warehouse expenses down but may be very costly to the firm because the truck's schedule is interrupted. Another common cause of suboptimization is a department not in the logistics area of responsibility causing another department to operate at less than full efficiency. For instance, the production department may desire to minimize the cost of production per unit of output. To achieve this goal, the production manager schedules long production runs with as few changeovers as possible. The result of this action lowers unit cost but creates excess inventory awaiting sale and the added cost of holding this inventory.

Another example involves the retailing industry. A regional traffic manager for a firm was recognized by senior management for his ability to reduce transportation costs. Top management wanted to know why other regional traffic managers were not so astute. What was later discovered was that the "star performer" was in fact crippling the sales activities of the firm. Both marketing and merchandising executives were ready to strangle the traffic manager. Why? Because the savings had been made possible by using slower and less reliable transprotation carriers. The result was store deliver-

---

[10] Warren Rose, *Logistics Management* (Dubuque, Iowa: Brown, 1979), p. 4.

[11] John F. Magee, *Industrial Logistics* (New York: McGraw-Hill, 1968), p. 31. See also, Paul T. McElhiney and Charles L. Hilton, *Introduction to Logistics and Traffic Management* (Dubuque: Brown, 1968), p. 340.

ies that were too late for seasonal sales. Many other shipments arrived in damaged condition. The overall result was that, although the traffic manager saved thousands of dollars, he was also responsible for millions of dollars in lost sales.[12]

A final illustration of potential suboptimization involved the National Engine Corporation. The replacement parts division of this firm had $160 million in sales, with total physical distribution costs of $26 million. This high cost of distribution was a result of the firm's high level of customer service, which involved a warehouse in every major market where the firm did business: fifty warehouses in all. Senior management was concerned that distribution costs were excessive and that customer service standards were unnecessarily high. Harvey N. Shycon, a noted management consultant, was retained to address the issue. He determined that twenty warehouses would result in the lowest distribution costs, with an annual savings of $2 million. However, with fewer warehouses, customers would not receive their products as quickly, and up to 20 per cent of total sales would be lost, according to Shycon's computer simulation. This potential loss of sales was not acceptable to the firm's senior management and they chose to continue their relatively larger number of warehouses.[13]

Cost Trade-offs. The third important concept that supports the total systems approach is cost trade-offs. This acknowledges that changing patterns or functions of distribution will cause some costs to increase and cause other costs to decrease. The net effect, however, should be an *overall cost decrease* for a given level of performance, whether for the customer or for another department of the firm. The concept of cost trade-offs can be well illustrated by the following two examples.

1. The Gillette Company, the world's largest producer of safety razors, was faced with an ever increasing assortment of products because it had expanded into a broad range of toiletry products. To give good customer service the company started using air freight, an expensive form of distribution. Upon studying their distribution system, they discovered that their problem was in the slowness with which orders were processed. By simplifying paperwork they were able to reduce the time required to process orders. Gillette was able to return to lower-cost surface transportation and still be able to meet delivery schedules. The cost trade-off was between order processing costs, which *increased,* and transportation costs, which *decreased;* the net result was that total distribution costs *decreased.*
2. The Montgomery Ward Company found that significant inventory reductions could be achieved by consolidating all slower-moving products into one central warehouse. This facility is located only seven miles from Chicago's O'Hare Airport. When a slow-moving product or part is needed, the Chicago warehouse is notified, and the requirement is often sent via air freight to the requesting party. Although this procedure greatly in-

---

[12] Thomas E. Foster, "Bowing Down to the Beancounters," *Distribution* (Sept. 1983), p. 5.
[13] Harvey N. Shycon, "The Folly of Seeking Minimum Cost Distribution," *Annual Proceedings of the NCPDM* (1982), pp. 523–538.

creases the transportation charges involved in sending a product or part to a customer, the inventory holding cost reduction more than offsets the increased per unit transportation charges.

The PD/L Concept

We have now discussed the three basic considerations of logistics and physical distribution: (1) total cost, (2) the avoidance of suboptimization, and (3) the use of cost trade-offs. These three subparts, when combined in the decision-making process, form what is commonly called the total PD/L concept. This concept is not unique because of the functions performed since each function (traffic, warehousing) is the same. Rather, the uniqueness comes from the integration of all of these functions into a *unified whole* that seeks to minimize distribution costs for a given level of customer and in-firm service.

Computer Applications in PD/L

One of the most important recent trends in PD/L management is the accelerating utilization of computers to assist distribution executives.[14] Throughout this book we will be examining numerous examples of computers assisting PD/L managers to become more efficient. In most situations it is *not* necessary for distribution managers to be proficient in computer programming. Why? Because this skill is so technical that only people who do it on a regular basis are really competent to perform the task efficiently. In large firms full-time programmers on the data-processing staff are available to help the logistics department. Small firms typically utilize consultants who will perform the specific programming necessary. Therefore, the PD/L executive, although not required to possess programming skills, *must* be fully familiar with the strengths and weaknesses of computers. He or she must know enough about computers not to be awed by them. They are, in fact, only machines that must be told *exactly* what to do. This is the role of the programmer. What is the minimum level of computer expertise that a future logistics executive should possess? These writers recommend a college-level introductory course in each of the following three areas: computer familiarization, operations research, and management information systems. A fourth helpful course, if the student's schedule permits, is an introduction to data-base management.

It is estimated today that there are literally hundreds of "canned" or general programs available by software companies that deal with every aspect of PD/L. Some involve very minute aspects of logistics, and others are

---

[14] See Tom Foster, "Computerization: Where Are We?" *Distribution* (Sept. 1983), pp. 85–90; and Thomas C. Dulaney, "Now's the Time to Get On-Line," *Distribution* (Feb. 1983), pp. 22–27.

massive programs that cost millions of dollars to purchase and involve total coverage of a PD/L system. Some programs can be up and running the day they are purchased, whereas others require the using firm to input millions of facts into a data base before the system will operate.[15]

All computer assistance is becoming more user-friendly, which means that the ability to program is becoming less and less important. The computer program literally tells the user what to do at each step in the analysis. All the user has to do is to follow the relatively simple and straightforward format that the program sets forth step-by-step. In fact, one of the tests of a good program is the ability of a "non-computer type" to be able to utilize it efficiently.

Four PD/L Systems in Action

This section provides partial descriptions of the PD/L systems of four well-known firms.

Firestone Tire and Rubber Company

Firestone, with annual sales greater than $4 billion, produces a wide variety of products besides tires, including industrial rubber products, polyurethane foam, synthetic rubber, synthetic yarns, and textiles. We will only examine their tire business, which involves seven U.S. manufacturing plants and ten production facilities in foreign countries. The great majority of tires are transported by truck, using for-hire carriers or Firestone's own fleet of private vehicles. Many of Firestone's customers are serviced on a regular weekly basis. Customer-service representatives call each customer weekly and record orders and check tire availability while the customer is on the phone. This is made possible by utilizing computer terminals that display the current tire inventory of every product at each warehouse location. Each customer's order is then combined with others located in the same general area, so full truck-load shipments can be made for the majority of the shipment.

For Firestone's larger customers, direct computer-to-computer ordering is becoming common. The customers enter their order into their computers, and the order is instantaneously transmitted to Firestone via phone lines. The purpose of this system is to give Firestone's customers better customer service and also allow the customer to operate with a lower level of inventory. Illustrative of this concept is the relationship of Firestone to one of its largest customers, the Ford Motor Company. Ford was an early proponent of just-in-time [JIT] inventory systems. The Ford plant at Louisville sends data every twenty-four hours by computer to Firestone's headquarters in Akron. Each night Ford transmits its tire requirements for the next day and

[15] See John A. Miller, "Survey of Software for Physical Distribution," *Annual Proceedings of the NCPDM* (1983), pp. 35–170; Richard C. Haverly, "Survey of Software for Physical Distribution," *Annual Proceedings of the NCPDM* (1984), pp. 717–886, and Jack W. Farrell, "The Micro: A Manager's Best Friend," *Traffic Management* (May, 1985), pp. 71–75.

its projected requirements for the next few days. The tires are shipped from either Firestone's main plant at Akron or from warehouses near Louisville—in any case, the tires arrive the next morning. At present this system allows Ford to operate with 50 per cent fewer tires in inventory than before JIT was initiated. Ford is not the only beneficiary of this system. Firestone, because it now knows Ford's tire needs for a number of days in the future, can set its own production levels much more accurately. Leon R. Brodeur, president of Firestone, noted "We are able to reduce our warehouse inventories because we do not have to maintain a 'safety level' of types and sizes of tires 'just in case' they're needed. Because we have more accurate production estimates, we are able to do a better job of controlling our own inventories of raw materials. . . . The JIT system is one of many activities designed to restructure our inventory and distribution system, and achieve the objective of *decreasing costs* while *meeting commitments* to the sales department."[16]

To achieve the above goal, Firestone from 1971 to 1983 has closed 33 warehouses. Results have been impressive. From 1979 to 1983, while sales have been increasing, Firestone has been able to decrease their level of finished goods inventory from $528 million to $332 million.

3M Corporation

In June 1983, 3M Corporation [annual sales of $7 billion, with $205 million spent on domestic transportation] invited eighty-five senior carrier executives to its St. Paul headquarters to discuss its "partners in quality" program. The one-day seminar was designed to alert its for-hire carriers that from then on 3M was going to expect specific service standards from all its carriers. Roy W. Mayeske, executive director of transportation, noted the theme of the meeting, "If you do it right, you're going to lower your cost of doing business. Hence, you'll lower your price to the customer."[17] Specifically, 3M noted that, for every carrier to be utilized in the future, performance standards would be established. Once the carrier agreed to the standards, the goal would be 100 per cent on-time, damage-free delivery. 3M noted that if it were the cause of the carrier missing the goal, the carrier would not be penalized for the system breakdown. Many carriers were at first skeptical about such a demanding goal. However, 3M found that the better carriers, upon reflection, were not afraid of having their service levels closely monitored. By the end of 1984, all three hundred carriers utilized, from all modes except pipeline, were covered by performance standards. 3M does not bluff—if carriers consistently do not meet their performance standards, the carrier is no longer used. How is compliance determined? Both delivery times and service standards are verified using customer surveys and electronic link-ups with its major customers. In addition, 3M has computer-to-computer links with twenty-seven trucking firms, and data from these sources can be uti-

[16] Leon R. Brodeur, "Streamlining Tire Distribution," *Handling and Shipping: Presidential Issue* (1983–84), pp. 20–26.

[17] James Aaron Cooke, "In Search of (Carrier) Excellence," *Traffic Management* (May 1984), pp. 32–39.

lized to determine if the carriers are meeting predetermined performance standards.

3M maintains that the overall goal of the PD/L system is to ensure predictable, consistent, and reliable service at a reasonable cost. In a number of cases 3M has not utilized the lowest-cost carrier because of service problems. The objective is a *quality* distribution system. 3M defines quality as "not having to redo things not done right the first time."

J. C. Penney Company

Prior to transportation deregulation, PD/L people were frustrated with their ability to "manage" the transportation aspect of their business. Jim Leach, manager of transportation services at J. C. Penney Company, noted, "For some time we had the feeling that we were not really a buyer of transportation. The government, the rate bureaus, and the carriers—everyone except us—were setting and controlling prices. We were forced to develop a transportation/distribution network based on what these outside influences chose to give us. Our hands were tied, we couldn't determine our own destiny."[18]

Deregulation, however, has opened the door to creativity in the transportation segment of PD/L. Carriers are now willing to negotiate specific price/service packages. Penney's has followed a common trend of consolidating the number of carriers it utilizes. The logic was that if a carrier received more business from Penney's, then Penney's became a more important customer and would therefore receive a better package of rates and service. To accomplish this goal Penney's PD/L people interviewed hundreds of trucking companies and eventually reduced its primary motor carriers from over five hundred to fewer than a dozen. Many carriers wanted to participate in Penney's program because its transportation requirements were substantial: over 536 million pounds to be shipped annually from over 10,000 suppliers to about 2,000 stores. Penney's director of distribution, Mike Todres, informed carriers that he was looking for creative concepts. "Over and over we stressed that we were looking for innovative thinking. We told the carriers we wanted to find out who the true leaders in the industry were. We wanted them to throw out the old ways and be as dynamic as their minds would allow."[19]

Deregulation made possible one new requirement demanded by Penney's: each trucking company was to obtain contract-carrier[20] status and then set forth exactly the rates and service each would provide for a one-year period. Rate determination was to be in a simplified format. Todres quipped, "I'm an engineer by background. I don't know how to look rates up in the old tariff books, and I don't want to learn how. I want rates that

[18] Joseph V. Barks, "The More Things Changed, the More Penney's Saved," *Distribution* (Sept. 1983), pp. 46–54.

[19] Ibid.

[20] A contract carrier does not hold itself out to serve anyone who requests service. Instead it serves customers with whom it has a specific contract that sets forth rates, services, how claims are paid, etc.

are so simple and easy that my thirteen-year-old daughter can tell me what they are."[21]

Penney's PD/L people note that, in the future, distribution activities will be wide open to innovative concepts in every aspect of the system. Once carrier-rate structures are stabilized, other system components will be carefully analyzed for additional service/cost improvements.

General Motors Corporation

General Motors, the largest U.S. auto maker, is committed to both improving the quality of its cars and reducing the cost of production.[22] The goal is clearly to become more competitive with Japanese auto companies. A key element in achieving this goal is utilizing the Japanese system of inventory control known as *Kanban*, or JIT. It involves greatly reducing the quantity of inventory that is stocked at each assembly plant. Production inputs arrive at the plant in the morning and in many cases are components of finished cars by the end of the day. Advantages of this system are many, but the basic two are that (1) inventory levels are reduced, so that inventory holding costs are greatly reduced because less money is tied up in inventory, less storage space is necessary, and so on; (2) quality problems involving production inputs are spotted almost immediately and can be quickly corrected. Historically, entire shipments of defective parts would sit around assembly plants for days and weeks before they were utilized and the defects noted. Robert D. Stone, the vice-president of the materials-management function at GM declared, "Inventory is evil."[23]

To accomplish JIT requires a substantial change in the logistical activities of GM's suppliers. Foremost among them involves numerous deliveries—often daily—compared to the former practice of large shipments that were delivered a few times per month. In many cases this revised delivery schedule mandated switching from rail to truck shipments. In addition, vendors that were located near to the GM plants were preferred because it was easier for them to meet the tight delivery schedules that GM was demanding. By late 1983, 94 per cent of all GM parts by volume in the Midwestern region were purchased from vendors who shipped them fewer than 300 miles to the GM plant. Sixty-eight per cent of production inputs were transported fewer than 100 miles to the GM production facility.

An example of GM's commitment to JIT is the Buick City plant in Flint, Michigan. This facility is over sixty years old, but it is now being rapidly modernized. Every 300 feet in the assembly plant, workers have punched holes in the plant walls for new truck-receiving docks. Production inputs will now be delivered directly from trucks to their appropriate position on the assembly line. Land is also being cleared for vendors to locate their plants

[21] Barks, *op cit.*

[22] This discussion is based on Gerald E. Bodrie, "Logistics Strategy Development at General Motors," *Annual Proceedings of the NCPDM* (1983), pp. 485–500; and Charles G. Burck, "Will Success Spoil General Motors?" *Fortune* (Aug. 22, 1983), pp. 94–104.

[23] Burck, *ibid.*, p. 97.

in the immediate area of the GM plant. This concept emulates the Japanese concept of having many vendors and customers located in close geographic proximity to each other. When Buick City is fully operational, the plant will have at most only *four* hours of any production input on hand at any given time. Thus, multiple daily supplier deliveries will become standard.

The railroad industry is *not* giving up this business to the trucking industry without a fight. Railroads have established minitrains (often five to ten cars in length) that operate on set daily schedules. GM is currently utilizing eighteen such dedicated trains that consistently meet the intricate delivery schedules required for JIT.

Responsibilities of PD/L Managers

The PD/L manager has a highly complex and challenging position.[24] The major reason is that he or she must be both a technical expert and a generalist. In the first capacity the PD/L manager must understand freight rates, warehouse layouts, inventory analysis, production, purchasing, and transportation law.[25]

As generalist, the PD/L manager must understand the relationship between all PD/L functions. In addition he must relate PD/L to other operations of the firm.

> The emphasis is on the importance of the modern distribution man thinking in terms of the whole business system with which he is concerned. He must not only think of a flow of materials within his company, his thoughts must go beyond the shipping dock to the customer's doorstep . . . sometimes backward to the sources of supply. His thinking must cut across traditional organization lines. It must reach out to include competitors, potential markets. . . . In short, the physical distribution manager must think big.[26]

George A. Gecowets, executive director of the NCPDM, observed, "Most people today at the higher levels in distribution are generalists. They are managers first and distribution professionals second. They could manage any of the corporate functions, not just transportation/distribution."[27]

At any level the PD/L manager must be concerned with profits. Burr Hupp, one of the nation's most respected PD/L consultants, has noted:

> Everyone realizes logistics can increase profits by operational efficiency that will cut costs. What we may overlook is that by the service it gives custom-

[24] James L. Heskett, "Challenges and Opportunities for Logistics Executives in the 80s," *Journal of Business Logistics*, (Vol. 4, No. 1, 1983), pp. 13–20.

[25] C. John Langley, Jr., and William D. Morice, "Strategies for Logistics Management: Reactions to a Changing Environment," *Journal of Business Logistics*, (Vol. 3, No. 1, 1982), pp. 1–16.

[26] Harry J. Bruce, "Distribution History in the Making," *Pacific Traffic* (Nov. 1973), p. 5.

[27] Lisa H. Harrington, "What It Takes to Succeed in Distribution," *Traffic Management* (Feb. 1984), p. 35.

ers, logistics can increase sales—and profits. But will logistics-generated profits be a significant magnitude. Again, the answer is "yes."

Logistics costs, according to the National Council of Physical Distribution Management (NCPDM), are about 20 per cent of GNP. But some of these expenditures are incurred by a company's suppliers and customers. Therefore, in companies in the food, chemical, pharmaceutical, appliance, and other industries where materials movement is important, logistics costs are usually about 10 per cent of the sales dollar. Profits before taxes vary widely by company, but average about the same percentage. So there's a seldom-appreciated relationship: that is, 5, 10, or 15 per cent improvement in logistics will increase pretax profits 5, 10, or 15 percent, definitely a significant increase.[28]

PD/L Careers

Career opportunities in PD/L are excellent.[29] Many firms, both large and small, actively seek two- and four-year college graduates and MBAs who desire to work in the PD/L area. Timothy P. Foley, general traffic manager of Algoma Steel Corporation, noted a recent change in personnel requirements, "A few years ago we drew our traffic people from the railroads and the motor carriers. Today there is a much greater inclination to bring in people from the universities and colleges on a theoretical basis and train them in-house."[30] James P. Falk, director of domestic transportation for Kaiser Aluminum and Chemical Corporation, made a similar observation, "We used to hire the best rate clerks from the carriers, but found we were developing no inner management. We ended up with a lot of technicians, and though we had a few people at the top, our personnel inventory revealed we had nothing in between and we weren't training anyone. As a result, we turned to the better universities—the University of Tennessee was one of our favorites—and hired people right out of school. We put them to work, but not in the home office, preferring to give them direct line exposure in the plants, warehouses, and distribution centers."[31]

In general there are two types of entry-level positions in PD/L. The first is often assisting a line supervisor in one of the functional activities such as traffic, warehousing, purchasing, materials management, or inventory control. The second, often staff in nature, is assisting in the coordination and management of several different functions. Large firms have training programs that expose their PD/L personnel to a variety of closely supervised job assignments.

[28] Burr W. Hupp, "Profit Opportunities in Logistics in the 1980's," *University of Tennessee Survey of Business* (Spring 1980), p. 5.

[29] Kofi Q. Dadzie and Wesley J. Johnston, "Skill Requirements in Physical Distribution Management Career Path Development," *Journal of Business Logistics*, (Vol. 5, No. 2, 1984), pp. 65–84.

[30] "How the Experts See Things," *Traffic Management* (Aug. 1983), p. 77.

[31] Ibid.

A further advantage of PD/L career professionals is that this aspect of business offers many opportunities for advancement. Charles Rader, general manager of corporate distribution for Cities Service Company, believes that PD/L is an excellent training ground for senior management because PD/L personnel have a high degree of visibility in the firm since PD/L is an "integrating" function and PD/L people are constantly in touch with the other functional areas of the firm such as marketing, production, finance, accounting, and research and development. Rader stated that because of this high level of contact outside the PD/L department a large percentage of his employees have the opportunity to be promoted to positions outside of PD/L.[32] PD/L training is also valuable for individuals who hope to work for carriers because it gives them a better understanding of shippers' needs.

Each year Professor Bernard LaLonde of The Ohio State University surveys career patterns in physical distribution and logistics. His findings, based on information from the highest ranking distribution executives in major firms, are reported at annual meetings of the NCPDM. What follows is a brief summary of his 1984 survey results of 139 executives. Ninety-three per cent of the respondents had college degrees; 44 per cent had a masters degree. The typical vice-president was forty-five years old, had an average salary of $93,900, and spent about 65 per cent of his or her time on PD/L activities and the rest interacting with other functional areas of the firm. The breakdown of their time spent on PD/L functions follows: traffic, 11 per cent; warehousing, 11 per cent; inventory, 7 per cent; purchasing, 5 per cent; order processing, 5 per cent; general administration, 14 per cent; plant and warehouse location studies, 4 per cent; and other activities, 8 per cent. The executives' nondistribution activities were spent in the following areas: marketing, 11 per cent; production, 9 per cent; data processing, 5 per cent; finance, 5 per cent; and "other," 5 per cent.[33]

Figures 1-3 to 1-6 are from a booklet published by the NCPDM, entitled *Careers in Distribution*. Each examines an individual in a specific job in the area of PD/L.

PD/L Professionalism

Because of the growing importance of PD/L, it has achieved a true professional status. There are a number of professional organizations in logistics that are dedicated to advancing the professional knowledge of their members. The rationale for these professional associations is that the state of the art is changing so rapidly that professionals must be constantly educating and reeducating themselves.

[32] Based on a telephone interview with Mr. Rader on July 15, 1980.
[33] Bernard J. LaLonde and Larry W. Emmelhainz, "Career Patterns in Distribution Profile: 1984," *Annual Proceedings of the NCPDM* (1984), pp. 1–20. See also: "Annual Salary Survey: Who's Making What?" *Traffic Management* (April, 1985), pp. 41–53.

Figure 1-3 PD/L Careers: Transportation Manager

"My college major was general business with extra courses in statistics, finance and accounting. My first position after graduation was a traffic coordinator and from there I became traffic manager.

"Currently, I am an associate director of distribution in corporate transportation, which means I am involved in all aspects of transportation for the corporation. This includes inbound, between facilities, and outbound. There are five functional areas for which I am responsible: transportation operations, transportation and rate analysis, transportation planning and control, transportation administration, and traffic services. Additionally, I work closely with the purchasing, international, marketing and sales divisions. Overall, my primary responsibilities include:

- supervision of the various functions and personnel
- negotiation of rates with warehousing and transportation companies
- planning, monitoring and implementing the distribution department's fiscal budget
- establishing the most beneficial routing of company shipments for satisfactory customer service
- determining pricing levels
- planning — on a quarterly, a yearly, and a five-year horizon

"If you were to consider today as one of my 'typical' days, my schedule includes negotiating for LTL commodities, checking the status of an air-freight-claim, implementing a plant distribution survey, training personnel about customs forms and detailing a change-over from truck to rail for one of our larger customers. I'll also be working on my production schedule and the fiscal budget, and I'll be attending a Trucking Association luncheon.

"I usually work about 10 hours a day but travel and after-hours meetings often bring the total hours worked closer to 60 per week.

"I love the excitement of something new each day and the sense of accomplishment. I also enjoy the interfacing with each of the different company divisions and the opportunity to work with many different companies outside the organization. Additionally, I like the level of authority on this position — in terms of staff, material resources and budget — and my compensation.

"I believe that one of the most important skills necessary for this position is adaptability — everything is in a constant state of change.

"And of course a basic understanding of transportation is essential. It's not just knowing the different modes of transportation; it's understanding how transportation affects all the other areas of the corporation. Knowledge of the computer, electronic data processing, customer service, inventory control and production scheduling are very helpful. The ability to communicate is most important — listening, speaking, writing and other non-verbal communication. Other attributes include the ability to plan, control, influence, motivate, lead, organize, select the proper employees and administer. Now, more than ever, it's important to know how to handle things from a resources standpoint.

"My advice to anyone interested in a career in transportation would be to get as broad a background as possible in addition to the traditional transportation courses. Try to get entry level experience prior to graduation and learn the jargon before looking for that first job."

Source: Reproduced with permission of the NCPDM.

National Council of Physical Distribution Management (NCPDM)

This organization is dedicated "to develop the theory and understanding of the physical distribution process, to promote the art and science of managing physical distribution systems and to foster professional dialogue in the field." Further information can be obtained by writing to NCPDM, 2803 Butterfield Road, Oak Brook, IL 60521. [Just as this book was going to press, NCPDM changed its name to the Council of Logistics Management.]

Figure 1-4 PD/L Careers: Customer Service Manager

"I grew up in a family that was in the motor carrier business, so I have always been intimately involved with and aware of the physical distribution industry. After college and graduate school, I accepted a position in customer service with a major pharmaceutical firm. At this time, I am a customer service supervisor. Reporting to me are the order entry and customer service departments. My manager is the customer service director.

"I enjoy being a customer service supervisor and being responsible for making certain that shipments take place as scheduled. I function as the liaison between the customers and the sales force.

"In this job I very rarely encounter the mundane. More than 60% of my time is spent in an administrative capacity such as reviewing performance standards. Approximately 10-15% is devoted to personnel matters — training, performance reviews and allocation of responsibilities. The remaining 30% is spent actually working in customer service. I normally work about 50 hours per week. Travel is minimal and I rarely find it necessary to work at home.

"One of the delights about this business is that I'm involved with so many different types of people and businesses. It is very rewarding to experience the variety of types of organizations, methods of production, marketing schemes and people. Changing relationships with people, positions, attitudes and philosophies is a continual learning process — and again, a rewarding one.

"The amount of paperwork that we process can be very frustrating. And this, as well as related administrative responsibilities and conflicting deadlines all contribute to a high level of job-related stress.

"A thorough knowledge of traffic is a primary skill necessary for success in this field. This includes knowing the nitty-gritty of tariffs and everything else that has to do with the traffic function itself. You also need to have a real understanding of sales. It is helpful to have an understanding of marketing, forecasting, product development and product capabilities. You have to be a good decision maker. You must be innovative in your presentations and skillful in your communications. It's extremely important that you are able to listen very carefully. The ability to follow through and to be detail-oriented are also important skills.

"When I'm interviewing a job candidate, I consider the individual's ability to learn. I normally inquire as to grade point average and am interested in knowing if the person was independent in obtaining that education.

"I would suggest that students start at the very bottom: in this company, that means beginning as an order entry clerk and then becoming first a customer service representative and then a key account representative. It also means working in the warehouse and directly with the freight companies.

"There really is a need in this industry for sharp, capable and creative young people. But it is extremely important for them to honestly evaluate their own needs and abilities and associate these with their career objectives before they seek a position in this industry."

Source: Reproduced with permission of the NCPDM.

American Society of Transportation and Logistics (AST&L)

AST&L was founded to help its members achieve "high standards of education and technical training, requisite to the proper performance of the various functions of traffic, transportation and physical distribution management." To become a certified member of AST&L, one must pass four comprehensive tests over various aspects of traffic, transportation, and PD/L and write an original research paper. For further information, write AST&L, P.O. Box 33095, Louisville, KY 40232.

Figure 1-5 PD/L Careers: Warehousing/Operations Manager

"I am a vice president of warehousing operations for a major U.S. food company. I am responsible for all activities in the warehouse that are outside the office area, including receiving, storing and shipping merchandise.

"My basic mission is to determine and develop distribution strategies and practices that will support our corporate objective. My major responsibilities are identifying areas within the company that offer some opportunity for improvement; optimizing our investment in all of our locations — in inventory, facilities, and people; and matching the corporate distribution support capabilities to the outlying marketing, business and operational needs.

"I am in the office by 7:15 a.m. and leave between 6:00 and 6:30 at night, so I spend about 50 hours a week on the job. It is not only planning which consumes a considerable amount of time, but also monitoring various activities and projects. Besides that, we do some entertaining of customers, which often involves evenings and weekends.

"There are very few average days in warehousing. Normally on Mondays, I get caught up on the paperwork from the previous week and I make a plan for the coming week. About 40% of my time is spent in planning for the future. Another 40% is spent on operational activities, and the final 20% on people/personnel related activities.

"What I like best about my job is that it's never dull. Just when I think I've seen or heard it all, something happens to prove I haven't. I have a lot of opportunity to work for the good of my company and to improve our status. The position involves coordinating the efforts of a lot of people so that the transition of our products from the time of production through their final disposition to the customer happens in the least amount of time and with the lowest costs possible. This job is competitive, but the very fact that it is competitive makes for an average day when there's never enough time to do what I want to do. It gives me a chance to use my head. I enjoy the challenge of identifying what appears to be a problem and solving it. I get satisfaction from preventing everyday problems and coming up with different ways to prevent them in the future. It is all done through people.

"My people do all the labor negotiations with the various unions that are involved with us, all the office administration, and the related data processing. They also do pricing. Other significant concerns include sanitary conditions of the facility, service, and the ability to consolidate merchandise.

"Generalizing about warehousing and the place it occupies on the organizational chart is difficult. Warehousing might be found under a distribution group, or as part of a customer distribution and services group, or as a separate entity. In my company, our domestic organization is centralized. It is made up of four principal groups which include transportation and field operations. (Field operations are comprised of outlying, regional distribution centers and the central distribution center which takes the finished product directly from manufacturing.)

"I began working in physical distribution when I was 20 years old. When I took the job in the warehouse, I had no intention of staying on. I didn't plan for it — I just happened into it. That was 15 years ago. With the competition for jobs the way it is today, fewer people just luck into a job anymore. It takes planning and preparation. Today, most of our new hires join the company through the estimating and planning organization or through our distribution systems organization. However, even our college graduates spend some time in the warehouse. From there, they might move into a supervisory position for their first taste of management. Their move could involve them in wide-ranging operations activities including planning and organization. The final step would be a position at corporate headquarters.

"Of all the skills necessary for success, organization is a must. Other definite assets are the ability to handle people and to solve problems. Considering the fact that most of physical distribution is unionized, it would be good to pick up something in school that would provide a basic knowledge of dealing with labor and negotiating. You do not have to know how to program the computer, but you will need to know the computer well enough to understand your involvement with it as well as how it interfaces with other people so that you will be able to spot a systems problem and what could be the cause of it.

"I think that a financial background is extremely helpful . . . being able to evaluate projects and allocate resources. It is helpful to have a systems orientation and to know how to set up a project. I think it is important to have a basic understanding of the sales forecasting process and the evaluation of statistical data to understand the total inventory management process. There are certain aspects of transportation that are helpful to any manager."

Source: Reproduced with permission of the NCPDM.

Figure 1-6 Careers in PD/L: Inventory Control Manager

"I was a marketing major in college. After graduation, I worked first as a marketing analyst and from there I moved into inventory.

"Presently, I am the vice president of inventory management and report directly to the president. Reporting to me are the inventory coordinators, inventory controllers and, the inventory managers for each product type. The department is divided into two parts: the basic responsibility is to make certain that all of our stock keeping units are in adequate supply — both components and finished goods. We work very closely with design and pre-production so that production can be contracted out. Also, we are responsible for the overall quality of the product. The objectives of this position are to maximize customer service levels, inventory investment and manufacturing efficiencies.

"On an average day, one of the major things I do is look at computer reports — just to get an overview and to see where we are — and follow through with actions as required. I spend a considerable amount of time evaluating reports on suppliers. And then, of course, other parts of my days are spent in writing, attending meetings, traveling and planning. About 45-50 hours per week are spent on the job. I do some work at home — correspondence and special reports.

"I probably have the most interesting job in the world. 'Perfect inventory' really is an unattainable goal but I feel that striving for it and getting close is very rewarding. It's a constant challenge and the politics are very difficult. Deadlines make the job stressful, as does change, but I love it.

"For this position you need a whole lot of patience and the ability to get along with people. Treating people fairly is very important — as is the ability to really listen. Computer skills would really be an asset. Communication is extremely important. In addition to the technical skills in your own field of interest, financial ability is very important and I would advise concentrating on finance, economics and marketing.

"Students interested in this area should consider examining all schools that have a formal inventory program. A summer job in warehousing or production would be very helpful. Join one of the professional organizations. And once you're out of college, I believe the best training you can get is to work for a large corporation."

Source: Reproduced with permission of the NCPDM.

American Production and Inventory Control Society (APICS)

The APICS attempts to develop professional, scientific approaches to methods of inventory control. In 1980 this group formed a special section to deal with the physical distribution aspects of logistics. For additional information, write APICS, Suite 504 Watergate Bldg., 2600 Virginia Avenue, NW, Washington, DC 20037.

Association of Transportation Practitioners (ATP)

The ATP is dedicated "to promote the proper administration of the Interstate Commerce Act and related Acts, to uphold the honor of practice before the Interstate Commerce Commission; to cooperate in fostering increased educational opportunities and maintaining high standards of professional conduct, and to encourage cordial communication among the practitioners." To belong to this organization, one must be an ICC practitioner. This is accomplished by passing a comprehensive test administered by the ICC on transportation law. For further information, write Association of Transportation

Practitioners, 1211 Connecticut Avenue, NW, Suite 310, Washington, DC 20036.

Delta Nu Alpha (DNA)

DNA is a transportation fraternity dedicated to the education of its members. DNA chapters are very active at the local level and stress the learning process by small educationally-oriented discussion groups. For further information, write DNA, 1040 Woodcock Road, Orlando, FL 32803.

Society of Logistics Engineers (SOLE)

The focus of SOLE includes military logistics as well as market-oriented products. For more information, write Society of Logistics Engineers, 303 Williams Avenue, Suite 922, Park Plaza, Huntsville, AL 35801.

Society of Packaging and Handling Engineers (SPHE)

SPHE is dedicated to improving the application of technology and management skills in the packaging and material-handling field by helping its members increase their knowledge, skills, and technical expertise. For additional information, write to SPHE, 11800 Sunrise Valley Drive, Reston, VA 22091.

Transportation Data Coordinating Committee (TDCC)

The TDCC's goal is to foster, develop, and maintain a program of action in the areas of standardization of descriptions and codes, reconstruction of tariff formats, and systems design to aid in the exchange of data between shippers and carriers. Further information can be obtained by writing TDCC, 1101 17th Street, NW, Washington, DC 20036.

Transportation Research Forum (TRF)

TRF is a "joint endeavor of interested persons in academic life, government service, business logistics, and the various modes of transportation. The Forum's purpose is to provide a common meeting ground or forum for the discussion of ideas and research techniques applicable to economic, management, and public policy problems involving transportation." Additional information can be obtained from TRF, 1133 Fifteenth Street, NW, Suite 620, Washington, DC 20005.

Warehouse and Education Research Council (WERC)

The purpose of the WERC is to provide education and to conduct research concerning the warehousing process, and to refine the art and science of managing warehouses. The Council will foster professionalism in warehouse management. It will also operate . . . in cooperation with other organizations and institutions." Additional information can be obtained by writing to WERC, 1100 Jorie Blvd., Suite 118, Oak Brook, IL 60521.

Summary

As used in this book, the phrase *materials management* refers to a firm's inbound movements, and the phrase *physical distribution management* refers to the outward flow of materials or services, in the direction of the customer. The term *logistics* covers both functions.

Many specific functions of the firm involve logistics. They include transportation, purchasing, warehousing, inventory management, order processing, protective packaging, materials handling, and warehouse and plant site selection. The objective of logistics within the firm is to provide the highest level of customer service and intrafirm cooperation, given the realities of budgetary and other constraints.

Logistics costs are a major cost item for the U.S. economy. A. T. Kearney estimated in 1982 that logistics costs equaled 21 per cent of the GNP, or $650 billion. The increasing importance of physical distribution and logistics is the result of several factors. These factors include: the significant increases in transportation rates since World War II; the fact that production had been overanalyzed while PD was ignored; the trend toward reduced inventories at all levels within the marketing channel; the proliferation of products in the marketplace, and the advancing prices of fuel that have driven up the costs of transportation.

The PD/L concept is comprised of three basic subparts: total-cost approach, avoidance of suboptimization, and utilization of cost trade-offs. Each of these aspects of PD/L would be difficult to implement without the assistance of computer technology. Executives in PD/L do not have to be proficient computer programmers, but they must be familiar with the basics of computer technology.

Four examples of successful PD/L systems have been noted: Firestone Tire and Rubber Company, 3M Corporation, J. C. Penney Company, and General Motors. The chapter concluded by examining career opportunities in PD/L.

Questions for Discussion and Review

1. "Traffic management and PD/L management are really the same thing! The latter term just sounds more sophisticated, but it's really nothing more than the purchasing of transportation services." Comment on the validity of this statement.
2. What are the technical differences between physical distribution, logistics, and materials management?
3. Discuss the functional areas that combine to form the PD/L department.
4. PD/L has become recognized as an important business function during the past decade. Discuss the reasons for this situation.
5. Why is the *phenomenon* of product proliferation so difficult from a PD/L manager's point of view?
6. Discuss the impact of computer technology on the development of the PD/L concept.
7. How did the increased usage of computer technology by customers affect the development of the PD/L concept?

8. Deregulation of transportation took place between 1977 and 1980. What has been the effect of this situation on PD/L managers?
9. What is the systems approach to problem solving? Why is this concept applicable to PD/L management?
10. Discuss the objectives of physical distribution, materials management, and logistics.
11. Discuss the total-cost approach to PD/L management.
12. What is suboptimization? Give an example.
13. Define a cost trade-off. Do you believe this concept is workable? Why?
14. Discuss the cost trade-off used by the Montgomery Ward Company.
15. PD/L managers must be both *generalists* and *technicians*. Why is this true? Does it help to explain why PD/L managers are in relatively short supply?
16. Discuss advantages to a career in PD/L management.
17. What computer skills are necessary to be an effective logistics manager?
18. Discuss logistical activities at Firestone Tire and Rubber Company.
19. What is the 3M "Partners in Quality" program? Do you believe this concept is sound? Defend your answer.
20. Discuss transportation rate changes that have taken place at the J. C. Penney Company in the last few years.
21. What is JIT? How has it been utilized by GM?

Additional Chapter References

Banks, Gary. "Logistical Systems at Bristol-Myers." *Annual Proceedings of the NCPDM* (1982), pp. 473–488.

Bowersox, Donald J. "Emerging from the Recession: The Role of Logistical Management," *Journal of Business Logistics* (Vol. 4, No. 1, 1983), pp. 21–33.

Bowersox, Donald J., Phillip L. Carter, and Robert M. Monczka. "Computer Aided Purchasing, Manufacturing & Physical Distribution Coordination Materials Logistics Management." *Annual Proceedings of the NCPDM* (1984), pp. 131–142.

Boyer, Paul, and George Wagenheim. "Physical Distribution Strategies in an Expanding Management Discipline." *Annual Proceedings of the NCPDM* (1982), pp. 845–859.

Campbell, John H. *Logistics: Issues for the '80s* (Shaker Heights, OH: Corinthian Press, 1982).

Charalambides, Leonidas C. "The Dynamic Transportation Job Shop—A Research Perspective." *Annual Proceedings of the Transportation Research Forum* (1982), pp. 659–667.

Corsi, Thomas M., and Curtis M. Grimm. "Transportation Education in the 1980s: An Examination of Teaching Materials," *Transportation Practitioners Journal* (Fall 1984) pp. 27–39.

Davis, Herbert W. "Physical Distribution Costs 1984: In Some Companies, a Profit Contribution, in Others, Cost-Price Margins Continue to Dwindle." *Annual Proceedings of the NCPDM* (1984), pp. 29–40.

Davis, James R. "Physical Distribution Costs: The 1982 Distribution

Cost/Service Database." *Annual Proceedings of the NCPDM* (1982), pp. 53–62.

Dorsett, Katie G., and Julian M. Benjamin. "Training and Career Opportunities for Minorities and Women." *Annual Proceedings of the Transportation Research Forum* (1984), pp. 177–181.

Ferguson, Wade. "An Evaluation of Journals That Publish Business Logistics Articles." *Transportation Journal* (Summer 1983), pp. 69–72.

———. "Logistics Education as a Career Field." *Transportation Journal* (Fall 1982), pp. 56–62.

Heskett, James L. "Challenges and Opportunities for Logistics Executives in the 80s." *Journal of Business Logistics* (Vol. 4, No. 1, 1983), pp. 13–19.

LaLonde, Bernard J., and David E. Lloyd. "Career Patterns in Distribution: Profile 1983." *Annual Proceedings of the NCPDM* (1983), pp. 171–192.

LaLonde, Bernard J., and Richard Brand. "Career Patterns in Distribution: Profile 1982." *Annual Proceedings of the NCPDM* (1982), pp. 25–52.

LaLonde, Bernard J. "A Reconfiguration of Logistics Systems in the 80s: Strategies and Challenges." *Journal of Business Logistics* (Vol. 4, No. 1, 1983), pp. 1–11.

———. "Distribution Careers: 1984." *Annual Proceedings of the NCPDM* (1984), pp. 1–20.

Langley, C. John. "Physical Distribution Management," *Annual Proceedings of the NCPDM* (1982), pp. 831–844.

———. "Strategic Management in Transportation and Physical Distribution," *Transportation Journal* (Spring 1983), pp. 71–78.

Lynagh, Peter M., and Richard F. Poist. "Womens' Perceptions Regarding Careers in Transportation and Distribution." *Annual Proceedings of the Transportation Research Forum* (1984), pp. 182–186.

Mahal, David G. "Compensation Trends in Distribution—The 1984 Survey." *Annual Proceedings of the NCPDM* (1984), pp. 21–28.

Mellios, George C. "Logistics Management: What, Why, How." *Journal of Business Logistics,* (Vol. 5, No. 2, 1984), pp. 106–122.

O'Neill, William J., and Charles B. Lounsbury. "Logistics: Change and Synthesis." *Annual Proceedings of the NCPDM* (1984), pp. 623–636.

Scott, Walt, and W. Elmer Hallowell. "Putting the Puzzle Together: Bringing Kodak Products to Market." *Annual Proceedings of the NCPDM* (1984), pp. 513–526.

Sherwood, Charles S., and William C. Rice, "Computer Literacy Needs in Transportation," *Journal of Business Logistics* (March, 1985), pp. 1–12.

Shycon, Harvey N. "The Folly of Seeking Minimum Cost Distribution." *Annual Proceedings of the NCPDM* (1982), pp. 523–538.

Stenger, Alan J. "Building the Computer Skills of Current and Future Logistics Managers." *Technological Challenge: Research and Educational Applications* (Columbus: Transportation and Logistics Research Fund, The Ohio State University, 1984), pp. 1–22.

Varrato, James D. "Physical Distribution Management: Career Path of Jim Varrato." *Annual Proceedings of the NCPDM* (1983), pp. 620–626.

Vellenga, David B., Benjamin J. Allen, and Cathleen D. Riley. "An Analysis of Author Affiliation for Publications in Transportation and Logistics

Academic Journals, 1967–1979," *Transportation Journal* (Fall 1981), pp. 44–53.

CASE 1-1

Superior Paper Products Company

Superior Paper Products Company is located in a medium sized southern city. The firm is sixty-five years old and has been controlled by the Sylvester family. Julius Sylvester (1888–1963) founded the firm and ran it until his death. His son George (1921–1966) ran it until his untimely death (struck by lightning on a golf course). Frank Sylvester (1953–) became president in 1979 and, with the help of Morris Blackman, who has been with the firm since 1937 and is currently executive vice-president, has managed to do a satisfactory job despite his youth and the fact that many of his grandfather's antiquated practices are still in force.

In 1985 the firm's sales were nearly $500 million. Products were marketed in all states east of the Rocky Mountains and about 3 per cent of the sales were exported to European markets. In 1985 profit margins were much lower than for the industry as a whole, and this was attributed to Superior's accumulation of embarrassingly large inventories.

In the early 1980s, several large customers who had carried both Superior's products and those of one or more of Superior's competitors dropped the Superior line claiming they wanted to reduce the number of different product lines they had to maintain in their own stocks. The reason given for dropping the Superior line was "poor customer service." Some of Superior's customers had been reading about some of the new inventory techniques that stressed smaller stocks and frequent, dependable shipments. In most instances these quantities were much less than either the railcar (Superior's favored mode of shipping) or even truck load. Some of Superior's competitors were enlarging their fleets of private trucks so that they could make timely deliveries of less-than-truckload quantities.

At the insistence of some of the family members who still owned large blocks of stock, Frank Sylvester (and Blackman) had retained Merlin Associates, a well-known physical distribution consulting firm. They paid Merlin Associates $100,000 to conduct a study of Superior's distribution system and recommend how it could be made more competitive.

Irwin Buchanan, sixty-three years old, had been traffic manager of Superior Paper Products since 1943. He had been with the firm since 1937 when, still in high school and working in a service station, he impressed Julius Sylvester with the enthusiasm he showed for washing the windows of the elder Sylvester's Packard. Even at washing windows on autos, Buchanan was a perfectionist. After finishing, he would ask permission to stick his head inside the car and then peer through each freshly washed window to make certain no streaks remained. Even though this was the depths of the depression and Superior Paper Products was not hiring, the elder Sylvester decided to make room for young Buchanan, who was assigned to Superior's three-man traffic department, which oversaw rates and dealings with rail carriers.

The elder Sylvester never regretted his choice. Buchanan was an outstanding traffic manager. He was one of the leading participants in the ICC's class rate investigations of the 1940s which ultimately resulted in a restructuring of the nation's entire rate structure so it was more equitable to the South. In 1953 the railroads in the Southern Territory named him "shipper of the year." In 1967 the state's chamber of commerce awarded him the title "Mr. Transportation."

Buchanan was an ICC practitioner and had participated in over two hundred ICC proceedings and an equal number of hearings held by state transportation regulatory bodies in states where Superior Paper Products had intrastate shipments. He had appeared numerous times before state legislative committees and congressional committees. He had represented both his industry and southern shippers before the various congressional committees that were considering legislation that finally became the Transportation Act of 1958. Later, he played a key role in the legislation that restructured the railroads in the northeastern United States. Currently he serves on several committees trying to "standardize" carrier and shipper terminology, in order to facilitate electronic data interchange and computerized preparation of shipping documents.

Because Superior Paper Products spent over $50 million annually for transportation, Buchanan had considerable leverage with carriers. He constantly strove to obtain the lowest rates possible. He had a "sixth sense" for knowing routes over which railroads had large "back hauls" of empty cars. Buchanan would advise Superior's timber buyers to buy timber at points near the beginning of the rail's empty haul and then would offer the rails a large tonnage if they would lower the rate. Surprisingly, after rail deregulation, Superior was not able to bargain with the railroads for much lower rates. The reason for this was actually a tribute to Buchanan's efforts over the years: the existing rail rates, which he obtained before deregulation, were already low and, by anyone's accounting, barely covered the railroads' out-of-pocket costs.

Buchanan had also seen to that Superior Paper Products' finished product warehouses were located in relatively isolated spots where, again, he could take advantage of a railroad back-haul situation and obtain low rates to the warehouse site because there was no other traffic moving to that community. Warehousing costs in these communities were also low; labor was nonunionized and very productive. Because of the large capacity of these warehouses it was possible to store large lots of Superior's finished products, and these large lots were the cushion between production and sales. Buchanan had developed a warehousing system with such large capacity that fluctuations in sales did not affect levels of production. The elder Sylvester had liked this system. It allowed him to run his plants at a constant pace for fifty weeks per year—no layoffs and no overtime. (The plant closed for two weeks in mid-August for vacations.)

When the Merlin Associates' report was completed, one copy was sent to Frank Sylvester, and both he and Blackman read it. It confirmed their suspicions that Superior Paper Products' distribution setup was too "transportation-savings" oriented. Sylvester and Blackman spent a long time discussing the report, whether to show it to Buchanan, and how to implement its recommendations. "I sure hate to move against Buchanan," said Frank Sylvester, sadly. "Both Gramps and Dad thought the world of him, and when I was growing up, he used to take me to Mobile and to Tampa to see car unloading equipment installations. I know you two are about the same age, but you realize that times have changed and some of Gramp's ideas no longer hold. Buchanan doesn't realize this. The Merlin report says we've got the lowest transportation rates and the biggest inventories in the industry. What am I going to do?"

"Irwin and I are old buddies," said Blackman, softly. "When I tell you what I recommend, I feel like I'm knifing my own brother."

"I appreciate that," said Sylvester, "but I think we're also agreed that something has to be done. Now, what do you recommend?"

Blackman responded: "First of all, I agree with the Merlin Associates' report. Second, we need a new logistics division, and Buchanan's traffic office will become part of the new division. Third, Buchanan will *not* head the new division."

"We're agreed," said Frank Sylvester. "Who's going to tell Buchanan?"

Question One: What do you think the contents of the Merlin Associates' report probably stated?

Question Two: How should Blackman and Frank Sylvester go about informing Buchanan of their decision? What should they say?

Question Three: Assuming a new logistics function were to be established, what functions should it cover?

Question Four: Where, if anywhere, in the new structure should Buchanan be placed? Why?

Question Five: You are Frank Sylvester. Prepare a brief statement to be presented at a meeting of your top subordinates to explain the new organizational changes.

Question Six: How might other employees view Buchanan's fate? If you are Frank Sylvester, should you take this into account? How, if at all, can you control or reduce ill feelings the entire situation with Buchanan is bound to generate?

CASE 1-2

Sudsy Soap, Inc.

Frank Johnson was physical distribution manager for Sudsy Soap, Inc. He had held the job for the past five years and had just about every distribution function well under control. His task was made easier because shipping patterns and volumes were unchanging routines. The firm's management boasted that it had a steady share in "a stable market," although a few stockholders grumbled that Sudsy Soap had a declining share in a growing market.

The Sudsy Soap plant was in Akron, Ohio. It routinely produced 100,000 48-ounce cartons of powdered soap each week. Each carton measured about ½ cubic foot, and each working day, 15 to 20 carloads were loaded and shipped to various food chain warehouses and to a few large grocery brokers. Johnson had worked with the marketing staff to establish prices so nearly all soap was purchased in carload lots. Shipments less than a full carload did not occur very often.

Buyers relied on dependable deliveries, and the average length of time it took for a carton of soap to leave the Sudsy production line and reach a retailer's shelf was 19 days. The best time was 6 days (mainly to chains distributing in Ohio) and the longest time was 43 days (to retailers in Hawaii).

Sudsy Soap's president was worried about the stockholders' criticism regarding Sudsy's lack of growth, so he hired a new sales manager, E. Gerard Beever (nicknamed

"Eager" since his college days at a Big Ten university). Beever had a one-year contract and knew he must produce. He needed a "gimmick."

At his university fraternity reunion he ran into one of his fraternity roommates who was now sales manager for an imported line of kitchen dishes manufactured in Hong Kong. Their quality was good, but competition was intense. It was difficult to get even a "toe-hold" in the kitchen dish market. He and Beever shared a common plight; they were responsible for increasing market shares for products with very little differentiation from competitors' products. They each wished they could help the other, but could not. The reunion ended and each went home.

The next week Beever was surprised to receive a telegram from his old roommate. It read:

> We propose a tie-in promotion between Sudsy Soap and our dishes. We will supply at no cost to you one hundred thousand each twelve inch dinner plates, seven inch pie plates, nine inch bread and butter plates, coffee cups, and saucers. Each week you must have a different piece in each package starting dinner plate in week one, pie plates in week two, and so on through end of week five. Recommend this be done weeks of October 3, October 10, October 17, October 24, and October 31 of this year. Timing important because national advertising linked to new television show we are sponsoring. We will give buyers of five packages of Sudsy Soap, purchased five weeks in a row, one free place setting of our dishes. Enough of your customers will want to complete table settings so they will buy three, five or seven more place settings from our retailers. Timing is crucial. Advise immediately.

Beever was pleased to receive the offer but realized a lot of questions had to be asked and answered before he could recommend that the offer be accepted. He sent a copy of the telegram to Johnson attached to an interoffice memo. The memo said:

> Note attached telegram offering "tie-in" with dishes. Dishes are of good quality. What additional information do we need from dish distributor and what additional information do you need before we know whether to recommend acceptance? Please advise quickly. Thanks.

Question One: Assume you are Frank Johnson's assistant, and he asks you to look into various scheduling problems which might occur. List and discuss them.

Question Two: What packaging problems, if any, might there be?

Question Three: Many firms selling consumer goods are concerned with problems of product liability. Does the dish offer present any such problems? If so, what are they? Can they be accommodated?

Question Four: Should the exterior of the Sudsy Soap package be altered to show what dish it contains? If so, who should pay for the extra costs?

Question Five: Assume you are another one of Johnson's assistants and your principal responsibility is managing the inventories of all the firm's inputs, finished productgs, and outbound inventories. What additional work will the dish proposal cause for you?

Question Six: You are Mr. Beever. Your staff has given many objections to the dish tie-in proposal, but you consider much of the problem is your staff's reluctance to try anything innovative. Draft a letter to the dish company that—although not accepting their proposal—attempts to clarify points that may be subject to misinterpretation and also takes into account some of your staff's legitimate concerns.

Recycling of useful materials causes a ''reverse'' flow in a firm's, or a channel's, functioning. The best-known example of recycling is of aluminum cans. Shown here is a device for crushing the cans and loading them into the truck body.

(Credit: Aluminum Company of America)

Physical Distribution and Logistics Interfaces Within the Firm

Purchasing and distribution have been working together more and more. Their goal is help our raw-materials and transportation vendors design superior delivery programs. This leads to significant reductions in inventory and warehousing requirements, while at the same time assuring the plants that they will have reliable material flows tailored to their production plans.

Joseph D. Williams
President, Warner-Lambert Corporation
Traffic Management
December 1984

In my opinion, EDI (electronic data interchange) may have as important an impact on distribution in this country as deregulation of transportation has already had.

John F. Wing
Handling and Shipping Management
January 1985

Key Terms

- Marketing channel
- Exchange function
- Transaction function
- FOB pricing methods
- Phantom freight
- Freight absorption
- Stock-out
- Materials requirements planning [MRP]
- Recyling

Learning Objectives

- To note the interaction between marketing and PD/L
- To examine the relationship of pricing activities to PD/L
- To identify the concept of MRP
- To relate the importance of recycling to PD/L
- To understand the impact of accounting and finance on PD/L activities

Introduction: Logistics and the Firm

As we mentioned in Chapter 1, logistics has gained increasing importance and recognition in corporate planning. It is no longer treated as an afterthought, something to be considered only after the "important" work of producing, selling, and promoting a product have been accomplished. Today it is at the center of most planning decisions, and as a result firms' logistics departments interact with all other major functional departments of their firms.[1] One of the greatest advantages of working in logistics is the high level of exposure the individual receives through contact with other areas of the firm. The purpose of this chapter is to examine the relationships between logistics and the other major areas of the firm.

Marketing Interactions

While the PD/L staff interacts with all departments, one of its most important contacts is with marketing. A 1984 survey by Professors Peter M. Lynagh and Richard F. Poist indicates that, with a few exceptions, marketing departments recognize the importance of physical distribution (PD) activities to achieving an effective marketing program.[2] This finding is encouraging, because a 1977 survey by Professors James C. Johnson and Donald L. Borger found that marketing departments often did not consider PD activities to be essential to the firm's marketing program.[3]

Figure 2-1 shows the integral relationship between physical distribution

---

[1] See Lynn C. Mallory, "Integrated Logistics: How to Make It Happen in Your Company," *Annual Proceedings of the NCPDM* (1983), pp. 731–750.

[2] Peter M. Lynagh and Richard F. Poist, "Managing Physical Distribution/Marketing Activities: Cooperation or Conflict?" *Transportation Journal* (Spring 1984), pp. 36–43.

[3] James C. Johnson and Donald L. Borger, "Physical Distribution: Has It Reached Maturity?" *International Journal of Physical Distribution*, **7**: 283–293 (1977).

Figure 2-1 Physical Distribution as a Step in the Marketing Process

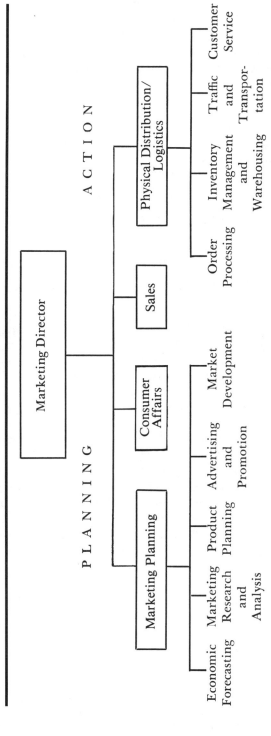

37

and the other parts of the firm's marketing "mix." Although Figure 2-1 looks like an organization chart—and it could be—it is also a form of flowchart where the earlier actions are shown on the left side. PD is the last step in the process.

The most important reason that those responsible for marketing have embraced physical distribution in recent years is that effective physical distribution is now recognized as a positive sales-generating asset. Professor George D. Wagenheim has noted:

> There are several opportunities for distribution to be a source of competitive advantage. Generally these are, but are not limited to, speed of delivery, consistency of delivery, availability of product, lowering purchasers' inventory, tracking inventory and generally working with the buyer toward mutual success. The key to competitive advantage is to offer something unique. Purchasers demand an industry level of competence [customer service levels equal to the industry average]. Thus, the challenge is not to offer what is normal among competitors but to offer something beyond.[4]

The following pages will examine how physical distribution interfaces with each of the four basic parts of the marketing mix: place, price, product, and promotion (sometimes known as the 4 P's).

Place Decisions

One important marketing concern is place. Place decisions involve two types of networks. The first network involves *physical distribution*. The second network involves *marketing channels*. PD decisions concern how most effectively to move and store the product from where it is produced to where it is finally sold.

The second type of network, the *marketing channel*, is the arrangement of intermediaries (wholesalers, retailers, brokers, manufacturer's representatives, etc.) the firm uses to accomplish its marketing objectives.[5] An effective physical distribution system can provide positive support by allowing the firm to attract—and utilize—the channel members believed to be the most productive. Frequently, the intermediary channel members are in a position to "pick and choose" which manufacturer's products they wish to merchandise. If a manufacturer is not able to consistently provide the right product, at the right time, in the right quantities, and in an undamaged condition, the channel members will either end their relationship with the supplier or—at least—will not actively promote that supplier's product.

Conflict is often present between channel members and the supplier's physical distribution department. Retailers and wholesalers want to "push" the inventory-holding function back onto the manufacturer in order to reduce their own inventory holding costs. The supplier's PD department, on

---

[4] George D. Wagenheim, "Distribution as a Source of Competitive Advantage," *Annual Proceedings of the NCPDM* (1983), p. 812.

[5] For further information on marketing channels, see Louis W. Stern and Adel I. El-Ansary, *Marketing Channels*, 2nd ed. (Engelwood Cliffs, N.J.: Prentice-Hall, 1982).

the other hand, wants wholesalers and retailers to maintain large inventories.

Professor Donald Bowersox has suggested a methodology for analyzing *place decisions.* He feels that there are two basic flows between the manufacturer and the ultimate consumer. The first involves the intermediaries engaged in physically moving the product from the manufacturer to the ultimate consumer. He calls this the *exchange function.* This includes the manufacturer's physical distribution/logistics department, as well as warehouses and carriers. The second flow, the *transaction function,* is devoted exclusively to selling the product to subsequent channel members. Figure 2-2 illustrates these two functions. While the goods physically move through the exchange channel, title to, or ownership of, the goods moves through the transaction channel at approximately the same time. (Geographic, or "place," decisions regarding movement of goods through the exchange channel are covered elsewhere in this book. Place decisions involving the transactions channel are not covered in this book.) Decisions about both of these movements follow the firm's overall marketing strategy of selecting the best channel member to serve each and every market.

It is both impossible and unwise to assume that either the exchange or the transaction function is the more important. They are *mutually dependent.* If either fails, the firm will not be able to sell its products.

Figure 2-2 The Exchange and Transaction Functions

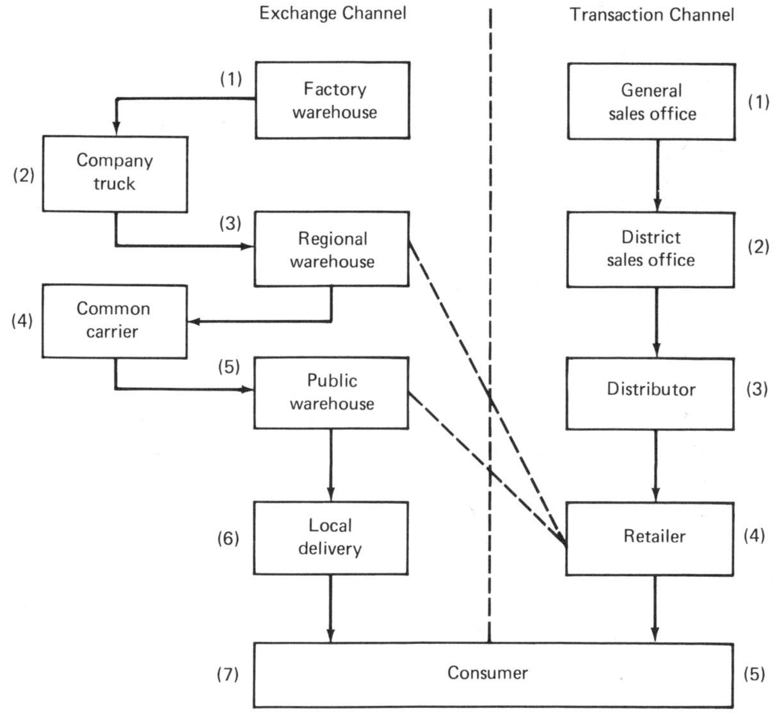

Source: Donald J. Bowersox, *Logistical Management* (New York: Macmillan Publishing Co., Inc., 1974), p. 49.

Physical Distribution and Logistics Interfaces Within the Firm   **39**

It is only good business sense to recognize that a firm cannot be profitable and grow—in fact it can be doomed—if it does not control its logistics costs.[6] Obviously, the price of a product must cover all costs associated with its production, and if a firm has serious waste in its logistics system, it will either have to pass these costs on to its customers—and thus make its price higher than its competitors—or cause the firm to reduce the quality of its product—and thus possibly lose customer loyalty.[7]

Transportation cost factors are especially important in determining the method used to quote the firm's selling price. A firm can handle its transportation costs by using one of several pricing methods, the two most common being FOB origin or a delivered-pricing system. An FOB-origin price does *not* include any transportation costs to the purchaser. With this type of pricing, the buyer is responsible for the selection of the transport mode because he or she assumes the expense of the transportation. This system of pricing is easy for the seller to administer and always yields the same net return from each sale.

FOB stands for "free on board." It comes from the days of shipping, when a price would be quoted FOB vessel, meaning the buyer had to arrange for delivery away from the ship.

A drawback of FOB-origin pricing is that it complicates marketing strategies that call for a uniform retail price for the product on a regional or national basis. Retailers are reluctant to follow the manufacturer's suggested retail price for a product because their "landed" price varies depending on the distance between them and the manufacturer. Because retailers typically have a predetermined margin based on total landed costs, the result is that each retailer has a different retail price.

Landed price includes the price of the product at the source *plus* the transportation costs to wherever it is delivered.

Another, more subtle problem is probably the most important. Donald V. Harper observed that "it may mislead the manufacturer into thinking that outbound transportation costs are of no concern to him although, in fact, they are still quite important to him to the extent that the buyer of a product is concerned with the total landed cost of the product, rather than just the price of the product alone."[8]

---

[6] See Graham Sharman, "The Rediscovery of Logistics," *Harvard Business Review* (Sept.–Oct. 1984), pp. 71–79.

[7] Edward W. Smykay, *Physical Distribution Management,* 3rd ed. (New York: Macmillan, 1973), pp. 36–37. See also, Jerome J. Wienfuss, "Distribution and Marketing Strategy Formulation," *Annual Proceedings of the NCPDM* (1983), pp. 829–831.

[8] Donald V. Harper, *Price Policy and Procedure* (New York: Harcourt, 1965), p. 208.

If the seller quotes the purchaser a price that includes both the price of the product and the transportation cost of the product to the purchaser's receiving dock, this is known as *delivered pricing*. The seller has the prerogative to select both the mode and the carrier to deliver the product.

An average amount of transportation costs is added to the cost of each product the firm makes to determine the *uniform delivered price*. The transportation component of this price reflects the cost of shipping the goods to a point that is the average distance from the seller's place of business. Buyers located relatively close to the seller's point (closer than the average) pay more than their share of freight charges. (It is said that these buyers pay *phantom freight.*) The opposite situation occurs when the buyer actually pays less freight than the seller incurs in shipping the product. This situation is known as *freight absorption* because the seller actually pays part of the transportation costs involved in the shipment. Freight absorption and phantom freight are illustrated in Figure 2-3 for shipments originating in Omaha.

Sellers find delivered pricing advantageous for several reasons. The first is that it allows a manufacturer to expand the geographic area to which his or her product is sold because distant customers in a region do not pay the full costs of transportation. Second, this system of pricing simplifies the usage of suggested retail pricing by the manufacturer. It is more feasible because each retailer in a region pays the same landed cost. Third, delivered pricing is favored by the manufacturer's salespeople because they can easily quote the total cost of the product to the buyer. Finally, product distribution is managed by the seller who can control the exchange network, making it function in a manner that is most beneficial to the firm's overall objectives.

There are also some *negative* aspects to delivered pricing systems. The first is that the firm does *not* receive the same net for each purchase because an average transportation cost rather than actual cost is added to the purchase price of each product. Second, over time, the locational "mix" of customers can change. This can be especially troublesome if sales continue to increase in the more distant markets in which the firm is already absorbing a portion of the freight charges. A problem also occurs when astute customers realize that since they are located relatively close to the vendor, they are being forced to pay phantom freight. Some sellers, to avoid alienating these customers, allow customers the option to order FOB origin if they so desire. FOB plant prices may be desired by buyers who have their own truck fleets and want to use them to pick up the seller's product. Buyers with their own truck fleets often ask vendors to quote both "FOB origin" and "delivered" prices and then decide whether to perform the haul themselves.[9]

Physical distribution managers play an important role in product pricing. They are expected to know the costs of providing various levels of customer service (see Chapter 3) and therefore must be consulted to determine the trade-offs between costs and customer service. Because many distribution costs produce per unit savings when larger volumes are handled, the physical distribution manager can also help formulate the firm's "quantity discount" pricing policies.

---

[9] See James C. Johnson and Louis E. Boone, "How Competitive Is Delivered Pricing?" *Journal of Purchasing and Materials Management* (Summer 1976), pp. 26–30.

Figure 2-3 Phantom Freight and Freight Absorption

National Single-Zone Pricing

Every customer in the U.S. pays $11 per unit.

Multiple-Zone Pricing

There are three zones, with the midwestern one paying $10.00 per unit while the east coast and west coast zones pay $11.95 per unit.

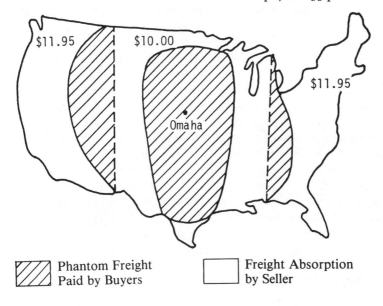

Phantom Freight Paid by Buyers

Freight Absorption by Seller

A final note about pricing involves determination of backhaul allowances, primarily in the grocery industry. Many retail grocery chains, such as Safeway, and wholesale grocery companies, such as Super Value, have extensive private truck fleets that are utilized to deliver products to their retail stores or to their customers. Prior to 1980 there was little incentive for these trucks to backhaul grocery products from food vendors. For example, assume that a Safeway truck delivered food products from a Safeway warehouse in Tucson to a Safeway store in Yuma. In most cases the truck would run empty back to Tucson to repeat the process. This was true even if there was a food supplier in Yuma that sold products to Safeway in Tucson. The reason Safeway would not backhaul the Yuma products was that there was no price advantage to Safeway. Why? Because the *Robinson–Patman Act* was generally interpreted by the Federal Trade Commission (FTC) to prevent a seller from giving a buyer a backhaul allowance for providing its own transportation. (In the great majority of cases, the grocery trade sold its products on an FOB-delivered basis.)

The FTC believed that backhaul allowances could be utilized to give buyers an unfair price advantage. Therefore, because Safeway did not receive a lower price from its vendors for backhauling, there was little incentive to engage in this type of activity. However, the 1980 *Motor Carrier Act* amended this aspect of the Robinson-Patman Act. Therefore, backhaul allowances are common today. In 1982 it is estimated that grocery backhaul allowances saved firms more than $160 million.[10] An example of this type of program involves the Borden Company. John G. Sarefield, the director of distribution for the Grocery Product Group, said, "It's nothing more than passing on to our customers a savings that we derive when our customers come in and pick up their own orders."[11] After the logistics and marketing people determined the level of backhaul allowances to be available to their customers, Sarefield was involved in educating the firm's sales force—both their own sales people and independent brokers—about how the backhaul program worked. Sarefield declared:

> We knew going in that most sales people were not transportation experts—we didn't expect them to be. But we did hear from our customers about their problems with untrained sales reps wasting the buyers' and the merchandisers' time. We were determined not to let that happen to our program. We held extensive training sessions designed to make our brokers the best informed sales organization in the food industry on the subject of backhaul. As a result, we haven't had customers complaining that our people don't know how to sell backhaul.[12]

Product Decisions

The most important interface between the firm's production and physical distribution/logistics departments is to insure that the product itself arrives where and when it is needed in an undamaged state. If this objective is not met, a *stock-out* may occur. There are three possible outcomes when a stock-out takes place. The first is that the retail customer is extremely brand loyal and refuses to purchase a substitute. This customer will wait until the stock-out has been corrected. A second and more likely event is that the customer

---

[10] Nancy Entwisle, "Super Market Strategies: Grocery Trucking Comes Full Circle," *Distribution* (Feb. 1984), p. 54.

[11] "Borden's Aggressive Backhaul Program," *Distribution* (Feb. 1984), p. 58.

[12] Ibid.

purchases a substitute product. However, when that substitute product needs replacing, the customer goes back to the original brand. The third potential outcome is when the customer purchases a competitor's substitute product and later decides he or she *prefers* the competitors product.

Both the production and physical distribution/logistics departments must agree on protective packaging and other materials-handling procedures that will result in a minimum of product damage. The subject of freight loss and damage control is discussed in Chapters 5 and 6, and protective packaging is covered in Chapter 10. At this time, note Figure 2-4, which shows a packaging-marketing-distribution interface.

Promotional Activities

Many situations require close coordination between the promotion department and physical distribution/logistics personnel. One important situation, a PD/L support function, concerns the availability of highly advertised products, such as "specials." Marketing experts contend that few things are more damaging to a firm's good will than being stocked-out of an item that is being heavily promoted in a large sales campaign. Another involves quantities being sold in large lots, such as cases. Peter R. Attwood, a British consultant, related the following situation, which would be amusing if it weren't so serious:

> An example to illustrate the need for unified planning concerns an American manufacturer who ran a massive sales promotion campaign a few years ago. Customers were given a large discount for orders requiring twenty-five cases of goods at one time. It had been planned that this discount would be covered by the savings from processing large orders. Unfortunately, the campaign flopped, because distribution costs increased out of proportion. These increases were due to handling in uneconomic batches, because a pallet load of goods comprised twenty-four cases.[13]

The physical distribution system is not simply a neutral factor in promotion. Outstanding distribution is a positive selling point. This is especially true for such commodities as paper products. For example, the Scott Paper Company continually monitors the size of shipments being sent to its customers. Whenever it appears that a relatively small increase in an order will substantially lower the freight charge per unit, the sales department is notified.[14]

The opposite happens too often. As Professors Sampson and Farris have pointed out, sales personnel always prefer to sell large orders but will sell in a smaller quantity if they cannot get a larger order. If the traffic department establishes too many esoteric rules about minimum order sizes, consolidated shipments, and the like, the sales people will simply ignore these rules.[15]

[13] Peter R. Attwood, *Planning a Distribution System* (London: Gower, 1971), p. 55.

[14] Janet Bosworth, "What Does a Traffic Manager Do?" *Distribution Worldwide* (March 1971).

[15] Roy J. Sampson and Martin T. Farris, *Domestic Transportation: Practice, Theory and Policy*, 3rd ed. (Boston: Houghton, 1975), p. 294.

Figure 2-4 A Product Protection Program

AS PART OF a continuing program designed to insure that its customers receive the best quality possible when they purchase its electric and gas appliances, the Caloric Corporation, a subsidiary of Raytheon Company, undertook a complete finished goods packaging evaluation program in 1971.

Top management initiated and gave its full support to the program, assigning to Paul A. Cloutier, packaging engineer, the task of organizing and coordinating it. His first step was to call a meeting of the company's major packaging material suppliers to discuss the aims and requirements of this program. All suppliers agreed to submit to a competitive design procedure whenever a new or revised package was needed. The following criteria were established:

1. Vendors would be furnished with finished goods samples whenever required.

2. They would be advised of ancillary packaging requirements as well as the testing parameters which had to be met.

3. Vendors could submit as many concepts as they desired.

4. All concepts and samples had to be submitted within 15 days from receipt of prototypes.

5. In addition to testing requirements, the proposed concept had to be able to withstand testing equivalent to double (X2) that required by the National Safe Transit Committee.

6. The proposed concept had to be priced competitively.

7. Vendor submitting the winning concept would be guaranteed a full year as sole supplier of the required material.

Next step was to talk to the Quality Assurance and Consumer Relations departments, which are in close contact with Caloric's sales force and its service people, as well as in direct contact with end product users. A letter from the company's president is included with every item shipped. It invites direct customer comment of the product, including its packaging. A review of such records and the "Product Quality Reports," which are a communication medium between the field and the factory, was instituted to determine the most pressing protective packaging problem area. This turned out to involve the "built-in" product line.

Two specific problems were discovered concerning built-in units. First, oven door kits, which are shipped separately from the ranges, were experiencing a high rate of enamel chippage. At the time, Caloric was using an expensive combination of molded Styrofoam end caps and accordian-pleated inserts within a corrugated carton. Subjecting these kits to the standard NSTC preshipment test indicated the packaged product could not pass the prescribed drop test. Inspection of the dropped kits revealed exactly the damage pattern being evidenced in the field.

Sample kits were taken to the company's vendors, and specific parameters were established. Two vendors submitted samples, and testing began immediately. End result was an all-new corrugated package able to withstand repeated drops from 36 inches. Two side benefits were realized: The overall size of the exterior container, a 200-pound test, C-flute, full overlap carton, was reduced by one-fourth, and a substantial material and labor savings also resulted.

Sales people in the high-volume areas were then contacted and advised of the changes. A group of test shipments were set up under control conditions, and arrangements were made for personal follow-up.

"The test shipment results were outstanding," reports Mr. Cloutier, "and not one of the kits in the new package was damaged, while 25% of those in the old one were. Since we started using the new package, we have shipped in excess of 12,000 kits and have had only 43 cases of reported damage."

Source: Lowell E. Perrine, "A Product Protection Program," *Traffic Management* (April 1973), pp. 44–45.

Inbound Logistics and MRP

In Chapter 1 we implied that traffic functions become subordinate to physical distribution functions. This is true, but in many instances it only applies to outbound shipments. For many firms, the logistics management problem associated with inbound materials is as important—if not more important—than that of outbound products. Sometimes managing movement of materials between various plants of the same firm is a major undertaking. Figure 2-5 shows the travels of raw materials that eventually become a DuPont toothbrush. The movements to the DuPont Texas plant are classified as inbound raw materials. Responsibility for coordinating these moves is shared by the firm's purchasing and production staffs. The moves from the Texas operations to West Virginia and then to Massachusetts involve company-owned material in semiprocessed form. These moves are under the direction of the traffic and production departments. Finally, the movements of finished product from the DuPont Massachusetts plant are classified as being physical distribution.

Traditionally, a firm's traffic department handled inbound, interplant, and outbound shipments. With the historical emphasis on production efficiency, inbound and interplant shipments were both considered to be of higher priority than were outbound shipments destined for customers. In many firms, one of the bureaucratic struggles that occurred when the PD/L concept gained acceptance was between marketing and traffic. The traffic department had to be convinced that outbound shipments were fully as important as inbound and interplant movements.

The initial emphasis of PD/L thinking had dealt with the outbound flows of finished products, but more recently the concepts have been broadened to include concern for inbound movements. Part of the reason for this has been the substantial increases in costs of transportation that made it necessary for firms to coordinate inbound and outbound movements of freight and thus increase their utilization of transportation equipment. Second, many of the operational research tools devised for improving control over outbound movements were adaptable to inbound movements, and vice versa. Third, for interplant transfers of semiprocessed goods or for regular shipments to customers, an obvious overlap developed in the activities of individuals trying to schedule movements to the shippers' advantage and others trying to schedule the same shipments to meet the receivers' needs.

A classic area of conflict between production and physical distribution/logistics regards the length of production runs. Production managers prefer long runs in order to minimize the "down" time between runs when the equipment is being retooled. PD/L personnel, while appreciating large runs from a transportation savings point of view, must consider the ramifications of the increased inventory holding costs that also result. The longer the product run, the greater the average length of time between the manufacturing of the product and its ultimate sale. As will be discussed in Chapter 7, inventory holding costs can be very substantial, often running 25 per cent per year of the value of the products and even higher in times of extremely high rates of interest.

Figure 2-5 From Doorstep to Doorstep: The Travels of a Toothbrush

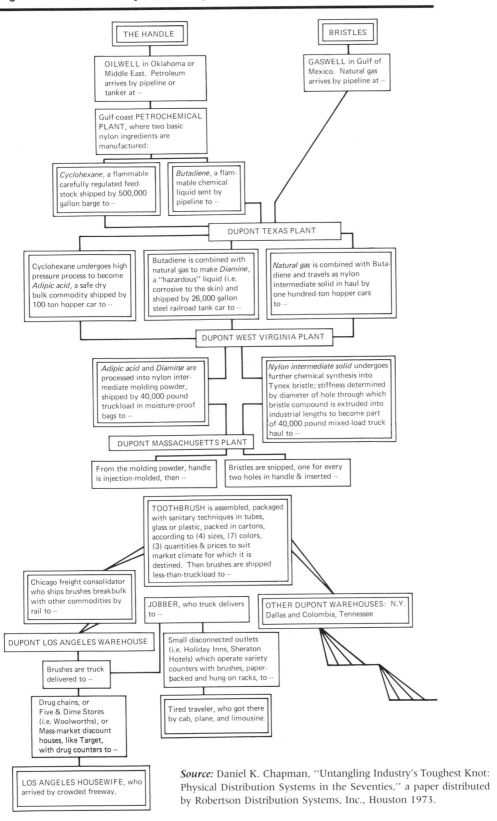

Source: Daniel K. Chapman, "Untangling Industry's Toughest Knot: Physical Distribution Systems in the Seventies," a paper distributed by Robertson Distribution Systems, Inc., Houston 1973.

Production scheduling is carried out at a fairly high level of management within the firm. Customer orders and sales forecasts determine what should be made and when. A bill of materials for all components and subassemblies needed to manufacture the desired item is drawn up. Orders are placed with vendors with delivery dates specified.

MRP is a computer-assisted method of managing production inventory, whereas distribution requirements planning (DRP) uses computer techniques to minimize inventory levels for manufactured/finished products. When MRP and DRP are combined, they provide a carefully monitored system of inventory control from when the firm receives production inputs from its vendors to when finished products are sold to customers.[16] DRP will be examined in Chapter 7, in the division of inventory control of finished products.

MRP recognizes that the demand for all components and subassemblies depends upon final demand for the finished product. "The basis of the MRP approach in a multiple-stage operation is the recognition that the demand for the finished product may be uncertain but there is no need to treat the demand for parts and subassemblies as being uncertain," and after "the planner establishes the number of finished items he wants to have available in future weeks . . ., he can establish exactly how many of each subassembly and part he will need and when he needs it."[17]

Traditionally firms have maintained substantial quantities of production inputs during the production cycle. These inventories were believed necessary as buffer stock because of slow deliveries or unexpected surges in demand for specific products. MRP directly challenges this concept: it maintains that very limited production inputs are required to have an efficient system that can respond to most production situations.[18] First, the firm establishes its master production schedule (MPS). This is based on a sales forecast or it may be generated from orders that have already been received. From the MPS a bill of materials (BOM) can be ascertained, which are the specific inputs required to produce the products called for in the MPS. Remember that, when producing a number of products simultaneously, there is a strong likelihood that the same component will be utilized in a number of different products. Therefore, a computer is typically necessary to keep track of the exact number of parts required for all products to be produced during a particular time period, typically one week. The computer thus "explodes" the production inputs needed for each product and then "aggregates" each part needed for all products to be produced during each MRP cycle. This MRP planning cycle takes place a number of weeks prior to the actual production. At this point, the firm places orders with its vendors for production inputs, and delivery is scheduled for arrival just before the inputs

---

[16] James Aaron Cooke, "A Dynamic Approach to Distribution," *Traffic Management* (July 1983), pp. 55–58.

[17] Alan J. Stenger and Joseph L. Cavinato, "Adapting MRP to the Outbound Side—Distribution Requirements Planning," *Production and Inventory Management* (Fourth Quarter 1979), p. 1.

[18] This discussion relies heavily on Donald W. Dobler, Lamar Lee, and David N. Burt, *Purchasing and Materials Management*, 4th ed. (New York: McGraw-Hill, 1984), pp. 245–247 and 272–278.

are required in the production process. If the firm manufacturers its own inputs, they are scheduled to be produced so that they are available shortly before the final assembly of the finished product.

Professors John C. Anderson and Roger G. Schroeder have surveyed MRP users and they estimate that MRP is currently being utilized by over one thousand firms and that the number is growing rapidly.[19] However, the degree of satisfaction is less universal. The professors found that less than 10 per cent of all MRP users were receiving full benefits from the concept. About 30 per cent of respondents reported that they were achieving "good" results from MRP, but less than had been expected. Finally, more than half of the MRP users contacted in the survey noted that they received at best modest or no benefits from MRP. What explains this lack of success in many companies? Anderson and Schroeder have concluded the following:

> MRP requires different policies and a new set of values for management. The system is seen only as a means to an end. The computer system and production and inventory control functions are not the heart of material requirements planning. Rather, these are only the tools for formalizing and systematizing a new way of managerial planning and control. MRP is a concept of management which must focus on the need to change the way decisions are made and the resulting manufacturing philosophy. Looking at MRP as a concept requires that we go beyond systems and engage the various functions of the business in this process. Putting together a crack technical team, buying a Cadillac software system, and focusing on production and inventory control is not sufficient. Decisions relating to plans, activities, and priorities of the entire business must be engaged in a team effort.
>
> Without this commitment to concept, we have accomplished little short of spending a great deal of money and time creating a tool that has merely the potential of being used. Performance is not improved, and may even be decreased because of the preoccupation with the system itself. Not enough companies have paid the price to implement MRP as a concept. This is a major force, we believe, behind MRP failures.[20]

Figure 2-6 presents a case study of a firm that successfully implemented an MRP system. A firm's logistics staff fits into the production scheduling and MRP processes in at least three ways. First, order processing (a PD/L function to be discussed in Chapter 3) often gives the firm its most accurate data regarding actual sales. This information can be read by skilled market analysts in a manner similar to that of a physician listening to a pulse or heartbeat. For example, Snap-on Tools Corporation receives orders from its branches via WATS telephone lines. The information on the order forms is processed so that goods will be shipped and, of interest here, the data on the order are fed into the firm's forecasting equations and then into its master production scheduling process. This then triggers raw materials purchase orders for materials needed to either manufacture the precise items that the

---

[19] John C. Anderson and Roger G. Schroeder, "Getting Results from Your MRP System," *Business Horizons* (May–June 1984), p. 57.
[20] Ibid., p. 59.

Figure 2-6 A Case Study of a Successful Application of MRP

Company X is a $100-million-a-year company engaged in the manufacture of light industrial equipment. About five years ago Company X decided to implement an MRP system. As a first step the company sent its top management—the president, the V.P. of manufacturing, the chief engineer, and the data processing manager—to a one-week school to gain a better understanding of MRP concepts. After returning, the president appointed a task force to develop an implementation plan for the MRP system. The task force consisted of representatives from manufacturing, purchasing, data processing, and engineering. The vice president of manufacturing chaired the task force and held weekly progress meetings. After three months the task force had developed a plan to implement the system over eighteen months. These steps included purchase of software, updating the company's bills of materials, revising the inventory records, and improving the accuracy of routings. The plan also specified a complete educational program, provided by outside and inside personnel, for shop personnel, purchasing, and production and inventory control people. The plan specified results to be achieved by the MRP system, including data accuracy specifications, inventory turnover improvements, delivery lead times, and delivery performance goals. Finally, the plan stated who would be responsible for each part of the implementation plan and the frequency of review by top management.

The plan was approved by senior management and put into effect. A key principle was active weekly involvement by the vice president of manufacturing who set this project as his number two priority, second only to continued manufacture of the product. Senior management also committed the necessary resources. All members of the task force were assigned full time to the project and funds were provided for software, hardware, and training.

After eighteen months the MRP system was up and running on the computer with reasonably accurate data. Management realized, however, that full benefits from the system were not being achieved since the master schedule was a "wish list" developed by marketing and not a true manufacturing plan. Although materials were being brought in the door at the right time, the plant was still expediting on the shop floor to get the orders out and to keep final assembly loaded.

At this point, management decided to continue system implementation by adding capacity planning and shop floor control. The same implementation task force and planning effort was used and another eighteen months was required to get these additional systems up and running. After three years, management now had the capability to load the shop in advance and to release and monitor orders on the shop floor.

Next, a management policy decision was made to load the master schedule only to available capacity. This was accomplished in two ways: first, all orders were frozen inside the production lead time, unless parts had been planned in advance for insurance. Second, marketing was instructed to check with manufacturing before promising delivery due dates. Once manufacturing accepted the due date, it was their job to get the order out on time. It took another year to iron out all of these policy changes and to eliminate the hot lists and expeditors from the shop. After four years, Company X had progressed to a class A MRP user.

Results in Company X were quite dramatic. Inventory turns increased from 3.2 per year to 6.5, on-time delivery performance increased from 75 percent to 95 percent, lead time was reduced from twelve to eight weeks, and shop throughput was increased from $8 million to $10 million per month in sales. All of this was accomplished with an investment of $450,000 in software, hardware, training, and personnel time.

Source: John C. Anderson and Roger G. Schroeder," Getting Results From Your MRP System," BUSINESS HORIZONS (May–June, 1984), pp. 61–62. Reprinted with permission.

customer has just ordered or to replenish stocks that will be depleted once his order is filled.[21]

Second, the logistics staff is concerned with scheduling and managing inbound products that have unique handling or storage characteristics. The logistics staff might also have contingency plans for finding and moving critical parts in cases where the initial source of supply proves to be inadequate or unsatisfactory. An example of this deals with Ford Motor Company's problems in 1964 of keeping up with demands for the newly introduced Ford Mustangs. The Ford plant in San Jose

> was nearly out of a certain part which was necessary to the assembly of the car. A rush order was placed to a plant in the midwest which supplied this part. Because of the necessity of having the shipment arrive quickly, it was sent by air freight to the West Coast. An order clerk who was responsible for assigning the destination of the order got confused and had it placed on a plane going to Los Angeles where Ford also has a large plant. By the time San Jose realized that the parts were in LA, time was running so short they were forced to charter a plane to Los Angeles which delivered the parts to the Oakland airport. Time was so critical that a helicopter was chartered from Oakland to deliver the parts to the San Jose plant. After all this confusion and expense, a shutdown was avoided by less than one hour!
>
> These are the types of emergencies that make a logistics expert a little nervous.[22]

Third, the logistics staff is responsible for all movements of materials between a firm's various plants and warehouses. For the toothbrush example shown on Figure 2-5, this would include movements from the DuPont plant in Texas, to its plant in West Virginia, to its plant in Massachusetts, and to its Los Angeles warehouse.

A longer-range issue in which production and logistics staffs must work together concerns warehouse and plant location. As will be examined in Chapter 8, a major input in any plant location decision is the cost of transportation. The structure of the transportation industry, which is examined in Chapters 4, 5, and 6, reveals a highly intricate system that can have substantial impact on facility location decisions.

Recycling: Its Impact on a Firm's Logistics

The interest in the recycling—reuse—of materials started as a protest against our "throwaway" society with its empty beverage containers littering the landscape. In the decade of the 1970s, recycling obtained more of an eco-

---

[21] "Fitting It All Together," *Handling and Shipping Management Presidential Issue,* 1978–1979, pp. 4–9.

[22] M. S. McLaughlin, "Problems of Success," *Business Logistics in America* (Stanford, Calif.: Stanford Graduate School of Business, 1968), pp. 282–283.

nomic rationale when it was discovered that use of recycled materials could reduce significantly our economy's use of energy.

> Recycling aluminum, steel, and copper scrap, compared with processing virgin ores, results in energy savings of approximately 90 percent. Processing aluminum takes only 4 per cent of the energy required to form bauxite into aluminum. Also consider that when 1,000 tons of steel ore are produced from scrap, rather than from virgin ore, the following benefits occur: 6.7 million gallons of water are saved because water usage is reduced from 16.6 million to 9.9 million gallons; 104 tons of air pollution effluent are avoided because pollutant discharges are reduced from 121 to 17 tons; and 2,754 tons of mining waste are avoided as these wastes are reduced from 2,828 tons to 64 tons. Another source states that every ton of steel scrap returned to the steel mills conserves 1½ tons of iron ore, a ton of coke, and a half ton of limestone.[23]

The value of—and necessity for—recycling is becoming more fully recognized by managers of business. It is mentioned here because of both its importance and the fact that—when used—it modifies (or creates additional) channels through which materials flow and goods are marketed. In some instances, recycling may also create additional competition for sales of the firm's product (for example, recapped tires compete with new tires).

Sometimes, recycling is carried on completely within a firm with the result being that additional arrows must be drawn on charts showing the flow of a firm's inbound materials and outbound products. Figure 2-7 shows the same information as depicted in Figure 1-1. We show some additional flows which might take place if the firms began instituting some internal recycling procedures.

Example A shows the recycling of a retail product. A real-world example is old loaves of bread that have not yet been sold at their end-of-shelf-life date. This bread is removed from the shelves, returned through reverse channels to a facility near the "finished goods inventory," where it is further dried, cut up into small cubes, packaged as croutons, and placed again into the firm's outbound new products channels.

> Packages of food products, film, and other perishable items often have a printed expiration date, beyond which they are not to be considered as possessing "top" quality. This is their *shelf life.*

Example B shows the recycling of glass beverage bottles. In this instance the firm has two sources of bottles: the bottle manufacturer and used bottles returned through the reverse distribution channels (or bottle collection).

Example C shows the re-use of pallets between the plant creating subassemblies and the main factory. Drivers returning to the subassembly plant are expected to return with as many empty pallets as pallets they had deliv-

---

[23] Vincent G. Reuter, "Management Tools for Materials Conservation," *Production and Inventory Management* (Fourth Quarter 1979), pp. 54–55.

Figure 2-7 Completed Diagram of Flow of Inbound and Outbound Movements

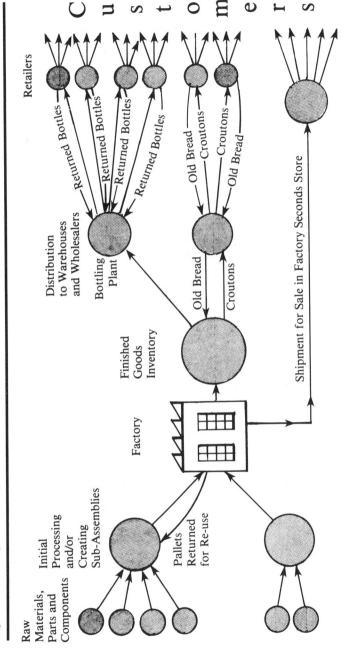

Source: Adapted from Richard A. Lancioni, "The Physical Distribution Concept and Its Implementation," in *Papers, NCPDM Annual Meeting,* 1978 (Chicago): 102; and Alan J. Stenger and Joseph L. Cavinato, "Adapting MRP to the Outbound Side," in *Production and Inventory Management* (Fall 1979):2–4.

53

ered loaded to the factory. The shipping dock foreman at the subassembly plant has two pallet sources: the pallet manufacturer and the pallets that drivers bring back. If the returned pallets are damaged, the foreman can either buy new pallets or assign a worker the task of repairing them.

> *Pallets* are usually flat wooden racks, 40 inches by 48 inches, upon which cargo is piled and strapped.

Example D, another form of recycling, shows the results of a decision to market factory "seconds" through a special store. In this instance, the product might be clothes, and the seconds may be products that did not pass final inspection because of stains or minor defects in the fabric. This factory seconds store bypasses the firm's conventional exchange and transaction channels and, to a limited degree, competes with them.

Sometimes a firm may rely on other firms that specialize in buying scrap materials suitable for recycling. Some of these firms also buy sorted waste products of factories, warehouses, and offices. Markets exist for buying used metals, glass, paper, rubber, plastics, and wood.

While recycling can present a firm many attractive possibilities, it can be troublesome. One problem is handling. Recycled products must be separated into and maintained as different groups or grades, and each grade must be relatively free of other materials. For example, there are five grades of used glass and nearly seventy grades of used paper and paper stock.

Rising prices of recyclable materials make it increasingly desirable for a firm to "manage" its flow of recyclable materials. This process occurs throughout the entire production and distribution network and must become an additional concern of managers at all levels. In a sense, the one-time scrap is assembled, baled, placed on the firm's shipping dock, sold, and loaded aboard the recycler's trucks in a manner similar to that by which many of the firm's other—more major—products are handled.

Financial and Accounting Interfaces

The PD/L departments constantly interface with both the financial and accounting departments. A key reason for this interdependency is that distribution and logistics managers' decisions are only as good as the quality of the cost data with which they are working. The finance staff, which is always predicting future cash flows, may be dependent upon the PD/L staff for information concerning the status of finished products that are somewhere between the end of the firm's production line and the purchaser's receiving dock.

The finance staff often is charged with the responsibility of allocating the firm's limited funds to projects desired by the various operating departments. Finance personnel use several methods such as the return on invested capital method to determine which projects should be funded.[24]

Assume, for example, that the physical distribution department wants to purchase pallet storage racks that allow loaded pallets to be stored higher since they are not resting on the pallets below them. While the racks and their installation will cost $10,000, it will allow the firm to avoid using additional public warehouse space that would cost $2,000 per year. Therefore, the pallet racks yield an annual return on invested capital of 20 per cent. If this project has a relatively high enough return on invested capital, compared with all other investment opportunities being considered, the finance department will authorize this expenditure.[25]

PD/L personnel are constantly interacting with the accounting department. Dr. Michael Schiff, of New York University, was commissioned by the NCPDM to study and write a report regarding suggestions as to how accounting can assist PD/L. The final report, entitled *Accounting and Control in Physical Distribution Management,* stated that at present most data required for efficient control of PD/L were already available. The problem was that the required information was scattered in many sundry accounts and difficult to assemble. Schiff argued that the best procedure would involve a controller (senior accountant) who would work directly for the manager of the physical distribution/logistics department. This person would then assemble the accounting data for presentation and analysis by the senior physical distribution executives.[26]

In mid-1981, the NCPDM, in conjunction with the National Association of Accountants, announced they were undertaking a study of "the status of accounting and control over inbound and outbound transportation activities." These two groups contracted with Ernst and Whinney and Cleveland Consulting Associates to conduct the required research. The study was completed in 1983 and was entitled *Transportation Accounting and Control: Guidelines for Distribution and Financial Management.* The study indicated that a continuing problem, as noted already by Professor Schiff, was that the required accounting information, although generally available somewhere in the firm, was often scattered in many different departments. Gene R. Tyndall, project manager for Ernst and Whinney's Transportation and Distribution Consulting Group, noted: "I think the single most important message that emerged is that you have to know your transportation costs before you can do something about them. There are major opportunities in all industries to do a better job of transportation financial management."[27] The report concluded that responsibility to ensure good financial decisions rested

[24] See John T. Mentzer, "A Modeling Approach to Strategic Distribution Planning: The Logistics, Marketing and Financial Interfaces," *Annual Proceeding of the NCPDM* (1981), pp. 193–201.

[25] For a good discussion of the preparation of a return on investment report, see Creed H. Jenkins, *Modern Warehouse Management* (New York: McGraw-Hill, 1968).

[26] Michael Schiff, *Accounting and Control in Physical Distribution Management* (Chicago: NCPDM, 1971).

[27] Francis J. Quinn, "Don't Be Afraid of Accounting," *Traffic Management* (Nov. 1983), p. 45.

on *both* logistics and financial executives working together to achieve a data base so that logistical decisions could be based on full and complete financial/accounting data.

Accounting systems that are attuned to the needs of physical distribution/logistics can be extremely beneficial.[28] George L. Stern reports that in many cases effective physical distribution (supported by proper accounting reports) can switch a sales territory from operating in the "red" to one in the "black." In one situation a firm consolidated orders into a sales territory, and it was able to produce a 25 per cent freight savings.[29] In addition, accounting can help to determine the cost of lost sales resulting from a stockout of the firm's product. Also, they can provide valuable inputs in establishing a zone-type delivered pricing system.

Accounting is a powerful tool for controlling a firm's operations. This is discussed in more detail in Chapter 14, which deals with physical distribution/logistics system controls.

PD/L Firms

At the risk of oversimplification, this book is written to make it appear that PD/L functions are performed within a firm. In many cases this is true. However, there are some exceptions and they will be mentioned briefly here. First, there are firms that contract to perform physical distribution/logistics services for others.[30] One such firm is Martin-Brower, which handles all distribution functions for food chains such as McDonalds and Baskins Robbins. Martin-Brower operates hundreds of tractors and trailers and also controls the inventory levels for their customers. The firm also handles purchasing, pricing, sales analysis, and planning functions for its clients.

Public warehouse personnel perform many assembly and distributing functions and in some states also perform deliveries. These channel members act as intermediaries between a manufacturer and the ultimate consumer. Some intermediaries perform more PD/L functions for the manufacturer than do others. And, of course, for doing this, they expect to be additionally compensated.

Chapter 11, which deals with international distribution, will discuss additional types of firms that specialize in handling all or portions of a firm's overseas distribution operations.

Summary

This chapter examined the fundamental interfaces between logistics, physical distribution, and the other functional areas of the firm. An important relationship exists between marketing and physical distribution. There are

[28] See Ron E. Cummings, "Monitoring Distribution Cost Service Performance," *Annual Proceedings of the NCPDM* (1982), pp. 625–651.

[29] George L. Stern, "Traffic: Clear Signals for Higher Profits," *Harvard Business Review* (May–June 1972), p. 79.

[30] See Richard C. Norris, "The Components of a Fully Integrated Physical Distribution Service," *Annual Proceedings of the NCPDM* (1983), pp. 778–789.

four basic aspects of the marketing mix: place, price, product and promotion.

Place decisions involve channels of distribution and physical distribution. Place decisions can be thought of as either part of the *exchange* function or as part of the *transaction* function.

Pricing activities are affected by physical distribution costs. The firm's products can be sold either FOB origin or a delivered pricing system can be used. Because an average amount of freight is added to each product sold in the zone, *phantom freight* and *freight absorption* are encountered. Since 1980, determination of backhaul allowances has become another important pricing activity that must be jointly determined by marketing and logistics executives.

Product decision interfaces involve insuring that the product arrives at its destination at the right time, in the correct quantities, and in an undamaged condition. If this objective is achieved, a *stock-out* can be avoided.

Promotional activities center around assuring that when highly advertised "specials" are held, the products involved will be physically available in the stores to meet customers demand.

The logistics function interfaces with purchasing and production activities. Logistics staff assist the purchasing department in arranging for the most advantageous transportation of the inputs into the production facility. Production and logistics staffs are primarily responsible for new plant and warehouse location analysis. MRP is another interface between production and logistics personnel. MRP offers great potential to reduce the inventory levels required for production, but at present it has often achieved less than optimum results because top management has not supported the concept with sufficient commitment.

Many firms are becoming more involved in recycling activities. This is done either within the firm or is contracted to specialized firms. In either event, additional "flows" of materials and products are created.

The finance department is often responsible for deciding what capital expenditures should be authorized by the firm each fiscal year. Therefore, whenever PD/L personnel request capital improvements, they must work closely with the financial people.

In the past the accounting department and physical distribution group have not supported each other properly. Effective accounting systems can help allocate sales incentive programs, develop delivered pricing systems, and help "control" PD activities.

Questions for Discussion and Review

1. PD/L necessarily interfaces with all the other functional areas of the firm. Which interaction do you believe is: (a) the *most* important? (b) the *least* important?
2. Discuss briefly each of the four basic aspects of the marketing mix and how *each* interfaces with the physical distribution department.
3. It has been suggested by many marketing executives that PD/L activities are really a subpart of the overall marketing function. Take a position regarding this issue and argue your case.

4. How can PD/L activities provide positive sales-generating situations? Discuss.
5. What is a channel of distribution? What is the relationship between it and PD?
6. Compare and contrast the *exchange* function versus the *transaction* function.
7. Regarding the exchange and the transaction functions, which do you believe is ultimately the more important to the long-run success of the firm? Defend your answer.
8. What does FOB-origin imply? What are the *pluses* and *minuses* of using this type of a pricing system? Discuss.
9. Are there any viable alternatives to FOB-origin pricing? If so, discuss them briefly.
10. What is the basic theory or rationale of zone pricing? Why is it done, and what information is necessary to implement such a pricing system?
11. Discuss briefly the concepts of phantom freight and freight absorption.
12. It is often said that zone pricing systems have the potential to produce customer ill will. Discuss why there may be validity to this statement.
13. The importance of coordinating PD with product decisions is well known. Discuss briefly why this situation is true.
14. Does PD interface with the firm's promotional activities? How, if at all?
15. Discuss the basic interfaces between inbound logistics and the production department?
16. What is MRP? Discuss the interface between MRP, purchasing, and logistics.
17. Many firms that have utilized MRP have experienced problems. Discuss why this situation took place.
18. Discuss factors responsible for successful implementation of an MRP system.
19. What is a backhaul allowance? Why have they become more important in recent years?
20. Discuss the relationship between recycling and a firm's logistical operation.
21. What activity is typically assigned to the finance group that directly affects PD activities? Discuss.
22. Discuss a number of situations in which PD/L and accounting can assist each other in performing more efficiently.
23. What is a PD firm? Are they very common? Discuss.

Additional Chapter References

Abrahams, Sanford. "Managing Change in Distribution and Transportation Carrier Corporation: A Case History." *Annual Proceedings of the NCPDM* (1982), pp. 331–354

Ayers, Allan F. "Improving Productivity Through MRP." *Annual Proceedings of the NCPDM* (1982), pp. 455–472.

Beimborn, Edward A., Robert P. Schmitt, and Julie P. Weitman. "Techniques for Effective Transportation Information Transfer." *Annual Proceedings of the Transportation Research Forum* (1982), pp. 524–531.

Bodrie, Gerald E. "Logistics Strategy Development at General Motors." *Annual Proceedings of the NCPDM* (1983), pp. 485–500.

Drumm, William H. "Economics of Distribution: Changing Distribution Strategies." *Annual Proceedings of the NCPDM* (1982), pp. 665–680.

Dunn, Richard L. *Practical Purchasing Management* (Barrington, Ill.: Purchasing World, 1984.)

Fischer, E. F. "Electronic Business Data Interchange (EBDI)." *Annual Proceedings of the NCPDM* (1984), pp. 707–716.

Haverly, Richard C. "Survey of Software for Physical Distribution." *Annual Proceedings of the NCPDM* (1984), pp. 717–886.

Heise, Fred H., Jr. "Integrated Logistics Management: Chemical Industry Issues." *Annual Proceedings of the NCPDM* (1982), pp. 275–280.

Hutchinson, Win. "Bar Coding for Data Entry—A User's Perspective." *Annual Proceedings of the NCPDM* (1984), pp. 461–463.

Lynagh, Peter M., and Richard F. Poist. "Managing Physical Distribution/Marketing Interface Activities: Cooperation or Conflict?" *Transportation Journal* (Spring 1984), pp. 36–43.

Meyburg, Arnim H., and Alfred M. Lee. "Electronic Message Transfer: The Impact on USPS Resource Requirements." *Annual Proceedings of the Transportation Research Forum* (1982), pp. 532–540.

Miller, John A. "Survey of Software for Physical Distribution." *Annual Proceedings of the NCPDM* (1983), pp. 35–170.

Miller, Robert W. "Managing the Physical Distribution Department's Human Resource for Strategic Results." *Annual Proceedings of the NCPDM* (1982), pp. 595–610.

MRP II Implementation and Operations Handbook Abstract (Hunt Valley, Md.: R. F. Alban, 1982).

Nelson, Gene R. "Electronic Data Interchange Developments in Distribution: WINS—Warehouse Information Network Standards." *Annual Proceedings of the NCPDM* (1984), pp. 427–436.

O'Neill, William J., John H. Campbell, and Masao Nishi. "Maximizing Distribution's Contribution to Corporate Performance: Major Messages from the 1983 Logistics Resource Forum." *Annual Proceedings of the NCPDM* (1983), pp. 317–330.

Parsons, Kathleen J. "Verification: The Key to Successful Bar Coding Systems." *Annual Proceedings of the NCPDM* (1984), pp. 437–446.

Pilnick, Saul, Jo Ellen Gable, and Michael Julian. "Line Supervisors." *Annual Proceedings of the NCPDM* (1984), pp. 527–534.

Pollock, Ted. "Integrated Logistics Management In the Food Industry." *Annual Proceedings of the NCPDM* (1982), pp. 247–274.

Ruetten, James E. "Developing, Articulating and Implementing a Physical Distribution Strategy." *Annual Proceedings of the NCPDM* (1983), pp. 501–508.

Strickler, Charles P., Omar Keith Helferich, Patrick Gallagher, and Craig M. Gustin. "How to Publicize Your Distribution Accomplishments." *Annual Proceedings of the NCPDM* (1984), pp. 585–602.

Voorhees, Roy Dale, John C. Coppett, and Eileen M. Kelley. "Telelogistics: A Management Tool for the Logistic Problems of the 1980s." *Transportation Journal* (Summer 1984), pp. 62–70.

Weinfuss, Jerome J. "Distribution and Marketing Strategy Formulation."
Annual Proceedings of the NCPDM (1983), pp. 814–835.

CASE 2-1

Eden Prairie Industries

Eden Prairie Industries was located in Eden Prairie, West Virginia. The firm manufactured "hard hats"—reinforced plastic and metal protective hats used by construction workers and other people who need head protection from falling objects.

Emil (Slim) Souba is the director of logistics for Eden Prairie. The firm is privately owned and had sales of $23 million in 1984. Although 1984 had been a disappointing year in regard to sales, the five-year average increase in annual sales was 14 per cent.

September 1, 1985, was approaching, and Slim did not look forward to the annual ritual of preparing his request for new equipment and other long-term projects. In prior years they were almost automatically approved if the requests seemed "reasonable." This year, however, two factors were different. Because business had not been as good as expected, there were fewer capital (long-term) project dollars available for 1986. Second, in an attempt to increase overall productivity, there were many more requests—companywide—for long-term capital expenditures than the firm could fund.

All 1986 capital budget requests had to be submitted to Patricia Johnson, vice-president of accounting and finance, by September 1. Pat told Slim that projects were ranked by using the "average payback" technique. Slim remembered that his college PD/L text contained a description of the payback method. That night, at home, he found the old text, blew the dust off of it and read:

> *Average Payback Period.* This is another commonly used capital budgeting technique. It is the average number of years required to recover the initial investment. The average payback period formula is:

$$\text{Average payback period} = \frac{\text{Cost of investment}}{\text{Average annual cash inflow or average annual cash savings}}$$

As Slim put the book down, he hoped the recession would soon be over because he did not like to have to formally "justify" his capital budget requests. This year he had four specific capital projects that he was asking to be funded for. Each will be briefly summarized:

1. Aerodynamic devices that reduce "drag" on an over-the-road tractor that pulls a semitrailer. Eden Prairie has 18 tractors for their private truck fleet. Each air deflector costs $875 installed, and one is used per tractor. Each deflector saves 3 per cent of the fuel bill of that tractor. Slim's records indicate that his typical tractor is driven 105,000 miles per year, and it averages 3.75 miles per gallon of diesel fuel. The average cost of diesel fuel—for calculation purposes—is $1.05 per gallon. Each device, which can be transferred from one tractor to another, has an estimated life of nine years.

2. Insulation for the warehouse roof. This would include a special foam applied to the roof to a depth of 12 inches. The foam would then be painted with a special silver paint that would reflect heat. The cost of this project is $27,000. The added insulation and heat reflective paint will save 4 per cent of the combined electric (used for air conditioning) and natural gas (used for heating) bills. The average electric bill per month for the warehouse is $1,340, and the average natural gas bill per month is $713. The estimated economic life of these improvements is 11 years.

3. New automatic sprinklers can be installed in the warehouse. The present sprinkler system is activated by heat from a fire that melts a heat-sensitive metal, and this activates the automatic sprinkler system. The proposed system detects smoke particles from a fire and sets off the sprinklers significantly sooner than the present system. Along with the new sprinkler system, additional fire retardant materials would be added to the warehouse. The total cost of both is $13,200. The new antifire system will reduce the warehouse insurance bill $850 per year. In addition, the safer work environment will reduce the firm's workman's compensation insurance $275 per year. These improvements have an estimated economic life of 14 years.

4. The warehouse currently employs seven order pickers—people who assemble each order for shipping. At present, each worker can assemble about forty orders each eight-hour day. A computerized order-picking program would tell each picker the exact order in which each product should be selected. This will minimize the pickers' travel time through the warehouse. With this computer program, each order picker can average 49 orders per eight-hour day. The net effect is that one fewer order picker will be needed, which will result in annual savings of approximately $15,000. The computerized order-picking system, including a minicomputer and software package, will cost $68,200 and have an estimated economic life of eight years. Maintenance of the system is guaranteed by the seller for two years, and will be provided for every year after the first two at a charge of $1,000 each year.

Slim was uncertain how to handle the tax calculations when he made his computations, so he asked Pat. She responded that—in a general way—the investment could be written off in a "straight-line" manner over its entire life. For example, the $27,000 insulation project for the warehouse could be written off over 11 years at a straight line rate of $2,454 per year. Eden Prairie paid corporate income taxes at the 50 per cent rate, so its tax payments for each of the 11 years would be reduced by $1,227. Pat told Slim that the tax savings or reductions are entered into the denominator (along with other savings) when calculating the payback period. She cautioned Slim that all calculations should be on an "after-tax" basis. If the insulation cuts the monthly fuel bill by $82, only half of this is an after-tax saving because operating costs are reduced by $82, which increases taxable income by the same amount, and results in an after-tax saving of only $41 per month. Pat concluded that this after-tax saving would go into the denominator—after it was converted into an annual figure—along with the $1,227 annual after-tax reduction in income tax payments resulting from equipment depreciation.

Slim responded that he would attempt to calculate, on an after-tax basis, the average payback period for all four proposals.

Question One: On an after-tax basis, what is the average payback period for the air deflectors for the trucks?

Question Two: On an after-tax basis, what is the average payback period for the warehouse roof insulation?

Question Three: On an after-tax basis, what is the average payback period for the sprinkler system?

Question Four: On an after-tax basis, what is the average payback period for the computerized order-picking equipment?

Question Five: After calculating the answer to question four, Slim was at a neighborhood party and was chatting with Sid Karecki, an investment specialist. Sid said he had a group of dentists who, as a group, often invested in capital equipment and leased it to users, and enjoyed for themselves the tax advantages of depreciation. The advantage to the user was that the user had to make no large investment, merely a long-term commitment to use the equipment. To the user, the lease payments were operating expenses and, in the case of Eden Prairie Industries, these lease payments would reduce their taxes by half the amount of the payments. How much a month should Eden Prairie be willing to pay to the inventors' group for an eight-year lease on the computerized order-picking equipment?

Question Six: Pat called Slim and told him that she thought that new federal tax incentives allowed firms to increase the depreciation rate on energy-saving investments. Pat thought that the new rules would make it possible to depreciate the wind deflectors over 4½ years, on a straight-line basis. What is their new average payback period? (Note that depreciation is compressed into a 4½-year period while the savings in fuel costs will continue for 9 years. Will this yield the save average annual payback period? If it does, how can Slim measure the advantage of the accelerated depreciation?)

Question Seven: Pat also believes that the new federal tax incentives will allow the insulation for the warehouse roof to be written off over 5½ years on a straight-line basis. Answer *all* the queries in question six, but answer them in regards to the warehouse roof insulation proposal.

CASE 2-2

The Bay Area Newsprint Case

The San Francisco Bay area contains approximately five million people. Water, mountains, and other natural features have influenced the patterns of urban and suburban growth. The city of San Francisco is the focal point of the region, but, while prosperous, is not growing in population. Growth is in the suburbs, and in urban areas to the east and to the south. San Francisco's port has lost ground to other ports in the Bay area that have more modern facilities. Land values within San Francisco are very high, often too high to allow the land to be used for port or cargo-handling purposes.

One cargo still handled through San Francisco's port facilities is newsprint. There are several reasons for this. First, the principal user of newsprint within the Bay area is still located in downtown San Francisco, only a few miles from the port area. Second, newsprint moves on small, specialized vessels that can still use the old-fashioned finger piers one finds along San Francisco's waterfront. Third, newsprint inventories move through ports more slowly than most other products, so they require low-cost

Overview of Physical Distribution and Logistics

storage—which happens to be available in the area in the form of underutilized port cargo-handling sheds.

Stinson Newsprint, Ltd. of Vancouver, B.C., was a principal supplier of newsprint to the San Francisco Bay area. (This, and several other statements in this case, are fictitious.) Stinson relied on water transportation to carry the newsprint; he employed a Swedish-flag vessel. His U.S.-based competitors in the Pacific Northwest used trucks to carry newsprint to San Francisco. (Because of the Jones Act, cargo between U.S. ports must move on U.S.-flag vessels, which have much higher labor costs than do vessels flying foreign flags.) Stinson used one vessel that sailed south from Vancouver every three weeks, fully loaded with newsprint, part of which was discharged in San Francisco and the rest in Los Angeles.

Stinson sold about 50,000 tons of newsprint in the San Francisco Bay area each year. The market was oligopolistic, and his market share had remained the same for years. He and his competitors all charged the same delivered prices to each user's plant, so Stinson could only hope to save on costs. Presently Stinson sold 20,000 tons in downtown San Francisco; 10,000 tons in Oakland; 10,000 tons in Hayward; and 10,000

Exhibit 2-1 San Francisco Bay Area

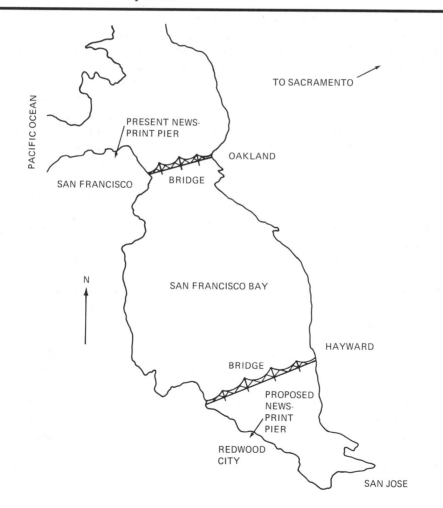

tons in San Jose. (The location of these markets is shown in Exhibit 2-1.) Stinson presently absorbed trucking costs from his San Francisco pier to each user's plant. Trucking costs to each user, per ton of newsprint, were San Francisco, $5; Oakland, $8; Hayward, $7; and San Jose, $9.

Stinson's market projections indicated that by 1995 he would be selling 65,000 to 70,000 tons per year in the Bay area. This would include 22,000 tons to downtown San Francisco; 15,000 tons to Oakland; 12,000 tons to Hayward; 15,000 tons to San Jose; and the remainder to new markets expected to develop in Sacramento, which is east of Oakland.

One day the Stinson firm was approached by a representative of a warehouse complex in Redwood City, located on San Francisco Bay, about 25 miles south of San Francisco. The firm was trying to develop additional business for its port and was hampered by its lack of navigable depths, which most large ocean-going vessels require. However, they had examined records of vessels of various drafts that called at San Francisco on a regular basis and found that the Swedish-flag vessel used by Stinson was of sufficiently shallow draft that it could call at Redwood City. The Redwood City firm promised to build Stinson a sprinklered warehouse of the same total size as the ones he was using in San Francisco. It also indicated that vessel- and cargo-handling charges would be the same as Stinson paid in San Francisco. They even told him that their dock workers' motto was "Redwood City Stevedores Do It Quicker."

The Stinson firm was glad to have a competing offer because shortly they would have to renegotiate their San Francisco lease. Trucking costs from the Redwood City site would, of course, be different. Stinson estimated them to be $8 per ton to San Francisco; $9 to Oakland; $4 to Hayward; and $6 to San Jose.

The Redwood City site had only one disadvantage that worried Stinson; it was much farther from the ocean. The vessel was already on a tight schedule. Its costs of operation averaged $2,400 per day. If it called at Redwood City, rather than San Francisco, five hours would be added to the total trip time, and pilotage charges for operations within the Bay would increase from $400 to $700 for each trip.

Question One: What are the present costs of trucking the newsprint from the San Francisco pier?

Question Two: What would be the estimated costs in 1995 of trucking the newsprint from the San Francisco pier?

Question Three: If Stinson relocated to the Redwood City site, what would his trucking costs be?

Question Four: This is the same as question three, but answer for the year 1995.

Question Five: What additional costs would there be to Stinson if he were to use the Redwood City facility?

Question Six: Assume Stinson's vessel was currently fully utilized and unloaded and/or loaded immediately upon arriving in the various ports at which it called. By how much would relocation of Stinson's Bay area facility cut into the vessel's annual productivity? Discuss.

Question Seven: When discussing the year 1995, reference is made to some tonnage that will be shipped to Sacramento, which is beyond Oakland to the east. How high would this tonnage have to be to make the Redwood City site less desirable than the one in San Francisco?

Question Eight: Should Stinson accept the Redwood City proposal? Why or why not?

Here's an ad from an aviation trade magazine stressing an element of customer service.

(Credit: Aviation Sales Company, Inc.)

Customer Service and the Order Cycle

Customer service, if not already, will be the most important consideration for vendor selection in the 1980s. We Physical Distribution managers have an obligation to formulate sound customer service strategies for our organization to ensure a competitive advantage in the market place.

Randall L. Hanna
Siemens-Allis, Inc.
NCPDM Annual Proceedings (1983)

Customer service also affects the bottom line. In a recent survey, for example, Ford Motor Company found that a loyal customer is worth more than $100,000 in repeat purchases during his or her lifetime. Clairol, Inc. reports that a satisfied customer will buy a particular hair-coloring product every four weeks for the rest of her life!

John J. Franco
Xerox Learning Systems
Marketing News (Sept. 14, 1984)

I think that during the next five or ten years, customer service will offer us the greatest opportunity we've ever had for logistics advances.

C. Lee Johnson
Warner-Lambert Company
Traffic Management (Sept. 1984)

Key Terms

- Customer service
- Order cycle
- Order transmittal
- Order processing
- Order picking and assembly
- Order delivery

Learning Objectives

- To understand the importance of customer service to a firm's marketing activities
- To relate the role of PD/L in the customer service area
- To examine why customer service standards should be specific and measurable
- To distinguish the four parts of the order cycle
- To describe how a customer service program is established and maintained
- To understand potential problems when customer service standards are not achieved

What Customer Service Is All About

Customer service is the collection of activities performed in filling orders and "keeping customers happy." One company notes that its definition of customer service "is creating in your customer's mind the perception of an organization that is being 'Easy To Do Business With'."[1] It is an excellent competitive weapon.[2] It has a special advantage over price competition. If a firm cuts its selling price, its competitors can initiate a matching price reduction immediately and eliminate the first company's comparative advantage. Customer service improvements take longer to establish; they are much more difficult for competitors to imitate. (Figure 3-1 examines two firms that have effectively utilized customer service to enhance their marketing goals.) Raymond R. Murray, director of distribution for Litton Microwave, noted:

> Through sound packaging, reliable delivery schedules, and efficient order processing, a distribution department makes an important hidden contribution to the bottom line by protecting against lost sales.[3]

Timothy P. Foley, general manager of traffic at Algoma Steel agrees with this. He has declared, "Where there is a customer service problem, we want

[1] Randall I. Hanna, "Customer Service Strategies," *Annual Proceedings of the NCPDM* (1983), p. 524.

[2] See Graham Sharman, "The Rediscovery of Logistics," *Harvard Business Review* (Sept.–Oct. 1984), pp. 71–79; and Douglas M. Lambert and Douglas E. Zemke, "The Customer Service Component of the Marketing Mix," *Annual Proceedings of the NCPDM* (1982), pp. 1–24.

[3] Jack W. Farrell, "Distribution Dynamics at Work: Litton Microwave Division," *Traffic Management* (April 1980), p. 59.

Figure 3-1 Case Examples of Customer Service Enhancing
Marketing Effectiveness

> ● Recognizing the competitive advantage of a sound information system, one
> company developed and implemented a state-of-the-art on-line order entry
> and information access system. Two features of the system are particularly
> relevant: a sophisticated substitutability program which enables capturing
> sales that may otherwise be lost; and an early-warning system which detects
> unusually large orders and arranges direct plant shipment so that warehouse
> stocks are not depleted and a domino effect created on other accounts.
> ● A company which found that completeness of orders was more important
> than actual speed of delivery was able to reduce the number of warehouses
> where it stocked the product. In so doing, it lengthened the order cycle by
> a few days but by consolidating stock it increased the ratio of complete
> orders dramatically—and this is what customers wanted. (The company
> was also able to wipe out substantial duplicate inventory in safety stock
> in slow-moving items, at a considerable saving in itself.)

Source: Davis Database (April, 1984), p. 3. Used with permission.

one of our distribution people to go out with the marketing or sales people,
identify the problem, and seek its resolution."[4] Figure 3-2 illustrates the
hidden potential for future problems when there are customer-service glitches.

Whereas Chapter 2 dealt with intrafirm relationships, this chapter will
show how PD/L affects the firm's relations with those outside of it. It will
first examine the basic aspects of customer service standards for which PD/L
personnel are sometimes held responsible. In addition, a key aspect of customer service, the order processing system, will be analyzed in order to show
its relationship to customer service standards.

The Importance of Standards

Customer service has traditionally been a frustrating area of PD because of
the problems involved in obtaining a specific, all inclusive, statement of objectives. An NCPDM task force dealing with customer service noted, "No
apparent means exist to specifically measure customer service performance
in a total sense. *Therefore, individual 'elements' must be defined and measured.*"[5] (Emphasis added.)

Elements of customer service occur in three phases. Some occur before
the transaction, some are involved as part of the transaction, and others
occur after the transaction has been completed. Professor Paul H. Zinszer
has divided all customer service elements into eight major activities.[6]

Two activities are in the pre-transactional phase. They are, one, devel-

---

[4] Jack W. Farrell, "Logistics Know-How," *Traffic Management* (Sept. 1984), p. 83.

[5] NCPDM news release, n.d.

[6] Paul H. Zinszer, "Customer Service: The Customers' Perspective," *Applied Distribution
Research* (1977), pp. 39–43. See also Bernard J. LaLonde and Paul H. Zinszer, *Customer Service:
Meaning and Measurement* (Chicago: NCPDM, 1976); and Paul H. Zinszer, "Customer Service:
Handling Limited Product Availability," *NCPDM 1980 Papers,* pp. 257–263.

Figure 3-2 The "Hidden Potential" of Customer Service Glitches

Case 1: A harried insurance claims rep tells a woman caller there is "nothing he can do" to check the status of her claim and advises her to "be patient". The next day her husband cancels a seven-figure corporate policy written by that insurance company.

Case 2: Mr. Z, a high-level executive with a large company, finds what he believes to be improper finance charges on his monthly credit-card statement and contacts the customer-service department of the credit-card firm.

The customer-service rep checks the file and determines that the interest charges are, in fact, correct and informs Mr. Z that he is "getting angry for nothing," since he is the one who is wrong. "Next time calm down and we'll take care of the problem right away," the rep says.

There is no "next" time. Even though the error was his own, Mr. Z, angered at what he considers rude treatment by the customer-service rep, converts all 73 of his company's business credit cards to a competing credit-card company.

Source: John J. Franco, "Proper Training of Customer-Service Reps Enhances Marketing Performance," *Marketing News* (September 14, 1984), p. 10. Used with permission.

oping a corporate customer service policy and, two, explaining the policy to customers.

Activities three, four, and five are related directly to the sales transaction phase. Three, the seller must have up-to-date status reports of his own inventory, which enables the customer to immediately make a substitute order if a first choice is not in stock. Activity four includes all the elements of the order cycle, which will be discussed later. Five concerns those elements of the transaction that deal with invoicing the buyer, handling returns, and making adjustments in cases of error.

Zinszer groups the last three activities into the post-transactional phase. They cover provision of additional technical services the customer may need, support materials and supplies, and repairs.

Establishing Specific Objectives

Some companies distinguish *goals* from *objectives* when establishing customer service standards. *Goals* tend to be broad, generalized statements regarding the overall results that the firm is attempting to achieve. *Objectives* are the means by which the goals are achieved. These objectives have certain minimum requirements. Usually, a company will determine a minimum set of requirements needed to meet an objective and then attempt to improve on it. The E. I. duPont de Nemours & Company's *goals* and *objectives* illustrate this difference.

> Our *Primary Goal* is to provide a level of service equal to or better than major competition in select area markets of opportunity, and in other areas, improvements requiring little or no physical system change.
>   Our *Secondary Goal* (in support of the primary goal)
>   —adequate stock available at all times to satisfy customer requirements promptly.
>   —dependable shipments and delivery service of products within the established objectives or the date specified by the customer.
>   —prompt notification to customer upon any deviation from standard terms.[7]

Their objectives are much more specific in nature. One example of an objective is to reduce the number or rate of errors in shipment from three per 1,000 to two per 1,000 shipments. Although many measures can be used to achieve specific objectives, we believe the following four areas deserve special attention:

1. The total elapsed time from when the customer places an order until the customer receives the order.
2. The percentage of customer orders that can be filled immediately and completely from stock located in the warehouse.
3. The total elapsed time from receipt of the order until the shipment is tendered to the transport mode for delivery to the customer.
4. The percentage of customer orders that are picked and sent correctly.

Unfortunately, many firms' statements of customer service goals are couched in platitudes lacking specific objectives defining how the goals are to be achieved. This is a serious problem because if the customer service objectives or standards are not stated in specific terms, they may be ignored or else will be so vague that they will not provide real guidance to operating personnel. In addition, the logistics department may then become the scapegoat for the marketing department. If a new product "flops," the marketing department might argue that the new product introduction failed because customer service standards were too low. Without specific guidelines the customer service staff lacks a base to prove that acceptable levels of customer service were maintained.

---

[7] T. R. Elsman, "Export Customer Service," *Annual Proceedings of the NCPDM* (1972), p. 172.

The solution to the above quandry is obvious. Customer service objectives or standards should be similar to the DuPont statement—very specific. When this is done, it becomes easier to determine whether the customer service staff did, in fact, "drop the ball." With specific customer service standards, the customer service department is in a better position to refute allegations if the established objectives had been met.

The Order Cycle

The order cycle is an important part of customer service, but its meaning depends on one's perspective. From the seller's standpoint, it is the time from when an order is received from a customer to when the goods arrive at the customer's receiving dock. From the buyer's standpoint, the order cycle is from when the order is sent out to when the goods are received. (This is also known as the *replenishment cycle* for goods needed on a regular basis.) The shorter and more consistent the order cycle is, the less inventory one's customers have to maintain. (See Chapter 7.) In 1983 the average order cycle for all types of companies was eight days.[8]

Herbert W. Davis, a management consultant who has specialized in physical distribution, has noted:

> Most managements (there are some notable exceptions) think of customer service as the time it takes an order to reach a customer once it's been shipped. They fail to realize that customer service is not a simple event, but rather a chain of events which, like any chain, is only as good as its weakest link.
>
> Transportation is a key link in that chain of events, to be sure. But the best transportation in the world cannot make up for the . . . lag between receipt of an order and shipment of the goods to the customer. And even automating the order processing function cannot overcome a stockout situation that started with inaccurate forecasting and compounded itself with inventory policies and production plans laid down far from the customer service scene.[9]

Many firms analyze their customer service standards in terms of four aspects or stages of the order cycle: order transmittal, order processing, order picking and assembly, and order delivery.

Order Transmittal

Order transmittal is the series of events that occurs from the time a customer places or sends an order until the time the seller receives the order. In recent years this aspect of the order cycle has received increasing attention for two reasons. First, many firms have calculated that the order transmittal time is

---

[8] Davis Database (April, 1984), p. 3.
[9] Herbert W. Davis, "4 Reasons Why Customer Service Managers Can't Manage Customer Service," *Handling and Shipping* (Nov. 1971), p. 51.

from two to five days if the U.S. Postal Service carries the order, and some feel that this is unreasonably long. Second, there are unpredictable variations in mail service. This high degree of variability makes it difficult to provide any sort of overall consistency when fulfilling orders. (Unfortunately, a buyer assumes that the seller receives the order almost immediately after it is mailed.)

To correct these deficiencies, many companies have their salespeople and customers order directly by phone or some other electronic method of order transmittal. The use of telephone order placement—including the use of "800" numbers—has grown considerably in recent years.[10] This kind of placement is instantaneous, but it does not provide "hard copy" or written information, which means that it is possible to make errors when transcribing orders from the phone to order sheets. This problem can be substantially reduced by having the recipient of the order read it back to the sender in order to verify its accuracy.

> For phone numbers with the "800" prefix, the party receiving the call pays the telephone charges.

Many companies now use CRTs to process phone orders. The CRT screen displays a blank order form with blank spaces for all processing-related information. The operator records all necessary information, such as name and address and then takes the order, typing in a product identifying number and the quantity desired. The CRT is linked to computers that maintain active records of the company's inventory. As the operator types the order, the computer indicates what is available for shipment now and when unavailable products can be shipped. The operator gives this information to the buyer, who is still on the phone. The buyer may make some changes that are recorded by the operator. The buyer then says to process the order, and the operator converts the material on the CRT to an actual order for processing.

> CRT is a cathode ray tube. It looks like a television screen and displays lines and columns of letters and numbers. The letters and numbers are produced by computers to which the CRT is linked and by a typewriter-like keyboard in front of the operator.

During the last five years, one of the major changes in order transmittal has been the increased utilization of computer-to-computer ordering.[11] Fig-

---

[10] See Roy Dale Voorhees, "Communications: A New Logistics Factor in Location Decisions and Patterns of Regional and National Development," *Transportation Journal* (Summer 1976), pp. 73–84; and Roy Dale Voorhees, John C. Coppett, and Eileen M. Kelley, "Telelogistics: A Management Tool for the Logistics Problems of the 1980's," *Transportation Journal* (Summer 1984), pp. 62–70.

[11] See "Order Processing and Inventory Control—The On-Line Revolution," *Traffic Management* (May 1983), pp. 33–42.

ure 3-3 discusses the advantages of this type of ordering. One problem for many companies is that the buyer's computer is programmed to record the purchase order in one format and the seller's computer requests the order in a different format. In effect, the information must be recorded twice to satisfy each party. To correct this problem in the grocery industry, a standard system of order communication is being developed. It is known as UCS (Uniform Communications System). It allows the buyer to enter the order into its system while exactly the same information is automatically sent— usually via a telephone line—to the seller. A number of software vendors have programs utilizing UCS.[12]

Another method of order transmittal that is also becoming more common utilizes scanners and bar codes. McKesson Corporation, a wholesale company supplying drugstores, utilizes this concept. It provides each of its retail customers with an electronic ordering machine that is only somewhat larger than a hand-held calculator. The store employee walks through the store at a regular time and notices which products are low on inventory. He or she then passes a pencil-like scanner, which is attached to the ordering device, across a label that McKesson has affixed to the shelf. The scanner automatically reads the label. After all products with low inventory have been scanned, the employee places the order by dialing McKesson's phone number and then placing the phone in a device (known as an acoustic coupler) that sends information from the ordering machine. The order is received by McKesson and they check each product code ordered against the predetermined quantity to send to each customer for each product. Orders are shipped to the drugstore the next day.[13]

Order Processing

Between the time a firm receives an order and the warehouse is notified to ship the order is the period of order processing. This time frame typically includes such factors as (1) verifying if all order information is complete and accurate; (2) a credit check by the credit department; (3) the marketing department crediting the salesperson with the sale; (4) the accounting department recording the transaction; (5) the inventory department locating the closest warehouse to the customer, telling it to pick the shipment, and updating the firm's master inventory controls; and (6) the traffic department arranging for the shipment's transportation from the warehouse site. These activities are shown in Figure 3-4.

One additional situation that every firm must contend with is a stockout. In most cases, the best procedure is to notify the customer of this situation as soon as possible. This can be done immediately if the customer is ordering via computer or a phone call-in system—assuming the seller has its inventory system computerized. If the order has been mailed, the cus-

[12] Richard C. Norris, "Uniform Communications System," *Annual Proceedings of the American Society of Traffic and Transportation* (1982), pp. 99–126; and, in the same publication, Ron E. Cummings, "Installing Order Entry Systems," pp. 127–135.

[13] "Retailers Depend on Their High-Tech Middlemen," *San Francisco Chronicle*, 3 September 1984, p. 52. See also, Sean MacAllister, "Micro Processings Applications and Order Processing," *Annual Proceedings of the NCPDM* (1982), pp. 653–664.

Figure 3-3 Communicating Via Computer By Bernard J. Hale, Vice-President, Bergen Brunswig Corporation

Computerization, one of the single biggest factors in productivity improvement in physical distribution, can be of significant benefit to manufacturers who use computers to communicate with distributors or large customers.

This has been the experience of the wholesale drug industry, which has been using such computer linkups between wholesalers and large manufacturers for about 10 years. I'd like to share some of the benefits of these links, from both the manufacturer's side and the wholesaler's side. Many of them could be enjoyed by other types of wholesalers, or direct customers and manufacturers.

Advantages for manufacturers include:
- Higher retail, in-stock positions, resulting in fewer lost sales.
- Fewer emergency orders because of more reliable order cycle time, and more accurate order information.
- Order consolidation, resulting in far more economical processing and picking by the manufacturer. Computerized communication has also led to more efficient handling within manufacturers' distribution centers, and more economical delivery through freight cost savings. This has also meant more profit per shipment for carriers, making the shipping of pharmaceutical products even more enticing. Consequently, service is more consistent, so everybody has gained.
- Better scheduling of distribution center workloads.
- Reduced order processing time and costs. Receiving orders via computer has lowered manual, clerical processing costs, and the need to re-submit — and re-process — orders.
- Notable improvements in accuracy, thus eliminating errors and their inordinately high costs.
- Increased sales, a function of having the right product in the right place at the right time. Minimizing back orders clearly is an objective for both wholesalers and manufacturers, because it prevents the loss of retail sales.
- Fewer problems for sales personnel to handle, minimizing long distance telephone calls, which are frequently charged to manufacturers.

Wholesaler benefits of computerized communications have included.
- Reduced lead time from the manufacturers — significant because the more reliable the figure for days involved in order cycle time, the more control over investment in inventory.
- Greatly improved customer service levels. The drug industry generally uses a system known as "fill or kill," so it is important that the product be in stock when the customer orders it; otherwise, it will be back-ordered and the sale will be lost.
- Out of stocks have been reduced significantly.
- The reliability of delivery has been greatly improved. Since wholesalers now know that the manufacturers are shipping on a far more consistent, reliable schedule, any major variances in lead time can be more easily pinpointed. This means all members of the distribution channel — manufacturers, carriers and consignees — can solve the problems.
- Reduced operating expenses. Eliminating clerical steps in the manual processing and transmission of purchase orders to the manufacturers is a very big plus.
- Wholesalers have also enjoyed greater receiving accuracy because there are fewer errors on the orders.

Many of the larger wholesalers have computerized communications with *their* customers, and are thus sharing these advantages with them.

The most exciting challenge to those of us in wholesale pharmaceutical distribution is stretching our imaginations to find more uses for computers to help our customers and ourselves improve profitability.

Source: Bernard J. Hale, "Communicating Via Computer" a commentary in *Handling and Shipping Management* (September, 1983), p. 11.

Figure 3-4 Flow Chart of Order Processing System

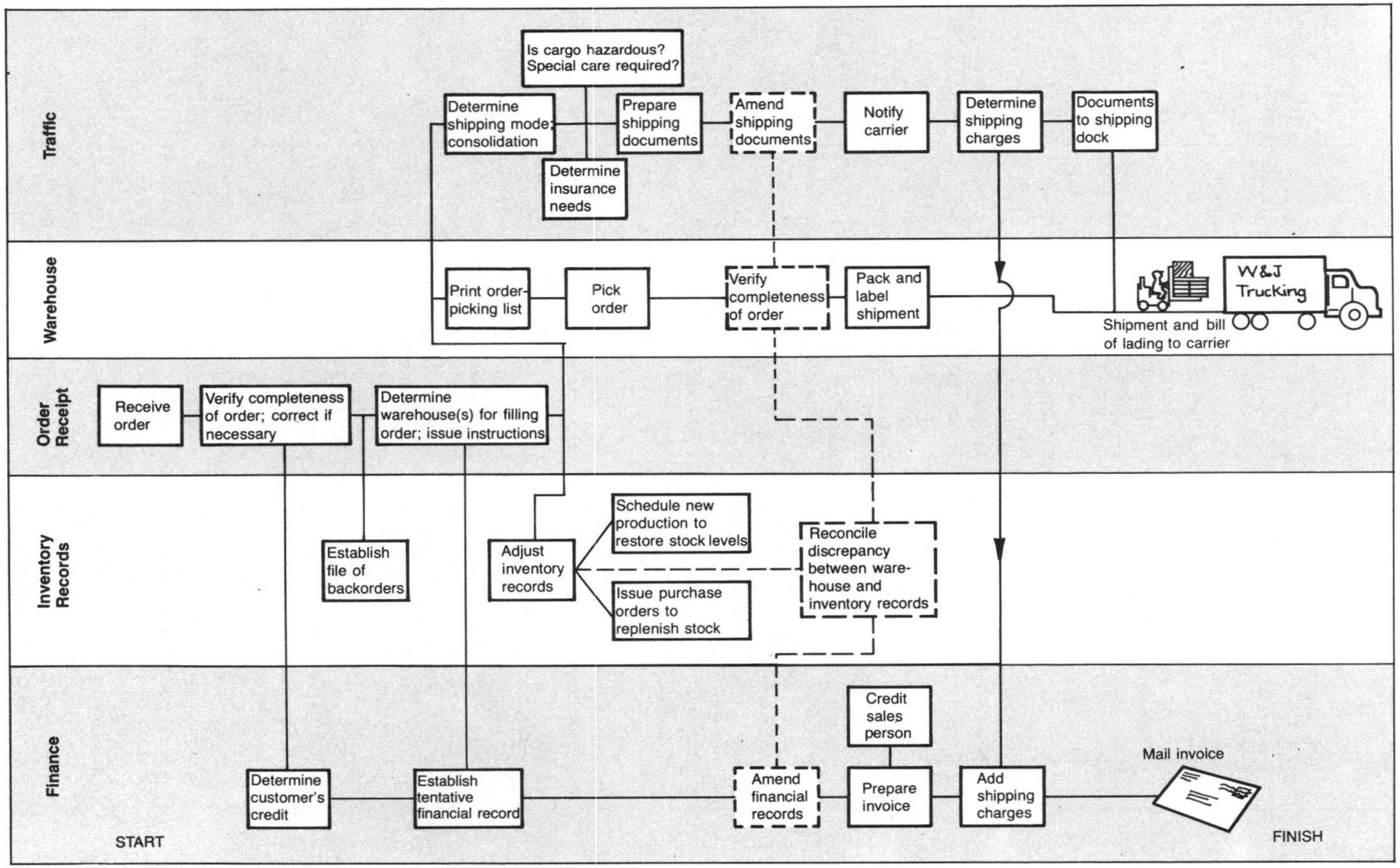

tomer should be contacted via phone or mail. In any case, the customer should be notified about when the order will be shipped and also given the option of accepting similar products that are currently in stock. Many firms have computerized certain aspects of their order processing systems. Order forms, themselves, are designed and printed in a manner that facilitates the use of computers by both the customer and the vendor.

Some companies centralize their order processing while others use a decentralized system. The system of the William Underwood Company, which manufactures B & M Beans and other food products, is an example of a centralized approach. Orders for products are received from seventy-five independent food brokers located throughout the United States. The brokers teletype their orders via Western Union facilities to Underwood's main distribution center in Westwood, New Jersey. Once an order is received, a computer verifies the credit standing of the customer, prepares an invoice, and updates inventory level records; one of thirty public warehouses is notified to ship the order, and sales and accounting records are updated. David Tarr, director of distribution, noted that centralized order processing is efficient because

> we will have less paperwork. Our data will only be entered into the system once, and that basic information will be expanded on as other events occur. There is also an excellent opportunity for a reduction in transportation expenses because now we can optimize our carrier selection whether it is rail or truck. This can be achieved because orders are entered in the system sooner, giving us a larger shipping perspective to determine the best method of shipment. This also will allow us to consolidate shipments more effectively. We believe we will increase the use of less expensive modes of transportation.[14]

The A. B. Dick Corporation, one of the country's largest producers of copying and duplicating equipment and supplies, has a decentralized order processing system. Customers phone in their orders to one of five regional distribution centers located in New York City; Los Angeles; Columbus; Washington, D.C.; and Suffield, Connecticut. As the order is entered into the computer, inventory files are updated, customer's credit standing is checked, shipping labels are prepared, a bill of lading is produced, and the customer invoice is completed. At the end of each day the computer at each distribution center transmits its daily activity directly to the firm's main computer facility at the corporate headquarters in Niles, Michigan.[15]

A major problem area in achieving an efficient order processing system (either centralized or decentralized) is "bunching." Bunching results when a high percentage of customers make their orders at approximately the same time. Such an overload on the order processing system causes delays in handling. The result, of course, is that the entire order cycle time is increased, and the firm's customer service is lowered.

[14] David Tarr, "Choosing and Implementing a Distributed Distribution System," *Annual Proceedings of the NCPDM* (1978), p. 301.

[15] John Bigelow, "The Benefits of Using Distributed Processing in a Modern Distribution System," *Annual Proceedings of the NCPDM* (1978), pp. 551–557.

The key to reducing bunching problems is to control when customers place their orders. If its customers' ordering schedules can be influenced, a firm will then be able to balance them out and minimize the peaks and valleys in the order-processing work load.

Three techniques are commonly used to control customer ordering patterns. The first is the use of "field" or "outside" salespeople, who take orders when they call on customers. Many customers prefer the ease of ordering directly from salespeople because of their extensive knowledge of the product lines. Thus, when a customer knows that a firm's representative arrives the first Monday of every month, he usually will hold his orders for the salesperson.

A second procedure involves the use of phone salespeople (called inside salespeople). A firm's representative calls the customer at a given time(s) during the month and takes the customer's order. This method is especially attractive because it is easy to operate. The final technique is to offer a substantial price discount to customers who place their orders on certain dates, such as every fourth Monday. Avon Products, whose representatives make sales on a door-to-door basis, uses this method. Each representative has "a specific day to submit the order every two weeks. By selecting the day of the week an order is submitted, we are able to balance the workload in our branches and consolidate orders into truckload quantities for maximum service at a reasonable expense."[16]

Order Picking and Assembly

One of the functions of order processing is to produce a document telling a specific warehouse to assemble a given order for a customer. An actual *order picking* list, indicating which items are to be assembled, is given to a warehouse employee. The order picking and assembly function includes all activities from the time the warehouse receives an order to ship items until goods are loaded aboard an outbound carrier.

The trend today is for the order pickers' activities to be scheduled by computer. At the L. L. Bean distribution center in Freeport, Maine (the firm is a national supplier of sporting goods, such as outdoor apparel, camping goods, and footwear), each order picker is given a computer printout that specifies what products to pick, where to find them, and in what sequence the products should be gathered for each order. This system has provided impressive results. During the peak of Bean's shipping season, the firm's sixty order pickers select from 13,000 products in a 50,000 square-foot picking area and can process over 33,000 orders per day.[17]

A further refinement in the use of computers in the order-picking process is reported by the E. J. Brach Company, a large manufacturer of candy. Each order picker carries a hand-held computer that functions as an order-picking terminal. It tells the picker what to pick, the quantity to pick, and

---

[16] Comments by W. R. Dykes, director of corporate transportation for Avon Products, Inc., at the American Package Express Carriers Meeting, San Francisco, June 7, 1979.

[17] "A Truly Outstanding System for Manual Order Picking," *Modern Materials Handling* (March 1980), pp. 66–71.

the location of the product. When each product has been picked, the employee presses the button labeled "task done." The warehouse computer then shows the employee his or her next assignment on the hand-held terminal.[18]

After orders have been picked, the assembled orders are checked to ensure that they were accurately picked. If there is a stock-out on a particular item, the information is sent back to the order-processing department so that original documents can be adjusted. Often, a "packing list" is enclosed with each outgoing order, indicating what items were picked and the initials of the individuals who prepared the order for shipment. The consignee is expected to check the packing list when he or she receives the order and verify that all items are present.

> In a shipping transaction, the *shipper* sends the goods to the *consignee* via a *carrier*.

Order Delivery

The final phase of the order cycle is order delivery, the time from when a carrier picks up the shipment until it is delivered to the customer's receiving dock. The factors that affect the speed and reliability of transportation service will be examined in the following three chapters.

Carriers have established their own service standards, and shippers using them have to incorporate the carrier's estimated delivery times into calculations of the entire length of the order cycle. Chapters 4 through 6 examine various transportation alternatives available for order delivery. In some situations carriers will guarantee a delivery schedule. This indicates that the carrier will pay a penalty payment to the shipper if the delivery is later than a specified time.

Importance of the Order Cycle

When the four stages of the order cycle—order transmittal, order processing, order picking, and order delivery—are carefully run and skillfully coordinated, impressive gains in performance can be realized, and the firm will have a potent marketing and sales tool.

An efficient order cycle can also be a valuable internal tool. Many of the same steps occur for intrafirm transactions, although some steps, such as credit verification, can be eliminated or modified. Intrafirm movements can also be conducted at very high service levels. As Avon's director of corporate transportation has said:

[18] Geoffrey P. Clark and Morgan F. Bryan, "Minicomputer Systems Demonstration of Paperless Order Entry and Order Picking," *Annual Proceedings of the NCPDM* (1978), pp. 355–371. See also Hal Wilson and Tony DeMaria, "An Evaluation of Alternative Techniques for Order Fulfillment," *Annual Proceedings of the NCPDM* (1983), pp. 628–644; and "One Company Scans Its Distribution Operations," *Traffic Management* (Oct. 1983), pp. 95–98.

Avon's policy is a maximum seven-day order turnaround to the sales representative; i.e., an order is submitted to Avon on Monday *must* be delivered not later than the following Monday, but consistently on the same day of the week each time. This system allows two days for order submission, one day for Avon branch processing, and one to four days for delivery of the order to the sales representative's residence, dependent upon the distance to the representative. Our entire marketing program is very service oriented, and the minimum acceptable on-time delivery performance is 99 per cent.[19]

Returned Products

One post-transactional customer service activity deserving additional mention is the handling of "returned" materials or merchandise. Somewhat like recycling, which was discussed in Chapter 2, one of its effects is to set up new "flows" of products. (A very specialized type of return movement, the "product recall," will be discussed in Chapter 13.)

Goods and materials are returned for a variety of reasons. Sometimes the shipper made an error when filling an order. Sometimes the goods are damaged in transit and the carrier responsible for the damage wants the shipper to determine costs of repairs. Sometimes the customer makes an error in ordering, such as writing down the incorrect part number.

The three examples given thus far are straightforward. The next example is the most difficult with respect to maintaining "happy" relationships between channels. It deals with the return of "defective" goods. Defects discovered by the customer immediately after unpacking a shipment usually are easy to handle, but sometimes defects are not discovered until later, such as when a retail customer attempts to return a purchased good, often after heavy use, claiming it is defective. Or, a merchant has overordered an item that is not selling well and decides to examine the materials again and again until he discovers defects and then has a "reason" for returning the entire lot.

Companies, as part of their customer service policy, should have procedures established for handling, inspecting, and allowing claims on returned materials. A hypothetical example from the sporting goods field of such a policy follows:

Returns of merchandise for credit or exchange will not be accepted under any conditions unless a Return Authorization Form obtained from and signed by John Doe Co. is enclosed with the items. A minimum of 10 per cent restocking charge will be made on all return merchandise unless it is for reasons caused by the John Doe Co. Any cost for work or repairs necessary to put returned merchandise into new, saleable condition will be made in addition to the 10 per cent restocking charge. Include the invoice number and the price of the merchandise returned. Returns must be shipped prepaid and insured. If a return is made because of John Doe Co.'s error, carrier fees will be credited. Returns will always be credited at your whole-

[19] Comments by W. R. Dykes.

sale or current wholesale cost, whichever is lower. Claims must be made within four weeks of invoice date.[20]

This policy seems strict, but the industry is one where over 85 per cent of merchandise returned to the manufacturer is claimed to be "defective."[21]

Another reason for returned goods relates to spare parts. The customer may know "something's wrong with the clutch" and order a new, complete clutch assembly. After disassembling the defective clutch, he discovers he needs only a small bearing and then wants to return all the other parts for credit.

Logistics personnel dealing with customer service can expect to confront problems arising from claims and must be able to develop procedures for handling them. Retailers making claims against manufacturers are often caught between a customer who has returned the good, claiming it is defective and wanting his or her money back, and the manufacturer claiming that nothing is—or was—wrong with the good in question.

Returned goods must be examined by the manufacturer to determine whether they can be placed back in the finished goods inventory or whether they require some additional repairs. Other alternatives are to dispose of them as "seconds" or to disassemble them, saving the usable parts.

PD/L's Role in Establishing Customer Service Goals and Objectives

Because customer service standards can significantly affect a firm's overall sales success, establishing goals and objectives is an important senior management decision. Distribution is closely related to customer service, so that the PD/L department plays an important role in the establishment of customer service goals and objectives.

PD: Advisors to Marketing

Generally, the marketing department is very influential in establishing customer service standards. As a part of marketing, the PD operation serves a particularly important advisory function. Marketing executives occasionally are guilty of equating *sales maximization* and *profit maximization*. Some marketing practitioners still believe that the most important objective of a firm is to increase sales. The result is that customer service goals and objectives are set at unreasonably high levels that ignore the costs incurred to achieve them.

The PD/L department then must act as marketing's conscience by asking "Are you aware that the goals and objectives you want established are going to cost $$$?" Relatively small increases in the overall level of customer ser-

---

[20] "Return Goods Haunt Dealers," *The Sporting Goods Dealer* (May 1980), p. 50.
[21] Ibid., p. 49.

Figure 3-5 The Relationship Between Inventory Levels and Customer Service Levels

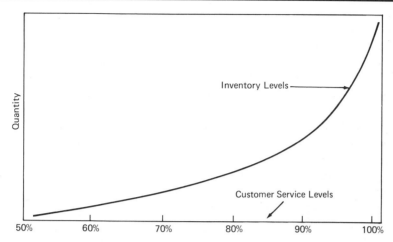

Source: Mason and Dixon Lines, Inc., "Needed: Credible Measures of Customer Service Costs and Penalties," *Procurement/Distribution Ideas and Methods,* p. 101. Used with permission.

vice objectives can substantially increase the costs of maintaining the increased level of customer service. Management consultant John F. Magee noted, "Approximately 80 per cent or more inventory is needed in a typical business to fill 95 per cent of the customers' orders out of stock than to fill only 80 per cent."[22]

Figure 3-5 illustrates what Magee's statement can mean to a company. Up to 90 per cent, the line indicating the necessary inventory to meet a customer service goal, goes up at an increasing, though only slightly higher, rate. But by the time the line reaches 95 per cent, it is going almost straight up. This example shows the need to consistently keep the *costs* of the firm's customer service goals and objectives in mind. Most firms have delegated this authority to the physical distribution/logistics department. Noted PD/L consultant Warren Blanding observed that the physical distribution group must

> *Help set customer service standards.* Note the word *help*. Physical distribution can outline the alternative means of delivering products to customers and calculate the cost for different levels of customer service: the size of inventories, the number of shipping points, the order-processing requirements, warehousing, and transportation. It can do all this, but it cannot (or at least should not) set actual customer service standards. That is management's job, with sales and marketing helping to determine the levels of customer service that the competitive situation requires—and that pricing policies and profit objectives will permit.[23]

[22] John F. Magee, "The Logistics of Distribution," *Harvard Business Review* (July–Aug. 1960), p. 92.

[23] Warren Blanding, "Yes, There Is Such a Thing as Too Much Customer Service," *Sales Management* (Oct. 14, 1974), pp. 41–42.

Overview of Physical Distribution and Logistics

Figure 3-6 An Analysis of Customer Profitability

He always orders in carload or truckload lots, always gives you plenty of lead time, and uses a purchase order your customer service personnel can understand. He accepts substitutions and back orders, pays his invoices promptly, and doesn't harass you to trace and expedite when shipments are a few days late. In short, he's a model customer.

Yet you may not even know he exists in those terms. To a sales manager, he may seem to be a moderately attractive account but relatively small potatoes in terms of total volume; certainly far down the priority list for allocating a scarce product. That oversight could be costing you more than you realize.

For today's shortages are largely the result of limited plant capacity, and when you're selling all the product you can get your hands on at sky-high prices, there's only one way to increase profits. That's by systematically identifying and concentrating your sales efforts on the accounts that (individually and in the aggregate) show the greatest margin between what you are paid for the product and what it costs you to get it. Discrete physical distribution costs are often a critical factor in separating the sheep from the goats.

For example, Customer A buys 80,000 lb. of product a year from you, Customer B, 240,000. Obviously, you would term Customer B the "better" customer. But wait a minute. Customer A buys two truckload lots a year—40,000 lb. each—which means you get full use of your truck. Also, he happens to be located only a few miles from one of *your* suppliers, so that further savings can be realized by having the truck stop and backhaul materials ordered by your purchasing department.

Meanwhile, you discover that Customer B's 240,000 lb. are spread over some 30 orders, a few for truckloads, to be sure, but a surprising number for 500 lb. or less. What's more, fully half the total orders required expediting because he simply hadn't given you enough lead time. Customer B's erratic and unpredictable manner of ordering made it virtually impossible to set up backhaul movements for your truck fleet. In fact, there were half a dozen instances when a truck was dispatched with a "rush" order of less than 10,000 lb.—and then had to deadhead home.

By the time you add on the comparative amounts of salesman expense involved in each of the two accounts, plus the relative demands on your customer service personnel, you will start wondering how many more Customer B's you have getting unwarranted red-carpet treatment. You may also decide to upgrade the likes of Customer A.

Source: Warren Blanding, "Sizing up Customers This Way Can Gain You Nothing But Profits," *Sales Management* (May 27, 1974):31.

Figure 3-6 discusses a situation where it becomes extremely important to carefully analyze costs of serving each customer. As Blanding points out, the obviously good customer upon scrutiny may turn out to be a "loser" and vice versa. Sales maximization is often not compatible with profit maximization, and the "devil's advocate" role of consistently pointing out this fallacy often falls upon the PD/L department. Sam R. Goodman, controller for the Nestle Company, sums it up by observing:

It may be that we can go to the sales force and say, "Don't sell to this customer," or "Let's reduce our volume, we will be better off for it." Now, this is a no-no to the accountant and to the marketing man. . . . You might make a lot more profit for the company by having a lower volume and fewer customers. It's not very different from having a lovely rose bush growing in your garden. If you want it to be lovelier, you prune it.[24]

Establishing a Customer Service Program

A central element in the establishment of customer service goals and objectives is determining the customer's viewpoint. This means asking customers what they feel is important about service. Bertrand Klass's research showed what value purchasing agents place on customer service. He found that customer service considerations were second only to product quality as the basic determinants of which vendors to patronize.[25] Professors William D. Perreault and Frederick A. Russ noted that purchasing agents are frequently instructed to consider the physical distribution service offered by suppliers when computing vendor evaluation analysis.[26]

William M. Hutchison and John F. Stolle described how a comprehensive survey can be used to identify three basic aspects of customer service.[27] The first aspect involves asking questions about additional elements of service. What services would he like to receive that are presently not available? For example, could the method of order transmittal be improved? If yes—how? Would it be helpful to have order shipment notification? If yes—why?

The second aspect involves determining which aspects of service are most important to the customer. Is the present speed of the order or replenishing cycle acceptable? If not—why? A key question for those who indicated that some aspect of the current customer service level is unsatisfactory is: are they willing to pay more to receive a higher level of service?[28]

The third aspect, which we believe is very important, is, how the customer evaluates the service levels of competing vendors. Some purchasing agents will release this information. (An example from a college bookstore is given in Chapter 12.) This type of information can be helpful in establishing the necessary minimum levels of customer service.

When all of the above information has been gathered and analyzed, management can establish the firm's customer service goals and objectives. Professor James L. Heskett has identified three basic categories of informa-

[24] Sam R. Goodman, "Improving Productivity Measurement and Control for Physical Distribution," *Annual Proceedings of the NCPDM* (1971), sect. X, pages not numbered.

[25] Bertrand Klass, "What Factors Affect Industrial Buying Decisions?" *Industrial Marketing* (May 1961), pp. 33–35.

[26] William D. Perreault and Frederick A. Russ, "Physical Distribution Service: A Neglected Aspect of Marketing Management," *MSU Business Topics* (Summer 1974), p. 38. See also Jack W. Farrell, "Get to Know Your Customers . . . and Vendors," *Traffic Management* (Sept. 1984), p. 83.

[27] William M. Hutchison and John F. Stolle, "How to Manage Customer Service," *Harvard Business Review* (Nov.–Dec. 1968), p. 89.

[28] See Carl H. Majeczky and Peter A. Smith, "Competitive Customer Service Planning at Sara Lee," *Annual Proceedings of the NCPDM* (1983), pp. 602–607.

tion: *economics, the nature of the competitive environment,* and the *nature of the product.*[29]

Economic considerations involve the costs of different levels of customer service. Higher levels of service, of course, are more expensive. Rapid order delivery generally requires premium transportation and its higher rates. Or, if all orders are to be picked in the warehouse within twenty-four hours of receipt, then it is necessary to maintain a larger work force to fill such orders. Do customers want this level of service? Do they want it enough to *pay* for it?

The *nature of the environment* relates to industry standards. Information about customer expectations and the customer service standards rendered by competitors is invaluable in establishing competitive standards.

The *nature of the product* also affects the level of customer service that should be offered. Substitutability is one aspect. It refers to the number of products that a firm's customers can choose from to meet their needs. If a firm has a near monopoly on an important product, then a high level of customer service is not required because if the customer needs the product he will buy it under any reasonable customer service standard. On the other hand, if there are many products that basically perform the same task, then customer service standards become very important from a competitive marketing point of view.

When customer service information has been thoroughly analyzed, it is possible to put customer service goals and objectives in writing. It has been said that "talk is cheap and actions dear." In other words, grandiose statements regarding a firm's level of customer service represent little more than rhetoric unless the customer service standards are actually implemented. To accomplish the latter, a systematic program of measurements and control is required.

Measurement and Control of Customer Service

The ability to measure is the ability to control. And effective control is what management is all about. The value of any corporate objective or goal depends to a large extent on the tools used to measure them. A firm's customer service program must be written and monitored.

A problem encountered when measuring actual customer service standards is determining what factors are to be measured. Many firms prefer to measure those aspects of customer service that are the easiest to measure instead of those that may be the most important from the customer's point of view. Instead of measuring the complete order or replenishment cycle, some firms only measure order processing and order picking times because these elements are readily available to them. The problem, of course, is that

---

[29] James L. Heskett, "Controlling Customer Logistics Service," *International Journal of Physical Distribution* (June 1971), pp. 140–145.

measurement of these aspects tells nothing about the quality of other parts of the order cycle, such as order transmittal and delivery, which are more difficult to measure and, consequently, most susceptible to problems.

How can a firm most effectively measure those aspects of customer service that the *customer* values? One technique that appears to be gaining in popularity is the performance model. It is based on a questionnaire that determines the percentage of times the firm is accomplishing its customer service goals and objectives. This can be done on a sampling basis.

Measuring the order delivery segment of the order cycle has been an especially difficult problem. John F. Sweers, physical distribution manager for Western Publishing Company, has established a simple and proven method.[30] Using a carefully prepared sampling procedure, the firm places a stamped post card in each selected order. The customer is asked to supply only the date of arrival and condition of the goods at destination. Sweers found that the customers are willing to return the cards. This technique allowed his firm to build a valuable data base that is used to identify good carriers.

Another way of measuring performance is by auditing "credit memos," the documents that must be issued to correct errors in shipping and billing. Comparing them with the volume of error-free activity gives a measure of relative accuracy in performance. This system is not foolproof, however, since customers who receive more than they are billed for may not call that type of error to the shipper's attention.

Meeting Customer Demands

So far this discussion has dealt almost exclusively with *measurement* of customer service goals and objectives and very little on *control*. Control is the process of taking corrective action when the measurements indicate that the goals and objectives are not being achieved. Measurement by itself is merely wasted time and effort if no action is taken based on the feedback received. The actions taken after the deficiencies have been identified makes for a strong and effective customer service program.

Firms are demanding higher levels of customer service for a number of reasons. First, reliable service enables a firm to maintain a lower level of inventory, especially of safety stocks. The lower average level of inventory produces lower inventory holding costs.

Second, the increased use of *vendor quality control programs* has necessitated higher levels of customer service. In recent years many firms, especially retailers and wholesalers, have become more inventory conscious. This emphasis has resulted in computer-assisted analysis to identify vendors who consistently give either good or bad levels of service. In the past, with manual systems, it took repeated and serious customer service errors before a vendor's activities would be singled out for corrective action. Today, these

---

[30] John F. Sweers, "A Standard to Beat the Carrier's Clock," *Handling and Shipping* (Oct. 1973), pp. 54–55.

factors are automatically programmed into the computer, and companies are able to closely monitor the *quality* of service received from each vendor.

> *Safety stocks* are additional units of inventory maintained to meet additional demands for the product or for use in case deliveries of replenishment stocks are delayed.

Ronald P. Willett and P. Ronald Stephenson attempted to verify the importance of customer service as perceived by purchasing executives. They surveyed 480 drugstore retailers and found that their buyers were able to consistently discriminate between even relatively small differences in the consistency and length of the order cycles offered by their vendors.[31]

Third, in our automated and computerized world, the relationships between customers and vendors often become *dehumanized.* This situation is both frustrating and often inefficient from the customer's viewpoint. The firm that can offer a high level of customer service, especially on a personal basis, finds it has a powerful sales advantage in the marketplace. A senior physical distribution practitioner has noted:

> We are right in the middle of another "backlash"—the computer number backlash. Depersonalized mechanization and centralization have the buyer at all levels rebelling. Have you tried to write a letter or telephone a computer system to correct an error? It simply cannot respond. As human overrides have been lessened and lowered in discretionary action, the buyer becomes frustrated. Even the industrial buyer, using tools of value analysis, and—all things being equal, and they are equal to a growing extent for a long list of products—will use the supplier that somehow treats him as a person, not only in the sales contact, but in order entry, tracing, physical delivery, invoicing, and follow-up. These are the coming measures of service.[32]

What happens to a supplier who consistently provides less than acceptable levels of customer service? This question was asked of a large number of companies and Figure 3-7 summarizes their answers. The most common response is that the customer reduced the volume of business it gave to the vendor involved. Almost one-in-five respondents stated that they have stopped all purchases with suppliers who provide inadequate levels of customer service.[33]

---

[31] Ronald P. Willett and P. Ronald Stephenson, "Determinants of Buyer Response to Physical Distribution Service," *Journal of Marketing Research* (Aug. 1969), pp. 279–283. See also Graham Sharman, "The Rediscovery of Logistics," *Harvard Business Review* (Sept.–Oct. 1984), pp. 71–79.

[32] James R. Davis, "Customer Service—PD's Newest Responsibility," *Annual Proceedings of the NCPDM* (1973), p. 447.

[33] Roy T. Sanford and Jack W. Farrell, "A Study of Customer Service Perceptions, Requirements, and Effects on American Industry," *Annual Proceedings of the NCPDM* (1982), pp. 234–245.

Figure 3-7 Penalties for Customer Service Failures

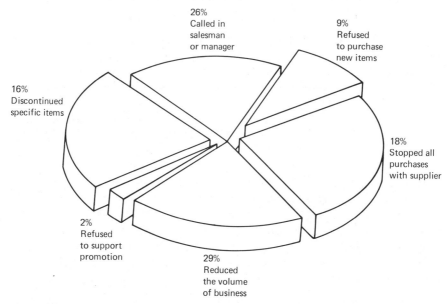

Source: "Does Your Customer Service Program Stack Up?" *Traffic Management* (September, 1982), p. 57. Used with permission.

Overall Customer Service Policy

So far, we have touched on many elements of customer service. Figure 3-8, developed by Warren Blanding, is an overall checklist to apply to a company's internal and external customer service policies. A firm that can handle all situations posed by statements on the form will have a fairly complete customer service policy. (An alternative is to adopt the calendar shown in Figure 3-9.)

Summary

Customer service standards can provide a firm with an important competitive advantage. They are often established in terms of *goals* and *objectives*. In order to determine whether these goals and objectives are being accomplished, they must be stated in specific, written, and measurable terms.

The *order cycle* is the critical series of functions that makes up a good customer service program. It is the time from when a customer places an order to when the order is received at the customer's freight dock. The order cycle is composed of four separate parts: order transmittal, order processing, order picking, and order delivery.

The PD/L department should act as an advisor to the marketing department when establishing the firm's level of customer service. In this capacity, the *costs* of achieving the various levels of customer service are indicated by the PD department.

Customer service goals and objectives are often based on the results of a customer survey that determines the importance of the various elements of customer service. The actual establishment of the customer service "package" is achieved by combining the survey information into three basic categories: economic considerations, the nature of the competitive environment, and the nature of the product.

Once the customer service goals and objectives have been established, it is important that periodic measurement and control be initiated. This will ensure that the firm's customer service standards are being implemented and not reduced to mere rhetoric.

Customer service considerations are becoming increasingly important in recent years because customers are *demanding* higher levels of service. The basic factors responsible for this are: customers are able to reduce their inventory holding costs and "vendor quality control" programs.

Questions for Discussion and Review

1. Discuss *why* customer service is often considered an important aspect of PD management.
2. Who in the firm should establish the customer service goals and objectives? What departments should assist in arriving at this decision? Why?
3. Define, in general terms, customer service *goals* and *objectives*. Then give a specific example of each one.
4. What are the most commonly used specific objectives for customer service programs?
5. The text argues that customer service objectives should be as specific as possible. Do you agree? Why?
6. Define and discuss the *order cycle*. Why is it considered to be an important aspect of customer service?
7. Discuss fully the four basic subparts that combine to form the order cycle.
8. Which of the four subparts of the order cycle do you believe is the most important? Why?
9. Discuss the customer service aspects of "returned products." Do you believe returned products will become a more or less serious problem in the 1980s? Why?
10. The establishment of customer service goals and objectives is a basic corporate responsibility. What information should the various departments in the firm provide for making this important decision? Why? Be specific in your answer.
11. The text stated, "The role of the physical distribution department is to act as an advisor to the marketing department regarding customer service standards." Explain the rationale of this statement.
12. Assume that you are asked to establish the firm's customer service goals and objectives. What information should you collect and how would you gather it?

Figure 3-8 Customer Service Policy Checklist

CUSTOMER SERVICE POLICY CHECKLIST

Published as a special supplement to CUSTOMER SERVICE NEWSLETTER by
Marketing Publications Inc., National Press Building, Washington, DC 20045

NOTE: This checklist is intended only as a general guide to formulation of customer service policy and makes no attempt to separate elements of external policy from those of internal policy. It also recognizes the overlap between terms of sale and customer service policy. Some elements of customer service policy may be influenced by legal requirements and/or trade customs, and in that respect should be interpreted by individual firms in the light of their own situation.

☐ CREDIT RULES AFFECTING CUSTOMER SERVICE

☐ Must credit be established prior to acceptance of orders?
☐ If open account orders are acceptable, are there limits?
☐ Are there credit limits for established accounts?
☐ When will orders not be filled for credit reasons?
☐ Is a responsible credit person readily accessible to customers?

☐ CONDITIONS GOVERNING ACCEPTANCE OF ORDERS

☐ Are there any restrictions on method of receiving orders? (These might include requirements for placing orders through salesmen, brokers, etc., or a prohibition of phone orders.)
☐ Will the customer be required to order from a specific order-receiving location?
☐ What information is required on the order?
☐ What authority is required? (Formal purchase order, or restrictions on phone or verbal orders.)
☐ Are COD orders accepted?
☐ Are there legal limitations? (This would cover restrictions applicable to controlled substances, export-import, licensing or other credentials required by the purchaser.)
☐ What is the policy when purchase orders conflict with terms of sale?

☐ MATERIALS IN SHORT SUPPLY

☐ Is there a suitable allocation policy?
☐ Is it legal?
☐ Is there a single person in charge who is accessible to customers, customer service personnel and salesmen at all times?

☐ CUSTOMER SERVICE ORGANIZATION AND PERSONNEL

☐ Has the mission of the customer service organization been fully defined?
☐ Do the managers have the tools necessary to accomplish their tasks, including personnel, information systems, communications, etc.?
☐ Do they have sufficient authority?
☐ Are there formal selection and training policies for personnel?
☐ Are customer service reps to be assigned by account, or by product line?
☐ Is there a policy whereby customer service managers spend a certain amount of time in the field contacting customers on-location?

☐ Are there provisions for monitoring customer service reps' contacts with customers, i.e., by phone or in correspondence?
☐ Are managers and personnel compensated in line with comparable positions elsewhere in the firm?

☐ JURISDICTION OF SALES VS. CUSTOMER SERVICE

☐ Are salesmen permitted to set shipping dates, or does a standard lead time apply?
☐ Are salesmen permitted to determine shipping locations, or do standard decision rules apply?
☐ Have guidelines been established for the respective participation of salesmen and customer service personnel in each of the following areas?

Prospect inquiries	Credits
Product inquiries	Carrier claims
Product complaints	Reorders
Delivery complaints	Order processing
Shipment tracing	Order status reporting
	Billing problems

Merchandising service
Technical support
Credits
Inside selling

(and other jurisdictional areas specific to the individual firm)

☐ COMPLAINT PROCEDURE AND RIGHT OF APPEAL

☐ Is there a standard procedure for handling complaints?
☐ Is there a policy for automatic resolution of complaints involving payments or replacement below a certain dollar level?
☐ Is the authority to resolve complaints placed at the lowest level consistent with good business practice?
☐ Is there a standard policy of keeping customers informed of the progress of complaints or claims?
☐ Is there an established routine for moving complaints to higher levels of authority when they can't be resolved initially to the customer's satisfaction?
☐ Are customers made aware of their "right of appeal?"

☐ MINIMUM ORDER AND STANDARD ORDER QUANTITIES

☐ Is minimum order size set by unit of shipment, or by dollar value?
☐ If it is set by unit of shipment, does the unit reflect current distribution economics?
☐ If it is set by dollar value, is it a reasonable figure?
☐ Is the minimum order size large enough to discourage costly hand-to-mouth buying by customers, but not so large as to discourage them from buying at all?
☐ Are there standard order quantities which the customer can translate to palletloads, truckloads, carloads, etc.?
☐ Is there provision for overflow truckloads or carloads, i.e., where there is more than enough for one full load but not enough for two?
☐ Does the seller retain the option to add or subtract "variance items" to achieve best transport utilization?
☐ Are there penalties or extra charges for non-standard orders?
☐ Are customer service reps charged with upgrading orders and advising customers of most economic order quantities?

☐ ORDER CYCLE AND LEAD TIME

☐ Are salesmen and reps given a standard lead time to quote to customers?
☐ Is the lead time realistic in terms of materials availability and production capacity?
☐ Is it realistic in terms of finished goods inventories?
☐ Is it based on maximum transportation economies consistent with competitive requirements?

page 2

90

Has a consolidation and pool shipment program been investigated and implemented if practical?

Have order cutoffs and schedules been established and made known to reps, salesmen and customers?

Has a plan been developed to sell such a program to customers on the basis of increased reliability?

Is it in fact more reliable?

Have standard times been developed for the following:

Inbound transmission of orders / Non-exception order processing
Order assembly and shipping / Invoicing
Transit and delivery

SPECIAL ORDERS AND VARIANCES

Are there extra charges for emergency shipments?

For telephone orders (where phone is nor normally used)?

Have rules been established governing change orders, including cutoff or lead time requirements in terms of originally promised shipping date?

What are the conditions under which the order will be recycled?

Have rules been set forth on changes in order cycle caused by addition of items to order which have a longer cycle than other items already ordered?

Has a schedule of penalties been established for cancellation or reduction in order size?

HANDLING OF STOCKOUTS AND BACKORDERS

In the case of partial or complete stockouts, does the policy indicate whether the seller will:

a) Hold order until all items are available?
b) Make partial shipment, with balance to follow?
c) Make partial shipment and cancel balance?
d) Make substitutions for out-of-stock items?
e) Cancel entire order?

Have subroutines been developed for order processing systems to handle stockouts and other exceptions in terms of individual customers' requirements?

If substitutions are acceptable, have criteria been established in terms of pack, size, color, style, model, value, etc.?

Has provision been made for effective monitoring of stockouts?

Has provision been made for timely notification of customers regarding stockouts?

If substitutions are acceptable, have criteria been established in terms of pack, size, color, style, model, value, etc.?

TIME DELIVERIES (IF APPLICABLE)

Has a clear statement of the company's extent of liability in the case of time deliveries to jobsites and elsewhere been formulated and made known to customers?

Have conditions imposed on customers (e.g., 24-hour phone contact) been made known?

Have rules been established for handling chargebacks imposed by customers for late deliveries?

CLAIMS, RETURNS AND CREDITS (see also COMPLAINTS)

Have clear rules been established for acceptance of returns?

Have similar rules been established for filing of non-carrier claims and/or chargebacks and subsequent issuance of credits?

page 3

Has responsibility for filing of carrier claims been established as between seller and buyer?

Has the seller company established a dollar cutoff below which it will not dispute claims or chargebacks by customers?

Has it established a similar dollar cutoff for carrier claims?

ORDER PICKUP BY CUSTOMERS IN THEIR OWN VEHICLES

Is customer pickup permissible?

Are lead time and advance notification requirements set forth so as to minimize disruption to warehouse operations?

Has a minimum order size been established for pickup?

If a freight allowance is granted, is it legal?

PROVISION FOR PRODUCT RECALL

Is lot identification and control adequate to permit efficient product recall as required by the Consumer Product Safety Act?

Are the full requirements of the Act known to all concerned?

Are buyers made aware of their responsibility under the Act to participate in recall activities?

Are communications and information systems adequate to perform product recall as required?

MADE-TO-ORDER PRODUCTS

Has policy been established for acceptable overruns and underruns?

Have penalties been set forth for cancellations and changes?

INVENTORY POLICY

Has a comprehensive inventory policy been developed, based on desired levels of customer service?

Is it adequate?

Have decision rules been developed covering all likely events?

Have adequate monitoring and feedback systems been developed to adjust production schedules and inventory levels as necessary?

Has the firm committed itself to an effective forecasting system?

Has it decided on acceptable stockout levels? By line item fill? By dollar fill?

Have the inventory investment requirements and profit contribution implications been fully explored and spelled out?

Have alternatives like air freight and centralized warehousing of low-volume, high-value items been considered?

CUSTOMER SERVICE LEVELS AND STANDARDS

Have customer requirements in terms of service levels, shipment mode, etc., been fully researched using accepted market research techniques?

Have customer service levels of competitors similarly researched?

Have customer service levels and standards been formulated accordingly?

Have investigations been conducted to determine customers' willingness to trade speed of delivery for improved reliability?

Have standards been established for speed of response to order status and other inquiries from customers?

Has provision been made for an ongoing system for monitoring customer service performance according to standards, and communicating the information in timely fashion to the appropriate quarters?

page 4

Figure 3-9 A Humorous "Solution" to Customer Service Complaints

PSYCHO
CALENDAR

NEG	FRI	FRI	THU	WED	TUE	MON
8	7	6	5	4	3	2
16	15	14	13	12	11	9
23	22	21	20	19	18	17
31	30	29	28	27	26	24
38	37	36	35	34	33	32

1. Every order is RUSH! Everyone wants his material shipped yesterday. With this calendar a customer can place his order on the 7th and have it delivered on the 3rd.
2. Most customers want their orders shipped by Friday, so there are two Fridays in every week.
3. There are seven extra days at the end of the month to take care of shipments which MUST go before the first of the following month.
4. There are no "first of the month" bills to pay because there isn't any "first." We've omitted the "tenth" and "twenty-fifth" so that you won't have to pay our invoices in accordance with our terms.
5. There are no bothersome non-productive Saturdays and Sundays. In that way we can manufacture your rush orders requiring week-end production without time-and-a-half or double-time overtime charges.
6. There's a new day each week called Negotiation day. Requests for improved delivery can be reviewed and discussed once weekly.

13. Does it ever make sense to purposely curtail sales to certain customers? Why?
14. Discuss fully the importance of *measurement* and *control* in achieving an effective customer service program.
15. A potential weakness in the measurement of customer service standards

is that the wrong elements may be measured. Discuss why this could happen.

16. It has been said that customers are demanding higher and higher levels of customer service from their vendors. Discuss fully the reasons that explain this situation.

17. Examine the extensive "Customer Service Policy Checklist" compiled by Blanding. Which major section do you believe is the most important? Why? Which do you believe is the least important? Defend your answer.

18. Look at the introductory quote at the beginning of this chapter by Randall L. Hanna. Do you agree with his statement? Why? Be specific.

19. Discuss the importance of the trend involving computer-to-computer order transmittal. (Be sure to incorporate information from Figure 3-3 in your answer.)

20. Read Figure 3-2. Can you think of any similar situations? If yes, discuss.

21. Study Figure 3-7. How do you think this chart will change by 1990?

22. What is the UCS? Discuss its importance to the grocery industry.

Additional Chapter References

Baritz, Steven G., and Lorin Zissman. "Researching Customer Service: The Right Way." *Annual Proceedings of the NCPDM* (1983), pp. 608–619.

Cooper, M. Bixby, John C. Jeidy, and George D. Wagenheim. "Surveying Customer Perceptions of Distribution Service at Ciba-Geigy." *Annual Proceedings of the NCPDM* (1984), pp. 165–178.

Davis, James R. "The Economic Benefits of a Fully-Integrated Physical Distribution Service." *Annual Proceedings of the NCPDM* (1983), pp. 759–777.

Hanna, Randall L. "Customer Service Strategies." *Annual Proceedings of the NCPDM* (1983), pp. 522–531.

Krenn, John M., and Harvey N. Shycon. "Modeling Sales Response to Customer Service for More Effective Distribution." *Annual Proceedings of the NCPDM* (1983), pp. 581–601.

Kuah, Geok-Koon. "Teleconference/Intercity Business Travel Substitution: Some Problems." *Annual Proceedings of the Transportation Research Forum* (1983), pp. 733–741.

Lambert, Douglas M., and Douglas E. Zemke. "The Customer Service Component of the Marketing Mix." *Annual Proceedings of the NCPDM* (1982), pp. 1–24.

MacAllister, Sean. "Micro Processing Applications and Order Processing." *Annual Proceedings of the NCPDM* (1982), pp. 653–664.

Majeczky, Carl H., and Peter A. Smith. "Competitive Customer Service Planning at Sara Lee." *Annual Proceedings of the NCPDM* (1983), pp. 602–607.

Norris, Richard C. "The Components of a Fully-Integrated Physical Distribution Service." *Annual Proceedings of the NCPDM* (1983), pp. 778–789.

Philip, Craig E., and Emmitt J. Posey. "Improving Railroad Marketing Effectiveness Through Management of the Customer Interface." *Annual Proceedings of the Transportation Research Forum,* (1982), pp. 541–548.

Polzello, Richard. "How Customer Service Policies Impact Inventory Management Decisions." *Annual Proceedings of the NCPDM* (1982), pp. 489–522.

Restaino, Thomas J. "International Order Processing: The Ingersoll-Rand Story." *Annual Proceedings of the NCPDM* (1983), pp. 751–758.

Ritz, Christopher J. "Analytical Methods for Measuring the Effect of Customer Service on Sales." *Annual Proceedings of the NCPDM* (1982), pp. 539–544.

Ronen, David. "Measures of Product Availability." *Journal of Business Logistics* (Vol. 3, No. 1, 1982), pp. 45–58.

Sanford, Roy T., and Jack W. Farrell. "A Study of Customer Service Perceptions, Requirements and Effects on American Industry." *Annual Proceedings of the NCPDM* (1982), pp. 233–246.

Sanford, Roy T. "The Cost/Benefit Approach to Designing Better Customer Service Strategies." *Annual Proceedings of the NCPDM* (1982), pp. 545–562.

Shycon, Harvey N. "How Customer Service Impacts Sales Growth and ROI and How Distribution Can Help Increase Corporate Success." *Annual Proceedings of the NCPDM* (1982), pp. 563–580.

Wagenheim, George D. "Distribution as a Source of Competitive Advantage." *Annual Proceedings of the NCPDM* (1983), pp. 807–813.

Weiss, Martin A. "Implications of Electronic Order Exchange Systems for Logistics Planning and Strategy." *Journal of Business Logistics* (Vol. 5, No. 1, 1984), pp. 16–39.

Wilson, Hal, and Tony Dmaria. "An Evaluation of Alternative Techniques for Order Fulfillment." *Annual Proceedings of the NCPDM* (1983), pp. 627–644.

CASE 3-1

KidieLand and the Super Gym[1]

KidieLand is a retailer of toys located in the Midwest. Corporate headquarters is in Chicago with 70 stores located in Minnesota, Wisconsin, Michigan, Illinois, Indiana, Ohio, Iowa, and Kentucky. Their two distribution centers are located in Columbus (for Kentucky, Indiana, Michigan, and Ohio) and Chicago (for Illinois, Iowa, Minnesota, and Wisconsin).

KidieLand markets a full range of toys, electronic games, computers, and playsets. Emphasis is on a full line of brand name products together with selected items sold under the "KidieLand" brand. KidieLand's primary competitors include various re-

---

[1] This is a disguised case, prepared by Dr. Michael A. McGinnis and Mr. Frank Burinsky, Shippensburg University, and reproduced with permission. This case was prepared as a basis for class discussion rather than to illustrate effective or ineffective handling of an administrative issue.

gional discount chains. A key to KidieLand's success has been a comprehensive product line, aggressive pricing, and self service.

Donald Hurst is KidieLand's Distribution Manager. He is responsible for managing both distribution centers, for traffic management, and for inventory control. Don's primary mission is "to make sure all stores are in stock at all times without maintaining excessive levels of inventory."

One morning in late January, Don was reviewing the new year's merchandising plan when he discovered that starting in March, KidieLand would begin promoting the "Super Gym Outdoor Childrens' Exercise Center." Mr. Hurst was particularly interested that the new set would sell for $715. In addition, the Super Gym is packaged in three boxes weighing a total of 450 pounds. "Holy Cow!," thought Don, "the largest set we have sold to date retails for $159 and weighs only 125 pounds."

"There must be some mistake," thought Don as he walked down the hall to the office of Olga Olsen, KidieLand's buyer for playsets. Olga was new on her job and unusually harassed because both of her assistant buyers had just resigned to seek employment on the West Coast.

As soon as Olga saw Don she exclaimed, "Don, my friend, I have been meaning to talk to you." Don knew right then that his worst fears were confirmed.

The next morning Don and Olga met with Randy Smith, Don's traffic manager; A. J. Toth, General Manager for KidieLand's eight Chicago stores, and Sharon Rabiega, Don's assistant for distribution services. Since the previous year had been unusually profitable, everyone was in a good mood (for once) because this year's bonus was 50 per cent larger than last year's.

Nevertheless, A. J. got to the point, "You mean to tell me that we expect somebody to stuff a spouse, three kids, a dog, and 450 pounds of Super Gym in their Vega station wagon and not have a conniption?"

Randy chimed in, "Besides, we can't drop ship Super Gyms from the manufacturer to the consumer's address because Super Gym ships only in quantities of ten or more."

Olga was now becoming worried, "We can't back out of the Super Gym now," she moaned, "I have already committed KidieLand for 400 sets and the Spring-Summer playset promotion went to press last week. Besides," Olga continued, "I am depending on the Super Gym to make my gross margin figures."

By now the scope of the problem had become apparent to everyone at the meeting. At 3 p.m. Don summarized the alternatives discussed. They are summarized below.

1. Purchase a two-wheeled trailer for each store.
2. Find a local trucking company who can haul the Super Gym from the store to the customer.
3. Stock the Super Gym at the distribution centers and have the truck deliver during the delivery runs to the retail stores.
4. Charge for delivery if the customer can't get the Super Gym home.
5. Negotiate with the Super Gym manufacturers to drop ship to the customer's address.

When the meeting adjourned, everyone agreed to meet the following Monday to discuss the alternatives. Thursday morning a record breaking blizzard hit Chicago; everyone went home early. KidieLand headquarters was closed Friday because of the blizzard. By Wednesday the same group met again except for A. J. Toth who was still stranded on a skiing trip in Colorado. However, A. J.'s assistant, Mary Anne Ainsworth, was in attendance.

Don started the meeting. "O.K.," Don began, "let's review our options, Sharon." Don continued, "What did you find out about buying trailers for each store?"

"Well," Sharon began, "the best deal I can find is $1800 per trailer for seventy trailers, plus $250 per store for an adequate selection of bumper hitches, and an additional $50 per year per store for licensing and insurance."

"Oh, no," moaned Olga, "we only expect to sell 5.7 sets per store—that means $368 per Super Gym for delivery," as she punched her calculator, "and $147,000 in lost gross margin!"

Next, Randy Smith summarized the second option. "So far we can get delivery within 25 miles of most of our stores for $38.21 per set. Actually," Randy continued, "$38.21 is for delivery 25 miles from the store. The rate would be a little less for under 25 miles and about $1.50 per mile beyond 25 miles."

Mary Anne chimed in, "According to our marketing research department, 85 per cent of our customers drive less than 25 minutes to the store so a flat fee of 40 dollars for delivery would probably be O.K."

Randy continued, "Most delivery companies we talked to will deliver twice weekly, but not daily."

Next, Sharon spoke, "The motor carrier that handles shipments from our distribution centers is a consolidator. He said that squeezing an eighteen wheeler into some subdivision wouldn't make sense." She continued, "Every time they try they knock down a couple of mailboxes and leave truck tracks in some home owner's driveway."

Olga added, "I talked to Super Gym about drop shipping to the customer's address and they said forget it. Whenever they have tried that," Olga continued, "the customer gets two of one box and none of another."

"Well, Olga," Don interrupted, "can we charge the customer for delivery?"

Olga thought a minute. "Well, we have never done that before but then we have never sold a 450 pound item before. It sounds like," Olga continued "that our choice is to either absorb $40.00 per set or charge the customer for delivery."

"That means $16,000 for delivery," added Olga.

"One more thing," Don spoke, "if we charge for shipping, we must include that in the copy for the Spring-Summer brochure."

Olga smiled sheepishly, "We can make a minor insert in the copy if we decide to charge for delivery. However," she continued, "any changes will have to be made to the page proofs—and page proofs are due back to the printers next Monday."

Question One: List and discuss the advantages and disadvantages of purchasing a two-wheeled trailer for each store to use for delivering Super Gyms.

Question Two: List and discuss the advantages and disadvantages of having local trucking companies deliver the Super Gym from the retail stores to the customers.

Question Three: List and discuss the advantages and disadvantages of stocking Super Gyms at the distribution centers, and then have the truck which makes deliveries from the distribution center to the retail stores also make deliveries of Super Gyms to individual customers.

Question Four: List and discuss the advantages and disadvantages of charging the customer for home delivery if the customer is unable to carry the Super Gym home by himself or herself.

Question Five: Which alternative would you perfer? Why?

Question Six: Draft a brief statement (catalog copy) to be inserted in the firm's Spring-Summer brochure which clearly explains to the potential customers the policy you recommended in question five.

CASE 3-2

The Cheezy Wheezy Case

Starting as a small retail store in New Glarus, Wisconsin, the Cheezy Wheezy firm had slowly grown into a chain of nine retail shops located in both southern Wisconsin and northern Illinois. In recent years nearly all of its competitors had begun issuing catalogs, widely distributed in late October, advertising gift packages of cheese, jam, jellies, and other fancy food items. Henry Wilson, son of the firm's founder, had convinced his father that Cheezy Wheezy should also issue a catalog.

It was then March, and the last snows were melting. Henry Wilson had called his third staff meeting in as many weeks to discuss the catalog project. Present were Henry (whose title happened to be vice-president); Susan Moore, the sales manager; Jeff Bell, the inventory manager; and Robert Walker, the traffic manager. Also present was Robert Caldwell, from a Milwaukee-based ad agency that was handling many aspects of the catalog project. Moore and Caldwell had just finished describing the catalog's tentative design and the allocation of catalog pages to various product lines. Caldwell then said: "We are up to the point where we must design the order form, which will be stapled inside the center pages. It will be a single 8½- by 11-inch sheet. The customer will remove it from the catalog, complete it, fold it into envelope shape, lick the gummed lines, and mail it in. The order form will be on only one side of the sheet. On the reverse will be the instructions for folding and Cheezy Wheezy's mailing address in New Glarus; the remainder of the space will be ads for some 'impulse' items. Right now we're thinking of a Santa Claus-shaped doll molded out of cheese."

"Enough of that," said Wilson, "this group isn't here to discuss Santa dolls. We're here to design the order form. We may also have to talk a little about selling terms. Susan?"

Responding to her cue, Moore said: "Our biggest problem is how to handle the transportation and shipping costs. We've studied all of our competitor's catalogs. Some absorb the costs into the product's price; some charge by weight of the order; some charge by money value of order; and some ship COD."

"How important are shipping costs, Susan?" asked Bell.

"Plenty," was her response. "They run two to $3.00 for a one- or two-pound package. If you take a pound of cheese that we sell in our retail stores for $2.00, here are our costs if it goes by catalog: our cost of goods, $1.00; order processing, 50 cents; overhead, including inventory carrying costs, 50 cents; packaging for shipment, 50 cents; and transportation costs to any point in the United States ranging between $1.75 and $3.20. If, however, we're dealing with bigger shipments, the relative costs vary."

"I'm not following you," said Wilson.

"It's like this," responded Moore: "The wholesale cost of cheese is the same per pound, no matter how much is sold. Order-processing costs are approximately the same for each order we'll be receiving by mail. Overhead and inventory carrying costs are always present but may be allocated in a variety of ways. Packaging costs are also about the same per order. They go up only a few cents as we move to larger cartons. Transportation costs are hard to describe because of their tapers. Right now our whole catalog project is bogged down with the problem of transportation cost tapers."

"Tapers?" said Wilson, turning to Walker. "You've never told me about tapers before. It sounds like some sort of animal."

"That's tapir, t-a-p-i-r," said Walker. "We're talking about tapers, t-a-p-e-r-s."

"Oh," said Wilson. "What are they?"

"When one ships small packages of cheese," said Walker, "rates are based on two factors, the weight being shipped and the distance. As weight or distance increases (or both), the rates go up, but not as quickly. This is called the tapering principle. To ship two pounds of cheese from New Glarus to St. Louis costs $2.40; three pounds cost $3.30; five pounds cost $4.60, and so on. A hundred pounds, no, fifty pounds is a better example because some of the parcel services we'll be using won't take one hundred pounds, fifty pounds would cost $21.00. There's also a distance taper. The two-pound shipment that costs $2.40 to St. Louis is $3.40 to Denver and $4.15 to LA."

"Can't we use the 'average' transportation costs?" asked Bell. "That's what we do with inventory carrying costs."

"Won't work," said Caldwell. "You'll be overpriced for small short-distance shipments and will lose sales. For heavy long shipments you'll be underpriced and will make so many sales that you might soon go 'belly up.'"

Wilson shuddered and inquired: "Does that mean we charge by weight and by distance?"

Moore answered. "It's not that easy. In the cheese business, people buy by the pound, but shipping weights—which include packaging—are actually more. A customer who orders three pounds of cheese is—in fact—shipping three pounds of cheese plus six ounces of packaging materials. I wish we could sell a 'pound' of cheese that consisted of fourteen ounces of cheese and two ounces of packing material, but that would be illegal at worst, and of questionable ethics, at best."

"We have the same problems with distance," added Walker. "We're trying to sell in fifty states, but who knows how far they are from New Glarus? We could have tables and maps in the catalog, but they take up valuable selling space. Also, if it looks too complex, we may just cause some potential customers to 'turn off' before completing their order."

"There's another problem some of our clients have," added Caldwell, "and that is 'split' orders. The customer will want ten pounds of cheese, but it will be five two-pound packages sent to five different locations. That has an impact on both packaging and transportation costs."

"So, what do we do?" asked Wilson.

Question One: Assume Cheezy Wheezy goes into the catalog order business. What policy should they adopt for handling stock-outs—that is, what should they do when they receive mail orders they cannot completely fill because one or more of the desired items are out of stock?

Question Two: Some mail customers will complain that the items Cheezy Wheezy shipped never arrived. What policy should Cheezy Wheezy adopt to deal with this?

Question Three: Should the order form, which will be stapled into the center of the catalog and be addressed to Cheezy Wheezy, be of the "postage-paid" type, which means that Cheezy Wheezy will pay the first-class postage rate plus a few cents on each envelope delivered to them, or should the customer be expected to add a first-class stamp to the order before he or she mails it? Discuss.

Question Four: Cheezy Wheezy's headquarters are in New Glarus, but they also operate in southern Wisconsin and northern Illinois. Is New Glarus the best address to use for receiving mail orders for cheese? Might there be advantages, perhaps, in having the mail addressed to a more major city—say, Madison or Milwaukee, Wisconsin, or Chicago? Discuss.

Question Five: From the facts that have been presented in the case, how would you handle the matter of charging for *packaging* costs of each shipment? Why?

Question Six: How would you handle the matter of charging for the *transportation* costs of each shipment? Why?

Question Seven: Taking your answers to questions five and six, write out—in either text or tabular form—the explanation of "shipping" charges that your catalog customers will read. (Note: as used here, *shipping* includes both packaging and transportation.)

Question Eight: On a single 8½- × 11-in. sheet of paper, design a catalog order form for use by Cheezy Wheezy.

Part **II**

The Elements of Physical Distribution/Logistics Systems

Part II presents a detailed examination of elements of PD/L systems.

Chapter 4 analyzes each of the U.S. transportation modes—railroads, motor carriers, pipelines, water transportation, and air freight. Chapter 5 builds on this analysis by examining the complex regulatory environment that is characteristic of the transportation industry and by exploring the subject of freight rate determination. Chapter 6, the final chapter dealing exclusively with transportation, examines the multifaceted functions of the traffic manager.

Inventory control and analysis are discussed in Chapter 7. Distribution logistics, by its very nature, involves spatial differences that are often of considerable magnitude. Chapter 8 examines locational and geographical considerations that directly interface with PD/L departments.

Warehousing is discussed from a PD viewpoint in Chapter 9, while Chapter 10 is devoted to an analysis of the fundamental aspects of materials handling and protective packaging. Chapter 11, the final chapter in Part II, presents a comprehensive discussion of the complexities and challenges inherent in international PD management.

The Exxon Maine *is a sea-going tug which operates along the Coast in the area between Boston and Baltimore. The top photo shows her pulling a barge. Since tugboats sometimes push* their loads, it is possible to elevate the Exxon Maine's *bridge, in order to improve visibility. This is shown in the lower photo.*

(Credit: *The Lamp*, Exxon Corporation)

The Transportation System

Meanwhile, worn-out locks continue to deteriorate, bottleneck locks restrict traffic on commercially important rivers, and a transportation mode which moves 16 per cent of the nation's freight at 3 per cent of the freight bill is deprived of the improvements which would make it even more efficient.

Harry N. Cook
Letter to the editor
Wall Street Journal
November 29, 1984

In my opinion, it is time to stop talking of rail or truck or barge or pipeline transportation in isolation and to start talking about transportation.

Hays T. Watkins
Chairman, CSX Corporation
Railway Age
November 1983

One of the brightest prospects for creating a competitive alternative in hauling coal [slurry pipelines] has been felled by the guerilla tactics of the railroads.

Carl E. Bagge
President, National Coal Association
Traffic World
August 13, 1984

We think the trucking industry is going to continue to be a fierce competitor with the rails, and we want to participate.

Luino Dell'Osso, Jr.
Senior VP, Planning and Finance
Burlington Northern
Minneapolis Star and Tribune
February 6, 1985

- Conrail
- Union work rules
- Unit train
- Run-through train
- Interstate system
- Gathering pipeline
- Trunk pipeline
- Product pipeline
- Slurry pipeline
- Towboat
- LASH vessel
- Combination airline
- Belly freight
- Freight forwarders
- Brokers
- Shippers' agents
- Shippers' cooperatives
- Auxiliary carriers
- Intermodal transportation
- Piggyback/TOFC/COFC
- Transportation companies

- To understand the role of transportation in a PD/L system
- To comprehend the size of the transportation industry in the United States
- To explain the railroad alternative for PD/L managers
- To describe the role of trucking in PD/L
- To identify the importance of pipelines to PD/L
- To note the position of domestic water carriers in the transportation system
- To comprehend the air freight options available to PD/L executives
- To differentiate other transportation alternatives, including transportation companies
- To distinguish criteria for selecting among transportation modes

Transportation and Logistics

The transportation system is an integral part of life in this country. Although most people don't realize how important the transportation system is, they become painfully aware of its existence when a segment of it malfunctions. Table 4-1 shows the nation's 1983 estimated freight bill for each of the major modes of transport. The nation's total estimated freight bill accounts for about 7½ per cent of the GNP. Transportation is pivotal to the successful operation of any logistics system:

1. Transportation costs are directly affected by the location of the firm's plants, warehouses, vendors, and customers.
2. Inventory requirements are influenced by the mode of transport used. High-speed, high-priced transportation systems require smaller amounts of inventories near customer locations.
3. The transport mode selected determines the packaging required.
4. The type of carrier used dictates a manufacturing plant's materials–handling equipment, such as loading and unloading equipment and the design of the receiving and shipping docks.

Table 4-1 The Nation's Estimated Freight Bill
(in millions of dollars)

	1983
Highway	
Truck—Intercity	
ICC-Regulated	46,500
Non-ICC Regulated	62,333
Truck—Local	80,946
Bus	246
	190,025
Rail	
Railroads	27,318
Water	
International	8,545
Coastal, Intercoastal	3,791
Inland Waterways	1,763
Great Lakes	660
Locks, Channels, etc.	1,158
	15,917
Oil Pipe Line	
ICC-Regulated	7,472
Non-ICC Regulated	830
	8,302
Air	
Domestic	3,671
International	1,170
	4,841
Other Carriers	
Forwarders	628
Other Shipper Costs	
Loading and Unloading Freight Cars	1,698
Operation of Traffic Departments	927
	2,625
Grand Total	249,656
Gross National Product (Billions of Dollars)	3,304.8
Grand Total % of GNP	7.56

Source: "Transportation in America" (Washington, D.C.: Transportation Policy Associates, March 1985), p. 4. Used with permission.

5. An order-processing methodology that encourages maximum consolidation of shipments between common points enables a company to give larger shipments to its carriers and take advantage of volume discounts.
6. Customer service goals influence the type of carrier selected by the seller. (See Chapter 3.)
7. Transportation costs represent the single highest cost element of a logistics system. (See Table 4-2.)

Table 4-2 Major Elements of
Physical Distribution and
Logistics Costs, 1984 (in %)

Transportation	45
Warehousing	20
Inventory Carrying Costs	20
Order Processing	6
PD/L Administration	4
Other	5
	100%

Source: Derived from *Davis Database* (October 1984), a newsletter published by Herbert W. Davis and Company, Englewood Cliffs, N.J. Used with permission.

Transportation Modes

The transportation sector of the United States economy is generally competitive both among and within modes. Table 4-3 shows the ton-mile distribution of freight between the various modes for 1984 and earlier years.

> *Ton-mile* is a transportation measure meaning one ton of freight moving one mile. Ten tons traveling one mile counts the same as one ton moving ten miles. Speed is not taken into account.

Table 4-1 shows the dollar distribution by mode. Perhaps the most interesting comparison between Tables 4-1 and 4-3 is the relationship between the railroads and the motor carriers. While railroads transported about 50 per cent more intercity ton-miles than motor carriers in 1984, the motor carriers received seven times more revenue than did the railroads. The reasons for this disparity are the types of products carried and the quality of service offered.

Railroads

Figure 4-1 shows the current railroad network. In 1982, there were 159,000 miles of railroad *line,* and approximately 263,000 total miles of *track* in the United States. (The figure for the latter is greater than the figure for the former because it counts switching yard trackage and situations where there are parallel tracks.) The total miles of railroad line has been declining since 1916, the peak year, when there were 254,037 line miles. Today railroads are actively attempting to abandon some rail lines for two reasons. First, as industries move and as population shifts, many railroad lines are no longer economically feasible to operate. Second, growth in the highway system,

The Elements of Physical Distribution/Logistics Systems

Table 4-3 Volume of U.S. Intercity Freight Traffic (millions of revenue freight ton-miles and percentage of total)

Year	Railroads	%	Trucks	%	Great Lakes	%
1929	454,800	74.9	19,689	3.3	97,322	16.0
1939	338,850	62.4	52,821	9.7	76,312	14.0
1944	746,912	68.6	58,264	5.4	118,769	10.9
1950	596,940	56.2	172,860	16.3	111,687	10.5
1960	579,130	44.1	235,483	21.7	99,468	7.6
1970	771,168	39.8	412,000	21.3	114,475	5.9
1980	932,000	37.3	565,000	22.6	113,000	4.6
1984	936,000	36.6	602,000	23.6	80,000	3.1

Year	Rivers and Canals	%	Oil Pipelines	%	Air	%	Total
1929	8,661	1.4	26,900	4.4	3	—	607,375
1939	19,937	3.7	55,602	10.2	12	—	543,534
1944	31,386	2.9	132,864	12.2	71	—	1,088,266
1950	51,657	4.9	129,175	12.1	318	—	1,062,637
1960	120,785	9.2	228,626	17.4	778	—	1,314,270
1970	204,085	10.5	431,000	22.3	3,295	0.2	1,936,023
1980	307,000	12.3	575,000	23.0	5,000	0.2	2,497,000
1984	324,000	12.7	605,000	23.7	6,526	0.3	2,554,000

Source: Association of American Railroads, *Yearbook of Railroad Facts* (1984), p. 32; and Transportation Policy Associates, *Transportation in America* (March 1985), p. 6.

Figure 4-1 United States Railroad Network

Source: Association of American Railroads.

especially the Interstate System, has made it very difficult for the rail industry to compete for short-haul traffic.

The railroad industry is dominated by 32 Class I railroads—an Interstate Commerce Commission (ICC) classification for railroads with greater than $50 million in annual operating revenues. They produce more than 98 per cent of the railroad ton-miles. While there is a considerable variation in size among the Class I railroads, the typical Class I rail carrier has about 12,000 employees and approximately 5,500 miles of rail line.

Railroads specialize in transporting raw materials and unprocessed products in car-load (CL) quantities, which usually are 30,000 pounds or more per shipment. Less-than-carload (LCL) quantity shipments are less than 1 per cent of all railroad freight car loadings and in many states not handled at all. In 1983, mining products, such as metallic ores, coal, stone, gravel, nonmetallic minerals, clay, and coke, accounted for 42 per cent of all CL shipments. Coal is the largest commodity transported by rail, amounting to 28 per cent of all shipments in 1983.[1] Unprocessed agricultural products account for 8 per cent of all shipments. Other products that use the railroad system extensively are processed foods, forest products, paper, chemicals, oils, metals, automobiles, and scrap. The average rate charged by the railroads in 1983 was about 3.1 cents per ton-mile. This reflects the efficiency of transporting commodities in bulk movements.

The current overall financial condition of the railroads is difficult to examine, although for the most part it is not good. In 1983, all railroads averaged only 3.89 per cent return on net invested capital. In the early 1970s there were a dozen rail carriers in bankruptcy proceedings, mostly in the Northeast region of the country. In an attempt to solve the crisis precipitated by the Penn-Central collapse, Congress passed the Northeast Regional Rail Reorganization Act of 1973. This initial legislation provided for more than $2 billion of federal loan guarantees and outright grants. On April 1, 1976, a new government-sponsored railroad, the Consolidated Rail Corporation (Conrail), took over the essential operations of the Penn-Central and other bankrupt eastern railroads.

Originally, Congress had believed that the new entity would need only the trackage necessary to create a slimmed-down railroad capable of being supported by the region's traffic and would become profitable by 1979. Conrail received federal subsidies and loans totaling $6 billion since 1976.[2] However, with the appointment of L. Stanley Crane as president of Conrail in 1980, the carrier has achieved remarkable success. Crane, former president of the Southern Railway, fully utilized the marketing flexibility made available by rail deregulation of 1980. In addition, Conrail recently transferred its passenger commuter business to state and local governments (this aspect of rail business almost always operates at a loss) and it has negotiated favorable wage and work-rule agreements with the unions. The result is that

---

[1] Approximately 12 per cent of coal production was being exported in 1983. See Thomas C. Campbell and Amy Dalton, "Coal Exports: A Problem in Energy and Transportation," *Transportation Journal* (Spring 1983), pp. 34–46. In late 1984, U.S. coal exports were declining.

[2] See James C. Johnson, "Lessons from Amtrak and Conrail," ICC *Practitioners' Journal* (March–April 1982), pp. 247–256.

Conrail in 1981 achieved its first profit of $39 million. Profitability has grown every year; in 1984 it was $495 million.[3] The Reagan administration desired to return Conrail to the private sector of the economy as soon as it was consistently operating profitably. In 1984 the Department of Transportation (DOT) accepted bids for Conrail and in February 1985 selected Norfolk Southern Corporation's $1.2 billion bid. Since NS already controls about one-third of the rail traffic in the Conrail service area, there is potential antitrust problems with the proposed merger. Congress has to authorize the sale of Conrail and as this book went to press, the merger with NS was still being debated.[4]

Railroad Operating Problems.   Three major problems confront rail management in the last half of the 1980s: continued loss of manufactured products to the trucking industry, union work rules, and union wage rates. Note that two of the three problem areas involve labor issues.

The food industry exemplifies the service/rate problem experienced by the rail industry. General Mills in the early 1970s shipped over 70 per cent of its finished food products via rail. Today that number is less than 30 per cent. The main reasons for this shift are that rail rates have increased while truck rates have decreased and their service levels have improved. Rail service levels typically cannot compete with the trucking industry. James Mann, director of transportation for Quaker Oats Company, declared, "In the grocery trade, acceptable rail delivery time has been plus or minus a day of the requested arrival date, whereas motor carriers are there usually on the hour. You have to consider the cost, safety, and inventory factors if you're going to deliver by rail."[5] Fleming Foods of Pennsylvania also is using less rail than in past years. The firm's distribution manager, Ken Collins, noted, "The company keeps rail to a minimum because using motor carriers is more productive, cheaper, and there is less damage."[6] Collins also stated, "The railroads are too independent. They're rarely on time—they're either too early or way too late—and when *they* make a mistake, they charge *you* to take care of it! Our industry can't stand it."[7] (Collins is referring to demurrage when he says that the railroad makes the consignee [receiver] pay for the railroad's mistakes. Demurrage, which is examined in Chapter 6, involves a penalty payment paid to a railroad for not loading or unloading a rail car within specified time periods.)

Railroads typically ship general merchandise in boxcars, and because this portion of their business is in a long-term decline, the industry finds itself with excess general-purpose boxcars. It has been speculated that the

[3] Don Byrne, "Conrail Budget Sees '85 Almost Equal In Profitability To Record '84 Levels," *Traffic World* (Jan. 28, 1985), p. 13.

[4] Richard Koenig and Daniel Machalaba, "Norfolk Southern Faces Number of Challenges To Its Conrail Purchase," *Wall Street Journal* (Feb. 11, 1985), pp. 1, 12, "Derailing the Conrail Deal," an editorial in *Wall Street Journal* (March 26, 1985), p. 34, and "NS-Conrail: The Fight is Just Beginning," *Railway Age* (March 1985), p. 23.

[5] Nancy Entwisle, "Super(Market) Strategies: The Boxcar's New Role," *Distribution* (March 1984), p. 36.

[6] Ibid.

[7] Ibid.

rail industry will never again purchase this type of car. One railroad, the Norfolk Southern, is converting its excess boxcars into flatcars to haul high-way trailers.[8]

Union work rules is the second operating problem.[9] This situation has been exacerbated by the declining level of rail employment.[10] In 1929 there were 1.7 million rail employees.[11] By 1980 the number was reduced to 459,000 and by 1984 to 330,000, and the trend will undoubtedly continue.[12] This declining total railroad employment has made rail unions generally unwilling to innovate and compromise with railroad management, especially in areas involving work rules and crew sizes. The majority of today's railroad work rules were developed prior to 1900. For example, a day's pay for line-haul train employees is computed as being equivalent to 100 miles traveled. The mileage factor was equitable in 1880, when trains often could not average 15 miles per hour. Now, however, many railroads are able to achieve freight train speeds of 50 miles per hour so that a crew is paid for a full day's work after only two hours. One writer noted that "these 'make-work' or 'featherbedding' practices produce a misallocation of resources, prevent further innovations, and further exacerbate the deteriorating competitive position of American railroads."[13]

The crew-size controversy has been a perennial problem area for railroad management. On line-haul freight trains, the unions require a four-person crew, whereas management believes that a three-person crew should be the maximum and that even two employees would be feasible. A number of railroads have recently negotiated three-person crews if the train is below a certain length. On the Burlington Northern, this reduced crew is utilized on trains with fewer than seventy cars.[14] In a limited number of cases, trains are operating without cabooses and with two-person crews. The Canadian National (CN) has been experimenting with ETUs (end-of-train-units that ride on the last rail car and monitor brake-line air pressure and transmit this information to the engineer by radio); they were found to be 98 per cent reliable in all types of weather. CN management points out that German National Railroads have not used cabooses for thirty years and the Quebec

[8] "Norfolk Southern Corp.," *Modern Railroads* (June 1984), p. 26.

[9] This problem has been a perennial issue for rail management. See I. Leo Sharfman, *The American Railroad Problem* (New York: Century Company, 1921).

[10] The decline in rail employment is primarily the result of improved labor productivity. One book was highly influential in achieving this result. See James C. Nelson, *Railroad Transportation and Public Policy* (Washington, D.C.: The Brookings Institution, 1959).

[11] Railroad workers were once so numerous and powerful as a political force that they were able to convince Congress that the federal government should become involved in creating a pension plan for retired rail employees. This retirement program was—and is—paid for by both rail employees and the employer. This program was a forerunner of today's Social Security system, which covers the rest of the work force. Even today rail employees are still covered by their retirement plan and are not contributors to Social Security.

[12] Gus Welty, "The Search for Productivity," *Railway Age* (Nov. 1984), p. 43.

[13] Marvin J. Levin, "The Railroad Crew Size Controversy Revisited," *Labor Law Journal* (June 1969), p. 373.

[14] For a complete discussion of this issue, see Carl D. Martland, "Workload Measurement and Train Crew Consist Adjustments: The Boston and Maine Experience," *Transportation Journal* (Spring 1982), pp. 34–57.

Cartier Railway stopped using cabooses in 1963.[15] The Union Pacific railroad has eliminated cabooses on about 25 per cent of its trains between Salt Lake City and Los Angeles.[16]

The last operating problem is the high wage rate of unionized labor relative to their competitors, especially the trucking industry. In 1983, for the first time, the average compensation package (wage and fringe benefits) for the average rail employee became the highest of any transport mode. For many years the airline industry had held this position. The average rail employee received $41,310 versus $38,951 for the airlines.[17] In terms of actual wages paid to union labor, in 1982 the average road locomotive engineer was paid $43,800, compared to the average teamster over-the-road driver of $32,000 and the typical nonunion over-the-road driver who was paid $26,500.[18] What concerns rail management most is that the rate of increase for rail labor is increasing faster than for the trucking industry. In the ten years from 1974 to 1984, rail wage increases grew 53 per cent faster than in the trucking industry.[19] Darius M. Gaskins, Jr., senior vice-president of the Burlington Northern (BN) railroad, has warned that railroads will be squeezed out of more and more markets in the future unless rails can control the rate of increase in their unionized wages. At present the BN can be cost competitive with trucks on hauls of over 700 miles. But Gaskins has noted that if the rate of future labor-cost increases continue at the previous rate, by 1986 the carrier will need a shipment of nearly 800 miles to be cost competitive. Gaskins observed, "If a nonunion railroad could come along, the rest of us would be in trouble."[20] Rail management will be negotiating for a two-scale wage system in 1985. New employees will be paid substantially less than existing workers. Rail unions point out that rail carriers are profitable and they are seeking a 30 per cent wage increase in the 1985–87 period with a cost-of-living escalator and improvements in the fringe-benefit program.[21]

Railroad Service Innovation. Most railroads are profitable and through service innovations and aggressive marketing are recapturing some lost traffic. The key to the railroads' attempts to increase levels of customer services has been their commitment to capital improvements. There are numerous examples. Because trains are traveling faster with heavier loads, the rail carriers have been replacing their rails with heavier track. Instead of pre-World War II rails, which came in 30-foot sections and weighed 70–90 pounds per yard, today's rail weighs 115–130 pounds per yard and is welded into con-

[15] Don Phillips, "One Step on a Long Journey," *Trains* (Sept. 1984), p. 10.

[16] *Railnews Update,* Association of American Railroads (Oct. 17, 1984), p. 2.

[17] "Rails Replace Airlines in Top Spot in Employee Earnings-Fringe Levels," *Traffic World* (Sept. 24, 1984), p. 78. See also Robert Roberts, "Job Security is Bargaining Chip," *Modern Railroads* (March 1985), p. 23.

[18] Don Phillips, "Haven't We Been Here Before," *Trains* (June 1984), p. 14.

[19] Welty, op. cit., p. 33.

[20] Robert J. Kursar and DeMaris A. Berry, "Distribution Professionals Focus on Future at NCPDM Conference," *Traffic World* (Oct. 1, 1984), pp. 17–18.

[21] Don Byrne, "Rail Management Seeking Showdown On Work Rules in This Year's Talks," *Traffic World* (Aug. 13, 1984), pp. 20–21.

tinuous sections, often a quarter-mile or longer in length. The continuous welding helps to eliminate vibration caused by the rail cars rolling over joints of the individual sections of rail, which was a major reason for product loss and damage. Railroad classification yards are complexes where rail cars are brought, separated, and then switched to a new train traveling in the direction of the car's destination. Computerized classification yards are speeding up this function.

Augmented by the preceding capital improvements, some railroads have started to offer shippers a number of innovative services. Only a few examples will be mentioned here, although there are others.[22] One new service is the *unit train*. This is a train of permanently connected cars that carries only one product nonstop from origin to destination. It can be thought of as a conveyor belt. Once the product is delivered, the train returns empty to its origin and makes another nonstop run. Unit trains benefit both the railroads and their customers: the trains achieve a very high percentage of car utilization and usually provide less expensive and more dependable service. Currently, over 90 per cent of all coal movement is by unit trains. General Motors uses a unit train from Chicago to Los Angeles carrying assembled autos and auto parts.

Another new service is the *run-through train*. The emphasis here is on saving time. These trains typically involve long-distance moves, so that two or more railroads will combine to offer this service. These trains bypass most classification yards and hence "run through" from origin to destination. They often only stop for crew changes or safety checks. The locomotives generally include power units from each of the participating carriers, and even they are not changed. One such train operated on a 40-hour schedule between Chicago and San Francisco, averaging better than 60 miles per hour. They have helped rails recapture tonnage from truckers.

Motor Carriers

The highway system of the United States includes approximately 3.9 million miles of roads that vary from ungraded dirt surfaces to multilaned divided highways. The back bone of the highway system is the 42,500 miles known officially as the National System of Interstate and Defense Highways, commonly referred to as the *Interstate System*. Figure 4-2 shows this system, which is about 1 per cent of the total highway mileage but carries more than 20 per cent of all automobile and truck traffic.

The most important business user of the highway system is, of course, the trucking industry. The trucking industry can be broken into two parts, one governmentally regulated and the other nonregulated. The distinction between these two carriers will be discussed more in Chapter 5, as will the 1980 legislation that "deregulated" trucking.

---

[22] Each year *Modern Railroads* magazine conducts a contest involving railroad service improvements. The winning railroad is awarded the "Golden Freight Car" award for marketing excellence. For the last several years, one of this book's co-authors has served as one of the competition judges who select the winner. See "Annual Golden Freight Car Award," *Modern Railroads* (June 1985), pp. 26–34.

Figure 4-2 The National System of Interstate Highways

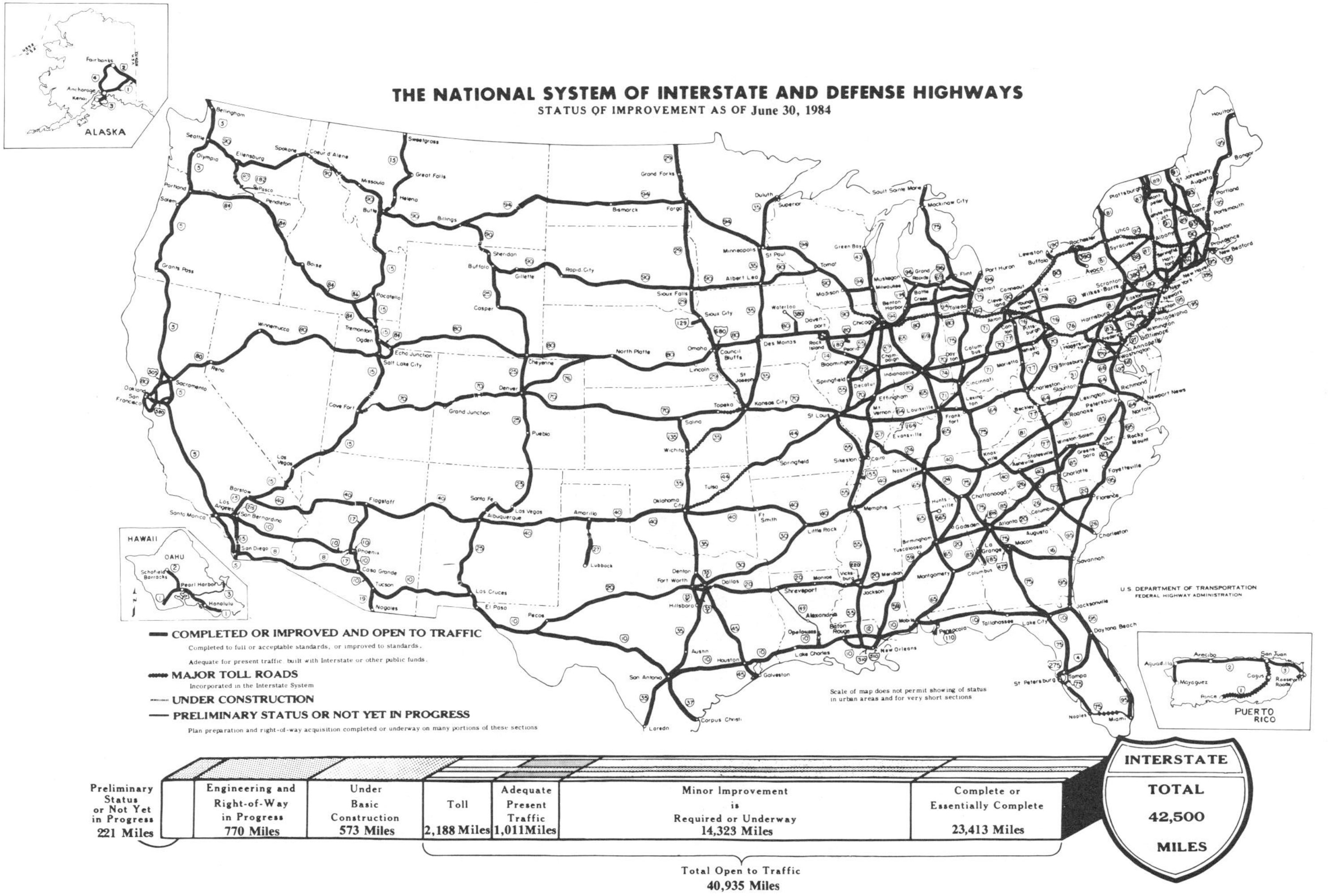

THE NATIONAL SYSTEM OF INTERSTATE AND DEFENSE HIGHWAYS
STATUS OF IMPROVEMENT AS OF June 30, 1984

COMPLETED OR IMPROVED AND OPEN TO TRAFFIC
Completed to full or acceptable standards, or improved to standards.
Adequate for present traffic, built with Interstate or other public funds.

MAJOR TOLL ROADS
Incorporated in the Interstate System

UNDER CONSTRUCTION

PRELIMINARY STATUS OR NOT YET IN PROGRESS
Plan preparation and right-of-way acquisition completed or underway on many portions of these sections

Scale of map does not permit showing of status
in urban areas and for very short sections

U.S. DEPARTMENT OF TRANSPORTATION
FEDERAL HIGHWAY ADMINISTRATION

ALASKA

HAWAII   OAHU

PUERTO RICO

Preliminary Status or Not Yet in Progress 221 Miles	Engineering and Right-of-Way in Progress 770 Miles	Under Basic Construction 573 Miles	Toll 2,188 Miles	Adequate Present Traffic 1,011Miles	Minor Improvement is Required or Underway 14,323 Miles	Complete or Essentially Complete 23,413 Miles

Total Open to Traffic
40,935 Miles

INTERSTATE
TOTAL
42,500
MILES

113

Table 4-4 Products Shipped by Truck

Item	Per Cent of Tons Moving by Truck
Clothing	84
Furniture and fixtures	84
Rubber and plastic products	83
Leather and leather products	91
Fabricated metal products	80
Machinery	81
Food and kindred products	73

Source: *1977 Census of Transportation Commodity Transportation Survey* (Washington, D.C.: U.S. Bureau of the Census, 1977).

There are three main size categories, or classes, of regulated truckers. In 1984 there were 1,088 Class I truckers (a carrier with annual revenues over $5 million), 1,554 Class II truckers (operating revenues between $1 million to $5 million) and 27,370 Class III truckers (operating revenues less than $1 million).

The trucking industry is the major transportation mode for a surprisingly large variety of products. Table 4-4 illustrates the large percentages of manufactured products and processed food products carried by truck.

Regulated motor carriers concentrate their activities in transporting small shipments, defined as those that weigh fewer than 10,000 pounds. For example, in 1983 the average shipment received by Roadway Express, the largest trucking company in terms of total revenues, was 974 pounds and it was transported 1,132 miles. Shipments under 500 pounds represented 66 per cent of Roadway's total number of shipments. Thirty-three per cent of their shipments weighed between 500 and 9,999 pounds and 1 per cent weighed 10,000 pounds or more.

The financial condition of the trucking industry can best be described as two-tiered. Many of the larger—and some smaller—carriers[23] have prospered under deregulation and they continue to report satisfactory profit levels. However, the great majority of trucking companies have experienced greatly reduced—or negative—profits that have resulted from price discounts brought about by the great influx of new carriers. This situation will be examined in the next chapter. Truckers receive a relatively high rate per ton-mile transported because their cost structure is high and they provide a superior level of customer service. Illustrative is the 22.7 cents per ton-mile received by Yellow Freight System in 1983. Remember that the average revenue per ton-mile for the railroad industry was 3.1 cents.

Motor Carrier Problem Areas.   From the regulated trucker's viewpoint, there are a number of basic problems, the most important of which are road taxes, Teamster wage rates, and the car-truck safety issue. Each will be examined briefly.

[23] See Albert R. Karr, "Iowa Trucker Prospers After Deregulation Eases Rules on Routes," *Wall Street Journal,* 13 February 1984, p. 1.

The controversy over road taxes for the trucking industry is related to the idea that heavy trucks are responsible for substantial damage to the highway system. A 1976 California study concluded that trucks weighing over 6,000 pounds caused 99 per cent of the structural damage to pavement.[24] Another study determined that one truck weighing 80,000 pounds utilizing the Interstate System causes the same damage to the pavement as 9,600 passenger cars.[25] Although the trucking industry states that most highway structural damage is caused by weather, this does not explain why the right-side lane on most Interstates is in worse shape than the passing lane. A *Wall Street Journal* reporter took a ride with Jerry Davis, a driver for the Maryland-based Preston Trucking Company:

> Exasperated at the rough ride, Mr. Davis pulls to the left and joins a line of other trucks high-balling it in the smoother, passing lane.
>
> "Riding the hammer lane," as truckers call it—the hammer is the gas pedal— is frowned upon as dangerous by some states, although in Maryland it isn't illegal. "Most truckers would rather stay in the right-hand lane anyway," says Mr. Davis. "So when you see them all out here in the hammer lane, you can be pretty sure the right-hand side of the road is so beat up they just can't stand it."[26]

Because of truck damage to roadways (see Figure 4-3), both federal and state governments have increased user taxes for highway carriers. At present the trucking industry pays substantial road-use taxes. In 1982 all trucks (including pick-up trucks), which represented 21 per cent of all motor vehicles, paid 39 per cent of all state road taxes and 50 per cent of federal road taxes. However, at the federal level, the Highway Trust Fund (which receives all federal highway taxes and then pays this money to states for highway construction and maintenance) reported that unless federal highway taxes were increased, the fund would run out of money by 1989. The primary use of the trust fund in recent years has not been construction, but maintenance.[27] Therefore, the Surface Transportation Assistance Act of 1982 greatly increased federal highway taxes for heavy trucks. An 80,000-pound truck paid an annual tax to the federal government of $210 in 1982. The new law increased this once-a-year payment to $1,900 by 1988. The trucking industry has always preferred to pay user taxes on a pay-as-you-go basis. This type of tax is not paid if the vehicle is not used. To counter this new emphasis on annual taxes, the trucking industry established an organization known as ASERTT (Alliance for Simple, Equitable, and Rational Truck Taxation). This organization, plus a massive lobbying effort by the trucking industry, was successful in changing the 1982 law. In July 1984, Congress passed an act that amended the 1982 law. It called for an additional tax of

[24] Coleman McCarthy, "The Big Rigs Keep on Trucking," *Minneapolis Star and Tribune,* 4 October 1983, p. 11A.

[25] Bill Richards, "Cracks, Bumps, Holes Make Many Highways Agonizing for Truckers," *Wall Street Journal,* 4 January 1983, p. 1.

[26] Ibid.

[27] "New Tax Threat Worries Truckers: CBO Projects Shortfall in Trust Fund," *Traffic World* (Aug. 27, 1984), p. 7.

Figure 4-3 It Is Alleged That Large Trucks Cause Serious Road Damage

Source: Reproduced by permission of the artist and the *Minneapolis Star and Tribune.*

6 cents per gallon for diesel fuel. This tax will be paid by all truckers using diesel vehicles. (Diesel car users must pay the additional 6 cent-tax, but they receive a tax credit for it.) The one-time annual tax for the heaviest trucks was reduced from a maximum of $1,900 to $550.[28] The trucking industry is currently concerned that many states either have or are planning to substantially increase their taxes on the trucking industry.[29]

Teamster wage rates and work rules are major problems for the trucking industry. As noted earlier, deregulation has allowed thousands of new trucking companies to enter this industry. Most of the new firms are nonunion. This allows management to have lower wage rates and allows workers to perform multiple tasks, which often are not allowed by the Teamsters. Illustrative is Overnite Transportation, the largest nonunion trucking company. Both company drivers and office workers occasionally sort freight in freight terminals when they become overly crowded. This would not be allowed in a Teamster contract.[30] In terms of wages, many trucking companies using Teamster labor have already been allowed by the union to reduce wages 10 to 15 per cent below contract levels so the firm can compete against nonunion carriers. It is estimated that union wage rates in some sections of the United States are about 50 per cent higher than what nonunion trucking companies are paying their drivers.[31] In March 1985 the latest Teamster contract was negotiated. It called for one of the most modest increases in the 21 year history of the National Master Freight Contract. Drivers won wage and benefit increases of about 10 per cent over the three years of the contract. Management gained the right to virtually eliminate annual cost-of-living increases, a 30 per cent lower starting wage for new full-time hires (these workers reach full scale in three years) and an 8 per cent wage decrease for part-time workers (these employees never reach full union scale). Although this contract was far from universally embraced by Teamster rank-and-file, it was ratified by the membership.[32]

The final trucking problem is the highway safety issue. There is a growing sentiment in many states to restrict the utilization of certain highways to large trucks. The American Automobile Association (AAA) wants to restrict the length of trucks (see Figure 4-4) and their weight because the AAA believes that large trucks are hazardous to people traveling in automobiles (see Figure 4-5). In 1977, according to the Insurance Institute for Highway Safety, "A car occupant was 22.9 times more likely than a truck occupant to be killed in a fatal large truck-car crash; in 1980, 30.6 times more likely."[33] The National Highway Traffic Safety Administration reported in 1982 that 30 per cent of tractor-trailer trucks had been involved in accidents. This compares with 7.6 per cent for all cars. In terms of accidents per mile of driving, tractor-trailer units had 594 accidents per 100 million vehicle miles

[28] "Congress Sends Truck Tax Bill to Reagan," *Traffic World* (July 2, 1984), p. 7.

[29] Bruce Heydt, "Road Tax Revolt," *Distribution* (Aug. 1984), pp. 12–21.

[30] Daniel J. McConville, "An Uncommon Carrier: Low Costs, 'Spirit' Keep Overnite Trucking," *Barrons* (Nov. 19, 1984), p. 41.

[31] "What Threatens Nationwide Truck Bargaining," *Business Week* (Oct. 15, 1984), p. 46.

[32] Leonard M. Apcar, "Teamsters, Trucking Companies Reach Tentative Agreement on 3-Year Contract," *Wall Street Journal* (April 1, 1985), p. 4.

[33] McCarthy, loc. cit.

Figure 4-4 The Trend is Toward Longer Trucks

" . . . Now there's a long rig!"

Source: Reproduced by permission of *Heavy Duty Trucking Magazine.*

traveled, compared to 517 for cars. When an accident does involve a tractor-trailer truck and a car, it is more than twice as likely to involve a fatality as when two cars crash. Finally, the Bureau of Motor Carrier Safety, an agency of the U.S. Department of Transportation, annually conducts about 30,000 roadside safety inspections. In recent years about 30 per cent of the trucks stopped had such serious safety problems that they had to be corrected on the spot before the truck could leave under its own power. The most serious problem was bad brakes, followed by defective tires, wheels, stop lights, and steering.[34] The American Trucking Associations (ATA) is working to correct these safety problems. Lana Batts of the ATA noted, "We've got a problem with some drivers, but we're trying to win back the knights-of-the-road image."[35]

Motor Carrier Service Innovations. The Interstate Highway System allowed truckers to perform faster service. In addition, the motor carrier industry is expanding its use of specialized equipment, such as double thermos shells to transport oxygen and hydrogen in liquid form. With this equipment, temperatures can be kept between 300 and minus 423 degrees F. Similar trucks haul liquid asphalt at plus 400 degrees F. directly to construction sites. Another equipment innovation involves the use of pneumatic systems for rapid loading and unloading of dry-cargo truck trailers. Approximately one hundred flowable commodities, such as cement, chemicals, and grains are now carried in this type of truck equipment.

Because of the thousands of new trucking companies that have entered this industry, the quality of trucking service has generally increased. Carriers

Figure 4-5 It Is Alleged that Trucks Cause an Excessive Number of Accidents

Source: Reproduced by permission of the artist and the Masters Agency.

are much more willing to negotiate specific rate/service packages for shippers. These agreements (typically with contract carriers) often call for specific service requirements at agreed rates. They also commonly contain penalty payments for poor service and bonuses for exemplary service levels, with *service* generally meaning "on-time" pickups and deliveries.

Pipelines

The oil pipeline system of the United States is extensive. There were 143 oil pipeline companies reporting to the ICC in 1981. In 1977, regulation of common carrier oil pipelines was transferred from the ICC to the new Federal Energy Regulatory Commission (FERC).

There are two types of oil pipelines: *crude oil* and *product.* Crude oil lines transport petroleum from wells to refineries. There are approximately 150,000 miles of crude oil pipelines (Figure 4-6). There are two types of crude oil lines. Somewhat more than half of the crude oil line mileage is *gathering lines,* which are 6 inches or smaller in diameter and are frequently laid on the ground. These lines start at each well and carry the product to concentration points. *Trunk lines* are larger diameter pipelines that carry crude oil

---

[34] Thomas G. Donlan, "No Crash Program: Truck Safety Takes a Back Seat in Washington," *Barrons* (Aug. 6, 1984), p. 26.

[35] "As Those Big, Big Trucks Hit the Road," *U.S. News and World Report,* (June 4, 1984), p. 37.

Figure 4-6 Crude Oil Pipelines

Source: The American Oil Company.

from gathering line concentration points to the oil refineries. They vary in diameter from 3 to 48 inches. However, 8- to 10-inch pipe is the most common size.

Product lines transport refined petroleum products from refineries to population centers. There are approximately 75,000 miles of product line, shown in Figure 4-7. The diameter of product lines is the same size or somewhat smaller than trunklines.

Figures 4-6 and 4-7 show that the oil pipeline system in the United States is not evenly dispersed throughout the country. Texas has one quarter of all the nation's pipeline mileage, and Oklahoma, Kansas, and Illinois combined have another quarter.

In 1984 the oil pipeline industry produced 605 billion ton-miles of transportation service. This was 24 per cent of all intercity ton-miles. In Canada, with the terrain less conducive to other modes of transportation, pipelines produce 30 per cent of all intercity ton-miles.

The pipeline is a very efficient means of transporting oil products, and almost 90 per cent of petroleum products are transported this way. An example of this efficiency is that the oil pipelines generate seventeen times as many ton-miles per employee as do the railroads. A large pipeline's capacity is also impressive. The 48-inch Trans-Alaska pipeline, which is 789 miles long, has a discharge capacity of two million barrels (42 gallons each) per day, although in 1984 it was operating at only 1.7 million barrels per day.[36]

The typical petroleum pipeline company in 1981 had gross revenues of approximately $52 million and had 153 employees. As these employment

[36] Walter K. Wilson, "TAPS Revisited," *The Lamp of Exxon Corporation* (Fall 1984), pp. 2–11.

The Elements of Physical Distribution/Logistics Systems

Figure 4-7 Oil Product Pipelines

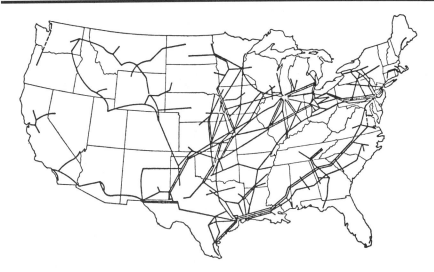

Source: The American Oil Company.

figures indicate, pipelines are very capital intensive. Labor costs are 59 per cent of total operating expenses for the motor carrier industry, 53 per cent for the railroads, and only *10 per cent* for the oil pipeline industry. Oil pipelines can carry products for less than one cent per ton-mile.

Nonpetroleum Products.   A number of other products are also transported by pipelines. Chief among these is natural gas. There are approximately 180,000 miles of intercity natural gas pipelines. This aspect of pipelining is also regulated by the FERC. Prior to 1977, interstate gas pipelines were regulated by the Federal Power Commission, an independent regulatory body.

One kind of nonpetroleum pipeline that appears to have significant potential is the *slurry* pipeline, which can be used to transport bulk products. Several steps are involved. The product is ground into a powder, mixed with water, and sent through the pipeline in suspension. At present, the most extensive use of slurry pipelines is for the transport of coal. Other products that are adaptable to slurry technology include iron ore, limestone, Gilsonite, sulphur, potassium chloride, and waste commodities. The largest and longest coal slurry line in operation today is the Black Mesa pipeline, which transports pulverized coal in an 18-inch pipe 273 miles from strip mines in Northern Arizona to an electric generating station on the Colorado River near Davis Dam, Nevada. The $35 million project, owned by the Southern Pacific Company, started operation in 1971. The slurry line was constructed because unit-train operation was not feasible over the terrain involved. The 50 per cent water, 50 per cent coal mixture moves at four miles per hour and makes the trip in three days. The speed of the movement must be carefully maintained because excessive speed makes the coal powder act like sandpaper on the inside of the pipe, and insufficient speed causes the coal powder to fall out of suspension and build upon the bottom of the pipe. When the slurry solution reaches destination, centrifuges spin the water out. The coal then is fed into the furnaces.

Pipeline Problem Areas. Although the pipeline industry is healthy, it does have some problem areas. The recent concern for ecology and environmental protection has greatly increased the cost of pipeline construction. Many of the delays and cost overruns on the Trans-Alaska pipeline system were caused by environmental protection requirements. Original cost estimates for the project were about $2 billion; however, final costs were over $9 billion.

A second problem area involves the difficulty of acquiring the rights-of-way for new pipeline construction. Some states do not give pipelines the ability to condemn property for their right-of-way, which is known as the *right of eminent domain*. Without right-of-way, pipelines are forced into circuitous routes. A recent coal-slurry pipeline right-of-way controversy involved a projected 1,030-mile pipeline from Wyoming to Arkansas, known as the Energy Transportation System, Inc. (ETSI) line. The coal would be consumed by a number of electric public utilities in the southeastern United States. The builders of the slurry line were attempting to win federal congressional action in order to secure the interstate right of eminent domain. Without this authorization, construction was stymied because it would cross railroad properties in forty-four places. The railroads, because of their dependence on coal tonnage, have refused to grant slurry pipelines the right of crossing their properties.

The ETSI line was dealt a serious blow when Arkansas Power and Light awarded a twenty-year coal transportation contract to the Chicago & North Western Railroad in August 1983. ETSI had also bid on this contract, and it was generally assumed that it would win this key contract.[37] ETSI next tried to shift the line from Wyoming to Texas. But the pipeline backers were not optimistic. One executive noted why: "After fighting slurry lines for two decades, the railroads can easily afford to make a losing bid for that contract. They will . . . drive ETSI into the ground, by making sure they come in with a low bid [for the Houston market]."[38] The next setback for ETSI and all proposed coal-slurry pipelines came in October 1983. The U.S. House of Representatives defeated, by a 53-vote margin, a bill to allow slurry lines the right of eminent domain.[39] ETSI was crippled, after having spent over $150 million in legal, surveying, and other expenses. In August 1984, ETSI announced that the project was being terminated. Paul Doran, the president of ETSI declared, "The decision to terminate is a result of protracted railroad opposition that has brought about costly delays in securing all necessary permits, rights-of-way, and other clearances for the project."[40]

[37] Bill Richards, "Lost Contract Raises Doubts on Coal Slurry," *Wall Street Journal*, 22 August 1983, p. 17.

[38] Carol E. Curtis, "End of the Line for Coal Slurry?" *Forbes* (Jan. 30, 1984), p. 94.

[39] "Railroads Win Big in House Vote Dooming Coal Slurry Pipelines," *Traffic World* (Oct. 3, 1983), p. 54.

[40] "ETSI Cancels Plans for Coal-Slurry Pipeline Project," *Minneapolis Star and Tribune*, 2 August 1984, p. 4M.

There are domestic movements of freight by water on our Great Lakes and on our inland waterways—or barge—system. There is also waterborne commerce via ocean-going vessels between the mainland ("lower 48") states and Alaska, Hawaii, and Puerto Rico. (International ocean transportation will be covered in Chapter 11.)

The inland waterway system, not counting the coastal routes, the Great Lakes, or the St. Lawrence Seaway System, is made up of about 16,000 miles that are dredged to a depth of nine feet, which is the minimum required for most barges. Figure 4-8 shows most of this system, which is concentrated in the southeastern region of the United States. In 1983, 270 inland and coastal water carriers had gross revenues of greater than $100,000, an *average* freight revenue of $28 million, and 700 employees each. In 1982 barge operators on the inland waterways received about 0.82-cent per ton-mile, making them the least expensive mode.

In general, the domestic water percentage of all intercity ton-miles has not changed significantly from 1929 to 1983. However, there has been a shift in the composition. In 1929, the Great Lakes accounted for 16 per cent of the total, while rivers and canals were only 1.4 per cent. By 1983 the former was 3.1 per cent and the latter was 12.4 per cent of all intercity ton-miles. In 1983 inland water carriers received only 3 per cent of all freight revenue for transporting about 17 per cent of all intercity ton-miles.

Domestic water carriers have specialized in transporting bulk products at very low prices at slow average speeds (six miles per hour). Petroleum and related products account for 36 per cent of total barge commerce. Coal is second, with 28 per cent. Other products that move extensively in the inland waterway system are grain and grain products, industrial chemicals, iron and steel products, forestry products, cement, sulphur, fertilizers, paper products, sand and gravel, and limestone. In most cases these products are tendered to the carriers in barge-load lots, which range from minimums of 500 to 2,500 tons on the rivers and canals up to 60,000 tons on individual vessels in ocean-going, coastal, or Great Lakes service.

Towboats, with powerplants from 1,000 to 9,000 horsepower, *push* the loaded barges, which are lashed together to make, in effect, one large mass of floating freight. As many as fifty barges are secured and operated as one "tow."

Inland Water Carriers Problem Areas. Domestic water carriers, like the other providers of transportation, have their share of problems. One serious quandary is that environmental groups have taken a strong stand against the expansion of the inland waterway system. Environmentalists believe that the dredging and the disposal of materials dredged from channels will upset the "balance of nature," and in some cases they have exerted considerable influence. For example, environmentalists generated sufficient pressure to halt the construction of the cross-Florida segment of the intercoastal waterway.

An operational problem plaguing the water carriers is the time needed to get through the locks on the waterway system. Many of the older locks

Figure 4-8 Waterways of the United States

Courtesy The American Waterways Operators, Inc., Arlington, Virginia.

are 600 feet long, but newer, larger tows often are considerably longer than this and must be broken and put through the lock in two parts. Thomas J. Barta, president of the Valley Line Company, reports that because of congestion, tows on the Upper Mississippi at Alton, Illinois, sometimes have to wait 24–36 hours to go through the locking system.

During the 1970s congestion at Alton was a focal point of a controversy between inland water carriers and various opposition groups. Railroads and environmental groups joined to prevent congressional approval of funds to expand the locks at Alton. The inland waterways industry was able to obtain enough votes in Congress to fund the needed expansion at Alton (sometimes referred to as Locks and Dam #26) only after it agreed to submit to a fuel tax, currently at 10 cents per gallon.

Another problem faced by inland waterway carriers operating in the northern states and on the Great Lakes is the fact that ice closes their systems and prevents year-round operation. This means their customers must stockpile inventories in the fall to last through the winter months. Studies are under way to determine the feasibility of extending the open navigation system into the winter months.

Inland Water Carrier Service Innovations. The typical carrying capacity of a barge tow has increased from 150,000 to more than three million ton-miles per day while improvements in propulsion, navigation, and control have reduced crew sizes by 50 per cent. Today, barge carriers are introducing new services made possible by equipment innovations. The Federal Barge Lines offers specially equipped barges that regulate both temperature and humidity for the shipment of anhydrous ammonia and sulphur. This equipment is running between Chicago and Houston on a 17-day schedule. Peter Fanchi, president of Federal Barge, stated that his company will supply the transportation services that their customers demand: "If somebody comes around here tomorrow and says, 'I'm going to move steel at 1,200 degrees,' why we'll build a barge to conform with that man's needs."[41]

An equipment innovation that is revolutionizing much of the inland water transportation system is the *LASH (Lighter Aboard Ship)* concept. (A lighter is a small ship or barge.) *LASH* barges are very similar to typical inland barges. What makes the system so unique is that ocean-going ships are equipped to take these barges directly on board ship by elevator systems. This greatly reduces the cargo transfer costs at the ocean port. Instead of the product having to be unloaded from the barge and then loaded onto the ocean going ship, the loaded barge is loaded into the "mother" ship. For many products bound for export or import, an all water route is now feasible.

Air Freight

The air freight industry is growing at a slow but steady rate. Revenues increased 5 per cent from 1980 to 1983, while ton-miles flown increased 6 per cent during this time period.

[41] "Barge Lines: No Trimmings," *Transportation and Distribution Management* (March 1972), p. 25. See also Denis J. Davis, "Waterways: A Long Struggle to Stay Afloat," *Distribution* (March, 1985), pp. 18–25.

Table 4-5 Ten Busiest Cargo
Airports in the United States, 1983
(thousands of metric tons
[2,204.6 lb])

New York (J F Kennedy)	1,280,700
Los Angeles	965,591
Chicago (O'Hare)	897,749
Miami	590,901
Atlanta	540,152
San Francisco	472,122
Dallas/Fort Worth	368,001
Dayton	322,850
Seattle	238,381
Honolulu	236,528

Source: Air Transport Association of America.

The structure of the air freight industry is not like other modes of transportation. One important difference is the character of the airline business. The great majority of the air freight ton-miles flown are performed by airlines whose primary business is passenger operations. Often, only about 10 per cent of their revenue comes from air freight. The top ten U.S. airlines in freight ton-miles included only one all-cargo air carrier, Flying Tiger. The other nine airlines were combination passenger and air freight carriers. The general level of air freight rates is very high compared to the other modes of transportation, averaging 47 cents per ton-mile.

The air freight industry transports a remarkable variety of products. The following product groups represent the largest users of air freight: wearing apparel; electronic/electrical equipment and parts; printed matter; machinery and parts; cut flowers and nursery stock; auto parts and accessories; phonograph records, tapes, TVs, radios, and recorders; fruits and vegetables; metal products; and photographic equipment, parts, and film. As this list illustrates, products that are air freighted tend to be high in value, of a perishable nature, or possessing "emergency" characteristics.

Table 4-5 lists the ten busiest airports in the country measured in terms of their 1983 air cargo tonnage. About seven hundred communities in the U.S. receive some form of scheduled airline service, and trucks connect just about every community in the country with an airport offering air cargo service.

Air Freight Problem Areas. Two major problems dominate this industry in the mid-1980s: air freight does not appear to be important to passenger airlines and the shift of passenger airlines out of the utilization of all-cargo aircraft. Each will be discussed briefly. As noted before, the air cargo industry is dominated by combination airlines—those that fly both people and cargo. Because people are much more important to airlines in terms of revenues received, the air freight side of the business is often treated as a stepchild. One West Coast air freight forwarder declared:

Figure 4-9 Air Freight Capabilities

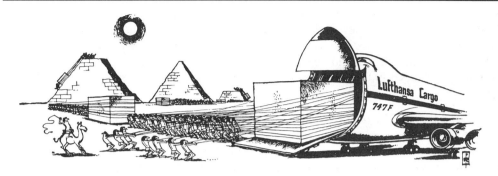

Source: Compliments of Lufthansa German Airlines.

> I'm not saying freight should be more important than passengers, since people are far more precious commodities. . . . All I'm saying is scheduled carriers don't give a damn about freight. If someone tenders them a shipment, fine, they'll take it on their terms. If their passenger load factors are strong, then they couldn't care less, and I think the situation with American and United—two of the strongest—proves my point.[42]

This quote alludes to the second problem. In late 1984 two of the largest combination carriers, United and American, announced that they were ceasing to operate all-cargo aircraft. Both firms noted that the profitability of air freight did not make it feasible to re-engine their freighters, which would have been necessary in order to comply with the federal noise regulations that were to become effective on January 1, 1985. Why were freight rates so low that combination carriers choose to get out of the all-cargo aircraft? One important factor is the increase in the number of all-cargo airlines, which has depressed the overall rate structure. Another reason involved *belly freight,* which is cargo that is flown in freight compartments on scheduled passenger flights. Historically, the airlines priced their air freight relatively low, and the volume of business generated was more than could be transported exclusively as belly freight. Therefore, all-cargo freighters were introduced. However, the established air freight rates were so low that an all-cargo aircraft, full of cargo, lost money. Further complicating the picture for the all-cargo aircraft has been the introduction of the wide-body jets, the Boeing 747, the McDonnell-Douglas DC-10, and the Lockheed 1011.

A quandary is associated with the wide-bodied passenger jets and their belly cargo. Traditionally, all-cargo aircraft flew during the night to avoid passenger plane congestion at airports and because their customers appreciated overnight freight service. However, demand for passenger service is during daylight hours and airlines soon had excess capacity of belly cargo space on their daylight flights. They cut down on their overnight service—

---

[42] Mark B. Solomon, "Airlines Drop Freighters, Force Change on Forwarders, Shippers," *Traffic World* (Nov. 5, 1984), p. 87.

to the distress of many of their cargo customers. In a few instances, freight forwarders chartered entire aircraft for night flights to satisfy the needs of customers who had become dependent upon the overnight freight service once offered by the airlines. Federal Express, an air carrier providing small-package overnight service between hundreds of cities utilizing 61 jet aircraft, grew because of this void in regular airline night-time service. Today the company delivers 350,000 parcels daily.[43]

Overnight freight service is important to users of air freight. For most of them, it means that late in the afternoon, at the close of their business day, a truck picks up their outbound air freight and carries it to the airport where it's loaded aboard aircraft. The planes move at night, arriving in the destination city before daylight. It is then delivered by truck to the customer at the start of the business day. Users of air freight desire overnight service because—in the sense of scheduling work at different locations and shipments between them—virtually no working time is lost.

With less overnight service being offered by scheduled airlines, how are shippers and air freight forwarders reacting to the new environment? The answer is that the air freight forwarders are going into the all-cargo airline business. Illustrative are four of the largest forwarders: Emery, Purolator, Airborne, and United Parcel Service (UPS). These four companies own, lease, or control the scheduling of at least 150 all-cargo freighters. These firms are in the process of expanding their "captive" lift capacity, and even firms that had stated they did not want to be involved in actually operating aircraft, such as Burlington Northern Air Freight, are now looking for aircraft. The size of the forwarders' fleets are impressive. UPS owns three Boeing 747s, 12 Fairchild Expeditors (small turbo-prop planes designed for short-distance cargo operations), 17 DC-8s, and 34 Boeing 727s. The firm also controls the scheduling of 75 other cargo planes owned by small airlines operating under exclusive lease to UPS.[44]

Air Freight Equipment Innovations.   To meet their problems, airlines have attempted two kinds of innovations. First, new equipment is being installed at air cargo-handling terminals to speed the flow of freight. More and more air freight is moved in large containers that the shipper loads. Some terminals are redesigning their operation to handle these large containers rather than individual pieces of freight. At this writing, however, some airlines are questioning the increased use of containers since the savings in labor are often *less* than the increased aircraft fuel costs for carrying the tare (empty) weight of the containers.

---

[43] Cindy Skrzycki, "An Industry That Keeps Promises—Overnight," *U.S. News and World Report* (Oct. 22, 1984), pp. 53–54.

[44] Stan Chapman, "Air Freight on a Different Plane?" *Distribution* (Nov. 1984), pp. 85–87. See also Michael J. Walker, "Air Freight Industry Changes For the Better," *Pacific Traffic* (Feb. 1985), pp. 20–23.

128   The Elements of Physical Distribution/Logistics Systems

The second innovation involves the use of aircraft. Virtually all aircraft are designed for the passenger business, but several passenger aircraft have been equipped so that they can be converted from passenger to freight operations and back again, as markets dictate. One such plane is the wide-body DC-10CF (convertible freighter). Although this plane is not designed to be changed every day, it can be converted from primarily passenger service to an all-cargo configuration. This would perhaps be done on a seasonal basis. For example, during the summer months, when tourism is at a high level, the plane is used as a passenger aircraft, able to accommodate 380 passengers. During periods of slack passenger demand, it can be changed into an all-cargo plane. World Airways has a Boeing 747 with similar conversion capabilities. Another version of the Boeing 747, becoming popular in international markets, is equipped with removable seats and a bulkhead on the main deck of the aircraft. Depending upon the relative demands for passenger seating and cargo space, the bulkhead can be moved fore or aft, with seats ahead of the bulkhead and cargo space behind.

Freight Forwarders, Brokers, and Shippers' Agents

Freight forwarders are not "modes," but from the shipper's viewpoint they are analogous to other carriers. The two types of domestic freight forwarders—surface and air—can best be thought of as consolidators of freight.

Freight forwarders operate as middlemen. Both surface and air carriers give volume discounts to customers shipping large quantities of freight at one time. For example, the motor carrier rate from City A to City B might be $5.00 per 100 pounds for shipments less than 20,000 pounds. This is called an LTL (less than truck load) rate. The TL (truck load) rate might be $2.00 per 100 pounds when 20,000 or more pounds are tendered. The freight forwarder exists by offering his service to shippers who must use LTL rates because they do not generate enough volume to use TL rates. Without the freight forwarder, the small shipper has to use the $5.00 LTL rate. The freight forwarder, however, offers the same transportation service for a rate between the LTL and TL rate, say, $4.00. This is possible because the freight forwarder consolidates all the small shipments it has and gives them to the carrier (a trucker in this case) and hence qualifies for the $2.00 TL rate. The freight forwarder typically offers pickup and delivery service, but he does not perform the line-haul service. This is done by the motor carrier or railroad involved. Forwarders also function as "traffic departments" for small firms, performing other traffic management functions.

Surface freight forwarders, as an industry, in 1983 had 231 firms, each of which *averaged* gross revenues of $2.1 million. Because they do not perform any line-haul transportation, their level of invested capital is not great. The surface freight forwarders do *not* represent a growing industry. In 1980 this industry accounted for $721 million in revenues, whereas in 1983 its business had dropped to $490 million.

The air forwarding industry works with the air carriers. The forwarders consolidate shipments and tender them, in containers that are ready for aircraft loading. This results in significant ground-handling time savings for the airlines. Therefore, airlines encourage forwarder traffic since it results in an agreeable division of labor: the forwarders provide the "retailing" function and deal with each individual shipper and consignee, and the airline concentrates on "wholesaling"—moving the forwarders' loaded containers between major cities. This industry appears to be growing at a robust rate.[45]

There are also barge-oriented freight forwarders offering services on the inland waterways system. Their main sales tool is to offer a smaller minimum tender requirement to shippers. One forwarder bases its rates on shipments as small as 100 tons, whereas common carrier barges serving the same area require minimum shipments of 800 tons.[46]

Brokers are a growing transportation alternative. They are companies that take a shipper's freight and find a carrier to transport this cargo. They are not considered common carriers like a freight forwarder and they do not issue tariffs or bills-of-lading. They can best be thought of as a consultant to both shippers and carriers. For shippers they secure the best transportation rate/service package available. For carriers—both for-hire and private—they help to insure that each load is operated close to maximum capacity. Brokers are licensed by the ICC and in 1985 there were about 4000 of these firms. Brokers are usually paid a commission by the carrier but can also be compensated by the shipper.[47]

Shippers' agents are not licensed with the ICC and they can best be thought of as retailers for piggyback service (which is discussed subsequently). They typically purchase large quantities of piggyback service from railroads at a discount and then they sell this service to shippers in smaller packages. It is estimated there are 600 shippers' agents, and this number is growing every year.[48]

Shippers' Cooperatives

Shippers' cooperatives perform basically the same function as surface and air freight forwarders, except they do not operate as profit-making organizations. All profits achieved through their consolidation program are returned to members. This type of consolidation program has been well received by shippers. One study of shippers' associations found that "97 per cent of the associations surveyed had lower rates than freight forwarders and motor carriers offering comparable services. The net savings to users of shippers' co-ops was $162 million."[49]

It is estimated that there are currently from 200 to 300 shippers' co-ops. According to the American Institute of Shippers Associations, their rev-

[45] Lisa H. Harrington, "Freight Forwarders: Living with Deregulation . . . and Liking It," *Traffic Management* (Nov. 1984), pp. 57–64.

[46] Letter from River Forwarders, Inc., of New Orleans, to authors, January 18, 1980.

[47] Robert C. Dart, "Freight Brokers Seek New Identities as Transportation Options Multiply," *Traffic World* (April 4, 1983), pp. 15–17; Joseph V. Barks, "Brokers Close In," *Distribution* (Nov. 1984), pp. 48–54 and Judith A. Fuerst, "Sorting Out the Middlemen," *Handling and Shipping Management* (March 1985), pp. 46–50.

[48] Terence A. Brown, "Shippers' Agents and the Marketing of Rail Intermodal Service," *Transportation Journal* (Spring 1984), pp. 44–52; and "Questions and Answers with Gary I. Goldstein, President, Interstate Consolidation Service," *Pacific Traffic* (July 1984), pp. 10–12.

[49] *Handling and Shipping Management* (June 1980), p. 15. The study was conducted by Terence A. Brown, of Pennsylvania State University.

enues are currently running 50 per cent higher than those of the surface freight forwarder industry.[50]

Auxiliary Carriers

The primary transportation alternatives have now been discussed. However, a number of auxiliary services are available, which generally specialize in small shipment transportation. These will now be mentioned.

Parcel Post is a service of the U.S. Postal Service. There are definite size and weight limitations (approximately 70 pounds). Charges are based on weight and distance and are relatively low. In most cases, the parcel must be carried to the post office, but it will be delivered to the receiver. The postal service also offers various levels of mail and parcel service.

Bus Package Service is offered by intercity bus companies. The maximum weight per package is 100–150 pounds. The packages travel in special compartments on the intercity buses. The service is fast, reliable, and packages delivered 30 minutes before a bus's departure will be aboard that bus. There is no pickup or delivery service.

Other Parcel Services include UPS, which has specialized in parcels of up to 70 pounds. This company has experienced growth because it has earned a reputation for very reliable service at rates that are equal to or less than parcel post. UPS rates include both pickup and delivery.

Intermodal Transportation

To this point we have discussed the modes of transportation available to the PD/L manager as individual services. In reality, many shipments are made on a combination of two or more modes. This is known as intermodal transportation.

Rail/Truck Service

Piggyback service, also called Trailer on Flat Car (TOFC), is by far the most important intermodal transportation service. It involves the transportation of highway trailers on railroad flatbed cars, each of which can handle two standard 45-foot highway trailers. When this service is used to transport containers, it is called Container on Flat Car (COFC). This service is less expensive than all motor carrier movement, and, especially in the mountainous western region of the United States, TOFC is faster than truck service. There are at least seven basic kinds of piggyback service available. Each alternative is known by its respective number. (See Figure 4-10.) Plan II½ is the most popular alternative, being commonly utilized by freight forwarders, shippers' associations, and shippers' agents. Plan III is the second most widely

---

[50] *Distribution Worldwide* (June 1979), pp. 28–29. See also, "Reshape Shipping," *Inc* (April 1984), p. 188.

Figure 4-10 Various Piggyback Alternatives Offered by Missouri Pacific Railroad

PIGGYBACK PLANS

Illustrated here are the Standard Piggyback plans. Each provides coordinated transportation services . . . utilizing trucking and Mo-Pac rail line haul in a variety of efficient combinations.

■ MO-PAC

☐ MOTOR COMMON CARRIER

▥ SHIPPER/CONSIGNEE

plan 1: Motor common carrier handles door-to-door service . . . using Mo-Pac Piggyback Rail Service as the long distance carrier.

PLAN II: Mo-Pac picks up trailers at your door, delivers them to the ramp, handles rail transport and delivers trailers to final destination. Door-to-door service.

PLAN II½: Mo-Pac provides trailers, flat cars and rail transportation; shipper and consignee arrange motor pick-up and delivery from ramps. (*)

PLAN III: Mo-Pac provides ramp-to-ramp rail transport . . . shipper/consignee handles motor delivery of trailers to and from ramps.

PLAN IV: Mo-Pac provides ramp-to-ramp rail haul . . . shipper provides motor delivery to and from ramps.

PLAN V: Mo-Pac or common carrier provides trailers, pick-up or delivery. Mo-Pac provides ramping and de-ramping.

NOTE: All plans also apply to container shipments.

*PLAN 11¼: Mo-Pac provides trailers, rail service and EITHER door-to-ramp or ramp-to-door motor carriage.

Source: Missouri Pacific Railroad.

132

used alternative.[51] In early 1980, the ICC started studying the possibility of exempting piggyback traffic from economic regulation. (Under the 1976 4R Act the ICC can—on its own initiative—exempt rail service from regulation when it is believes regulation is no longer necessary to protect the public interest.) Piggyback deregulation took place in March 1981. Piggyback service has enjoyed a healthy growth, both in absolute terms and as a percentage of rail carloadings. In 1964 there were 920,927 TOFC/COFC carloadings and this was 3.0 per cent of all rail carloadings. In 1983 the comparable figures were 2,338,527 and 12.4 per cent. Only one other traffic group, coal, accounts for more rail carloadings than piggyback.

In an effort to help its grain shippers, the Iowa Department of Transportation developed a combined rail-barge tariff. The purpose was to achieve better coordination between rail and barge movements on shipments moving from Iowa to New Orleans. A single rate was established for the entire movement (actually there were three rates, each dependent upon the season of the year, reflecting changes in rates charged by barge operators). The shipper had to deal only with the railroad because the railroad coordinated its operations with the barge line. Only one shipping document was required. Both the railroads and the barge lines made some special concessions with respect to providing and moving equipment. The barge lines agreed to absorb demurrage charges levied by the railroads in case a barge was not available—as scheduled—for receiving the grain to be unloaded by the railcars.[52]

Demurrage is a penalty payment the railroads must collect from users who fail to load or unload equipment within specified times. *Detention,* which has a similar meaning, is used in other transport modes.

The intermodal relationship between trucks and airlines has already been referred to. Specialized truck bodies have been developed for handling the aircraft containers in the move between the air cargo terminal and the customers. Airlines are allowed to offer truck service to pick up and deliver cargo, and the Motor Carrier Act of 1980 removed all regulations on domestic airlines' use of trucks for this purpose.

Canadian Intermodal Policy

One logical extension of the intermodal approach to transportation has been the idea of the "total transportation company"—one company owning more than one transportation mode. This idea has been put into practice in Canada, and the Canadian experience is instructive. The best example is Cana-

---

[51] "Piggyback Potentials and Problems Are Probed at Atlanta Conference," *Traffic World* (April 23, 1984), pp. 25–29. See also Judith A. Fuerst, "Piggyback Goes To Market," *Handling and Shipping Management* (April 1985), pp. 46–50.

[52] David J. Marshall, "Iowa's Consolidated Rail/Barge Tariff," Paper submitted in partial fulfillment of the requirements for the certificate of membership in the American Society of Transportation and Logistics, 1979.

dian Pacific Limited, which includes an international airline, transcontinental trucking and railroad service, a telecommunication system, and a fleet of ships that circle the world.[53]

The theoretical advantage of a total, or multimodal, transportation company is that because it operates various modes of transportation, it will use each mode most advantageously to minimize transportation costs while meeting the service requirements of its customers.[54]

Although Canadian governmental policy has no restrictions on multimodal transportation companies, two royal commissions that have studied this issue have concluded that multimodal ownership has not adversely affected the vigor of intermodal competition in Canada.[55]

What has been the overall effect of multimodal transportation companies in Canada? Most people who have studied this issue conclude that it has been a positive benefit to the Canadian economy for three reasons. First, it has allowed the railroads to expand their operations into newer forms of technology. Thus management that is knowledgeable in the transportation sector of the economy can diversify its operations where it already possesses expertise. Second, the railroads can substitute high-cost services with more efficient ones. The Canadian Pacific has basically eliminated less-than-carload traffic, using, instead, its trucking subsidiary. Third, customers benefit from being able to select the exact service-cost combination they desire. Trevor D. Heaver of the University of British Columbia has observed:

> The marketing of transport by a multimodal company offers service advantages to the shipper. Through transport is more likely to be possible with advantages in documentation and clear responsibility in cases of loss and damage. "One stop shopping" is possible for rate quotations and advice concerning physical distribution design.[56]

United States Intermodal Policy

A number of U.S. carriers have started to establish one-stop transportation companies. Tiger International was an early advocate of the multimodal concept. The firm's traditional business was air freight provided by Flying Tiger Line. The company then added Seaboard World Airlines (air freight), Hall's Motor Transit (motor carrier), Warren Transportation (motor carrier),

[53] Frank MaLone, "CP Rail: The Marketing Approach to Railroading," *Railway Age* (March 26, 1979), pp. 22–32.

[54] See Robert S. Tripp, Norman L. Chervany, and Frederick J. Beier, "An Economic Analysis of the Multi-Modal Transportation Company: A Simulation Approach," *The Logistics and Transportation Review* 9:69–84 (1973). See also, R. B. Taylor, "Canadian Transport Competition—Advantages and Limitations: A Shipper's Perspective," *The Logistics and Transportation Journal* (Summer 1973), p. 14.

[55] John M. Munro, "A Comparative Evaluation of Canadian and U.S. Transport Policy," *Transportation Journal* (Summer 1973), p. 14; W. Graham Clayton, Jr., "A Single Intermodal Transportation Company," *Transportation Journal* (Spring 1972), p. 36.

[56] Trevor D. Heaver, "Multi-Modal Ownership—The Canadian Experience," *Transportation Journal* (Fall 1971), p. 18. See also, Karl M. Ruppenthal, ed., *Issues in Transportation Economics* (Columbus: Merrill, 1965), chap. 5, "The Question of Common Ownership"; and H. L. Purdy, *Transport in Canada* (Vancouver: University of British Columbia Press, 1972), chap. 7, "Intermodal Ownership and Transport Competition."

North American Car Corporation (leases rail cars), and Bi-Modal Corporation (leases transportation equipment to truckers and railroads). Tiger International experienced losses from 1981 to 1983, and some of its subsidiaries have been sold. The firm remains committed to combining air freight with trucking.[57]

The Denver and Rio Grande Western Railroad became the first railroad to apply to the ICC for "unrestricted" operating rights for a trucking company. In September 1983, the Commission granted the D&RGW trucking subsidiary 48-state authority with no restrictions.[58] In the same year, United States Lines, a large ocean carrier, received ICC approval to establish a nationwide trucking company that will act as a feeder to the shipping company. They plan to utilize owner-operators[59] to provide the line-haul transportation service.[60] In addition, Consolidated Freightways (CF), one of the largest trucking companies in the United States, has been expanding into the air freight forwarder business. Raymond F. O'Brien, chairman of CF, noted, "CF has no intention of becoming a railroad, but we do plan to offer various types of intermodal service as well as virtually any other kind of service a customer might want."[61]

Criteria for Selecting Transportation Modes

We have surveyed the essential operating characteristics of each transportation alternative available to the user. Every logistics manager must decide which transportation "mix" will best meet the company's objectives. The four basic—and most important—characteristics will be discussed here.[62]

Speed

Without question the fastest transport mode from airport to airport is the *jet aircraft,* which often cruise at 550 miles per hour. However, ground-handling delays often significantly reduce this impressive speed.

[57] Peter Brimelow, "Where Those Hybrid Haulers Are Headed," *Fortune* (March 19, 1984), pp. 115–116.

[58] "DRGW Truck Subsidiary Approved by Commission," *Railnews,* Association of American Railroads (Sept. 21, 1983), p. 2.

[59] Owner-operators are independent businesspeople who own and operate their own trucks. They frequently sign contracts to work for common carriers and provide the line-haul transportation service for them. Typically they receive about 75 per cent of the revenue that the carrier collects for each shipment. See D. Daryl Wyckoff and David H. Maiston, "The U.S. Owner-Operator Trucker: A Transportation Policy Based on Personal Bankruptcy," *Annual Proceedings of the Transportation Research Forum* (1977), pp. 291–297.

[60] Bill Paul, "Freight Transportation Is Being Transformed in Era of Deregulation," *Wall Street Journal,* 20 October 1983, p. 1.

[61] "Total Transportation: Just Around the Corner," *Traffic Management* (Aug. 1983), p. 70.

[62] This section is based on James L. Heskett, Nicholas A. Glaskowsky, and Robert M. Ivie, *Business Logistics,* 2d ed. (New York: Ronald, 1973), pp. 110–118; and Donald F. Wood and James C. Johnson, *Contemporary Transportation* 2nd. ed., (New York: Macmillan, 1983), chaps. 4–8.

Motor carriers generally offer the next most rapid service. *Railroads*, especially in the western region of the United States, are able to approach motor carrier service standards, especially on runs of 1,500 to 2,000 miles in length.

Inland water carriers and the *pipelines* are clearly in last place regarding speed. Both average 3–6 miles per hour.

Dependability

Obviously, the ability to deliver a product when promised usually is an important concern. Dependability of service, as previously noted, is generally of much greater concern to shippers and consignees than is speed.

Pipelines know no equal in this respect because weather does not affect them and because they require so little labor. If a strike takes place, supervisory management can continue to operate the system. *Motor carriers* are the next most dependable. The basic reason for this is the small operating unit involved. Once a truck is loaded for shipment, only the drivers involved can cause the shipment to be late, barring equipment breakdowns and bad weather.

Air carriers have significantly improved their dependability. Weather is still a problem, but the jet aircraft is a very dependable piece of equipment.

The *railroads* have historically done a lackluster job in respect to dependability. A source of delay has been the bottlenecks involved at classification yards. Railroads are spending millions of dollars to correct this deficiency.

The *inland water carriers* are the least dependable mode. This is caused by the vicissitudes of weather and the unpredictable delays encountered at the locks on the waterway system.

Table 4-6 presents the results of a DOT survey that dealt with the quality of service offered by the various modes as perceived by shippers.

Capability

Capability refers to the size, weight, and variety of products that the mode can physically accommodate. *Barge carriers* clearly are in first place in this respect. The Valley Line Company possesses covered barges that are 200 feet long, 35 feet wide, 12 feet deep, and can transport 80,000 cubic feet of cargo. Barges, for example, have been responsible for transporting the Saturn and other space program rockets to Cape Canaveral.

Railroads are next in capability. Some rail cars can support over 500,000 pounds of freight, but they are limited in height by their bridges and tunnels. *Trucks* are limited by the state and federal weight restrictions on the highway system. *Air carriers* have recently increased their overall capacity, with such planes at the 747F. It has 23,690 cubic feet of capacity and can lift payloads in excess of 220,000 pounds. *Pipelines* are the least capable of transporting a variety of products, although what they can do, they do without equal.

Table 4-6 Shippers' Performance Ratings of Each Mode

| Performance Factor | Mode | Number and Percentage[1] of Shippers Ascribing Each Level of Performance for Each Mode | | | | | | | | | | Total Usable Responses |
| | | Excellent | | Quite Good | | Adequate | | Minimally Acceptable | | Unsatis- factory | | |
		N	%	N	%	N	%	N	%	N	%	
On-time pickup	Motor	51	27	79	42	47	25	9	5	3	2	189
	Rail	23	23	31	31	19	19	20	20	7	7	100
On-time delivery	Motor	26	15	65	37	70	39	12	7	4	2	177
	Rail	7	7	26	25	33	32	22	22	14	14	102
	Air	32	29	47	42	22	20	8	7	2	2	111
	Water	13	32	12	30	11	27	3	7	1	2	40
Arrivals without loss, short, or damage	Motor	58	31	82	44	33	18	9	5	3	2	185
	Rail	21	20	42	39	25	23	12	11	6	6	106
	Air	55	49	42	37	11	10	2	2	1	1	111
	Water	21	51	12	29	6	15	2	5	0	0	41
Specified equipment availability	Motor	52	31	58	35	41	25	9	5	4	2	164
	Rail	17	16	24	23	25	24	19	18	18	17	103

[1] Percentages calculated on basis of total number of shippers using each mode and rating it for the specific performance factor.
Source: *1974 National Transportation Report, Summary* (Washington, D.C.: U.S. Department of Transportation, Dec. 1974).

Fuel Efficiency

Fuel that is expensive today and will become more expensive tomorrow seems to be a permanent part of the business climate, and since it is such an important part of transportation, fuel efficiency is a critical part of every PD/L manager's calculations.

Fuel efficiency can be difficult to determine. For some carriers, especially barges, greater output in terms of ton-miles carried per gallon of fuel can be achieved by reducing the speed at which the vessel moves, but this kind of calculation tends to be the exception, not the rule. One factor complicating calculations of fuel efficiency is that domestic carriers' routes between specific points are often circuitous—that is, they must follow the highway, rail tracks, or waterway. In any particular situation being studied, the road, rail, and water mileage between two points usually differs. Even aircraft often do not fly directly from city to city. Pilots attempt to avoid areas of airspace congestion, and if they use navigational aids, they will fly from navigation marker to navigation marker, which is not quite the same as going from city to city.

Another factor complicating fuel efficiencies is that loads and load patterns of vehicles continually change, as does their load factor. Some transportation equipment moves loaded in one direction only and returns empty for another load. Fuel consumed in repositioning the empty equipment must also be taken into account.

Load factor means the percentage of capacity utilized. An airplane with 100 seats carrying 62 passengers is operating at a load factor of 62. Capacity of a vehicle is sometimes difficult to determine. For example, a beverage truck may be loaded with bottled soft drinks as it starts the day. During the day, the driver picks up cases of empty bottles in place of full ones he has delivered. In terms of cubic load factor, the truck's load factor remains at 100 for the entire day. In terms of weight load factor, the load factor decreases during the day.

Summarizing several studies, and acknowledging that spokesmen for different modes continue to disagree on this issue, we would say that pipelines are the most efficient. Barges are next. For each gallon of fuel a pipeline consumes, barges require 1.2 to 2.3 gallons to move the same load the same distance. Then come railroads, which require 1.5 to 2 gallons; trucks, which need 6.2 to 10 gallons; and airplanes, which require 43 to 93 gallons to perform the same amount of work. Vehicle speed is not taken into account (and we assumed all modes burned the same type of fuel).

Summary

This chapter has surveyed the transportation system available to logistics managers. A basic understanding of transportation is vital to logistics management. Transportation directly affects the other components of PD/L, and it is the largest single cost category of most operations.

The *railroads* transported 37 per cent of all ton-miles in 1984. Railroad companies tend to be relatively large compared to the other transport modes, averaging 12,000 employees per Class I railroad. This mode specialized in transporting carload quantities (greater than 30,000 pounds) of raw materials and bulk products. Their average revenue per ton-mile is 3.1 cents.

There are approximately 30,000 regulated interstate *motor carriers*. All truckers (regulated and private) produced 24 per cent of all intercity ton-miles. The regulated truckers' average revenue per ton-mile is 23 cents. The motor carrier industry has specialized in relatively small shipments (less than 10,000 pounds) that are typically high in value manufactured products. The three most serious problem areas are road taxes, Teamster wage rates, and the car-safety issue. In order to improve customer service, the truckers have introduced specialized equipment and computer-assisted programs to monitor shipment status in their system.

The *oil pipelines* are responsible for almost one fourth of all intercity ton-miles. There are three basic types of oil pipelines; crude gathering lines, crude trunklines, and product lines. The average revenue per ton-mile is 1.3 cents. Pipelines also carry solid products in slurry lines. Problem areas include the public's concern for the environment and the availability of rights-of-way.

The *inland water carriers* produce about 16 per cent of intercity ton-miles. They specialize in bulk movements of raw materials. The share of water traffic carried on the Great Lakes has declined while the share carried on the Mississippi River and other inland waterways routes has increased.

Air freight no longer grows at a healthy rate. The great majority of air freight is performed by combination passenger-cargo airlines. In 1984, air freight accounted for only 0.3 per cent of intercity ton-miles. One reason for this is the expense involved. The average revenue per ton-mile is 47 cents. Air carriers are currently experiencing some financial difficulties.

The *freight forwarder,* who specializes in the consolidation of small shipments, is an important transportation intermediary. The shippers' nonprofit association and a number of auxiliary carriers also play important roles in the transportation industry.

The final section examined each mode of transportation according to these four modal selection criteria: speed, dependability, capability, and fuel efficiency.

Questions for Discussion and Review

1. After reading this chapter, which mode of transportation do you believe has the greatest growth potential? Defend your answer.
2. It has been said that the transportation segment of the PD/L system is the most important. Is this true? Why?
3. Discuss briefly the *structure* of the railroad industry. Be sure to include in your answer the approximate number and size of the carriers, the products that they specialize in, and their current financial condition.
4. Why have railroads continued to lose finished [manufactured] products to the trucking industry?
5. Labor relations has historically been a difficult area for rail management. What are the problem areas involved?
6. The U.S. railroads have achieved some very definite service improvements during the last few years. Discuss briefly a number of these service innovations.
7. Discuss briefly the *structure* of the motor carrier industry. Be sure to discuss the approximate number and size of the carriers, the products that they specialize in, and their current financial condition.
8. Discuss the current financial condition of the trucking industry. What has caused this situation? When do you believe it will change? Why?
9. Examine briefly a number of areas in which the trucking industry has been able to achieve significant improvements in customer service levels.
10. Discuss the *structure* of the pipeline industry. Your answer should include the approximate number and size of the carriers, the products that they specialize in, their current financial condition, and the basic types of oil pipelines.
11. What is a slurry pipeline? How do they operate and what products are

currently being transported in slurry lines? Do you believe slurry pipe-lines have significant growth potential?

12. Discuss or define briefly each of the following:
    a. The Black Mesa project
    b. A LASH ship
    c. A user-tax or user-fee
    d. Wide-body jets
    e. Belly cargo
    f. Load factor
    g. Conrail
    h. A freight forwarder
    i. A shippers' nonprofit association
    j. TOFC/COFC

13. Discuss briefly the *structure* of the inland waterway system. Be sure to mention the products that they specialize in and their current financial condition.

14. Discuss briefly the three major problem areas of the inland water carriers.

15. Discuss the *structure* of the air freight industry. Cover the types of firms offering air cargo service, the products that they specialize in, their current financial condition, and the future of this industry.

16. What is the basic problem of belly cargo versus the jet freighter?

17. From an air freight point of view, discuss the current problem areas.

18. What function does an air freight forwarder provide? Is this a growth industry? Why?

19. Discuss the Canadian experience with "total" transportation companies. Would you recommend that the U.S. government encourage this concept in the United States? Why?

20. Regarding transportation modal selection criteria, which modes do the *best* and the *worst* for speed, dependability, and capability. Why?

21. Regarding the proposed ETSI pipeline, take a postition *for* or *against* this project and write a 300-word essay defending your position.

22. What is the difference between a broker and a shipper's agent?

Additional Chapter References

Adams, Sylvia, and William Heidelmark. "State and Local Taxation of Rail-roads and Other Transporation Companies: A Survey of Statutory Treatment." *Transportation Journal* (Summer 1984), pp. 50–61.

Agar, Michael. "Toward an Owner-Operator Theory of Carriers." *Annual Proceedings of the Transportation Research Forum* (1984), pp. 410–414.

Allen, Benjamin J., and David B. Vellenga. "Public Financing of Railroads Under the New Federalism: The Progress and Problems of Selected State Programs." *Transportation Journal* (Winter 1983), pp. 5–19.

Allen, Benjamin J., and Gary L. Maydew. "The Impact of Financial Accounting Standard No. 44 on Selected Motor Carriers." *ICC Practitioners' Journal* (July–Aug. 1983), pp. 532–541.

Allen, Benjamin J. "Rail-Barge Coordination: An Example and Evaluation of Its Potential." *ICC Practitioners' Journal* (March–April 1983), pp. 286–309.

Altshuler, Alan (ed.) *Current Issues in Transportation Policy* (Lexington, Mass.: Heath, 1979).

Baldwin, Peter, L. Lee Lane, and Thomas M. McNamara. "Congestion and Congestion Tolls on the Inland Waterways." *Annual Proceedings of the Transportation Research Forum* (1983), pp. 758–766.

Beier, Frederick J. "Electric Utilities and the Movement of Coal." *Transportation Journal* (Summer 1982), pp. 15–24.

Beilock, Richard. "Toward a Balanced Delivery System for Fresh Fruits and Vegetables." *Transportation Journal* (Winter 1981), pp. 28–36.

Berry, Thomas D., and Tad M. Walters, "Criteria for Selection of Transportation Rating Systems." *Annual Proceedings of the NCPDM* (1982), pp. 713–734.

Boberg, Kevin B. "Track Structure Accounting and Reported Earning of U.S. Railroads," *Transportation Journal,* (Spring 1985), pp. 18–25.

Bronzini, Michael S., Craig E. Phillip, and Charles J. Drobny. "Strategic Management of Vessel Movements on the Inland Waterways." *Annual Proceedings of the Transportation Research Forum* (1984), pp. 337–346.

Brown, Terence A. "Freight Brokers and General Commodity Trucking." *Transportation Journal* (Winter 1984), pp. 4–14.

———, "Shippers' Agents and the Marketing of Rail Intermodal Service." *Transportation Journal* (Spring 1984), pp. 44–52.

———, "Shippers' Associations: Operations, Trends, and Comparative Prices." *Transportation Journal* (Fall 1981), pp. 54–66.

Bruning, Edward R., and Larry E. Oberdick. "Market Structure and Economic Performance in the Commuter Airline Industry." *Transportation Journal* (Spring 1982), pp. 76–86.

Bunting, P.M. "Highway Cost Recovery and Intercity Trucking." *Annual Proceedings of the Transportation Research Forum* (1983), pp. 90–99.

Burdg, Henry B., and James M. Daley "Shallow-Draft Water Transportation: Marketing Implications of User and Carrier Attribute Perceptions," *Transportation Journal,* (Spring 1985), pp. 55–67.

Buxton, Freeman K. "Railcar and Barge Equipment Needs for Future U.S. Grain Movement." *Annual Proceedings of the Transportation Research Forum* (1982), pp. 599–607.

Carroll, Joseph L., and Kant Rao. "Financing the Inland Waterway System: A Role for the States?" *Annual Proceedings of the Transportation Research Forum* (1983), pp. 173–182.

Carroll, Joseph L. "Tennessee-Tombigbee Waterway Revisited." *Transportation Journal* (Winter 1982), pp. 5–20.

Casavant, Ken L., and Jeanne Hehringer. "Impact of Waterway User Fees on Pacific Northwest Wheat Movement: Before and After Staggers Act." *Annual Proceedings of the Transportation Research Forum* (1983), pp. 319–330.

Chow, Ming H., Michael W. Babcock, L. Orlo Sorenson. "The Changing Logistics Structure for Grain Marketing: A Case Study of Export Wheat in Northwest Kansas," *Transportation Journal* (Spring, 1985), pp. 37–46.

Clayton, A., and F. Nix. "Owner- Operators in Canadian Trucking—Their Role and Status and Implications of their Future Use." *Annual Proceedings of the Transportation Research Forum* (1984), pp. 1–11.

Constantine, James, A., and Marie Adele Hughes. "Motor Carriers and Marketing." *Annual Proceedings of the NCPDM* (1984), pp. 464–484.

Creedy, John A. "Why a Congressional Investigation of the Rail Land Grants?" *ICC Practitioners' Journal* (Jan–Feb. 1983), pp. 156–162.

Crew, James, and Kevin H. Horn. "The Impact of Inland Waterway Lock Congestion upon Barge Shippers." *Annual Proceedings of the Transportation Research Forum* (1983), pp. 779–787.

Crum, Michael R. "A Critique of and Recommendations for the ICC's Evaluation of Proposed Railroad Mergers." *ICC Practitioners' Journal* (May–June, 1984), pp. 368–390.

Cunningham, Lawrence F., and Wallace R. Wood. "Diversification in Major U. S. Airlines." *Transportation Journal* (Spring 1983), pp. 47–63.

Daley, James M., and Henry B. Burdg. "An Assessment of Shippers' Perceptions in the Modal Selection of Shallow-Draft Waterway Transportation." *Annual Proceedings of the Transportation Research Forum* (1983), pp. 751–757.

Davis, Grant M., John E. Dillard, Jr., and William Cunningham. "Motor Carrier Strategic Planning: Price and the Monopsonistic Shipper." *Annual Proceedings of the Transportation Research Forum* (1983), pp. 201–207.

Due, John F. "Government Versus Private Financing of the Railroad Industry." *Transportation Journal* (Spring 1982), pp. 16–21.

Early, Rollie W. "Innovative Purchasing of Transportation to Solve Distribution Problems." *Annual Proceedings of the NCPDM* (1984), pp. 571–584.

Fitzsimmons, E. L. "A Statistical Sketch of the Demand for Rail Transport of Grain and Soybeans." *Transportation Journal* (Spring 1981), pp. 59–65.

Flood, Kenneth U., Oliver G. Callson, and Sylvester J. Jablonski. *Transportation Management*, 4th ed. (Dubuque: Brown, 1984).

Folk, J. F., and R. E. Lindquist. "Reducing Excess Train Crew Members on Conrail." *Annual Proceedings of the Transportation Research Forum* (1983), pp. 507–513.

Gaskins, Darius W. "Intermodal Business Opportunities: An Analysis of Truck vs. Rail Costs." *Annual Proceedings of the NCPDM* (1983), pp. 245–252.

Germane, Gayton E. *Transportation Issues for the 1980's* (Menlo Park, Calif.: Addison-Wesley, 1983).

Ghoshal, Animesh. "Price Elasticity of Demand for Air Passenger Service: Some Additional Evidence." *Transportation Journal* (Summer 1981), pp. 93–96.

Goicoechea, Ambrose, Don Sweeney, Francis M. Sharp, and John J. Burns. "A Transportation Model for Economic Policy Analysis of National Inland Waterways Navigation." *Annual Proceedings of the Transportation Research Forum* (1983), pp. 767–778.

Goldschmidt, Neil. "The U.S. National Transportation Policy: Is it for Real?" *Annual Proceedings of the NCPDM* (1982), pp. 219–232.

Gritta, Richard D. "Air Carrier Financial Strategies: A Contrast—Pan Am and Delta." *Annual Proceedings of the Transportation Research Forum* (1983), pp. 684–691.

Hauser, Robert J., and Steven A. Neff. "The Pricing Efficiency of the Barge Freight Call Session." *Annual Proceedings of the Transportation Research Forum* (1984), pp. 331–336.

Hazard, John L. "Transitional Administration of National Transportation Policy." *Transportation Journal* (Spring 1981), pp. 5–22.

Hoffer, George E. "Estimating the Impact of Changes in Recent Cost Allocation Methodology and Highway User Fees on the Allocated Cost and Revenue Responsibility of Motor Carriers." *Transportation Journal* (Fall 1983), pp. 31–37.

Horn, Kevin. "Characteristics and Opportunities of Minority-Owned Interstate Motor Carriers of Property." *Annual Proceedings of the Transportation Research Forum* (1982), pp. 135–144.

———, "Pricing of Rail Intermodal Service: A Case Study of Institutional Myopia." *Transportation Journal* (Summer 1981), pp. 63–77.

Jennings, Kenneth M., Jay A. Smith, Jr., and Earle C. Traynham, Jr. "Transit Boards and Labor-Management Relations." *Annual Proceedings of the Transportation Research Forum* (1982), pp. 208–215.

Johnson, James C., and David J. Thomas. "Railroad Standard Time: A Centennial Remembrance." *Traffic World* (Jan. 2, 1984), pp. 53–57.

Johnson, James C. "Going, Going, Gone!—The ICC's Regulation of Trucking Mergers." ICC *Practitioners' Journal* (May–June 1984), pp. 391–407.

———, "Lessons from Amtrak and Conrail." ICC *Practitioners' Journal* (March–April 1982), pp. 247–256.

———, "Railroad Management's Myopia." *Journal of Business Logistics* (Vol. 3, No. 1, 1982), pp. 114–118.

Jones, J. Richard, and Sheila I. Cocke. "Commuter Airline Service to Non-Hub Airports." *Annual Proceedings of the Transportation Research Forum* (1983), pp. 692–699.

Kahn, Fritz R. "Restoring Brown Shoe: Railroad Mergers and the Antitrust Laws." *Transportation Practitioners Journal* (Fall 1984), pp. 40–50.

Kaminski, Peter F., and David R. Rink. "Industrial Transportation Management in a Systems Perspective." *Transportation Journal* (Fall 1981), pp. 67–76.

Kohon, Jorge C. "Cost and Subsidies in Railway Transport." *Annual Proceedings of the Transportation Research Forum* (1983), pp. 429–437.

Lancioni, Richard A., and Michael P. Coyle. "A Comparison of Two Methods for Measuring Motor Carrier Market Potential." *Transportation Journal* (Fall 1982), pp. 63–74.

Liba, Carl J. "Definition of the Inland Waterways Hinterland." *Annual Proceedings of the Transportation Research Forum* (1982), pp. 153–161.

Lieb, Robert C. "Intermodal Ownership: The Perspective of Railroad Chief Executives." *Transportation Journal* (Spring 1982), pp. 70–75.

———, "The Changing Nature of Labor/Management Relations in Transportation." *Transportation Journal* (Spring 1984), pp. 4–14.

Martland, Carl D. "Workload Measurement and Train Crew Consist Adjustments: The Boston & Maine Experience." *Transportation Journal* (Spring 1982), pp. 34–57.

Maze, T. H., Allen R. Cook, and Max Carter. "Restoring Rail Service Along the Old Chisholm Trail: The Oklahoma Brokerage Approach." *Transportation Journal* (Spring 1984), pp. 15–23.

McCabe, Douglas M. "The Railroad Industry's Labor Relations Environment: Implications for Railroad Managers." ICC *Practitioners' Journal* (Sept.–Oct. 1982), pp. 529–608.

McGee, Michael P., and Richard A. Lancioni. "A Case Study in Market Strategy Development for a Motor Carrier in Uncertain Times." *Annual Proceedings of the NCPDM* (1984), pp. 197–206.

McLeod, A. D. "A Grain Industry's Requirements for Rail Capacity." *Annual Proceedings of the Transportation Research Forum* (1983), pp. 66–73.

Metz, Peter K. "The Evolution of the Carrier Industry in the 80's." *Annual Proceedings of the NCPDM* (1982), pp. 355–376.

Meyer, Neil L. "Field to Market Transportation of South Idaho Wheat: Implications for Rural Transportation." *Annual Proceedings of the Transportation Research Forum* (1983), pp. 341–351.

Mitchell, Susan C. "The Alaska Railroad Transfer." *Annual Proceedings of the Transportation Research Forum* (1984), pp. 390–396.

Musick, Virgil O., Bill Huie, and Jerry A. Glawson. "Purchasing Texas Intrastate Transportation," *Annual Proceedings of the NCPDM* (1984), pp. 679–683.

Myers, Stewart C., A. Lawrence Kolbe, and William B. Tye. "Regulation and Capital Formation in the Oil Pipeline Industry." *Transportation Journal* (Summer 1984), pp. 25–49.

Oliver, David C. "A Framework for an International Multi-modal Transportation Policy Based upon the Concept of the World Ocean." ICC *Practitioners' Journal* (Jan.–Feb. 1983), pp. 196–208.

Petri, David L., Robert McKay Jones, Walter D. Todd, and Donald A. Wright. "Motor Carrier Transportation Costs can be Reduced through the Use of ICC Property/Transportation Brokers." *Annual Proceedings of the NCPDM* (1983), pp. 434–468.

Potter, Ronald S., and Robert M. Sutton. "Transportation Cost and Rate Forecast." *Annual Proceedings of the NCPDM* (1982), pp. 789–816.

Rao, Kant, and Thomas D. Larson. "Capital Investment, Performance, and Pricing in Highways." *Transportation Journal* (Spring 1982), pp. 22–33.

Roberts, Merrill J. "Railroad Maximum Rate and Discrimination Control." *Transportation Journal* (Spring 1983), pp. 23–33.

Ross, Richard K., Jr. "The New Era of Motor Carrier Marketing: Meeting the Challenge." *Annual Proceedings of the Transportation Research Forum* (1983), pp. 193–200.

Rowe, John W. "Perceptions of Failure and Collective Bargaining in the Railroad Industry." *ICC Practitioners' Journal* (March–April 1984), pp. 245–274.

Sampson, Roy J, Martin T. Farris, and David L. Shrock. *Domestic Transportation: Practice, Theory, and Policy,* 5th ed. (Boston: Houghton, 1985).

Sauter, John. "Airline Data Reporting Requirements: Costs and Benefits for Large Carriers and Aircraft Manufacturers." *Transportation Journal* (Winter 1982), pp. 74–83.

Selva, Regina T., and Richard F. Poist. "An Examination of Planning and

Organizational Responses to the Energy Crisis: A Survey of the Nation's Largest Motor Carriers." *Annual Proceedings of the Transportation Research Forum* (1983), pp. 716–723.

Schlesinger, Gale. "Working Women's Travel Issues." *Annual Proceedings of the Transportation Research Forum* (1982), pp. 436–442.

Shrock, David L., and Mary Ann Stutts. "A Comparative Analysis of Carrier Print Advertising." *Transportation Journal* (Fall 1981), pp. 77–88.

Sloss, James, and Carl D. Martland. "Government Intervention in Railroad Freight Car per Diem: An Historical Perspective." *Transportation Journal* (Summer 1984), pp. 83–95.

Smith, Daniel. "The Evolution of Rail Merger Policy." *Annual Proceedings of the Transportation Research Forum* (1983), pp. 558–565.

Smith, Jay A., Jr., Kenneth M. Jennings, and Earle C. Traynham, Jr. "Analysis of the Grievance/Arbitration Process in the Transit Industry." *Annual Proceedings of the Transportation Research Forum* (1984), pp. 397–402.

Southern, R. Neil. "Motor Carrier State Taxes: The Solution?" *Annual Proceedings of the Transportation Research Forum* (1984), pp. 380–381.

——— "Structure of the Private Motor Carrier Industry." *Annual Proceedings of the Transportation Research Forum* (1982), pp. 129–134.

"Special Issue; Transportation." *Business History Review* (Spring 1984).

Stephenson, Frederick J., and John W. Vann. "Air Cargo: A Marketing Technique and Strategy to Stimulate Primary Demand." *Annual Proceedings of the Transportation Research Forum* (1983), pp. 483–489.

Sugrue, Paul K., Manfred H. Ledford, and Nicholas A. Glaskowsky, Jr. "Operating Economies of Scale in the U.S. Long-Haul Common Carrier, Motor Freight Industry." *Transportation Journal* (Fall 1982), pp. 27–41.

Talley, Wayne K. *Introduction to Transportation* (Cincinnati: South-Western, 1983).

Vann, John W., and Frederick J. Stephenson. "Air Cargo—One Market or Three?" *Transportation Journal* (Fall 1981), pp. 14–23.

Vollmers, A. Clyde, and Stanley Thompson. "An Economic Evaluation of State Ownership of Grain Hopper Cars." *Transportation Journal* (Summer 1982) pp. 59–65.

Voorhees, Roy D., and Benjamin J. Allen. "Rail/Barge Ownership: A Baseline Estimate of Its Potential Effects." ICC *Practitioners' Journal* (Jan.–Feb. 1984), pp. 152–167.

Voorhees, Roy D., and Richard D. Reed. "The Rock Island Divorce Case." *Journal of Business Logistics* (Vol 3, No. 1, 1982) pp. 102–113.

Voorhees, Roy D., and John Coppett. "New Competition for the Airlines." *Transportation Journal* (Summer 1981), pp. 78–85.

Walters, Robert J. "Brokers," *Annual Proceedings of the NCPDM* (1984), pp. 643–646.

Wood, Donald F., and James C. Johnson. *Contemporary Transportation,* 2nd. ed. (New York: Macmillan, 1983).

Wood, Wallace R. "A Robust Model for Railroad Costing." *Transportation Journal* (Winter 1983), pp. 47–60.

Yarusavage, George A. "Carrier Evaluation and Selection." *Annual Proceedings of the NCPDM* (1983), pp. 852–868.

CASE 4-1

Sheboygan Pickle Company

Sheboygan Pickle Company was located in Sheboygan, Wisconsin, a small Great Lakes port. The firm was over one hundred years old, and its location could be considered as "resource oriented" since it was on the eastern edge of one of the largest cucumber-growing areas in the nation. It produced sweet pickles, relish, dill pickles and Kosher dill pickles. It sold nationwide under both its own brand name and under more than fifty different "private" labels of large food chains and buying co-ops. Nationally, its sales were increasing about 3 per cent a year; sales under private labels were increasing much faster than sales with its own label.

Its best sales area continued to be upstate New York, in the area from Albany to Buffalo. Sheboygan Pickle had never penetrated into the New York City market. Although some of the large buyers in Albany did ship some pickles to the New York City area, these usually bore "private" labels, rather than the Sheboygan Pickle label.

The reason Sheboygan pickles sold well in upstate New York is somewhat historic. Many settlers in Wisconsin had originally settled in upstate New York before moving west again. Hence many original family and trade ties still existed. Sheboygan pickles destined for upstate New York had been a major cargo on many Great Lakes "package" freighters through the 1920s, when the freighters dropped out of business. Since then, Sheboygan Pickle Company relied on railroads to reach its upstate New York customers. Indeed, nearly all of its outbound shipments moved by rail. Rates varied, of course, although the average rail rate on a 60,000-lb carload shipment to points in upstate New York was $450.

The firm purchased labels, bottles, and some spices from nearby Milwaukee. Cucumbers were purchased locally from about fifty growers who would truck them directly to the plant. Each year the pickle factory bought 5,000 tons of sugar. Currently the best arrangement was to buy it in New Orleans for $400 per ton and ship to Sheboygan by rail carload. The rail rate was $283 for each 50,000-lb carload. The sugar was needed during only four months of the year, July, August, September, and October, when most of the production occurred.

Sales were spread fairly evenly throughout the year, although they were a bit higher during the summer months and around the Thanksgiving and Christmas holidays. By August 15 of each year, Sheboygan Pickle Company produce buyers would have a good idea of the entire harvest of cucumbers for the season, and the remaining production for the season would be scheduled. In most "good" crop years, Sheboygan Pickle Company would start offering "deals" to buyers about September 1, offering them lower prices for larger-than-average orders. The buyer, then, would assume responsibility for warehousing the pickles, rather than Sheboygan Pickle Company.

George Abernathy had been traffic manager of Sheboygan Pickle Company since 1965. Since the late 1960s he had been troubled by the continual decline in the quality of rail service in the northeast. Buyers tended to blame him, rather than the carriers, when cars were delayed or lost. Additional "lead times" had been assigned to cars destined to upstate New York markets although, on rare occasions, the car would arrive too early and the consignee would have to unload it before he wanted it just to avoid demurrage charges. Truck transportation from Sheboygan was too expensive. The motor common carrier cost would be about $400 for a 40,000-lb shipment; contract truck rates would be about 10 per cent less. In the early 1980s, after both rail and motor carriers were deregulated, Abernathy attempted to negotiate contracts with both modes but was unable to obtain agreements that would substantially upgrade the dependability of deliveries without costing far too much.

Several of the large customers in upstate New York, including one firm that had been buying Sheboygan pickles since 1913, indicated they would drop the line unless better delivery service could be provided. Top management of Sheboygan Pickle Company became concerned because the upstate New York market was one where "brand loyalty" to the Sheboygan label still existed. If that market were lost, Sheboygan Pickle would be one large step closer to becoming merely a supplier to chain stores, and all of its products would be sold under chain labels.

Abernathy cancelled his regular Saturday golf game and went into the office to see if he could figure whether Sheboygan Pickle Company should locate a distribution center in upstate New York, supply it by rail, and make deliveries by truck. He had just completed tallying 1985 shipments from Sheboygan to upstate New York. They totaled 20,000 tons. The phone rang. He answered it. It was Bob Benson, one of his regular golfing partners. Benson worked for a neighboring shipyard where he was a sales engineer.

"You missed a good game today, George," said Benson. "If we'd played for our usual stakes, you would be three dollars richer this very moment!"

"Playing with you three for money is like plucking chickens," retorted Abernathy, "but you know why I had to work."

"That's why I called," said Benson. "Up in Escanaba, we may have the answer to your problems."

"What do you mean?" asked Abernathy.

"Up there is a converted World War II landing craft which has new adjustable loading ramps on both sides. We were converting it for what we thought was a 'CIA front' for possible use in Latin America when we got a stop-work order. We got paid for our work and then bought it on speculation. We just about had it sold to a paper company for picking up shipments of logs from small Lake Superior islands, when their financing fell through. I thought of you right after you called to cancel the golf game because the vessel is small enough to pass through the New York State Barge Canal."

"The what?" asked Abernathy.

Benson answered: "The New York State Barge Canal is the successor to the old Erie Canal. It stretches from Buffalo to Albany and is presently used mostly by pleasure boaters. Its locks are too small to handle conventional barges. I remembered you said once that your upstate New York markets had been influenced by the location of the old Erie Canal. We worked out cost figures for the paper company and I'd be glad to show them to you. How about Monday?"

Benson appeared in Abernathy's office at 9 A.M. Monday with a map of the Great Lakes and the barge canal (Exhibit 4-1); a batch of marine engineering drawings; photos of the vessel and its new loading ramps; and a packet of cost figures. Benson and Abernathy calculated that the vessel could carry 2,000 tons of pickles that would lower the vessel to its maximum allowable draft of 12 feet. The vessel could travel at 10 knots in open sea. Benson explained that the side loading ramps meant that conventional

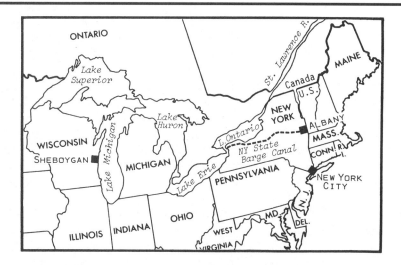

fork-lift trucks could be used to load and unload pallet loads of pickle cases. Once the cargo was stowed, it could be protected from the weather and from heavy seas.

"Do we have 12 feet of water alongside our plant?" Abernathy wondered. He called the pickle company's plant engineer and asked him. An answer was promised later that day.

Benson said operating costs would be about $700 per day for a 240-day season. (The northern extremities of the Great Lakes are closed to navigation during the period from December to March, although studies are underway to determine whether the navigation season could be extended.) These operating costs were exclusive of depreciation. "How much for depreciation?" asked Abernathy.

"That depends on what you pay for it and how long you plan on keeping it," said Benson. "For the paper company, we had said the vessel would sell for $150,000 and they could count on its use for ten years. I'd have to check, but I'm sure you could use the $150,000 figure in your calculations. I've got to go now to a luncheon appointment. I'll leave all this material with you. We should get together by the end of the week." He left and Abernathy was alone. The phone rang.

It was the plant engineer who reported that the U.S. Army Corps of Engineers maintained the navigation channel adjacent to the plant at a depth of 18 feet. The area right next to the plant had silted to nine feet, and it would be Sheboygan Pickle Company's responsibility to dredge alongside its bulkheading. A contractor had estimated that it would cost $8,000 to perform the dredging and dump the spoil in an approved spill site. The contractor said one dredging would last for several years; he did not think much silt would accumulate at the site, especially if it were being used. He also thought that the bulkheading was in satisfactory condition to accommodate the dredging and any shoreside storage and cargo-handling activity.

During the following week Abernathy and his assistants were busy. They assembled the following facts.

1. Sugar could be purchased in New York for $404 per ton and in Albany for $406 per ton. Costs of loading the sugar aboard the vessel in either port would be $1 per ton.

2. A route could be set up from Sheboygan to Buffalo and then through the canal to Albany. Pickles could be unloaded at Buffalo, three intermediate points (Rochester, Syracuse, and Utica), and Albany. The trip eastbound, including the loading of a backhaul of sugar at Albany, would take fourteen days. The trip from Albany to Sheboygan would take five days. At Sheboygan the sugar would be unloaded in one day and the pickles loaded in one day. Costs of unloading and loading at Sheboygan would be the same as presently experienced for loading and unloading rail cars. Loading and unloading during rainstorms would be an occasional problem. Tarpaulins would have to be thrown over each pallet. Aboard ship, there would be no problem with moisture. In the fourteen-day trip estimate just given is a one-day delay factor to cover the possibility of inclement weather.

3. During the eight-month season, eleven or twelve round trips could be made. (Two days could be saved when sugar was not a return haul.)

4. Costs for operating longer than the eight-month season climbed swiftly. Wage rates were higher, insurance was higher, and Coast Guard regulations did not allow the vessel to load as heavily. It would increase the time required to move through the canal.

5. The costs of carrying pickles inland from the five points along the canal was very low, averaging only $2 per ton. They were low for two reasons. In some instances they represented a desirable "back haul" for motor carriers. In two instances, large buyers had their warehouses adjacent to the canal and could unload the vessel as easily as rail cars.

Question One: Based on the information given so far, do you think Abernathy should recommend purchase of the vessel? Give your reasons.

Question Two: If you were Abernathy, what additional information—not given here—would you like to have?

Question Three: The vessel can apparently carry all of Sheboygan Pickle Company's pickles going to upstate New York. If they obtain the vessel, should they stop completely all use of rail and/or truck service to carry pickles from Sheboygan to upstate New York? Why or why not?

Question Four: The federal government is studying the possibilities of extending the navigation season on the Great Lakes and inland waterways. Assume they were planning on keeping navigation channels open one additional month in the November–December period. How would this 270-day navigation season, rather than a 240-day season, affect Sheboygan Pickle Company and its use of the vessel?

Question Five: Fuel costs are expected to increase, adding $100 per day to the vessel's operating costs (an additional $24,000 for the 240-day season of eleven or twelve round trips). By operating at slower speeds and making only nine round trips per 240-day season, this $24,000 can be saved. Given these new fuel costs for the vessel, how many round trips would you schedule per season?

Question Six (continuation of question five): Competing modes also must pay more for fuel. Assume rail rates increase by 20 per cent and truck costs and rates increase by 30 per cent. Assume further that demand for Sheboygan Pickles in upstate New York stays the same. How many round trips per year would you schedule for the vessel? Why?

CASE 4-2

Microcomputers for Talbot Industries?

Jack Talbot looked out of his office window, past the lawn sprinkling equipment that bore his name, to his production building. Talbot Industries (TI) of which Jack was president and founder, had indeed made great progress over the last seven years. TI now manufactured and sold annually slightly over $50,000,000 worth of lawn and agricultural sprinkling equipment. To the company's original home base in the Midwest has been added a major new agricultural market in California. In addition, there appeared to be a good chance of new business from Saudi Arabia, as a result of the good offices of Aziz Tarbi, a former college classmate of Jack's, who was presently deputy director of irrigation planning for the Saudi Agricultural Development Agency. The firm's current organization chart is shown as Exhibit 4-2.

Although he was proud of his company's performance to date, Jack knew that there were significant near-term decisions he would need to make that would have a major impact on the continued expansion of his sales and profits. One of the most unsettling of those decisions was related to TI's data-processing capabilities.

Within two years of its founding, TI leased, and later bought, a minicomputer. This machine had a direct-access memory of one million bytes and was sufficient to handle the data-processing needs of a small- to medium-sized company desiring largely commercial (record processing) applications. (Present-day microcomputers are distinguished by much smaller memory sizes—64,000 to 256,000 bytes—and a different intended use—namely, by an individual rather than by an entire firm.)

The data-processing section at TI consisted of a director, two programmers, and four data-entry clerks. The director's job was mainly as liaison with other departments to determine coming needs for data-processing services and to straighten out problems as they surfaced. The programmers were almost entirely engaged in the maintenance

Exhibit 4-2 Organization Chart for Talbot Industries as of July 30, 1986

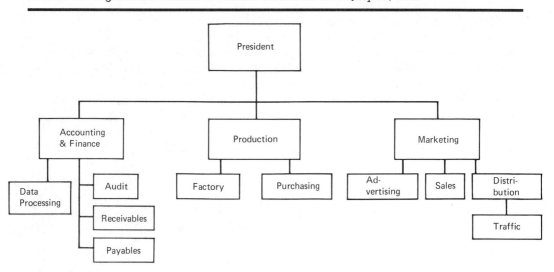

The Elements of Physical Distribution/Logistics Systems

and adaptation of existing programs to company needs. Note that they did no new program production. The data-entry section had one main task: to maintain the large data bases required for marketing (customer files), accounting, purchasing, and the traffic operations. Typically, there was a backlog of at least one week's work for the data-entry section, whereas one of the programmers was usually off on an internal consulting mission explaining to a department head what could or could not be done with existing data and capacities.

The section was organizationally part of the accounting department. This position was largely historical in its origins. Initially, the accounting department had been by far the greatest user of the computer, both for such tasks as printing pay checks and for producing various financial reports. Recently, the marketing, production, and traffic operations had developed a need for large data bases of their own, which were also resident in the company's system. That this organizational location had been largely successful was a credit to the firm's director of accounting, who had taken great pains to ensure that other departments felt that they were getting their fair turn at the computer's increasingly limited capacity.

Jack Talbot, himself an engineer by training and a manager by choice, was initially more than happy to have computer matters taken care of without having to hire an expensive director of data processing. He was not excited by business computers, per se, and considered them to be in the nature of necessary utilities—like the phone system.

Over the last several years, Jack's almost continuous contact with buyers, sellers, and manufacturers of products similar to his had convinced him that his own company's computer capacity was not being wisely used. Major problems included the following:

1. Capacity problems during the weekdays. If accounting were using the machine, there was little option for the others but to wait.
2. Late management reports. Even reports requested specifically for a given date were often late.
3. Access of nonaccounting personnel. Complaints were received from other departments that it was difficult even for senior people in production or marketing to gain timely access to the computer, even though they had terminals in their offices. Jack himself often had to be brought in to mediate some of these arguments.
4. Many of the younger employees on the production, marketing and traffic staffs had suggested that the use of the present company computer for purposes of data analysis, planning, and, more generally, as a direct decision support tool for departmental planning efforts was far too low. For example, there were several statistical programs that marketing wanted to use to plan promotion campaigns—programs that analyzed the type of customer who bought their product and the product features that related sales to each group of buyers, and then generated sales projections from time-series data. These programs required access to relatively large data files and a significant amount of the company's processing capacity. Traffic had become very concerned recently about the updating of its rate files, which provided the basis for contract negotiations with carriers, and for planning future movements.

The company computer was more than adequate to handle each of these tasks sequentially but not simultaneously. Thus, a question of priorities arose. Partly this issue may be laid to early decisions on which software to buy and which to design in-house. The accounting package was purchased from a nationally known vendor shortly after the acquisition of the computer. It was a large program that was not designed to accommodate many alternative configurations. When the accounting program was running, most other programs could not be used simultaneously. Other programs—such as those that controlled the customer files for the marketing department or the rate files for the traffic department—had been designed as the need arose. They were, therefore, considerably less efficient than the accounting software. Moreover, there was a tendency on the part of the programmers within TI to consider data bases from nonaccounting sources as a subset of the existing accounting data base. This was largely in order to copy routines that managed the accounting package and thus save programming time.

5. Although the accounting program was still adequately supported by its original vendor, the in-house products were in much more precarious states with regard to their maintenance. For example, when the systems analyst who developed the traffic department's planning tool (a simulation) departed for another job, there was no one in the data processing section who could make modifications in the program to make it applicable to TI's expanding transport requirements. Hence, the traffic department was left with a tool less and less applicable to its problems.

6. Recently the marketing department and the purchasing division had begun to realize that they had a need for many data that had been given a relatively low priority by the data-entry section of the data-processing operation. One reason for this backlog was a disagreement as to whether maintenance of the data bases for other divisions was a responsibility of the data-processing section or it was being done as a favor. As these specialized data bases grew in number—to about a dozen—this became a source of considerable friction between data processing and the other departments that used the computer. Complaints of "How can we plan with three-month-old data?" were met with, "You're lucky we took the time to get as much of your information recorded as we did!"

7. Finally, the data processing section was very conservative about permitting direct access and file modification by anyone outside their section. Their rationale was straightforward: The existing data bases represented a considerable investment by the company, and there was always the possibility that the untrained user would damage the data structures. Effectively, this meant that outside users' stored data was available to them when the data-processing section had time to get it for them.

Jack knew that things were coming to a head when he was confronted by the heads of his production department and his marketing department. The two had formed an ad hoc committee to get their message across: TI was not an accounting firm, it was an industrial manufacturer whose profits were highest when a quality product was shipped economically to customers. There were critical advantages available from computers to those charged with marketing and production, and they were not benefiting from them at present. What was Jack going to do about this state of affairs? Frankly, the two department heads were very angry.

Jack considered his options. He could establish an independent data-processing department, which would be more evenhanded in its treatment of other department heads. He could also invest in additional capacity for his existing system. This would cost roughly $100,000 and would probably eliminate most of the capacity problems. Recently, during his attendance at major industry meetings, Jack has been considering a third option: He could purchase a set of upper-end microcomputers for each of the departments concerned, along with appropriate printers and storage devices. This last course of action was of particular interest because it was much less expensive than mainframe conversions and it gave the rebellious departments some control over their own machines. (Jack estimated that ten micros were needed at $6,000 each, including peripheral devices.)

Jack decided that, prior to introducing the idea of microcomputers at his weekly staff meeting, he would request a memo on the subject from the data-processing section and several other departments. In this way he would have a better idea of the issues to be raised. Some of the responses he received are shown as Exhibits 4-3, 4-4, 4-5, 4-6, and 4-7.

Exhibit 4-3 Memorandum from Data Processing Section

TO: Mr. Jack Talbot　　　　　　　　　　　　　　　　　　　　May 14, 1986
FROM: Jeff Andrus, Chief, Data-Processing Section
Subject: Microcomputer Acquisitions

There can be no doubt that TI has outgrown the data-processing (DP) systems that we set up ten years ago during our early stages of growth. In retrospect, there may be some aspects of our decisions at that time we would like to undo if we could. The purpose of this memo is to suggest that the best means for improved DP operations and service is probably not to add a large number of amateur operators all trying to use our central storage capacity. Rather, the more efficient approach is to add one, perhaps two at most, additional staff to our data-processing section whose sole responsibilities would be to maintain nonaccounting software and data bases. With this additional staff, the bottlenecks experienced in recent weeks would have been eliminated. Moreover, the scope of existing software for marketing and production could be enhanced.

If a large number of (i.e., over ten) microcomputers are to be introduced into the offices of major departments at TI, the following points should be noted:

A. Training costs for new operators spread throughout TI will be significant. It costs the DP section about $10,000 to train new operators now. This is the cost of the four months it normally takes to introduce them to our particular hardware configuration and the programs we run. How much training would the new "operators" require? How specialized will it be? Will the data-processing division have any responsibility for such an effort?

B. Coordination will be needed between large and small computers. The existence of a number of untrained operators on their own micros will create the need for considerable in-house consulting. Most importantly, untrained operators must not be permitted access to our data bases without professional supervision. Very serious damage could be done to our data bases by untrained personnel. In the worse case, it would be possible to destroy our accounts-receivable files. Therefore, I strongly recommend that the interface between the main computer and the new micros be in the hands of the DP section. This should include technical supervision of the machines themselves.

C. Security will need to be greatly strengthened. With a micro in a number of insecure offices, the possibility of loss of our proprietary and confidential information increases. Therefore, it is suggested that a locking cover be purchased for each machine, and that a member of the data-processing section be assigned to check them.

D. Quality control of the software used will become much more difficult. A large number of inefficient programs, or inefficient uses for purchased software, will be developed by company personnel working on their own. Then data-processing will be asked to help find the bugs. Because we will not have the personnel to handle this work, it may be months before we can check a given program. This will lead to frustration among those given micros and will probably result in many remaining unused. More important, there will be the possibility that potential inaccuracies will remain unrecognized, leading to poor decisions based on bad output.

Finally, I would suggest that if the decision is made to buy micros for other departments, sufficient funding should be provided to data processing to manage the transition and to train personnel.

Exhibit 4-4 Memorandum from the Marketing Department

TI Interoffice Memo   May 16, 1986

TO: Jack Talbot

FROM: Jim Neto, Director, Marketing Department

SUBJECT: Microcomputers

An outstanding idea, long overdue! As you probably know, there are currently storage devices on the market called hard disks that can provide up to ten-million bytes of storage that the computer can get to quickly. It would be very valuable for us here in marketing to have one such device that we could use for our customer data files. Although there is no way we could get all the stored material into the personal computer at the same time, we would be able to look at the parts of the data base we wished to without going through TI's main computer (a time-consuming process)!

There are two basic functions that these computers would perform in marketing. First, they would provide ready access to data that have been increasingly difficult to get in a timely manner from our data-processing section. As you know, our expansion into the California market and potential business in Saudi Arabia present exponentially greater decision options both for our sales force and for our physical distribution and customer-service activities. We have no choice but to achieve immediate access to the information necessary to make these decisions correctly.

The second major function is in planning and data analysis. Particularly with the penalties for late deliveries built into the proposed Saudi contract, we simply must do the best possible job in projecting lead times for our shipments. This can be done very readily with the aid of simulations of our product flow that could be run on the proposed micro computers.

Specific functions of the micros might include tracking our shipments, route selection, rate analysis, sales forecasting, and analyses of specific groups of customers. Certainly all of these functions cannot be performed entirely on the micros we buy. However, we could store the results of such analyses in our own department and gain direct access to them there. In fact, there are a great many types of marketing and transportation analysis that can now be performed entirely on the micro.

Another benefit of the proposed purchase would be the possibility of performing our own maintenance and updating for those data bases that are still stored on the main computer. Frankly, Jack, you are as aware as I that we have not been able to get the maintenance we need on our data bases from the DP section. Not surprisingly, maintaining our bases gets relatively low priority over there. With the micros, we will be able to do it ourselves and then transmit it directly to the main computer as necessary.

Morale would also be very positively impacted. As you know, many of our new employees, hired over the last several years are very oriented toward computer applications in marketing and physical distribution. They consider the DP facilities as a needed support for doing their jobs right. Several have personal computers at home and have brought in the results of job-related programs that they developed on their own. There is tremendous willingness to spend personal time learning whatever is needed to use these new machines. In fact, I anticipate a real diplomatic challenge in determining who gets one on his or her desk. I could also identify two or three employees who could be detailed as "departmental training persons" in the area of microcomputers.

I would anticipate several areas where your direct mediation/policy-making efforts would improve the transition to micros, especially with the DP section. We will need to work out, on a companywide basis, procedures for access for departments other than accounting to the main computer. The new machines will not do much good if we have to wait days for access to needed data bases. Also, it should be clear that the machines themselves, and the policies regarding their use inside the marketing department, are the responsibility of marketing alone, not DP. Finally, I would like some top-level decision as to the extent we may expect to get help from DP when we do have a problem.

Exhibit 4-5 Memo from Purchasing Department

TI Interoffice Memor   May 17, 1986

TO: Mr. Jack Talbot

FROM: Susan Moore, Purchasing Manager

SUBJECT: Microcomputers

The purchasing function would be significantly benefited by the introduction of microcomputers into our office. In my view, the most important benefit would be an ability to obtain information immediately on past vendor performance and current prices as an aid in our negotiations with potential suppliers. Presently this function is performed using our DP division and our vendor data base, which is stored on our main computer. The time required to get the information at present precludes direct use in our negotiations. Because many of the best purchasing opportunities come up quickly, often over the phone, it is not very handy to have the data in the main computer.

A second major use for our personal computers would involve our ability to track the quality characteristics of the parts we do order. In conjunction with production, we would like to be able to identify quality problems as a function of inputs wherever possible. This, again, requires a good deal of direct access to our data base, which is not presently practical.

Finally, you are aware of the issues surrounding the maintenance of nonaccounting data bases in this firm. If we had our own micros, and one storage device large enough to put our information on, we would be very happy — even anxious — to keep our own files up-to-date. The only reason we do not do so now is that there are strong feelings in DP that we might "damage" the data bases if we "amateurs" got direct access to them.

Exhibit 4-6 Memorandum from Traffic Manager

MEMO

May 21, 1986

TO: Mr. Jack Talbot

FROM: Michael Hardesty, Traffic Manager

SUBJECT: Computer needs

I've seen copies of the several memos sent to you and have little to add. Many shippers now have "personal-sized" computers for operations smaller than mine. I learned this from carrier sales reps who now will give us diskettes with their rates on them. Also, the traffic magazines I read indicate there's a lot of software available.

There is one thing I must point out, however, and that is our present reliance on the "big" computer in the accounting department, although not always prompt, it has given us much better control over making sure that shipments leaving our dock are being billed to customers. It's my understanding that a shipping document won't be printed unless the items described are simultaneously being billed to some account. As you may recall, this reduced our "shrinkage" considerably.

P.S. As you suspect, my knowledge about computers is very limited, so I asked Dan Schroeder, whom we recently hired, to send you a memo also. He's just completed his six-month probationary period and I intend for him to become our "computer man."

Exhibit 4-7 Memorandum from Assistant Manager

MEMORANDUM: May 22, 1986

TO: Jack Talbot

FROM: Dan Schroeder, Assistant Traffic Manager, Outbound.

I've looked at some of the material put out by other departments on this microcomputer question, and a lot of it makes good sense. From our perspective in traffic, there are certainly a lot of uses we could find for these little machines. Let me first mention a few dangers, however:

1. As you know, we have some very tough competition for our product on the West Coast. Much of the business we have there stays with us because of our good record on customer service. Establishing new computer-based methods relating to our purchase of transportation services must not be done at the expense of either our service or the good relations we have built up with our westbound carriers. We should plan very carefully just when these new machines are to be introduced and how much time is likely to be lost during the training period.

2. It appears that several of the memos I saw on this subject said, in effect, that now we can get on with our computing without waiting for the DP section in accounting. From our standpoint, we would like to make sure that the accounting department is very much involved in the preparation of invoices for the customer and our own shipping documents. It is also important that accounting has a very good idea of just what was shipped by which carrier when carrier invoices come through our office on their way to be paid.

3. I suspect that our traffic people will continue to look on the computer, whether a terminal or a micro, largely as a user. That means that, if we move toward micros, we will need to make sure there is someone who can both train and consult with us as to how to use these machines. I know of no one in my shop who has the skill — or the time — to do this at the moment, although I'm willing to try.

4. When I go to professional meetings, I am swamped with demonstrations and brochures on new software that will help us do our job. I would be very hard pressed to select from among the various vendors for the best product, especially if there are technical factors involved. To whom in TI should I turn for help in this area?

Turning to possible applications, I would like to see our access to data bases greatly improved — whether on our own micros or on better terminals from our large machine. When I negotiate with a carrier, it would be valuable to have information on his costs (this can be obtained on software commercially) to help in developing our proposals. We would like the software to help us identify trade-offs between costs and service for the transportation we are buying.

I would also like to develop a readily accessible base for monitoring carrier performance. Again, at contract time, it would be handy to have figures as to the percentage of on-time deliveries, number of claims for damage, and other items that come into play as we discuss terms.

Finally, when we get the time to do so, we might eventually use the computers to develop an evaluation method for our distribution pattern. Could we save money with a new set of warehouse locations? Or perhaps a new modal mix? This type of analysis, which I have seen used to good advantage in other shops, is likely to require that we hire someone who is very much more talented with the micro than anyone we now employ. Although, an outside consultant might be able to help.

All in all, I feel that the micros would be fine so long as they do not upset our important existing relationships with our main computer and the DP section.

Question One: To what extent are the problems with data processing at TI organizational in nature?

Question Two: Discuss the explicit and implicit reasons for the DP section's attitude toward the move to microcomputers.

Question Three: Which problems are probably underestimated by the marketing manager?

Question Four: How would the role of the DP section change if the project went forward?

Question Five: How might Jack Talbot best initiate the change so as to maintain morale in both the DP section and other departments?

Question Six: You are a salesperson for a major manufacturer of microcomputers that is coincidentally the supplier of the minicomputer TI uses. Develop a sales presentation that both reassures your old friends in the DP section, and sells your micros to marketing and production.

Question Seven: Draft a memo, for Talbot's signature, announcing his decision and how it will be implemented.

One of the problem areas regarding regulation of U.S. carriers dealt with coordinating different modes of transportation. This was especially true when one mode represented domestic moves connected with another mode which was international in nature. These interfaces were also often focal points of technological change. Shown here are some of the advances in truck-to-ship transfers of cargo. The upper picture is from the Library of Congress. Taken in 1926, its title is ''New port of St. Petersburg on Florida's west coast.'' The bottom photo, taken in 1983 in Seattle, shows one of American President Line's new container ships, the President Lincoln.

(Credit: Library of Congress, and Don Wilson, Port of Seattle)

Transportation Regulation, Deregulation, and Rates

Forget your effete Harvard Business School strategies; this is crush-the-competition market-ing in the John D. Rockefeller style. Unshackled from government regulation and financial hardship, the giant U.S. [air] carriers are muscling each other for every passenger and every scrap of turf. The battle, which could last years and cost billions of dollars, is no game for the meek.
"The only guys who'll survive are those who eat raw meat," a Boeing official says.

> **William M. Carley**
> *Wall Street Journal*
> June 18, 1985

As far as the motor carrier industry is concerned, we've certainly wanted the continuation of regulation. We had it made. We could sit on our yachts, or whatever, and just let the world go by, for our profits were secure. They were absolutely guaranteed under the old regulation that existed five to ten years ago. It wasn't just the ICC, but teamwork between the Teamsters, the rate bureaus and the old ICC that gave this guaranteed protection to the established motor carrier.

> **Herald A. Smith, Jr.**
> Chairman, CRST Trucking, Inc.
> *Traffic World*
> April 2, 1984

I can say without hesitation that the Staggers Act has been the primary force of change. Staggers was the most important piece of railroad legislation in one hundred years. It not only allowed—it actually forced—the railroads to become modern corporations and to learn the meaning of a few new words—words like marketing *and* innovation. *It did not really give us deregulation; what it gave us was an area of pricing freedom within which we could adjust rates without prior ICC approval. It forced us to learn what competition was. It taught us to compete in the open market.*

> **Hays T. Watkins**
> Chairman, CSX, Inc. (A major railroad)
> *Railway Age*
> February 1984

I don't know how to look rates up in the old tariff books, and I don't want to learn how. I want rates that are so simple and easy that my thirteen-year-old daughter can tell me what they are.

> **Michael Todres, Director of Distribution**
> J.C. Penney Company
> *Distribution*
> September 1983

Key Terms

- **Common law**
- **Common carrier obligations**
- **Rate bureaus (conferences)**
- **Market dominance**
- **Embargo**
- **Contract carrier**
- **Exempt carrier**
- **Private carrier**
- **Tariff**
- **Value-of-service pricing**
- **Full-cost pricing**
- **Class rate**
- **Exception rate**
- **Class rate**
- **Hierarchy of rates**

Learning Objectives

- **To explain why transportation regulation was established**
- **To examine the traditional obligations of common carriers**
- **To identify why each mode of transportation became federally regulated**
- **To analyze the reasons for transportation deregulation**
- **To discuss each major deregulation act and the *effects* each has had on PD/L operations**
- **To contrast the legal obligations of the various types of carriers**
- **To understand the complexity of freight rate determination**
- **To note the importance of computerization in freight rate determination**

Introduction

One of the most controversial subjects in the history of American business has been the regulation of business, a subject often closely associated with the transportation industry. With deregulation, transportation has again been near the center of controversy. This chapter covers these two issues, as well as rate determination.

A Brief History of Transportation Regulation

Governmental regulation of transportation dates back to England. In 1670 Lord Chief Justice Hale, in his treatise *De Portibus Maris,* stated that when private property is used in such a way that the majority of the public has a vital economic interest in its usage, then the owner of the property "grants to the public an interest in that use, and must submit to be controlled by the public for the common good." It was felt that the transportation system was so basic to the efficient operation of the economy that it should be regulated by the court system according to the *common law* rather than *statutory law*. During the 1600s and 1700s in England the common law system of regulation of the transportation systems prevailed with respect to unreasonable rates and service practices. Statutory laws were not considered necessary because of the prevailing attitudes of *laissez-faire* (that which governs least governs best).

> *Common law* developed as grievances decided by the court system
> on a case-by-case basis. Over extended periods of time, the courts
> made similar rulings in cases that had approximately the same cir-
> cumstances. This consistency of judicial interpretation and findings
> is known as common law. The stability and continuity of the sys-
> tem basically made it unnecessary to establish statute law, which is
> often nothing more than the common law precedents being written
> and enacted into law by legislative bodies.

This system of common law transportation rate and service regulation
was adopted in the United States. Because the public's demand for transportation regulation was not acute, common law regulation worked reasonably well until the 1870s. Typically, the state government would give limited
monopoly rights to a ferry, a stage coach line, or a railroad—meaning that
government would not allow another competitor to operate in the same
area. In return the carrier would agree to assume the traditional common
carrier obligations, summarized on Figure 5-1.

After the panic of 1873, the United States experienced depression.
Farmers, who were at best irritable because of the depressed agricultural
prices, became incensed by a number of railroad activities. These railroad
practices included:

1. Rate discrimination, which meant that shippers who had services of
   competing railroads paid low rates, while shippers served by only one
   railroad paid high rates.
2. The farmers were often heavily taxed to pay for gifts that had been
   formerly pledged to the railroads by local and state governments. When
   a railroad was being built into an area, it was a matter of life-and-death
   for communities to be located on the rail line. The railroads knew this
   and would survey as many as four or five alternative routes from City
   A to City B. Then the railroads would play the communities along one
   proposed route against those on the others. The winning communities
   would be those which pledged to build a free terminal, grant the railroad a number of years of no taxation, and give it the largest cash
   bonus. These gifts necessitated the subsequent taxation of the farmers
   and other landowners.
3. The railroads were the first major industry to extensively sell their stock
   to the general public. Many farmers had mortgaged their farms to buy
   the securities, which often turned out to be worthless because the rail
   management had "watered" their stock—i.e., issued more stock than
   the firm's assets justified.
4. The arrogant attitude of railroad management and the ease with which
   they "bought" legislators enraged the public. This was the era when
   Commodore Vanderbilt's son, William, uttered his famous statement,
   "Let the public be damned."

By the mid-1880s farmers were insisting that the federal government
correct the abuses listed here. Various state governments had attempted to
solve the railroad problem, but because of legal complications dealing with

Figure 5-1 The Traditional Common Carrier Obligations

Federal and state laws that regulate carriers often place on the carriers a responsibility known as the *common carrier obligation.* Based on English common law and spelled out in our statutes, the obligation on the carrier has four parts:

Service Obligation. Common carriers have a legal obligation to serve *all* customers who request their service. This assumes the requested service is one the carrier has the authority and equipment to serve. For example, a motor common carrier of general commodities may refuse to accept a 10,000-gallon bulk shipment of sulfuric acid if he does not have the proper equipment to handle this type of commodity.

Delivery Obligation. The common carrier has a strict obligation to deliver the products entrusted to it to the consignee (receiver). This delivery must be accomplished with reasonable dispatch, and the products must be in the same condition as the carrier received them. It is this obligation under which the *law of loss and damage* (L&D) is founded. It is generally believed that this duty is the oldest common carrier obligation. Writing in 1703, Lord Holt stated:

> The law charges this person thus intrusted to carry goods, against all events, but Acts of God, and the enemies of the King. For though the force be ever so great, as if an irresistible multitude of people should rob him, nevertheless, he is chargeable. And this is a political establishment, contrived by the policy of the law, for the safety of all persons, the necessity of whose affairs oblige them to trust these sorts of persons, that they may be safe in their ways of dealing: for else these carriers might have an opportunity to undoing all persons that had any dealings with them, by combining with thieves, etc., and yet doing it in such clandestine manner as would not be possible to be discovered. And this is the reason the law is founded upon that point.[*]

Today, all a shipper or consignee has to prove to have a valid claim against a common carriers is that: (a) the goods were tendered to the carrier in good condition, and (b) when received by the consignee the product was damaged, or (c) the product was lost. When this occurs, the carrier is liable for a loss and damage claim.

Reasonable Rates. Because the number of competitors is limited, it is only logical that the rates of existing carriers be kept at a reasonable level.

Avoidance of Discrimination. The final common carrier obligation is to treat all customers, products, and geographic locations the same when similar circumstances are present.

[*]Richard R. Sigmon, *Miller's Law of Freight Loss and Damage Claims,* 4th ed. (Dubuque, Iowa: Wm. C. Brown, 1974), p. 3.

interstate commerce, no one state could adequately address the issue. The stage was set for federal intervention.

Railroad Regulation (1887)

In 1887 Congress passed the *Act to Regulate Commerce,* whose name was changed in 1920 to the *Interstate Commerce Act.* This legislation was designed to control the most serious railroad abuses. The 1887 act called for the following federal regulation: (1) all rail rates had to be "just and reasonable" as determined by a federal agency, (2) all shippers were to receive similar rates and services when the transportation service was performed under similar conditions, (3) no person, locality, or product was to receive undue preference or prejudice, and (4) all rail rates for both passengers and freight had to be published and made available for all to see. (The act contained many other provisions.)

The 1887 act created the ICC to administer the act on a day-to-day basis. Congress had given the ICC broad overall guidance, and the commission was expected to interpret and implement these mandates.

Oil Pipeline Regulation (1906)

The Hepburn Act (1906) brought *oil pipelines* under the 1887 act, although they are not regulated as strictly as the railroads. The rationale for this legislation was that the Standard Oil Company appeared to control railroad transportation of all oil products. The rail rates for oil were kept relatively high, and Standard Oil negotiated (illegally) to receive rebates both on the oil they tendered the railroads and also on the oil tendered by other, competing oil companies. Furthermore, Standard had a virtual monopoly on all existing oil pipelines and did not allow its competitors to use its system. Congress reacted by declaring in the Hepburn Act that all oil pipelines are common carriers, and hence they had to accept all oil shipments tendered to them. This legislation broke the Standard Oil monopoly on oil transport.

Trucking Regulation (1935)

In 1935 the Motor Carrier Act placed the trucking industry under federal safety controls and economic regulation administered under the Interstate Commerce Act. The key aspect of this legislation was *entry control*. Thereafter, anyone who wanted to enter the interstate trucking business as a common carrier had to obtain a *certificate of public convenience and necessity* (commonly called a certificate) from the ICC. The existing truckers in 1935 were able to continue in business under a *grandfather* provision. The existing truckers, in return for this protection from competition, were regulated with respect to both rates and service.

Airline Regulation (1938)

Airlines became federally regulated for safety, rates, and services by the 1938 Civil Aeronautics Act. Virtually all economic aspects of their operations were regulated by the Civil Aeronautics Board (CAB). (The airlines were the first industry to be deregulated and, in early 1985, the CAB went out of existence.)

Domestic Water Carrier Regulation (1940)

Five years after federal trucking regulation was enacted, Congress again passed another significant piece of transportation legislation. The *Transportation Act of 1940* brought some *inland water carriers* under federal economic regulation. As is turned out, the inland water carriers are at best nominally regulated because of the extensive exemptions from economic regulation that were allowed. The most important exemptions include all dry bulk commodities and all liquid commodities shipped in bulk. The ICC has estimated that only 10 per cent of all tonnage shipped by inland water carriers is subject to federal economic regulation.

Freight Forwarder Regulation (1942)

Forwarders are intermediaries between small shippers and carriers. This law recognized them, defined their responsibilities, and prohibited them from owning intercity common carriers. (However, intercity common carriers could own freight forwarders.)

Reed-Bulwinkle Act (1948)

The Reed-Bulwinkle Act rounded out our nation's regulatory system for transportation. The law authorizes the use of rate bureaus (conferences) for all land common carriers. Rate bureaus establish rates, but each carrier is guaranteed the right to establish its own rates, which may differ from those set by the bureau. This is known as taking "independent action" or "flagging-out." Finally, the *Reed-Bulwinkle Act* states that rate bureaus which fully conform to the ICC's rules and procedures will be exempt from the antitrust laws. Supposedly, they were to deal only with rates; but sometimes (and, possibly, illegally) they discussed other items of common interest.

This was the last piece of regulation to strengthen the transportation regulatory system. In essence, this is the set of rules by which the carriers competed (or did not compete). Brief mention should also be made of state regulation. States usually regulated intrastate operations of rail, motor, and water carriers, and a few even regulated intrastate airlines. Often, but not always, state regulations followed the federal pattern. In any event, the traffic manager must be aware of state regulations whenever she or he deals with an intrastate shipment.

Transportation Deregulation

The regulatory system described so far did not function well after World War II, for many reasons. One was that the "coverage" of regulation—especially of motor and inland waterways carriers—was incomplete. Unregulated firms would continually take traffic away from the regulated modes, weakening their financial condition, and making it more and more difficult for them to meet their common carrier obligations. Railroads were especially vulnerable, and many were bled white. There also were frequent technological changes in transportation, and many of them were not in harmony with the transportation regulatory climate. Regulatory board members and their staffs had lost their crusader zeal, eventually concluding that "free-market" forces could better protect the public interest than they—the regulators—could.

We have discussed the move toward deregulation in some detail in another book.[1] We will do little more here than mention the major laws and some of their impacts. Deregulation in the United States has come quickly and in many forms. There exists a patchwork of what is regulated, what is not regulated, and what is partially regulated. In addition, some of the new rules and laws bringing about deregulation are currently being challenged in the courts, so it may be some time before we know exactly how to interpret them. Presently the ICC's members tend to agree with deregulation, so when issues are brought before them, they choose a solution that further relaxes the regulatory burdens on carriers. Individual states are also in the process of reducing the amount of regulations they have over intrastate movements.

All-Cargo Aircarft Deregulation (1977)

In late 1977, all-cargo aircraft operations became free from CAB regulations. After an initial transition stage, anyone wanting to enter this business could do so automatically, assuming they met the safety standards established by the FAA. Freight rates were freed from CAB controls.

An *all-cargo aircraft* is one that carries cargo only. Hence, the law applied to those few airlines that carried only freight; to the all-cargo planes operated by some of the major airlines, such as United and American; and to a few commuter or local airlines that happened to qualify because they flew some night flights carrying mail only.

The effects of cargo aircraft deregulation have been many. The initial response was the establishment of many new all-cargo airlines. More new companies would have been established, except that there was a shortage of used propeller-driven aircraft, which are the best for flights of less than 500 miles. With rates no longer regulated by the CAB, and many new carriers competing for air freight, the inevitable took place: rates shot downward. By late 1983 rates were so low that Senator Mark Andrews proposed federal legislation to eliminate predatory pricing in the air cargo industry.[2] Although rates are relatively low, service levels have improved as a result of deregulation because of the increased competition offered by new firms.[3]

---

[1] Donald F. Wood and James C. Johnson, *Contemporary Transportation*, 2nd ed. (New York: Macmillan, 1983), pp. 108–122.

[2] See Stephen A. Alterman, "Air Freight Association: A Broad-Brush Perspective," *Traffic World* (Nov. 7, 1983), p. 39.

[3] Jim Tanchon, "Air Freight and 'Just in Time' Go Together Like Love and Marriage," *Traffic World* (Nov. 4, 1984), pp. 38–40.

One additional result, mentioned in Chapter 4, is that the depressed level of air freight rates has forced many combination air carriers out of all-cargo aircraft operations. They will only transport air freight as a by-product on their passenger planes. In this situation, air freight becomes relatively "profitable," but only because the expenses of operating the aircraft are being paid by passengers. The problem is that passenger aircraft are used primarily in the daytime, and therefore it is difficult to offer much overnight service on combination carriers. To meet the need for overnight service, some air freight forwarders are purchasing their own aircraft. They believe they can operate these planes profitably for two reasons: (1) they can charge a higher rate for guaranteed overnight service, and (2) because cargo is their only business, they will be more efficient in this type of service than combination carriers.[4]

Passenger Airline Deregulation (1978)

President Carter signed the law to deregulate the airlines on October 24, 1978. It deregulated the passenger side of airline operations, along with the air freight service provided by combination carriers. After a transition period that is now over, rates have become totally deregulated for both passenger and freight service. Entry control has been abolished, so any new carrier can enter this industry. The CAB no longer exists; its noneconomic regulatory functions are now administered by the DOT. These include such factors as smoking regulations, compensation for passengers denied boarding who had confirmed seats, and baggage liability.

The airline industry has been turned upside down by deregulation. The primary reason has been the influx of new carriers. The CAB had historically been protective of "its" industry and utilized entry control to limit price and service competition. From 1938, the year federal regulation was established for the airline industry, to 1978, not one new trunk (large national) airline was authorized by the CAB.[5] However, with entry control barriers now removed, fourteen new jet airlines have commenced operation. Over one hundred new smaller airlines using propeller planes have also entered this industry.[6] Many fundamental changes have occurred in the area of rates and services, each of which will be discussed briefly.

Change was necessitated because new carriers were typically nonunion, which benefited carrier management in two ways: (1) wages were lower and (2) nonunion workers performed more than one type of duty. In 1983, Trans World Airlines, for example, paid its pilots an average of $87,000 and its mechanics $32,000. Nonunion carriers, such as Southwest Airlines, People Express, Muse Air, New York Air, and New Continental, typically pay

---

[4] Stan Chapman, "Air Freight on a Different Plane," *Distribution* (Nov. 1984), pp. 85–87.

[5] James P. Rakowski and James C. Johnson, "Airline Deregulation: Problems and Prospects," *Quarterly Review of Economics and Business* (Winter 1979), p. 68.

[6] "Airlines: Survival of the Fittest," *U.S. News and World Report* (Nov. 26, 1984), p. 52.

their pilots in the mid-$30,000 range; their mechanics average about $21,000.[7] In terms of work rules, pilots at People Express work forty hours per week. Because they are not allowed to fly that many hours per week because of FAA regulations, they also sell tickets and work on plane scheduling.

The new low-cost airlines started to charge substantially lower rates than the older established carriers. The result was price wars: older carriers matched the lower rates of new carriers. From 1980 to 1982, U.S. air carriers lost almost $1.4 billion. Donald May, president of Republic Airlines, noted in dismay, "Our industry has shown itself completely incapable of pricing its product."[8] More recently, order has begun to emerge. All carriers are pricing their services closer to the cost of production. Older carriers have worked with their unions and salaried employees, and in most cases labor costs have been frozen or "give-backs" have been established.[9] The result is that domestic airlines made all-time record earnings of $1.5 billion in 1984. Douglas W. Caves, Laruits R. Christensen, and Michael W. Tretheway have presented a summary of the impact of new carriers on the airline industry:

> As deregulation proceeds, lower-cost carriers will either force efficiency on the others or, eventually, drive them out of business. The competitive pressures applied by People Express, Pacific Southwest, and the other low-cost carriers, along with efficient commuters and the expanding locals (and even such efficient trunks as Delta), will be a spur to productivity improvement under deregulation. Ultimately, all carriers will be low-cost carriers and all of us, as consumers of airline services, will benefit. Our findings show that the benefits are already substantial.[10]

Service levels have been substantially increased because of new competitors. Smaller cities typically are served by commuter airlines that feed passengers and freight to airports served by larger carriers.[11] Larger cities that traditionally did not receive much attention are now being sought out by carriers to establish new centers of operations, called hubs. Spokes are the routes between smaller cities and each airlines' hubs. An example is Piedmont Aviation. Not being one of the largest airlines in the country, it did not want to compete directly against the giants of the industry in the cities they dominate: New York, Chicago, Los Angeles, Dallas, and Atlanta. Instead, Piedmont looked for cities that could utilize additional service. They chose three: Charlotte, North Carolina; Dayton, Ohio; and Baltimore, Maryland. This concept has worked well for Piedmont.

Air freight service is now available on a much larger number of flights as a result of deregulation. Why? Passenger service offerings have increased,

---

[7] William M. Carley, "How TWA Is Trying to Get Some Workers to Take Big Pay Cuts," *Wall Street Journal,* 10 January 1984, p. 1.

[8] David Stamps, "Fare Game," *Minnesota Corporate Report* (July 1983), p. 47.

[9] Kenneth Labick, "Fare Wars: Have the Big Airlines Learned to Survive?" *Fortune* (Oct. 29, 1984), pp. 24–28.

[10] Douglas W. Caves, Laruits R. Christensen, and Michael W. Tretheway, "Airline Productivity Under Deregulation," *Regulation* (Nov.–Dec. 1982), p. 28.

[11] Anthony P. Ellison, "The Structural Change of the Airline Industry Following Deregulation," *Transportation Journal* (Spring 1982), pp. 58–69.

and because passenger planes also transport freight, additional freight capacity has been added. In addition, rates can be negotiated for every shipment. Robert W. Baker, freight marketing vice-president for American Airlines, has noted:

> We can negotiate a rate over the telephone with a shipper, and we don't have to wait days and even months for regulatory approval. This flexibility gives us more opportunity to negotiate rates to meet specific shipper requirements, and it also enables pricing to reflect actual costs of fuel and labor on a more timely basis.[12]

In summary, airline deregulation has been traumatic for the industry. Nevertheless, most carrier managers prefer the free-market environment to the previous regulated system. A spokesperson for the Air Transport Association, which represents most of the larger airlines, has stated: "All our members oppose economic reregulation." Another observed, "Having tested its wings in the brisk wind of competition, the airline industry is confident it can fly."[13]

Trucking Deregulation (1980)

On July 1, 1980, President Carter signed the Motor Carrier Act of 1980. This law was long and complicated—its purpose was to free the trucking industry from most of the economic regulation administered by the ICC. The net effect of this law was to allow virtual open entry into interstate trucking and to allow carriers almost complete freedom to price their services as they wish. In most cases after July 1, 1984, carriers could no longer establish rates together in what are known as rate bureaus. In addition, contract carriers were allowed to have as many customers as they desired. (Previously the ICC had limited their customers to eight).

The effects of the 1980 act have been as significant as in the airline industry. We will look briefly at (1) the structural change in the industry precipitated by deregulation, (2) rate changes, and (3) service implications.

The 1980 act opened the floodgates to the interstate trucking industry. In 1980 there were 17,721 truckers, whereas in 1983 this number had increased to 27,181.[14] Illustrative of the change taking place is the specialized market for truck transportation of explosives. Prior to deregulation, the ICC had allowed only four interstate carriers of explosives—now there are more than twenty.[15]

Besides the new carriers that have entered the industry, the majority of

---

[12] Robert W. Baker, "Future Role of Distribution and Transportation," *Annual Proceedings of the American Society of Transportation and Logistics* (1979), p. 192.

[13] "Battling It Out in the Skies," *Time* (Oct. 8, 1984), p. 58.

[14] *ICC Annual Reports,* (1980) and (1983).

[15] Bill Richards, "Independent Truckers Who Hailed Deregulation Reconsider," *Wall Street Journal,* 31 March 1983, p. 44.

existing truckers have applied to the ICC to expand the services and geo-graphic regions they wish to serve. The ICC has granted these requests al-most without exception. Overnite Transportation used to serve the south-eastern United States. Today the firm serves Utah, Colorado, and California markets, in addition to adding service to states contiguous to its traditional service area. Almost one thousand new employees have been added to serve the new regions of the country. Yellow Freight System also is expanding its service area. In 1983 the firm opened sixty new freight terminals in cities where the company had not served. The following year, seventy-five new terminals were added. Its employees have increased by over 2,200 since 1980. Overnite and Yellow[16] illustrate that the trucking industry has be-come more competitive because most existing trucking firms have expanded their service area.

No industry could absorb these increases in competitors without a trau-matic impact on many of its members. This has indeed happened. From 1980 to 1983, 305 trucking companies either went out of business or de-clared bankruptcy. Together they represented $3.2 billion in sales and em-ployed 64,000 workers.[17] One reason for these failures was that many of the new companies are nonunion, and their employees receive, according to one estimate, about 43 per cent less in wages than the current Teamsters' scale.

Trucking rates have dropped as a result of the increased number of carriers. Previously it was mentioned that the number of trucking companies hauling explosives had substantially increased: rates for this cargo had dropped in some cases up to 47 per cent. Although this decrease is unusual, a 1983 study found that all truckload rates had dropped about 25 per cent since 1977, while shipments weighing under 10,000 pounds had rate decreases averaging 12 per cent.[18] The federal General Accounting Office looked at all sizes of shipments from 1980 to 1983 and found that rates had dropped about 15 per cent.[19]

There is general agreement that service levels have increased to the shipping public as a result of trucking deregulation. One shipper in Janes-ville, Wisconsin, had ten carriers call on him before 1980. Today he has fifty-one truckers fighting for his business.[20] Professor Donald V. Harper conducted a detailed survey of shippers in Minnesota and concluded that they now receive improved levels of customer service as a result of deregu-lation.[21] Kenneth C. Williamson, Marc G. Singer, and Roger A. Peterson conducted a national survey of shippers and reached the same conclusion

[16] The information about these two companies comes from their 1983 annual reports.

[17] "Truck Industry on Recovery Route," *Traffic World* (Dec. 26, 1983), p. 14.

[18] Thomas Gale Moore, "Rail and Truck Reform—The Record So Far," *Regulation* (Nov.–Dec. 1983), p. 39.

[19] "GAO Says Motor Carrier Act of 1980 Putting Downward Pressure on Rates," *Traffic World* (Jan. 30, 1984), p. 41.

[20] Parry Desmond, "Churchill: Making Money the Old-Fashioned Way," *Commercial Car-rier Journal* (Nov. 1984), p. 90.

[21] Donald V. Harper, "Consequences of Reform of Federal Economic Regulation of the Motor Trucking Industry," *Transportation Journal* (Summer 1982), pp. 35–58.

as Harper.[22] It was often thought that the service available to small cities would be less if deregulation took place. In fact, the opposite has taken place. Richard Beilock and James Freeman studied this issue and concluded that, at a minimum, service levels have not decreased, and that in some regions of the country service levels are higher to nonurban shippers.[23] The ICC surveyed 1,500 small-town shippers and the majority reported that service levels had improved after deregulation.[24]

W. B. Watkins, chairman of Watkins Motor Lines, summed up the current situation in trucking when asked what was the most important factor impacting on the trucking industry in recent years:

> In my opinion, the number one factor is the Motor Carrier Act of 1980. It certainly changed the way trucking executives had to approach the business. We had to look to marketing our services instead of simply operating our services. In addition, we were no longer able to pass the cost of any inefficiency onto the public. All trucklines have had to find more efficient ways to operate.[25]

As the dust settles in the trucking industry, it is more and more imitating other service industries in the economy. Each carrier is trying to find the best niche for itself relative to its customers and competitors. Some carriers will offer a bare-bones, no-frill service at very low rates. Other carriers will offer many services to the shipper besides just transportation. They will act as a consultant to the shipper, a warehouser, and they will design their service and equipment to meet exactly the shippers' unique requirements. This type of service will command a premium price.[26]

Railroad Deregulation (1980)

The Staggers Rail Act of 1980, named after Representative Harley O. Staggers of West Virginia, was signed into law by President Carter on October 14, 1980. This law is complicated: it contains sixty-one sections and is seventy-one pages long.[27] For our purposes, it accomplished the following: (1) The ICC was ordered to give railroads more pricing freedom. In situations or markets where railroads are *not* the dominant carrier, there will be no ICC controls on maximum rates. In situations or markets where railroads

---

[22] Kenneth C. Williamson, Marc G. Singer and Roger A. Peterson, "The Impact of Regulatory Reform on U.S. For-Hire Freight Transportation: The Users' Perspective," *Transportation Journal* (Summer 1983), pp. 27–54.

[23] Richard Beilock and James Freeman, "Deregulated Motor Carrier Service to Small Communities," *Transportation Journal* (Summer 1984), pp. 71–82.

[24] Reese H. Taylor, Jr. "Viewing the Motor Carrier Act of 1980 with 20/20 Hindsight," *Annual Proceedings of the NCPDM* (1982), pp. 209–217.

[25] "Watkins Motor Lines Talks with Pacific Traffic," *Pacific Traffic* (Oct. 1984), p. 19.

[26] See Colin Barrett, "Trucking Moves Closer to Form," *Distribution* (Jan. 1984), pp. 73–79.

[27] See Ernest W. Williams, Jr., "A Critique of the Staggers Rail Act of 1980," *Transportation Journal* (Spring 1982), pp. 5–15.

are the dominant carrier, the ICC's jurisdication covers only those rates that are approximately 1.75 times the railroad's variable costs. (2) Railroads were allowed to establish specific contracts with shippers in terms of rates, services, and the obligations of each party.

> *Market dominance*, a term that has crept into transportation regulatory parlance, is believed to exist when one carrier or mode carries a minimum of approximately 60 per cent of the traffic within a specified market.

A major difference between rail deregulation and that found in the trucking and airline industries is the rationale for passing the laws. The latter two industries were often thought to lack effective competition because of entry control. Therefore, barriers to entry were relaxed to encourage new competitors to enter the industry. Exactly the opposite reason was involved in rail deregulation. The rail industry was financially "sick," and the purpose of the law was to establish an environment in which the railroads could prosper. No new carriers entered this market after deregulation. (In fact, no new major railroad has been started in decades, because it would cost billions of dollars to acquire the land, bridges, and other structures necessary to establish a new sizable carrier. However, existing rail trackage segments, which are perceived as not profitable because of low traffic volumes, have been sold to cities, states, and groups of investors who hope to either operate the track as a public service or to make a profit on the operation.)

What has happened to rail rates after deregulation? The general consensus was that rail rates, once freed from the ICC, would shoot upward. This did not take place. The General Accounting Office studied the issue and noted that the rate of increase of rail rates *slowed* after deregulation.[28] Another survey of rail rates found that, from 1978 to 1982, rail rate increases were below the general level of inflation.[29]

Railroads have enjoyed their new pricing freedom. An example involves fresh fruits and vegetables, which the ICC deregulated in 1979. Rail rates were promptly lowered when demand was low and equipment available. Conversely, rates were increased when the demand for transportation service was high and equipment shortages were present. Railroads also offered low backhaul rates to fill containers and cars that traditionally returned empty. Thus, a rail car of oranges from Florida to New York typically returned empty to start the process over. Rails now offer discounts for return-haul freight that is compatible with this type of car—cargo that will not contaminate a freight car that is used to haul edible products. The pricing flexibility obtained by the railroads in this area allowed them to participate more actively in this traffic. From 1980 to 1982, rail car loads of edible commodities more than doubled.[30]

[28] Don Phillips, "No Smoking Guns," *Trains* (Nov. 1983), p. 6.
[29] Moore, op. cit., pp. 36.
[30] Ibid., p. 35.

In terms of the railroads' most important single product—coal—rail rates increased 28 per cent from 1980 to 1983, while the inflation rate advanced 26 per cent.[31] It is estimated that future coal rate increases will be further moderated because of increased rail competition to transport coal to the Midwest and Southwest. Western coal up until 1984 was primarily transported by the Burlington Northern. In 1984 a new competitor entered this market when a new 107-mile track was built by the Chicago and Northwestern Railroad (C&NW) out of the Powder River Basin coalfields in Wyoming. The C&NW transfers this coal to the Union Pacific Railroad for delivery to the Southwest. Also competing against the BN for Midwest coal delivery will be the CSX railroad when it combines with the American Commercial Lines barge carrier.[32]

What happened to service levels after deregulation? The general consensus is that it has improved or remained the same, according to a survey by the General Accounting Office.[33] One shipper noted, "The benefits to railroads and shippers are only limited by the imagination of the parties."[34]

The primary service advantage noted by shippers is the utilization of contracts. Since 1980, over 22,000 rail contracts have been filed with the ICC. These contracts generate over 30 per cent of total rail revenues. The ICC estimated that traffic subject to contracts will increase 5 to 10 per cent per year for the next ten years.[35]

Let us look at two examples of how shippers have utilized railroad contracts. The Ford Motor Company has an annual transportation bill of over $1 billion, and 55 per cent of its traffic is shipped by rail. Ford is an extensive user of contracts according to Richard Haupt, director of transportation and traffic for the company. He stated, "Contracts have paid off very well for us. There's been a dramatic improvement in efficiency; transit times have never been better." He noted that one contract states that the railroad must pay Ford a penalty payment for every 15 minutes a train is late. "Out of 600-odd trains, only one's been late. That *never* happened before."[36] The Adolph Coors Company has an annual freight bill of more than $100 million. Prior to deregulation, about 60 per cent of Coor's beer was shipped by rail. Today that figure is 80 per cent, which equals about 50,000 carloads per year. Lou Bonner, vice-president of physical distribution, noted, "Coors has entered into several hundred railroad contracts which assure equipment supply and in many cases lower rates."[37]

A final note about rail deregulation is that some shippers, especially those who use rail almost exclusively, believe that the rail's monopoly po-

[31] Daniel Campbell, "Assault on Rail Deregulation Gains Steam," *Wall Street Journal,* 4 October 1984, p. 34.

[32] Bill Richards, "Midwest, Southwest Utilities See Savings from New Coal-Shipping Competition," *Wall Street Journal,* 4 September 1984, p. 10.

[33] Phillips, loc. cit.

[34] "Railroads: On a Fast Track," *U.S. News and World Report* (Nov. 26, 1984), p. 53.

[35] "Contracts: The Big Leap Forward," *Railway Age* (May 1984), p. 19. See also, "ICC Survey of Rail-Shipper Contracts Shows Fast Growth, Mutual Benefits," *Traffic World* (March 26, 1984), pp. 10–17 and "New Service for TW Readers," *Traffic World* (April 8, 1985), p. 1.

[36] Joseph V. Barks, "Some Words of Caution Arrive Just in Time," *Distribution* (Jan. 1984), p. 30.

[37] "For Starters, Try Detroit," *Railway Age* (Aug. 1984), p. 16.

sition with them has meant that their rates and service levels have suffered as a result of less federal regulation. These shippers are trying to convince Congress to reregulate certain portions of the rail industry.[38] At this time, there did not seem to be great support for the action.

Legal Obligations of Carriers

We have examined briefly the history of transportation regulation and deregulation. It is now appropriate to analyze the specific regulatory obligations of the transportation modes. *Common carriers, contract carriers, exempt carriers,* and *private carriers* will be defined and discussed in turn. This is particularly important because the new transportation deregulation measures have blurred some of the traditional distinctions between common, contract, and private carriers. Also, some of their responsibilities for meeting obligations may have been changed.

Common Carrier Obligations

The common carrier system is the backbone of the transportation industry. Virtually all railroads are common carriers, and common carriers are also found in trucking, water carriage, air freight, and pipelines. The key factor that separates a common carrier from the other forms of transportation is the specific obligations that the common carrier assumes: to serve, to deliver, to charge reasonable rates, and to avoid discrimination. These were outlined in Figure 5-1.

Common carriers have a legal obligation to serve *all* customers who request their service. This assumes the requested service is one the carrier has the authority and equipment to serve. In theory these service obligations were enforced by the ICC by means of removing a carrier's operating rights for repeated violations of the service obligation of common carriers. In fact, it was seldom utilized. Herald A. Smith, Jr., chairman of a large common carrier trucking company, declared:

> The ICC was protecting the carriers with the misguided idea that they were protecting the consumer. The common carrier obligation is the most worn-out phrase that I have ever heard in my life. For years and years I've listened to it. . . . This confused the public into thinking that this common carrier obligation has forced us to serve the whole industry and that without this obligation our transportation services would collapse.
>
> But this was a misguided conception, and as a common carrier obligation certainly was a wrong obligation. In the many years I've been in the trucking business—my entire working life—not once have I heard of a carrier losing his franchise because he didn't serve his franchise or full obligation. Nor, if I may state, could it have ever been possible for him to serve his full franchise. . . .

[38] See Campbell, loc. cit.; and "DOT Vows to Fight Staggers Act Repeal," *Traffic World* (Oct. 29, 1984), pp. 31–32; and Craig C. Carter, "Railroads Fight to Fend Off Re-Regulation," *Fortune* (Jan. 7, 1985), p. 90.

So I guess the common carrier obligation is now disappearing. Anyway, I think now that it's all over but the shouting.[39]

There was some concern in the motor carrier industry that the Motor Carrier Act of 1980, which removed many restrictions on the operations of motor common carriers, might be a two-edged sword: the removal of restrictions on their operations can also be interpreted as an increase in their responsibility to serve. In March 1983 the ICC resolved this potential problem by ruling that common carriers must provide service to the public consistent with their operating *capabilities;* not their operating *certificates.*[40]

One other allowable exception to the service obligation is an *embargo.* This usually happens when excessive congestion is found at a destination or when delivery is impeded because of storm-related damage to the carrier's right-of-way or terminals. In 1970 many common carrier truckers embargoed shipments bound for Chicago because there was a Teamsters strike in Chicago. The truckers embargoed Chicago shipments because both the shipper's freight and the carrier's equipment would arrive in Chicago and sit idle until the strike was settled. Railroads occasionally embargo grain products bound for export if there is excessive congestion in port cities caused by too much traffic or a strike. After the initial Mount St. Helen's eruption in 1980, both the Burlington Northern and the Union Pacific railroads had to place embargoes on traffic destined to several ports because ash and mud from the volcano had blocked the navigation channels between the ports and the ocean and had snarled all transportation facilities.

Embargoes do not violate common carrier obligations when they have been approved by the ICC. The ICC has noted, "Carriers have the right, in order to prevent complete paralysis of their operating facilities, to protect themselves by embargo against acceptance of freight."[41] Embargoes are even more common in international shipments. Even mail to Canada will not be accepted if there is a Canadian postal workers' strike.

Contract Carrier Obligations

Contract carriers are found extensively in the motor carrier and inland water carrier industries and more recently in the rail industry. A contract carrier offers a specialized service to a limited number of clients on a contractual basis. The contracts specify in detail the compensation the carrier will receive, the services it must render, etc. Because of the tailor-made individual nature of the contract between each contract carrier and its customer, this type of service is almost the same as a private transportation system for a company. Another item to be negotiated is the carrier's financial liability in case it fails to perform the contracted service.

An important difference between contract and common carriers involves discrimination. The contract carrier is under no legal obligation to render any service to the public and only has to serve those customers with

---

[39] Robert M. Butler, "Motor Carrier Issues and Answers Viewed," *Traffic World* (April 2, 1984), p. 23.

[40] "ICC Limits Obligation of Trucking Companies," *Traffic World* (March 21, 1983), p. 89.

[41] 73 ICC 749, 752 (1922).

whom it has contracts. Also, the contract carrier is under no obligation to treat all of its contract customers on an equal basis. Westmeyer explained the rationale for this provision:

> The amount a contract carrier charges any given shipper will vary with the volume of traffic the shipper can offer, the regularity of the traffic, the possibility of obtaining a back haul for trucks which would otherwise have to return to their point of origin without a payload, the cost and practicality of a shipper providing his own motor transport facilities, and possibly other factors which vary from shipper to shipper. To attempt to establish a uniform schedule of rates under such conditions would destroy the peculiar advantage of this type of transportation.[42]

Contract carriage is growing because these carriers are no longer subjected to the ICC "Rule of Eight," which limited them to having contracts with no more than eight shippers. Before the 1980 deregulation act, there were about 7,000 contract motor carriers—by 1983 the number had increased to 10,000.[43]

Exempt Carriers

Exempt carriers can legally transport any commodity that is specifically "exempted" from regulation in the Interstate Commerce Act. Important exempt commodities include unprocessed agricultural products in trucking and bulk and liquid products transported in barges. In other words, *any* trucker can transport unprocessed agricultural products in interstate commerce. However, when they haul the exempt commodity, they become for that haul an *exempt carrier*. Exempt carrier rates and services are not regulated—they must be negotiated directly between the carrier and the shipper.

Private Carriers

Private carriage is often called do-it-yourself transportation. A company buys (or leases) its own vehicles and operates its own cartage service. Private carriage is used most extensively in the motor carrier mode, but it is also used in all other modes. There is no economic regulation of private carriage by the ICC. Private carriage is subject to safety regulations. This subject will be examined in detail in the next chapter.

Freight Rate Determination by Shippers

A key aspect of regulation—the logic and determination of just and reasonable freight rates charged by common carriers—is incredibly complex. To the uninitiated, it would appear the height of folly to state that it is very difficult

---

[42] Russell E. Westmeyer, *Economics of Transportation* (Englewood Cliffs, N.J.: Prentice-Hall, 1952), p. 403.
[43] Francis J. Quinn, "Contract Carriers Start to Flex Their Muscles," *Traffic Management* (Sept. 1983), p. 84.

to determine the correct carrier rate for a 30,000-pound shipment of shoes from Norfolk, Virginia, to Reno, Nevada. However, the discussion that follows will illustrate just how difficult rate determination can be.

The complexity of freight rate determination is related to *tariffs,* which are often 1,000 pages or more in length, and are used to determine the applicable freight rate. Tariffs are known as "official publications" because when the carriers properly file them with the ICC, or FMC, they take on the force and effect of law. In 1960, one tariff expert estimated that there were 43,000,000,000,000 (that's 43 trillion!) rates on file with the ICC.[44] Another indication of this unbelievable complexity is that there are over 200,000 active tariffs on file with the ICC. The *1984 ICC Annual Report* noted that the commission receives 4,782 new tariffs every working day!

One veteran observer of transportation noted:

> "There are certain things," said a General Attorney for one of the Western Railroads, "spiritual and material, in the presence of which ordinary mortals stand dumb. When I stood at the tomb of Napoleon, first viewed the Washington Monument, gazed into the Grand Canyon, words were superfluous.
>
> "Feeling akin to this arises within me when I contemplate a freight tariff, with its exceptions, items, notes, commodities, distances, proportionals, disproportionals, gateways, basing points, arbitraries, and God knows what. If the thing itself amazes, what must be the feeling when one views from afar the mind that conceived it?
>
> "I can approach a Superintendent, a General Manager, a General Solicitor, or a President, if you will, with a certain amount of assurance, and composure; but when I approach the portals of a Traffic Expert's office, I not only remove my hat, but also my shoes, and like the devout ancient Greek, chant as I near the throne:
>
> "Great is Zeus but greater is the man who understands the freight tariff."[45]

An entire profession has developed merely to catch mistakes made in trying to determine the proper freight charge. These individuals are known as *freight bill auditors.* They provide an independent check of the individual company's ability to determine the correct freight rate. After a shipper has paid the freight rate, he turns over the paid bills to the freight bill auditor who checks to make sure the lowest rate has been paid. An auditor who discovers an overpayment generally receives 50 per cent of the overcharge, which the shipper recovers from the carrier.

Even after deregulation, an understanding of traditional freight rate determination is still necessary. The reason is that carriers, as they compete, often quotes prices in terms of percentage discounts from existing, or published, rates.

---

[44] Herbert O. Whitten, "Why Freight Rates Must Be Computerized," *Distribution Age* (March 1966), p. 30.

[45] Anonymous quote in Paul T. McElhiney and Charles L. Hilton, *Introduction to Logistics and Traffic Management* (Dubuque: Brown, 1968), p. 229.

Full-Cost vs. Value-of-Service Rate Making

The complexity of the freight rate structure is related to the extensive use of "value-of-service" pricing as opposed to full-cost pricing. *Full-cost pricing* refers to setting a price that covers both fixed and variable costs plus a margin for profit. *Value-of-service pricing*, which is also called *differential* pricing, *discriminatory pricing*, or *charging what the traffic will bear*, involves using variable costs only to establish a floor below which rates normally will not go. The objective is to set rates that will maximize the contribution received over and above the variable costs incurred for carrying each shipment. The result is that a ton of steel, a ton of gravel, a ton of canned goods, a ton of liquor, and a ton of furniture, each moving from City A to City B, pay different rates. In fact, one commodity may just barely cover variable costs involved, while another product pays as much as 100 to 200 per cent more than the full costs of carriage.

The extensive use of value-of-service rate making is a result of the precedent established by the railroads during the nineteenth century. The railroads, which had no effective competition during this period, established a pricing structure that called for high rates for relatively high-valued commodities (i.e., liquor, manufactured products, etc.) and low charges for products of lower value (sand, gravel, coal, pulp wood, etc.). This pricing system was sanctioned by the ICC. "The theory behind this method of pricing was to maximize the total movement of goods in the United States, and profits derived from the transportation of high valued and high rated commodities were expected to offset the carriage of other commodities at less than their full cost."[46]

Value-of-service pricing, which was started by the railroad industry, has been adopted to one degree or another by all of the other modes of transportation. Truckers use it the least because their very high variable cost structure leaves little room to cut prices and still cover variable costs. Rates far above full cost are impractical because this forces shippers into private transportation.

Basic Freight Rates

The specific rate for shipping a product from City A to City B is determined by the use of tariffs. There are three basic types of freight rates: *class*, *exception*, and *commodity*.

Class rates are standard rates that can be found for almost all products or commodities shipped. These rates are found with the help of a *classification tariff*. This tariff gives each shipment a *rating* or *class* ranging from 400 to 13 in the widely used *Uniform Freight Classification* (UFC). It contains 31 separate ratings or classes and is used extensively by the railroads and many truckers and water carriers. The other widely used classification tariff is the *National Motor Freight Classification* (NMFC), which has ratings or classes from

---

[46] Paul M. Zeis, "Competitive Rate Making in the United States," *Transportation Journal* (Summer 1969), p. 36.

500 to 35, with 23 separate ratings. The higher the rating or class, the greater the relative charge for transporting the commodity. A multitude of factors are involved in determining a product's specific class or rating. However, the ICC in recent years has stated that the following four factors should be primary inputs to determine a freight classification: (1) density of the product (how heavy it is in relationship to its size), (2) stowability, (3) ease or difficulty of handling, and (4) liability for damage or theft.

Once the commodity rating or class is determined, it is necessary to establish the rate bases number from the applicable tariff. This number is the approximate distance between any two city pairs. With the commodity rating or class and the rate bases number, the specific rate per hundred pounds can be located in another tariff. Finally, to establish the specific cost of moving commodity A between City B and City C, the formula—*weight* (in hundred pound units) × *rate* (per hundred pounds) = *charge*—must be used.

An example will help to clarify the situation. Assume that a professor of archeology is retiring and moving from Sioux Falls, South Dakota, to Hannibal, Missouri. He had collected 30,000 pounds of bones during his long career. The railroad serving his town uses the UFC. To establish the rating (class), it is necessary to find the commodity in the UFC index. Figure 5-2 contains the appropriate page from the index which contains human bones. Note that the letters *noibn* follow human bones. This stands for Not Otherwise Indexed By Name. We are referred to item number 13350. Figure 5-3 is the page in the UFC that contains item number 13350. This tariff also specifies how the human bones are to be packaged for presentation to the carrier. On the right-hand edge of Figure 5-3 are the appropriate ratings or classes. The first rating of 200 is the less than carload (LCL) rating. Then it states that if 20,000 or more pounds of bones are tendered to the carrier, then the carload (CL) rating is 100. Because this shipment involves 30,000 pounds, the CL rating of 100 will be used. The next requirement is to determine the rate bases number. Figure 5-4 illustrates a typical tariff page containing this information. The appropriate rate bases number between Sioux Falls, South Dakota, and Hannibal, Missouri, is 448. Finally, it is necessary to establish the specific rate per hundred pounds. Figure 5-5 contains a tariff page that uses the rating (class) and rate bases number to determine the rate, which is $3.07 in this example. The total charge can now be determined using this formula:

Rate (per hundred pounds) × weight (in hundred pound units) = charge

$$\$3.07 \times 300 = \$921$$

Exception rates can best be thought of as modified class rates. They are designed to produce a less expensive rate than the class rate. The class rate formula, however, is still used to calculate the freight charge. The exception rate is lower than the class rate by taking "exception" to some aspect of the class rate. Thus, the exception tariff may provide for a lower rating or class than the class tariff, it may provide for less expensive packaging requirements, or it may require a lower minimum weight to qualify for a TL or CL rate. An exception rate, since it produces a lower overall charge, has priority

Figure 5-2 Index Page from Freight Classification

UNIFORM FREIGHT CLASSIFICATION 7

INDEX TO ARTICLES

STCC No.	Article	Item	STCC No.	Article	Item
	Hulls┬Concluded:			Huskers┬Concluded:	
20 914 45	Cottonseed,mixed with meal 37130		35 225 23	Corn,and fodder shredders, combined,ot hand,	
20 914 25	Cottonseed,not ground. . . .31250,131270			SU	3370,†4050
20 939 46	Fleaseed (psyllium). 33800,80090		34 236 79	Corn,hand	
34 412 15	Launch,steel 11690			(husking gloves) 36260	
37 329 12	Launch,wooden,in the white,		35 225 60	Corn,noibn,ot hand,	
	KD. 11490			KD. . . . . .3360,†4050	
37 329 13	Launch,wooden,in the white,		35 225 59	Corn,noibn,ot hand,SU,	
	SU. 11490			on wheels. . . . . .3360,†4050	
20 939 55	Nut,noibn. 86140		35 227 30	Green corn. 62530	
20 418 30	Oat. 47110		34 236 79	Husking gloves,corn	
20 999 25	Peanut,crushed or ground 37530			(corn huskers) 36260	
20 939 20	Peanut,not crushed nor ground. 37540		34 236 80	Husking pins. 36500	
20 939 46	Psyllium seed (fleaseed) . . 33800,80090		01 199 30	Husks,corn (shucks) 37350	
20 449 15	Rice,ground and rice bran,		33 219 16	Hydrants,or sections. 29520	
	feed. 37580		28 311 51	Hydrastis canadensis (golden seal)	
20 449 20	Rice,ground,feed 37590			roots,ground or powdered . . 33590,33800	
20 449 25	Rice,unground (rice chaff),		01 915 13	Hydrastis canadensis (golden seal) roots,	
	feed. 37600			not ground nor powdered. . . 33620,33800	
09 131 55	Shrimp . . . . δ		35 329 10	Hydraulic accumulators,mining,	
20 923 16	Soybean,ground 37640			ore milling or smelting. 63480	
20 923 17	Soybean,not ground 37640		32 411 15	Hydraulic cement. . . . . .21680,†77130	
20 939 56	Sunflower seed 83440		35 999 16	Hydraulic cylinders,ot rotary,steel 60780	
20 939 27	Tung nut 52790		35 691 45	Hydraulic rams. . . . .†61240,64890	
20 939 64	Velvet bean,ground 95550		35 329 10	Hydraulic rotary swivels,oil,	
20 939 66	Velvet bean,not ground 95560			water or gas well. 72070	
28 311 21	Human blood,liquid,frozen or		29 912 10	Hydraulic system fluid,ot,	
	chilled.. 11355			petroleum. 14690	
39 998 21	Human bones,noibn. 13350		34 434 38	Hydraulic wheel presses . . . . .†66800	
39 994 10	Human hair 48320			Hydro-pneumatic tanks,copper,	
39 994 20	Human hair goods,noibn. 48390		34 434 40	cylindrical closed at both ends. . 89040	
39 994 15	Human hair samples,mounted on			Hydro-pneumatic tanks,silicon	
	cardboard 48360			bronze,cylindrical closed at	
40 291 47	Human hair waste,not stumps nor			both ends. 89050	
	combed hair 95490		34 434 42	Hydro-pneumatic tanks,steel,14	
	Humidifiers:			gauge or thicker,cylindrical,	
41 111 10	Air and blowers or fans combined,			closed at both ends. 89060	
	mounted on freight		38 213 15	Hydrobarometers 32990	
	automobile. 73400		28 139 92	Hydrocarbon gas,noibn 45630	
35 857 20	Air and blowers or fans combined,		35 599 78	Hydrocarbon recovery systems. . . . δ	
	noibn,. . . . . . †30740,58510		28 194 50	Hydrochloric (muriatic)	
35 857 45	Air bakers',cast iron. . . .58610,†58720			acid 2340,33800	
37 142 12	Coolers and filters,air,		28 194 34	Hydrocyanic acid. 2260	
	automobile,non-electric 8125		28 194 42	Hydrofluoric and sulphuric acid,	
34 336 49	Hot air house heating			mixed. 2280,33800	
	furnace,automatic 12700		28 194 38	Hydrofluoric acid 2270,33800	
34 299 30	Humidors,ot display. 52800		40 251 65	Hydrofluoric acid waste,	
14 917 15	Humus. 27320			aqueous. . . . . δ	
33 992 50	Hungarian nails,noibn,brass,		28 194 46	Hydrofluosilicic acid 2290,33800	
	bronze or copper. . . . . .†49771,50810		28 139 20	Hydrogen bromide,anhydrous,	
33 152 25	Hungarian nails,noibn,steel,with			liquefied. 45410	
	ot steel or zinc		28 139 22	Hydrogen chloride,anhydrous,	
	heads . . . .†49781,50820			liquefied. 45420	
33 152 30	Hungarian nails,noibn,steel,		28 199 31	Hydrogen dioxide. 24020,33800	
	with steel heads. . . . .†49781,50830		28 134 60	Hydrogen gas. 45640	
33 152 35	Hungarian nails,noibn,steel,		28 199 31	Hydrogen peroxide 24020,33800	
	with zinc heads . . . . .†49781,50840		28 139 46	Hydrogen sulphide 45650	
	Hurdles,track,steel with		20 469 10	Hydrol (corn,sorghum grain	
	wooden cross bars,			or wheat sugar final	
	noibn 7580			molasses). 37360	
	Hurdles,track steel with		38 219 14	Hydrometers 33000	
	wooden cross bars,uprights		28 186 20	Hydroxy acetic acid 2300,33800	
	folded to base,or SU nstd,		40 251 62	Hydroxy aldehydes,waste,	
	in nests of five or			containing not less than	
	more. 7580			40% water. 96090	
22 995 73	Hurds,hemp or ramie. 52810		28 612 20	Hypernic extracts,dry 35860	
35 225 29	Huskers and pickers combined,		28 612 21	Hypernic extracts,liquid or	
	corn. . . . . .3390,†4050			paste. 35870	
35 225 61	Huskers and shellers,combined,		40 291 57	Hypo-mud,photo silver 95720	
	corn,ot hand. . . . . . . .3380,†4050				
	Huskers:				
35 225 24	Corn and fodder shredders,				
	combined,ot hand,KD . . . .3370,†4050				

over a class rate. Exceptions are generally the result of competitive factors, either between modes or between individual carriers of the same mode. They also are established because of unusual regional or local operating conditions.

Commodity rates can be thought of as custom-made economy rates that a carrier makes available because a specific commodity is shipped in large

Figure 5-3 Page Showing Classification of Articles

Item	ARTICLES	Less Carload Ratings	Carload Minimum (Pounds)	Carload Ratings
	BOILERS, FURNACES, RADIATORS, STOVES, RELATED ARTICLES OR PARTS NAMED (Subject to Item 11960)—Concluded: Group No. 1			
13250	Coal hods (scuttles) or vases, steel; cookers or steamers, stock feed, noibn; furnaces, house heating, hot air, with or without equipment of air conditioning apparatus or thermostats; griddles, kettles, pots, skillets or spiders, sheet steel; holloware, cast iron, as described in Item 49880; house heating furnace casing parts; sugar or syrup evaporator kettles, iron; stove or range cabinets, closets or high shelves, steel; stove or range ovens; stove or range parts, iron or steel, other than castings, noibn; stove pipe drums or drum ovens; stove pipe or elbows, sheet iron, steel or tin plate, side seams closed; stove pipe thimbles, plate or sheet iron or steel or tin plate, side seams closed; stove or range reservoirs or reservoir attachments; tee joints and draft regulators combined, stove pipe.			
	Group No. 2			
13260	Air registers, noibn, including air louvres, iron or steel; andirons, iron; ash scrapers; heating furnace pipe or elbows, sheet iron, steel or tin plate; house heating furnace castings, iron; burners, gas, for coal, oil or wood stoves, see Note 58, Item 13271; oil burning outfits for brooders or coal or wood stoves; pans, baking, dripping or frying, sheet steel; fire pokers, iron; sad irons, with or without stands, other than self-heating; stove boards, iron or metal clad wood or fibreboard; stove cover lifters, iron; stove or range castings, iron; stove pipe, sheet iron, steel or tin plate, side seams not closed, nested; dampers, cast iron or plate or sheet iron or tin plate, side seams not closed, nested; stove shovels, sheet steel; water heaters, noibn			
13261	Note 52.—Weight of articles in Group 2, Item 13260, must not exceed 50% of weight upon which charges are assessed.			
13265	Mixed CL of two or more of the following articles, viz.: Stoves or ranges, iron or steel; dampers, noibn, iron; electric logs, see Note 54, Item 13266; fireplace grates or grate baskets, with or without heating units; fireplace grate parts, noibn; gas logs; heaters, gas, with or without clay radiants; andirons (fire dogs); fenders or fireplace guards or screens, brass, see Note 54, Item 13266; fenders or fireplace guards or screens, iron or steel, plain or brass or brass coated or plated, or with brass trimming; fireplace sets (shovels and tongs), with or without hearth brushes, holders or pokers, brass or brass and iron combined, see Note 54, Item 13266; fireplace sets (shovels and tongs), with or without hearth brushes, holders or pokers, iron; lighters, fire, brass or iron, see Note 54, Item 13266; or wood holders or racks, fireplace, see Note 54, Item 13266...	......	24,000R	45
13266	Note 54.—Aggregate weight of articles subject to this note must not exceed 50% of weight upon which charges are assessed.			
13267	Note 56.—Section 2 of Rule 34 is not applicable.			
13270	Superheaters, other than locomotive: SU, loose or in packages..	70	24,000R	40
13271	KD, or superheater parts, KD, loose or in packages....................................	65	24,000R	40
	Note 58.—Ratings apply only on burners for converting coal, oil or wood stoves into gas stoves.			
13272	Note 60.—Weight of articles subject to this note shall not exceed 10% of weight upon which charges are assessed.			
13280	Tanks, oil stove, sheet steel, 26 gauge or thicker, capacity not exceeding 5 gallons, in boxes or crates..	110	16,000R	60
13281	Note 66.—Ratings also apply on stoves or ranges designed for separate permanent installation of oven and surface cooking units.			
13282	Note 68.—CL ratings will include iron or steel garbage or offal incinerators, not exceeding 25% of the weight upon which freight charges are assessed.			
13295	Bolster rolls for beds, couches or lounges, fibreboard with plywood ends and reinforcing ribs, upholstered, in Package 9F...	150	10,000R	100
13300	Bolster rolls for beds, couches or lounges, noibn, in boxes or crates....................	200	10,000R	100
13310	Bone, charred filtering (animal charcoal), other than spent, in bags or barrels..................	70	36,000	35
13320	Bone, charred filtering (animal charcoal), spent, in bags.............................	50	40,000	20
13330	Bone, charred filtering, synthetic, in bags or barrels..................................	70	36,000	35
13340	Bone ash, in bags, barrels or boxes..	55	36,000	30
13350	Bones, human, noibn, prepaid, in barrels or boxes.....................................	200	20,000R	100
13360	Bones, noibn, ground or not ground, LCL, in bags or barrels, or in barrels with cloth tops; CL, loose or in packages..	50	40,000	22½
13370	Book ends, moulded wood or plaster, in boxes..	85	24,000R	55
13380	Book stacks, library, consisting of iron brackets, floor framing, stairs, railings, standards, and shelves, in packages; also CL, loose..	70	36,000	40
13390	Boot or shoe arch supports or arch support insoles, in boxes.........................	100	20,000R	70
13400	Boot or shoe forms or trees, in barrels or boxes......................................	85	20,000R	55
13410	**BOOTS, SHOES, OR BOOT OR SHOE FINDINGS:**			
13420	Boot or shoe findings, noibn, in bales, barrels or boxes, or in barrels with cloth tops..........	100	16,000R	70
13430	Boots or shoes, noibn, see Note 1, Item 13431, in boxes; in trunks in crates; in salesmen's sample trunks, locked; in Packages 277 or 1197; also in straight CL in Package 1126.................	100	24,000R	70
13431	Note 1.—Ratings also apply on Huaraches (Mexican leather sandals) in bamboo baskets or hampers, tops securely closed.			
13440	Boots or shoes, old, used, leather, having value other than for reclamation of raw materials, prepaid, see Note 2, Item 13441, in packages; also CL, loose.............................	85	36,000	50
13441	Note 2.—Old used shoes rebuilt or repaired, will be rated as shoes, noibn.			
13450	Boots or shoes, plastic, rubber or rubber and canvas, felt or wool combined, in bales or boxes.....	100	15,000R	70
13460	Boots or shoes, wooden or leather with wooden soles, in packages...........................	92½	24,000R	65
13470	Box toe boards, in packages; also CL, loose..	70	36,000	35

Reproduced by permission of tariff publisher.

quantities and/or at frequent intervals. These rates, which are found in commodity tariffs, are specific in nature. They state the commodity, the origins, and destinations involved and the minimum weight required for the commodity rate.

Figure 5-4 Tariff Page Showing Point-to-Point Rate Bases

Freight Tariff No. W-1000

APPLICATION OF RATE BASES

BETWEEN (See Item 100) / AND (See Item 100)

RATE BASES APPLICABLE

BETWEEN — AND	Greeley Centre, Neb.	Green Bay, Wis.	Greenbush, Minn.	Grenville, S.D.	Grinnell, Iowa	Grover, Colo.	Hallock, Minn.	Hannaford, N.D.	Hannibal, Mo.	Harvard, Ill.	Havarden, Iowa	Hartun, Colo.	Hays, Kan.	Hazen, N.D.	Herington, Kan.	Hermanaville, Mich.	Hermosa, S.D.	Herrick, S.D.	Hettinger, N.D.	Hibbing, Minn.
Rugby....N.D.	716	716	233	340	680	944	202	128	855	768	465	914	939	306	824	687	609	714	461	372
Rulo....Neb.	240	619	712	627	237	546	718	621	251	477	244	438	318	699	179	715	619	347	669	636
Russell....Kan.	335	844	919	834	479	474	925	828	457	606	451	482	27	906	121	941	695	506	875	868
St. Cloud....Minn.	489	350	262	223	317	828	287	241	495	401	250	737	712	433	596	367	558	487	461	193
St. Francis....Kan.	309	918	935	850	568	502	941	844	620	809	467	363	363	922	332	985	646	487	892	884
St. Ignace....Mich.	937	256	681	735	619	1277	713	722	659	392	713	1186	1098	914	959	166	1064	935	966	477
St. James....Minn.	358	380	430	345	220	697	436	363	408	388	133	607	581	488	465	414	498	356	457	314
St. Joseph....Mo.	284	579	737	652	213	587	743	646	207	437	269	479	293	724	154	676	657	383	694	614
St. Louis....Mo.	583	458	854	812	305	890	880	833	⊕	⊕	545	783	561	983	414	553	940	668	952	719
Sabetha....Kan.	223	640	740	655	273	524	747	649	267	498	272	414	277	727	155	736	604	349	697	666
Sabula....Iowa	492	246	639	597	146	832	665	618	⊕	⊕	364	741	625	792	486	343	756	572	762	504
Sac City....Iowa	250	464	545	460	143	589	552	472	317	362	115	499	462	561	347	540	510	302	530	442
Salem....S.D.	330	539	456	359	313	670	442	304	488	512	76	579	553	383	438	572	340	328	352	437
Salina....Kan.	258	767	842	757	402	526	848	751	380	619	374	405	104	829	44	864	618	429	798	791
Salisbury....Mo.	412	515	778	734	201	720	804	757	91	362	383	612	393	838	253	611	771	497	808	649
Sanborn....Minn.	376	407	396	311	238	715	402	329	427	415	151	625	599	454	483	430	470	374	423	325
Sanish....N.D.	793	817	368	428	768	962	336	247	942	871	543	933	1016	227	901	815	628	791	447	506
Sargent....Neb.	102	750	766	681	408	475	773	675	530	641	298	389	406	754	308	816	538	314	723	716
Sauk Centre....Minn.	517	392	234	181	359	857	254	199	537	443	279	766	740	391	625	409	546	515	419	228
Sault Ste Marie....Mich.	955	273	685	739	664	1294	717	726	708	452	730	1203	1144	918	1004	184	1082	953	984	481
Sawyer....Kan.	405	872	987	903	522	656	994	897	480	719	520	552	210	975	158	968	765	576	944	923
Schley....Minn.	648	427	146	276	476	988	178	258	654	518	409	897	871	450	756	399	670	646	522	82
Scott City....Kan.	461	959	1044	959	594	437	1051	953	572	811	576	486	244	1032	228	1055	726	632	1001	993
Scottsbluff....Neb.	365	980	897	804	638	175	883	746	729	871	529	145	565	765	467	1046	222	544	735	946
Sedalia....Colo.	490	1105	1095	1001	762	130	1081	943	832	996	554	180	361	963	505	1171	420	669	932	1071
Sedalia....Mo.	413	568	831	787	254	709	857	792	144	415	415	603	371	870	224	664	794	529	840	702
Seney....Mich.	891	210	605	660	601	1231	637	646	644	388	667	1140	1080	838	941	120	1012	889	906	401
Severy....Kan.	375	757	920	835	410	643	926	829	364	605	452	522	231	907	114	854	735	521	877	811
Sharon Springs....Kan.	355	965	982	897	608	317	988	891	623	851	514	366	140	969	287	1031	606	534	938	931
Shawano....Wis.	690	38	553	544	403	1030	585	507	447	190	498	939	882	956	743	107	860	721	763	351
Shawnee....Wyo.	479	1023	864	771	731	165	850	677	843	948	539	259	612	732	581	1056	190	575	702	940
Sheboygan....Wis.	700	63	613	604	356	1040	645	631	397	129	522	949	835	817	696	159	905	745	822	411
Sheldon....Ill.	653	275	802	760	304	986	828	781	⊕	⊕	533	881	717	962	578	372	925	738	931	601
Sheldon....Iowa	267	471	464	379	216	607	471	392	395	415	43	516	490	480	375	505	429	265	449	404
Shenandoah....Iowa	218	571	657	572	189	547	663	566	268	429	189	441	383	644	243	556	577	303	614	562
Sheridan Lake....Colo.	536	1034	1120	1035	669	361	1126	1029	647	886	652	411	319	1107	303	1131	651	707	1077	1069
Sidney....Neb.	328	943	908	815	601	102	894	757	691	834	492	73	504	776	429	1009	233	507	746	909
Simpson (Johnson Co.)....Ill.	733	552	995	953	446	1040	1021	974	⊕	⊕	686	933	711	1123	564	649	1081	818	1093	835
Sioux City....Iowa	211	527	512	427	236	550	518	421	398	453	44	459	434	499	318	561	444	209	468	461
Sioux Falls....S.D.	299	499	437	340	273	639	444	337	448	473	46	548	522	422	407	533	380	297	392	397
Sisseton....S.D.	537	503	318	193	439	831	304	230	627	552	284	786	760	385	645	521	496	535	354	370
Smithboro....Ill.	625	432	858	816	309	932	884	837	⊕	⊕	549	825	604	987	464	528	944	710	956	711
South Beloit....Ill.	588	150	634	592	242	928	660	613	⊕	⊕	433	837	721	805	581	247	819	653	802	434
Sparta....Ill.	637	490	908	866	359	944	934	887	⊕	359	599	537	607	1036	460	587	994	722	1006	769
Spencer....Iowa	303	443	500	415	180	643	507	428	379	⊕	79	552	527	516	411	496	465	302	486	386
Spooner....Wis.	570	253	353	379	473	909	385	394	510	328	345	818	786	586	659	247	697	568	599	149
Springfield....Ill.	580	369	794	752	261	894	820	773	⊕	⊕	501	786	584	938	445	466	895	665	908	642
Stafford....Kan.	360	841	942	858	479	568	949	852	449	688	475	507	165	930	113	937	720	531	899	880
Stanley....N.D.	795	804	348	419	759	1023	317	214	934	856	544	993	1018	315	903	799	688	793	535	486
Stapleton....Neb.	212	827	843	759	485	423	850	753	575	718	376	365	411	831	313	893	519	391	800	973
Sterling....Colo.	343	958	948	855	616	106	934	796	707	849	507	33	460	816	443	1024	273	522	785	924
Stiles Jct....Wis.	722	28	576	575	419	1061	607	602	463	207	332	780	805	257	690	75	892	753	794	371
Stockton....Kan.	271	838	867	782	481	539	874	776	477	707	399	418	217	854	157	914	630	442	824	817
Strasburg....Colo.	477	1086	1003	1015	730	144	1094	957	779	973	635	194	299	977	443	1153	434	656	946	1053
Stratton....Neb.	256	866	883	798	516	275	889	792	586	757	415	202	329	870	298	932	442	435	839	832
Streator....Ill.	583	297	732	690	231	916	758	711	⊕	⊕	460	811	648	888	503	370	852	668	858	556
Streeter....N.D.	582	630	304	241	547	810	290	134	721	687	332	780	805	257	690	448	475	580	327	411
Studley....Kan.	330	923	956	871	558	388	963	865	536	775	488	398	157	944	200	1006	677	409	913	906
Sturgeon Bay....Wis.	762	58	630	621	449	1102	662	648	492	236	570	1011	928	834	788	154	934	793	535	488
Sublette....Kan.	479	971	1062	977	606	473	1069	971	580	819	594	523	261	1049	240	1067	763	650	1019	1007

⊕For rates refer to I. F. A. Tariff No. I-1002, I. C. C. No. 757, R. G. Raasch, Agent.

Reproduced by permission of tariff publisher.

In March 1984 the ICC authorized, for the first time, trucking commodity rates that specify a specific shipper and consignee at their respective locations. Prior to this the commission had rules that this type of rate was inherently discriminatory. The ICC stated that the purpose of the 1980 Mo-

Figure 5-5 Tariff Page Showing Application of Rate Bases to Charges

Tariff W-1000

CLASS RATES IN CENTS PER 100 POUNDS

RATE BASIS NUMBERS	400	300	250	200	175	150	125	110	100	97½	95	92½	90	87½	85	82½	80	77½	75	73½	72½	70	67½	66
5	328	246	205	164	144	123	103	90	82	80	78	76	74	72	70	68	66	64	62	60	59	57	55	54
10	356	267	223	178	156	134	111	98	89	87	85	82	80	78	76	73	71	69	67	65	65	62	60	59
15	384	288	240	192	168	144	120	106	96	94	91	89	86	84	82	79	77	74	72	71	70	67	65	63
20	408	306	255	204	179	153	128	112	102	99	97	94	92	89	87	84	82	79	77	75	74	71	69	67
25	420	315	263	210	184	158	131	116	105	102	100	97	95	92	89	87	84	81	79	77	76	74	71	69
30	448	336	280	224	196	168	140	123	112	109	106	104	101	98	95	92	90	87	84	82	81	78	76	74
35	460	345	288	230	201	173	144	127	115	112	109	106	104	101	98	95	92	89	86	85	83	81	78	76
40	480	360	300	240	210	180	150	132	120	117	114	111	108	105	102	99	96	93	90	88	87	84	81	79
45	492	369	308	246	215	185	154	135	123	120	117	114	111	108	105	101	98	95	92	90	89	86	83	81
50	504	378	315	252	221	189	158	139	126	123	120	117	113	110	107	104	101	98	95	93	91	88	85	83
55	524	393	328	262	229	197	164	144	131	128	124	121	118	115	111	108	105	102	98	96	95	92	88	86
60	536	402	335	268	235	201	168	147	134	131	127	124	121	117	114	111	107	104	101	98	97	94	90	88
65	556	417	348	278	243	209	174	153	139	136	132	129	125	122	118	115	111	108	104	102	101	97	94	92
70	564	423	353	282	247	212	176	155	141	137	134	130	127	123	120	116	113	109	106	104	102	99	95	93
75	572	429	358	286	250	215	179	157	143	139	136	132	129	125	122	118	114	111	107	105	104	100	97	94
80	588	441	368	294	257	221	184	162	147	143	140	136	132	129	125	121	118	114	110	108	107	103	99	97
85	600	450	375	300	263	225	188	165	150	146	143	139	135	131	128	124	120	116	113	110	109	105	101	99
90	616	462	385	308	270	231	193	169	154	150	146	142	139	135	131	127	123	119	116	113	112	108	104	102
95	624	468	390	312	273	234	195	172	156	152	148	144	140	137	133	129	125	121	117	115	113	109	105	103
100	636	477	398	318	278	239	199	175	159	155	151	147	143	139	135	131	127	123	119	117	115	111	107	105
110	656	492	410	328	287	246	205	180	164	160	156	152	148	144	139	135	131	127	123	121	119	115	111	108
120	676	507	423	338	296	254	211	186	169	165	161	156	152	148	144	139	135	131	127	124	123	118	114	112
130	700	525	438	350	306	263	219	193	175	171	166	162	158	153	149	144	140	136	131	129	127	123	118	116
140	720	540	450	360	315	270	225	198	180	176	171	167	162	158	153	149	144	140	135	132	131	126	122	119
150	740	555	463	370	324	278	231	204	185	180	176	171	167	162	158	153	149	144	139	136	134	130	125	122
160	756	567	473	378	331	284	236	208	189	184	180	175	170	165	161	156	151	146	142	139	137	132	128	125
170	784	588	490	392	343	294	245	216	196	191	186	181	176	172	167	162	157	152	147	144	142	137	132	129
180	796	597	498	398	348	299	249	219	199	194	189	184	179	174	169	164	159	154	149	146	144	139	134	131
190	812	609	508	406	355	305	254	223	203	198	193	188	183	178	173	167	162	157	152	149	147	142	137	134
200	828	621	518	414	362	311	259	228	207	202	197	191	186	181	176	171	166	160	155	152	150	145	140	137
210	852	639	533	426	373	320	266	234	213	208	202	197	192	186	181	176	170	165	160	157	154	149	144	141
220	868	651	543	434	380	326	271	239	217	212	206	201	195	190	184	179	174	168	163	159	157	152	146	143
230	884	663	553	442	387	332	276	243	221	215	210	204	199	193	188	182	177	171	166	162	160	155	149	146
240	900	675	563	450	394	338	281	248	225	219	214	208	203	197	191	186	180	174	169	165	163	158	152	149
260	940	705	588	470	411	353	294	259	235	229	223	217	212	206	200	194	188	182	176	173	170	165	159	155
280	964	723	603	482	422	362	301	265	241	235	229	223	217	211	205	199	193	187	181	177	175	169	163	159
300	996	747	623	498	436	374	311	274	249	243	237	230	224	218	212	205	199	193	187	183	181	174	168	164
320	1032	774	645	516	452	387	323	284	258	252	245	239	232	226	219	213	206	200	194	190	187	181	174	170
340	1060	795	663	530	464	398	331	292	265	258	252	245	239	232	225	219	212	205	199	195	192	186	179	175
360	1092	819	683	546	478	410	341	300	273	266	259	253	246	239	232	225	218	212	205	201	198	191	184	180
380	1116	837	698	558	488	419	349	307	279	272	265	258	251	244	237	230	223	216	209	205	202	195	188	184
400	1148	861	718	574	502	431	359	316	287	280	273	265	258	251	244	237	230	222	215	211	208	201	194	189
420	1180	885	738	590	516	443	369	325	295	288	280	273	266	258	251	243	236	229	221	217	214	207	199	195
440	1204	903	753	602	527	452	376	331	301	293	286	278	271	263	256	248	241	233	226	221	217	211	203	199
460	1228	921	768	614	537	461	384	338	307	299	292	284	276	269	261	253	246	238	230	226	223	215	207	203
480	1260	945	788	630	551	473	394	347	315	307	299	291	284	276	268	260	252	244	236	232	228	221	213	208
500	1288	966	805	644	564	483	403	354	322	314	306	298	290	282	274	266	258	250	242	237	233	225	217	213
520	1308	981	818	654	572	491	409	360	327	319	311	302	294	286	278	270	262	253	245	240	237	229	221	216
540	1344	1008	840	672	588	504	420	370	336	328	319	311	302	294	286	277	269	260	252	247	244	235	227	222
560	1368	1026	855	684	599	513	428	376	342	333	325	316	308	299	291	282	274	265	257	251	248	239	231	226
580	1396	1047	873	698	611	524	436	384	349	340	332	323	314	305	297	288	279	270	262	257	253	244	236	230
600	1420	1065	888	710	621	533	444	391	355	346	337	328	320	311	302	293	284	275	266	261	257	249	240	234
620	1448	1086	905	724	634	543	453	398	362	353	344	335	326	317	308	299	290	281	272	266	262	253	244	239
640	1476	1107	923	738	646	554	461	406	369	360	351	341	332	323	314	304	295	286	277	271	267	258	249	244
660	1508	1131	943	754	660	566	471	415	377	368	358	349	339	330	320	311	302	292	283	277	273	264	254	249
680	1532	1149	958	766	670	575	479	421	383	373	364	354	345	335	326	316	306	297	287	282	278	268	259	253
700	1560	1170	975	780	683	585	488	429	390	380	371	361	351	341	332	322	312	302	293	287	283	273	263	257
720	1592	1194	995	796	697	597	498	438	398	388	378	368	358	348	338	328	318	308	299	293	289	279	269	263
740	1616	1212	1010	808	707	606	505	444	404	394	384	374	364	354	343	333	323	313	303	297	293	283	273	267
760	1640	1230	1025	820	718	615	513	451	410	400	390	379	369	359	349	338	328	318	308	301	297	287	277	271
780	1672	1254	1045	836	732	627	523	460	418	408	397	387	376	366	355	345	334	324	314	307	303	293	282	276
800	1700	1275	1063	850	744	638	531	468	425	414	404	393	383	372	361	351	340	329	319	312	308	298	287	281
825	1724	1293	1078	862	754	647	539	474	431	420	409	399	388	377	366	356	345	334	323	317	312	302	291	284
850	1756	1317	1098	878	768	659	549	483	439	428	417	406	395	384	373	362	351	340	329	323	318	307	296	290
875	1784	1338	1115	892	781	669	558	491	445	435	424	413	401	390	379	368	357	346	335	328	323	312	301	294
900	1812	1359	1133	906	793	680	566	498	453	442	430	419	408	396	385	374	362	351	340	333	328	317	306	299
925	1840	1380	1150	920	805	690	575	506	460	449	437	426	414	403	391	380	368	357	345	338	334	322	311	304

Reproduced by permission of tariff publisher. Note: On this table, interpolation is not used. Instead, if you cannot find the exact number in the left-hand column, use the next higher printed value.

tor Carrier Act was to encourage competition, and this ruling was consistent with the intentions of the new law.[47]

Hierarchy of Rates

Class, exception, and commodity rates have been discussed. It is important to note that there is a priority or *hierarchy of rates* regarding which of these rates to use at any given time. The Interstate Commerce Act stated that *commodity* rates have the highest priority. In other words, whenever a shipment is tendered to a carrier, the commodity rate should be used if it is available. If it does not exist, then an exception rate should be used. If it is not available, the *class* rate can always be found for any product, even if it is a new product that is not currently located in the class tariffs. A procedure known as the *rule of analogy* is used. This states that if a product is not described in the tariff, then the shipper and carrier will agree to use the rating or class of the most similar existing product in the tariff. Eventually, they will arrange to have the new product placed in the classification tariff. A class rate is sometimes referred to as the old standby because it is possible to find a class rate for every product.

There are many additional types of commodity rates, but they are slowly being phased out for two reasons: (1) more and more rates are being negotiated between the carrier and the shipper that are unique to the parties involved, and (2) tariffs are becoming more computerized, which means that standardization of rate determination is becoming less Byzantine. Tariffs are the subject of the next section.

Computerization of Freight Rates and Tariffs

One of the most dismal problems of our transportation system has been the enormousness and the complexity of its rate structure. So complex (and frequently illogical) is the system that it was once believed to be impossible to computerize. This meant that a shipper's traffic department was the last bastion within the firm to resist the timesaving advances that computers were providing to all other aspects of business enterprise. In 1975, while addressing a Delta Nu Alpha meeting, one of the authors of this book lamented:

> Tariff complexity and the difficulties of applying computer logic thereto is making the firm's entire traffic section more and more isolated from other management. . . . Transfers and promotions into and out of the traffic department are less likely to occur.[48]

Fortunately, things have begun to change. Considerable progress is finally being made to render carrier and rate bureau tariffs into a form that

---

[47] "ICC Drops Prohibition Against Truck Rates Naming Shippers, Sites," *Traffic World* (March 5, 1984), p. 7.

[48] "Transport Schools Seen Lagging Behind the Times," *Transport Topics* (Oct. 20, 1975).

computers can accommodate. In general terms, the industry is revising its description of commodity items, its listing of routes and junctions, and its listing of geographic points, so that they are amenable to computer processing. Several precise steps include:

1. The removal of minor differences in the place and commodity descriptions used by different modes.
2. The removal of peculiarities in working of tariffs and tariff rules that are difficult to convert to computerized format—one example being overuse of the word *except.*
3. The requirement that new tariff and tariff rule submissions to the ICC for approval be in a specific computer-oriented format.

Much of the credit for creating the framework that will make computerized freight rates possible should go to the Transportation Data Coordinating Committee (TDCC). The TDCC was started in 1968 as a nonprofit corporation designed to develop, foster and maintain a program of action to achieve coordination of transportation data and information systems by standardization of descriptions and codes, tariff formats, systems and procedures for transportation and distribution. Its membership is composed of both shippers and carriers, and its goals are endorsed by federal agencies, including the ICC and the DOT. Additional participating organizations include the National Industrial Traffic League, the Association of American Railroads, and the American Trucking Associations.

The initial thrust of the TDCC was to encourage further development of standardized code categories. Four codes will be briefly mentioned—each has been tentatively accepted by the TDCC. They will be the "building blocks" of the TDCC Tariff Modernization Program. The objectives of this program are to *simplify* and further *computerize* transportation documentation and rate determination.

1. *Commodity Code.* The Standard Transportation Commodity Code (STCC) is designed to accurately represent all products and commodities being transported.
2. *Carrier Code.* The Standard Carrier Alpha Code (SCAC) lists all common carriers by rail and motor carrier firm.
3. *Geographic Code.* The Standard Point Location Code (SPLC) is a six digit number that is a unique identifier to individual locations.
4. *Patron Code.* Patron codes identify both shipper and receivers. *Dun's Code,* based on Dun and Bradstreets' customer codes, is the choice of the TDCC because it provides an alphabetical listing of more than 2.4 million businesses in the United States.

Many large shippers and carriers have computerized certain aspects of their freight and passenger moving activities. One of the reasons that the TDCC exists is to encourage all these individual users of transportation-related computer applications to adopt a universally used code system. This way, carriers and shippers could interchange computer-generated information. Also, if different transportation modes adopted similar coding, shippers would be more likely to introduce computers into their documentation and rate determination procedures.

Deregulation of the trucking and rail industries has also stimulated interest in computerizing freight rates. Why? Because transportation rates now change more rapidly to reflect market conditions. However, the astute traffic manager must devise a system to cope with this fluid rate situation. Computerization of rates has proven to be a successful solution. Walter W. Slaughter, Jr., manager of traffic services at Borg-Warner Corporation, noted one reason why his firm has moved rapidly to computerize rate determination: "Deregulation promises to make rates increasingly unstable. Competition may bring opportunities to cut costs, but only if traffic personnel have the timely knowledge to take advantage of fast-changing conditions."[49]

Assume that a traffic department decides to computerize the carrier rate determination function. Then a basic issue becomes: Should the computerization be performed internally or externally? An internal system implies that the firm will own or lease their own computer facilities and that the entire rate retrieval operation will be performed by employees of the company. The use of an outside contracting company is the key aspect of the external system. Here the computer itself (known as *hardware*) and its rate retrieval or other programs (known as *software*) are operated and continually updated by the contracting company. Their business is to provide accurate and expeditious rate determination for their traffic manager customers.

The general trend for firms first utilizing computer rate retrieval is to use the services of an external rate specialist. Illustrative of this situation is the General Tire and Rubber Company. This company prepares between 11,000 to 15,000 bills of lading per month and it utilizes the services of Distribution Sciences, Inc., a firm that has been a pioneer in computerized rate determination. Why did Joseph Vatalaro, General's corporate director of transportation, decide to utilize an outside firm? "The decision was made after General Tire researched the project of building its own data base and keeping it up to date. We didn't want to reinvent the wheel. Our study showed that tariff maintenance is a monumental task even after the gigantic effort of putting the tariff on system initially."[50]

Another reason many firms choose to use an external computerized rate service is that it is both less expensive to start up and can be operational in less time (a few months) than an internal service. Mr. Slaughter of Borg-Warner stated that it normally takes about two years to fully implement an internal automated rate system. In addition, the old manual system and new computerized system must operate in parallel for a few months. This is designed to insure that the new system has become fully "debugged," that is, all errors in the software have been located and corrected, before full reliance is placed on it. Slaughter noted, "Only larger companies are likely to find the internal service a practical alternative because there will be a need for programmers who are tariff specialists, a complete and renewable tariff library, experienced data entry personnel, and priority access to company

---

[49] "Traffic Computerization: Internal or External," *Traffic Management* (Nov. 1980), p. 64.

[50] Tom Dulaney, "Computers Turn On to Rating and Routing," *Distribution* (Feb. 1981), p. 36.

computers. Data storage capacity must be ample. Backup personnel must be available, so that if key personnel are absent the system does not break down."[51]

Firms that choose to have an internal rate automation system can purchase "canned" software packages. These involve detailed programs that have been fully checked for "bugs"—errors—and therefore they can be utilized almost immediately. In late 1980 the McDonnell Douglas Automation Company announced that it had developed and completely tested a computerized freight rate retrieval system. The program, known as FREIGHT, is designed for relatively large shippers. With this program, the shipper uses a centralized data base of transportation rates and routes. A McDonnell Douglas spokesman stated:

> Use of this system will lower a shipper's operating costs, reduce paperwork and prevent overbilling.
>
> Inquiry into the transportation data base can be either from a CRT terminal or by automated request from user-written programs. All inquiries for rates must include mode of shipment, date of shipment, weight, origin, destination and product. Optional inquiry data can include pallet weight, delivering carrier, container code and specific routes.
>
> FREIGHT searches the data base for a point-to-point rate. If none applies, a scale rate is calculated based on mileage and supplied to the requestor. Primary and alternate routes also can be furnished by the system if not specified with the inquiry.
>
> With FREIGHT, a shipper's traffic department can update the rate file from on-line CRT terminals immediately on receipt of new tariffs. This new rate data is available immediately to all company personnel having computer access through CRT terminals.[52]

The cost of the FREIGHT computer program, all necessary documentation, training materials and training of user's personnel is $125,000.

Some international freight rates are also computerized and made available to shippers and other carriers. The *Journal of Commerce,* a New York based daily shipping paper, now provides a service with the acronym RATES (rapid access tariff expediting service). This service stores the equivalent of 200,000 tariff pages and updates them nightly. Subscribers maintain terminals in their own offices.

An increasingly common solution to small shipments (under 10,000 pounds) transported via common carrier trucker is the utilization of a computerized rate system that can be run on most shippers' personal computers. These rate systems are being used by each of the following trucking companies: Roadway Express, Carolina Freight, Arkansas Best Freight, Murphy Motor Freight, and Ryder/PIE Nationwide as well as many others. Each of these systems emphasize three main inputs: distance, weight of shipment, and class—which is determined from the *National Motor Freight Classification.* This factor was previously discussed when determining a class rate. (Figure 5-3 is an example of a rail classification tariff.) The National Motor Freight

[51] "Traffic Computerization: Internal or External," op. cit., p. 65.
[52] "Large Shippers Can Now Use Centralized Data in Computing Freight Charges," *Traffic World* (Oct. 20, 1980), p. 43.

Classification is similar to this tariff in format. Note that in Figure 5-3, the word *rating* is used, which is the same as a "class."

Let us examine one of these simplified rate systems. Carolina Freight's system is known as SNAP. It is available in these formats: paper (manual), diskettes for personal computers, program inserts for hand-held computers, and programs for mainframes (large computers). The system was primarily designed to be used on an IBM Personal Computer. It is now also available in other personal computer formats. The user only inputs four numbers to determine the applicable rate: (1) the ZIP code of the shipment origin, (2) the ZIP code of the shipment destination, (3) the shipment weight, and (4) the "class" of the product being shipped.[53]

Note that this rate determination takes the mystique out of the function. What previously took six or more steps to determine a class rate can now be accomplished in a matter of seconds by keying a few numbers into one's personal computer. Shippers like this concept. Trucking companies report that a high percentage of their customers utilize the simplified rate systems. It is estimated that within a year of its introduction by one large trucking company, over 60 per cent of its customers were using the system.[54]

Carrier rate bureaus, which are rapidly losing many of their traditional functions, are developing and marketing rate-retrieval systems for computers. Figure 5-6 is the cover sheet from a folder describing one such system. The initial diskette and operating manual cost about $130; file maintenance will cost about $70 per year.

Summary

This chapter has presented an overview of transportation regulation and rates. The transportation industry, because of its public nature and importance to commerce, has been regulated since the 1600s in England by the common law. The United States followed this precedent until the 1870s, when an agrarian revolt against the railroads led to the enactment of the Granger laws and eventually the 1887 Act to Regulate Commerce. This vanguard legislation was designed to promote "just and reasonable" railroad rates and to eliminate unreasonable personal, place, and commodity discrimination. The law was administered by the ICC, an independent regulatory body, and was subsequently strengthened by legislation as problem areas developed.

Starting with the railroad industry in 1887, the other modes of transportation were subsequently brought under federal regulation. The 1906 Hepburn Act regulated the oil pipeline industry. The trucking industry became regulated under the 1935 Motor Carrier Act. Inland water carriers were added with the Transportation Act of 1940. The air carriers came under federal regulation with the 1938 Civil Aeronautics Act, which created the CAB.

The first industry to be deregulated was all-cargo aircraft, in 1977. This was followed by airline passenger deregulation in 1978. The latter resulted

---

[53] Ripley Watson, "Carrier Pricing Systems Offer Varied Options," *Journal of Commerce* (Feb. 15, 1984).

[54] Ripley Watson, "Rate Systems Change Truck Industry," *Journal of Commerce* (Feb. 13, 1984).

Figure 5-6 Example of Transportation Rate Diskette Sales Announcement

PRODUCT DEVELOPMENT
FROM
CENTRAL STATES

THE CMB 575 ═══ *ACCELL-A-RATER* ©

"An Efficient Automated Rating and Billing System
for shipments moving under
Class Rates within Central Territory"

- Rating of Mixed Shipments
- Rating of Discounted Shipments
- Applies Percentage Factors
- Requires only Origin and Destination Zip, Class and Weight
- Monochrome or Color screen option

New! ➜

- Error Message Routine to alert user of invalid input data
- Continuous Processing unless user wishes to exit program
- File Maintenance on a Quarterly basis or Upon Request
- Rate Quotation Enhancement reflects all weight breaks and minimum charge

EQUIPMENT REQUIRED:
IBM PC or IBM XT (IBM-Compatible machines may be used, but should be tested before purchase)

(For specific costs, see Application on next page)

Source: Central States Motor Freight Bureau. Used with permission.

in rates decreasing and more service available to the traveling public. Trucking deregulation followed in 1980. Many new carriers entered this industry, and the results have been greatly reduced rates and increased service levels to shippers. The last major mode to be deregulated was the rail industry, also in 1980. Although rail rates have continued to increase, their rate of increase has been less than the rate of inflation. A major change legalized by deregulation has been the utilization of rail contracts, with over 22,000 in use.

Common carriers can be distinguished from other carriers because of their four fundamental duties: to serve, to deliver, to charge reasonable rates, and to avoid discrimination. *Contract carriers* are also "for-hire" in nature, although they only serve a limited number of customers under specific contracts. *Private transportation* involves a company performing its own transportation in its own vehicles.

Freight rate determination is complex. A primary reason for this situation is that value-of-service pricing is extensively used relative to cost-of-service pricing. The three basic types of freight rates are: class, exception, and commodity.

Computerization of rates is becoming more common. For commodity rates, the TDCC has been the leader in trying to standardize the documentation that will render computerization feasible. Many trucking firms offer their customers diskettes for determining class rates.

Questions for Discussion and Review

1. The transportation industry has been subjected to governmental regulation in England since the 1600s. What factors warranted this action during a period where the basic concept of *laissez-faire* was predominant?
2. Farmers were very active in demanding both state and federal regulation for the railroad industry. Discuss why farmers took this position.
3. Common carriers have four basic obligations. Discuss each.
4. Discuss briefly the key elements of the 1887 Act to Regulate Commerce.
5. Why was the Reed-Bulwinkle Act passed in 1948?
6. Discuss why transportation regulation did not appear to work well after World War II.
7. Discuss the effects of deregulation of the airline passenger business.
8. Do you believe airline passenger deregulation has been successful? Defend your answer.
9. Discuss the impact of trucking deregulation on this industry.
10. Do you believe trucking deregulation should have taken place? Why?
11. Discuss the changes that have taken place in the railroad industry because of deregulation.
12. Would you have deregulated the railroad industry? Defend your answer.
13. Discuss an embargo.
14. What is a contract carrier? How are they doing in today's deregulated motor carrier industry?
15. Compare and contrast full-cost versus value-of-service pricing.

16. Discuss briefly the steps involved in determining a class rate.
17. What is the hierarchy-of-rates concept?
18. Discuss the computerization of rates. Why do you think this concept is growing so rapidly?
19. Discuss how carriers are using personal computers in the rate determination area.
20. As you look back over this chapter, which subject did you find the most interesting? Why?

Additional Chapter References

Allen, Benjamin J., David B. Vellenga, and Bruce Ferrin. "A Review and Analysis of the Iowa Railway Finance Authority Legislation: An Example of Defederalization of Transport Policy." *Annual Proceedings of the Transportation Research Forum* (1982), pp. 383–390.

Barrett, Colin. "If Regulation's Sun Sets. . . ." *Annual Proceedings of the Transportation Research Forum* (1983), pp. 552–557.

Beilock, Richard, and George Fletcher. "Exempt Agricultural Commodity Hauler in Florida." *Annual Proceedings of the Transportation Research Forum* (1983), pp. 444–450.

Beilock, Richard, and James Freeman. "Carrier and Shipper Perceptions of Motor Carrier Deregulation in Florida." *Annual Proceedings of the Transportation Research Forum* (1982), pp. 250–257.

———. "Deregulated Motor Carrier Service to Small Communities." *Transportation Journal* (Summer 1984), pp. 71–82.

———. "Motor Carrier Perceptions of Intrastate Motor Carrier Regulations and Regulators." *ICC Practitioners' Journal* (March–April 1984), pp. 275–285.

Beilock, Richard, and J. Scott Shonkwiler. "An Analysis of Rate Variations Across Time for Identical Hauls of Unregulated Commodities." *Annual Proceedings of the Transportation Research Forum* (1982), pp. 300–305.

Beilock, Richard, and Richard Kilmer. "Regulations and Empty Mileage." *ICC Practitioners' Journal* (May–June, 1983), pp. 433–439.

Boisjoly, Russell P., and Thomas M. Corsi. "Shifts in Indicators of Motor Carrier Bankruptcies: Before and After the Motor Carrier Act." *Annual Proceedings of the Transportation Research Forum* (1984), pp. 454–463.

———. "The Aftermath of the Motor Carrier Act of 1980: Entry, Exit and Merger." *Annual Proceedings of the Transportation Research Forum* (1982), pp. 258–264.

Borghesani, William H. "Regulatory Reform and Recession: Their Not So Obvious Impact on Private Carriage Planning." *Annual Proceedings of the NCPDM* (1982), pp. 377–406.

Bruning, Edward R., and Edward A. Morash. "Deregulation and the Cost of Equity Capital: The Case of Publicly Held Motor Carriers." *Transportation Journal* (Winter 1983), pp. 72–81.

Bunce, Elliott. "Special Problems Relating to Collective Ratemaking." ICC *Practitioners' Journal* (Sept. 1984), pp. 583–590.

Cavarra, Leslie A., Roger D. Stover, and Benjamin A. Allen. "The Capital

Market Effects of Airline Deregulation." *Transportation Journal* (Spring 1981), pp. 73–78.

Cavinato, Joseph L. "An Analysis of Impacts from Possible Carrier Credit Rule Deregulation." *ICC Practitioners' Journal* (Jan.–Feb. 1982), pp. 132–143.

Chow, Garland, and Kenneth Button. "The Economic Regulation of Road Haulage (Trucking) in Canada and the United Kingdom." *Annual Proceedings of the Transportation Research Forum* (1982), pp. 642–652.

Corsi, Thomas M., and Merrill J. Roberts. "Patterns of Discrimination in the Collective Ratemaking System." *Annual Proceedings of the Transportation Research Forum* (1982), pp. 621–630.

Corsi, Thomas M., and Russell Boisjoly. "The Long-Run Effects of Merger in the Motor Carrier Industry: The Implications of Deregulation," *ICC Practitioners' Journal* (March–April 1982), pp. 280–293.

Corsi, Thomas M., J. Michael Tuck, and Leland L. Gardner. "Minority Motor Carriers and the Motor Carrier Act of 1980." *Transportation Journal* (Fall 1982), pp. 42–55.

Cunningham, Lawrence F. "Transportation and Distribution Management: New Options." *The Distribution Handbook* (New York: Free Press Division of Macmillan, 1985), pp. 497–510.

Davis, Grant M., and John E. Dillard. "Collective Ratemaking—Does It Have a Future in the Motor Carrier Industry?" *ICC Practitioners' Journal* (Sept.–Oct. 1982), pp. 619–625.

———. "Financial Stability in Motor Carrier Industry—The Role of Collective Ratemaking." *Annual Proceedings of the Transportation Research Forum* (1983), pp. 241–248.

———. "The Professional Traveler and the Airline Deregulation Act of 1978: An Appraisal." *Annual Proceedings of the Transportation Research Forum* (1982), pp. 419–426.

Davis, Grant M. "One Regulatory Agency for Transportation?" *ICC Practitioners' Journal* (Sept.–Oct. 1983), pp. 624–640.

———. "The Collective Ratemaking Issue: Circa 1984." *Transportation Practitioners Journal* (Fall 1984), pp. 60–68.

Douglas, N. J. "An Econometric Investigation into the Demand Function for U.K. Express Coach Travel During a Period of Deregulation." *Annual Proceedings of the Transportation Research Forum* (1984), pp. 194–203.

Edles, Gary. "The Strategy of Regulatory Change." *ICC Practitioners' Journal* (Sept.–Oct. 1982), pp. 626–637.

Ellison, Anthony P. "Regulatory Reform in Transport: A Canadian Perspective." *Transportation Journal* (Summer 1984), pp. 4–19.

———. "The Structural Change of the Airline Industry." *Transportation Journal* (Spring 1982), pp. 58–69.

Emrich, Richard S. M. "Improper Use of Review Board Appellate Powers in Recent Market Dominance Decisions." *ICC Practitioners' Journal* (July–Aug. 1984), pp. 490–495.

Enis, Charles, and Edward A. Morash. "The Economic Losses from the Devaluation of Motor Carrier Operating Rights." *ICC Practitioners' Journal* (July–Aug. 1983), pp. 542–555.

Ezard, P. H. B., and R. J. Lande. "Computerization of Railway Freight Tariffs." *Annual Proceedings of the Transportation Research Forum* (1984), pp. 415–419.

Farris, Martin T., and Norman E. Daniel. "Bus Regulatory Reform Act of 1982." *Transportation Journal* (Fall 1983), pp. 4–15.

Farris, Martin T. "The Multiple Meanings and Goals of Deregulation: A Commentary." *Transportation Journal* (Winter 1981), pp. 44–50.

Ferguson, Wade, and Louis W. Glorfeld. "Modeling the Present Motor Carrier Rate Structure as a Benchmark for Pricing in the New Competitive Environment." *Transportation Journal* (Winter 1981), pp. 59–66.

Freeman, James W. "A Survey of Motor Carrier Deregulation in Florida: One Year's Experience." *ICC Practitioners' Journal* (Nov.–Dec. 1982), pp. 51–83.

Frey, N. Gail, Reuben H. Krollck, Leone Nidiffer, Jay L. Tontz. "Effects of Reregulation of the California Intrastate Trucking Industry," *Transportation Journal*, (Spring 1985), pp. 4–17.

Fuller, Stephen, Larry D. Makus, and Jack T. Lamkin. "Effects of Intrastate Motor Carrier Regulation on Rates and Service: The Texas Experience." *Transportation Journal* (Fall 1983), pp. 16–30.

Grimm, Curtis M., and Robert G. Harris. "Vertical Foreclosure in the Rail Freight Industry: Economic Analysis and Policy Prescriptions." *ICC Practitioners' Journal* (July–Aug. 1983), pp. 508–531.

Grimm, Curtis M. "Promoting Competition in the Railroad Industry: A Public Policy Analysis." *Annual Proceedings of the Transportation Research Forum* (1984), pp. 222–227.

Guandolo, John. *Transportation Law* (Dubuque: Brown, 1983).

Harmatuck, Donald J. "The Effects of Economic Conditions and Regulatory Changes upon Motor Carrier Tonnage and Revenues." *Transportation Journal* (Winter 1984), pp. 31–39.

Harper, Donald V. "Consequences of Reform of Federal Economic Regulation of the Motor Trucking Industry." *Transportation Journal* (Summer 1982), pp. 35–58.

———. "Economic Regulation of For-Hire Trucking in the 1980s: The Case of Minnesota." *Transportation Practitioners' Journal* (Fall 1984), pp. 69–92.

———. "The Marketing Revolution in the Motor Trucking Industry." *Journal of Business Logistics* (Vol. 4, No. 1, 1983), pp. 35–49.

Heaver, T. D., and S. LeFebvre. "Management Strategies Under Railway Deregulation: The Case of the British Columbia Forest Industry." *Annual Proceedings of the Transportation Research Forum* (1984), pp. 44–53.

Heaver, Trevor D. "The Canadian Experience with Limited Regulation of Maximum Railway Rates." *Transportation Journal* (Fall 1981), pp. 5–13.

———. "The Regulation of Railway Access to Shippers Through Interswitching." *Annual Proceedings of the Transportation Research Forum* (1982), pp. 43–50.

Horn, Kevin, and John E. Tyworth. "The Impact of Railroad Boxcar Deregulation: A Case Study of Transcontinental Lumber." *Annual Proceedings of the Transportation Research Forum* (1984), pp. 280–289.

Horn, Kevin H. "Entry into Regulated Interstate Trucking: Shipper Perspectives and Carrier Prospects." *Transportation Journal* (Winter 1984), pp. 55–72.

———. "Federal Preemption of State Transportation Economic Regulation: Conflict Versus Coordination." *Transportation Journal* (Winter 1983), pp. 28–46.

Huie, Bill W. "Texas Trucking Regulation." *Annual Proceedings of the NCPDM* (1984), pp. 684–691.

Jacobsen, Thomas R. "Railroad Exemption Procedures under Section 213 of the Staggers Act." *ICC Practitioners' Journal* (May–June, 1984), pp. 360–367.

Jones, J. Richard, and Sheila I. Cocke. "Deregulation and Non-Hub Airports: Discriminant Analysis of Economic, Demographic and Geographic Factors." *Annual Proceedings of the Transportation Research Forum* (1984), pp. 251–257.

Katzman, Owen B. "The Bus Regulatory Reform Act of 1982: What It Does and How It Works." *Transportation Practitioners Journal* (Winter 1985), pp. 221–255.

Keyes, Lucile Sheppard. *Regulatory Reform in Air Cargo Transportation* (Washington, D.C.: American Enterprise Institute for Public Policy Research, 1980).

Lande, Richard. "Advantages of Collective Ratemaking for Railways: A Canadian Perspective." *ICC Practitioners' Journal* (Sept.–Oct. 1982), pp. 609–618.

Lande, Richard. "How Collective Ratemaking Improves the Canadian Economy." *Transportation Practitioners Journal* (Winter 1985), pp. 198–220.

Lande, Richard. "Possible Remedies to Reconcile the Differences between Canada and U.S. Rail Regulation." *Annual Proceedings of the Transportation Research Forum* (1983), pp. 293–299.

Lazar, Lee A. "Alteration of Private Changes as a Result of Motor Carrier Deregulation." *Annual Proceedings of the NCPDM* (1984), pp. 647–660.

Lieb, Robert C. "Regulatory Reform in Transportation: Some Interim Observations." *ICC Practitioners' Journal* (March–April 1982), pp. 273–279.

Ludwick, E. M., and Miro Bukal. "The Regulatory Reform Debate on Railway Pricing in Canada: The Impact of U.S. Deregulation from the Shipper's Perspective." *Annual Proceedings of the Transportation Research Forum* (1984), pp. 446–453.

McBride, Michael F. "Interstate Commerce Commission Certification of State Regulatory Bodies and Review of Interstate Rail Rate Decisions: The Need for Reform." *ICC Practitioners' Journal* (July–Aug. 1984), pp. 476–489.

Merkel, Philip L. "The Origins of an Expanded Federal Court Jurisdiction: Railroad Development and the Ascendancy of the Federal Judiciary." *Business History Review* (Autumn 1984), pp. 336–358.

Meyer, John R., Clinton V. Oster, Ivor P. Morgan, Benjamin A. Berman, and Diana Strassmann. *Airline Deregulation, The Early Experience* (Boston: Auburn, 1981).

Ming, Dennis, Denver Tolliver, and Daniel Zink. "Effects of Airline Deregulation on North Dakota Fares and Service." *Annual Proceedings of the Transportation Research Forum* (1984), pp. 265–274.

Morash, Edward A. "A Critique of the Household Goods Transportation Act of 1980: Impact and Limitations." *Transportation Journal* (Winter 1981), pp. 16–27.

———— and Charles Enis. "The Effects of Motor Carrier Deregulation: A Stock Market Perspective." *Annual Proceedings of the Transportation Research Forum* (1982), pp. 265–271.

Pustay, Michael W. "Intrastate Motor Carrier Regulatory Reform in South Dakota." *Transportation Practitioners Journal* (Fall 1984), pp. 93–107.

————. "Regulation of the Intrastate Motor Freight Industry in Ohio." *ICC Practitioners' Journal* (May–June 1983), pp. 415–432.

Pautsch, Gregory R., Cathy A. Hamlett, and C. Phillip Baumel. "Impact of Alternative Changes in the Surface Transportation Assistance Act of 1982." *Annual Proceedings of the Transportation Research Forum* (1983), pp. 331–340.

Phillips, Karen Borlaug. "The Role of Research in Transportation Policy: The Case of Motor Carrier Regulatory Reform." *Annual Proceedings of the Transportation Research Forum* (1983), pp. 399–409.

Pickett, Gregory M., and Marilyn G. Kletke. "The Motor Carrier Act of 1980: An Industry Profile of Its Effects in the Southwestern United States." *Journal of Business Logistics* (Vol. 5, No. 2, 1984), pp. 48–64.

Rose, Warren. "Three Years After Airline Passenger Deregulation in the United States: A Report Card on Trunkline Carriers." *Transportation Journal* (Winter 1981), pp. 51–58.

Sanders, Malcolm S. "Deregulated Environment: Crisis or Opportunity? The Conrail Story." *Annual Proceedings of the NCPDM* (1983), pp. 232–244.

Schuster, Allan D. "The Effects of Intrastate Motor Carrier Regulation upon the Texas Agricultural Industry." *Annual Proceedings of the Transportation Research Forum* (1983), pp. 461–472.

Seiden, Elliot M. "Competition in the Motor Carrier Industry—The Battle Is Not Over." *Annual Proceedings of the NCPDM* (1984), pp. 321–332.

Smith, Jon L. "Market Performance in Domestic Airline Markets." *Transportation Journal* (Fall 1984), pp. 51–57.

Stephenson, Frederick J., and Frederick J. Beier. "The Effects of Airline Deregulation on Air Service to Small Communities." *Transportation Journal* (Summer 1981), pp. 54–62.

Stephenson, Frederick J., and John W. Vann. "Air Cargo Liability Deregulation: Shippers' Perspective." *Transportation Journal* (Spring 1981), pp. 48–58.

————. "Deregulation: The Elimination of Air Cargo Tariff Filing Requirements." *Journal of Business Logistics* (Vol. 3, No. 1, 1982), pp. 59–72.

Talley, Wayne K., and William R. Eckroade. "Airline Passenger Demand in Monopoly Flight Segments of a Single Airline," *Transportation Journal* (Winter 1984), pp. 73–79.

Taylor, Reese H. "Viewing the Motor Carrier Act of 1980 with 20/20 Hindsight." *Annual Proceedings of the NCPDM* (1982), pp. 209–218.

Thompson, Michael. "The Relevance of Revenue/Variable Cost Ratios to

Market Dominance Determinations." *Annual Proceedings of the Transportation Research Forum* (1982), pp. 362–368.

Tye, William B., A. Lawrence Kolbe, and Miriam Alexander Baker. "The Economics of Midstream Switches in Regulatory Treatments of Deferred Income Taxes Resulting from Accelerated Depreciation." *ICC Practitioners' Journal* (Nov.–Dec. 1983), pp. 24–53.

Tye, William B. "Balancing the Ratemaking Goals of the Staggers Rail Act." *Transportation Journal* (Summer 1983), pp. 17–26.

Tye, William B., A. Lawrence Kolbe, and Miriam Alexander Baker. "The Economics of Revenue Need Standards in Motor Carriers General Increase Proceedings." *Transportation Journal* (Summer 1981), pp. 5–28.

Tye, William B. "On the Effectiveness of Product and Geographic Competition in Determining Rail Market Dominance." *Transportation Journal* (Fall 1984), pp. 5–19.

———. "Revenue/Variable Cost Ratios and Market Dominance Proceedings." *Transportation Journal* (Winter 1984), pp. 15–30.

———. "The Role of Revenue/Variable Cost Ratios: Determinations of Rail Rate Reasonableness." *Annual Proceedings of the Transportation Research Forum* (1984), pp. 214–221.

Wagner, William B. "Exit of Entry Controls for Motor Common Carriers: Rationale Reassessment." *ICC Practitioners' Journal* (Jan.–Feb. 1983), pp. 163–175.

Walter, C. K. "Analysis of Railroad Contract Provisions and the 1980 Staggers Act." *Journal of Business Logistics* (Vol. 5, No. 1, 1984), pp. 81–91.

Waring, Dabney T. "Motor Carrier Regulation—By State or by Market?" *ICC Practitioners' Journal* (March–April 1984), pp. 240–244.

Williams, Ernest W. "A Critique of the Staggers Rail Act of 1980." *Transportation Journal* (Spring 1982), pp. 5–15.

Williamson, Kenneth C., Lawrence F. Cunningham, and Marc G. Singer. "Scheduled Passenger Air Service to Small Communities: A Role for State and Local Governments." *Transportation Journal* (Summer 1982), pp. 25–34.

Williamson, Kenneth C., Marc G. Singer, and Roger A. Peterson. "The Impact of Regulatory Reform on U.S. For-Hire Freight Transportation: The Users' Perspective." *Transportation Journal* (Summer 1983), pp. 27–54.

CASE 5-1

Boone Shoe Company

"Red" Boone founded the Boone Shoe Company in St. Joseph, Missouri, during the 1930s. Unable to find work as a sheet metal worker, Red started to make moccasins for friends who had always admired the ones he had made for himself. Over time, the reputation of Boone's shoes spread, and Red expanded his product line and hired additional employees. The real growth of the company took place during World War II. In 1942, almost as a joke, Red submitted a bid to the War Department to produce

100,000 pairs of combat boots. Much to his surprise, the contract was accepted, probably because Red noted in the bid that a sufficient noncombat labor force (females and retirees) existed in the area to produce the boots.

The main production input, leather, was easily obtained at the nearby Kansas City stockyards. After the war, the Boone company expanded its production of civilian shoes and related products and also continued to supply the military services with all types of leather footwear. Red Boone's son, Barry, was in charge of all marketing and distribution activities.

Larry Gitman functioned as the firm's warehouse, purchasing, and traffic manager. After two years experience as a management trainee with a large motor common carrier, Larry had accepted the position at Boone Shoe Company. Because of the firm's steady annual growth rate of 15 per cent, Barry Boone had authorized Larry to hire an assistant.

Steve Knapp, although just out of high school, was working part time from 1:00 to 6:00 P.M. and also attending the local community college. Steve had progressed so rapidly that Larry felt comfortable taking a three-week vacation, his first extended vacation in some years.

During Larry's vacation, Steve assumed Larry's responsibilities. As Steve sat in his office, the intercom buzzed and Barry asked Steve to pick up line #3 and take part in the conversation. The call was from Tom Cook, Boone's salesman for Minnesota and Wisconsin. Tom stated, "I'm calling from the buying office of Lawson department stores in Green Bay. Although they're currently overstocked in shoes, they are interested in buying a sizable quantity of our 'Light Stride' arch-support insoles. They plan on giving them away with their shoes in order to stimulate shoe sales. They want to buy FOB destination. I need to know in the next few minutes the cost of sending 17,000 pounds of the arch supports from St. Joseph to Green Bay."

Steve asked, "Will they accept a rail shipment? It's less expensive, and we usually receive fairly good rail service on our northbound shipments."

Tom replied, "The buyer said he expected the shipment to come via rail."

Barry came on the line and asked, "Steve—can you look up this info for Tom?"

Steve said, "No problem. I'll call you back with the answer in 15 minutes or less."

Question One: Assume there are no commodity or exception rates in effect for this shipment. Using Figures 5-4, 5-5, and 5-6, calculate the applicable charge.

Question Two: Steve remembered that he had heard Larry speak of shipping "wind." This involved paying the CL minimum weight in order to receive the CL rate, even if the shipment actually weighed less than the carload minimum weight. Should this technique be used for the shipment? Why or why not?

Question Three: The buyer will pay upon receipt of the shipment, which is valued at $21,000 plus any transportation charges. Boone Shoe Company borrows money from the bank regularly on an open line of credit and currently is paying interest on its debt at the rate of 15 per cent per year. If rail LCL service is used, delivery time to Green Bay will be about ten days. If rail CL service is used, delivery time will be six days. What is the additional advantage to Boone Shoe Company if it chooses to use CL service?

Question Four (continuation of question three): Boone Shoe Company also owns several large trucks, although Steve is uncertain whether they are available for immediate use. He knows that they could make the delivery to Green Bay in two days. He checks the highway distance from St. Joseph to Green Bay and finds it is 588 miles.

Larry had once told Steve that it cost the company 85 cents per mile to operate its highway trucks. Do you think that a truck should be used if it is available? Why?

Question Five (continuation of questions two and three): Another alternative is to make the shipment by rail from Boone's St. Louis warehouse. Rail delivery time will be four days. What price should Tom Cook be told to quote to Lawson's?

Question Six: Boone Shoe Company often sells large quantities—from 10,000 up to 30,000 pounds—of arch-support insoles on an FOB delivered basis. After referring to Figure 5-4, do you think there is a minimum weight (in this 10,000 to 30,000 pound range) that customers should be encouraged to order? If so, what is it?

CASE 5-2

Chippy Potato Chip Company

Located in Reno, Nevada, since 1947, the Chippy Potato Chip Company manufactured potato chips and distributed them within a 100-mile radius of Reno. It used its own trucks for delivery in the Reno, Carson City, and Lake Tahoe area and common carrier trucking for all other outgoing shipments. All of its common carrier shipments were on an LTL (less than truckload) basis. The applicable motor carrier freight rating or classification for LTL potato chips was 200. The classification (200) was high although potato chips are often given as textbook examples of bulky freight that will cause a truck to "cube-out" (reach cubic capacity before weight capacity). Even after much of the motor carrier industry was deregulated, Chippy had difficulty finding contract truckers interested in negotiating specific contract rates. This was because potato chips—as a result of their bulk—were not a desirable cargo from the truckers' point-of-view.

At present, the potato chips were packed in bags containing eight ounces of chips. Twenty-four eight-ounce bags were packed in cartons which were 12 inches by 12 inches by 36 inches. The packed carton weighed 14 lb. The eight-ounce bags of chips wholesaled FOB plant for 40 cents each and retailed at 59 cents.

Recently the Chippy firm acquired rights to produce a new type of chip, made from powdered potatoes yielding chips of identical shape that could be packed in tubular shaped containers. A five-ounce paper tube of chips would wholesale (FOB plant) at 40 cents and retail for 59 cents. The new chips were much less bulky: 24 five-ounce containers could be packed in a carton measuring one cubic foot. The filled carton weighed ten lb. (The differences between weight of chips and cartons is because of packaging materials. The carrier is paid on the basis of carton weight.)

Chippy management believed that since the new chips were less bulky, the LTL classification of 200 was too high. They decided to ask the motor carrier tariff and classification bureau for a new, lower classification. (Common carrier rates for a movement are the classification multiplied by a distance factor. If the classification were lowered, the rate would be lowered proportionally for all shipments.)

Question One: If you worked for Chippy, what new classification would you ask for? Give your reasons.

Question Two: Classifications are based on *both* cost and value of service. From the carriers' standpoint, how has cost of service changed?

Question Three: Given the existing LTL classification of 200, how has value of service to the customer changed?

Question Four: The new tubular containers are much sturdier. If you worked for Chippy, how—if at all—would you argue that this factor should influence classification?

Question Five: You work for the motor carrier rate bureau and notice that the relationship between the weight of potato chips and the weight of packaging has changed. How, if at all, should this influence changes in the product's classification?

Question Six: One of Chippy's own trucks, used for local deliveries, has two axles, an enclosed body measuring (inside) 7 feet by 8 feet by 20 feet, and limited by law to carrying a load of no more than 8,000 pounds. Because the truck is not supposed to be overloaded, what combinations, expressed in terms of cartons of each, of new and old style chips can it legally carry? (Hint: use a piece of graph paper.)

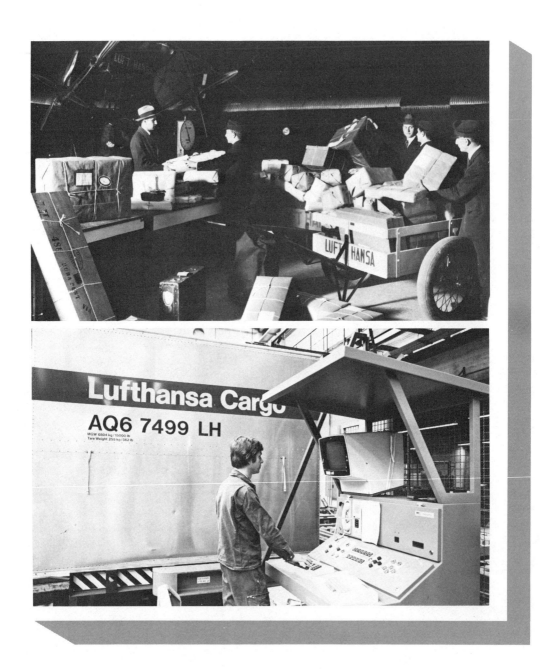

Once little more than a curiosity, air freight has developed to a point where it is an integral part of many shippers' daily operations. Today, airlines offer—and charge for—a premium service; and many of their cargo handling techniques are the most modern in use anywhere. These two photos, both from Lufthansa, illustrate some of these changes. In the upper photo, taken in Berlin in 1929, parcels are accepted on the tarmac while the plane, a Junkers tri-motor, waits. The bottom photo, taken in Frankfurt in 1982, shows an operation at Lufthansa's automated terminal. The worker records the container's number. It will be automatically moved to a slot where it will be held until the plane is ready for loading.

(Credit: Lufthansa German Airlines)

The Traffic Management Function

Fortunately—or maybe unfortunately, for some—deregulation removes many of the complexities and mysteries of transportation. We can no longer hide behind esoteric government regulations and tariffs. The spotlight can be very hot for the unprepared actor [traffic manager].

Charles L. Taylor
Director of Transportation
Nabisco Brands, Inc.
NCPDM Annual Meeting (1982)

Yes, there is a new freedom. There is a new feeling that you and I must be more responsible. No longer do we have strict regulatory reform. As I look back, wasn't it a straight jacket that you as carriers and we as shippers were involved with?

J. Robert Morton
Vice-president, Transportation and Distribution
Combustion Engineering, Inc.
Traffic World (April 2, 1984)

Key Terms

- **Rate determination**
- **Rate negotiation**
- **Consistency of service**
- **Bill of lading**
- **Transit privilege**
- **Law of loss and damage**
- **Reparations**
- **Demurrage/Detention**
- **Tracing**
- **Expediting**
- **Bank payment plans**
- **Hazardous materials**
- **Shipment consolidation**
- **Break-bulk distribution center**
- **Make-bulk distribution center**
- **"Toto" operating rights**
- **Compensated intercorporate hauling**
- **Single-source leasing**

Learning Objectives

- **To examine the background of the traffic management function**
- **To discuss the traditional functions of traffic management**
- **To describe how transportation deregulation has impacted the traffic management function**
- **To identify the crucial role negotiation plays in the traffic management function**
- **To relate the importance of computers to the traffic department**
- **To examine the new options available for private carriage**

[handwritten annotations in margin: "Jim", "Tom" (struck through), "ME", "Tom", "Matt"]

Traffic Management: Background and Scope

Senior management is concerned about traffic management more than ever before because transportation represents a major expense item and will continue to increase. In 1983 United States business firms spent more than $251 billion on freight transportation, which represented about 7½ per cent of the gross national product.

Prior to federal transportation regulation of rates and services in 1887, the real job of the traffic manager was to negotiate the largest possible rebates from the railroads. A business using a particular railroad often chose its traffic managers from among people who worked for that railroad. Hence, the newly appointed traffic managers could "negotiate" the best "deals" with their prior cronies. When the Act to Regulate Commerce was enacted into law in 1887, the traffic management position fell upon hard times. Because rebates and other discriminatory practices became illegal, the special "services" of the traffic manager were no longer needed. Nor was the job of purchasing transportation service considered to be complex because the railroad was the only viable mode of inland transportation. Instead, the traffic manager was replaced by a shipping clerk who notified the railroad when shipments were ready.

After World War I the traffic management function began to grow in stature as competitive transport modes developed. Significant federal government funding was provided for the dredging and expansion of the inland waterway system. The truck had proven its dependability in World War I, and a highway system was being built to accommodate the traffic caused by new trucking companies as well as firms that owned their own fleets. Oil pipelines and freight forwarders were emerging as additional alternative choices for traffic managers. Along with these many new alternatives the regulatory environment and carrier rate structures started to assume their present-day complexity. These factors all worked together to reestablish the importance of the traffic management function. Today, riding on the crest of enthusiasm for the PD/L concept, the traffic manager is considered to be an important member of the distribution/logistics team. Deregulation of carriers has also sparked management's interest in transportation issues. The following sections will discuss the primary activities of the traffic department.

Rate Determination and Negotiation

As used here, the phrase *rate determination* means locating the lowest rate charged by a common carrier. This task is often not as easy as it sounds because of the large number of existing tariffs. Large shippers, with somewhat regular movements, are computerizing those rates that are applicable to their routine business. The ICC is requiring tariffs to be converted to a format that makes them more adaptable to computerized handling. (See Chapter 5 and Figure 6-1.)

The phrase *rate negotiation* has two applications. For *common carriers*, it means attempting to obtain a new, usually lower, rate within the regulated system. The service offered by the common carrier meets the traditional common carrier obligations (as discussed in Chapter 5) along with other service requirements imposed by the ICC or other regulatory body. When dealing with *contract carriers*, negotiation can include both rates and levels of service.

Common Carrier Rate Determination and Negotiation

It is, at best, extremely difficult to determine the correct freight rate for a shipment. A noted transportation rate consultant has mused:

> The able lawyer who may never have engaged in practice before the Interstate Commerce Commission has learned to approach the freight tariff warily and with distrust. Even the experienced traffic manager has at times found his own tools, the freight tariffs, reaching a state of baffling complexity.[1]

Rate determination is very important to every traffic manager. Although the carrier has a legal obligation to determine the correct rate, this is an extremely complex process that usually is open to a broad range of interpretations.

In most situations many applicable rates can be found in the tariffs. If the carrier representative is left to determine the correct rate, he has no

[1] Edward A. Starr, *The Interpretation of Freight Tariffs* (Fort Worth: Transportation Press, 1961), p. 1.

Figure 6-1 Shippers' Traffic Departments Are Computerizing

"Thank God there's one thing they'll never be able to computerize..."

Cartoon by E.A.C. Wren from *Air World*, 31, no. 4, © 1979, Exxon Corporation.

incentive to actively search the tariffs for the *lowest* applicable rate. Instead, the carrier representative will typically use the rate that is easiest to find. Experienced consultants know the industry rule of thumb that the "correct" freight charge quoted by the carrier averages about 10 per cent higher than the lowest applicable legal rate.

Freight tariffs and rates are not engraved in stone. Given sufficient lead-time and patience, freight rates can be and frequently are altered by negotiations between the carrier and the shipper. After additional, often routine, procedures have been followed, the rate can be officially changed.

One general principle must always be kept in mind when negotiating with a carrier: the proposed arrangement must also be beneficial to the carrier. Michael Uggens, traffic analyst with Chevron, USA, has noted:

> The single most important question in a rate negotiation is "What is in it for the other party?" Everything else is secondary. Unless there is a specific incentive for the carrier to take the shipper's desired action or for the shipper to use the carrier's proposed rate, both parties are basically wasting their time. The greater the incentive, the higher the probability for success.[2]

Before considering strategies helpful in negotiating with a carrier, the shipper must remember that only a Pyrrhic victory can be achieved if the

[2] Michael W. Uggen, "Negotiating with Carriers: Rates," *Distribution* (March 1983), p. 66. See also, Donald R. Souza, "Shipper-Carrier Rate Negotiation: A New World for the Traffic Manager," *Traffic World* (March 19, 1984), pp. 34–38.

negotiated rates are so low that they sap the financial strength of the carrier and lead to the carrier's demise. When a carrier fails, this will involve service interruptions—freight that has been accepted by the carrier may not be delivered when the system shuts down—and the shipper will need to establish a new relationship with a new carrier.[3]

Although numerous factors influence the shipper to negotiate lower rates with the carrier, there are three situations in which the shipper's arguments are most likely to prevail. The first, and generally conceded to be the most important situation, is the volume of new business—for both the shipper and the carrier—that would result from a rate change. Assume, for example, that the existing commodity rate of widgets from Knoxville, Tennessee, to San Antonio, Texas, is $1.80 per CWT [100 pounds] and at the current rate the shipper ships 100,000 pounds per year. Assume further that the shipper has determined by market research that if freight costs can be reduced 30 cents per CWT, he can increase sales in San Antonio to 300,000 pounds per year. The carrier would probably see real merit in this lower rate (assuming it covers the variable costs of carriage) because its total revenue would increase from $1,800 to $4,500. Therefore, the carrier undoubtedly would favor the proposed rate change before the appropriate rate bureau.

A second situation that encourages lower carrier rates is to compare the present rates with the existing rates on similar and often competing products. Assume the railroad commodity rate for apples from Saint Joseph, Michigan, to Greenville, South Carolina, is $2.85 per CWT and that you are the traffic manager for a firm that ships pears, and the rate for pears is $3.71 between the same two cities. Because these two products compete, and the value of each is roughly the same (as are costs of carriage), an argument can be made that the rate on pears should be closer to the rate on apples. If the railroad will not support the proposed rate reduction, as traffic manager you can take your case to the ICC, complaining that Sections 1 and 3 of the Interstate Commerce Act have been violated.

The final situation that will bring about carrier rate reductions involves the rates of competing forms of transportation. If another transport mode has a lower rate and is actively participating in the carriage of freight based on this lower rate, then this factor is often very influential regarding a carrier's decision to lower its existing rate. Related to this is the shipper's threat of using or expanding the usage of private transportation. Figures 6-2 and 6-3 discuss rate and service negotiation at Apple Computer and Mead Data General.

Rate and Service Negotiation with Contract Carriers

When dealing with contract carrier negotiation, both rates *and* service are subject to negotiation. In 1978 the ICC allowed railroads to enter into contracts with shippers, a move that helped make the railroads more competi-

---

[3] Thomas A. Foster, "Financial Profile 1982: Motor Carriers," *Distribution* (June 1983), pp. 59–66.

Figure 6-2 An Example of Rate Negotiation at Apple Computer

The traffic department's cost-reduction efforts focus largely on what Mr. Briody calls the most readily controllable freight...as opposed to every single piece of cargo that moves in the far-flung Apple network. "I would absolutely lose my mind if I tried to control 100 percent of the freight," he says.

This "controllable freight" represents some 60 to 70 percent of Apple's total transportation bill. These are the regular, high-volume movements from vendors to manufacturing plants, and from the plants to the distribution centers. Until recently, much of this freight moved via costly premium transportation, with little or no coordination provided at the corporate level. Today, however, the high-volume freight moves under tight traffic-department control, and often at low, negotiated rates.

Here is a good then-vs.-now illustration. In the past, components moving from Singapore to the Dallas manufacturing plant went by air all the way—from Singapore to San Francisco, and from there to Dallas. The freight charges were staggering. Upon examining the freight bills, the traffic department discovered that Apple was paying more to fly the cargo from San Francisco to Dallas (1,780 air miles) than from Singapore to San Francisco (7,338 miles).

The department further found that with as little as 6,000 pounds, it could send the San Francisco-to-Dallas shipments by truck and save money. As it turned out, Apple had little trouble amassing the 6,000 pounds. In fact, the company now ships more than 160,000 pounds a month between the two points. Most of this traffic moves in full truckloads under negotiated rates.

The switch from air to truck necessitated a one-time adjustment to the Dallas production schedule. Once that adjustment was made, however, the truck deliveries proved sufficiently timely to keep production running smoothly. The cargo moves mostly via two-man driver teams; typical transit time is under 48 hours.

"We saved $450,000 in freight costs in the first three months alone," says Mr. Briody, adding that now only about 5 percent of the Singapore-to-Dallas traffic still goes all the way by air. These kinds of programs further establish the department's credibility, he says, by demonstrating that cost-effective transportation-purchasing decisions need not upset the production applecart.

Source: Francis J. Quinn, "The Manager as Diplomat," *Traffic Management* (October, 1984), p. 82. Used with permission.

tive with contract motor carriage. However, because of legal challenges, rail contracts were of questionable legality until 1980, when they were specifically authorized by the Staggers Rail Act. Since 1980 over 22,000 rail contracts have been filed with the ICC, and this number continues to grow rapidly. What follows are summaries of some contract elements in agreements that have been negotiated between railroads and individual shippers.

- In an agreement between the Western Pacific Railroad and Sierra Pacific Industries involving the movement of woodchips moving to California ports for export, the shipper agreed to pay an additional $150 per month per

The Elements of Physical Distribution/Logistics Systems

Figure 6-3 Rate Negotiation and Analysis at Mead Data Central

At first glance, Mead Data Central would seem to have little concern with traffic. The Dayton, Ohio-based company provides instant research services to its subscribers, who include lawyers and news reporters, through on-line access to its specialized data banks. By using such programs as LEXIS and NEXIS, the company's clients can avoid maintaining extensive libraries and spending precious time looking up bits of information.

To gain access to these data bases, however, a subscriber needs a terminal or personal computer. Many choose terminals manufactured at Mead Data Central's Dayton plant. Until a couple of years ago, only a modest number of these terminals were produced. Yet as more and more professionals became sold on the virtues of on-line access to data, production increased. Currently, the company ships several hundred units daily. Because the units weight only about 40 pounds apiece, overall tonnage is small. Even so, the speed requirement and the high value of the goods shipped run Mead Data Central's annual freight bill up well over $1 million.

By mid-1981, the company recognized that it needed more adequate traffic and distribution control. In September of that year, it added Kathryn Greene to the staff as traffic manager.

With 15 years of distribution experience, Mrs. Greene immediately set out to fulfill a threefold mission:

- To establish procedures and controls for managing all outbound shipments.
- To analyze shipping patterns and optimize use of modes.
- To negotiate the lowest rates possible while ensuring fast service and adequate protection of the high-value equipment.

Starting From Ground Zero

"We introduced shipping controls in steps," Mrs. Greene recalls, explaining that she felt the other departments would accept the new procedures more readily that way. "In the past anyone with a shipment to make simply called the carrier and ordered a pickup. Virtually all freight moved via air forwarder and no records were maintained.

"Step one," Mrs. Greene continues, "was to ask the departments to make their calls instead to the traffic unit, where we logged them in on newly created forms so that data for review, analysis, could be maintained properly. This also opened the door for the first time to commodity freight-cost analysis."

To measure existing distribution patterns, Mrs. Greene's group then sought to identify which companies supplied transportation services. This had to be done through a manual analysis of

Mead Data Central's vendor file to determine which carriers were used and what they transported.

The analysis revealed that data terminals and printer units constituted most of the freight. Armed with this information, the traffic department called in potential carriers and invited them to bid on this traffic. The companies included all airlines and airfreight forwarders serving the Dayton area. CF Air Freight made the most competitive bid and was awarded the air portion of the traffic.

By analyzing past shipping patterns and current data, Mead Data Central also created a more cost-effective modal mix. "Our goal was to continue with fast deliveries, but with significant cost reductions," says Mrs. Greene of this effort.

One-fourth of Mead Data Central's outbound shipments now qualify for deferred air shipment via CF Air Freight. UPS now handles another third of the company's shipments. The remaining traffic still moves via regular air-forwarder service. Yet costs for this traffic, too, have been cut thanks to rate negotiations conducted by the traffic department. Through these changes, Mead Data Central has reduced its shipping cost per unit by 45 percent. Moreover, because carriers are directly accountable to the traffic unit, service performance has improved perceptibly.

Source: "High-Tech Company Stresses Cost-Control Basics," *Traffic Management* (June, 1984), pp. 39–40. Used with permission.

car in return for the railroad's agreement to assign twenty-five cars for the exclusive use of the shipper.[4]

- In an agreement between the Chicago and Northwestern Railroad, and Woodchem, Inc., regarding the movement of lignin liquor from Peshtigo, Wisconsin, to Fremont, Nebraska, the shipper agreed to route at least 90

---

[4] All these examples are from an ICC announcement, dated July 11, 1980, that a "contract advisory service" had been established by the ICC to aid shippers.

per cent of this business, and also to meet an annual minimum volume requirement, via the railroad. In return, the railroad charged a lower rate. If volume requirements were not met, the railroad could assess additional charges.

- In an agreement between the Chicago and Northwestern and General Foods Corporation involving the carriage of grocery products from Northlake, Illinois, to eight consignees in the St. Louis area, the shipper agreed to pay the railroad an additional amount (ranging from $117 to $159 per car) when the car was delivered on a precise, previously scheduled, day.
- In an agreement between Ford Motor Company and the Missouri Pacific Railroad involving the movements of new autos and auto parts between several specified points, the railroad agreed to give the shipper an allowance if thirty or more cars were tendered at one time or if the cars arrived at their destinations late. In return Ford agreed to ship 95 per cent of this business via Missouri Pacific.
- In an agreement between Del Monte Corporation and the Western Pacific Railroad, the railroad agreed to grant allowances ranging from $50 to $125 per car if the customer utilized the cars in both directions to carry canned goods. The shipments had to be routed via the Western Pacific Railroad, and established tariff rates (less the allowance) would apply.
- In an agreement between the Santa Fe Railroad and General Foods Corporation for shipments of grocery products moving in trailers aboard flatcars from Houston to Chicago, the shipper agreed to ship a minimum of six million pounds per year. The shipper further agreed to pay an additional $75 per trailer when 90 per cent or more of the trailers completed the rail movement within 96 hours. The railroad agreed to furnish sufficient trailers to meet the six million pounds per year volume requirement.

The contract provisions illustrate different aspects of service that are important to the shipper and may be subject to negotiation. Also, they indicate that shippers are willing to pay for improved quality of railroad service. Once a contract is entered into, the burden of meeting the shipper's obligations and monitoring the carrier's performance rests on the shipper's traffic manager.

Contracts with other modes of transport can follow some of the objectives indicated in the rail examples just given. Another form of service is for the carrier to assign one or more vehicles to the exclusive use of the shipper for a specified amount of time. A retail store may contract with one or more truckers to help with holiday deliveries.

An additional aspect of a contract between carrier and shipper is illustrated by the 3M Corporation. Roy W. Mayeske, director of transportation, uses what he calls a competitive service clause in contracts with carriers. It is used for cargo moving between specific cities. Part I of the "competitive service clause" states:

> If, at any time during the term of this contract, seller [carrier] should sell to any other customers, except affiliates or subsidiaries of seller, service of at least equal quality at a rate lower than in effect hereunder, buyer [ship-

per] shall receive the benefit of the lower rate on all deliveries of service which are made during the period when such lower rate is in effect.

Part II reads:

If buyer is offered service of equal quality at a rate lower than that in effect hereunder, seller agrees to *discuss* [the] *possibility* of reducing his rate hereunder.

A final important clause used by 3M is the following:

It is the further intent of the parties hereto that they shall mutually benefit from the terms, conditions and provisions of this agreement and, in the event that either party shall suffer a gross inequity resulting from the terms, conditions, or provisions, the parties shall negotiate in good faith to resolve or remove such inequity. If (after negotiation in good faith, including annual charge and volume negotiations), the parties are unable to agree upon new terms prior to the expiration of the period, either party may terminate this agreement by giving ———— days written notice.[5]

Carrier Selection

The selection of the mode and then the specific carrier within that mode is another of the fundamental activities of the traffic department. However, the decision regarding which transport mode or modes to actually use may not be exclusively determined by the traffic manager. In many corporations, the decision to use more expensive forms of transportation (i.e., air freight) is decided by more senior management. A survey by *Distribution Worldwide* found that the traffic department typically initiated the research on the modal choice and then presented its findings to the vice-president of physical distribution, or materials, or manufacturing, who made the decision. The same survey found that once the modal decision has been decided, then the traffic department was charged with the responsibility of selecting the specific carriers.[6]

While there are numerous factors to consider when selecting a carrier, the following five tend to be the most important: rates, consistency of service, speed, loss and damage record, and special services available. Three of these factors will be examined here. Loss and damage and special services will be covered later in this chapter.

[5] Roy W. Mayeske, "Contracting—A Partnership," *Annual Proceedings of the Northwest Shippers Advisory Board* (Feb. 1983), pp. 16–17. See also: Lisa H. Harrington, "Negotiating With Motor Carriers: Think Long-Term!" *Traffic Management* (May, 1985), pp. 58–65.

[6] Janet Bosworth Dower, "Will the Real Airfreight Buyer Please Stand Up?" *Distribution Worldwide* (Jan. 1974), pp. 28–29. See also, Roger E. Jerman, Ronald D. Anderson, and James A. Constantin, "How Traffic Managers Select Carriers," *Distribution Worldwide* (Sept. 1978), pp. 21–24; Edward R. Brunning and Peter M. Lynagh, "Carrier Evaluation in Physical Distribution Management," *Journal of Business Logistics,* 5:30–47, (1984), and George A. Yarusavage, "Carrier Evaluation and Selection," *Annual Proceedings of the NCPDM* (1983), pp. 852–868.

Rates

Rates vary substantially today between different modes of transportation *and* between carriers of the same mode. The latter is a result of less collective rate making—a procedure that allowed carriers to establish rate bureaus that set common rates between cities for their members—which has forced carriers to establish their own rates. Remember that all modes today will negotiate rates for each customer. Diane H. Greenwood, vice-president of the Miami-based Industrial Traffic Consultants, Inc., noted that for her clients, the rate charged is the most important factor in carrier selection.[7]

Consistency of Service

Inventory holding costs are expensive and, if a high degree of dependability of service is offered by the carrier, smaller inventories would be sufficient at each location. Assume a retailer sells 100 units per day and when reordering, places an order for 1,000 units. Assume that one day delivery is possible and always achieved. Then the retailer would reorder when inventory was at 100 units. The next day the 100 units remaining would sell, and the following day the new order of 1,000 units would arrive. Now assume instead of taking the usual one day for the order to arrive, it takes several days more. The retailer would be out of stock, and his customers would be unhappy. To avoid this happening again, the retailer would have to maintain, perpetually a larger *safety stock*—additional inventory designed to prevent an excessive number of stock-outs. This would be expensive. An alternative would be to find a more dependable delivery carrier.

Speed of Service

The specific time that it takes to transport a shipment is typically less important than the consistency of service that the carrier can offer. Nevertheless, if two competing carriers offer equally reliable service, then the actual speed or time of delivery is important because less money is invested in goods in transit. Speed is important for any type of perishable food.

While all freight on the airplane moves through the air at the same speed, various items and containers travel under different priorities. "First flight out" service guarantees that the freight will be on the next outbound plane. Other plans provide for "overnight" or "second-morning" delivery. Some new contract rates that one airline has with movers of household goods promise "five-day" delivery (which is very slow but fills up otherwise unutilized capacity). Passenger planes offer additional small parcel service, with the packages being checked in at the passenger counter, moving with passenger baggage, and being picked up by an individual at the destination airport. Individual courier services, which offer varying degrees of pickup, delivery, and escort services for packages, and air freight forwarders, which have their individual service agreements with shippers, also use the same airplanes.

---

[7] Lisa H. Harrington, "Carrier-Selection Criteria Change with the Times," *Traffic Management* (Sept. 1983), p. 60.

In important markets, or "corridors," carriers often attempt to introduce and operate faster equipment so that they can earn a reputation for speed. Figure 6-4 shows the Santa Fe Railway's "Fuel Foiler," a lightweight container train with special containers. These were introduced on the Santa Fe's Los Angeles-Chicago run. A train such as this will receive top priority when traveling on the Santa Fe system.

Documentation

The traffic department is responsible for completion of all documents necessary for the transportation of the firm's products. The most important single document is the *bill of lading*, which is the basic operating paper in the transportation industry.[8]

The bill of lading functions as a delivery receipt when products are tendered to common carriers. The carrier, upon receipt of the freight, signs the bill of lading and gives the original of this document to the shipper. The signed original of the bill of lading is the shipper's legal proof that the carrier received the freight.

The second function of the bill of lading is that it contains a binding contract specifying the duties and obligations of both the carrier and the shipper. When properly executed and signed by both the carrier and the shipper, the bill of lading is a contract. The bill of lading contract for surface carriers is basically standardized by law and greatly simplifies the traffic manager's job because it specifies exactly the duties of the traffic manager as the shipper and the duties of the carrier.

There are two types of bills of lading: the *straight* and the *order*. On a *straight* bill, which is printed on *white* paper, the name of the consignee is stated in the appropriate place and the carrier is under a strict legal obligation to deliver the freight to the named consignee and to no one else. Ownership of the goods is neither stated nor implied. On the *order* bill of lading, which is printed on *yellow* paper, the name of the consignee is not specified. Assume that a lumber company in Seattle has loaded a boxcar of plywood that it has not yet sold. It would use an order bill and tender the shipment to the Burlington Northern Railroad, which would start the car moving toward Chicago. Once a buyer for the plywood is found, the shipper would send via mail the original copy of the order bill to a bank near the buyer and would also tell the buyer which bank had possession of the order bill. The buyer would go to the bank and pay for the plywood, and the bank would give the original copy to the buyer. The buyer would take it to the railroad, and the railroad would deliver the carload of plywood. (Order bills are used in one other situation—that involving "slow payers"—because they guarantee that the customer must pay for the products prior to receipt.)

An additional classification of bills is the specific form—long, short, and preprinted. The long-form bill of lading, which may be either an order or straight bill, contains the standard information on the face of the bill (see

---

[8] See Colin Barrett, "Stay True to the Form!" *Distribution* (June 1984), pp. 30–32.

Figure 6-4 Santa Fe Railway's Fuel Foiler

The train is on the right. Car's frames are much narrower: wide areas hold the chassis' rubber tires. Containers can handle bulk goods, liquids, or packaged goods and can be stacked several high.

Credit: Santa Fe

Figure 6-5) and the reverse side contains the entire contract between the carrier and the shipper. The reverse side is printed in extremely small print. Because of the difficulty of reading the long-form contract and because of the printing costs of including the contract on all bills, in 1949, the railroads and motor carriers adopted the short-form bill of lading. Instead of printing the entire contract on the back of the bill, the short form has the following statement on its face: "Every service to be performed hereunder shall be subject to all the terms and conditions of the Uniform Domestic Straight Bill of Lading."

Another type of bill, which may be a long, short, order, or straight, is *preprinted.* In theory, the bill of lading is prepared and issued by the carrier. In fact, however, many shippers buy their bills and then have them preprinted with a list of the products that they regularly ship. Figure 6-6 illustrates a preprinted, short form, bill of lading. Shippers go to the expense of buying and printing their own bills because, in practice, they frequently prepare their own bills prior to calling the carrier. The preprinted bill can be prepared more rapidly and with less chance for error. The shipper can insert the correct rate rather than letting the carrier determine it. Shippers' highly computerized systems may generate the bill of lading document along with other documents that adjust their inventory control records (to take into account the items that have just been deleted) and prepare a separate bill for the goods, which is mailed to the customer.

The other basic document that the traffic manager must be familiar with is the freight bill. It is an invoice, submitted by the carrier, requesting to be paid. Often, the traffic manager must approve each freight bill before it is paid.

Routing

The top section of Figures 6-5 and 6-6 has a line entitled *route.* A rail shipper has an absolute right to route shipments to their destinations. This provision was added to the original 1887 act by the Mann-Elkins Act. The purpose was to give the shipper the ability to patronize rail carriers that were offering good services but did not serve the origin city.

The Interstate Commerce Act says nothing about the right to route a shipment via motor common carriage. It was always assumed that this privilege did not exist in the trucking industry. In recent years, however, the ICC has ruled that it is an unreasonable motor carrier practice to sign a bill of lading that has routing instructions on it and then ignore them. The trucker can refuse to accept a shipment with specific routing instructions. However, if the trucker signs the bill that specifies the routing on a shipment, he must follow the instructions.

Should the traffic manager specify routing instructions on the bill of lading? A helpful rule to keep in mind regarding this issue is that in the absence of any shipping directions, the carrier is legally obligated to use the least expensive available route. As a general rule, it is best not to specify

Figure 6-5 A Long-Form Bill-of-Lading

UNIFORM FREIGHT CLASSIFICATION 7

(Uniform Domestic Straight Bill of Lading, adopted by Carriers in Official and Western Classification territories, March 15, 1922, as amended August 1, 1930, and June 15, 1941.)

UNIFORM STRAIGHT BILL OF LADING
Original—Not Negotiable

Shipper's No..........

(To be Printed on "White" Paper)

Agent's No............

Company

RECEIVED, subject to the classifications and tariffs in effect on the date of the issue of this Bill of Lading,

at..., 19...

from...

the property described below, in apparent good order, except as noted (contents and condition of contents of packages unknown), marked, consigned, and destined as indicated below, which said company (the word company being understood throughout this contract as meaning any person or corporation in possession of the property under the contract) agrees to carry to its usual place of delivery at said destination, if on its own road or its own water line, otherwise to deliver to another carrier on the route to said destination. It is mutually agreed, as to each carrier of all or any of said property over all or any portion of said route to destination, and as to each party at any time interested in all or any of said property, that every service to be performed hereunder shall be subject to all the conditions not prohibited by law, whether printed or written, herein contained, including the conditions on back hereof. which are hereby agreed to by the shipper and accepted for himself and his assigns.

(*Mail or street address of consignee—For purposes of notification only.*)

Consigned to...

Destination...State of.........................County of...........................

Route..

Delivering Carrier...Car Initial.....................Car No......

No. Pack-ages	Description of Articles, Special Marks, and Exceptions	*Weight (Subject to Correction)	Class or Rate	Check Column	Subject to Section 7 of conditions, if this shipment is to be delivered to the consignee without recourse on the consignor, the consignor shall sign the following statement:
					The carrier shall not make delivery of this shipment without payment of freight and all other lawful charges.
					(Signature of consignor.)
					If charges are to be prepaid, write or stamp here, "To be Prepaid."
					Received $............ to apply in prepayment of the charges on the property described hereon.
					Agent or Cashier.
					Per................ *(The signature here acknowledges only the amount prepaid.)*

*If the shipment moves between two ports by a carrier by water, the law requires that the bill of lading shall state whether it is "carrier's or shipper's weight."

Note.—Where the rate is dependent on value, shippers are required to state specifically in writing the agreed or declared value of the property.
The agreed or declared value of the property is hereby specifically stated by the shipper to be not exceeding

Charges advanced:

$.....................

..................................per........................

.................................Shipper.   ....Agent.

Per.................................   Per.................................

Permanent postoffice address of shipper...

Reproduced by permission of tariff publisher.

routing instructions unless there is a good reason to do so. Railroads, for example, often work out expeditious interchange agreements with other railways at junction points that insure rapid transfer of the freight from one carrier to the next. This is also true of motor carriers.

Figure 6-6 A Preprinted Bill-of-Lading

NAME OF CARRIER

STRAIGHT BILL OF LADING — SHORT FORM — Original — Not Negotiable

RECEIVED, subject to the classifications and tariffs in effect on the date of the issue of this Bill of Lading,

the property described below, in apparent good order, except as noted (contents and condition of contents of packages unknown), marked, consigned, and destined as indicated below, which said carrier (the word carrier being understood throughout this contract as meaning any person or corporation in possession of the property under the contract) agrees to carry to its usual place of delivery at said destination, if on its route, otherwise to deliver to another carrier on the route to said destination. It is mutually agreed, as to each carrier of all or any of said property over all or any portion of said route to destination, and as to each party at any time interested in all or any of said property, that every service to be performed hereunder shall be subject to all the terms and conditions of the Uniform Domestic Straight Bill of Lading set forth (1) in Official, Southern, Western and Illinois Freight Classifications in effect on the date hereof, if this is a rail or rail-water shipment, or (2) in the applicable motor carrier classification or tariff if this is a motor carrier shipment.

Shipper hereby certifies that he is familiar with all the terms and conditions of the said bill of lading set forth in the classification or tariff which governs the transportation of this shipment, and the said terms and conditions are hereby agreed to by the shipper and accepted for himself and his assigns.

CARRIER'S NO.

SHIPPER'S NO.

FROM KILSBY - TUBESUPPLY   At TULSA, OKLA.   DATE   19

CONSIGNED TO

(Mail or street address of consignee—For purposes of notification only.)

DESTINATION   STATE   COUNTY

(To be filled in only when shipper desires and governing tariffs provide for delivery thereof.)

DELIVERY ADDRESS

No. Packages	KIND OF PACKAGE, DESCRIPTION OF ARTICLES, SPECIAL MARKS AND EXCEPTIONS			*Weight (Sub. to Corr.)	Class or Rate	Ck. Col.	FOB POINT
BOXES	PIPE OR TUBING WROUGHT STEEL, N.O.I.	☐ 20 GA. AND THINNER	HEAVIER THAN ☐ 20 GA.				
TUBES	PIPE OR TUBING WROUGHT STEEL, N.O.I.	☐ 20 GA. AND THINNER	HEAVIER THAN ☐ 20 GA.				Subject to Section 7 of Conditions of applicable bill of lading, if this shipment is to be delivered to the consignee without recourse on the consignor, the consignor shall sign the following statement:
PCS	PIPE OR TUBING WROUGHT STEEL, N.O.I.	☐ 20 GA. AND THINNER	HEAVIER THAN ☐ 20 GA.				The carrier shall not make delivery of this shipment without payment of freight and all other lawful charges.
BDLES	PIPE OR TUBING WROUGHT STEEL, N.O.I.	☐ 20 GA. AND THINNER	HEAVIER THAN ☐ 20 GA.				KILSBY - TUBESUPPLY
BOXES	PIPE OR TUBING ALUMINUM	☐ 2" DIA. AND UNDER	OVER ☐ 2" DIA.				(Signature of Consignor) If charges are to be prepaid, write or stamp here, "To be prepaid."
TUBES	PIPE OR TUBING ALUMINUM	☐ 2" DIA. AND UNDER	OVER ☐ 2" DIA.				Rec'd $
PCS	PIPE OR TUBING ALUMINUM	☐ 2" DIA. AND UNDER	OVER ☐ 2" DIA.				apply in prepayment of the charges on the property described hereon.
BDLES	PIPE OR TUBING ALUMINUM	☐ 2" DIA. AND UNDER	OVER ☐ 2" DIA.				Agent or Cashier Per (The signature here acknowledges only the amount prepaid.)
							Charges Advanced $
	☐ PACKING LIST						"Shipper's imprint in lieu of stamp; not a part of bill of lading approved by the Interstate Commerce Commission."
	☐ SMALL SHIPMENT SERVICE REQUESTED PREPAID / RELEASED VALUE NOT EXCEEDING 50¢ LB. SIGNED BY						The Fibre Boxes used for this shipment conform to the specifications set forth in the box maker's certificate thereon, and all other requirements of Rule 41 of the Consolidated Freight Classification.
							C.O.D.
	CUST. P.O. #						

KILSBY - TUBESUPPLY   SHIPPER, PER_____   _____

Permanent Post Office Address of Shipper

1819 NO. GARNETT ROAD   _____ A G E N T, PER_____
TULSA, OKLA. 74116

1

Transit Privileges

Transit privileges allow cargo to be stopped en route between its initial origin and final destination and to be unloaded, stored, and/or processed and then reloaded for shipment to its final destination. Key to the understanding of transit (or in-transit) privileges is the concept of tapering costs, which apply to all modes of transportation. As depicted in Figure 6-7, the rate increases with distance, but increases at a slower rate. A shipment from City A to City B, 200 miles, pays a rate of $2.90 per CWT, while a shipment twice as long from City A to City C pays only $4.10 per CWT instead of double the 200-mile rate. The logic of tapering rates is that some costs, such

The Traffic Management Function

215

Figure 6-7 Example of Tapering Rates for Sugar Beets

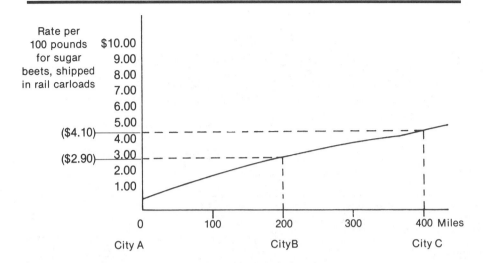

as most terminal operation costs, billing costs, and pickup and delivery costs, do not increase with distance. Therefore, as distance increases, these costs are spread over more miles, allowing the rate to increase less proportionately than distance.

> *Tapering* transportation *costs*, or *rates*, expressed in terms of cents per ton-mile, increase as distance increases, but at a slower rate of increase.

Assume City A in Figure 6-7 is in the center of a sugar beet producing area. A sugar beet dealer purchases sugar beets at relatively low prices in City A during harvest time, stores them, and then is lucky enough to resell them at City C, where prices are much higher. The merchant must decide where to store the sugar beets. Figure 6-7 illustrates that the logical storage point should be either in City A or City C but *not* in between because, with tapering rates, one long shipment is less costly than two shorter trips equal in distance to the long trip. Notice that storage in City A or City C results in one long shipment at $4.10 per CWT. If storage were at City B, the result would be a 200-mile shipment at $2.90. When the storage period ended, a second 200-mile shipment to City C would also cost $2.90 for a total transportation cost of $5.80. In other words, a decision to store at City B and ship twice would cost $1.70 per hundredweight more than storing at either City A or City C and shipping only once.

The result of the tapering rate structure is to keep freight moving and to discourage stopping, storing, or doing anything to the freight en route. This discourages producing intermediate goods or otherwise processing the product at any point between City A and City C. Railroads, in an attempt to disperse storage and other activities—often onto land that they owned be-

The Elements of Physical Distribution/Logistics Systems

cause of the federal land grant program—initiated the transit privilege concept. It allows products or raw materials to be shipped to an intermediate location, where they can be stored, compressed, blended, mixed, milled, inspected, refined, reconditioned, fabricated, assembled, etc. The regular freight rate is the rate from origin to the intermediate location. Then, generally up to one year later, the products can be shipped from this intermediate location to destination and only pay the *remainder* of the long-haul through rate. In Figure 6-7 $2.90 is paid from City A to City B. Upon shipment from City B to City C, only $1.20 is paid, so that eventually the total transportation cost equals $4.10, which is the same as the long-haul rate from City A to City C.

This is a *greatly simplified* explanation of how transit privileges work. They are a complex aspect of traffic management; there are traffic managers who work exclusively in this demanding area. (Just three of many complicating factors are rate changes during the interim period; rates for finished products are different than the rates for the raw materials used as production inputs; or the total weight of the products leaving the intermediate point can be significantly less or greater than what was originally shipped to the intermediate location.)

Loss and Damage

"Cargo loss and damage has been the bane of the transportation industry since the invention of the wheel."[9] Common carriers traditionally were slow in handling loss and damage claims. Therefore, in 1972 the ICC issued a new regulation,[10] which placed three requirements on all surface common carriers. First, common carriers must acknowledge receipt of each loss and damage claim within 30 days. Second, carriers are charged with the responsibility of promptly investigating all new claims. Third, all claims must be resolved within 120 days of their receipt or else the claimant must be given a written explanation as to the reasons why the carrier has neither paid the claim nor officially rejected it. Time limitations on various types of claims and appeals vary by carrier and by the fault for which he is allegedly responsible. Table 6-1 shows different applicable time limits for shipper action. Filing claims against carriers is a routine matter; Figure 6-8 shows a loss and damage claim form used by Zellerbach Paper Company.

If the carrier and the shipper are not able to resolve a dispute regarding a loss and damage claim, the dispute is handled by the court system, not the ICC. The law states that the claimant has nine months from the date the shipment is delivered to file a claim with a carrier. If the carrier and claimant cannot settle the issue, then the claimant has two years and one day from the date the claim is denied (in whole or in part) to file a claim in the appropriate federal district court. If the claim is not filed within this time

---

[9] Carlo J. Salzano, *Traffic World* (April 7, 1975).

[10] For further information, see *Loss and Damage Claims,* 340 ICC 515. See also the *86th ICC Annual Report,* pp. 59–61.

Table 6-1 Time Limits for Filing on Shipments Moving in Interstate or Foreign Commerce

VIA	Claims				Suits	
	Loss Damage or Delay	Concealed Damage	Non-Delivery	Overcharges	Loss, Damage or Delay	Overcharges f/
Air Freight (Domestic)	9 months & 9 days from shipping date (see exceptions) a/	Report in Writing within 15 days of delivery	9 months & 9 days from shipping date (see exceptions) a/	2 years from shipping date (see exceptions) a/	2 years from disallowance of claim	2 years from delivery or 6 months from disallowance, whichever is later. i/
Air Freight (International)	Damage 7 days from delivery Delay 14 days	7 days from delivery	120 days from shipping date. b/	2 years from arrival or scheduled arrival	2 years from arrival or scheduled arrival	2 years from arrival or scheduled arrival
Air Freight Forwarder	NOTE: Under Investigation by CAB	No Uniform Rules—Consult Individual Tariffs of Forwarder Used Before Selecting Forwarder			No Uniform Rules—Consult Individual Tariffs of Forwarder Used Before Selecting Forwarder	
Bus	9 months from delivery	If written notice not given within 15 days of delivery, claimant has burden of proving it did not cause the damage. c/	9 months and 15 days from shipping date	3 years from delivery	2 years plus 1 day from disallowance of claim	3 years from delivery or 6 months from disallowance, whichever is later. h/
Rail	9 months from delivery	If written notice not given within 15 days of delivery, claimant has burden of proving it did not cause the damage. c/	9 months after a "reasonable time" for delivery	3 years from delivery	2 years plus 1 day from disallowance of claim	3 years from delivery or 6 months from disallowance, whichever is later. h/
Steamship	1 year from delivery or scheduled delivery	Report in Writing within 3 days of delivery	1 year from scheduled delivery	2 years from shipping date or payment of charges whichever is later. d/	1 year from delivery unless extended in writing	6 months from shipping date or payment of charges, whichever is later, unless formal complaint filed with Federal Maritime Commission within 2 yrs. d/
Truck and Freight Forwarders	9 months from delivery	If written notice not given within 15 days of delivery, claimant has burden of proving it did not cause the damage. c/	9 months after a "reasonable time" for delivery	3 years from delivery	2 years plus 1 day from disallowance of claim	3 years from delivery or 6 months from disallowance, whichever is later. h/
UPS	9 months from acceptance by UPS	If written notice not given within 15 days of delivery, claimant has burden of proving it did not cause the damage. c/	9 months from acceptance by UPS	3 years from delivery	2 years plus 1 day from disallowance of claim	3 years from delivery or 6 months from disallowance, whichever is later. h/

a/ Exceptions filed for account of individual airlines in CAB No. 96, Official Air Freight Rules Tariff No. 1-B, Rule 60
b/ Airbill provision, but not authorized in Warsaw Convention.
c/ Former rules requiring notice in writing within 15 days held UNLAWFUL in Ex Parte 263, 340 ICC 515 586/
d/ Tariff rule requiring claims for adjustment of weights or measurement errors to be made before shipment leaves custody of carrier held UNLAWFUL by U.S. Court of Appeals in Dist. of Col. 7/13/76.
e/ Applies only to common carriers. For contract carriers and exempt commodity shipments, see individual contracts. If any, and/or state statutes.
f/ Also applies to filing complaints with the ICC against surface carriers.
h/ The extra 6 month period starts from the first disallowance by the carrier following the last resubmission of the claim by the claimant within the claim filing period. If the carrier brings an action to collect charges or collects same, an additional 90 days is granted from that date.

Source: Courtesy, *Distribution Worldwide* (June, 1977), pp. 38–39.

Figure 6-8 Claim Form Used by Shipper

(revised 12/28/80)

IF HANDWRITTEN—BEAR DOWN FIRMLY—THIS IS A 5 PART FORM.

CLAIM FOR LOSS and/or DAMAGE

This claim is made against the carrier named below by **ZELLERBACH PAPER COMPANY** for Loss and/or Damage in connection with the following described shipments:

R. R. Code: 26055301

OVER, SHORT AND DAMAGE

REPORT NO.________

Z P Co CLAIM NO. ________

REPORTED BY________ DATE OF REPORT________

CARRIER ________ DELIVERY DATE________

VENDOR ________ PURCH. ORD. NO. ________

INVOICE DATE ________ AMOUNT ________

CONSIGNOR	ORIGIN	ORIGINAL CAR NUMBER	TRANSLOADED AT:
CONSIGNEE	DESTINATION	Received at Destination in Car	
FREIGHT BILL (PRO) OR S/S B/L NUMBER: DATE:	WAY BILL NUMBER: DATE:	BILL OF LADING DATE: ISSUED BY:	

ROUTE

DETAILED STATEMENT SHOWING HOW AMOUNT CLAIMED IS DETERMINED

QUANTITY OR WEIGHT			DESCRIPTION OF GOODS	COST	DISC.	EXTENSION
OVER	SHORT	DAMAGED				

REMARKS:

	WEIGHT RATE	
PLUS FREIGHT		
LESS FRT. ALLOW		
PLUS LABOR	MAN HRS. RATE	
PLUS MATERIALS		
Total Amount Claimed		$

DATE TRANSP. CLAIM FORWARDED TO HDQTRS.	DEBIT NO.	ACCOUNT NOS.
PREPARED BY:	DATE	

INSPECTION CALLED FOR	DATE INSPECTED	COMPLETED

DISPOSITION OF SALVAGE: (√)

RETAINED		PICK UP	By:
DUMPED			Date:
HELD FOR CARRIER			Sales Order No.:

GUARANTY AND CERTIFICATION

The undersigned binds and guarantees, to reimburse the ________ whatever amount it may be required to or may pay on other claims of overcharge or for loss or damage on same shipment, or for damages, cost or expenses, incident to or growing out of such payments, or out of refusal to pay such claims made by any parties in case of presentation of claim at any time hereafter, accompanied by the missing original Freight Bill and/or Bill of Lading. The undersigned hereby certifies that this claim, if for loss or damage, does not exceed the destination value of the property, in the quantity shipped at time of delivery, or invoice prices less discounts or allowances, if any, and that the salvage allowance, if any, represents the actual amount realized from sale or use of damaged property, and that missing articles have not been received from any other source.

The foregoing statement of facts is hereby certified to be correct and reasonable.

Enclosure (check)

1–FB
2–BL
3–Invcice
4–Inspection Reports
5–Assignment
6–Salvage Report
7–

____
MANAGER TRAFFIC DEPT

ZB 174 REV. 7-73

PLEASE ADDRESS ALL CORRESPONDENCE AND PAYMENT TO: **ZELLERBACH PAPER COMPANY**
Headquarters Traffic Dept.
P.O. Box 7748 • San Francisco, Calif. 94120

(SHOW ZPCO. CLAIM NO.)

This Company will not be responsible for payments made other than by check payable to its order.

Courtesy Zellerbach Paper Company, San Francisco, Calif.

period, the statute of limitations is binding, and no further action can be taken against the carrier.

One of the most difficult and challenging aspects of claim work is the determination of the exact dollar amount of the damage. The law states that the *common* carrier is responsible for the *full actual loss* sustained by the shipper or consignee. How can this figure be determined? A common rule of thumb is the following:

The basic thought underlying the federal statutes which define the liability and prescribe the measure of damages in cases of this kind is that the owner shall be made whole by receiving the proper money equivalent for what he has actually lost, or, in other words *to restore him to the position he would have occupied, had the carrier performed its contract.* (Emphasis added.)[11]

A key factor in determining the value of the "full actual loss" is the word *earned.* Assume that a retailer owned the products shipped via a common carrier and that they were damaged beyond repair. The question arises, should the retailer recover the wholesale price or the retail price? If the products destroyed were going into a general inventory replacement stock, the retailer would receive only the wholesale price plus freight costs (if they had been paid) because the retail price has not been *earned.* Assume instead, that a product is ordered especially for a customer. When the product arrives, it is damaged and the retailer's customer states that he will wait no longer and cancels the order. In this situation, the retailer is entitled to the retail price because the profit would have been *earned* if the carrier had properly performed its service.

Another very difficult area for both shippers and carriers alike involves concealed loss or damage. If a shipment arrives in damaged condition and the damage is detected before the consignee accepts the goods, then the issue is not whether the carrier is liable but the dollar amount of the claim that the carrier must pay. However concealed loss and damage cases are more difficult to handle because the exterior package does not appear to be damaged or tampered with. At a later date, the consignee opens the package and finds that the product is damaged or missing. As can be appreciated, carriers are reluctant to pay concealed loss and damage claims for two reasons. If the package came through the shipment with no exterior damage, then there is a strong possibility that the product was improperly protected on the inside. If this is the case, the carrier is exempted from liability, since improper packaging is a *fault of the shipper.* Second, the possibility also exists that the consignee's employees broke or stole the products. One writer noted that "carriers do not have a monopoly on damaging freight or on employing 'light-fingered' employees."[12]

An important ally of the traffic manager who also wants to reduce freight claims is the carriers themselves. The railroads, for example, have been actively involved in the claim prevention area. Apparently their efforts are paying off, because 1982 represented the lowest loss and damage payout in fifty years.[13] Railroads are accomplishing these improvements via a number of techniques. The Southern Railway analyzes loss and damage claims on a computer for similarity of problem area occurrences and when they are discovered, corrective action is taken. The Bangor & Aroostook Railroad uses

[11] *Atlantic Coast Line Ry. Co.* vs. *Roe,* 118 So. 155.

[12] Richard R. Sigmon, *Miller's Law of Freight Loss and Damage Claims,* 3rd ed. (Dubuque: Brown, 1967), p. 141. See also, William J. Augello, *Freight Claims in Plain English,* 2nd ed. (Huntington, N.Y.: Shippers National Freight Claim Council, 1982) and "The Great Claims Debate," *Distribution* (May, 1985), pp. 39–46.

[13] "Win Some, Lose Some," *Railway Age* (June 1983), p. 43.

The Elements of Physical Distribution/Logistics Systems

a radar system to ensure that rail cars do not couple at excessive speeds.[14] (This entire discussion of loss and damage relates only to common carriers. In contract carriage, loss and damage are negotiated issues.)

Reparations

The preceding discussion just illustrated the importance of the traffic manager working closely with the carriers to solve mutual problems. In other cases, the traffic manager must be assertive to protect the interests of his or her company even if it involves alienating the carriers. Such is the case with *reparations*. These are payments made to a shipper by a carrier who has charged illegally high rates in the past.

To understand the procedure involved in securing a reparation payment, it is necessary to distinguish between a *legal* rate and a *lawful* rate. A *legal* rate is any rate that is filed with the ICC and subsequently published in a tariff. If a rate can be located in an official tariff, then by definition it is legal. A *lawful* rate, on the other hand, is a legal rate that does not violate any provision of the Interstate Commerce Act. Because the ICC processes thousands of rate changes daily, it is not possible for the commission to determine whether each rate change is lawful. Therefore, it is possible to have a legal rate that is not lawful.

Assume that a traffic manager of clay bricks is paying the legal commodity rail rate of $5.17 per CWT from San Diego to Philadelphia. However, he has located in another tariff that concrete bricks transported between the same cities pay only $3.67. The traffic manager believes that since there is no substantial difference between the two products, he—as a shipper—has been discriminated against. Therefore, he files a complaint with the ICC alleging that the $5.17 rate violates Sections 1 and 3 of the Interstate Commerce Act. Assume further that the ICC rules that the rate in question is unlawful. In this case only, the ICC will determine what the lawful rate should be. Finally, assume that the commission notes that clay bricks are subject to greater breakage than concrete bricks, and therefore should have a higher rate, say, $3.77 per CWT.

At this point, the traffic manager is eligible to receive a reparation from the railroad, because the carrier has been unlawfully overcharging the shipper in the past. The shipper or consignee can be reimbursed for the difference between the past legal rate and the new lawful rate for all shipments during the past 24 months.

Demurrage and Detention

Demurrage is a penalty payment made by the shipper or consignee to a railroad for keeping a rail car beyond the specific length of time when it should be released back to the carrier. Demurrage is also collected by inland water

[14] William S. Criss, "Damage Prevention Works on Conrail," *Traffic World* (March 21, 1983), pp. 39–47.

carriers if their barges are kept by the shipper or consignee for a longer period than allowed. Pipelines are also involved with demurrage if oil stored in tanks at destination is not removed within specified time limits.

Detention is basically the same concept as demurrage, except that detention usually refers to the trucking industry. Users of containers owned by the airlines are subject to similar charges.

For many traffic managers, handling demurrage and detention are important responsibilities. The rail demurrage tariffs typically state that demurrage payments will start after the expiration of the applicable "free time." For most cars, the receiver or consignee has 48 hours of free time (starting at the first 7:00 A.M. after the car has been delivered) to *unload* the freight car. The "free time" for *loading* a car is 24 hours. "Free time" does not count Saturdays, Sundays, or holidays. For example, if a rail car is delivered to the consignee at 10:00 A.M. on Thursday, the first day of free time starts on Friday at 7:00 A.M., Saturday and Sunday are not counted, and then the second day starts at 7:00 A.M. on Monday. The consignee must release the car to the carrier by 7:00 A.M. on Tuesday or else pay demurrage charges. The current ICC-authorized demurrage payment schedule, increased in early 1979, is $20 per day or any part of a day for the first four penalty days. During *penalty* days, all days, including weekends and holidays, are counted. For the next two penalty days the payment is $30 per day, and thereafter it is $60 per day. The railroad collecting the demurrage can keep only $10 per day if it is not the railroad which owns the car, with the remainder over $10 per day going to the railroad which owns the rail car.

Many traffic managers who are large users of rail cars have found it advantageous to enter into *averaging agreements* with the railroads. In an averaging agreement an accounting system of debits and credits is established. A credit is received every time the shipper or consignee releases a car one day early, and a debit is recorded each time a car is surrendered to a carrier one day late. Debits and credits can only be applied to the loading of the car, or to the unloading, but they cannot be transposed; i.e., credits earned for rapid loading cannot be applied against debits charged for slow unloading. At the end of each month the debits and credits are added. If there is a credit balance, the carrier does not pay the shipper or consignee. If, however, there is a debit balance, the shipper or consignee pays the carrier the appropriate payment based on the size of the debit balance. Each month the average agreement starts again; credits from a prior month cannot be brought forward.

Detention, as mentioned earlier, is the similar penalty payment assessed by the motor common carriers. In the case where the driver waits with the vehicle, the detention penalty often starts after one or two hours. If the trucker delivers a trailer for loading, the "free time" before detention begins is generally less than the railroads offer. This reflects the "faster pace" of the trucking industry. Detention charges are also assessed when either surface or air containers are held too long.

Tracing and Expediting

Tracing is a procedure that involves attempting to locate lost or late shipments. When the traffic department determines that a shipment has not arrived at destination on time, it may contact the carrier to whom it tendered the shipment and ask them to trace the shipment. This is a no-cost service offered by common carriers. Tracing should be requested only when a shipment is unreasonably late. Many of the airlines, larger trucking companies, and almost all of the railroads have computer systems that can be used to monitor the progress of all freight movements throughout their system. This allows the carrier's tracing procedure to be almost instantaneous.

Roadway Express, the largest common carrier trucking company in the United States, has recently established a tracing service known "QUIKTRAK PLUS." This sytem allows a customer to access Roadway's main computer to determine the exact status of a shipment. The customer dials a toll-free 800 phone number and can communicate with a computer anytime seven days a week. Roadway's computer is voice activated when the customer tells the computer its "pro" number, which is assigned to each shipment when a Roadway driver picks it up. The computer then checks its memory and a computerized voice response tells the customer exactly where the shipment is believed to be at that time.[15]

Expediting is another no-cost service of common carriers. It involves notifying the carrier as far in advance as possible of the need to expedite or rapidly move a shipment through the carrier's system. The carrier makes every effort to ensure that the shipment is delivered to destination with maximum speed. The carrier must have sufficient lead time to alert its employees regarding the shipment to be expedited. For the railroads this involves alerting the yardmaster at each relevant classification yard so that the expedited car can be singled-out when it arrives and immediately switched to the proper outbound train. Motor carriers generally notify the operations manager of each freight terminal that the product will be flowing through; in this way, the operations manager can ensure that the product will be quickly placed on the next outbound vehicle. (A specific responsibility sometimes assigned to a shift supervisor in a motor carrier terminal is to personally see that each piece of "expedited" freight is removed from the inbound truck and placed on the next outgoing truck.)

Over and Undercharges

The traffic manager is charged with the responsibility of not overpaying freight bills. Likewise, a carrier is legally bound not to undercharge customers, which is discriminatory. Therefore, both the carrier and the customer attempt to

[15] "New Computerized System Allows Roadway Shippers Direct Freight Tracking," *Traffic World* (Feb. 6, 1984), p. 27.

ensure that the correct freight rate is assigned the first time. However, due to the labyrinthine system of rates in the United States, the probability of errors is substantial. The Interstate Commerce Act states that both over and undercharge claims must be presented within three years from the delivery of the freight to the consignee.

The primary technique used to determine carrier overcharges (few traffic managers actively look for undercharges) is the freight-bill audit. There are two basic types of freight-bill auditing. The *internal audit,* as the name implies, is conducted by employees of the company involved. The *external audit* is performed by independent companies. Both types of audits are designed to detect current errors that result in overcharges and to correct these errors in the future.

Figure 6-9 is an example of a form letter used by a freight-bill auditor to request that a carrier reimburse him (on behalf of his client) for overcharges.

Figure 6-9 An Overcharge Claim Form

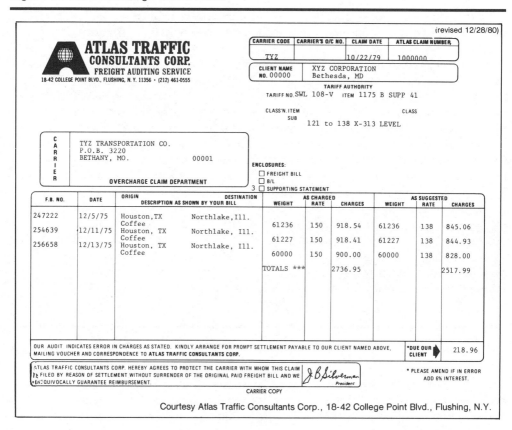

Courtesy Atlas Traffic Consultants Corp., 18-42 College Point Blvd., Flushing, N.Y.

Bank Payment Plans

The ICC requires that rail carriers be paid within five working days of receipt of the freight bill and that motor common carriers be paid within seven working days. Many traffic managers, in an attempt to meet these time limits conveniently, participate in what is known as *bank payment plans.* Once the traffic manager initiates this program with the nearest affiliated bank, the carriers submit their freight bills directly to the appropriate bank. The bank treats the freight bills as checks drawn on the shipper's freight account and pays the carriers by transferring the funds out of the shipper's account into the carrier's account. The bank sends the shipper the freight bills that were paid that day.

Bank payment plans are experiencing substantial growth because shippers appreciate the convenience of the bank handling the paperwork involved in paying freight bills. Carriers support the concept because of the ease and speed in which they are compensated for their transportation service rendered. Also, banks often present summaries of traffic activity that may be useful for further planning.

Transportation of Hazardous Materials

A hazardous material is defined in the Hazardous Materials Transportation Act of 1974 as "a substance or material in a quantity and form which may pose an unreasonable risk to health and safety or property when transported in commerce." Hazardous materials are very common, as indicated in Figure 6-10. In 1980 there were over 18,000 transportation-related accidents in-

Figure 6-10 Common Examples of Hazardous Materials

Products We Use	Component	Typical Waste	Type of Hazard
Electrical products	Printed circuit	Cyanides	Toxic
Televisions	boards	Metal sludges	Toxic
Micro-wave ovens	Wire	Caustics	Corrosive
Stereos		Acids	Corrosive
		Solvents	Flammable
Textile-mill products	Dyes	Waste organic	Toxic
Clothing	Materials	compounds	
Leather		Chromium shavings	Toxic
Synthetics		Solvents	Flammable
Paper products	Paper	Organic by-products	Toxic
Newspapers	Ink	Black liquor	Corrosive
Books		Waste ink/oils	Toxic

Source: Minnesota Waste Management Board, "Types of Wastes Generated During Production of Consumer Goods," (March 26, 1981), p. 1.

volving hazardous materials, the great majority involving the trucking industry.[16]

Most accidents involving hazardous materials do not involve loss of life, but there are exceptions. The *Wall Street Journal* of February 27, 1978, reported, "The 47-car derailment near the Florida Panhandle town of Youngstown caused a tank car to rupture, spewing a cloud of deadly chlorine gas across a busy highway. Authorities said at least seven persons were killed and about 67 were injured."

The potential danger involved in the transportation of hazardous materials has been recognized for a long time—the federal government has regulated this area since 1838—but the amount of hazardous materials being produced in this country has increased rapidly, especially in recent years. The 1838 law, entitled an "Act to Provide for the Better Security of the Lives of Passengers on Board Vessels Propelled in Whole or in Part by Steam," specified proper packaging, marking, and stowing requirements for such products as camphene, naphtha, benzene, coal oil, petroleum, oil of vitriol, and nitric acid. In 1866 Congress passed a law stating that the newly discovered superexplosive—nitroglycerine—could not be transported in the same vehicle or boat with passengers.

Since 1866 there have been literally hundreds of changes in federal statutes dealing with the transportation of hazardous materials.[17] The most important recent change was the Hazardous Materials Transportation Act, a subpart of the Transportation Safety Act of 1974. This law consolidated the regulation of hazardous materials into one DOT agency: the Materials Transportation Bureau. Major aspects of the 1974 law include (1) authorizing the DOT to regulate additional aspects of the transportation of hazardous materials, such as unloading procedures and the routing of shipments; (2) establishing training requirements for carriers, shippers and manufacturers of hazardous materials, and (3) increasing penalties for violating the law.

The training mandate in the 1974 act is a basic requirement for both shippers and carriers. Specifically, the DOT regulations state:

> It is the duty of each person who offers hazardous materials for transportation to instruct each of his officers, agents, and employees having any responsibility for preparing hazardous materials for shipment as to the applicable regulations.[18]

Westinghouse Corporation's training program illustrates the training requirements necessitated by the 1974 act. The firm periodically offers seminars on the packaging, marking, handling, and transportation of hazardous

[16] K. Eric Wolfe, "An Examination of Risk Costs Associated with the Movement of Hazardous Materials," *Annual Proceedings of the Transportation Research Forum* (1984), pp. 228–240.

[17] For an excellent history of federal regulation of hazardous materials, see Richard D. Hilton, "Consolidation of Hazardous Materials Regulation and Miscellaneous Proposals," *Transportation Journal* (Spring 1977), pp. 81–91. See also Bob Jordan, "Document the Danger," *Distribution* (May, 1985), pp. 23–29 and Stephen D. Strauss, "Regulation of Hazardous Waste Transportation In Ohio," *Transportation Practitioners Journal* (Spring, 1985), pp. 349–358.

[18] As quoted from, Don A. Boyd, "Current Status of Hazardous Materials Regulations," *Annual Proceedings of the NCPDM* (1977), p. 489.

materials. The meetings are attended by traffic people, engineers, warehouse people, and individuals involved in materials handling.[19]

It is imperative that every company's employees follow all federal safety regulations. Following regulations prevents accidents, lowers insurance rates, provides workers with a safer working environment, and minimizes fines from federal and state inspectors. The following are safety violations and the fines involved for not following federal hazardous materials regulations:

1. Lystad's, Inc., a shipper, gave improperly marked hazardous materials to a carrier. Fine: $3,000.
2. Buffalo Equipment and Chemical Company, a shipper, gave a carrier hazardous materials in nonauthorized containers. Fine: $3,000.
3. Harper Truck Service, a motor common carrier, transported poisons and foodstuffs in the same vehicle. Fine: $13,500.
4. Alamo Express, a motor common carrier, failed to use proper placards on a vehicle transporting hazardous materials. Fine: $2,500.[20]

Several federal agencies are considering adoption of additional regulations that would restrict trucks carrying hazardous chemical and radioactive materials to travel on certain routes. Such regulations, if enacted, would have a direct impact upon the traffic manager's routing decisions.

Consolidating Small Shipment Traffic

The small shipments problem represents one of the most bewildering situations faced by the traffic manager.[21] Small shipments are usually defined as those that weigh more than 50 pounds and less than 500 pounds. Shipments under 50 pounds can be handled relatively expeditiously and inexpensively by either the Postal System or by UPS. These shipments are transported almost exclusively by the trucking industry. Air courier services operate between many cities; they also specialize in small parcels.

Small shipments are problems for shippers for two reasons. First, truckers are reluctant to accept certain small shipments because of their physical characteristics. These products are often light in weight and called "balloon traffic." Typical products in this category are toys, stuffed animals, and furniture. Second, motor common carriers have been reluctant to accept small shipments based purely on the volume of the shipment or shipments tendered by the shipper. This action is usually a violation of the common carrier's legal obligation to transport all traffic that is specified by its certificates

[19] Joseph E. Levine, "Transportation of Hazardous Materials," *Annual Proceedings of the American Society of Traffic and Transportation* (1978), pp. 157–163.

[20] Howard J. Bosscher, "Transportation of Hazardous Materials," *Annual Proceedings of the American Society of Traffic and Transportation* (1978), pp. 173–174.

[21] See Walter L. Weart, "The Techniques of Freight Consolidation: An Area of Increased Interest Aided by Computers," *Traffic World* (March 19, 1984), pp. 46–60 and Walter L. Weart and Edward J. Marien, "Everybody Out of the Pool," *Distribution* (May, 1985), pp. 50–62.

and tariffs without discrimination. In some situations, motor common carriers dislike small shipments because they fail to cover costs.

The traffic manager must be innovative to compensate for the high cost and poor service given to small shipments. While there are numerous solutions, three primary approaches appear to be most readily used. The first involves the use of interfirm consolidation, or shipper cooperatives (see Chapter 4). The second type of solution involves *intrafirm consolidation*. In this case, the traffic manager seeks ways to consolidate shipments within his or her own firm. This typically involves a systematic study of the firm's past shipments in order to locate consolidation possibilities. The result of this analysis is the use of either *make-bulk* or *break-bulk* distribution centers. Products move rapidly through these facilities.

Figure 6-11 illustrates a break-bulk distribution center. Assume that a manufacturer of pharmaceutical products in Los Angeles has a number of wholesale customers in the Baltimore, Philadelphia, New York City, and Boston Areas. Previously each customer would place an LTL order from 300 to 1,000 pounds. The shipments would be sent at relatively high costs with low service levels because many motor common carriers believed that they were losing money on these shipments. To correct this problem, the traffic manager initiated a break-bulk distribution center in Philadelphia. Now, instead of numerous LTL shipments to the East Coast, one TL shipment is consolidated for delivery to the Philadelphia distribution center. Upon arrival of the TL shipment at Philadelphia, the products are distributed to other truckers who make the final delivery. The net result is that substantial trans-

Figure 6-11 A Break-Bulk Distribution Center in Philadelphia Receives Truckload Lots from Los Angeles and Then Distributes Less-Than-Truckload Lots to Points in the Northeast

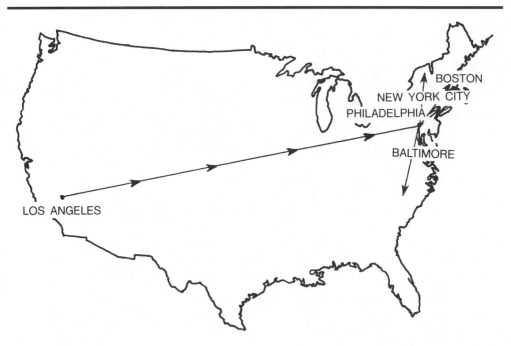

The Elements of Physical Distribution/Logistics Systems

portation savings are achieved, often with a corresponding *decrease* in the total delivery time of the product. This is because TL shipments, unlike LTL, travel to their destination with no intermediate stops.

One user of the break-bulk concept is Avon Products, which distributes cosmetics to its 375,000 representatives. W. R. Dykes, director of corporate traffic for the firm, described his distribution system this way:

> The Avon distribution system consists of two major components: line haul and delivery.
>
> *Line haul* service to the delivery company is practical since we control the shipping date for each order. A geographic area's orders are consolidated for truckload service to the city where the delivery company is located which ensures high-speed service at a reasonable expense.
>
> *Delivery company* service to the representative's residence is, obviously, the major factor in our distribution system since we are delivering to 375,000 representatives every two weeks. . . . The minimum acceptable level of on-time delivery performance is 99 per cent. We serve every city in the United States of 60,000 + population via an independent package delivery company. In doing this, we use the services of 185 delivery companies. The delivery companies are identified as local, extended or contract. Let me briefly explain the differences:
>
> • *Local delivery* companies serve the commercial zone of the city in which they are located. Their delivery market is urban/suburban.
>
> • *Extended delivery* companies, as the name implies, extend their service beyond the commercial zone. They serve the urban/suburban market plus other towns, rural routes, etc.
>
> • *Contract delivery* companies are generally dedicated to serving Avon exclusively. They operate five days each week for us and serve the largest metropolitan areas. Their delivery market includes urban, suburban, other town and rural routes.
>
> *UPS* is used in those markets which cannot practically be served by a delivery company.
>
> *Parcel Post or Bus* service is used for a very small percentage of our deliveries where delivery company service or UPS is not available.[22]

Commercial zones are established by the ICC in metropolitan regions to include all areas which should be considered the same as the central city for rate-making purposes.

Make-bulk distribution centers are illustrated in Figure 6-12. In this case, a multidivision firm near Seattle has a large customer in Dallas. Historically, each division would process its own orders and send them directly to Dallas, often in LTL quantities. The traffic manager now establishes a make-bulk distribution warehouse in Seattle. Each division now consolidates its shipments in Seattle, so that TL rates and service levels can be achieved for the Dallas movement.

---

[22] Comments of W. R. Dykes, director of corporate transportation for Avon Products, Inc., at the American Package Express Carriers Meeting, San Francisco, June 7, 1979.

Figure 6-12 A Make-Bulk Distribution Center in Seattle

Private Transportation

The final basic solution to the small shipments problem is the use of private "do-it-yourself" transportation. Traffic managers who become frustrated with the service inconsistencies on small shipments are often forced into private trucking. Some firms own and operate their own barges and ships, and airplanes. Some also own their own railcars and then contract with railroads to haul them, but in the field of domestic distribution and logistics, the term *private transportation* applies mainly to trucks.

The segments of the trucking industry not subject to ICC regulation are much larger than those segments that are. No precise statistics exist that accurately describe the extent of unregulated fleets of trucks. In the United States in 1983 there were 34.5 million registered trucks and 574,000 registered buses. However, the vast majority of trucks are small pickup body styles used by a family or individuals for personal transportation. There are only about 1.2 million truck-tractors registered in the United States. Truck-tractors pulling trailers or semitrailers are familiar sights on our highways. For-hire trucking companies operate about 421,000 truck-tractors. Other categories of firms that own large numbers of truck-tractors are leasing firms (which lease trucks to both regulated and unregulated truckers), food processors, manufacturing firms, retail chains, the construction companies, and petroleum distribution. ICC-regulated carriers also operate some two-axle trucks (known as bobtails) mainly to pick up and deliver shipments within urban areas. Over three million trucks are considered "farm" trucks. Some of these carry unprocessed agricultural commodities on highways and are exempt from ICC regulation. Other farm trucks are seldom on a highway; they are used mainly for work on the farm.[23]

The growth of private trucking can be equated to a number of factors. Without a doubt, the most important single factor is the improved level of customer service that private trucking makes feasible. The vice-president for trucking of Burlington Industries, which has a multimillion dollar private trucking operation, said:

> Private carriage was born out of necessity. The primary impetus was *service improvement*. If economies result it is a welcomed gain. We have found, however, that our private truck operations people have the ability to innovate and improvise on a day-to-day, hour-to-hour basis almost beyond imagination, and we are credited with a substantial improvement in sales in many product areas as a result of the service rendered to our customers.[24]

Another advantage is that private trucking vehicles can be rolling billboards which advertise the product. This factor can be important, especially if the vehicles look "sharp," have courteous drivers, and create a positive impression to the thousands of viewers who see the vehicles each day.

An additional factor comes into play if the traffic manager uses both private carriage and common carriage, which is often the case. The traffic manager has a good working knowledge of the costs of using both types of trucking service and is in a better position to evaluate merits of carrier rate increases. The traffic manager can threaten to take traffic from the common carrier and haul it in the in-house trucking operations.

Private trucking, for many companies, also offers the advantage of being less expensive than motor common carriers. This is typically the case when the private trucking operation is able to achieve full loads in both directions, although, it must be remembered that private truck operators do not have complete freedom in soliciting backhaul business. Private truckers can legally carry "exempt" commodities, such as unprocessed agricultural products. For example, a burial vault manufacturer in Minnesota has an extensive private trucking fleet, in which many of the trailers are equipped with "reefers" (refrigeration units). The sight of a burial vault semi-trailer with a refrigeration unit is somewhat unsettling. The logic is that empty burial vaults are transported to the southeastern and western regions of the United States and instead of "deadheading" (running empty) back, the trailers are loaded with vegetables and fruits for the return trip. Many private fleet managers use the services of a broker to insure a backhaul load of exempt agricultural products.[25] Until a few years ago, unprocessed agricultural products were about the only commodity that could be legally transported on the backhaul

[23] For additional information, see R. Neil Southern, "Structure of the Private Motor Carrier Industry," *Annual Proceedings of the Transportation Research Forum* (1982), pp. 129–134.

[24] Statement by George J. Agamemnon, in "PDM Challenged at Seminar," *Handling and Shipping* (July 1973), p. 57.

[25] See James A. Cooke, "Fleet Management: More for the Dollar," *Traffic Management* (Nov. 1983), p. 30.

for another company. Today, however, many new options exist. Six of which will now be examined.

In 1978 the ICC allowed, for the first time since the 1940s, a private carrier to also be a for-hire carrier. The company involved was known as the Toto Purchasing and Supply Company and, today, when a private carrier applies to the ICC to become a common and/or contract carrier as well, this is known as applying for "Toto" operating rights.[26] An example of this option is the Kleen Brite Laboratories private truck fleet. Located in Rochester, New York, the firm's major markets were in the Northeast. However, as the market expanded into the Southeast and Midwest, the firm started to experience longer empty backhauls. The firm has always benefited from excellent delivery schedules; therefore, the option of using common or contract carriers was eliminated. The solution to the empty backhauls came with the Toto decision by the ICC. The firm established K-B Transport and applied to the ICC for 48-state common carrier authority, which was granted in 1982. The result is that almost all empty backhaul miles have been eliminated.[27]

A second new option for private fleets is known as compensated intercorporate hauling. Until the 1980 Motor Carrier Act, it was illegal for two divisions of the same company to use the private fleet of one of the divisions or subsidiaries. Assume that a firm had a division in Oklahoma and another in North Carolina. The Oklahoma division had a private truck fleet that would send a truck to North Carolina and would have to return empty for lack of a backhaul. The North Carolina division simultaneously had cargo bound for the Oklahoma market, but it could not use the trucks of the Oklahoma division. This restriction was removed in the 1980 act to reduce the number of "deadhead" (empty) miles in the trucking industry. It is known as "compensated" intercorporate hauling because one division pays the other division for the service rendered. Over 1,000 companies have notified the ICC that they have taken advantage of this option once it was legalized.[28]

Another option available to private fleet managers is to establish an in-house brokerage service. Anyone can become a broker by applying to the ICC and paying a $350 application fee. A firm typically also applies to the ICC under Toto authority to become a contract and/or common carrier. The private fleet manager can now, acting as a broker, solicit additional business for its for-hire trucking service. It can also generate business for other for-hire carriers and be paid by them, usually 5 to 10 per cent of the transportation charges. An example of this concept is the Distron Division of Burger King Corporation, which has reduced its empty mileage to very low levels for its contract carrier operation.[29]

Single-source leasing is the fourth new alternative in private trucking. This allows a private trucking manager to lease *both* the vehicle and the driver from a single source, such as a leasing company or an owner-opera-

[26] 128 MCC 873 (1978).
[27] Lisa H. Harrington, "A Private Fleet Goes Public," *Traffic Management* (July 1984), pp. 37–40. See also, Joseph L. Cavinato, "Pricing Strategies for Private Trucking," *Journal of Business Logistics*, 3:72–84 (1982).
[28] "ICC Says It Is Following Mandate to Deregulate," *Traffic World* (Nov. 21, 1983), p. 12.
[29] "All Aboard to Be a Broker," *Distribution* (May 1983), p. 71.

tor. (This is an individual who drives a truck that he or she owns. In the past, these drivers typically transported unprocessed agricultural products.) This greatly simplifies a firm's ability to get into the private trucking business. Single-source leasing is usually an arrangement lasting over thirty days, but it is now legal to use this concept for shorter periods of time.[30]

A variation on single-source leasing is the fifth option, known as trip-leasing. It allows two types of activities to be legal: owner-operators can lease themselves and their vehicle to a private trucking operation for a single trip, and a private trucker can lease a truck and its driver to a for-hire (either a common or contract) carrier for a single trip. Both options allow private carriage more flexibility to operate with less empty mileage.[31]

The final alternative is for two firms to own and operate one private trucking fleet. A firm with shipments from Los Angeles to Kansas City is not able to find a backhaul. Another firm in Kansas City had the same problem when it ships to Los Angeles—deadhead trips to Kansas City. The solution, which until recently was not authorized by the ICC, is for the two firms to go together into the private carriage business. The result will be full trucks running in both directions.[32]

The decision to enter into a private trucking operation should be very carefully researched and analyzed. One factor often ignored in the cost calculations is the requirement that the private trucking operation be managed by a professional. All too often, the traffic manager assumes that, along with many other duties and responsibilities, he or she will also supervise the private trucking operation. When it becomes obvious that all but the smallest fleets require a full-time manager (who supervises vehicle scheduling, maintenance, labor relations, etc.), the firm finds itself with a large, unanticipated expense item.

Antitrust Considerations

As a result of deregulation, shippers are now subject to certain antitrust issues that were not applicable before 1980. This area is so new that it is difficult at this time to know what is legal and what is not. Two situations will be noted that *could* pose antitrust problems. The first involves a number of shippers in a particular area all agreeing not to use a carrier unless it establishes a certain rate or service for each shipper. This shipper strategy could be viewed as collusion to achieve rates or services not available to competitors. Another situation involves negotiating a contract that is so favorable to the shipper that it renders it difficult for a competitor to be able to compete because its transportation costs are so much higher than the

---

[30] "Appeals Court Affirms ICC Rules Permitting Single-Source Leasing," *Traffic World* (Feb. 27, 1984), p. 4. This decision was upheld by the Supreme Court in April, 1984.

[31] See James A. Cooke, "Proceed with Caution," *Traffic Management* (July 1984), pp. 22–24; and Joan M. Feldman, "Private Fleets Test Leasing Waters Slowly," *Handling and Shipping Management* (Nov. 1984), pp. 68–76.

[32] See Colin Barrett, "What Future for Private Trucking?" *Distribution* (Dec. 1984), p. 28.

favored company [33] Both of these situations *may* be innocent activities; but traffic managers are well advised to (1) learn the basics of the 1890 Sherman Act, the 1914 Clayton Act, and the 1914 Federal Trade Commission Act, and (2) seek the advice of an attorney who specializes in this area if any of the preceding or similar situations take place.

Summary

In all organizations the traffic manager's position is pivotal, and in some it is a life-and-death matter. While the traffic manager's activities involve nearly all aspects of a firm, the two most important areas of responsibility are (1) rate determination and negotiation and (2) carrier selection.

Because the rate-making process is so complex, the traffic manager must be vigilant to ensure that the firm is being charged the lowest rate possible. When negotiating with a carrier, the traffic manager's main tools are showing how a lower rate could increase volume, making comparisons with rates for similar commodities, investigating competing modes of transportation, and negotiating for different levels of service.

All of these responsibilities relate to the traffic manager's other main duty: carrier selection. Documentation is an especially important aspect of a firm's relations with its carriers. The main form of documentation, the bill of lading, functions as a delivery receipt, a contract for carriage, and evidence of title.

The problem of *loss and damage* claims is related to documentation. Common carriers are subject to pay the claimant the "full actual loss" sustained by either the shipper or consignee. Concealed loss and damage claims are undoubtedly the more difficult aspect of claims work. *Demurrage* and *detention* are penalty payments for keeping carrier equipment an excessive length of time. Averaging agreements often are a helpful method of reducing overall demurrage payments.

Two additional activities include *tracing*, which is a procedure to locate late shipments, and *expediting*, which involves insuring that a shipment arrives according to a prearranged schedule. The traffic manager is also responsible for detecting all over and under charges from the carriers. These are often detected by means of an internal and/or external audit. Bank payment plans are being extensively used because they greatly simplify the traffic manager's procedure for paying freight bills within the specified legal time frame.

Transit privileges, which are typically offered by railroads, allow intermediate cities between origin and destination locations to attract industrial activities. Because of the tapering principle, one long haul is less costly than two shorter movements. The transit privilege allows the two-part movement to be performed at the same charge as though one long haul had been performed.

The traffic manager can reduce the seriousness of small shipments prob-

---

[33] See Donald L. Flexner, "Potential Problem Areas for Shippers and Carriers Under Antitrust Laws," *ICC Practitioners' Journal* (Sept. 1984), pp. 571–582. This entire issue is devoted to antitrust issues in transportation.

lems by a program of freight consolidation. This typically involves the usage of shippers' cooperatives, make-bulk distribution centers, and break-bulk distribution centers. Some traffic managers decide to operate their own trucks: this is known as private carriage. Deregulation has resulted in many new options for the private truck fleet manager. Antitrust issues are a new area of concern to the traffic manager. Because penalties are harsh, the traffic manager is well advised to seek the assistance of an attorney who specializes in this area of the law.

Questions for Discussion and Review

1. Discuss briefly the major differences between the responsibilities and objectives of the traffic manager as opposed to the director or vice-president of physical distribution.
2. In recent years, senior corporate management has started increasingly to stress the importance of the traffic management function. Discuss briefly the factors responsible for this trend.
3. Why should a traffic manager be concerned with freight rate determination if the carrier is willing to tell him the correct rate? Discuss fully.
4. Discuss briefly the factors that are influential in negotiating with a carrier for a rate reduction. Be as specific as possible in your answer.
5. Summarize the rate negotiation activities that took place in either Figure 6-2 or 6-3.
6. Why do you think rail contract rates have become so commonly utilized in recent years?
7. What are some common factors that are typically addressed in rail contracts?
8. Discuss the features that 3M Corporation commonly uses in its contracts with both railroads and truckers. Do you think this is a good idea? Why?
9. Assume you are the traffic manager of a large furniture manufacturer. What information would you want to know before making your carrier selection decision?
10. Is consistency of service or overall carrier speed more important to traffic managers? Why? Defend your answer.
11. The bill of lading is the most important single document in transportation. Discuss the three basic functions of the bill of lading.
12. Discuss briefly the logic of the transit privilege. Be sure to mention why the railroads established them.
13. What is the basic rule of thumb regarding the determination of the *full actual loss* sustained by the shipper or consignee in a loss or damage claim situation?
14. Discuss completely the basic issues, conflicts, and problems involved in *concealed* loss and damage claims.
15. What procedure is necessary in order to collect *reparations* from a carrier? Be specific in your answer.
16. Discuss the basic idea of demurrage and how an averaging agreement can often be helpful in this area.

17. Discuss the basic types of freight bill auditing. Why is this procedure necessary in the first place?
18. Discuss the involvement of the federal government in the interstate transportation of hazardous materials.
19. The small shipments problem is one of the most perplexing quandaries in the transportation industry today. Discuss the *reasons* and *possible solutions* to this difficult problem.
20. Private transportation has been experiencing tremendous growth during recent years. Discuss completely the factors that have been responsible for this situation.
21. What is the significance of Toto operating rights? Do you think most private carriers should be involved in this situation? Why?
22. Do you believe private carriage will become more or less important in the future? Why?

Additional Chapter References

Allen, Warren H. "The Private Carriage Marketplace: Changing Times Reflect a New Purchase Logic." *Annual Proceedings of the NCPDM* (1984), pp. 153–158.

Altrogge, Phyllis D. "Railroad Contracts and Competitive Conditions." *Transportation Journal* (Winter 1981) pp. 37–43.

Bagby, John W., James R. Evans, and Wallace R. Wood. "Contracting for Transportation." *Transportation Journal* (Winter 1982), pp. 63–73.

Baker, Gwendolyn H. "The Carrier Elimination Decision: Implications for Motor Carrier Marketing." *Transportation Journal* (Fall 1984), pp. 20–29.

Blackwell, Richard B. "Pitfalls in Rail Contract Rate Escalation." *ICC Practitioners' Journal* (July–Aug. 1982), pp. 486–502.

Bradley, John C. "Antitrust Compliance Programs in the Motor Carrier Industry—A Primer on Why and How." *ICC Practitioners' Journal* (May–June 1982), pp. 395–412.

Bruning, Edward R., and Peter M. Lynagh. "Carrier Evaluation in Physical Distribution Management." *Journal of Business Logistics* (Vol. 5, No. 2, 1984) pp. 30–47.

Carr, Ronald G. "Railroad-Shipper Contracts Under Section 208 of the Staggers Rail Act of 1980: An Antitrust Perspective." *ICC Practitioners' Journal* (Nov.–Dec. 1982), pp. 29–41.

Cavinato, Joseph L., Alan J. Stenger, and Paul Novoshielski. "A Decision Model for Freight Rate Retrieval and Payment System Selection." *Transportation Journal* (Winter 1981), pp. 5–15.

Corsi, Thomas M., J. Michael Tuck, and Leland L. Gardner. "The ICC and Owner-Operators: Leasing Rules Modifications." *ICC Practitioners' Journal* (Nov.–Dec. 1983), pp. 54–76.

Courtney, J. L. "Technological Change and Multimodal Freight Competition." *Annual Proceedings of the Transportation Research Forum* (1984), pp. 116–121.

Cunningham, Wayne H.J. "Freight Modal Choice and Competition in

Transportation: A Critique and Categorization of Analysis Techniques.'' *Transportation Journal* (Summer 1982), pp. 66–75.

Daley, James M., and Raymond W. LaForge. ''An Analysis of Intercity Commuter Travel Behavior.'' *Annual Proceedings of the Transportation Research Forum* (1982), pp. 412–418.

Dowell, S., M.C. de Malherbe, I. H. Uhm, and R. de Halherbe. ''Risk Analysis of Hazardous Materials Transportation by Rail: A Comparative Study of Canada and the U.S.'' *Annual Proceedings of the Transportation Research Forum* (1984), pp. 23–33.

Due, John F. ''New Railroad Companies Formed to Take Over Abandoned or Spun-off Lines.'' *Transportation Journal* (Fall 1984), pp. 30–50.

Farris, Martin T., and R. Neil Southern. ''Federal Regulatory Policy Affecting Private Carrier Trucking.'' *ICC Practitioners' Journal* (July–Aug. 1982), pp. 503–529.

Flexner, Donald L. ''Potential Problem Areas for Shippers and Carriers under the Antitrust Laws.'' *ICC Practitioners' Journal* (Sept. 1984), pp. 571–582.

Freed, Charles, L. ''Current Status of the Keogh Doctrine.'' *ICC Practitioners' Journal* (Sept. 1984), pp. 599–608.

Hammes, Patrick J. ''Private Carriage Market Place: Changing Times Reflect a New Purchase Logic.'' *Annual Proceedings of the NCPDM* (1984), pp. 903–912.

Hoffman, Stanley. ''Transportation Contracts: Publication, Filing, and Adherence.'' *Annual Proceedings of the NCPDM* (1984), pp. 913–920.

Jackson, George C., ''A Survey of Freight Consolidation Practices,'' *Journal of Business Logistics* (March 1985), pp. 13–34.

Johns, Richard S. E. ''An Introduction to Predatory Pricing.'' *ICC Practitioners' Journal* (Sept. 1984), pp. 591–598.

Kalish, Steven J. ''Antitrust Considerations for Shippers In a Changing Environment.'' *Transportation Practitioners Journal* (Winter 1985), pp. 185–197.

Kromberg, P. N. ''Optimal Off-line Car Sourcing Under Deregulation.'' *Annual Proceedings of the Transportation Research Forum* (1984), pp. 275–279.

Linzer, Joel. ''Antitrust Year in Review: Recent Developments in Antitrust Defenses for the Transportation Industry.'' *ICC Practitioners' Journal* (Nov.–Dec. 1982), pp. 42–50.

Low, Christopher R. ''Computer Training for Physical Distribution: An Opportunity for Partnership.'' *Technological Challenge: Research and Educational Applications* (Columbus: Transportation and Logistics Research Fund, Ohio State University, 1984), pp. 23–35.

Marien, Edward J. ''Use of Personal Computers in Transportation, Today and in the Future.'' *Technological Challenge: Research and Educational Applications* (Columbus: Transportation and Logistics Research Fund, Ohio State University, 1984), pp. 91–108.

McGee, Michael P., and Margaret Carlock. ''Motor Carrier Market Segmentation: A Function of Shipper Cost Sensitivity.'' *Annual Proceedings of the Transportation Research Forum* (1982), pp. 202–207.

Mentzer, John T., and Robert E. Krapfel. ''Reactions of Private Motor Carriers to *Toto* and Compensated Intercorporate Hauling Rights." *Transportation Journal* (Spring 1981), pp. 66–72.

Morton, J. Robert. "Contract Rates by Rail—A Tool in Ratemaking." *ICC Practitioners' Journal* (May–June 1982), pp. 413–419.

Mulcahy, Francis. "Motor Carrier Cargo Liability—An Overview." *ICC Practitioners' Journal* (March–April 1982), pp. 257–272.

Nannes, John M. "What to Expect When the Department of Justice Calls." *ICC Practitioners' Journal* (Sept.–Oct. 1983), pp. 646–652.

Nordling, Mark R. "Demurrage Car Service Orders As A Car Service Tool: An Operational and Judicial Analysis," *Transportation Practitioners Journal* (Spring, 1985), pp. 332–339.

Ongman, John Will. "U.S. Antitrust Ramifications for the Canadian Transport Industry." *Annual Proceedings of the Transportation Research Forum* (1982), pp. 1–6.

Rosen, Stanley B., Essie Burnworth, Martin N. Chase, and Arthur Schwartz. "Planning Factors for Specialized Transportation Services." *Annual Proceedings of the Transportation Research Forum* (1982), pp. 216–223.

Schneider, Lewis M., "New Era in Transportation Strategy," *Harvard Business Review* (March–April 1985), pp. 118–126.

Stammer, Robert E. "Evaluation Models to Assess Fleet Vehicle Utilization." *Annual Proceedings of the Transportation Research Forum* (1982), pp. 145–152.

Statter, Bradley D. "A Model of Industrial Buyer Behavior: Physical Distribution Management and the Motor Carrier Selection—A Task Approach." *Annual Proceedings of the Transportation Research Forum* (1983), pp. 490–497.

Susser, Peter A. "Labor Relations Issues Raised by Alteration of Private Fleet Operations." *Annual Proceedings of the NCPDM* (1984), pp. 485–489.

Taylor, Charles L. "What Carriers Must Do to Recapture Traffic Lost to Private Carriers." *Annual Proceedings of the NCPDM* (1982), pp. 407–414.

Uhm, Ihn H. "Risk Analysis: Regular Implications for Dangerous Goods Transportations." *Annual Proceedings of the Transportation Research Forum* (1983), pp. 35–44.

Vandiver, Louis A. "Merchandise Transported in Private Carriage—A Tremendous Market Potential for Regulated Motor Carriers." *ICC Practitioners' Journal* (Jan.–Feb. 1984), pp. 168–179.

Voorhees, Roy Dale, Benjamin J. Allen, and Dale J. Pinnekamp. "An Examination and Analysis of the 'Invisible' Full-Service Truck Leasing Industry." *Transportation Journal* (Spring 1983), pp. 64–70.

Weiss, James R. "What to Do When the Department of Justice Calls." *ICC Practitioners' Journal* (Sept.–Oct. 1983), pp. 641–645.

Wolfe, K. Eric. "An Examination of Risk Costs Associated with the Movement of Hazardous Materials," *Annual Proceedings of the Transportation Research Forum* (1984), pp. 228–240.

Wyckoff, Daryl, Timothy Tardiff, and Bram Johnson. "Shippers' Preferences for Trucking Services: An Application of the Ordered Logit Model." *Annual Proceedings of the Transportation Research Forum* (1982), pp. 195–201.

CASE 6-1

The Rakowski Industrial Vacuum Co.

Headquartered in Chattanooga, Tennessee, the Rakowski Industrial Vacuum Co. made a high-quality industrial vacuum that was marketed throughout the United States. All sales were FOB plant (Chattanooga), so the only transportation of immediate concern was that of inbound materials and movements between plants. Rakowski had another plant in Birmingham, Alabama, and also a close relationship with a supplier in Atlanta, Georgia. So many of Rakowski's shipments moved between Chattanooga, Birmingham, and Atlanta that, after interstate motor carriage was "deregulated" in 1980, Rakowski decided to attempt to negotiate a contract with a single trucking firm to handle all of Rakowski's business between the three points. Exhibit 6-1 shows the weekly pattern of the movements Rakowski wants covered in the contract. Product type A is high priority and must be delivered the day after it is picked up. Product type B is material scheduled for recycling; it must be picked up at least once a week (to empty the storage bins) and, delivered within seven working days.

After a preliminary screening of about twenty carriers, Rakowski narrowed the field down to two large nationwide carriers with whom it had already done business. Both were reputable firms, both were unionized, and both were in fairly good financial condition. One was Sherwood Trucking, headquartered in California, and the other was Voorhees Express, headquartered in Iowa. Rakowski intended to negotiate a tentative contract with each of them and then select the one trucker whose contract was most favorable to Rakowski.

Exhibit 6-1 Weekly Inter-Plant Tonnages

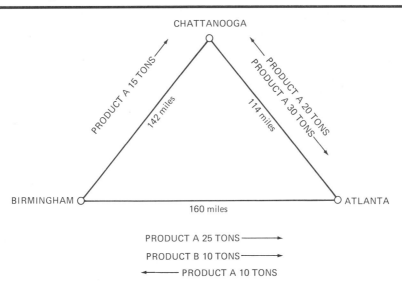

Source: Last year's tonnage divided by 52. Each week's activity is within ten per cent of figures shown above.

Exhibit 6-2

Issue	Rakowski's Position	Sherwood's Position	Voorhees's Position
I. Loss and damage to product	Product A is valued at $3 to $4 per pound. It is subject to pilferage and to damage in handling. Last year, when dealing with common carrier truckers, Rakowski filed loss and damage claims of $17,000. Product B is worth 25 cents per pound and is not subject to damage or theft. Rakowski wants claims paid promptly.	Willing to assume that annual loss and damage will be $17,000. Will build this into cost of carriage. Will pay claims promptly.	Wholesale value of product A is less than $2 per pound. Freight claims Rakowski refers to were settled for only $11,000. Prefers Rakowski assume risk up to a certain amount; this will eliminate petty paperwork.
II. Outside insurance	Rakowski wants truckers to carry insurance protection with an outside firm to cover loss of cargo as a result of a truck accident or fire, etc.	Agreeable. Already has coverage.	Agreeable. Already has coverage.
III. Scheduling of payments to truckers	Rakowski prefers to delay payments because working capital costs 1½ per cent per month interest.	Prefers prompt payment, with penalties for "late" payments.	Prefers prompt payment with an incentive, or "discount," for early payment.
IV. Packaging	The product is currently packaged according to rules of the Motor Carriers Freight Classification. Rakowski wants the contract to allow them to use less costly packaging.	No experience with other types of packaging for this product. Worried about additional claims for damaged freight.	Concerned about damage claims. Also, Voorhees's terminals are set up to handle palletized freight much more easily than nonpalletized items.
V. Next-morning delivery	For product A, Rakowski wants freight picked up one day to be delivered the next, with penalties if it is not. These penalties should be large because production would be upset.	Agrees, except for when cause of delay is beyond control of trucker.	Same as Sherwood's position.
VI. "Appointments" or "windows" for pickup and delivery of freight.	Wants to establish one-hour "openings" within which the trucks will show up. This is needed to help schedule the plant's work. Wants to assess penalties for trucks showing up before or after the 60-minute window.	Will agree reluctantly. Prefers to be penalized only after missing by an excessive number of minutes. Wants exemption when cause is beyond control of trucker.	Will agree very reluctantly. Prefers to be penalized after missing a certain number of windows per month. Wants exemption for causes beyond trucker's control.
VII. Charges for picking up and carrying freight	The tonnage to be carried is shown on Exhibit 6-1. Products are loaded on pallets; the trucker is responsible for loading and unloading. Note: all this freight is handled on an LTL basis,	Pickup charges (including carriage to local terminal) are $20 per stop, including the first five minutes; then $2 per minute. It takes one minute to load or unload a pallet. Line-	Pickup costs (including carriage to the local terminal) are $20 per stop, plus $1 per minute for each minute spent at the stop. It takes one minute to load each pallet. Line-haul

Item			
(no. VII, continued)	haul costs (from city to city) are 10 cents per ton-mile. Delivery costs and times are the same as pickup costs. All costs include normal profits.	costs are 11 cents per ton-mile for the first 100 miles covered; 10 cents per ton mile for miles over 100, up to 149; and 9 cents per ton-mile for miles over 149, up to 299. (A ton, moving a distance of 113 miles, would cost $100 \times 11¢ + 13 \times 10¢ = \$12.30$.) All costs include normal profits.	
VII-A. Charges for picking up and carrying freight. (Note: This is an optional item, which complicates the negotiations. The course instructor should decide whether it should be included. If it is, all conditions and statements made for VII hold as well.)	Although shipments of Product A are heavier toward the end of the week, Rakowski is willing to agree to ship the same approximate amount each day of the week: Monday through Friday. If truckers want even more of Product A to move early in the week, Rakowski will have to manufacture it the week before. The cost of manufacture is $2 per pound, and the rate of interest on borrowed working capital is 1½ per cent per month.	The average line-haul costs given in no. VII hold. However, in the Atlanta-Chattanooga-Birmingham area, Sherwood's line-haul trucks are only 40 per cent full on Monday nights and carry freight that pays only 5 cents per ton-mile. On Tuesdays and Wednesdays, trucks are half full and carry freight paying 10 to 15 cents per ton-mile. On Thursdays, they are nearly full and carry cargo paying about 15 cents per ton-mile. On Fridays, they are full and carry freight paying 25 cents or more per ton-mile.	The average line-haul costs given in no. VII hold. Voorhees has a policy of analyzing traffic in lanes between points and asking more in the direction of predominant flow, in an attempt to achieve balance. From Atlanta to Birmingham, Voorhees wants to charge about twice as much per ton-mile as for the reverse direction. From Atlanta to Chattanooga, it wants to charge at least 1.5 times as much for the reverse direction. In the lane between Birmingham and Chattanooga, there is no imbalance.
VIII. Special pickups of freight	Sometimes Rakowski will want the carrier to make an additional pickup of freight—in addition to the pickups already agreed to and scheduled.	Will allow a certain number of "freebies" a month; beyond this it will assess a charge.	Will charge for additional unscheduled pickups unless the shipment is above a certain weight.
IX. Annual volume of freight	Wants the contract to cover volume of freight shown in Exhibit 6-1, plus or minus 10 per cent.	Wants the contract to cover the amount of freight shown on Exhibit 6-1, with penalties if it drops below that volume. Penalties should be justified in terms of additional costs to the carrier.	Wants the contract to cover the amount of freight shown on Exhibit 6-2, with incentives if greater volumes are shipped. Incentives should be justified in terms of the savings to the carrier.
X. Subsequent adjustments to take into account: increase in costs of living (or inflation)	Recognizes that the contract is written in dollars. Inflation may drive carrier costs up, and it would be reasonable for them to be paid more dollars (of deflated currency).	In the mid- and late-1970s, fuel and labor costs climbed faster than the general cost of living.	Holds the same position as Sherwood. Believes that labor costs will have more of an influence on pickup and delivery costs; fuel costs will impact more on line-haul costs.

which means it moves to the trucker's terminal in the city, where it's picked up, on to a line-haul truck to a terminal in the city of destination, and then to a small truck for local delivery.) Product A must be delivered on a next-day basis. It should be picked up once a day. Shipments of Product A tend to be heavier later in the week. Product B must be picked up at least once a week. Each loaded pallet carries one ton.

As it turned out, there were many items to be negotiated. Rakowski and the two trucking companies knew all of the information presented in the case. (Although the two competing truck firms do not exchange information directly, they have been involved in enough competitive bidding situations that they know something about each other's costs and strategies.) The various contract items to be negotiated are listed, along with some data concerning the position of Rakowski Industrial Vacuum, Sherwood Trucking, and Voorhees Express.

(At this point, the instructor should divide the class into three negotiating teams: one representing Rakowski Industrial Vacuum Co., one representing Sherwood Trucking, and one representing Voorhees Express. Negotiations between the Rakowski and Sherwood teams must be conducted separately from negotiations between the Rakowski and Voorhees teams. It will be considered unethical for the Rakowski team to use a concession negotiated from one trucking company as leverage to obtain a greater concession from the other trucking company. The object of the exercise is to have a tentative contract drawn up with the Sherwood firm, and a tentative contract drawn up with the Voorhees firm. Then the instructor—with the assistance of the Rakowski team—selects the contract that is most favorable to Rakowski Industrial Vacuum Co. Note, however, that Rakowski Industrial Vacuum is very ethical and concerned about positive long-term relationships with its suppliers. Therefore, it will not knowingly enter into a contract that is obviously so disadvantageous to a trucker that the trucker is likely to lose money in performing the agreement.)

The items or issues to be negotiated are listed, along with the viewpoints of Rakowski and of the two truckers. Each should be negotiated separately and—to the extent possible—independently of the other issues. After the Rakowski team and a trucker's team agree on how to handle an issue, the agreement must be written or typed, as though it were to be one paragraph in a multiparagraphed agreement.

CASE 6-2

Arlington Heights Watch Repair Case

Mary Walstad, having raised her family, contemplated going back to her former occupation, watch repairing. She had not seriously considered going back to work, but she was asked by friends and relatives to repair their mechanical watches. (She did not have the ability to repair electronic digital watches.) The requests originated because the traditional watch-repairing business was in the declining stage of its life cycle. There were two factors that caused this situation: (1) most mechanical watches cost less than $40, and therefore, when they malfunctioned, their owners threw them away because the repair costs were often higher than the original cost of the watch; and (2) the sales trend indicated that electronic digital watches already commanded over 50 per cent of watch sales, and this trend was still growing. Electronic watches were totally different from mechanical watches—Mary laughingly said that the TV repairman had a better chance of fixing them correctly than she did.

Because of these trends there were relatively few traditional watch repair people available. Her nephew, Karl Schober, encouraged her to get back to work. He said, "I'll take care of everything except the actual repairing of the watches." Mary finally consented because of Karl's enthusiasm for this new business. (She really didn't think Karl would have the marketing ability to generate any significant business, so she said, "Why not humor my favorite nephew?")

Karl, to the surprise of everyone, worked diligently for many weeks finding jewelry stores that did not presently offer a traditional watch-repair service. When he had located eight customers in the northern Chicago suburbs, he decided that he had enough business to begin with. His operational plan was relatively simple. On Monday, Wednesday, and Friday, he would visit each jewelry store and pick up all the watches needing repairs. He would also drop off watches that had been repaired. Service would be relatively fast—in almost all cases it would take no longer than one week, from pickup to delivery of the repaired watch.

Exhibit 6-3 shows Mary Walstad's home town of Arlington Heights (she would repair the watches in her home), and the eight surrounding communities that Karl had located jewelry store customers. Exhibit 6-4 shows the average *driving time*, not distance, between the customers in all cities in Exhibit 6-3.

Karl's long-time girl friend, Brunnhilde, had mixed feelings concerning Karl's success. She was happy because, for once, he was earning enough so that they could consider marriage. However, Karl was gone long hours on his delivery route and could not figure out the shortest way to call at all the stores. Brunnhilde wished Karl could finish his route earlier so that they could have more time together. Brunnhilde mentioned her concern to some fellow workers during coffee, and one of them recalled having an old college physical distribution text they'd been unable to sell that had "something about routing" in the back. The next day, he brought the book in for Brunnhilde with the pages marked. Under the heading "Routing Techniques," Brunnhilde read:

The Listing Method.—A proven and uncomplicated procedure involves determining the time or cost involved between each point that has to be covered. We will only look at the travel times in the example because it is assumed that the delivery or service times are the same at each stop. Exhibit 6-5 illustrates the seven locations and the travel times between all six customers and the warehouse in a given city. The travel times are also listed in a matrix. Remember that *times* are listed and not miles. Thus, for example, the time from Customer A to Customer D is less than the time from Customer A to Customer B because the travel from A to D is on an all interstate route, whereas A to B is travelled on local roads.

The driver must start at A, the company warehouse, and return there after deliv-

Exhibit 6-3 Location of Jewelry Stores

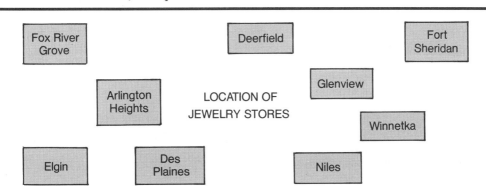

Exhibit 6-4 Driving Time (in Minutes) Between Locations

	Arlington Heights	Deerfield	Des Plaines	Elgin	Fort Sheridan	Fox River Grove	Glenview	Niles	Winnetka
Arlington Heights		22	25	25	21	43	20	43	39
Deerfield			43	29	36	31	43	39	25
Des Plaines				33	45	39	29	36	22
Elgin					20	24	40	34	29
Fort Sheridan						22	31	25	33
Fox River Grove							39	43	39
Glenview								34	45
Niles									20
Winnetka									

ering to each of the six customers. To start, add destination B to the route that must start and end with A. It is A-B-A and has a travel time of 40 minutes (A to B is 20 and B to A is 20). Next, add destination C and insert it between each point in the A-B-A route. A-C-B-A has a value of 61 (20 + 21 + 20). The other possible combination, A-B-C-A, also has a value of 61, (20 + 21 + 20). In the case of a tie, such as this, select either alternative and add destination D and insert it in all possible locations. (When one route yields a lower travel time than the other, of course, continue this method with the swifter route.) Exhibit 6-6 illustrates the addition of destination D to route A-C-B-A. The circled numbers are the times between locations. The route A-C-D-B-A has the *lowest* travel time and is used when destination E is added. Exhibit 6-7 indicates that route A-E-C-D-B-A has the lowest travel time. Destination F is added to this route in Exhibit 6-8. The lowest cost route is A-E-C-D-F-B-A. Finally, destination G is added in Exhibit 6-9. Notice that a tie results and that either route A-G-E-C-D-F-B-A or route A-E-G-C-D-F-B-A result in the lowest travel time.

This type of methodology is sometimes referred to as a *heuristic* procedure, meaning that it is a short-cut method of obtaining a satisfactory answer, although not necessarily the best answer. In this example, the optimum solution found by checking every possible alternative route is A-C-E-G-D-F-B-A or A-B-F-D-G-E-C-A. Each of

Exhibit 6-5 The Time (in Minutes) Between Each Location

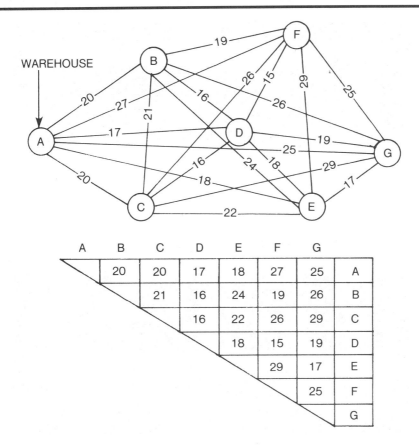

A	B	C	D	E	F	G	
	20	20	17	18	27	25	A
		21	16	24	19	26	B
			16	22	26	29	C
				18	15	19	D
					29	17	E
						25	F
							G

these solutions has a travel time of 132. The simplified heuristic procedure produced a solution (134) almost as accurate as the optimum solution. Remember that the value of a heuristic procedure is when the complexity of the problem is great. If the above problem had 156 destinations that had to be serviced, the problem would obviously be too complex to be performed manually. A computer would be utilized, and the program would be based on the heuristic methodology discussed.

Exhibit 6-6 Addition of Destination D

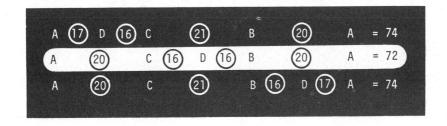

Exhibit 6-7 Addition of Destination E

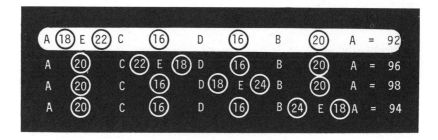

Exhibit 6-8 Addition of Destination F

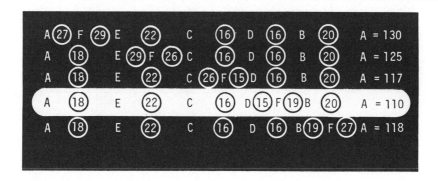

Exhibit 6-9 Addition of Destination G

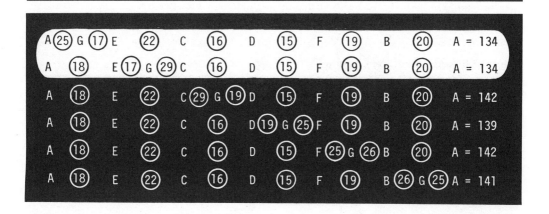

Question One: You are Brunnhilde. Determine the route that Karl should use to mimimize the travel time involved. Remember that he must start at Mary Walstad's house in Arlington Heights (to pick up repaired watches) and must finish his route at the same location (to drop off watches needing repairs). Use the heuristic "listing method" that is discussed here.

Question Two: The PX at Fort Sheridan decides to terminate its watch repair agreement, which eliminates the Fort Sheridan stop. What new routing should be followed?

Question Three: After the Fort Sheridan account is lost, the outlet in Niles announces that it will be closed for a month's vacation and that there will be no deliveries there for a while. What new routing is best (without Fort Sheridan and Niles)?

Question Four: According to Exhibit 6-4 the driving time between points is the same in either direction. How realistic is this assumption? Discuss.

Question Five: Service to both Fort Sheridan and Niles has been resumed, but there will be many road repairs in the vicinity of Fox River Grove for the next six months. This increases two of the times shown on Exhibit 6-4. The time between Fox River Grove and Arlington Heights has increased from 43 minutes to 58 minutes, and the time between Fox River Grove and Elgin has increased from 24 minutes to 40 minutes. All other times remain the same. What is the new routing, if any, which should be followed?

Question Six: Brunnhilde, despite her successful scheduling efforts, discovers that poor Karl is so exhausted after the days he makes deliveries that he nods off to sleep during the 6:00 P.M. news and sleeps through until the next morning. She decided to split his route into two, calling at some accounts on Mondays, Wednesdays, and Fridays and at the other accounts on Tuesdays, Thursdays, and Saturdays. Determine the two routes that will minimize Karl's weekly travel time.

Changes in transportation equipment have an influence on inventory management. Larger vehicles increase the lot size moved; more dependable equipment reduces the chances of missed deliveries. These two photos illustrate some changes in tank car equipment. The upper picture—from the early days of the oil industry—shows a tank car consisting of two wooden tanks made of staves bound by metal bands mounted on a rail flatcar. The bottom shows several types of present-day cars. The ones on the right have a curved shape—when viewed from the side—with the low point in the car's center.

(*Credit:* Union Tank Car Company)

Inventory Management

Inventory pressures at the retail level have increased dramatically. Our customers want faster inventory turns [they want very little inventory in stock except what is on the store shelfs], and they insist that suppliers provide the delivery support to make this possible. For Warner-Lambert, this has created a valuable opportunity—we now are out to sell service superiority as well as product superiority. To this end, we have materially improved our total logistics system. More than that, we are making logistics an integral part of our marketing effort.

Joseph D. Williams
President, Warner-Lambert Corporation
Traffic Management
December 1984

General Motors Corporation used to keep a 10-day supply of seats and other parts made by Lear Siegler Inc. on hand; now GM sends in orders at four- to eight-hour intervals and expects immediate shipment.

Business Week
May 14, 1984

Bit by bit we are moving our assembly operations adjacent to car assembly plants. We are taking more responsibility for inventory control. We assemble axles at night that are used the next day. We have nineteen regional centers offering overnight delivery on truck parts to assembly plants.

Gerry Mitchell
Chairman, Dana Corporation
Forbes
January 2, 1984

Key Terms

- Inventory carrying costs
- Stock-out costs
- Safety stock
- Economic order quantity (EOQ)
- Inventory flows
- Fixed-order-interval system
- Just-in-time inventory system (JIT)
- Kanban
- Bar code scanners
- Inventories in motion

Learning Objectives

- To determine the costs of holding inventory
- To identify the costs associated with a stock-out
- To understand the concept of EOQ
- To differentiate the various inventory flow patterns
- To note when a fixed-order-interval inventory system is appropriate
- To understand the JIT/Kanban system of inventory management
- To appreciate the role of scanners in inventory control

Introduction

Inventories are stocks of goods that are maintained for many purposes, such as resale to others, use in further manufacturing or assembling processes, or for the maintenance of existing equipment.[1]

The most prominent ongoing concern about inventories is cost. Inventories are carried as assets on a company's balance sheet. However, an increase in inventories cannot be automatically interpreted as desirable. A firm may manufacture much more than it can sell. One wellknown U.S. firm expanded too quickly in its European market and, in "achieving such hectic growth, the company committed a number of classic management errors, and so stumbled into that familiar booby trap: an excess of inventories. . . . It required a full year of ever more costly price cutting to dispose of the goods."[2] Carrying costs for the inventories are significant, and the return on investment to the firm for its funds tied up in inventory should be as high as the return it can obtain from other, equally risky, uses of the same funds.

If this was all there was to the "problem" there would be no problem. Firms would keep inventory costs down by keeping inventories extremely low. However, being understocked and having repeated stock-outs also can be expensive. One certain way to lose customers is to be an unreliable source of supply. The solution, then, is to determine the proper balance of inventory and maintain it. That is the subject of this chapter.

---

[1] See Larry H. Beard, Al L. Hartgraves, and Fred A. Jacobs, "Managing Inventories in a Small Business," *Business* (April–June, 1983), pp. 45–49; and Thomas C. Jones and Daniel W. Riley, "Using Inventory for Competitive Advantage Through Supply Chain Management," *Annual Proceedings of the NCPDM* (1984), pp. 309–320.

[2] "When Levi Strauss Burst Its Britches," *Fortune* (April 1974), p. 131.

Bearing or Sharing the Burden?

Inventory policy integrates all aspects of physical distribution management because the PD/L manager must determine the quantity and location of each item to be stored. Recall from Chapter 3 the discussion of rapid and accurate order processing; and from Chapter 6 the importance of carrier dependability. Buyers prefer situations where they can reduce their inventory levels because they are assured of rapid, on-time replenishment as a result of the supplier's and carrier's dependability.

Because of the high costs associated with maintaining inventories, it is usually desirable to have somebody else maintain the inventory. In a situation where one distributor supplies several dealers, the distributor will try to force the dealers to carry larger inventories so he or she can carry a smaller inventory, while the dealers would prefer an opposite policy. The distribution manager of a pharmaceutical company made the following observation: "Inventory management becomes a difficult thing when your customers take the position that they're not going to operate with any more inventory than they possibly have to. Then they push it back to us. We in turn try the same technique with our suppliers."[3]

Inventory order systems are sometimes classified as being either a *pull* or *push* type. In a pull situation, the channel members (retailers or wholesalers) request or order products as they are needed from the manufacturer. Push systems occur when manufacturers force products upon their channel members in an effort to reduce their own inventories.[4]

This phenomenon occurs even within a single firm. A plant's production manager incurs costs every time he or she changes the type, size, or model of product that a production line is making. The manager would prefer to wait until night or the weekend to make the changes on the line necessary to accommodate the next type of product. Until the change is made, the line will continue to manufacture the former product, possibly far in excess of the marketing manager's desires or needs.

This can become even more complex. In the auto industry, as the model year end approaches, the manufacturer has in stock many accessory components for the current year's model which have proven to be unpopular with buyers. Assume that 20,000 autos are still to be built and the following optional items are in inventory: 17,000 vinyl tops; 14,500 right-hand rearview mirrors; 6,000 radios with rear seat speakers; and 3,000 tinted windshields. If so, then the last 20,000 autos will contain one or more of these slow-moving optional items. The result is that none of the optional items are left when the 20,000th, and last, car rolls off the assembly line. The production manager's problem has been solved, but the marketing manager's problem has become more acute because dealers are reluctant to take autos containing an odd assortment of accessories for which buyers have already shown disdain.

[3] "Inventories: Which Way Now?" *Transportation and Distribution Mananagement* (May–June 1975), p. 27.

[4] See Roger L. Rosenberger, "Push or Pull Distribution?" *Handling and Shipping* (May 1972), pp. 62–64. Analogous examples of push systems exist in retailing. Some book and record clubs automatically mail their monthly selections to members unless the member has specifically advised the club not to send it.

Determining Inventory Levels

Inventory size determination deals with the amounts, or levels, of inventories a firm attempts to maintain. There are costs of maintaining inventories, and there are costs of being out of stock. The PD/L manager must maintain an inventory level that minimizes the total of both costs.[5]

The discussion in this chapter assumes that a firm has already decided on storage sites for its inventories. Site selection will be covered in Chapter 8 and in Chapter 12, which deals with system design. However, a firm determines the number and location of sites after it determines the desired level of customer service to be offered at a specific cost. Decisions about inventory levels are, in a sense, like a closed loop.

Inventory Carrying Costs

The costs of carrying inventories fall into several categories. *Storage* costs are those of occupying space in a storeroom or in a warehouse. Many inventories must be *insured* against fire, flood, theft, and other perils, and this is part of the expense of storing goods. Some products lose volume or size over time. *Inventory shrinkage* recognizes the fact that more items are recorded entering warehouses than leaving. *Obsolescence* recognizes that items in an inventory gradually become out of date. This can be a serious problem with some consumer products such as cosmetics. Related to obsolescence is *depreciation*, which is a form of deterioration that is a function of time, not usage. For example, upholstery may begin to fade in new automobiles that are stored outside. *Interest charges* for the money invested in inventories must be added to take into account the money that is required to maintain the investment in inventory.

Inventories are taxed, usually on the basis of the inventory on hand on a certain date, and considerable effort is made to have that day's inventory be as low as possible. Outgoing shipments are speeded up while suppliers are told to delay their deliveries. The inventory tax and most of the costs associated with avoiding or evading the inventory tax are all part of the inventory carrying costs.

Fresh fish or many types of fresh produce deteriorate (or depreciate) completely in only a few days. Hence, the depreciation portion of a produce company's carrying costs might be 25 per cent to 50 per cent per day. Dairy products, drugs, bread, and camera film are examples of items with a form of expiration date before which they must be sold or used. Their rate of depreciation can easily be calculated because at the expiration date, the unsold items must be removed from the shelf.

Some inventory items have other types of carrying costs because of their specialized nature. Pets or livestock must be watered and fed. Tropical fish must be fed and have oxygen added to the water in which they are kept. Precious items require additional security measures.

[5] See Brian F. O'Neil and Gerald O. Fahling, "A Liquidation Decision Model for Excess Inventories," *Journal of Business Logistics*, **3**: 85-103 (1982).

Table 7-1 Inventory Holding Costs
(in %)

Insurance	0.25
Storage facilities	0.25
Taxes	0.50
Transportation	0.50
Handling costs	2.50
Depreciation	5.00
Interest	6.00
Obsolescence	10.00
Total	25.00%

Source: L. P. Alford and John R. Bangs (eds), *Production Handbook* (New York: Ronald, 1955), pp. 396–397.

When added together, these costs are known as *inventory carrying charges.* They are usually expressed as a percentage of the inventory's value and sometimes are surprisingly high. One old, but still widely cited estimate is that carrying costs approximate 25 per cent per year of a product's value. Table 7-1 summarizes the component breakdown of the 25 per cent figure. The interest rate shown in the table is about one-half the level of rates which businesses had to pay in 1985. For each industry, or product line, the distribution of holding costs varies; in any event they are substantial.[6]

Stock-Out Costs

If avoiding an oversupply was the only problem associated with inventories, the solution would be simple: *store* fewer items. But not having enough is as bad as having too many. A stock-out occurs when the supply of an item is exhausted and a customer wants to buy the out-of-stock item. The determination of stock-out costs is difficult and inexact but nevertheless real.

Estimating the cost or "penalty" for a stock-out involves an understanding of customers' reactions to a seller being out of stock at the time the customer wants to buy an item. Assume the following customers' responses. How should they be evaluated?

A. The customer says, "I'll be back," and this proves to be so.

B. The customer says, "Call me when it's in."

C. The customer buys a substitute product, which yields a higher profit for the seller.

D. The customer buys a less expensive substitute, which yields a lower profit.

E. The customer asks to place an order for the item that is out of stock (known as a back order) and asks to have the item delivered when it arrives.

F. The customer goes to a competitor.

[6] For a discussion of how one firm determined its inventory-associated costs, see William R. Steele, "Inventory Carrying Cost Identification and Accounting," *NCPDM 1979 Papers*, pp. 75–86.

Table 7-2 Determination of the Average Cost of a Stock-out

Alternative	Loss*	Probability*	Average Cost*
#1 (Brand-loyal customer)	$ 0.00	.10	$ 0.00
#2 (Switches and comes back)	$ 37.00	.65	$ 24.05
#3 (Lost customer)	$1200.00	.25	$300.00
Average cost of a stock out		1.00	$324.05

* These are hypothetical figures.

The loss in situation A is negligible; the sale is only slightly delayed. In situation B, the information upon which to make a judgment is incomplete; it is not known whether the customer will, in fact, return. In situation C, the seller is actually better off than if the item the customer initially desired were in stock; the opposite situation occurs in situation D. Of interest would be the quality of the product the same customer requested the next time he comes in. Situation F is most difficult to evaluate because it is unknown whether the customer is lost temporarily or permanently. The competitor may also be out of stock.[7] If the customer is lost for good, then it is necessary to know the cost of developing a new customer to replace the lost customer.

For sake of simplicity, assume the responses can be placed into three categories: sale delayed; sale lost; customer lost. The third is the most critical. Assume further that over time, 300 customers who experienced a stock-out are queried. It was found that the first alternative occurred 10 per cent of the time, the second, 65 per cent of the time, and the third, 25 per cent.

These percentages or probabilities of each event taking place can be used to determine the *average* cost of a stock out. Table 7-2 illustrates the procedure. Each cost is multiplied by the likelihood it will occur, and the results are added. A delayed sale has no cost because the customer is brand-loyal and purchases the product when it is again available. The lost sale alternative results in the loss of the profit that would have been made on the customer's purchase. The lost customer situation is the worst. The customer tries the competitor's product and prefers it to the product originally requested. The customer is lost and the cost involved is that of developing a new brand-loyal customer.

Safety Stocks

Firms usually maintain safety or "buffer" stocks that will prevent an excessive number of stock-outs. Marginal analysis is generally used to determine the optimum level of safety stocks. (See Table 7-3.) Assume goods must be ordered from a wholesaler in multiples of 10. When adding 10 additional units of safety stock, the carrying cost of the *additional* or *marginal* 10 units is $1,200. However, by stocking an additional 10 units of safety stock and

---

[7] See Philip B. Schary and Boris W. Becker, "The Impact of Stock-out on Market Share: Temporal Effects," *Journal of Business Logistics* (Spring 1978), pp. 31–44.

The Elements of Physical Distribution/Logistics Systems

Table 7-3 Determination of Safety Stock Level

# of Units of Safety Stock	Total Value of Safety Stock ($480 per Unit)	25% Annual Carrying Cost	Carrying Cost of Incremental Safety Stock	Number of Additional Orders Filled	Additional Stock Out Costs Avoided
10	$ 4,800	$1,200	$1,200	20	$6,481.00
20	$ 9,600	$2,400	$1,200	16	$5,184.80
30	$14,400	$3,600	$1,200	12	$3,888.60
40	$19,200	$4,800	$1,200	8	$2,592.40
50	$24,000	$6,000	$1,200	6	$1,944.30
60	$28,800	$7,200	$1,200	4	$1,296.20
70	$33,600	$8,400	$1,200	3	$ 972.15

maintaining it throughout the year, the firm is able to prevent 20 stock-outs. Because the *average* cost of a stock-out has already been determined to be $324.05, preventing 20 stock-outs saves the firm $6,481.00 ($324.05 × 20). Savings far outweigh costs, and the next alternative is to maintain a safety stock throughout the year of 20 units. This adds $1,200 to the costs but prevents 16 additional stock-outs from occurring, thereby saving $5,184.80.

The optimum quantity of safety stock is 60 units. With this quantity, carrying cost of 10 additional units is $1,200 but $1296.20 is saved. If safety stocks are increased from 60 to 70 units, the additional carrying cost is again $1,200 while the savings is only $972.15. Therefore, the firm would be better off by permitting three stock-outs to occur each year. Note that these concerns determine a *level of customer service.*

Economic Order Quantity (EOQ)

The previous section has indicated the safety stock level, the minimum a firm always tries to have on hand. However, what determines how this level is maintained? How often should stocks be replenished? How much should be ordered each time?

The typical inventory order size problem deals with calculating the proper order size and attempts to minimize the total of two costs: (1) the costs of carrying the inventory, which are in direct proportion to the size of the order that will arrive; and (2) the ordering costs, mainly the paperwork associated with handling each order, irrespective of its size. Were there no inventory carrying costs, customers would hold an immense inventory and therefore avoid the details of reordering. If there were no costs associated with ordering, one would place orders continually, and maintain no inventory at all, aside from safety stocks.

Figure 7-1 shows the two costs on a graph and indicates the point at which they are minimized. Mathematically, EOQ is determined by using this formula:

Figure 7-1 Determining EOQ

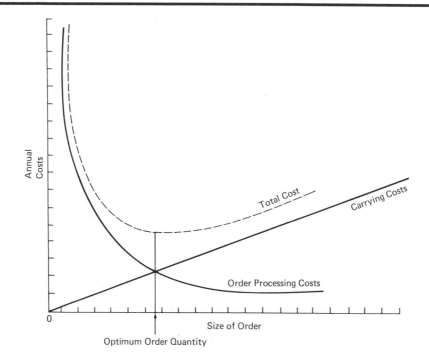

$$EOQ = \sqrt{\frac{2\ A\ B}{I}}$$

where EOQ = the most economic order size in dollars;

   A = annual usage in dollars;
   B = administrative costs per order of placing the order;
and I = carrying costs of the inventory (expressed as an annual percentage
       of the inventory's dollar value).

   If $1,000 of an item is used each year, if the order costs are $25 per
order submitted, and if carrying costs are 20 per cent, what is the EOQ?

$$EOQ = \sqrt{\frac{2 \times 1000 \times 25}{.20}} = \sqrt{250,000} = \$500 \text{ order size.}$$

Because of the assumption of even outward flow of goods, inventory carrying costs are applied to one-half the order size that would be the average
inventory on hand. (See Table 7-4.) *EOQs, once calculated, may not be the same
as lot sizes in which the product is commonly sold and bought.*
   EOQs can also be calculated in terms of number of units that should be
ordered. The formula is

Table 7-4 EOQ Calculations

No. of Orders Per Year	Order Size in $	Ordering Costs in $	Carrying Costs on Average Inventory in Stock in $	Total Costs in $
1	1,000	25	100	125
2	500	50	50	100
3	333	75	33	108
4	250	100	25	125
5	200	125	20	145

$$EOQ = \sqrt{\frac{2 \text{ (annual use in number of units) (cost of placing an order)}}{\text{annual carrying cost per item per year}}}$$

Assume that the item employed in the Table 7-4 example costs five dollars. Substituting numbers in the new formula would yield:

$$EOQ = \sqrt{\frac{2 \ (200) \ (25)}{5 \times .20}} = \sqrt{\frac{10,000}{1}} = 100 \text{ units}$$

The earlier EOQ formula and Table 7-4 showed that $500 was the best order size, and since the product is priced at $5.00 per unit, the answer is the same.

The simple EOQ formulation just given does not take into account the special discounts given to encourage larger orders or increased volumes of business.[8] (EOQ problems can be found in Case 7-1.)

Inventory Flows

At this point the figures from the EOQ and the safety stock calculations can be used to develop an inventory flow diagram. Assume the EOQ in this instance has been determined to be 120 units, the safety stock level is 60 units, that average demand is 30 units per day, and the replenishment or order cycle is two days. On day one (see Figure 7-2) an EOQ of 120 units arrives. Total inventory (point A) is 180 units (one EOQ plus 60 units of safety stock). Demand is steady at 30 units per day. On day three, total

[8] Carriers usually charge less per pound for larger shipments. In a simplistic sense, this can be handled as another form of discount, but—in reality—incorporating this into actual use is difficult. See Alan J. Stenger, John J. Coyle, and Marshall Price, "Incorporating Transportation Costs and Services into the Inventory Replenishment Decision," *Applied Distribution Research* (Columbus: Transportation and Logistics Research Fund, Ohio State University, 1977), pp. 22–26. Another concern is inflation—i.e., the problem that costs for the materials one is ordering continue to increase. See Sumer C. Aggarwal, "Economic Ordering in Periods of Uncertainty," *Journal of Purchasing and Materials Management* (Fall 1979), pp. 13–18; and Shyam S. Sethi and Robert M. Sutton, "Inventory and Warehouse Cost Forecasting," *Annual Proceedings of the NCPDM* (1982), pp. 817–830.

inventory has declined to 120 units (point B), which is the reorder point, because it takes two days to receive an order and during this time 60 units would be sold. Because safety stock is *not* to be used under normal circumstances, reordering at 120 units means that 60 units (safety stock) will be on hand two days later when the EOQ arrives. The EOQ of 120 units arrives at point C and then total inventory increases to 180 units at point D.

If the rate of sales doubles to 60 units per day, the reorder point is hit at 120 units (point E) and an additional EOQ is ordered. However, it will not arrive for two days. A day after the reordering, the regular inventory is exhausted, and at point F the safety stock is starting to be used. At point G the EOQ arrives just as the safety stock is about to be exhausted. If the EOQ arrived later than day 8, a stock-out would have occurred. The new EOQ boosts the inventory to 120 units, which is also the reorder point. Therefore, at point H another EOQ is ordered. Starting on day 8 the demand settles back to the old average of 30 units per day.

If it appeared that the demand rate of 60 units per day was going to become the average demanded rate, the firm would have to redetermine its EOQ. Recall that a basic input into the EOQ formula is the annual sales of the product. If this figure changes, then the EOQ must be recalculated.

Starting at point H, demand is again 30 units per day. The next EOQ arrives on schedule at point I, and total inventory increases to 180 units at point J. The reorder point is at 120 units, and an EOQ is ordered on day 12. Demand stays constant, but the transportation mode delivering the EOQ is delayed one day. Instead of arriving on day 14, it arrives on day 15. Safety stock is entered at point L on day 14. A stock-out is again prevented because the EOQ arrives at point M. Note that safety stock protects against two problem areas—increased rate of demand and an increased replenishment cycle.

When an EOQ system is used, such as illustrated in Figure 7-2, *the time*

Figure 7-2 Inventory Flow Diagram

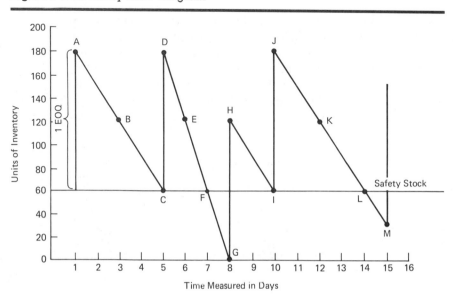

The Elements of Physical Distribution/Logistics Systems

between orders varies. The normal time between orders was four days, but when sales doubled the time between orders was only two days. One requirement for the utilization of an EOQ system is that the level of inventory in the system must be monitored constantly. Then, when the reorder point is hit, an EOQ is ordered. With the advent of computerization, many firms have the capability to constantly monitor their inventory and hence have the option of using an EOQ system. A reorder point for each item can be established in the computer's memory so it can indicate when the stock has been depleted to a point where a new order should be placed. Sophisticated computer systems even print the purchase order leaving only the signature space blank so the purchasing agent can sign it.

A variation of the EOQ method is the *fixed order quantity* method, used in the repetitive purchases of the same commodity. An example would be a lumber/construction materials retailer located along the Mississippi River who buys gravel by the barge load (of approximately 1,000 tons per load). The retailer would wait until his gravel stockpile was nearly exhausted and then order another barge load.

Fixed-Order Interval System

An alternative inventory concept that is also commonly used is known as the *fixed-order interval system.* In this system, EOQs are not used. Instead, orders are placed at fixed intervals, such as every three days or twice a month. In the EOQ system, the time interval fluctuated, with order size remaining the same. Under fixed interval systems, the opposite holds, and order sizes may vary each time. Fixed interval systems are used in three situations.

The first is when the firm does *not* maintain automatically updated stock levels. Such firms typically have a clerk manually check the level of all items and determine which stocks are running low. This task is assigned on a regular basis.

A second situation is that vendors may have offered the firm significant discounts if it will place its orders at certain fixed time intervals. Because the discounts are greater than the advantages of using the EOQ system, the fixed order interval ordering system is utilized.

The third reason is that the firm buys FOB origin and tries to utilize its own private trucking fleet whenever possible. If one of the firm's trucks normally deadheads from a point near a supply source back to the firm's plant on a regular basis, the firm may decide to buy FOB origin and carry the supplies in its own truck.

The fixed order interval system also is used in conjunction with a safety stock and usually requires *more* safety stock than the EOQ system because an EOQ system constantly monitors the inventory levels. In an EOQ system, if sales start to increase, the reorder point will be hit earlier and a new order for an EOQ will be placed automatically. Stock-outs can still take place, but only during the replenishment cycle after the new order has been placed. With the fixed-order interval system, since the inventory levels are not monitored, a stock-out can occur during both the order cycle and the time before order placement.

Most fixed-interval order systems do borrow one element from EOQ systems. Next to each bin or slot in the warehouse is a card indicating the minimum quantity for that product. When the order pickers note that the stocks have been drawn down to this level, they are to notify their supervisor, who decides whether the reorder should occur immediately or on the next scheduled date.

Cyclical buying is a very specialized form of fixed-order interval ordering. This practice occurs in the women's fashion industry where retailers place their orders directly with the manufacturer for each season's fashions, and there is almost no possibility of reorder. Another example is a grocery retailer's purchase of Halloween pumpkins or Christmas trees.

Just-in-Time Inventory System

An inventory system that has received attention recently is known as just-in-time (JIT), or by its Japanese name, *Kanban*. This concept has been effectively utilized by Japanese manufacturers and now it is being widely implemented in the United States. The concept is related to the fixed-order interval system previously discussed, in that customers place orders with their suppliers on basically set schedules that frequently involve daily or hourly delivery by suppliers to their customers. It is also related to the EOQ system, in that the concept assumes that ordering costs are negligible; hence, firms order frequently in order to minimize inventory holding costs.

Although JIT is often thought to be a new inventory system, the concept actually started in the United States with Henry Ford's integrated production and assembly plants in Detroit in the 1920s. Iron ore would arrive by barge and within one day it would be turned into steel in one of Ford's steel plants and then stamped or molded into auto parts that were assembled within days of the ore's arrival from Minnesota. In 1926 Ford stated, "Waste is that stock of materials and goods in excess of requirements that turns up in high prices and low wages."[9] American businesspeople lost track of Ford's JIT system in the affluence that followed World War II. Professor Bernard J. LaLonde explains why this took place:

> For thirty-five years, most businesspeople in the United States solved most problems by throwing inventory at the problem. And if they throw enough inventory at the problem, everybody in the organization is happy; sales people don't complain, vendors don't complain, customers don't complain, and so on.[10]

This traditional system worked well until two things happened: (1) interest rates started to increase greatly, causing the cost of holding inventory to skyrocket, and (2) foreign products actively started to enter the U.S. market.

Even though U.S. firms were not overly concerned about inventory costs in the 1950s, Japanese manufacturers were trying to rebuild their industrial capacity. Because their war damage had been so great, they effectively started

[9] Brian C. Kullman and Robert W. Haessler, "Kanban, American Style," *Annual Proceedings of the NCPDM* (1984), p. 101.

[10] R. Scott Whiting, "Public Warehousing and the 'Just-in-Time' Production System," *Warehousing Review* (Distribution Executive Issue, 1982), p. 3.

from scratch. They invited Professors Edward Deming and Joseph Juran from the United States to instruct them on quality-control techniques and on how to minimize production costs. (Appropriately, Japan's most coveted industrial honor is the Deming award for quality.[11]) The firm that most vigorously adopted Kanban in the 1950s was the Toyota Motor Company.[12] Kanban, as used in Japan in the 1950s and in the 1980s, is *not* a computerized inventory system. Kanban literally means "card" and the system involves two basic types of cards, or placards. The first is the *move card*, which is utilized by assembly workers to indicate that they are getting low on an input. This card is given to workers who bring inventory stored in the plant to the assembly line so employees can easily reach the parts necessary to assemble the product being manufactured. When the move card requires a container of inputs to be brought to the assembly line, the *production card* is taken from the container. The production card is initially placed in the container by the manufacturer of the production input. This production card is then sent back to the manufacturer so the input can be replaced before another move card calls for more parts at the assembly line. (In some cases the firm manufacturers its own inputs, so the production card is sent to the section of the plant that produces the input so that it can be manufactured.[13])

General Concepts. Today the terms *Kanban* and *JIT* are used interchangeably, although, as we have seen, Kanban is a specific type of JIT system. Let us look at how Toyota uses Kanban and contrast their production system with the traditional methods used in the United States. Toyota looks at inventory as "waste."[14] In the United States, inventory has traditionally been considered "insurance." One U.S. management consultant put it this way:

> In the United States, we've sold our soul to Murphy's law [if something can go wrong—it will]. We believe that there's some mystical force out there that's going to do us in—that's going to shut down a [production] line—and so we protect ourselves with inventory. The Japanese believe that human error, machine breakdowns, and defective parts can be prevented, and that inventory simply hides the problems and keeps companies from achieving their goals.[15]

The key to reducing inventory, the Japanese believe, is to look at suppliers as partners in the production process. In the United States, suppliers are often viewed as adversaries, hence the buyer should constantly play one against another to get lower prices. Multiple suppliers (vendors) are frequently utilized in the United States, to encourage price competition; it is

[11] Craig R. Waters, "Why Everybody's Talking About 'Just-in-Time'," *Inc* (March 1984), p. 80.

[12] George C. Jackson, "Just-in-Time Production: Implications for Logistics Managers," *Journal of Business Logistics,* **4:** 1–2 (1983).

[13] Jinichiro Nakane and Robert W. Hall, "Management Specs for Stockless Production," *Harvard Business Review* (May–June, 1983), pp. 85–87.

[14] Walter E. Goddard, "Kanban Versus MRP II—Which Is Best for You?" *Modern Materials Handling* (Nov. 5, 1982), p. 42.

[15] Waters, op. cit., pp. 78–79.

considered "safer" because, if one vendor is shut down with a labor dispute or a fire, the other vendor can supply the firm's requirements. In Japan, one supplier for each production input is the rule. Thus, Toyota has 250 vendors and General Motors has 4,000.[16] Toyota uses the following method, which is typical of Kanban. Vendors are included when the firm establishes its ninety-day production schedule. Each vendor receives an "informal" order for inputs required during this time period—but only the first thirty days is an actual order from Toyota. The production schedule tells exactly what will be needed each day for the next thirty days. Then at the first of each month, another ninety-day schedule is given to each vendor, with the first thirty days again a "firm" order and the next sixty days Toyota's best estimate of what production will be during this time period. Notice that this system allows vendors to be able to carefully plan their production schedules to coincide with Toyota's. The result is that each level of production uses the Kanban system of small lot sizes that are shipped frequently to customers when a production card is received.

As previously noted, in the United States we have traditionally utilized safety stock to protect against defective parts, late deliverys, or incorrect inputs sent to the manufacturer. Because each of these problems will shut down an assembly line, safety stock was looked at as a necessary, but expensive, requirement. Kanban says that safety stock only covers up problems. The time to key in seriously on problems, identify them, and correct them quickly is when assembly lines stop.

Kanban works best in two situations, both of which are found at Toyota. First, the product produced should have relatively few variations. This allows the ninety-day production schedule to be accurate. This is why Toyota offers so many "luxury" items on their cars as standard features. It is actually cheaper to produce cars that are all about the same and then "brag" about the impressive list of typically extra-cost options being standard on Japanese cars. U.S. car companies are starting to copy this idea, offering fewer options and many more standard features. The second condition is vendors that are physically located close to their customers. In Japan almost all auto production parts and the cars themselves are assembled in three city clusters: Tokyo, Nagoya, and Hiroshima.[17] Almost all of Toyota's vendors ship their products, often many times per day, less than 60 miles to the assembly plants. Many vendors are located in the same industrial parks as the Toyota assembly plant.

The Advantages of Kanban/JIT. There are two primary advantages that accrue when the JIT inventory system is used. The first involves a reduced level of production inputs on hand at any given time. With inventory holding costs high, reduced levels of inputs can be a major cost reduction program. This involves less money tied up in inventory, less storage space required, and less physical deterioration. The net effect is more inventory turns, indicating that inventory sits around less waiting to be assembled. Assume, for example, that a firm needs 9,000 units in a year of a given input. If the

---

[16] Kullman and Haessler, op. cit., p. 105.
[17] Whiting, op. cit., p. 4.

firm has three inventory turns, it means the firm has an average inventory—assuming steady production and no safety stock—of 1,500 units (9,000 divided by three; and half of this is 1,500. We take half because, when the 3,000 units are received, we start to use them immediately and, on the average, we have half the order on hand.) However, if a firm can achieve an inventory turn of 10, the average level of inventory in stock is then reduced to 450 units. (Ten deliveries of 900 units divided in half.) Toyota, using Kanban, has been able to achieve an average of 100 inventory turns per year for its production inputs. The best that an U.S. auto industry firm has achieved is an inventory turn of 15 times annually.[18] Another example is the Bendix Corporation when it established Kanban/JIT at a production facility in Japan that supplied Toyota. Within two years after the new inventory method was established, inventory turns increased from ten to thirty times annually.[19] Another illustration is Harley-Davidson, a U.S. motorcycle manufacturer. In order to compete with Japanese manufacturers, H-D started to use JIT. Inventory turns increased on an annual basis from 3 to 16—this decreased the firm's costs so much that their prices could be reduced, and their market share increased from 10 per cent of all motorcycles sold in the United States to 16 per cent.[20] A final illustration of the savings possible with Kanban/JIT is General Motors, which is actively starting to utilize this concept. A comparison of 1984 and 1982 shows that 30 per cent *more* cars were produced with 20 per cent *less* inventory of production inputs.[21]

The second advantage of Kanban/JIT is quality control, which is explained by James Harbour, a management consultant to the auto industry:

> Use your own logic. If you're a supplier and you ship me junk and I have no inventory, guess what happens? The [production] line shuts down. Guess what happens next? Everybody is aware of the quality problem and it gets fixed then and there. If you ever ship junk again, you're done. . . . We get a new supplier.[22]

With previous inventory systems that utilize high levels of inventory, defective production inputs could sit around the plant for months before the quality problems were spotted. In early 1984 at two General Motors JIT assembly plants—Pontiac, Michigan, and St. Louis, Missouri—production ceased when the factories received defective bumpers and molding trim. The problems were quickly corrected by vendors. 3M Corporation now utilizes JIT at some production facilities, and the results have been impressive. In 1981, 13 per cent of inputs were found to be defective—by 1984 the defective rate was reduced to 1 per cent.[23]

[18] Jackson, op. cit., pp. 8–9.

[19] Ibid., p. 9.

[20] James Cook, "Kanban, American Style," *Forbes* (Oct. 8, 1984), p. 66.

[21] Demaris A. Berry, "Reliable Transportation Termed Vital in Making 'Just-in-Time' System Work," *Traffic World* (Sept. 10, 1984), p. 22.

[22] Whiting, op. cit., p. 3.

[23] Mike Meyers, "Low-Inventory Manufacturing Arrives Just-in-Time," *Minneapolis Star and Tribune*, 11 March 1984, pp. 1D and 4D.

Carrier Reaction to JIT. The greatest beneficiary of JIT is the trucking industry. This mode is well equipped to provide a high-quality service in terms of on-time pickup and delivery for relatively small shipments. Richard Haupt, director of transportation and traffic for Ford Motor Company, has noted:

> Trucks seem to fit in with JIT, as they are smaller conveyances than rail boxcars, operate direct from door to door generally in less time than trains, and are less subject to variations in transit time.[24]

Some trucking companies work exclusively with manufacturers providing JIT service.[25] Other large common carriers, such as Roadway Express, stress their service levels as being an ideal solution to the shipper who has customers that require JIT delivery schedules. Paul Greene, Roadway's vice-president of sales, has declared, "Just-in-time means zero defects—no early shipments and no late shipments."[26] At General Motors' new Buick City plant in Flint, Michigan (this facility was discussed in Chapter 1), only truck deliveries can be accepted on inbound shipments because there are no rail sidings. The plant has 300 truck-receiving docks to accommodate the almost constant stream of trucks delivering production inputs.[27]

Railroads are not typically as well suited to daily (or hourly) delivery of production inputs over relatively short distances. L. Stanley Crane, chairman of Conrail, noted the JIT trend in the auto industry and declared, "Now that strikes right at the heart of the railroads' capabilities because we're a volume business. It was more convenient for us to gather a bunch of material and dump it in their plant rather than running little mini-trains each day."[28] Nevertheless, Conrail has been able to work with General Motors to operate "mini-trains" at selected assembly plants that provide daily service, typically with ten cars per train.[29]

Air carriers have also benefited from JIT. One supplier in Indianapolis, Indiana, uses Burlington Northern Air Freight to supply, on a daily basis, its customer (Hewlett-Packard) in Greeley, Colorado.[30] Figure 7-3 discusses an international example of JIT using air freight.

Plant and Warehouse Location and JIT. The surest way to ensure timely delivery to customers utilizing JIT is to locate a production facility close to one's customers. At Pontiac Motor Division of General Motors, the Fiero model is produced in a new production plant that utilizes JIT. The firm

---

[24] Berry, op. cit., p. 21.

[25] "From Rages to RAMS," *Forbes* (Dec. 17, 1984), pp. 78–79.

[26] Francis J. Quinn, "Just-in-Time: No Room for Error," *Traffic Management* (Sept. 1984), p. 29.

[27] Joan M. Feldman, "Transportation Changes—Just in Time," *Handling and Shipping Management* (Sept. 1984), p. 47.

[28] "The Rail Report," *Passenger Train Journal* (March 1983), p. 40.

[29] "1982 Golden Freight Car Awards," *Modern Railroads,* mimeographed (1982).

[30] Margaret Grande, "Flying for Just-in-Time," *Handling and Shipping Management* (Oct. 1984), p. 45. See also, Jim Tanchon, "Air Freight and Just-in-Time Go Together Like Love and Marriage," *Traffic World* (Nov. 5, 1984), pp. 38–40.

Figure 7-3 Global Just-in-Time—A Whole New World

Just-in-time has increased air cargo business internationally as well as domestically. "But it's hard to differentiate whether it's because of JIT or not," comments Emery's Richard Steiner.

That may be so, but there are strong indications that air carriers have found a place in the international transport of JIT shipments.

For example, last fall Burlington Northern Air Freight (BNAF) put on its own aircraft and began JIT delivery of automotive parts to four General Motors (GM) plants in Mexico City. "Currently, we're running a 727 stretch freighter with a 42,500-lb capacity every night, says BNAF's Muggins Richards.

The flight originates in El Paso, Texas and travels a Chicago-Detroit-Laredo loop back to El Paso. "Once it makes it to Laredo down at the U.S. border, it's still one more day before it makes it to the plants, "Richards states. Even so, the arrangement to fly in the freight shaves several days off the transport time compared to trucking the freight in all the way.

The Greeley, Colo. division of Hewlett-Packard also relies on international air carriers for JIT shipments. Greeley receives tape drives and disk drives from Japan, subassemblies from Hong Kong, and controller boards from Singapore, plus parts from Europe.

The Singapore arrangement is probably the most interesting. Every Friday, an air freighter leaves the peninsula bound for a major U.S. airport on the West Coast. On Sunday, the freight clears customs. On Monday it's broken down, and on Tuesday at 6:30 a.m. it's delivered to the Greeley plant, courtesy of BNAF.

"We set up this arrangement with Burlington because of the urgent need for parts from Singapore," explains Jerry Gavaler, traffic assistant. The arrangement works so well that there are no plans to switch to sea containers. Greeley has slowly been phasing in these containers for its other overseas shipments, as JIT schedules are refined.

"To a degree, value of the product and speed of delivery take precedence over the cost of transportation," said Gavaler about the company's decision to continue the Singapore arrangement.

Baker Material Handling Corp. also relies on air carriers for its overseas JIT shipments. The company has no plans to alter service either, according to Gene Shuster, material planning and procurement manager. The reason: it saves money.

"People don't want to have their money tied up in transit," he said, referring to the inventory that's sitting in a sea container while the ship carrying it moves slowly across the ocean. "They're looking at the dollars now, whereas before they took them for granted."

For this reason, Shuster expects management of the future will more seriously consider using air carriers for JIT shipments.

Source: Margaret Grande, "Flying For Just-in-Time," *Handling and Shipping Management* (October, 1984), p. 46. Used with permission.

purchases 75 per cent of its inputs from suppliers that are located within 200 miles of the plant. At the new "Buick City" plant, GM has suggested to vendors that they will receive more favorable consideration if they are located close to the plant, preferably in the industrial park located next to the assembly plant.[31] Illustrative is Kasle Steel Corporation of Dearborn, Michigan. Although it had two plants within 70 miles of the Buick City facility in Flint, Michigan, the firm decided it had to locate closer for perfectly timed delivery of steel products to Buick. Kasle's new production plant cost $6 million and is located 300 yards from the Buick assembly plant. Kasle itself is using JIT with its vendors. Whereas it used to have six suppliers of the steel it fabricated into car parts, it now utilizes only one firm, Jones and Laughlin Steel.[32] Another subsidiary of GM, Delco Electronics, is using JIT at its production plant in Kokomo, Indiana. Many of Delco's eight hundred suppliers are moving their production plants closer to Kokomo. At another GM plant in Baltimore, JIT will be utilized. Once this was announced, vendors started to look for nearby sites. Maryland's director of business and economic development stated, "One company phoned the other day and said it wanted help finding a site 20 minutes by truck from GM."[33]

An alternative to actually moving production plants closer to customers is to ship the firm's production inputs to a warehouse located close to the customer. As already noted, a GM plant in Baltimore is using JIT. For customers of this plant, Raymond J. Dallas has established the Just-in-Time Warehousing Company in Baltimore near the GM plant. He also offers truck service to the facility on an hourly basis.[34]

Inventory Reordering Procedures

In addition to the JIT inventory system already noted, there are several more traditional systems for replenishing inventory stocks that vary in sophistication. Nearly all inventory systems require some formal sort of stock-level monitoring capability. This section discusses the more common reorder processes.

A separate listing of what the inventory levels *should be* is usually maintained, and then the actual stock levels are checked against it. A common problem caused by beginning stock clerks is that they assume that when they see the level of some item is low, they will reorder. However, if the stock is exhausted, the clerk forgets completely about the item, especially if adjoining stocks overflow into the empty space. Hence a separate list must be kept, and, usually, each bin must be labeled. (However, reserving empty space for an out-of-stock item consumes considerable warehouse space or shelf space.)

In chain grocery stores one frequently sees a code number on the shelves,

[31] Feldman, loc. cit.

[32] Amal Nag, "Auto Companies Push Parts Makers to Raise Efficiency, Cut Prices," *Wall Street Journal*, 31 July 1984, pp. 1, 27.

[33] Robert Johnson, "An Idea from Japan May Offer Cities a Way of Recruiting Industry," *Wall Street Journal*, 23 August 1983, pp. 1, 29.

[34] Robert L. Simison, "Auto Parts Buying: Businessman Offers Nuts-and-Bolts Idea," *Wall Street Journal*, 5 October 1983, p. 7. See also, Delbert S. Conner, "Public Warehouse Industry Maps Strategies to Meet Just-in-Time Production Demands," *Traffic World* (March 19, 1984), pp. 62–66.

Figure 7-4 Bar Code Scanners

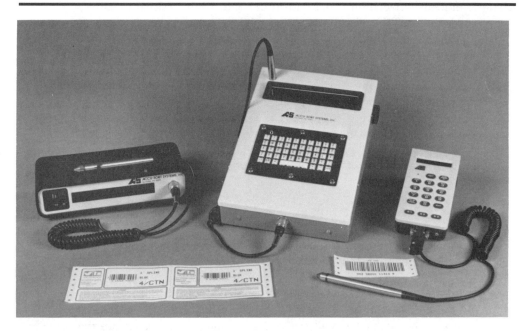

Credit: Weber Marking Systems, Arlington Heights, Illinois. Used with permission.

next to the price listing for each item. Each day, an employee walks up and down each aisle, checking the stocks of items the store is supposed to be carrying. The employee pushes along what looks like a grocery cart with a desk-top calculator. Attached to the device is a small box, with a wire and "wand" connected. (Some examples are shown on Figure 7-4.) The wand is used to scan, or read, the bar codes for each product on the shelf front. Then, after scanning the code—and depending on how the system is programmed—the employee punches in either the number of items in stock, or the number he or she wishes to reorder. The tape produced by this machine can be read by a device attached to a telephone so that the order is transmitted to the firm's warehouse, where the new order is made up for shipment.

A more complex variation of this order system is used for automobile parts. Manufacturers of some popular auto makes establish and enforce rigid repair parts inventory requirements, specifying the minimum number of each item that dealers must keep in stock. On a specified day each month (it varies by dealer so that orders reaching the distributor's warehouse are spread out), the dealer must report inventory to the distributor, who then determines what parts the dealer needs to bring his stock up to the minimum levels. This is the first type of dealer order.

The second type of order is for accessories, sales of which depend on the efforts of new car salespeople. Because these demands are less predictable, the dealer places a *supplemental* order once a month for accessory items. Parts can be placed on this order, which must be submitted two weeks before or after the next monthly parts order. Note that the dealer has this one chance, midway between his other parts order date, to request parts that are being used quickly. The distributor pays freight charges on both types of orders that have been mentioned.

Two other order systems are available, but the dealer must pay the freight charges. *Emergency* orders reach the dealer two or three days after being placed (compared with the normal time of two weeks). A *car-down* parts order is handled with even higher priority, and the fastest mode of transportation is used for delivery. Frequently the dealer will phone in the order and come in and pick it up. For all types of orders except the *car-down* order, the distributor handles the paperwork and billing at the same time as processing the order. For a *car-down* order, paperwork is handled after delivery of the part.

Suppliers' Systems

In some industries, especially retailing, the supplier provides the order system. The supplier employs an "order taker" who surveys the stocks on the shelves, in the storeroom, and in the warehouse and writes out a "suggested" order for the retailer to sign. If the retailer has a favorable relationship with the order taker, he or she will sign the order without questioning it. Sometimes the order taker will make a small sales pitch for one of the supplier's items and try to get the retailer to order more of that particular item. Rack salespeople operate in a similar manner. A rack salesperson may maintain the hardware rack in a grocery store and reach an agreement with the retailer on the rack's initial inventory. The rack salesperson comes back every other week, replenishes the items that have been removed from the rack, lists the items being replenished on a form, calculates the wholesale prices, and presents the completed form to the retailer as a bill.

Reorder System Shortcomings

Although PD/L thinking has generally held that lower inventory levels are desirable, in 1972 and 1973 there developed in the United States a so-called "shortage" economy, which meant that certain materials were in very short supply. Users of these supplies started stockpiling them to avoid both further price increases and stock-out situations. "As vendor backlogs increased, they once again quoted longer leadtimes. Their customers, in turn, had to order earlier and consequently backlogs increased again."[35] Then, as the economy slowed in 1974, orders dropped and leadtimes decreased. Buyers—noting the decreased lead times—reduced or delayed their orders. Lead times decreased further. "In no time at all those unbelievable backlogs melt[ed] away like the snow in Spring."[36]

This situation illustrates two shortcomings in the inventory replenish-

[35] Oliver W. Wight, "Where Did All the Backlog Go?" *Modern Materials Management* (May 1975), p. 17.
[36] Ibid.

ment practices of many firms. First, as vendors' quoted delivery times increase, the buyers' order systems (frequently computerized) respond by placing the order for the next needed batch a bit earlier. This increases again the vendors' leadtimes, and the buyers' systems again respond by placing the order for the next batch even earlier, which further increases the vendors' quoted leadtimes. Second, in times of shortage, many buyers place identical orders with different vendors, intending to accept only the first order that is delivered and canceling the others. This creates a "phony" backlog of orders for many vendors, although they may engage in the same practice when ordering from their own sources of supply. Both practices tend to create bubbles that can easily burst.

Is inventory level maintenance an art or a science? An article in the *Wall Street Journal* in 1980 started with these words:

> The 1973–75 recession taught most American businessmen all they needed to know about inventory control. Or so, as late as last year, they thought.
> Now they know better. . . .
> Inventory control gains in importance when interest rates and inflation run high. That's because inflation raises the value of goods in inventory and high interest rates raise the cost of financing, cutting into current profits. Keeping the warehouse all but empty can cost future profits. Despite all the attention inventory has got in the past five years, however, keeping just the right amount of goods on hand has proved neither simple nor painless.[37]

The article went on to explain that firms were trying to place upon others the burden of carrying inventories.

> But not buying anything until it's absolutely necessary means somebody has to wait for what he wants. "This is the strangest recession I've ever heard of," a purchasing man for a Midwest utility company says. "You can't buy anything. Whether I want an electric transformer or a special utility truck, I have to wait for it. Nobody wants to stock anything."[38]

This is, in effect, the same old inventory problem we have been discussing throughout this chapter: maintaining the proper balance between too much and too little. The *Wall Street Journal* report merely illustrates how policy appears to have gone from one extreme to the other. Although various management tools can be extremely helpful, it seems that maintaining proper inventory levels is like a ballet: *maintaining* balance means having a *sense* of balance.[39]

---

[37] *Wall Street Journal,* 15 August 1980, p. 15.

[38] Ibid.

[39] See "Business Gets a Grip on Inventories," *Business Week* (May 14, 1984), pp. 38–39; Mark L. Fagan, "Inventory Management: Organizing for Success," *Annual Proceedings of the NCPDM* (1984), pp. 447–460; and Douglas M. Lambert and Douglas E. Zemke, "Reducing Channel Inventories by Improving Information Flows," *Annual Proceedings of the NCPDM* (1983), pp. 998–1009.

Only in a few instances can an individual look around and see the entire inventory with which he or she must be concerned. A physical distribution manager of a large firm may be responsible for an inventory list of 10,000 or 100,000 different items located at 50 or 100 locations all over the globe. Much of the "inventory" may not be at a fixed location; it may be aboard a moving ship, a truck, or a rail car. In order to effectively manage an inventory, the PD/L manager must maintain records that indicate the current inventory and tell where it is located. These tallies must be adjusted continually to take into account purchases, sales, deliveries, and shrinkage.

The simplest record for duplicating an inventory was known as the "scratch-in, scratch-out" method. A sheet of paper, usually on a clipboard, lists all different items down the left-hand margin. Using hatch marks, a mark is added every time a case is received, and a mark is erased or crossed out every time a case is removed. The number of hatch marks on the sheet is the same as the number of cases in the storeroom. On occasion, it is necessary to take the tally sheet into the storeroom and to reconcile the number of hatch marks with the number of cases.

A somewhat later example of the same system can be seen in retail operations selling tires. The inventory is large and is kept near the shop area where the new tires are mounted on vehicles. It is not necessary to display many sizes or styles of tires in the salesroom. A customer who makes a purchase probably wants to have the tires mounted immediately. Thus, the salesperson on the floor must know what tires are in stock. This is done through use of computer punchcards with one card for each tire in the storeroom. The cards are printed and key-coded to represent each different type of tire, and the cards are kept in a tray with divider file tabs between each type of tire. If a salesperson wants to know whether four tires of a particular type and size are in stock, he checks the tray and if at least four of the cards for that type and size are in the tray, he can assure the customer that four tires are in stock. If the customer then decides to buy, the salesperson removes the four cards from the tray and places them in a reorder basket. The original tray correctly reflects the depletion of four tires from the storeroom, and the cards in the reorder basket can be sent to the wholesaler who will replenish the stock. Today, functions similar to this are often performed by using small computers.

Multiple Locations

More sophisticated systems keep track of inventories that are scattered in many locations. For example, United Air Lines stocks various aircraft repair parts at its maintenance stations throughout the United States. Because it has numerous commercial flights scheduled between these points every day, it can easily carry a part from one airport location to another. A maintenance mechanic in Chicago who needs to replace a coffee warmer in the food galley of an aircraft goes to the stock clerk who in turn goes to a computer at the maintenance station and finds out where the needed replacement item is located in United's repair parts inventory. Even if the part is in Chicago—possibly just on the other side of the wall from where he is standing—it is quicker for the clerk to ask the computer than to go wandering through the parts room. The computer, in seconds, tells him where the part is stocked. If none is in Chicago, he notes where they are located. If the only ones are in Detroit and San Francisco, he can ask the computer when the next United flight from each city will leave for and arrive at Chicago and then arrange to have the item placed aboard the flight that will get the part to Chicago most quickly.

Identification Numbers.   Some items, such as office equipment, automobiles, cameras, and firearms, are easier to keep track of because they contain serial numbers. In the case of autos or firearms, governmental agencies also keep close control over transfers of the items. Frequently, a governmental agency also has what amounts to a record of each inventory.

Pharmaceutical drugs and some food items must now have "batch" numbers on each carton and on each individual container. In case of product recall, the recall is by batch or lot number, and all such items must be removed from warehouse stocks and from retailers' shelves.

Scanners.   Another recent development has been the use of printed codes that can be read by electronic scanners. The scanners record data and may even be directly attached to a computer, which makes use of the data to adjust inventory records.

The most widely known scanner system is the one associated with the Universal Product Code (UPC). The UPC was designed to increase the overall efficiency of grocery stores at the retail level. IBM, NCR, Sperry Univac, and other computer firms are manufacturing computer check-out systems at grocery stores. The ubiquitous black and white vertical stripe label is now found on almost all grocery products.

The system involves passing the UPC label on each product over an optical scanner at the check-out counter. The UPC is "read" and recorded in a computer which supplies such information as the product's price, tax, if food stamps can be used, and whether it can be legally sold on Sundays. The specific price of each product and its description is then flashed onto a television-type screen positioned near the counter. When all the products have been recorded, the customer receives a tape that lists the products purchased, the price of each article, and the total bill. The system was also intended to monitor stock levels, trigger reorder procedures, etc.,but, to date, grocery stores have not adapted the UPC-scanner system to a complete, storewide, inventory management system. However, the UPC-scanner system is used in many specific ways, such as tracking the sales of a limited number of items to test the effectiveness of an advertising campaign featuring specific items. Retailers in nongrocery fields are also close to adopting universal requirements for product coding and labeling.

The UPC is used at only the retail level, but similar scanner systems have been developed for other applications. Figure 7-5 shows the use of labels and scanners in manufacturing and warehousing. Figure 7-6 shows a truck-mounted scanner used to inventory containers in outside yards.

Figure 7-5 Use of Scanners in Manufacturing and in Warehousing

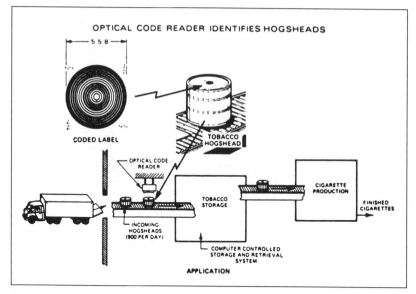

A circular code pattern utilizing overhead readers identifies and counts hogsheads of tobacco entering a large tobacco plant in Virginia.

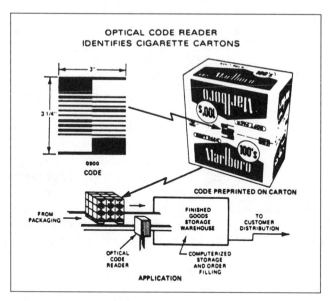

Vertically mounted readers are utilized to read and identify the preprinted bar code on corrugated cartons.

Figure 7-6 Truck-Mounted Scanner for Inventorying Container Yards

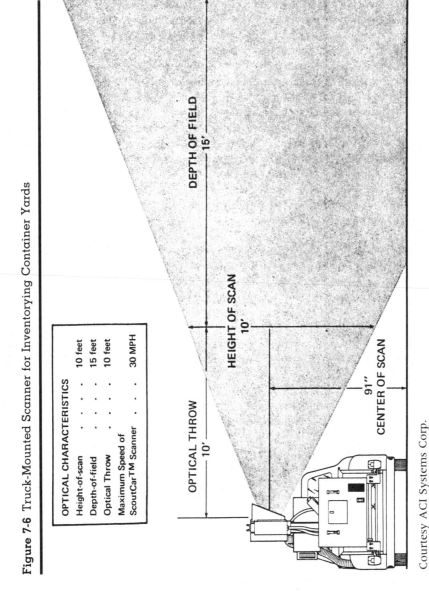

OPTICAL CHARACTERISTICS

Height-of-scan	. . . .	10 feet
Depth-of-field	. . . .	15 feet
Optical Throw	. . . .	10 feet
Maximum Speed of ScoutCar™ Scanner	. . . .	30 MPH

OPTICAL THROW
10'

HEIGHT OF SCAN
10'

DEPTH OF FIELD
15'

91"
CENTER OF SCAN

Courtesy ACI Systems Corp.

273

The utilization of scanning outside the retail area was given a significant boost in 1982 when the U.S. Department of Defense ordered all defense contractors—there are some 50,000—to start using bar codes on all products purchased by the Pentagon. In the same year, the General Services Administration, the purchasing agent for most federal agencies, issued a similar

Figure 7-7 Industries Utilizing Bar Codes

Industry required to bar code products	Users of the bar code	Code	Program name	Development level	Applications
Suppliers of Ford, Chrysler, Volkswagen, American Motors, General Motors	Used internally by large suppliers and all five auto manufacturers; eventually used by auto dealers and anti-theft service outlets	Code 39	Automotive Industry Action Group Bar Code Program	Growth Stage	Material tracking and inventory control; automated re-ordering and warehousing operations associated with Just-In-Time inventory systems; cycle checking and production counting
Suppliers of General Service Administration (GSA) and Department of Defense (DoD)	Presently used by Army, Air Force, Navy, Marines, and GSA activities, as well as large manufacturers supplying these agencies	Code 39	LOGMARS Bar Code Program	Early implementation stages	Inventory control and material tracking
Grocery Retail Product Manufacturers	Grocery retailers, and national brands manufacturers	UPC	Uniform Product Code	Mature; over 60% of all commodity volume (ACV) sold in U.S. stores is scanned	Inventory control, marketing effectiveness evaluation, and pricing
Pharmaceutical Product Manufacturers; Hospital Supplies Manufacturers; Hospitals	Hospitals, health care centers, and large health related items manufacturers	Code 39	Health Industry Bar Code Task Force (HIBC) Bar Code Program	Early Implementation stage	Monitoring patient care; inventory control and material tracking; automated production control; warehousing and distribution
Corrugated box makers	Food retailers, national brands manufacturers, warehousers/distributors of grocery products; near future—used by non-grocery product manufacturers and retailers	I2 of 5	UPC Shipping Container Symbol Marking Program	Early Growth Stage	Inventory control, material tracking and warehousing operations; soon, automated production processes
Producers of printing-writing paper, newsprint	Paper manufacturers; publishers of periodicals, dailies, books	Code 39	American Paper Institute Bar Code Program	Early Growth Stage	Material tracking and inventory control; receiving/forwarding; automated ordering, billing, crediting
Music recording industry	Used internally by record, tape, and laser disc manufacturers; record retailers	UPC	Recording Industry Association of America (RIAA) Bar Code Program	Growth Stage	Material tracking, warehousing operations, inventory control, billing, receiving and forwarding
Magazine publishers	Magazine distributors	UPC with 2-digit addendum	Council for Periodical Distributors Association (CPDA)	Mature Stage	Inventory control and material tracking; issue identification; automated billing and crediting; forwarding and receiving
Book publishers	Book distributors	UPC with 5-digit addendum	CPDA	Mature Stage	Inventory control and material tracking; issue and price identification; automated billing and crediting; forwarding/receiving

Source: Kathleen Parsons and Christopher Maginnis, "Verification: Key To Effective Bar Coding," *Handling and Shipping Management* (November, 1984), p. 40. Used with permission.

The Elements of Physical Distribution/Logistics Systems

Figure 7-8 A Bar Code Label Printer

Credit: Intermec Corporation. Used with permission.

dictum to its myriad of suppliers.[40] Figure 7-7 summarizes the various bar codes being utilized today. A bar code label printer is shown on Figure 7-8. As shown, it is printing the label for a cam shaft to be placed into stock.

Inventories in Motion

The person who needs the inventory (while never forgetting the adage that "a bird in the hand is worth two in the bush") assumes that his or her inventory consists of what is in stock *plus* what is on order. He or she assigns varying probabilities or likelihoods to goods on order showing up in time to avoid stock-outs. The narrowest permissible margin occurs when a salesperson, with a customer out front, discovers the bin empty, but before returning empty-handed to the customer, notices that the stock clerk is coming down the aisle from the receiving dock with goods to replenish the empty bin. In fact, inventory includes all completed but unsold products, including those that are on their way from the point of manufacture to the point of sale.

Products moving in rail cars, truck trailers, or vessels are considered inventory in motion. For example, rail car diversion and reconsignment

[40] Elizabeth Sanger, "No Magic Wands: A Scan of the Hand-Held Laser Scene," *Barrons* (April 4, 1983), pp. 15–20. See also "Is Bar-Coding Right For You," *Traffic Management* (April 1985), pp. 89–93.

privileges are used in the marketing of fresh produce. California lettuce is loaded into rail cars and started moving east. As it moves eastward, the owner sells it by long-distance telephone. Once it is sold, the owner notifies the railroad to deliver it to the buyer.

According to Exxon Corporation, the free world's oil inventory—between the point of production and the point of consumption—is about ten billion barrels, which equals about six-months' consumption.[41] So large is this inventory, that one of the aspects of its management is to alter the speed at which it flows through pipelines and tankers at sea. In mid-1981, this tanker fleet—at any one time—was carrying 750 million barrels of oil. If its average speed were increased by one knot, there would be a decrease of approximately 100 million barrels in the amount of oil being aboard the free world's tanker fleet at any one time.[42]

An example that shows the flowing nature of an inventory comes from a description of Quaker Oats' computerized system for inventory control. Their computer "prepares a daily stock status report as of 7 A.M. each morning . . . as to goods available, committed and in-transit at all of the distribution centers." The report includes month-to-date experience plus a listing of planned shipments. "It gives those concerned with inventory an effective running picture of how things are moving in every line item that the distribution centers handle."[43]

Another example of the "inventories in motion" concept was described by a transportation writer who said, "mobility replaces dead storage" and gave as an example the experience of a southern meat packer who closed several warehouses and substituted in their place truck containers that were continually in motion. The refrigerated containers were 15 feet long and equipped with self-contained legs. A larger truck would carry three containers and make individual stops where it would meet smaller trucks, capable of carrying only one container. (Both the large and small trucks had the capability for lifting into place or discharging a container.) At the meeting point between the large and small truck, the small truck unloaded an empty container and took on a full container. This operation was repeated at two other sites with two other small trucks; the small trucks then made deliveries from the full containers while the large truck headed back with empty containers to the packing plant. The process was repeated each day.

Actually, it was not necessary for the large and small trucks to meet because it was possible to leave the containers in a stationary position. Figure 7-9 shows these transferable containers in use.

There are limitations to the inventory-in-motion concept. For example, legal restrictions may keep an inventory from being in motion. If the goods are kept in a public warehouse and are being used as collateral for a loan, the warehouse manager will not release them without approval of the lender. Liquor or cigarettes in a bonded warehouse may not be released until the

[41] "World Oil Inventories," (New York: Exxon Corp., 1981), pp. 3–8.

[42] Ibid., pp. 8–10. Fewer tankers would be needed to *move* the same amount of oil.

[43] "Flexible Inventory Control Fights Shortages and Inflation," *Traffic Management* (Jan. 1974), pp. 50–52.

Figure 7-9 Truck Transferrable Container System

A tractor-trailer with three, separate, refrigerated containers. The containers have folding legs which also can be elevated. This makes it possible for the truck driver to leave loaded containers in various locations and to pick up empty ones as well.

A smaller truck backing under a parked container. Once the truck is in position the container will be lowered, the legs folded up, and the container will be locked to the truck's chassis.

Both photos courtesy Kidron Body Company, Kidron, Ohio and Lakeland, Florida.

owner purchases and affixes various tax stamps. Last, where rail transit privileges are being used and the freight is at the intermediate stopping point, there are limitations as to where it can be shipped from the intermediate point, unless the shipper is willing to surrender some of the freight rate savings that were anticipated.

Inventory Management

Inventory Management—Special Concerns

Generalizations concerning inventory management are often hard to make. Each commodity has its own handling characteristics, and the framework through which each product is marketed also varies. What follows is a discussion of factors that affect the management of some but not all inventories.

The inventory manager must divide all materials into stock-keeping units (or SKUs). Each SKU represents a type of individual item or product for which separate records will be maintained. A coal yard, carrying five differ-

> The phrase *line item* is analogous to SKU. It means that a separate horizontal line on inventory record forms is devoted to that product type.

ent grades of coal, has five SKUs. A large grocery store has between 10,000 and 15,000 SKUs. In addition to designating each product and product variation or size as an SKU, the inventory manager must also designate the quantity—or minimum lot size—with which the inventory records will deal. The retail grocer thinks—or keeps records—in terms of individual items or case lots (a case usually holds 12 or 24 or some other number of individual items). The warehouse serving that retail store may deal only with case lots or pallet loads (a pallet load contains 25 to 50 cases, depending on the product). If the smallest SKU quantity the warehouse wishes to deal in is cases, it will accept orders for one or more cases only. If the distributor selling to the warehouse wants to deal only in pallet loads, it will accept orders for one or more pallet loads only, and so on. Thus, a retailer taking inventory would consider the following as a SKU:

• *Lori's tomato paste, 10 oz. can, number of cans* . . .

The warehouseman stocking the same product would list the following as his SKU:

• *Lori's tomato paste, 10 oz. can, number of 24-can cases* . . .

The distributor of the product who sells to wholesale warehouses would consider the following as his SKU listing:

• *Lori's tomato paste, 10 oz. cans, in 24-can cases, number of pallets of 42 cases* . . .

Many firms stock hundreds or thousands of items, and to them the problem is one of determining the relative importance of each item. A rule of thumb that can be applied to most inventories is that 20 per cent of the items account for 80 per cent of the sales. The other 80 per cent of the items are much less active. This is known as the 20/80 rule.

The term *ABC* is frequently applied when analyzing large inventories. An application of ABC analysis might place the top, or fastest-selling, 10 per cent of inventory items in category A, the second fastest-moving group is B, and the slowest is C. Each of the three groups would be handled separately, and the system designed would take into account their differing inventory-related characteristics. In a repair parts inventory, an additional consideration would be how "critical" a part might be to customers. Hence, category A might include fast-moving repair parts plus a few slow-moving—but extremely important—repair parts. The reason for including both in category A is that their stock levels require closer surveillance. A stock clerk might be expected to check A category items daily, B items weekly, and C items every three weeks.[44]

Complementary Inventory Items

An example of inventory items with a complementary relationship occurs if they are subject to demand in different seasons. Skis are sold for winter use, but scuba equipment is sold during the summer. When goods complement each other in this way, their carrying costs are lower since costs of storage assigned to them are only for a fraction of the year.

Items that are complementary from the retail customer's viewpoint may only intensify the pressures on the retailer or wholesaler concerned with stock maintenance. In the summer, picnic items, such as catsup and mustard or weiners and buns, sell together. Almost any time that an item requiring subsequent purchase of a refill is sold, the refills must be marketed alongside the initial item to demonstrate to buyers that they will not be impossible to find later. Also, customers want to know the price they will have to pay for refills. An example is filter bags for vacuum cleaners. A store carrying an inventory of vacuums will also carry filters. An initial analysis of inventory procedures might lead the PD/L manager to recommend dropping the line of filters because of high costs involved. Marketing people would then point out that the sale and display of filters is necessary to the sale of new vacuums.

Sometimes it is necessary to stock items that have no market value but which must be used as customer service tools, such as sales literature that a wholesaler supplies to retail outlets, spare copies of instruction manuals, or extra copies of book jackets that can replace soiled and torn originals. These are justified on the basis of "customer service."

The most frequent complementary relationship between goods in an inventory occurs when incoming goods come from one supplier or outgoing goods go to one receiver or consignee. In these situations, the controlling factors may be the dollar, weight, or cubic volume of the entire order. The individual items in the inventories may be of secondary consideration, except to the extent they contribute to totals. A chain food store schedules a truck to go to a specific retail store on Tuesdays and Fridays. The order to go on Tuesday's truck is small, leaving both cubic and weight capacity of the truck underutilized. The warehouse will add to the store's order (with-

---

[44] See David P. Herron, "ABC Data Correlation," in *Business Logistics in American Industry* (Stanford, Calif.: Stanford University Graduate School of Business, 1968), pp. 85–95.

out consulting the store) and fill the truck, usually with steady-moving, nonperishable items such as paper towels. In this instance the chain owns the inventory, the retail outlet, and the warehouse, so its costs of maintaining the inventory remains the same. However, by utilizing the truck's unused carrying capacity, the chain manages to reduce its transport costs.

When using common carriers there are "weight breaks" that are points in tariffs where the charges per hundred pounds drop as the size of shipment increases. If an inventory manager's order were just under one of these points, he or she might save money by ordering more to get the freight savings. Or if the seller pays the freight, a quantity discount may be offered to entice the buyer to purchase a quantity above the weight break involved.

"Deals"

Sometimes a manufacturer or wholesaler will have an unbalanced inventory with too many slow-moving items. To clear the warehouses the manufacturer or wholesaler may offer retailers a "deal" that is a specific lot of merchandise combining desirable and less desirable items. The price is set so that the retailer will buy in spite of the fact that some of the items will be hard to resell except at a low price. This is offset by the fact that the lot also includes some fast-moving items and that its total price is relatively low. When this lot arrives at the retailer's storage facility, it tends to run counter to inventory management objectives because it contains some unpopular, slow-moving items that may be the same as unpopular, slow-moving items already in stock. An example of a "deal" occurred after the introduction of color TV, which proved to be more popular than expected. Manufacturers had many unsold black and white sets and could get dealers to take them only if they were part of a specially priced "deal" including color sets.

In retailing, the term *carload sale* was often used to mean that the retailer had purchased an entire rail carload of a product and wished to pass the savings in both quantity and discounts from the manufacturer and rail transportation costs on to the retail customer. (Figure 7-10 shows the delivery of a carload of tires to a Miami retailer in the early 1920s.) Moving larger quantities than usual through the system may have many advantages from a retailing standpoint, but it may or may not be related to the goals of inventory management.

Substitute Items

A more complicated relationship between goods in an inventory occurs when some are substitutes for each other. Because of this, many food stores are relatively unconcerned about temporary stock-outs of food items. They realize that the shopper will not hesitate to substitute a 75-watt light bulb for a 60-watt bulb or one cut of meat for another. Sometimes these substitutions could occur in either direction, but in other cases only a one-way relationship exists. For example, a bolt $7/16$-inch in diameter could be used in place of a bolt that was $1/2$-inch in diameter, but the reverse may not hold.

The relationships between goods discussed in this section have implications with respect to determining stock-out costs and the sizes of safety

Figure 7-10 Gearing Up for a Carload Tire Sale

This photo was taken in Miami in 1921. Note that the center truck, and the one on the left, have solid rubber tires.

Credit: The Florida Photographic Collection, Florida State Archives

stocks to be maintained. If the consumer has no hesitation about making substitutions, it would appear, initially, that there were no penalties for a stock-out. However, a point will be reached where customers become sufficiently annoyed at having to make substitutions that they decide to take their business elsewhere.

Informal Arrangements Outside the Distribution Channel

Competing dealers of the same manufacturer may, in some instances, group their respective inventories for certain purposes. All dealers of a certain make of auto in a city often circulate among themselves a list of each other's inventory of new cars. If one dealer has a ready buyer for a specific model and color of auto that he does not have in stock, he will check the list of other dealers' inventory to see whether they have the model. If one of them does, he will arrange a trade between himself and the other dealer; and then he will have the auto in stock that his buyer wants.

In industries with spirited competition between dealers, there is usually little or no competition between them when it comes to supplying each other with needed repair parts. Informal channels of distribution benefit all parties concerned, including the consumer. They indicate some of the hazards in applying formal inventory analyses to some situations since the informal relationship between dealers may be overlooked.

Major U.S. airlines and many foreign airlines that fly U.S.-built aircraft belong to an organization that lists spare parts they have for sale:

The listing merges the separate data of participating airlines so that items bearing the same manufacturer's part number are grouped together. As an example from a recent printout, Pratt & Whitney's part No. 484637, an engine strainer, is noted as being offered for sale by five airlines. Also listed are the quantities each seller has available (ranging in this case from 72 to 3,967). Buyers negotiate directly with the sellers.[45]

This procedure does, of course, compete directly with parts sold by the manufacturer although the manufacturers refer to this same listing for two purposes. They find it cheaper to buy back some parts they originally sold rather than to reopen their production line. Second, by noting the quantities available of surplus parts on the airlines' listing, the manufacturer can make a more accurate prediction of needed production of more units.

Repair Parts

Repair part inventories cause many problems. A truck manufacturer, with a nationwide market in mind, may advertise that there are one thousand dealers who offer specialized parts and service. This will assure truck buyers that, no matter where in the United States their trucks operate, they will typically be near parts and service. The individual truck dealer sees things differently. To the individual truck dealer the profits come from the sale of new trucks locally, and the dealer feels that the only customers who must be kept satisfied are those local firms who buy new trucks from him or her. The dealer is less concerned about stocking parts for models of trucks he or she does not sell. If a cross-country trucker has a breakdown and must wait several days for the repair part to reach the dealer in question, this makes little difference to the dealer. Thus, the manufacturer may *require* the dealer to maintain a certain basic inventory, which often includes items the dealer would typically not choose to carry. This relieves the manufacturer of a portion of the burden of maintaining inventories. In situations where the manufacturer requires dealers to maintain a parts inventory, special incentives are frequently offered. The manufacturer may agree to buy back inventory items at cost in situations where obsolescence or depreciation of the items occurs. The manufacturer may absorb shipping charges on items needed to maintain the dealer's required levels of stock.

Note the problem cited here started out as being one of marketing; i.e., the truck manufacturer wanted to advertise a nationwide network of service and parts. Nearly all inventory policies have a relationship to marketing and to customer service. Few, if any, decisions are made without speculating about customer reaction.

Federal Express, an airline specializing in rapid delivery of parcels throughout the United States, maintains a warehouse for use by its customers near the airline's Memphis hub. Customers maintain inventories of repair parts at this warehouse and then instruct Federal Express to carry or ship them to where they are needed.

[45] "Worldwide Supermarket for Aircraft Parts," *Exxon Air World* (1979), p. 28.

Return Items—Recycled Materials

Inventory systems are designed so goods can flow from the manufacturer to the ultimate consumer. However, in some instances provisions must be made for accommodating a flow, although a lesser flow, in the opposite direction. If a customer is unhappy with a defective item and returns it to the store where it was purchased, should the store return it to the wholesaler? Who is authorized to make repairs and then place the item back into stock? If it is not worth returning items, what controls are necessary to avoid fraudulent claims?

Wholesalers who desire to have retailers increase their inventories can offer to buy back unsold items at a later date. A distinction has to be made between returned goods that can be placed back into the wholesaler's stocks and those that are no longer salable. Some products are repackaged or recycled.

In industries where return items are a major consideration, driver/salesmen are sometimes employed. They are paid on a salary plus commission basis and perform more services than the typical delivery personnel. One of these services is to check display cases for dated merchandise, remove soiled items, and collect returnable items (such as bottles). Chain food stores frequently rely on driver/salesmen employed by other suppliers to continue to handle items that involve returns. This means that the chain's distribution system need not be concerned with the return flow.

An earlier section described the parts order system used by a foreign automobile manufacturer. There are also return flows within that system. Some automobile parts are considered rebuildable, and the customer who buys the rebuilt part must be assured that it meets the manufacturer's factory specifications. The manufacturer rebuilds motors in its own country but allows parts such as speedometers to be rebuilt by specific firms in the United States. When a mechanic at the dealer goes to the parts room and asks for a speedometer, the parts clerk notices that the bin containing speedometers has a special-colored tag that tells him to ask the mechanic for the old speedometer. If there is no old speedometer to be traded (such as might occur because of auto accident) the parts clerk charges a higher price to the customer for the new (or rebuilt) speedometer he has just handed to the mechanic. The used speedometers are sent to the distributor who sends them to the plant where they are rebuilt. When finished, they are returned to the distributor and become part of the regular inventory. In this instance the distributor has two sources of supply for speedometers: his factory and the rebuilder.

Distribution Resource Planning (DRP)

DRP is an inventory method helpful in determining inventory requirements at branch warehouses. Whereas MRP (which was discussed in Chapter 2) dealt with production inputs, DRP involved finished products. They key to

DRP is centralized order processing by a manufacturer. Many firms receive orders at their regional warehouses, but this can result in an unbalanced inventory of finished products throughout the firm's regional warehouses. With DRP all orders are processed at one location and then finished products are sent to the appropriate warehouse to replenish inventory that was just sent to the customer who had placed the order. The effect is that inventory is balanced throughout the warehouse system. The central inventory planner can also ensure that, if shortages do occur, they can be evenly spread among warehouses, so that no customer must accept complete stockouts while others are receiving almost all of their requested shipments.[46]

Summary

Inventory policy is affected by the attitude of the other channel members, inventory carrying or holding costs, and the ramifications of a stock-out. The EOQ is a trade-off between inventory holding costs and ordering costs. Safety stock is extra inventory that is kept to protect against stock-outs. The consequences of a stock-out can be negligible or very serious. The optimum level of safety stock can be calculated using marginal analysis.

Inventory flow is the sequence of events in which inventory arrives and is depleted. Reorder points indicate the time to place an inventory replenishment order. The EOQ system involves varying time between orders but each order is for a fixed quantity indicated by the EOQ formula. An alternative approach is the fixed order interval system in which the EOQ formula is not utilized. The time between orders is fixed, but the quantity varies. ABC analysis is often used in conjunction with this approach.

Kanban/JIT is an inventory system that stresses keeping a minimum of production inputs on hand at any given time. This concept has been successfully utilized by Toyota Motor Company of Japan and now U.S. auto manufacturers (and many other types of firms) are using this idea. JIT works best when production involves making large numbers of products with relatively few product variations. Suppliers are frequently located in close geographic proximity to their customers who utilize JIT.

It is important that inventories be physically accounted for and this can be accomplished using a number of techniques. Inventory ordering procedures involve the methods used to place replenishment orders.

Inventories in motion refers to products which have been ordered but have not yet been received. The chapter concluded by examining the key relationships between items in inventory. These included complementary inventory items, "deals," substitute items, informal arrangements outside the distribution channel, repair parts, and recycled materials. DRP tries to balance the level of finished goods inventory held in regional warehouses. This is accomplished by centralized order processing.

[46] See Andre J. Martin, *Distribution Resource Planning* (Essex Junction, Vt.: Oliver Wight, 1983).

Questions for Discussion and Review

1. One section of the chapter was entitled, "Bearing or Sharing the Burden?" What was the issue involved here?
2. Discuss the costs of holding inventory.
3. Discuss the concept of stock-out costs. How can a stock-out cost be calculated?
4. What is safety stock? How can it be calculated?
5. What is the logic of the EOQ model?
6. Study Figure 7-2. Present a brief explanation of the inventory flow in this diagram. Be sure to mention the role of the reorder point.
7. "Only unsophisticated inventory managers would prefer a fixed-order interval system to the EOQ system." Do you agree? Discuss.
8. What is the basic theory of JIT inventory systems?
9. Discuss briefly the Kanban system of JIT.
10. How have Japanese companies utilized JIT? Give an example.
11. Discuss the two primary advantages of the JIT system.
12. How have carriers reacted to JIT in the United States?
13. What will be the impact of JIT on the railroad industry?
14. Can JIT be used for international shipments? Discuss.
15. What has been the impact of JIT on plant and warehouse location decisions?
16. Discuss the utilization of scanners in inventory control.
17. One section of this chapter was entitled "Inventories in Motion." What did this section discuss?
18. Discuss the concept of complementary inventory items.
19. Do you believe JIT will become more or less important in the future? Defend your answer.
20. Do you believe the area of inventory management will become more or less important relative to the other areas of PD/L in the future? Why?

Problems to Work Out

1. Assume you operate a cigar stand. Your customers must request the brand of cigars they want, and you usually sell cigars on a one-at-a-time basis. You sell El SMOKOs for 15¢ each; they cost you only 10 cents apiece. You are out of EL SMOKOs, and on a tally sheet you record the responses of 100 customers who ask for an EL SMOKO and are told that you are out of stock.
   a. Thirty walk away without making a purchase.
   b. Twenty buy an EL SUPREMO cigar that sells for 25 cents (and costs you 18 cents).
   c. Forty buy an EL CHEAPO at 10 cents (that costs you 8 cents).
   d. Ten say they can wait and will check with you later in the day to see whether the EL SMOKOs have arrived.

   What has it cost you to be out of stock of the 100 EL SMOKO cigars you could have sold? What is your best estimate? What other information, if any, do you still need to know?

2. Assume as a retailer you order $5,000 worth of SUPER GLO toothpaste per year and it is sold in an even flow. It costs you $40 to place and receive an order of SUPER GLO. Your annual inventory carrying costs are estimated to be 30 per cent of the inventory you have on hand. What is your EOQ?

3. You are a retail coal dealer and buy $300,000 worth of coal from the mines each year, and your sales are fairly evenly distributed throughout the year. Order-processing costs (including rental of equipment to unload the cars at your yard) are $1,000 per order; and carrying costs are 20 per cent per year for the inventory on hand. What is your EOQ?

Additional Chapter References

Aggarwal, Sumer C. "Economic Ordering in Periods of Uncertainty." *Journal of Purchasing and Materials Management* (Fall 1979), pp. 13–18.

Closs, David J., and Wai-Kin Law. "Modeling the Impact of Environmental and Inventory Management Policy on Material Management Performance." *Journal of Business Logistics* (Vol. 5, No. 1, 1984), pp. 57–80.

Blumenfeld, Dennis E., Randolph W. Hall, and William C. Jordan, "Trade-offs between Freight Expediting and Safety Stock Inventory Costs," *Journal of Business Logistics* (March 1985), pp. 79–100.

Collins, Robert S., and D. Clay Whybark, "Realizing the Potentials of Distribution Requirements Planning," *Journal of Business Logistics* (March 1985), pp. 53–65.

Fagan, Mark L. "Inventory Management: Organizing for Success." *Annual Proceedings of the NCPDM* (1984), pp. 447–460.

Gill, Lynn E., George Isoma, and Joel Sutherland. "Inventory and Physical Distribution Management." *The Distribution Handbook* (New York: Free Press Division of Macmillan, 1985), pp. 615–733.

Gundrum, Lawrence J., and Raymond J. Casey. "Improving Inventory Productivity." *Annual Proceedings of the NCPDM* (1984), pp. 692–700.

Jackson, George C. "Just-in-Time Production: Implications for Logistics Managers." *Journal of Business Logistics* (Vol. 4, No. 2, 1983), pp. 1–19.

Jones, Thomas C., and Daniel W. Riley. "Using Inventory for Competitive Advantage Through Supply Chain Management." *Annual Proceedings of the NCPDM* (1984), pp. 309–320.

Kullman, Brian C., and Robert W. Haessler. "Kanban, American Style." *Annual Proceedings of the NCPDM* (1984), pp. 99–108.

Lambert, Douglas M., and Douglas E. Zemke. "Managing Inventories in Uncertain Times." *Annual Proceedings of the NCPDM* (1983), pp. 998–1009.

Martin, André J. *Distribution Resource Planning* (Essex Junction, Vt.: Oliver Wight, 1983).

Mentzer, John T., and R. Krishnan, "The Effect of the Assumption of Normality on Inventory Control/Customer Service," *Journal of Business Logistics* (March 1985), pp. 101–120.

Nelson, Benjamin A. "On Site Printing of Bar Code Symbols." *Annual Proceedings of the NCPDM* (1984), pp. 661–678.

Schneider, Paul H. "Warehousing, Transportation, and Finished Goods Inventory Strategies." *Annual Proceedings of the NCPDM* (1983), pp. 509–521.

Sethi, Shyam S., and Robert M. Sutton. "Inventory and Warehousing Cost Forecasting." *Annual Proceedings of the NCPDM* (1982), pp. 817–830.

Whiting, R. Scott. "Making Just-in-Time Work!" *Warehousing Review* (Oct. 1984), pp. 14–16, 23–25, 46–48.

"Why Everybody Is Talking About 'Just-in Time.'" *Warehousing Review* (Oct. 1984), pp. 4–6, 26–29.

Zinszer, Paul H. "An Examination of the Cost of Capital and Inventory Stocking Policy." *Annual Proceedings of the NCPDM* (1984), pp. 603–606.

——— "Inventory Costing." *Journal of Business Logistics* (Vol. 4, No. 2, 1983), pp. 20–39.

CASE 7-1

The Low Nail Company

After making some wise short-term investments at a race track, Chris Low had some additional cash to invest in a business. The most promising opportunity at the time was in building supplies, so Low bought a business that specialized in sales of one size of nail. The annual volume of nails was two thousand kegs, and they were sold to retail customers in an even flow. Low was uncertain how many nails to order at any time. Initially, only two costs concerned him: that of order processing, which was $60 per order, without regard to size; and warehousing costs, which were one dollar per year per keg space. This meant that Low had to rent a constant amount of warehouse space for the year, and it had to be large enough to accommodate an entire order when it arrived. Low was not worried about maintaining safety stocks, mainly because the outward flow of goods was so even. Low bought his nails on a delivered basis.

Question One: Using the EOQ methods outlined earlier in Chapter 7, how many kegs of nails should Low order at one time?

Question Two (continuation of situation in Question One): Assume all conditions in Question One hold, except that Low's supplier now offers a quantity discount in the form of absorbing all, or part, of Low's order-processing costs. For orders of 750 or more kegs of nails, the supplier will absorb all of the order-processing costs; for orders between 249 and 749 kegs, he will absorb half. What is Low's new EOQ? (If you are assigned this, or later questions, it might be easiest to lay out all costs in tabular form.)

Question Three (continuation of situation in Question One; ignore—temporarily—your work on Question Two.) Instead of the conditions mentioned in Question Two, assume that Low's warehouse offers to rent Low space on the basis of the *average* number of kegs Low will have in stock, rather than on the maximum number of kegs Low would need room for whenever a new shipment arrived. The storage charge per keg remains the same. Does this change the answer to Question One? If so, what is the new answer?

Question Four (continuation of situations outlined in Questions One, Two, and Three.) Take into account the answer to Question One *and* the supplier's new policy outlined in Question Two *and* the warehouse's new policy outlined in Question Three, and determine Low's new EOQ.

Question Five (continuation of situation in Question One; ignore—temporarily— your work on Questions Two, Three, and Four.) Low's luck at the race track is over; he now must borrow money in order to finance his inventory of nails. Looking at the situation outlined in Question One, assume that the wholesale cost of nails is $40 per keg, and that Low must pay interest at the rate of 1½ per cent per month on unsold inventory. What is his new EOQ?

Question Six (continuation of situation in Questions One, Two, Three, and Five.) Take into account all the factors listed in Questions One, Two, Three, and Five, and calculate Low's EOQ for kegs of nails.

CASE 7-2

Sandy's Candy

Sandy Nykerk was an operations analyst for Mannix Model Markets, a food store chain headquartered in Omaha, Nebraska, with fifty-five food stores in an area that extended as far east as Des Moines, Iowa, as far north as Sioux Falls, South Dakota, as far west as North Platte, Nebraska, and as far south as Emporia, Kansas. All of the stores were served by daily deliveries five days a week from a large complex of Mannix warehouses in Omaha. There were two exceptions. Each store's produce department could buy some produce locally, which they usually did during the summer and autumn months. The second exception was that some goods were delivered to the stores by vendors, usually operating through driver/salesmen who would stock the goods on the shelves. Examples of these goods were dairy products, soft drinks, bakery items, "name-brand" snacks, beer, panty hose, candy and yogurt. Vendors delivered ice cream directly to the stores west of Grand Island; in part this was because Mannix was short of trucks with freezer capacity, especially in summer months.

Mannix Markets was a member of a buying cooperative. The buying cooperative had forced many name-brand manufacturers to make their goods available to the co-operative, in which case they would be delivered to each chain's warehouse, and then via chain trucks to individual retail chain stores, where store personnel would place them on the shelves and treat them as any other product. The only goods that could not be purchased through the cooperative was beer. This was because some states had stricter regulations regarding the wholesaling of beer (and other alcoholic beverages) initially to insure that the state received all of its beverage tax receipts (although beer wholesalers oppose legislation to relax these regulations).

Sandy knew that most of the vendor-delivered goods were ones that Mannix Markets did not want to handle through its own distribution system. Milk, for example, would be very expensive to handle because it was costly to ship and had a short shelf life. Bakery products had similar characteristics although Mannix Markets did buy some bread from a private bakery and sold it in Omaha stores under the "Mannix" label. Snack foods were also best handled by driver/salesmen working for vendors because they were handled roughly in the Mannix distribution system, and by the time pretzels or potato chips reached the shelves, they were mostly broken and filled only the bottom third of the bag.

The buying cooperative had recently entered into an agreement with Schoenecker's Candies, a well-known regional firm that produced eight different types of candies and caramels sold in cellophane bags. The experience of Mannix Markets was that Schoenecker's candies sold much better than any competing brand, almost irrespective of price, so Schoenecker's was the only brand that Mannix Markets would carry. Sandy had received a note from her boss saying that Schoenecker's candies could now be purchased directly through the buyers' cooperative and handled through Mannix Markets' regular distribution system. Her boss wanted her to calculate whether Mannix Markets should stop having Schoenecker's candies delivered by driver/salesmen and, instead, purchase through the buying cooperative.

If the cost comparisons were close, Mannix Markets would prefer using its own system for several reasons. The reasons were generalities regarding driver/salesmen and not specifically referring to the Schoenecker driver/salesmen. The three objections to deliveries by driver/salesmen were:

1. Their deliveries could not be scheduled, and sometimes their trucks would tie up an unloading dock, which could delay a Mannix truck waiting to discharge 10 or 20 tons of groceries.
2. Some driver/salesmen needed space in the stock room, and this meant more "unknown" people were wandering an area where pilferage was sometimes a problem.
3. When a driver/salesman appeared, this interrupted the store manager or assistant manager, who routinely would have to approve the next order and also have to check in the new merchandise and agree on the amount of "returned" merchandise the driver-salesman was removing from the store.

Store clerks disliked some driver/salesmen, claiming that they took shelf-stocking work away from store personnel. Store management discounted this argument because they thought that many store clerks did not like to see how quickly the driver/salesmen worked. (The driver/salesmen were mostly nonunion and worked on a commission basis.) Also, the shelves stocked by driver/salesmen were always neater than those stocked by ordinary store personnel. On occasion, when store clerks disliked a specific driver/salesman, they would sabotage him by rearranging the shelves after he had left, hiding all of his products behind those of a competitor.

Sandy started working on her assignment and found that she was comparing the efficiency of Mannix Markets' distribution system, which handled 10,000 line items, with that of the Schoenecker Candy Company, which handled only eight types of candy in several different sizes of packages. Soon Sandy's project became known as the Sandy Candy Puzzle among her fellow workers. Finally, to organize her thoughts and provide a basis for comparison, Sandy took a sheet of paper, drew a line down the middle, and tried to tally as many comparisons as possible. Her analysis is shown in Exhibits 7-1 and 7-2.

Sandy completed her tally sheet and wondered why sales per store should be higher when driver/salesmen service the merchandise. She was told that this was because they did a better job of arranging the goods on the shelves, they kept abreast of changes in demand, and that they sometimes placed posters and other small displays on the candy shelves.

Question One: Using those items of comparison for which costs can be calculated, determine the cost difference between the two systems.

Exhibit 7-1 Sandy's Worksheet #1

PRESENT SYSTEM	ALTERNATE SYSTEM
Schoenecker Candy Co. has driver/salesmen deliver and stock shelves	Purchase Schoenecker's Candies through buying cooperative and distribute to stores through Mannix Markets' own distribution system
BUYING TERMS	
Every Friday, the d/s tallies sales for past seven days and store manager approves. Then three days later a bill comes from Schoenecker with 2% discount if paid within ten days (i.e. 13 days after the d/s makes his tally). The entire amount is due within 30 days (or 33 days of d/s tally).	Schoenecker must be paid within seven days after candy is received at Mannix warehouse. No discounts.

WHOLESALE AND RETAIL PRICES OF CANDY

package size	wholesale price paid to Schoenecker	retail price	package size	wholesale price paid to Schoenecker	retail price
3½ oz.	13¢	19¢	4 oz.	10¢	19¢
8 oz.	28¢	39¢	9 oz.	20¢	39¢
12 oz.	42¢	57¢	13 oz.	30¢	57¢

AVERAGE TIME IN INVENTORY	
Goods were actually on consignment which meant Schoenecker's owned them and only collected for those which had been sold.	Candy would be in the Mannix warehouse for an average of two weeks and on a retail store shelf for an average of one week.
AVERAGE SALES PER STORE PER WEEK	
110 3½ oz. pkgs., 70 8 oz. pkgs., and 40 12 oz. pkgs.	100 4 oz. pkgs., 60 9 oz. pkgs., and 30 13 oz. pkgs. (Sales were somewhat lower because store personnel do not take as good care of merchandise on shelves.)
SHRINKAGE ON STORE SHELF	
(unaccounted-for loss): 2 percent per week, paid for by Mannix Markets	2 percent per week, paid for by Mannix Markets

Question Two: List and compare those factors to which it is difficult to assign precise costs.

Question Three: Given the data that Sandy Nykerk has, do you believe that Mannix Markets should get its Schoenecker Candy through the buying cooperative or continue to rely on direct deliveries by Schoenecker's driver/salesmen? Give your reasons.

Question Four: If you were Ms. Nykerk, what additional information would you like to have before being asked to make such a recommendation?

Exhibit 7-2 Sandy's Worksheet #2

PRESENT SYSTEM	ALTERNATE SYSTEM
SPOILAGE	
(package torn open on shelf which cannot be sold): 1 percent a week, absorbed by Schoenecker Candy	same rate, paid for by Mannix Markets
ORDERING COSTS	
Absorbed by Schoenecker Candy Co. However store manager or assistant must approve order, twice a week, taking a total of 10 minutes time. Assistant manager makes $16,000 per year plus 15% fringe.	1½¢ per day, 4 days a week, for each of 24 items (8 types of candy in three sizes of package)
SHELF STOCKING	
Absorbed by Schoenecker Candy Co.	20 minutes of clerk's time per week. (Clerk's hourly rate is $3.75 plus 10% fringe.) For every 10 stock clerks there is one supervisor paid $13,000 per year plus 15% fringe.
WAREHOUSING COSTS	
Absorbed by Schoenecker Candy Co.	The Mannix warehouse costs $10,000 per day to operate. Its "thru-put" is 750 tons per day, five days a week.
DELIVERY TO STORE COSTS	
Absorbed by Schoenecker Candy Co.	Only available cost figure is 3¢ per ton mile and the average distance from Mannix warehouse to a retail store is 50 miles.
CHECKING IN GOODS AT STORE	
Takes 10 minutes per week of manager's or assistant manager's time.	No check-in necessary; controls are at warehouse, and truck is sealed in between warehouse and store.
BILLING AND BILL PAYING COSTS	
Mannix Markets pays $1.00 per week to process and pay the Schoenecker Candy Co. invoice.	Believed to be less since rather than spot-checking forms from each store, only the Mannix warehouse receipt form need be checked.

Question Five: Candy sales increase during holiday seasons. Which of the two candy distribution systems do you think will do a better job of anticipating and supplying these seasonal increases? Why?

Question Six: Assume you are in charge of labor relations for Mannix Model Markets. Would you like to see continued reliance on driver/salesmen to supply the markets' candy needs? Why or why not?

Users of bulk materials like waterfront sites so that they can use low-cost water transportation. Here, a number of barges are tied up, waiting to be unloaded. The materials are unloaded by a crane-mounted bucket which drops them into a hopper, feeding them on to a conveyer belt moving toward the camera.

(*Credit:* Barber-Greene Company)

Figure 8-1 Advertisement Showing a Site's Location as an Advantage in Reaching British and European Markets

MORE FOR DISTRIBUTION

Location and access to Britain,
Ireland and Europe are the
reasons why . . .

Sanyo
Fiat
Woolworth
Safeway
Nestle
Marks & Spencer
Rowntree-Mackintosh
Goodyear
Dresser
Koehring
Bostitch
Travenol
Becton-Dickinson
Anixter
Snap-on-Tools
Avdel
Compair
Inmac
Allied Breweries
Schweppes

are serving their customers in Britain and Europe through
the Warrington-Runcorn centered motorways, railways,
seaports and airport complex of Manchester-Liverpool.
Freehold Sites - Ready Space - Custom Premises

For information, please contact: The Estates Department, Warrington
& Runcorn Development Corporation. P.O. Box 49, Warrington,
England WA1 2LF ■ Telephone (0925) 51144 ■ Telex 627225

**Warrington & Runcorn
Development Corporation**

WARRINGTON & RUNCORN DEVELOPMENT CORPORATION
P.O. BOX 49, WARRINGTON, ENGLAND WA1 2LF

(*Credit:* Warrington and Runcorn Development Corporation, England)

second focus is more precise and usually involves selection of the metropolitan area or community in which the facility will be located. This is illustrated on Figure 8-1, which is from a brochure describing a site in the Manchester-Liverpool area of England.

Final analysis involves a detailed inspection of various sites of land. As an alternative, one might look at available space in existing buildings.

Factors Influencing Location

Most products are the result of combining raw materials and labor and are made for sale in specific markets. Thus, these factors—raw materials, labor, and markets—all influence the decision to locate a manufacturing or processing facility. Distribution warehouses exist to facilitate the distribution of products. Their location is between, and influenced by, the location of plants whose products they handle and the markets they serve. The discussion that follows covers the location of manufacturing, processing, and distribution facilities. The relative importance of each factor varies with the type of facility, the product being handled, its volume, and the geographic locations being considered. Although much of the discussion deals with single facilities, the decision process often involves a combination of facilities, and one must take into account the relationships between or among them.

Natural Resources

The materials used to make a product must be extracted directly from the earth or the sea, as in the cases of mining or fishing, or indirectly, as in the case of farm products. In some instances, these resources are located great distances from the point where the materials or their products will be consumed. If the materials must be processed at some point between where they are gathered and where they are needed, their *weight-losing* characteristics become important. For materials that lose no weight in processing, the processing point can be anywhere between the raw material source and the market. If the materials lose considerable weight in processing, then the processing point will be near the point where they are mined or harvested. Or, if they gain weight, the processing point will be close to the market (for example, bottled soft drinks).

Many products are a combination of several material inputs and labor. Traditional site location theory can be used to show that one (or several) locations will minimize total transportation costs. Figure 8-2 shows a laboratorylike piece of equipment that could be used to find the "lowest cost" location for assembling a product consisting of inputs from two sources and a market in a third area. This equipment, as shown, can only be used to minimize transportation costs.

Population Characteristics

Population can be viewed as either a market for goods or a potential source of labor. Distribution planners for consumer products follow shifts in population carefully. Not only are changes in numbers of interest, so are changes in the characteristics of the population—especially when those characteristics can be translated into buying power. In the United States, a comprehensive census is conducted each decade by the U.S. Bureau of the Census. Between decades, one must rely on data such as estimates made by moving companies of the numbers of households whose goods are moved from state to state. Figure 8-3 is based on one moving company's 1984 records. State and regional planning bodies possess additional information concerning population within their areas of jurisdiction.

In the United States between 1960 and 1980 three general trends were apparent. The first was from rural areas to urban areas; the second was from the central city to suburbia; the third was to the West Coast. The "flight" from the central city was relatively new. The other trends are very old. If

Figure 8-2 Example of Transportation Forces Dictating Plant Location

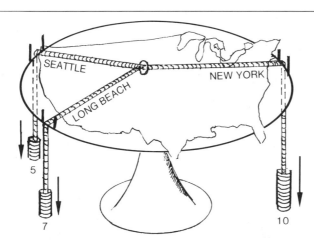

This is a simplified demonstration showing the various "pulls" which exist to determine the industrial location which minimizes the total ton miles of transportation used to transport both inputs and output. This method can be used for situations where there are "pulls" in three directions — either two sources of supply and one market, or one source of supply and two separate markets.

Assume we have two inputs, one produced in Long Beach and one produced in Seattle. The two inputs are combined to make a product which is sold in New York City. Assume further that to produce ten tons of the product consumed in New York, we must combine seven tons of the product which comes from Long Beach with five tons of the product which comes from Seattle. Assume finally that a transportation system is available anywhere and that the transport costs per ton mile are the same for either input or for the final product.

We take a circular table, placing a map of the U.S. on it and pairs of pegs on the table edge in the vicinity of Long Beach, Seattle, and New York as they are on the tabletop map. The pairs of pegs are so that a piece of string can pass between them.

We knot together three pieces of string, with all of them ending in one knot. To one of the pieces of string, which we pass through the pegs near Seattle on our map, we attach five identical metal washers (each one representing five tons). We attach seven washers to a second piece of string and pass it through the pegs in the vicinity of Long Beach on our tabletop map. To the third piece of string we attach ten washers and place it through the pegs in the vicinity of New York.

Then we take the knot and gently lift it to a point above the center of the table, with the washers on all three strings pulling down. We then drop the knot and it comes to rest at the spot on the map which represents the point in the U.S. where the manufacturing operation (for combining these two inputs into the single product) should locate. No other point will require less transportation effort — measured in ton-miles of freight moved.

(If transportation costs, or rates, differ on a per ton mile for each of the commodities or products involved, this can be taken into account by having the number of washers "weighted" to take into account the varying rates as well as the differences in weight being shipped. If for example in the situation described above carriers charged twice as much per ton mile to carry the finished product as they charged for carrying inputs, one would attach 20 washers (2 x 10) on the string reaching toward New York.)

Adapted from: Alfred Weber, *Theory of the Location of Industries,* translated by Carl J. Friedrich (Chicago: Univ. of Chicago Press, 1929).

you wanted to locate a facility at the center of 1970s population, you would choose Mascoutah, Illinois, near St. Louis. Between 1970 and 1980 the "center" crossed the Mississippi River and moved to DeSoto, Missouri, about 40 miles south of St. Louis. This shift of population to the South and to the West is expected to continue.

Figure 8-3 United States Migration Patterns in 1984

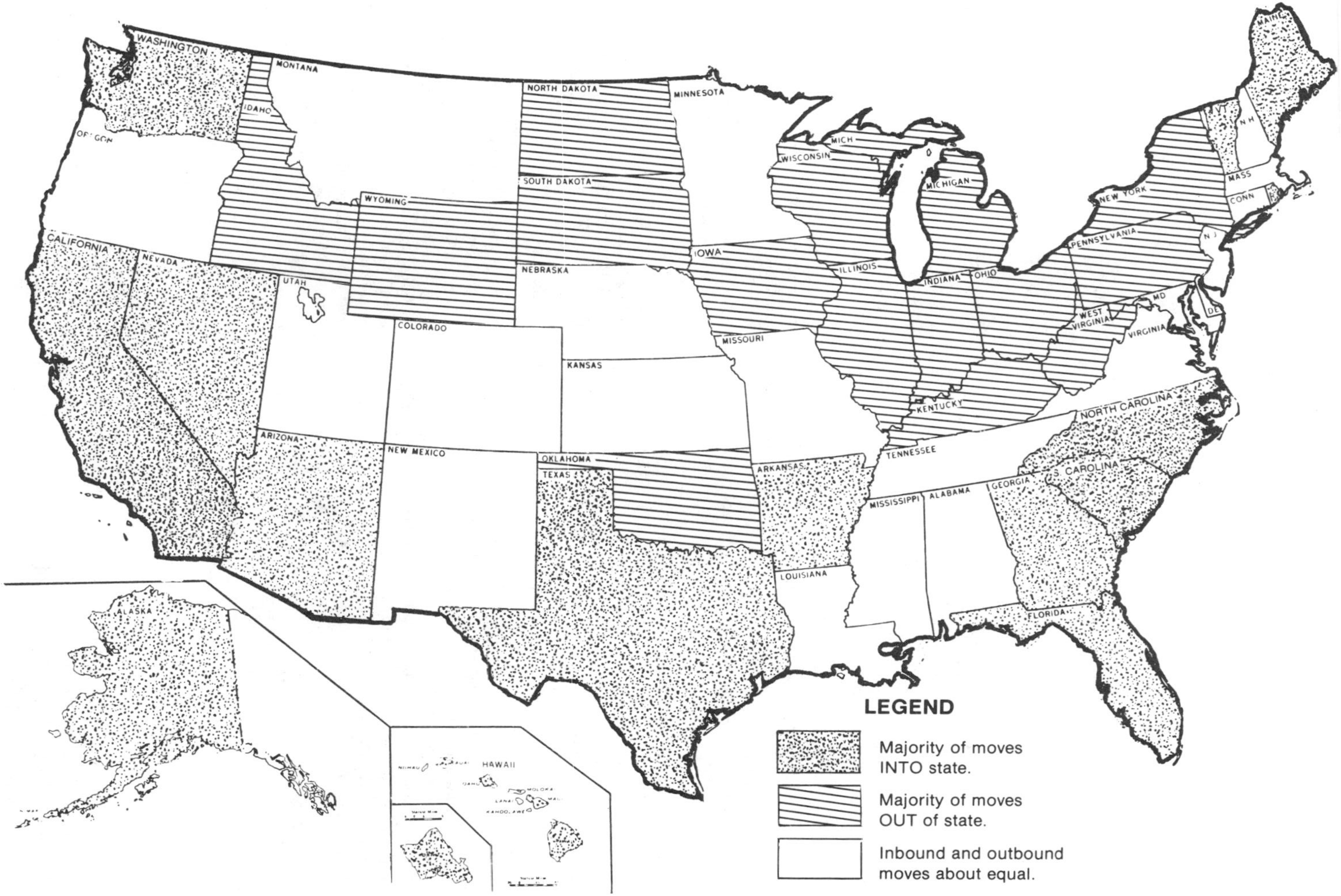

LEGEND

Majority of moves
INTO state.

Majority of moves
OUT of state.

Inbound and outbound
moves about equal.

Courtesy of United Van Lines.

298

Labor availability is of prime concern when selecting a site for manufacturing, assembling, and even warehousing. Businesses are concerned with the size of the available work force, its skills, the prevailing wage rates, and the extent to which the work force is, or will be unionized. Firms looking for sites often prefer areas where unions are not strong. Some states and communities pride themselves on the fact that unions in their area are not well developed. These states often have "right-to-work" laws, which means an individual cannot be compelled to join a union. At the same time, some unions are expanding their jurisdiction nationwide and making it more difficult for firms with union contracts to open nonunion operations elsewhere. "Industrywide" bargaining agreements result in fairly uniform wages and work standards, although there is often less uniformity nationwide than is commonly believed to be the case because so-called nationwide settlements have to be ratified locally, at which point both labor and management may bargain for additional terms. State labor laws must also be examined because often they are applicable. Such laws deal with such issues as minimum wages and management-labor disputes. Local economic conditions also can influence negotiated agreements. In the late 1970s and early 1980s, some unionized workers at plants that were about to be closed softened their demands in hopes of keeping their plant open.

In the United States, the skills of individuals seeking employment are fairly well catalogued. Therefore, someone who is comparing different communities in which to locate should work with representatives of the state employment office. An employer needing additional workers possessing certain skills could have state or federal agencies conduct job training courses that would provide the necessary skills. In some areas, unions will agree to supply the necessary labor force. In areas with chronic unemployment, job "retraining" programs are available. Vocational schools and community colleges frequently train individuals to work in various distribution functions, and these educational institutions can be relied upon to train additional personnel. Not all personnel at a new operation will be new employees of the firm. A small number of supervisory staff are frequently transferred from one location to another.

When expanding operations into foreign countries, there sometimes are limits as to the number of supervisory personnel that can be brought in. The foreign government may insist that its own nationals be trained for and employed in most supervisory posts.

Taxes and Subsidies

While labor availability and practices are an important consideration in any location decision, taxes are frequently more important, at least insofar as distribution facilities are concerned. The reason is that most distribution facilities, and especially the inventories they contain, are often viewed as "milk cows" by local tax collectors. From the community's standpoint, warehouses are "desirable" operations to attract because they add to the tax base without requiring much in the way of municipal services.

Warehouse and Plant Location

Tax burdens differ by location, and it is necessary to ask tax consultants to determine the actual tax burden associated with each site. Even when areas have what appear to be identical taxes, there are frequently significant differences in the manner in which assessments are made, or in which collections are enforced. Some localities are so anxious to attract "new" industries that they either formally or informally agree to "go easy" on the new operation for its first several years. The term "enterprise zone" or "free enterprise zone" is sometimes used to describe areas, often in declining regions or portions of cities, where special tax inducements are offered to industry.

Some localities even subsidize new industry by issuing "tax free" bonds

> *Tax-free* bonds in this instance refers to the fact that interest paid on state and municipal bonds is exempt from federal income taxation, meaning that these bonds can be sold at prices bearing a lower interest since the owner is not taxed on this interest income.

to prepare plant sites and to construct buildings. Municipalities can borrow money for less than private firms can, hence it is the firm's financial advantage to locate in such a subsidized setting and reimburse the local unit of government for its interest and debt retirement costs for preparing the site and building. While commendable insofar as attracting new industries, it frequently places a burden on existing taxpayers.

While no list of taxes is complete, a partial list would include sales taxes, real estate taxes, corporation franchise taxes, taxes associated with the exchange of real estate, business income taxes, motor fuel taxes, unemployment compensation taxes, and severance taxes (for the removal of natural resources). Of particular interest to logistics managers is the *inventory* tax, analogous to the personal property tax paid by individuals. In states with inventory taxes, the assessment date is usually in the spring (chosen by rurally dominated legislatures as the date for assessing all personal property and which would find farmers' holdings at a minimum). When only one date is used, it is to the advantage of logistics managers to have their inventories as low as possible at that time.

Most states have inventory taxes, although frequently they exempt items of political importance. Wisconsin exempts natural cheese in storage for aging, Virginia exempts tobacco still in possession of its producer, Georgia exempts all farm products, and Maryland exempts imported olive oil and coffee beans. Several states exempt property used for pollution abatement. Other exemptions deal more precisely with distribution functions. Some states exempt goods in public warehouses; one exempts goods brought into the state by water transport so long as they are still stored in the county of the entry port; and some states exempt goods passing through the state on a "storage-in-transit" bill of lading. Many states exempt goods moving on carriers passing through the state and covered by an "active" bill of lading.[1]

---

[1] "Tax Rates/Exemptions," *Distribution Worldwide* (Feb. 1974), pp. 34–37. See also, "Distribution Know-How," *Traffic Management* (March 1976), p. 37.

As if taxes are not difficult enough to understand, they are but one side of the coin in determining the costs that must be paid to governmental entities. The other is to know the value of services received from these same governmental entities. If water supply is inadequate or if fire protection is poor, the result will be higher fire insurance rates. If a plant cannot discharge its waste into a municipal sewage collection and treatment system, it may be forced to install facilities of its own. It may be difficult to attract workers to a community with a poor school system because they are concerned with their children's education. A poor school system ultimately places a greater training burden on employers, so the savings in taxes may not be as great as they initially appeared.

To complicate matters further, governments often "subsidize" new industries or firms as an inducement for them to locate. Use of a state or municipality's ability to issue tax-exempt bonds has already been mentioned. Other subsidies, common in the United States, are massive site improvements, including installation of roads and sewers. In early 1985, GM announced that it was looking for a site to build its new Saturn automobile. It was deluged with offers of concessions from states and cities. Company officials appeared surprised by the response. However, one magazine noted:

> GM, in fact, may simply be emulating its foreign competition. "GM is just doing what the foreign companies alerted it to," says Maryann N. Keller, a director at Vilas-Fischer Associates in New York City. Volkswagenwerk, she notes, announced publicly that it was looking for a U.S. manufacturing site in 1976 and wound up with concessions worth more than $75 million from Pennsylvania. Nissan, Honda, and Mazda have won generous incentives from Tennessee, Ohio, and Michigan in return for locating new plants in those states.[2]

On the international level, nations subsidize, or otherwise promote or protect, many types of commerce. The term *national competitive strategy* is employed when discussing a nation's attempts to adopt policies that will strengthen its economic position vis-à-vis the rest of the world.[3]

Transportation Services

When considering a new location, the individual performing the analysis must calculate the transportation costs between sources of supply and each proposed site and to markets that must be served from the site. Costs are calculated in terms of both money paid to carriers (or for one's own vehicles) as well as the investment in products while they are being carried. Figure 8-4 reflects this concern and shows distances, in *time*, for truck shipments leaving Oklahoma.

Competition among carriers is often important. Some electric utilities

[2] "Wherever GM Puts Saturn, It's Going to Get a Sweet Deal," *Business Week* (April 1, 1985), pp. 36–37. In July, 1985, GM announced that the plant would be located in Spring Hill, Tennessee.
[3] David Irons, "Inching Toward a National Competitive Strategy," *Harvard Magazine* (Nov.– Dec. 1983), pp. 44–49.

Figure 8-4 Map Showing "Time Distance" For Truck Shipments From Oklahoma

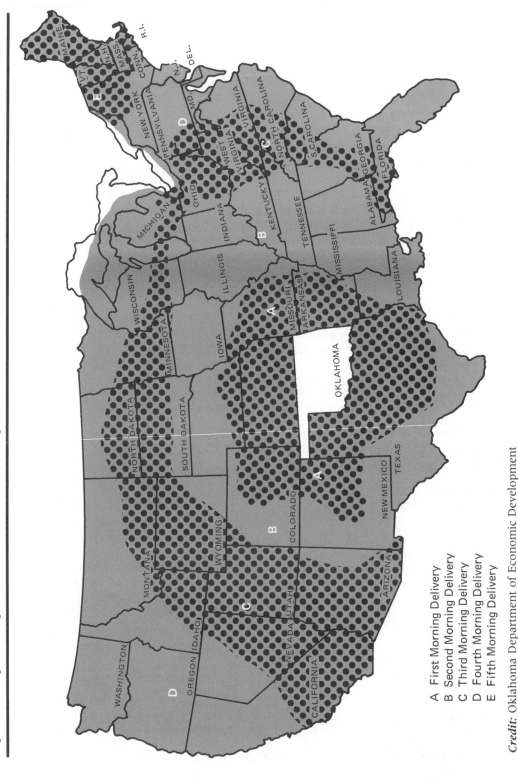

A First Morning Delivery
B Second Morning Delivery
C Third Morning Delivery
D Fourth Morning Delivery
E Fifth Morning Delivery

Credit: Oklahoma Department of Economic Development

located in Great Lakes ports adjacent to deep-draft navigation channels have not installed equipment to unload coal from vessels. However, their waterfront site allows them to obtain a lower rate from the railroad because they may threaten to install vessel-handling equipment and switch to water transportation. Service by several modes also means that a plant is less threatened by strikes in any one mode.

In addition to being served by more than one mode, it is advantageous to have several carriers of the same mode from which to choose. Even if there is not rate competition between carriers, they compete in terms of services. Railroads compete in terms of frequency or scheduling of switching service or in terms of "finding" specialized cars when they are scarce.

Transportation, as a factor in site selection, has become more important in recent years because its costs have increased more than have those of other factors. One consultant reported that, based on location assignments carried out between 1978 and 1983, "transportation costs for a representative national distribution warehousing facility have risen 120 per cent vs. comparable rates of increase for electric power (57 per cent), . . . labor (52 per cent), construction (47 per cent), industrial land (27 per cent), and real property taxes (19 per cent)."[4]

Customers

The order of presentation thus far in this chapter has stressed resource, labor, taxes, and transportation factors, rather than customers. Customers are, of course, of great importance. Most distribution facilities are oriented more toward customers than they are toward other factors. Finding and satisfying customers is discussed in basic marketing texts. For consumer products, a firm usually seeks a population with buying power and designs its distribution system so that it carries out the firm's marketing objectives.

Sellers of industrial products also locate near their buyers. A study of plant location decisions made by firms which located in Greensboro, North Carolina, described a specific type of customer orientation referred to as dovetailing.

> Dovetailing is the process whereby a supplier locates his plant in close proximity to a large customer. The most obvious examples of dovetailing in the United States are the several tin can plants abutting food or beverage packers. For this particular dovetailing situation the tin can conveyor belt is actually extended through a common wall so the finished cans are never touched before they are filled with product. . . . Nonelectrical machinery dominates the dovetailing orientation in Greensboro. These machinery factories were constructed to build machinery for use by the local textile and furniture industry. The other four plants dovetail as follows: the textile plant manufactures woven elastic for the apparel industry; the apparel plant does contract sewing for a large garment manufacturer; the chemical plant

---

[4] *Handling & Shipping Management* (March 1984), p. 60. The consultant is the Boyd Company of Princeton, N.J. In their analysis, shipping costs accounted for 11.9 per cent of total operating costs in 1978 and 16.5 per cent in 1983.

manufactures textile chemicals; and the furniture plant does contract upholstering for furniture assemblies.[5]

Energy Sources

All distribution and manufacturing facilities use electricity, and some manufacturing processes are very dependent upon other forms of energy as well. Questions should be asked about energy costs and the likelihood of shortages. Electric utilities rely on a number of sources of energy to generate electric power, and some of these sources are more likely to be subjected to price increases than others.

This is also another area where local subsidies to new industries are given. A study of factors influencing plant location in small Texas communities stated that it is important to determine "whether the utility company is owned by the city, a public organization or a private concern. The importance is that often cities may offer utility rebates to induce industries to locate there."[6]

Commodity Flows

Firms producing consumer goods follow the changes in population in order to better orient their distribution systems. There are also shifts in markets for industrial goods. Data on general sources of data regarding commodity flows would be studied, much like population figures, to determine changes occurring in the movements of raw materials and semiprocessed goods. Government data in these areas are generally complete, but the degree of coverage varies. There may be excellent reports concerning the supply and demand for a specific agricultural commodity, while there may be almost no data at all concerning other, more significant products. Some trade organizations report data concerning their members' activities. Figure 8-5 is a page from an annual report on coal traffic produced by the National Coal Association. This particular page shows the states from which coal is shipped to large coal-burning electric utilities and the mode of transportation used.

Although population shifts are especially important to marketing decisions, commodity flow data are related to production. Two vital pieces of information are (1) how much is being produced and (2) where it is being shipped. If a firm is concerned with a distribution system for its industrial product, this information would tell how the market is functioning, and, in many instances, how to identify both the manufacturers and their major customers. At this point, the researcher would understand the existing situation and would try to find a lower cost production-distribution arrangement. Should the firm join the existing patterns of trade (which is easier to

[5] Charles R. Hayes and Norman W. Schul, "Why Do Manufacturers Locate in the Southern Piedmont?" *Land Economics* (Feb. 1968), pp. 117–121.

[6] Ronald Linehan, C. Michael Walton, and Richard Dodge, "Variables in Rural Plant Location: A Case Study of Sealy, Texas," Memo 21 (Austin: U. of Texas Council for Advanced Transportation Studies, 1975), p. 21.

Figure 8-5 Excerpt from Trade Association Report Showing Movements of Coal to Electric Utilities in 1978

Annual Survey of Coal Transportation from Mine to Utilities
1978

State, Utility & Plant	Origin State	Share of Coal Shipments to Plant (% of Total Ton Miles)		
		Rail	Water	Truck
ALABAMA				
Alabama Elec Coop				
McWilliams*	AL-KY-TN	100.0 (u)	–	–
Tombigbee*[1]	AL-KY-TN	59.9	40.1	–
Alabama Power				
Barry[e]	AL-KY-TN	50.0	50.0	–
Gadsden[e]	AL-KY	80.0	–	20.0
Gaston[e]	AL-KY-TN	80.0 (u)	–	20.0
Gorgas*	ALABAMA	Rail, Truck & Conveyor	–	–
Greene County	ALABAMA	–	100.0	–
Miller	ALABAMA	–	–	100.0
Tennessee Valley Authority				
Colbert	KY-OH	38.0 (u)	62.0	–
Widows Creek	AL-KY-TN-WY	88.1 (u)	8.8	3.0
ARIZONA				
Arizona Public Service				
Cholla	NEW MEXICO	100.0 (u)	–	–
Salt River Project				
Navajo	AR-AZ	100.0 (u)	–	–
ARKANSAS				
Southwestern Electric Power				
Flint Creek	WYOMING	100.0 (u)	–	–
COLORADO				
Central Telephone & Utilities Corp.				
Clark	COLORADO	–	–	100.0
Colorado Springs, Dept. of Public Util.				
Martin Drake	COLORADO	100.0	–	–
Colorado-Ute Electric Assn.				
Bullock	COLORADO	100.0	–	–
Hayden*	COLORADO	–	–	100.0
Nucla*	COLORADO	–	–	100.0

Note: the (u)'s in the rail column mean that coal moved by unit trains.

Courtesy National Coal Association

do in an expanding market) or should it produce at a point where no other manufacturers of a similar product are located?

Determining the Number of Facilities

Very few firms start business on one day and need a nationwide distribution system the next. Distribution and production facilities are usually added one at a time. *Marginal analysis* is employed to test whether one more (or less) distribution facility is required. The drawback of marginal analysis is that one may miss the "big picture." Very painstaking analysis may be applied to the question, "Do we need a 37th distribution facility, and if so, where should it be located?" Instead, the question should have been, "Do we need approximately 35–40 distribution facilities? Is there some other total number that would serve us better?"

An example of this latter type of analysis was Firestone Tire and Rubber Company's system of "45 warehouses . . . being replaced by only 24 distribution centers."[7] In determining the numbers and locations of the 24 centers, labor attitudes, transportation costs, and inventory levels were all important:

> We developed a sales history for the 2,100 counties in which we sell. From that we built multicounty market zones. Then we started fitting distribution centers arbitrarily into our model. This was a no-strings simulation. We began with 12, then 16, then 20, and continued up to 45 locations. Transportation cost curves were made for each location. We also watched the changes in product mix, the average and peak inventory levels, the operating costs per distribution center, and for the whole system. That's basically how we settled on the figure of 24 centers.[8]

Most analytical procedures for determining the number of distribution centers are computerized because of the vast number of alternatives that must be considered. Through simulation techniques, varying hypothetical demands are forecast, and the ability of each facility and the system as a whole to avoid stock-outs and also to provide a specified minimum of service is tested. The difficulty in testing an entire system is that neighboring distribution centers, while each is designed to serve a specified number of locations, also serve as backup for each other. Hence, if a firm tests a system for upstate New York and one of the points being considered is Syracuse, it must also measure the ability of Syracuse to back up facilities at Rochester, Binghamton, and Schenectady, and vice-versa. Given these four points; Syracuse is probably the best back-up point because it is located between the other three. However, determining its *value* as a backup facility is difficult because Rochester could also draw on Buffalo, and Binghamton could rely on a facility at Scranton, Pennsylvania; thus this back-up value must be shared with other locations as well. One can see that the complementary relationship between adjoining distribution facilities makes manual analysis of distribution system design difficult. If, in addition, varying levels of service were being tested, one might find that for each level of service an entirely

[7] *Handling and Shipping* (Dec. 1971), p. 41. Note the old facilities were "warehouses," the new ones, "distribution centers."

[8] *Handling and Shipping* (Dec. 1971), statement of James F. Davis, Firestone's manager of inventory and distribution research. See also, "Do You Need All Those Distribution Centers?" *Distribution Worldwide* (April 1979), pp. 42–47; and John J. Kaufman, "The Central Warehouse: Solid Foundation for a National Distribution System," *NCPDM 1980 Papers*, pp. 143–150.

different series of distribution sites would prove to be ideal. Clearly, these are problems of a scope that only computers can handle.[9]

Finding The Lowest Cost Location

Most solutions to locational problems are reached through use of computerized analysis. Frequently, large geographic areas are under consideration, and, initially, all possible sites are considered eligible. But ultimately, the firm must decide where to locate *specifically*. A firm exporting into western Europe may decide that it must locate a manufacturing operation inside one of the Common Market countries so it can avoid the higher tariff barriers facing exports from outside. A U.S. firm, located in Pennsylvania, may decide that the time has come to locate an additional distribution facility west of the Mississippi River. This section illustrates a method for finding the low-cost location and discusses the various sources of geographic coding data, available in the United States, that might be needed for any computerized analysis of a locational problem. It assumes that the decision has been made that only one additional facility is needed and that the problem has been reduced to finding the "best" location for that facility.

Center-of-Gravity Approach

The center-of-gravity method is frequently used for locating a single facility at a site where the distance to existing facilities is minimized. Figure 8-6 shows a grid system placed over a map of five existing retail stores. Assuming that each store receives the same tonnage and that straight line (or "as the crow flies") distances are used throughout, the "best" location for a warehouse to serve the five retail stores is determined by taking the average north-south coordinates of the retail stores and the average east-west coordinates. On Figure 8-6 the grid system has its lower left (southwest) corner labeled point zero, zero. The vertical (north-south) axis shows distances north of point zero, zero, and the horizontal (east-west) axis shows distances to the east. In the example, the average distance north is $3 + 1 + 3 + 2 + 3$ divided by the number of stores, or 5, and the answer is $12/5$ or 2.4 miles. The average distance east is $1 + 2 + 3 + 4 + 6$ divided by 5 or 3.2 miles. The best warehouse location is one with coordinates of 2.4 miles north and 3.2 miles east of point zero. (The term *best* is used, but the method described here only approximates the most accurate solution.) Figure 8-7 contains additional problems of this type.

Approaches such as this provide approximate locations of centralized

---

[9] For a discussion of the mathematical concepts included, see, David M. Smith, *Industrial Location: An Economic Geographical Analysis* (New York: Wiley, 1971); and for a discussion of all the aspects of answering the question "How many warehouses should we have?" see Arthur M. Geoffrion and Richard F. Powers, "Facility Location Analysis Is Just the Beginning—If You Do It Right," *Interfaces* (April 1980), pp. 22–30.

Figure 8-6 "Center of Gravity" Location for Warehouse to Serve Five Retail Stores

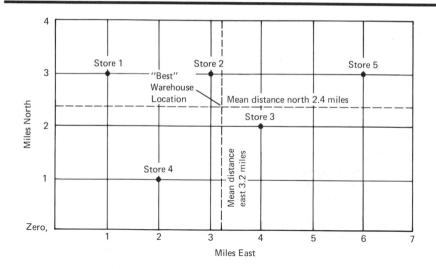

facilities, at least in a transportation sense. However, adjustments have to be made to take into account taxes, wage rates, volume "discounts," the cost and quality of transport services, and the fact that transport rates "taper."

Other Grid Systems

Grid systems are checkerboard patterns placed on a map (such as in Figure 8-6). Squares are numbered in two directions: horizontal and vertical. Recall from geometry that the length of the hypotenuse of a right triangle is the square root of the sum of the squared values of each of the right triangle's

Figure 8-7 "Grid" Problems Involving Location of a Single Facility

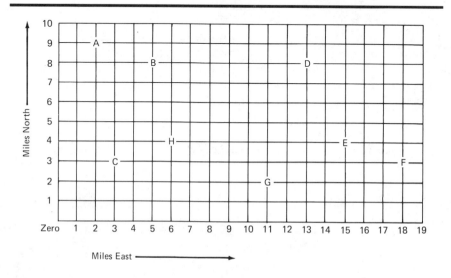

The Elements of Physical Distribution/Logistics Systems

two legs. It is easy for a computer to calculate the distance between any two points whose grid coordinates are known. Grid systems are placed so they will coincide with north-south and east-west lines on a map (although minor distortion is caused by the fact that east-west lines are parallel while north-south lines converge at both poles—a factor that sophisticated computer programs can take into account). Grid systems are important to locational analysis because they allow one to analyze spatial relationships with relatively simple mathematical tools. One may also group, and regroup, various areas for purpose of analysis.

At least one firm has placed varying types of geographic data on one record. Figure 8-8 shows a layout that uses 126 digits to record 23 types of information. Some of the types of information require additional explanation. Item 3, unit type, indicates whether the place is a city or a county or some other governmental unit. Item 4 refers to the airport code developed by the International Air Transport Association (IATA). Items 6 through 8 refer to a numeric code established by Dun and Bradstreet. Items 10 and 11 refer to a Standard Point Location Code developed jointly by the National Motor Freight Tariff Association and the Association of American Railroads for purposes of providing a scheme for identifying locations in "computerized" transportation tariffs and in other transportation and logistics systems. Items 15 and 18 are the mean latitudes and longitudes of the counties. Items 19 and 20 refer to a geographic coding system devised by IBM, and items 21, 22, and 23 refer to FIPS, or Federal Information Processing Standards, a system maintained by the National Bureau of Standards. The firm whose form is pictured lists over 132,000 "places" in the United States.

The discussion to this point has emphasized transportation data. Marketing data are equally important, and in a geographical analysis a locational researcher might include statistics concerning the population and buying power of areas for which distribution centers are being considered. This information is available from the Bureau of the Census or from private services. The marketing and transportation data could be combined and make it possible to search for distribution sites that meet both transportation requirements and are within reach of specified blocs of buying power.

Specialized Location Characteristics

To this point, the chapter has dealt with many general considerations concerning the selection of a site for manufacturing, distributing, or assembling. Mathematical techniques may indicate that if a facility is located in a certain spot, transportation costs will be minimized. More sophisticated models take other factors into account and indicate an "ideal" site. This section deals with some specialized considerations that must be recognized before deciding upon a specific area or site. Most of these considerations are "invisible" boundaries that are frequently of great significance.

Within municipalities most lands are "zoned," which means there are limits on the types of uses to which they may be put. Thus, a warehouse might be allowed only in areas set aside for wholesale or other specified

Figure 8-8 Example of U.S. Geographic Code Layout

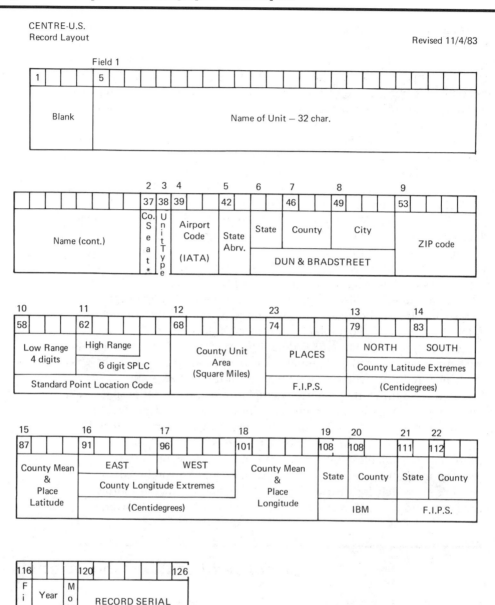

© 1984 Distribution Sciences, Inc., Des Plaines, Illinois.

commercial operations. Restrictions on sites for manufacturing are even more severe, especially if the operation in question is not considered to be a "desirable" neighbor because of the fumes, smoke, dust, and noise it creates. Distribution centers are believed to be more desirable, the only complaint against them being the volume of truck traffic they cause on neighboring streets. Zoning classifications can be changed, especially if the community in question is attempting to attract industry. Vacant land should not be considered without first checking out any possible land-use restrictions.

Controls on *environmental pollution* are a matter of increasing concern. While they affect mainly manufacturing and assembling operations, they also can affect distribution operations. Warehouses with incinerators for burning cartons may find an air pollution control inspector insisting that the incinerator chimney be modified. Gasoline distribution operations (including retail service stations) are being required to install devices to capture gasoline vapors that otherwise would escape into the air. The Delaware Coastal Zone Act of 1971 "barred heavy manufacturing industry from locating in a two-mile-wide strip along the state's 115-mile coastline . . . , and prohibited the construction in the bay of marine terminals for the transhipment of liquid and solid bulk materials."[10] Such examples are not restricted to the United States: a consultant's study for the Island of Cyprus, dealing with the possible substitution of coal for oil as the island's main energy source, discovered that ash production and disposal were a major impediment, despite the coal's lower price.[11]

Union locals have areas of jurisdiction. A firm's labor relation manager may have preferences as to which locals he would rather deal with; he should be consulted before any decisions are made. The firm's existing contracts may have some provisions regarding union jurisdiction over new sites. Sometimes unions battle for jurisdiction. For example, stevedores claimed the right to stuff and unstuff containers carrying exports and imports when the stuffing or unstuffing occurred within 50 miles of a port. Teamsters in the affected area dispute this because they felt that they should have an equal right to work in the growing container trade.

Free-Trade Zones

A very specialized site in which to locate would be a free-trade zone, (also known as "foreign trade zones") of which there are about eighty in the United States. A typical free-trade zone is an enclosed facility, under Customs security supervision, situated in or near an international port and into which foreign merchandise may be brought without being subject to formal Customs requirements. The merchandise is stored, exhibited, processed, or used in zone manufacturing operations, without being subjected to duties and quotas unless and until the goods or their products enter the Customs territory of the zone country. The most common advantage of a free-trade zone is that the payment of duties can be delayed until the goods are ready to deliver to retailers or customers. For example, liquor purchased in large quantities is stored in a free trade zone until needed. Then import duties are paid and federal and state liquor tax stamps purchased and placed on the bottles. Another distribution function performed in free-trade zones is to

[10] "Showdown on Delaware Bay," *Saturday Review* (March 18, 1972), pp. 34–39.
[11] Peter H. Van Gorp, Bechtel Civil & Minerals, Inc. A talk before the Northern California chapter of the Transportation Research Forum, San Francisco, January 18, 1984.

relabel canned and bottled foods that may be required before they can be sold in U.S. markets.[12]

A Site's Transportation Characteristics

Many "invisible" boundaries exist, and must be determined prior to site selection. A common one is a line dividing areas where different rates are charged. Figure 8-9 shows rate zones for trucking containers between the port of Galveston, Texas, and points in its immediate tributary area. Similar examples can be found for carriers making deliveries to and from airports or to and from railroad container-handling facilities.

Shippers benefit from intermodal competition, and often a site is believed to be more desirable if it has access to more than one mode of transport. One very long, historic trend has been a declining reliance on railroads. Transport users—influenced in part by modern physical distribution thinking—placed a higher value on motor carriers' superior level of service. It was once thought that waterfront cargo-handling facilities needed rail connections. However, a study completed in the mid-1960s that was based on inventorying 2,000 cargo-handling facilities adjacent to deep water navigation channels in the United States showed that, just after World War II, 81 per cent of the sites had rail connections. Ten years later this had dropped to 58 per cent.[13]

The traditional work rules of railroads made serving small shippers along lightly used lines very costly, and railroads effectively discouraged much of this traffic. However, the railroad deregulation statutes enacted in the early 1980s made it easier for railroads to turn these lightly used lines over to public bodies or to small "new" railroad lines (often consisting of the line's remaining shippers). Those new railroads have lower labor, equipment, and maintenance costs and feed traffic between their line and the major railroad(s). Table 8-1 shows the short-line railroads that "spun-off" of Conrail during the early 1980s.

Other Site Requirements

Once a precise site is under consideration, many other issues must be dealt with before proceeding. The title must be searched by attorneys to make certain that the seller can, in fact, sell the parcel and that there are no liens against it. Engineers must examine the site to ensure that it will properly drain and to ascertain the loadbearing characteristics of the soil. Architects

[12] See Pat J. Calabro, "Foreign Trade Zones— A Sleeping Giant in Distribution," *Journal of Business Logistics* (March 1983), pp. 51–64.

[13] *Waterfront Renewal: Technical Supplement* (Madison: Wisconsin Department of Resource Development, 1964), pp. 119–120. (A news item in the May 1974 issue of *Traffic Management* indicated that a number of plant-planning consultants believed that access to railroads was becoming more important because of the energy "crisis" and its adverse impact on trucks, although we have seen no more recent studies to verify this.) For a discussion of the relationship between railroads and their users who have their own rail sidings, see Frederick J. Beier, "Costs of Locating On-Rails: Perceptions of Shippers and Practices of Carriers," *Transportation Journal* (Fall 1977), pp. 22–32.

Figure 8-9 Rate Zones in the Galveston Area

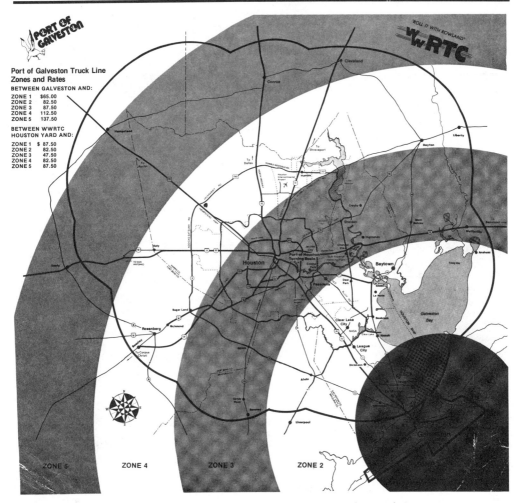

The Port of Galveston Truck Line begins operations on June 1, 1984. The Port has contracted with W.W. Rowland Trucking Company to provide competitive trucking services for container movements within the greater Houston-Galveston commercial zone. Container yard facilities are available in Houston and adjacent to the East End Container Terminal in Galveston for the marshalling of containers.

Credit: *Port Galveston Magazine,* May/June 1984.

may indicate what types of buildings can fit on the site and what types of alterations must be accomplished before a building can be started.

Knowledge of the weather is important because it will have some influence on the type of facility which is constructed. One large spice manufacturer/distributor located its facility in Salinas, California, because the area is dry and neither heating nor cooling apparatus is required. Abbott Laboratories, in its choice of a U.S. port at which to consolidate its export shipments, restricted its choices to ports where there was no freezing weather

Table 8-1 List of Short Lines That Have Purchased Former Conrail Trackage Under Northeast Rail Service Act (NERSA) of 1981 Abandonment Program (alphabetical by purchaser name)

Purchaser	Operator	# of Lines	Total Miles	State
Cattaraugus Co. NY IDA	New York & Lake Erie RR	1	16.1	NY
Central Rwy. Historical Society	*	1	1.0	PA
Chester Branch Co.	Morristown & Erie Railway	1	4.0	NJ
Commonwealth of Mass.	Bay Colony Railroad	5	46.8	MA
Commonwealth of Mass.	Lynn Industries	2	2.6	MA
Continental Rail Freight Co.	Sugarloaf & Hazelton RR	1	8.2	PA
Delaware DOT	Delaware Coast Line RR	1	6.8	DE
Delaware Otsego System	*	5	133.5	NY
Durabond Inc.	Turtle Creek Industries	1	9.3	PA
Essex Group Inc.	*	1	0.3	OH
Everett Railroad	*	1	7.9	PA
F.R. Orr Grain Co.	KB&S RR	1	3.1	IL
Genessee & Wyoming RR	*	2	16.55	NY
Henry Development Co.	*	1	1.3	NJ
Indiana Hi-Rail Corp.	Indiana Hi-Rail Corp.	1	6.3	IN
ITT Grinell	Middletown & Hummelstown RR	1	2.5	PA
IWK&J Railroad	*	3	28.68	PA
Long Island RR	*	1	9.8	NY
Michigan DOT	Lenawee County RR CO.	2	10.25	MI
Microdot Inc.	N/A	1	0.7	PA
Montel Metals	*	1	8.0	OH
Morrison's Cove RR Committee	Allegheny Southern RR	2	6.8	PA
O'Brien Machinery Co.	*	1	0.4	PA
ORTA, State of Ohio	Ashtab./Carson/Jefferson RR	1	6.3	OH
ORTA, State of Ohio	Ohi-Rail Corp.	4	36.7	OH
ORTA, State of Ohio	IIP Enterprise Inc.	5	32.6	OH
Pioneer Valley RR	*	2	24.2	MA
Pocono Northeast Railway	*	40	119.64	PA
Prairie Central Railway	*	1	25.25	IL
SEDA-COG Joint Rail Authority	Nittany & Bald Eagle RR	3	43.70	PA
SEDA-COG Joint Rail Authority	Northshore RR Co.	4	38.38	PA
Shore East Lines	*	2	8.9	NJ
So. Illinois Rwy. Investors Corp.	Cairo Terminal RR	1	2.5	IL
State of Ohio	AC&J Railroad Co.	1	6.18	OH
Sterling China Co.	Sterling Belt Line Railway	1	1.1	OH
Tonawanda Island Railroad	*	3	3.6	NY
Upper Deerfield, NJ	Jersey Southern Railway	1	2.9	NJ
Wayne County, NY	Ontario Midland Railroad	1	2.0	NY
West Shore Railroad Corp.	*	1	11.8	PA
Worchester County, MD	Maryland & Delaware RR	1	26.7	MD
Wye Transportation Co.	*	1	1.0	OH
TOTALS		110	724.33	

*In "operator" column denotes that the purchaser is operating the line.
Source: Conrail Regional Market Development Department, rev. Nov. 13, 1984. Chart courtesy Consolidated Rail Corporation. Used by permission. All rights reserved.

because some of its hospital and infant nutritional products were subject to freezing.[14]

Surveys of firms that have made locational decisions are sometimes conducted, such as one by the U.S. Department of Commerce entitled, "Survey of Industrial Locational Determinants—1971–75." More than 2,600 respondents indicated that the single most important consideration for both new plant and warehouse locations is *highway access,* defined as a location within 30 minutes of a major highway interchange. Three other factors were of significant importance: scheduled rail service, industrial water supply, and natural gas service.[15]

Facility Relocation

A specialized but frequent case of location choice occurs when a firm decides it can no longer continue operations in its present facility and must locate elsewhere. Sometimes the problem is merely lack of room for expansion. A common phenomenon in the United States since World War II has been the relocation of industrial plants and warehouses from the aging and crowded central cities to spacious sites in the suburbs. In these instances, the old site could not be expanded, and workers, who once rode mass transit to and from work, were now demanding private parking facilities for their autos. Trucking firms handling pickups and deliveries at the old site would claim that they could provide better service to suburban sites because there was less traffic congestion.

When relocation is being considered, all of the calculations with respect to selecting a new site must be made. In addition, one must compare all proposed alternatives with continuing operations at the existing site. Many existing sites of operation are in satisfactory, if not ideal, locations, and one must choose between expansion at a site that is not ideally located or closing down that site and starting a completely new operation at the "ideal" location.

There are special considerations regarding relocation to distant communities. The first deals with labor. Employees must be kept informed of any planned relocations that might affect them. If not, rumors will destroy morale, and workers at the old site will start seeking other employment immediately. Their departure will affect the output capability of the old operation at a time when it is nearly impossible to hire replacements. Policies must be decided and announced with respect to which employees will be asked to relocate to the new facility and have their relocation expenses paid. Others may not have their relocations expenses paid but will have the right to assume comparable positions at the new facility. Older employees may be granted earlier retirement benefits. Employees who are not going to re-

---

[14] They selected New Orleans. New Orleans *Port Record* (July 1984), pp. 16–17.

[15] Janet Bosworth Dower, "Choosing an Industrial Site," *Distribution Worldwide* (Feb. 1974), pp. 24–27. See also, T. E. McMillan, "Why Manufacturers Choose Plant Locations vs. Determinants of Plant Locations," *Land Economics* (Aug. 1965), pp. 239–246.

locate but will agree to stay at the old operation until it ceases operation will be given additional severance benefits.[16]

Difficult decisions must be made regarding equipment. What should be taken to the new site? What should be left behind? This is compounded by the need to maintain production in the old facility as long as possible. Inventories of manufactured products must be expanded at this time to offset the loss in production between the time the old plant or warehouse closes and the new one shifts into operation. There are delays at both sites. At the old site, fewer experienced workers remain, and those who do are not happy. At the new site, "bugs" have yet to be discovered.

The physical move of equipment must be timed so as to minimize total "down" time. When General Foods Corporation relocated some of its facilities, it calculated the trade-off between two costs necessary to maintain an adequate inventory of Jell-O's product lines. The first cost was accumulating a larger inventory produced at the older plants by use of overtime. Included in this were the higher (overtime) costs of labor, additional money invested in inventory, and payments for use of public warehouses. The alternative was to pay overtime to the work force installing the new and transferred equipment at the new site. The faster that work was completed, the less would be the down time when operations were halted at both the old and new plant. In this instance, use of additional shifts for installing equipment at the new plant was found to be the better alternative.[17]

Another type of problem occurs when it becomes apparent that a firm has overexpanded and must plan an orderly withdrawal from certain markets. The analytical techniques are the same as for location or relocation, except that the new alternatives involve service to a smaller area. While this is not the best situation to be in, it frequently occurs, especially during periods of economic downturns. In industries with very volatile markets, all locational decisions are made on a less permanent basis. Many examples can be found in today's electronics and computer industries.

Summary

This chapter has emphasized the qualitative aspects of site selection, although it indicated the paths that a more mathematically oriented approach would follow. We emphasized the basic considerations involved in plant and warehouse location decisions. Natural resource locations must be considered, especially if they are a weight-losing product in the manufacturing or processing stage. Another locational consideration is population shifts because they represent both demand for the firm's product and a potential source of labor. Not only is labor availability significant, the overall skill

---

[16] See Kurt R. Student, "Cost vs. Human Values in Plant Location," *Business Horizons* (April 1976), pp. 5–14. See also, "America's New Immobile Society," *Business Week* (July 27, 1981), pp. 58–62.

[17] Edmund S. Whitman and W. James Schmidt, *Plant Relocation: A Case History of a Move* (New York: American Management Association, 1966), p. 79. The study dealt with General Food's construction of a new plant at Dover, Delaware, that replaced four older plants in the northeastern United States.

level and the degree of unionization must be considered. The availability of energy to serve a site is also a matter of concern.

Taxes are a fundamental locational consideration that varies by state and local taxing authorities. Low tax rates may not be advantageous if the level of public services is substandard. Often, communities offer subsidies.

Other basic considerations involve the availability of transportation, especially motor carriers, and the location of the customers for a firm's product. Commodity flows help to indicate where products are being produced and where they are being consumed.

The center-of-gravity method of locating a facility was examined. Once the general area has been determined, specific locational considerations must be taken into account. These include the tax situation, zoning requirements, environmental considerations, union jurisdictions, and transport availability.

The problems involved in relocation of an existing facility were examined. These include employee transfer, equipment relocation, and planning to prevent stock-outs during the transition period.

Questions for Discussion and Review

1. What are the important factors influencing a decision to locate a distribution warehouse or plant?
2. What types of questions should be asked regarding transportation services to and from sites under consideration?
3. Figure 8-2 examined a physical model used to find the low-cost location for assembling a product. Discuss the strengths and weaknesses of this concept.
4. When an operating facility is moved from one location to another, what special considerations must be given to the labor force?
5. How do population shifts influence decisions to locate distribution or manufacturing facilities?
6. How might the factors considered important for locating a manufacturing facility differ from the factors considered important for locating a distribution warehouse?
7. What is a free-trade zone? What functions might be performed in one?
8. Discuss the usage of tax-free industrial revenue bonds. From a public policy point of view, do you believe they are a good idea? Discuss.
9. "Energy costs and availability are becoming fundamental aspects in production plant location analysis." Comment on the validity of this statement.
10. How do the recent environmental protection programs influence site selection?
11. What does the word *dovetailing* mean, when used in reference to industrial location? Give some examples.
12. Under what circumstances might a firm decide to reduce the number of facilities it operates?
13. Discuss the use of grid systems.
14. What are right-to-work laws? Do they influence decision locations? How?
15. Why do some states tax inventories? Do you think inventories should be taxed? Why or why not?

16. What mode of transport appears to be most important to firms evalu ating new sites? Why do you think this is so?
17. Discuss the basic aspects that should be considered when examining the labor environment of a particular geographical region.
18. Discuss the importance and types of taxes involved in a location decision.
19. How might climate affect the choice of a site for manufacturing or a warehouse? Discuss.
20. Discuss the basic considerations involved in a facility relocation decision.

Additional Chapter References

A Comparison of High Technology Centers in the U.S. (Annapolis: Maryland Department of Economic and Community Development, July 1983).

Cooper, Martha C. "Freight Consolidation and Warehouse Location Strategies in Physical Distribution Systems." *Journal of Business Logistics* (Vol. 4, No. 2, 1983), pp. 53–74.

Crosby, Robert, Steven Feldsott, and Wilbur A. Steger. "Tri-State Region Intermodal Terminal System Study." *Annual Proceedings of the Transportation Research Forum* (1982), pp. 224–232.

Perl, Jossef, and Mark S. Daskin. "A Unified Warehouse Location-Routing Methodology." *Journal of Business Logistics* (Vol. 5, No. 1, 1984), pp. 92–111.

Robinson, Raymond M. "Environment and Transportation—Avoiding the Traffic Jam." *Annual Proceedings of the Transportation Research Forum* (1982), pp. 84–89.

Taggart, Robert E., and Isaac McCrary. "Low-Cost Solutions to Rail/ Community Conflicts." *Annual Proceedings of the Transportation Research Forum* (1982), pp. 243–249.

Teal, Roger, and Mary Berglund. "Lessons from Urban Transportation Deregulation." *Annual Proceedings of the Transportation Research Forum* (1984), pp. 464–472.

CASE 8-1

Mom's Tacos

Mom's Tacos was a fast-growing food franchise chain. Its motto was "Mom's secret is the sauce," which applied to the sauce served with the tacos. There was no "Mom" as such. The firm was the creation of a group of college dropouts, living in Lubbock, Texas, who had been engaged in communal living and, as a commercial venture, had tried making large batches of tie-dyed shirts. The tie-dye shirt craze passed, and that market collapsed. However, some of the organic dye ingredients were left over, and the group used them in experimental cooking. They managed to produce an excellent tasting taco sauce and sold the sauce to various restaurants near college campuses. The group then purchased a rundown coffee house, changed its name to "Mom's Tacos," and a legend was born. Within nine years the group, now incorporated, of course, had over three hundred franchised restaurants along the west coast, in the Southwest, and in the Midwest. They were now considering expansion into the South.

Ms. Jenny Wong, logistics manager for the group, was also responsible for purchasing. Others supervised the construction and operation of the franchised restaurants. Restaurant operators were governed by very strict rules regarding cleanliness, personnel, amounts of food in each serving, etc. The restaurant operators were allowed to purchase all foods they needed locally, provided that specifications, set forth by Mom's Tacos, were met. The only ingredient the restaurant operators had to purchase from Mom's was the taco sauce itself. It allegedly was a combination of secret ingredients known only to "Mom." The sauce was manufactured at Mom's plant in Del Rio, Texas, where it was shipped by the rail carload, to Mom's distribution points in Los Angeles (for the West Coast) and Chicago (for the Midwest). There was also a distribution point in Del Rio. After careful market analysis prepared by the well-known marketing consultant, Edsel, Tucker, and Frazer (E T & F), Mom's was ready to move into the south. E T & F had recommended Savannah, Georgia, as the location for Mom's southern distribution point. Franchise agreements had already been signed for operations in Savannah, Atlanta, and Augusta, Georgia; Tallahassee and Jacksonville, Florida; and Columbia, South Carolina.

The phrase "Mom's secret is the sauce" was not true, at least in its reference to Mom. The rest of the phrase was true, however. The various herbal ingredients were kept secret, and some of them were still chemically active. They were added, at the last moment, and under the carefully monitored and guarded conditions, before the sauce left the distribution point bound for the various restaurants. Once mixed, the sauce had a useful life of only ten days, after which the restaurant operations were under the strictest instructions to destroy it. Hence the shipping pattern of the sauce was in the form of a small, steady, move from the distribution point to each restaurant.

The shipping container was a plastic bottle inside a fiberboard box. The cost of the containers to Mom's was $46.00 per hundred for the five-gallon size and $81.00 per hundred for the 20-gallon size. When shipped, the 5-gallon size of sauce weighed 47 pounds, and the 20-gallon size weighed 183 pounds. The 5-gallon container was an 18-inch cube. The 20-gallon container was 24 inches square at the base and 48 inches high. The main reason for using 5-gallon container was that, in some states, an employee could not be required to lift more than 50 pounds. The 20-gallon container required additional mechanical handling equipment in the restaurant. However, Mom's priced the taco sauce so that the restaurants had a strong incentive to use the 20-gallon container. At first, all of them would use the 5-gallon container, but within a year of starting operations, over half the restaurants moved to the 20-gallon container.

A small, or beginning restaurant would use a 5-gallon container every day or day and a half. The largest, and most successful, Mom's Taco Restaurant (in Lubbock, and referred to as the "Mother Mom's") was now using six 20-gallon containers per day.

Because of its interest in maintaining quality and its realization that restaurants would order fewer shipments of larger quantities of sauce in order to benefit from lower per pound shipping rates, Mom's Tacos paid the freight charges on shipments of taco sauce from distribution points to restaurants. Shipments were made to each restaurant twice a week. At any one time, a restaurant would have a three- to six-day supply on hand. In their weekly report to Mom's Tacos' home office, the restaurant operator would indicate the serial or batch number of each unused can in stock and would also indicate the amount to be shipped in the following week.

Warehouse and Plant Location   **319**

The present price of the taco sauce, as charged to each restaurant, consisted of three elements: (1) a charge for the sauce, (2) a discount for ordering in 20-gallon containers, and (3) a transportation charge based on "zone," each zone being a certain distance away from the distribution point. The ordinary zone map looked like a bull's-eye target with the distribution point in the center.

Restaurants that used over 40 gallons of sauce per week had the option of ordering in 20-gallon containers. The price in 20-gallon containers was somewhat lower and was to reflect the lower cost (on a per gallon basis) of the container and (on a weight or gallon basis) of shipping. It was Wong's assignment to work on a pricing zone system for distribution from the new Savannah facility. She was told to include the price of the sauce at $7 per gallon. In addition to this, she was to add charges for the container (taking into account that larger containers cost less per gallon) and to add charges for transportation, using the concentric rings or zone approach. The profits were already in the charge for the sauce, so the charges for the containers and for transportation were to (1) cover costs and (2) reflect the cost differences in reaching each restaurant as accurately as possible. While the initial zone system would apply only to Savannah, Atlanta, Augusta, Tallahassee, Jacksonville, and Columbia, it would be in effect for any other new restaurants that were opened in the area. In fact, Mom's Tacos' representatives would use Wong's cost chart when talking with potential restaurant operators in other southern cities.

Wong recalled that she had a file folder labeled "price zone construction" that she had put together after working out the price zones in the southwest from the Del Rio distribution center. In it she found three notes she had written to herself.

The first note said "use 50-mile rings" and was dated April 3, 1982. She remembered that, after long discussions with both Mom's Tacos' management and with some restaurant operators, it seemed most reasonable to draw circles around the distribution center with radii of 50 miles, 100 miles, 150 miles, and so on and then set the same price for deliveries inside each ring.

The second note, "Remember the Alamo," was dated March 31, 1983. Ms. Wong remembered that on that date Alamo Junior College in Brownsville, Texas, had won the state basketball tournament. The Mom's Taco Restaurant operator in Brownsville had promised free tacos to everyone in case Alamo Junior College won the tournament. That wild night he needed 700 gallons of Mom's taco sauce (his usual weekly usage was 75–80 gallons), and Mom's Tacos had to pay an air freight bill of over $1,000. The note was in Wong's file to warn her the next time zone prices were set up, some sort of rule would have to be set up so that the home office could avoid the excess freight charges in instances such as "the Alamo."

The third note said "newer operations cost more to reach" and was dated February 22, 1984. This was after a year-end audit had disclosed that Mom's Tacos was losing money on reaching most of its new restaurants being served out of Del Rio. The reason was that initial franchises were located in large cities to which transport rates from Del Rio were relatively low. However, newer restaurants were in smaller cities, and while still within 50, 100, or 150 miles of Del Rio, the costs of reaching them was somewhat higher, mainly because they were in areas with poorer transportation service, less carrier competition, and higher rates. The auditor has suggested to Wong that the next time rates be established, she calculate average rates to a number of points inside each ring, rather than just to points where restaurants were in operation or being planned for.

Exhibit 8-1

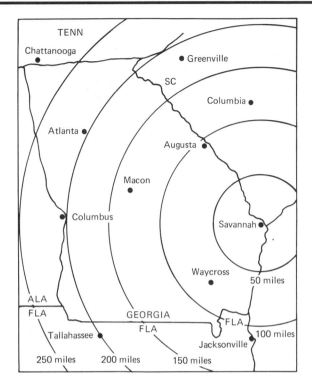

Wong then took a map of Georgia and the adjoining areas and, using a compass, drew circles with 50-, 100-mile, and longer radii, from Savannah. (See Exhibit 8-1.) She then got on the telephone and started tracking down the various types of motor carriers who would handle the deliveries from the Savannah distribution point. Some carriers were excluded from consideration because they did not provide both pickup and delivery service. Delivery service to restaurants was considered especially important because few restaurant operators had trucks of their own.

Within Savannah, there were several local drayage services who could operate anywhere within the city limits. Their rates were $5.30 per cwt for shipments up to 100 pounds; $4.30 per cwt for shipments between 100 and 499 pounds; and $3.30 per cwt for shipments between 500 and 999 pounds. The minimum charge for any shipment was $5.00, and they would not handle any shipment over 1,000 pounds.

Acme Parcel Service also served most cities in the South. Their rate would be $10 per week (irrespective of volume but which would guarantee that a truck of theirs would stop twice a day at Mom's Tacos' Savannah distribution point to pick up any outgoing orders). Mom's Tacos uses Acme Parcel Service for other shipments and thus already pays the weekly fee. Their rates would be: for deliveries within Savannah, $4.00 per cwt; for deliveries outside Savannah but within fifty miles, $4.50 per cwt; for deliveries within 50–100 miles, $5.75 per cwt; for deliveries within 100–150 miles, $6.50 per cwt; for deliveries within 150–200 miles, $7.50 per cwt; and for deliveries between 200 and 250 miles, $8.00 per cwt. They would not handle any single parcel

Exhibit 8-2 Rates for Shipments Outside Savannah

Rates are in Cents Per Hundred Pounds

Distance from Savannah in miles	If shipment is between			
	0-99 lbs	100-399 lbs	400-999 lbs	over 1,000 lbs
up to 50	650	600	500	400
50-100	750	700	500	450
100-150	850	800	600	500
150-200	950	850	650	550
200-250	1,000	900	700	600
250-399	1,100	1,000	750	650

*Note one, the minimum charge for any shipment is $6.00.

weighing over 50 pounds, which meant that, say, a 150-pound shipment would have to be made in three separate parcels, each one weighing 50 pounds.

Motor common carriers rates turned out to be: deliveries within Savannah, $5.00 per cwt for shipments under 200 pounds; $4.00 per cwt for shipments between 200 and 999 pounds; and $3.50 per cwt for shipments over 1,000 pounds. The minimum charge on any delivery within Savannah was $6.00. Exhibit 8-2 shows their rates for shipments outside Savannah. It was based on the applicable intrastate and interstate motor carrier tariffs in effect.

Question One: Ignoring the three notes Wong had written to herself, construct a price chart for varying amounts of sauce, delivered to different locations on Exhibit 8-1, using the lowest cost transportation.

Question Two: Modify the chart (which can be done by adding a note at its bottom) that will protect Mom's Tacos in case another "Remember the Alamo" type of situation occurs.

Question Three: How, if at all, would you modify the chart to take into account the fact listed on Wong's third note—i.e., the one saying "newer operations cost more to reach?"

Question Four: The text of the case says, "Mom's priced the taco sauce so that the restaurants had a strong incentive to use the 20-gallon container." Assume that another Mom's employee, looking at the price chart constructed in answer to question one, feels that there is not enough incentive in those prices to encourage use of the 20-gallon containers. What would you do to modify the chart—or other of Mom's practices—to take into account this criticism?

Question Five: Assume that Wong wants to have only certain carriers haul the sauce. Does the product have unique requirements that call for high-quality truck service? Outline what you think Wong should tell carriers to let them know what Mom's Tacos wants in terms of carrier service.

Question Six: What if some franchise holders want to carry the sauce on their own vehicles? Should Mom's allow this? If so, what price should be charged for Taco sauce sold FOB Mom's plant?

Question Seven: Assume Mom's want to recycle its containers—i.e., have them returned so they can be used again. Outline what should be studied to determine whether the idea is feasible.

CASE 8-2

Amanda's Commute

Amanda Johnson was sprawled on her family-room couch, deep in thought. Only a small portion of her mind was taking in the *Cagney and Lacey* detective program blaring out of the TV. The extra costs of her new commute drive to San Francisco from Santa Rosa, sixty miles north of San Francisco, concerned and perplexed her. The gas alone was costing her nearly $40.00 a week, even though she did get good mileage on her Toyota. Add the bridge toll and the horrendous downtown parking costs—Amanda hated even to add them all up—let alone the solitariness of the drive.

A noisy chase was in motion across the television now—with the two female detectives determinedly driving separate vehicles. Amanda was thinking of her own twelve years with Hektal. They had been good years; intriguing engineering projects with good job security and benefits. When the transfer from Boise, Idaho, to the head office in San Francisco was offered to her, she had been elated—here was a real chance to be where the core work and decisions were made. She and her family had quickly realized that they could not live in the immediate San Francisco area (the monthly payments on adequate houses were usually almost as much as her monthly take-home check), so they had settled on the North Bay town of Santa Rosa. The cost of living was still making things tight, though. Her husband was saying that he didn't think that he could be solely a house-husband any more, and that he was going to start looking for a job, especially now that the kids were in school.

Taking the bus from Santa Rosa was an option, Amanda thought. It would be a lot cheaper than driving. However, she realized that, even though she didn't talk much herself, she enjoyed having people around. And she really enjoyed driving. She heard a screeching of brakes and some gunshots. A Dodge van shot across the TV screen—the wild chase became worth watching.

"Hey, everybody, maybe that's it!" Amanda called out. Her family, immersed in their own Sunday evening activities, looked up in surprise. "What I mean is," Amanda attempted to explain, "maybe I could get a carpool together—look at that wonderful van!"

Unbeknownst to Amanda, there were other people at Hektal who wanted to do something about employee transportation problems. Just the very next day, Kathy Barrett, director of personnel for Hektal, sat in her office contemplating her upcoming meeting with Virginia Neto, a senior vice-president. Kathy knew that anything new, especially if it was going to cost more money, was going to put Virginia on the defensive. But Kathy also knew, from long experience, that Virginia would listen to good logic and would act in the best interests of the company. And Virginia Neto was the person whom Kathy had to convince. Kathy hoped that they would be able to reach some agreement as to whether to assign or hire a transportation coordinator.

There continued to be a raft of employee complaints about salary levels. And yet, thought Kathy, Hektal Company's salary ranges were quite competitive with other large corporations in the area. The factor they had been able to determine as the main cause of the wages discontent was the high cost of living in the San Francisco area. Hiring clerical and data-processing help was the most pervasive problem. Secretaries just could not afford to pay $600–$700 a month to rent a minimal apartment in San Francisco.

Results from the employee survey that they had specifically conducted to pinpoint transportation problems indicated unhappiness with the crowded city buses, downtown parking problems, and so on.

Too often a prospective bright young engineer would be flown into San Francisco for a Hektal interview and offered a job. Subsequently, however, the person would look in the want ads of the local newspaper and would discover how much it cost to live in the San Francisco area, and that would be the end of his or her interest. The company frequently recruited top-notch engineers and other scientists from all over the world for many special projects. The problems of housing costs and commuter needs just had to be dealt with.

"I hope that we can work something out," began Kathy, as she settled herself into Virginia's spacious office. "There are certainly a lot of issues here."

"You certainly seem convinced that we need a transportation coordinator, Kathy," began Virginia. "What does that mean to us in terms of spending?"

"Well, Virginia, I need to talk to you about hiring a coordinator—or maybe we could assign someone who's already working for Hektal—because there's that base salary to take into account. But, she or he would have to have a budget to work with to set up and run the program. I was thinking in the range of around $100,000 per year."

"That's a lot of change, Kathy," Virginia quickly responded. "What are we going to get for it?"

"Very, very simply, the benefit of being able to recruit and keep better employees!", Kathy replied, just as quickly. "Put it into perspective—how much money per year do we spend on advertising job vacancies in our firm, or, on other benefits?"

"Well, just what would you see this person doing?" asked Virginia.

"I've gotten some information from the Metropolitan Transportation Commission. They have helped people set up programs like this, and they have a training course, consisting of six half-day sessions. Apparently the course covers ride sharing, transit, parking management, bicycling, alternative work hours, marketing, and program maintenance. They have become familiar with various transportation strategies, such as shuttle buses, van pools, club buses, and so on."

Virginia was listening, almost in spite of herself. "What if we had an employee living in Sebastopol wanting to join a carpool? How would he find out about it? Also, do you think that many people would be interested? Don't you think that most people have worked things out for themselves?"

"That would be part of the transportation coordinator's role, to figure out ways to connect people up," replied Amanda. "The coordinator would also be responsible for providing guidelines for carpool etiquette, like smoking and talking, driving responsibilities, and reimbursement of driving expenses. We would expect her or him to work closely with those of us in management to develop a good employee commute program. I don't know—maybe we would experience some initial apathy from some employees. But we would hope that the coordinator would work on marketing the program, disseminating information, and providing personal assistance to employees in selecting the best commute alternative. As far as exactly what form of transit assistance we decide to offer—of course, that will have to be worked out."

Virginia Neto was not the sort of woman to make snap decisions. If she sanctioned a program like this, who knows what Hektal employees might keep asking for, thought Virginia. "I saw a petition on my secretary's desk this morning. Do you know that the joggers want showers installed in the office? That jogging business is a fad, at best.

Would that be part of the coordinator's job, to make sure that the joggers took their showers? And as far as helping all of the commuters, what about all of the employees who already pay high rent in the city?," she demanded of Kathy. "Aren't those people going to want to get some little goodie? You know that I live right downtown in Opera Plaza myself, and I *walk* to work. That's why I'm still a size 8."

"Yes, Virginia, I know that you live in Opera Plaza *and* pay high rent. But the joggers probably live in the city and pay high rent, too, and maybe they feel that the showers are their payoff. The bikers want cages built downstairs for their bicycles—and they probably live in the city, too. But, you know, someone was telling me that they have seen commuters who use BART (Bay Area Rapid Transit) with those new foldup bicycles. Apparently they use them to get from the station to their office building." But Kathy was realizing that she was going to need more constructive evidence to satisfy Virginia Neto further. "I know of employees who are really concerned about the costs of commuting. I got a call the other day from one of our engineers, who recently made a lateral transfer from Boise to San Francisco. She had to buy a house as far away as Santa Rosa and was all excited about the idea of starting a vanpool. There's just no question that we are going to have to work something out, and I think that we are going to have to start considering just how much subsidization the company will think of offering," Kathy continued. "Oh, and by the way, here's a brochure on van pooling." (See Exhibit 8-3.)

"All right, Kathy," replied Virginia. "I know I was being a little facetious. Why don't you get back to me with some more details, and I'll give the matter some real thought?"

Amanda Johnson had certainly given the matter some serious thought. The morning after the illuminating TV chase, she had been inching along Highway 101 to work when she became aware of the fast-moving traffic in the left lane. The lane was reserved during rush hours for buses and vehicles with three or more occupants. She saw a Dodge van with the letters "vanpool" lettered across its side. There was a large poster taped to the van's side door also. It read, "Call 861-POOL." "That might be just the ticket for me," she had muttered.

So that's why, a week later, she was sitting in Kathy Barrett's office. "Would you believe that I've been making inquiries about some kind of car pooling on my own?" she told Kathy. "And then when I heard through the grapevine the other day that personnel was thinking of hiring a transportation coordinator, I really wanted to talk to you about it. I'm still excited about my transfer to head office, but this commute situation is a real problem for me, as it must be for lots of other people, too." Amanda grinned, "I've already made some calls, as I mentioned to you, and talked to some people and found out about some pooling alternatives."

"Great!" smiled Kathy. "I've just started talking with Ms. Neto, who will have to find money for such a program. Tell me about it."

"Well," replied Amanda, "The Transit District buses offer good monthly rates for commuters, but the waits are long, and the buses are often packed, I hear. And to tell the truth, taking the bus just doesn't appeal to me. If I can drive, or ride in a car, I sure don't want to take a bus. And then I thought of car pooling, but when I found out about the possibility of van pooling—well, I think that would be an excellent solution."

"Well, that's fine," replied Kathy. "But buying a van, running it, and paying the insurance cost a lot of money."

"Have you heard of the "Rides for Bay Area Commuters" people to whom I spoke?" interjected Amanda. "That's what they do. They help firms set up van pools, and the

Exhibit 8-3

TODAY'S TRANSPORTATION ALTERNATIVE

- What A Van Pool Is And How To Get One Started
- Choosing The Right Van Size And Equipment
- Where To Go For Help And Information

Chevrolet Motor Division, General Motors Corporation

Credit: Brochure reproduced courtesty of Chevrolet Motor Division.

VAN POOLING:
TODAY'S TRANSPORTATION ALTERNATIVE

The Phenomenal Growth Of Van Pooling

According to the National Association of Van Pool Operators, in less than ten years the number of organized van pools has grown from just a few, to more than 20,000. That's because van pooling is a logical concept . . . a group of people travel in a single vehicle rather than each person commuting in separate automobiles. With ride sharing, fewer vehicles crowd the streets, highways, and parking lots—and the cost of commuting to and from work is drastically reduced.

Van pools range from simple operations—like a group of friends or neighbors sharing rides to and from work—up to sophisticated programs that companies sponsor for their employees. Van pooling not only reduces the costs of transportation for everyone involved, but helps conserve over 100,000,000 gallons of fuel each year. It also helps contribute to clean air by reducing the number of vehicles on the road during rush periods, thus reducing automobile exhaust emissions.

Company Sponsored Van Pooling Programs

A good-looking van with the company name on the side has a lot going for it. It's a travelling billboard, advertising the company to hundreds—perhaps even thousands—of people along the route each day.

It's a public relations emissary telling the community that the company is concerned with energy conservation and environmental responsibility.

And, it's an employee benefit that saves hundreds of dollars for those who participate. It can also help promote company loyalty and serve as an attractive fringe benefit when recruiting new employees. Instead of the usual headaches and frustration associated with individual commuting, van pool riders generally arrive at work refreshed, relaxed, and in a proper frame of mind conducive to a full productive day's work.

In this type of program, the company purchases or leases the vans and charges pool members on a monthly basis for the cost and operating expenses like fuel, maintenance, and insurance. Some companies use a payroll deduction plan. Usually, one of the pool members serves as driver. He or she maintains records and commutes for no cost along with the option of using the van for personal use on weekends and during evenings either free, or at a nominal cost.

Van Pool Growth

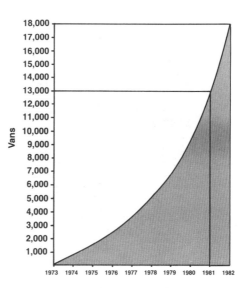

SOURCE: National Association of Van Pool Operators, November, 1982

Owner/Operator Van Pools

Many people own and operate their own individual vans as a small, part-time business in which they charge riders a monthly/weekly/daily fee. Instead of riding to and from their regular jobs by themselves, they enjoy the company of others and cut their own commuting costs to zero. The fees collected from the riders pay for the van and operating expenses.

Besides riding to and from work for free, the van pool owner/operator also enjoys owning the van outright at virtually no cost and has the use of this van for his or her personal use for the cost of gasoline alone.

This type of program can range from a simple share the ride arrangement with friends and neighbors that work together, on up to private businesses created specifically for van pooling for profit—in effect, small private bus companies with custom routes tailored to meet the exact needs of the riders. This type of van pooling is ideal for office and shopping center workers, students and even church groups.

Whether company sponsored or owner/operated, a critical element in any van pool operation is the vehicle itself.

Seating Capacity

A primary consideration in selecting a vehicle is passenger capacity. Besides saving money, a major feature of van pooling is convenience. Experience has shown that crowding too many people into a van is one of the best ways to destroy a van pool because too many people make the operation inconvenient. Too many stops have to be made, people have to wait too long.

That's why when it comes to van pooling, the smaller the number of passengers, the better it is from a passenger comfort and convenience point of view. On the other hand, from an economy point of view, the more people the van carries, the less it costs per person to operate. Chevrolet Vans and Sportvans are designed to seat the optimal number of passengers. Up to 12 adults can be transported in comfort.

Chevy Sportvan Seating Configurations

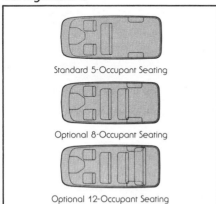

Standard 5-Occupant Seating

Optional 8-Occupant Seating

Optional 12-Occupant Seating

The "Van Alternative" For Van Pooling

Though not a van, a Chevrolet Suburban is a logical vehicle for ride sharing work. With optional seating for up to 9 adults, and the availability of both 2-and 4-wheel drive models, Suburbans are ideally suited for van pooling in areas where terrain and/or weather favor the need for the extra traction of 4-wheel drive.

Chevy Suburban Seating Configuration

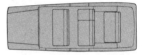

Optional 9-Occupant Seating

Economy And Performance

Another major consideration in selecting a van pool vehicle is economy and performance. For van pooling, the engine needs to be powerful enough to handle the extra weight of passengers and still be able to merge into freeway traffic or pass slower moving vehicles with ease. That's why Chevrolet offers a broad choice of engines

including the proven 6.2-Liter V-8 Diesel that offers unbeatable fuel economy and V-8 performance. Of course, a wide choice of conventional gasoline engines is available, too.

Overdrive Transmissions

Chevrolet Vans, Sportvans and Suburbans are available with a choice of transmissions including both manual and automatic 4-speed overdrive transmissions for enhanced fuel efficiency. The overdrive fourth gear lets the engine run at reduced RPMs at highway speeds.

Comfort and Convenience

A Chevy Van, Sportvan, or Suburban can be equipped to be as comfortable and luxurious as you want it to be. Your Chevrolet dealer can help you choose the options that are right for your particular needs. Some of the more popular options ideally suited to van pooling are shown and explained on this page.

Automatic Speed Control

This option allows you to maintain a constant road speed on the highway. It can help lessen driver fatigue, and adds to overall operating convenience.

Intermittent Windshield Wipers

With this option, you can adjust the timing of the windshield wipers. It comes in handy on misty days or when it's raining or snowing lightly.

Comfortilt Steering Wheel

With a tilt-wheel, you can adjust the angle of the steering wheel to six different positions. By varying the angle, you can suit individual driver needs or just change the angle to get a different "feel of the wheel."

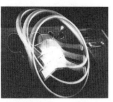

Choice of Audio Equipment

A wide range of audio options is available to meet your listening needs, from an AM push-button radio to AM/FM stereo radio with cassette tape player.

Power Windows And Door Locks

Power windows and door locks are convenient because they let the driver control the windows and door locks from a master control. This means the driver can open the window or un-lock the door with-out having to stretch across the seat. This convenience can really pay off in van pool operations.

Front And Rear Air Conditioning

For climate control in the heat and the cold, Chevy Vans, Sportvans and Suburbans are available with air conditioner/heater units for the front and the rear as well. This is an important consideration for van pooling, since passenger comfort is especially important.

Other Comfort And Convenience Options

- Power Brakes
- Power Steering
- Roof Vent
- Reclining Bucket Seats
- Deep-Tinted Glass
- Electric Clock
- Travel Bed
- 33-Gallon Fuel Tank
- Auxiliary Lighting Package
- And More! See your Chevrolet Dealer for details.

"Custom" Touches . . .

Your Cheverolet dealership can also help you create a truly custom vehicle for van pooling by helping with special touches that a "van conversion" company or special equipment manufacturer can supply. Things like recline and swivel seats, extra-plush carpeting, enhanced styling, special windows, etc.

Electric Step

One custom touch is an electric door step that automatically extends when the side door is opened, providing excellent footing for getting in and out. It automatically retracts when the door is closed.

Help For The Handicapped

Vans are easily adapted to meet the requirements of transportation for the handicapped like the wheelchair lift pictured.

329

THE BASICS OF STARTING A VAN POOL

Putting It All Together

Whether company sponsored or owner/operated, there are several considerations that need to be addressed. These include administering the program, promoting the operation to attract passengers, selecting the routes and pick-up/drop-off points, establishing a time schedule, setting fares, and for company-sponsored plans—choosing drivers and alternates.

Administration

Company-sponsored van pools are usually administered by the personnel department. The drivers report to the department or "van pool administrator." Monthly charges for riders are either collected by the driver or through a payroll deduction plan.

Successful van pool programs demand reliable, dependable vehicles. That means that preventive maintenance is a must. It also means that if a van requires service, it must be done as soon as possible. Over 5,000 Chevrolet dealers can provide factory-trained and certified technicians and genuine GM parts. The dealer can also help with backup vehicles so the driver can have a van to use when the pool van is in for service.

Promoting The Program

Company van pools can be promoted as a service to employees and as an expression of the company's willingness to do its share to help reduce traffic congestion, conserve energy resources, and limit vehicle exhaust emissions. Employees can be made aware of the program through company meetings, notcies on bulletin boards, an article in the company newsletter, memos, etc.

The best way for an owner/operator to get riders is by word of mouth. Other methods include placing ads in local papers, posting notices on office, church, shopping center, and barber/beauty shop bulletin boards. Once a van pool is established, the riders themselves will be the best source of new riders.

Selecting The Routes

For large company-sponsored programs, a computer can be used to "group" employees into van pools based on zip codes and addresses. Each employee interested in the program can fill out a simple form giving name, address, nearest cross streets, regular working hours, etc. Employees are then grouped in pools of 8 to 12 according to where they live and their working hours.

Routes should be laid out so that pickups and drop-offs can be made as efficiently as possible. In some cases it may be best to have a central pickup point such as a school or church parking lot. In many parts of the country, there are "Park and Ride" commuter lots in the outlying areas specifically for this purpose. If the riders live close together, it may be more convenient for the driver to pick up each person at his or her home.

Time The Routes

A big feature of van pooling is arriving to work on time. To do this, it's important that the exact route be timed. A good practice is for the driver to test drive the route to see precisely when the van will arrive at the established pickup points. It's important to time the route during the same time of day that the van pool will be operating. In other words, don't assume that because it takes 20 minutes to drive from point A to point B at 11:30 am, that it will take the same amount of time to make the same drive during rush hour. And since ride sharing requires cooperation, all riders should be made aware of the need for being prompt.

Setting Fares

Monthly fares may range from $30 for a 20-mile round trip each working day up to $50 or $60 for a longer trip. To get a basic idea of the fare schedule, you need to calculate the monthly costs of the van to include service and insurance. Estimate the costs for fuel by determining the mileage involved and the cost per gallon of fuel. Once you know the costs, simply divide that number by the number of riders.

It's recommended that each passenger pay the month's fee in advance, at the beginning of the month. That way, a seat can be reserved on the commuter van.

Choosing Drivers

In a company-sponsored van pool, selection of the driver should be on the basis of dependability and the ability to keep track of expenses and in some states, the need to obtain a chauffeur's license.

A back-up or alternate driver should also be appointed to cover the principal driver when required. The ultimate success of any van pool depends on the driver and his ability to maintain a clean van, be on time, and to settle things like smoking, listening to music, rolling down windows, and the like.

WHERE TO GO FOR HELP AND INFORMATION

This brochure is intended as an introduction to the subject of van pooling. It's not meant to make you an expert on van pooling. Chances are it's raised many issues that you haven't thought about before and that you need further information on.

For starters, you can talk with your local Chevrolet dealer. The dealership has experience in solving transportation needs of all types. It's a logical first stop.

Your state energy office can also provide information on van pooling. Many states encourage van pooling by offering tax incentives, designating special traffic lanes on highways for commuter vans, and by providing parking lots for commuters in outlying areas as pickup and drop-off points.

The U.S. Department of Energy can also supply information in the form of booklets and brochures that detail specifics on van pooling. "Starting a Driver-Owned and Operated Van Pool" is an 8-page brochure published by the department that contains worksheets to calculate van operating costs.

U.S. Department of Energy
1000 Independence Ave. S.W.
Washington, D.C. 20585

The growth of van pooling has also meant the growth of organizations that focus on van pooling. One such group is the National Association of Van Pool Operators (NAVPO). NAVPO publishes newsletters, sponsors van pooling conferences, and provides other services.

NATIONAL ASSOCIATION OF VAN POOL OPERATORS
12208 W. Kingsgate Drive
Knoxville, Tennessee 37922

This brochure was published by the Chevrolet Motor Division, General Motors Corporation. Chevrolet has also released a film entitled "Today's Transportation Alternative," that addresses van pooling in greater detail. See your Chevrolet dealer for details on the film.

Let's get it together... Buckle Up!

firms underwrite a certain percentage of the cost for it. The firm, for instance, might pay 10 or 20 cents per mile, or a certain percentage of the cost of the insurance. They told me about another company, Davy McKee Corporation, that moved its offices from San Francisco way over to San Leandro and wanted to keep most of their old employees. Davy McKee paid 75 per cent of the initial costs for the first year and 60 per cent for the following year. I guess that they hope that the van pools will eventually be self-supporting. They've got eleven van pools going now. Riders pay a fee depending on the distance traveled."

"It sounds as if it could be an answer to some of our commute problems, Amanda," sighed Kathy. "But first of all, there's Ms. Neto to deal with. She lives in the city herself, and she seems to think that it's just tough luck for people who don't choose to live here."

"Well, get some hard data for her, then," replied Amanda. "What percentage of Hektal employees live long distances from work because of real estate financial restrictions? What percentage of Hektal employees live within the city limits and choose to bicycle or jog to work, rather than have the usual hassles? Also, I've heard that some other companies will subsidize parking."

Kathy's phone rang three short bursts. Kathy picked it up and listened. "Okay, Virginia, sure, I'll meet you down in the cafeteria in a few minutes." Kathy put the receiver back down, looking at Amanda intently. "Do you know what? I wonder if we could get someone to help you with your project so that you could spend some time with us setting all of this up. That was Virginia Neto, asking me to join her downstairs for some lunch. Why don't you join us, and we can continue talking about this?"

"And another thing," said Amanda, as the two of them stood up. "Have you thought of the parking spaces that a van pool could save? If I had twelve people in a van, that would save eleven parking spaces. In fact, the van pools could even have preferential parking!"

Question One: Assume the firm appoints a transportation coordinator. On what basis should the costs be justified?

Question Two: What should her or his duties be?

Question Three: The brochure describes two forms of van pools: company sponsored and owner/operator. Which do you think Hektal should use? Why?

Question Four: Is it fair to other employees to give van-pool vehicles preferential parking spaces? Why or why not?

Question Five: Carpools are semiorganized groups of riders who take turns riding in each other's auto. How, if at all, might Hektal encourage them?

Question Six: Is it fair to Hektal employees who live in San Francisco where housing costs are high for the company to subsidize employees who choose to commute from distant suburbs where housing costs are lower? Why or why not?

Question Seven: Have your instructor divide the class into groups who live near each other. Assume you are organizing into car pools to commute to school. Each group should draw up a hypothetical agreement.

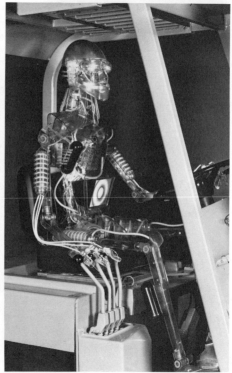

Warehouse lift trucks and tractors have evolved during this century. The top picture is from some 1920 advertising. The lower left photo shows some equipment currently used for reaching high-rise storage. Robots are also being introduced into warehouse operations, but they tend to look less human than the one pictured in the lower right photo. He (or she—?) is actually an imitation robot, constructed for display for a warehousing equipment trade film.

(**Credit:** Top and lower left pictures: Yale Materials Handling Corporation; lower right picture: Clark Industrial Truck Division.)

Warehousing and Distribution Centers

In their earliest days warehouses were places where goods and product waited at "zero miles an hour" to resume their journey toward the final consumers, but today they are not that at all. . . . The cost of money makes the old way of doing business quite obsolete.

Jerry Leatham, president
American Warehousemen's Association 1983

Warehouses are changing dramatically, according to John White of SysteCon, Inc., and the Georgia Institute of Technology, "from a conventional, labor-intensive activity, warehousing has transformed into a sophisticated, highly automated environment," he said. Several forces are behind these changes, such as smaller inventories to support just-in-time production, the continuing trend toward high-rise storage, and shifts in product-demand that have forced firms to either rely on public warehouses or lease space in general-purpose facilities.

Modern Materials Handling
Feb. 6, 1984

Many public warehouses have switched to computerized warehouse locator systems. The computer knows the exact location of each SKU. Nabisco reports that one of their public warehouses was thus able to keep "can't finds" to less than 1 per cent. And these were corrected every day.

Modern Materials Handling
March 19, 1984

Key Terms

Learning Objectives

Introduction

Warehouses are used to store goods, for varying amounts of time, on their journey between points of production and to wholesale or retail outlets. This chapter will discuss warehouses and their operations.

Inventory analysis can help individual retailers to determine whether they should stock all the items in question. Analysis may also have shown that if the items in question were stocked only at the factories where they were manufactured, customer service levels could be inadequate because it might take too long to supply customers. Therefore, distribution warehouses represent a compromise. They are justified on the basis of cost analysis that determines that a specified level of customer service can be achieved at minimum cost by locating inventories at certain intermediate locations.

The phrase *distribution center* is virtually synonymous with *warehouse* since most goods in a warehouse are in somebody's distribution system. In distribution channels, warehouses are intermediate storage points between the manufacturer and the retailers. A distribution center is a warehouse that places emphasis on the rapid movement of goods.

Donald J. Bowersox, in his thoughtful discussion of distribution channels, defines the *exchange* channel as "consisting of a number of independent firms [which] exists to deliver the specified product assortment to the right location at the right time. A number of functions must be performed jointly by all channel members in the exchange process."[1] The functions are: storage, transfer, handling, communication, and adjustment. The adjustment process occurs at a warehouse. Note that the warehouse is involved in four

---

[1] Donald J. Bowersox, *Logistical Management* (New York: Macmillan, 1974), p. 51. The "firms" need not be independent; they could be logistical components of the same corporation.

> As used here, the *adjustment function* consists of choosing a point or points in the exchange channel to concentrate the goods, making a selection from the concentration, and forming a new selection of goods to be dispersed to the next level in the exchange channel.[2]

of the five exchange channel functions; storage, handling, communications, and adjustment. Storage and adjustment features are unique to the warehouse. Storage is a somewhat passive function. The *adjustment* function is more dynamic and gets to the basics of logistics and physical distribution thinking. In how many places and at what locations should goods be concentrated so that new and different selections can be assembled and shipped to the next receiver?

Warehouses are also needed because production and consumption do not coincide; canned fruits and vegetables are examples at one extreme, where production occurs during a short period while sales are spread throughout the year. An example at the other extreme is Cleo Wrap, a large manufacturer of Christmas wrapping paper, which sells 90 per cent of its output during the last two months of each year.[3] In both instances warehouses serve to match different rates of flow. When goods are purchased, sometimes larger quantities are bought than can be immediately consumed. This may occur to prevent anticipated scarcity or to benefit from a seller's advantageously priced deal. Warehousing space is needed to store the surplus supplies.

Warehouses discussed in a distribution textbook would be thought of as primarily *market* oriented. However, some warehouses are production or raw material oriented. Manufacturers who stockpile some of the items they need consider *their* warehouse selection decision as being *production* oriented.

Implicit in many warehouse functions are assembling or light manufacturing processes. Goods are uncrated and tested. Some goods are repackaged prior to distribution to retail outlets. State tax stamps may be affixed. Minor damage to incoming goods may be repaired (and the carrier or party responsible for the damage billed).

Shipment Consolidation and Pooling

A warehouse's principal function is to receive goods, store and care for them, and then assemble and ship outgoing orders. This is the adjustment function. Consolidation is the adjustment function in action and involves arranging one's logistics system so that, as far as possible, goods arrive and leave in vehicle-load quantities. "Everything in today's distribution environment

---

[2] Ibid., p. 52.
[3] *Handling and Shipping Management 1978–79 Presidential Issue* (1978), p. 35.

favors volume shipments for as much of the distance between shipper and receiver as possible. Bear in mind that the carriers are doing whatever they can to avoid individual small shipments themselves, and shippers who want to maintain any semblance of customer service are generally going to be highly motivated to put it mildly—to plan volume shipments."[4] Thus, one approach to the warehouse number and location choice is to determine what configurations allow for maximum utilization of truckload, rail carload, container-load, or barge load lots.

Consolidation Analysis

Analysis of possible movements that could be consolidated is rather easy to describe, at least in manual terms. A traffic manager sets up tally sheets for each different origin and destination pair. Figure 9-1 is an excerpt from a 48-state worksheet that could be used for making preliminary tallies. For each day of the week, one lists the number of shipments that moved from the origin to the destination and notes the commodity description and weight. Weekly totals are calculated, and an attempt is made to determine whether

[4] Warren Blanding, "Thirteen Opportunities to Sell Public Warehousing Today," *Warehousing Review* (special issue, 1974), pp. 2–3. See also," Despite Problems, Warehousemen View Future with Optimism," *Traffic World* (May 6, 1985), pp. 27–32.

Figure 9-1 Excerpt of 48 State "Worksheet" for Preliminary Freight Consolidation Analysis

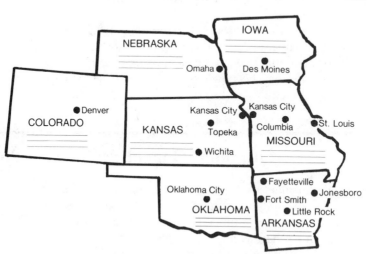

The user is instructed to list on the lines within each state the cities to which shipments from a common point are made, and their weights. The circles indicate cities where the carrier who supplies this form has terminals.

Source: Interstate System, Marketing Department, Physical Distribution Audit Map, (Grand Rapids, Michigan, 1978). Reproduced with permission.

The Elements of Physical Distribution/Logistics Systems

enough weight was involved that an entire truckload or rail carload could have been used.

The variations to this approach are usually more complicated. They would involve learning cyclical patterns in shipments and lead times that were necessary to fill orders. The key is to know what can be done to work up to truckload or carload minimums. While transportation savings may be considerable, one must also make certain that other costs—especially those associated with holding inventories—do not increase more. Other changes also occur. Many small shipments of different types of goods may be consolidated. Once consolidated, they move under an FAK (freight-all-kinds) rate, rather than the rate for a specific commodity. When moving goods in truckload or carload lots, transit times are reduced considerably because the goods do not have to move through the carriers' own small package terminals.

The vehicle-load concept is a very important determinant of warehouse location. A firm's managers look at its retail outlets and asks, "To and from which points can we most economically serve retail outlets in vehicle-load quantities?" The points selected will then be the sites for renting public warehouse space or, possibly, constructing a private distribution facility. Note that the warehouse sites are between the factory and the retailer; the factory-warehouse links and the warehouse-retail store links must be considered simultaneously. Alternatives would be to look at various arrangements of adjustment points (warehouses) to see if a lower total cost of combined freight rates and inventory changes could be achieved to meet some specified level of customer service. Today, there are many computer programs that assist in the analysis necessary to make such decisions.

Firms also use export and import warehouses to consolidate their foreign trade movements. In 1981 Abbott Laboratories chose New Orleans as the site for its export warehouse, and all of their exports now move through that facility. (Previously several export warehousing sites had been used and the "maintenance of multiple export warehouses caused several problems, including the inefficiency of packing and loading by personnel unfamiliar with international export operations and a crazy quilt shipping pattern from Illinois and North Carolina locations to ports on all three coasts plus Canada. Excess LTL—less-than-truckload—shipments and missed sailings were the rule, not the exception, with an average of 20 per cent in 1980 alone.")[5] Criteria involved in the choice of New Orleans included climate, frequency of sailings to world markets, and the availability of a full range of port-related services necessary to support a large-scale export operation. Since the consolidation in 1981, the company has noticed several favorable results. There has been "an 80 per cent reduction of order-dedicated inven-

---

Order-dedicated inventory is ready to be shipped but cannot be because it may be awaiting the arrival of other items to complete a shipment or be waiting for some other function to be completed so that it can be moved.

---

[5] New Orleans *Port Record* (July 1984). p. 16.

tory," and there has been a reduction in "transit time from point of manu-facturing to point of export (products funnel from Utah, Missouri, Illinois, and North Carolina to the New Orleans warehouse) because material is moving in truckload versus costly LTL (less-than-truckload) to the port."[6]

Less-Than-Vehicle Loads

Smaller lots should be considered. Some truck LTL rates have a "break" at 5,000 pounds, which means that it costs less per pound for shipments over 5,000 pounds than the cost per pound for shipments that weight less than 5,000 pounds. Thus, the planning specification for a distribution system may require that warehouses be located so that none of their outgoing shipments is under 5,000 pounds. In Chapter 10, packaging and material handling will be discussed and the "unit load" concept of using pallet loads of materials as the materials-handling "building block" will also be mentioned. A firm exploiting that concept would try to locate warehouses in a way that no outgoing shipment is less than a pallet load. In this instance the objective would be savings in materials-handling costs at both the warehouse and the consignee's receiving dock. Figure 9-2 is a distribution center's tariff showing assembly and distribution charges. Note the incentive for goods on pallets or skids and for larger shipments.

Carriers also have incentives for consolidation. They offer partial load-ing or unloading privileges so that a vehicle load can be assembled from several small sources of supply or can be dispersed among several consign-ees.

Public and Private Warehouses

A common distinction among warehouses is whether they are public or pri-vate. Distribution centers can be either, although they emphasize distribut-ing rather than storing goods.

Public Warehouses

Public warehouses are analagous to common carriers in that they serve all legitimate users. Also similar to the common carriers, they have certain re-sponsibilities to their uses. The Uniform Commercial Code provides that:

> A warehouseman is liable for damages for loss of or injury to the goods caused by his failure to exercise such care in regard to them as a reasona-bly careful man would exercise under like circumstances but unless oth-erwise agreed he is not liable for damages which could not have been avoided by the exercise of such care.[7]

[6] Ibid., p. 17.
[7] See "Liability of the Warehouseman," *Warehousing Review* (Summer 1979), pp. 2–4; and Kenneth B. Ackerman, "Warehousing Responsibility," *Distribution Worldwide* (Feb. 1978), pp. 42–46.

Figure 9-2 Excerpt from Warehouseman's Assembly and Distribution Tariff

ICC MEWC 601					3rd Revised Page 23
		METROPOLITAN DISTRIBUTION CENTERS, INC. Tariff MEWC 601			

SECTION 3	ASSEMBLY AND DISTRIBUTION RATES In Cents Per 100 Pounds	ITEM

COMMODITY

Freight as described in Item 170.

A
3000

APPLICATION

(A) For commodities classified over Class 100 the rate shown in this item shall become the given rate and the provisions of Section 2 shall apply.

(B) When one or more shipments require the full utilization of one or more units of carrier's equipment and equipment is used exclusively for transportation of shipment or shipments only, the charge shall be assessed by applying the applicable rate in this item to each shipment (when more than one shipment), subject to a total minimum charge of $154.65 per unit of carrier's equipment utilized. See Paragraph (C).

(C) A unit of equipment is one tractor and one semi trailer 35 feet or more in length.

(D) Minimum charge shall be the charge for 300 pounds, per component part, on Class 100, 400 pounds, per component part, on Classes 92½ through 65, and 500 pounds, per component part, for Classes 60 and lower.

BETWEEN

Assembler's or Distributor's Los Angeles, California Terminal

AND

Points within Assembler's or Distributor's Territory as described in Item 100

MINIMUM WEIGHT IN POUNDS	CLASSES					
	100		92½; 85; 77½; 70; 65		60; 55; 50	
	B	C	B	C	B	C
	RATES					
AQ	460	427	352	321	335	303
1,000	—	—	—	—	263	230
2,000	—	—	—	—	217	184
5,000	245	212	185	154	177	145
10,000	221	183	170	132	159	122
20,000	183	146	140	103	116	78
30,000	169	131	127	90	107	70

A — Rates in this item will not apply on shipments picked up or delivered at steamship docks or wharves.
B — Will not apply for which rates are prefixed by Reference C.
C — Applies only on shipments or portions thereof unitized on pallets or skids weighing an average of 1,000 pounds per pallet or skid per shipment or portion thereof.

ISSUED: March 8, 1982	EFFECTIVE: April 13, 1982
1070 WMT	ISSUED BY: CHARLES S. SHUKEN President 1340 East Sixth St.
RS/suz 23	Los Angeles, CA 90021

Credit: Metropolitan Distribution Centers, Los Angeles, Charles S. Shuken, Chairman of the Board.

Public warehouses are used by firms that either cannot justify the costs of having their own facilities, or prefer not making a commitment to owning and operating their own facilities. In most analyses of a firm's warehousing needs, public warehouses are considered as the initial alternative. They offer more in the way of flexibility in terms of both space needs and location than would be offered by any system of company-owned facilities. They require no capital investment, and space is rented as needed.

Some public warehouses are specialized. They may handle only refrigerated goods, steel, or household goods, or even be grain elevators. Maritime general cargo "transit sheds" in ports perform some public warehouse functions, although they are oriented more toward *moving cargo through* than they are to storage.

The following is a list of services that many public warehouses provide:

1. Bonded storage. There are several types of bonded storage. U.S. Customs-bonded warehouses will hold goods until import duties are collected. Internal Revenue Service (IRS)-bonded warehouses will hold goods until other federal taxes and fees are collected. (In addition, certain federal laws related to storing agricultural products and some state laws require warehousemen to be bonded in the sense they must carry insurance to protect their customers.)[8]

2. Office and display space. Firms that have large and complex inventory holdings in a warehouse may permanently station one or more of their own staff in the warehouse to perform some of the functions that otherwise would be provided by their warehouseman. Display space would be used by the selling staff in instances where they wanted to show products to prospective buyers.

3. Integrated data-processing equipment. Integrating data-processing equipment with user's equipment allows the user to communicate with public warehouses in the same manner as with his or her own. Often, the user merely has one of his or her computer terminals placed in the warehouse office, where it can issue queries or instructions to warehouse personnel.

4. Inventory-level maintenance. Users who specify the inventories they want stocked receive inventory-level maintenance.

5. Local delivery or tendering outgoing movements to carriers. The authority of warehousemen to perform delivery services is regulated and varies according to the state in which they are located. In any event, they can handle and prepay the outgoing shipment of goods.

6. Unpacking, testing, assembling, repacking, stenciling, and price marking. These are additional commonly performed services, as are break-bulk and assembling functions.

7. Securing collateral goods for loans. This can be done either on or off the warehouseman's premises. A *field* warehouse is a warehouse temporarily established at the site of an inventory of goods, often the premises of the good's owner. The warehouseman assumes custody of the goods and issues a receipt for them which can then be used as collateral for a loan. Using one's inventory of goods as loan collateral is helpful, although the

[8] See "What Is a Bonded Warehouse?" *Warehousing Review* (Summer 1981), pp. 23–24.

goods are temporarily "frozen" in the distribution channel. (One of the major business scandals of the 1960's resulted when a warehousing subsidiary of American Express Company failed to verify the existence of inventories of cooking oils for which they had issued warehouse receipts.) [9]

Many examples could be cited of a public warehouseman's functioning as an integral link in a product distribution channel. In a city with ten dealers for one make of electrical appliance, none of the dealers might stock an inventory. The only models they possess are on their showroom floors. Once they make a sale, they notify the public warehouse, which delivers a unit directly to the buyer's residence from the warehouse stock. The warehouse notifies the factory of the sale, and the factory replenishes the warehouse's stock. In this instance, the stock in the inventory in the warehouse belongs to the manufacturer, a factory distributor, or an areawide dealer. The warehouse performs functions that would otherwise have to be performed by the owner of the inventory; the principal advantage is that dealers do not have to maintain large inventories.

Public warehouses also serve as integral links for other logistical functions. Public warehouses are used by the auto industry; they feed components to the assembly plants on a daily and, sometimes, an hourly basis. With the growing interest in JIT inventory/production systems, there has been some concern as to what role, if any, the public warehouse might play. To a certain extent, the manufacturer may reduce inventories of in-bound materials on hand by accepting smaller, more frequent deliveries from stocks the vendor maintains—often in nearby public warehouses. This shift in responsibility for holding the inventory would result in little net savings unless the vendor were able to do a better job of managing the inventory in warehouses than the user could in the factory. However, the responsibility for inventory has been pushed back one step in the production/supply process. The more this can happen, the better, because each step back toward the original source represents a delay in the final user's having to pay certain costs.

It is too early to tell whether public warehouses in this country will benefit. One public warehousing leader said:

> It is revealing to note that it is in the Japanese makeup to consider inventory as inherently "evil." Carrying that train of thought further, one runs headlong into a perceptual problem: What is a warehouse then, but a place to keep inventory, and therefore a place that is inherently "evil"? It is precisely this type of logic that the public warehouseman is likely to encounter as he begins to market his services to an industry that has been preached to unremittingly about the "Japanese Miracle." [10]

The answer may be that better communications are needed. Marianne Warner, of Leaseway Transportation Corporation, has stated:

[9] "Who Was Minding the Store?" *Forbes* (Dec. 1965), pp. 21–23.

[10] R. Scott Whiting, "Public Warehousing and the 'Just-in-Time' Production System," *Warehousing Review (Distribution Executive Issue* 1983), p. 10.

The whole object of just-in-time systems is to reduce the amount of inventory needed to support a manufacturing and distribution process. And just how does a manufacturer or retailer accomplish this, if not simply by moving his suppliers closer? One important way is through more sophisticated information systems which, in essence, substitute timely information for inventory. These systems can then be linked to the larger logistics system to achieve greater inventory velocity.[11]

Private Warehouses

Private warehouses are owned or occupied on a long-term lease by the firm using them. They are used by firms who find that their warehouse needs are so stable that they can make long-term commitments to fixed facilities. (Private warehouse operation also requires commitment to a warehouse labor force.) The largest user of private warehouses is retail chain stores. They handle large volumes of merchandise, and one of their resulting economies of scale comes from integrating the warehousing function with purchasing and distribution to retail outlets.

Manufacturing firms also maintain their own warehouses. For a firm manufacturing related products at different locations, each plant ships its items to the firm's regional distribution warehouses so that each of them can stock a complete line of products. There are also products with unique handling characteristics such as steel beams or gasoline, that, in some areas, public warehousemen prefer not to handle. In these instances the manufacturer is forced to develop his own facilities.

Plant Warehouses

A warehouse associated with most manufacturing operations is the plant warehouse, usually located somewhere near the end of the assembly line. Its principal function is to accommodate the differences in production line output and product demand in the distribution network.

The plant warehouse may also be the single location where every line item in the firm's inventory is stocked. This is especially true for repair parts. Dealers may be required to stock certain items, and regional parts depots may be expected to stock all items. Another centrally located site could perform this function, but it is performed in the plant warehouse because part of the stock of repair parts is merely left-over components from the assembly process.

Distribution Centers

The phrase *distribution center* is applied somewhat loosely. Some public warehouses refer to themselves as distribution centers, which means they emphasize the distribution aspects of warehousing instead of the storage operations. The emphasis is on fast turn-over of goods. Service to retailers is required to be of such quality that the distribution center is relied upon to

[11] "Making Standards Pay Off in the Warehouse," *Modern Materials Handling* (Aug. 6, 1984), p. 64.

maintain the needed levels of inventory, rather than the individual retailers. The distribution center may also house other customer-oriented services such as sales, traffic, and credit.

Warehouse Design

Public warehouses are usually designed to handle a variety of items, while private warehouses are more specialized. Prior to designing a warehouse, the quantity and character of goods to be handled must be known.

Warehouse and Distribution Center Layout

The relative emphasis placed on the storage function and on the distribution function affect space layout. A storage facility having low rates of turnover is laid out in a manner that maximizes utilization of the cubic capacity of the warehouse devoted to storage. A distribution-oriented facility would attempt to maximize "throughput" rather than storage.

> *Throughput* is a term frequently associated with warehouse productivity. It is a measure of how much material passes through a facility within a given period of time.

Trade-offs. Trade-offs must be made between space, labor, and mechanization. Spaciousness may not always be advantageous since the distances that an individual or machine must travel in the storing or retrieving functions are increased. But cramped conditions also lead to inefficiencies. Before layout plans are made, each item that will be handled is studied in terms of its specific physical handling properties, the volume and regularity of movement, the frequency it is picked, and whether, compared to related items, it is "fast" or "slow" moving.

Many trade-offs are involved in designing both the structure and arranging the equipment inside. Several will be listed here. The trade-offs are often more complex than appear on the list since all factors on the list affect each other.

1. Fixed versus variable slot locations for merchandise. Should one slot always be assigned to each product, which results in a "logical" layout but also in low space utilization because many goods have seasonal characteristics? The alternative, which results in higher space utilization, is to assign empty slots in an almost random manner to incoming products.
2. Horizontal versus "high-rise" layout. The cubic capacity of a warehouse is a function of horizontal area times height. A later section in this chapter discusses "high rise" storage. The relevant trade-off in utilizing a high rise operation is between *building costs*, which decline on a cubic foot

Figure 9-3 An Example of Labor Displaced by Machinery

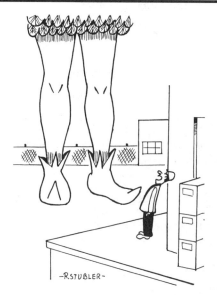

Sorry to let you go, but we've automated our
high-rise order picking.

Reproduced through the courtesy of *Handling and Shipping Management* magazine
and of Richard Stubler, the artist.

basis as one builds higher, and *warehouse equipment costs,* which increase.
Figure 9-3 shows what *might* happen to labor.

3. Order-picking versus stock-replenishing functions. Should workers who
   are picking outgoing orders and those who are restocking the warehouse
   work at the same time? Should they use the same aisles? How much
   space should be devoted to "active" or "live" stocks, which are stocks
   the order pickers pick from to fill orders? How much space is devoted to
   "reserve" stocks, which are stocks awaiting assignment to the active stock
   area? If too much space is devoted to active stocks, the bins are larger
   and the order picker's travel time from bin to bin is increased. If the bins
   are smaller, the active stocks must be replenished from the reserve stock
   more frequently.
4. Two dock versus single dock layout. Conventional warehouses have the
   receiving dock on one end, the shipping dock on the other end, and
   goods move through between them. An alternative uses one dock that
   receives in the morning and ships in the afternoon. Viewed from the top,
   the goods move in a U-shaped rather than a straight configuration. This
   reduces the space devoted to loading docks but requires carriers to pick
   up and deliver at more specific times.
5. Space devoted to aisles versus space devoted to racks. As aisle space increases, storage capacity decreases. Wider aisles make it easier to operate
   mechanical equipment, but they increase travel distances within the facility.

6. Labor-intensive versus highly mechanized. As labor costs increase, many warehouses place an increasing reliance on equipment to perform tasks that had once been performed manually. Union Carbide has a 12-million cubic foot warehouse in West Virginia that can hold 64,000 drums of chemicals. Two persons (one of whom is a computer programmer) handle the entire warehouse.[12]

7. Private ownership versus use of space in public warehousing. This choice influences design because of the tax considerations involved and because of the commitments that must be made to a public warehouseman if he is expected to invest in some very specialized handling equipment.

Three Examples of Layout. Distribution centers have varying layout objectives, as the following three examples illustrate:

1. A men's jeans manufacturer/distributor has only a few products. The main difference is in size of jeans. In laying out this facility, jeans could be arranged by size moving from smallest waist and pants length through all lengths with that waist, to the next waist size, through all the lengths for that waist size, and so on. This is the way they are displayed in retail stores. Instead, in order to minimize the time of order pickers, the jeans are arranged so that the most popular sizes are in the locations that are the easiest (i.e., least time consuming) for the order pickers to reach. The less popular sizes are placed on less accessible shelves.[13]

2. A different approach is taken by an auto accessories chain for their distribution center. First, they insist that all of their retail outlets have the same physical arrangement of merchandise. Goods in the warehouse are arranged in the same order. Inventory and reorder forms for use at the retail level are laid out in the same order, which is retained when they are converted to the order picker's form to be used in the warehouse. The warehouse order pickers use metal carts upon which metal baskets can be stacked. The order is picked in the same sequence as it appears in retail shelves, and the baskets are delivered to the retail stores. This allows the retail clerk to rapidly place the items from the basket onto the shelves.

3. A large food chain continually attempts to encourage its retail outlets to order the "optimum" lot size for a specific item. They may require or encourage the store to order ant poison by the tube, tomato puree by the 48-can case, and paper towels by the pallet load. Forms supplied to the retail store allow for orders in only these quantities or multiples thereof. The warehouse is split into three sections: for the individual items, for the items handled in case lots, and for the items handled in pallet lots. When assembling an order for a retail store, a computer separates the three types of orders and assignments are made to order pickers who have different equipment, depending upon the section of warehouse in

---

[12] "Automated Storage," *Distribution Worldwide,* (Feb. 1976), pp. 21–27.

[13] For a discussion of placement of stocks with relationship to order-picking frequency, see Arthur L. Davies, Michael C. Gabbard, and Ernst F. Reinholdt, "Storage Method Saves Space and Labor in Open-Package-Area Picking Operations," *Industrial Engineering,* (June 1983), pp. 68–74.

which they are working. During the course of the year, some items move from one category of minimum lot size to another, and the computer is programmed to make the adjustment readily.

Two Working Systems. Figure 9-4 shows a top view and end view of a distribution center. In this example the replenishment and order-picking functions are completely separated. Order pickers work in the center aisle. Stock replenishers work in the outer aisles, moving goods from "reserve" to "live" or "active" storage. As order pickers empty cartons, they place them and other wrapping materials on the trash conveyer. The trash is carried to another room, where it is probably separated into different types of materials, and each type is baled and then sold to a paper-products recycling plant.

Figure 9-5 illustrates a much more complex, high-rise distribution center that receives pallet loads, breaks them down into carton lots, then reassembles the carton lots into new, outgoing pallet loads. In that figure, pallet loads are received at point 2 where a computer-controlled stacker takes each pallet and stores it in one of 17,200 openings in the 10-aisle, 65-foot high storage area (point 1). As goods are needed to replenish stocks on the lane loaders (point 4—to be discussed shortly), they are retrieved from area 1 and taken by the pallet carrier to one of several depalletizing stations (point 3). At point 3 the pallets are *manually* unloaded and the cartons placed aboard a conveyor system, which takes them to the lane loaders (point 4). At the lane loaders at least one lane is assigned to each product and cartons are loaded into the top of each lane. The bottom of the lane feeds on to a moving conveyor belt, which is at right angles to the lanes. The lanes slope downward toward the belt and at the bottom of each lane (near the conveyor belt) an electrically triggered escapement device releases one case at a time on to the conveyor belt. The lane is of sufficient slope that gravity forces the case out on to the conveyor belt. As orders are assembled on the conveyor belt, they move toward point 5, where they are routed to one of four loading stations and are placed aboard pallets for outgoing shipments. This is also done manually. Hence loading and unloading pallets are the only two manual operations; the other operations are by machine. All operations are computer-controlled.

Other Space Needs

In addition to space for the through-put of merchandise, areas must be set aside for other warehouse activities. They require some detailed analysis in terms of space requirements and layout. Examples are

1. Areas for vehicles waiting to be unloaded or loaded and employee parking.
2. Receiving and loading facilities for each mode of transport serving the facility.
3. Staging, or temporary storage areas, for both incoming and outgoing merchandise.

Figure 9-4 Top and Side View of a Distribution Warehouse

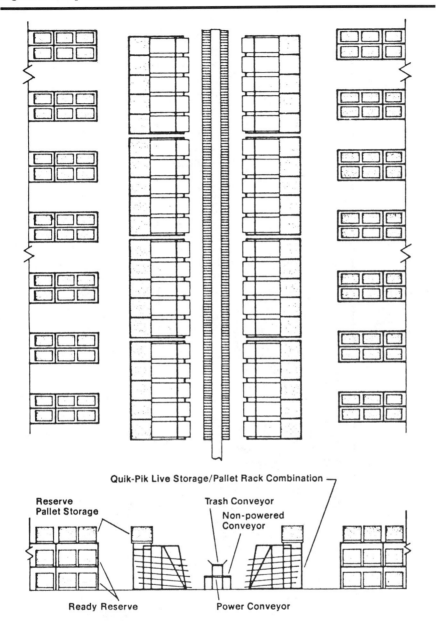

Quik-Pik Live Storage/Pallet Rack Combination

Reserve
Pallet Storage

Trash Conveyor

Non-powered
Conveyor

Ready Reserve

Power Conveyor

Note: The live storage racks slope downward toward the center so that gravity will force cartons to move toward the center.

Courtesy: North American Equipment Corp.

4. Office space including an area for whatever computer facilities may be involved.
5. Employee washrooms, lunch rooms, etc.
6. Pallet storage and repair facilities. (A large distribution facility that re-

Warehousing and Distribution Centers

349

Figure 9-5 Large Automated Distribution Center

Courtesy of SI Handling Systems, Inc.

ceives unpalletized materials, but ships on pallets may require a pallet-assembly operation.)

7. An area to store damaged merchandise that is awaiting inspection by the carrier's claim representative.
8. An area to salvage and/or repair damaged merchandise.
9. An area for repacking, labeling, price marking, etc.
10. A room for accumulating and baling waste and scrap.
11. An area for equipment storage and maintenance. For example, battery-powered lift trucks must be plugged-in to battery chargers overnight.
12. Specialized storage areas for hazardous items, high-value items, warehouse supplies, or items needing other specialized handling such as freezer or refrigerated space.

Retail Storerooms

Distribution center design is not an end in itself. It is but one link in the distribution process. The next link is the retail store itself. Some retail stores no longer have storerooms, which means that the goods go from the distribution center directly to the retailer's display shelves. A retail chain will often own two or three times as many trailers as it does tractors. Each time a tractor makes a delivery to a retail store, it will leave a trailer for the store to unload within 24 hours. It will also pick up the trailer that it had left the previous day to be unloaded. Hence, the parked trailer serves as a storeroom and reduces the "truck-to-storeroom" and "storeroom-to-shelves" movements to only one because the goods will go directly form the parked trailer to the shelves.

This practice does not hold for all industries, however. One successful furniture retail chain utilizes existing warehouses in urban areas. Part of the warehouse is converted to display space and if the customer selects the item, an identical one is given him from the adjacent storage space.

Warehouse Equipment

This section will discuss computers, scanners, and handling equipment used in warehouses. Much of the equipment discussed in this section is more likely to be found in larger warehouses or in specialized distribution centers.

Computers

Warehousing is one field where the use of computers has virtually "exploded" in the last decade. At the public warehousing level, the American Warehousemen's Association (AWA) has developed for its members considerable software for personal computers. One program can develop and analyze the costs of handling a client's potential public warehousing needs. The cost analysis is built on data inputs from nine separate warehousing functions: inbound truck, inbound rail, stocking, order filling, checking, outbound truck, outbound rail, elevator use, and repacking. "Standard" times are applied to each function, and a 15 per cent allowance is added to cover unexpected delays.[14]

A more detailed AWA program for personal computers deals with storage-rate analysis and focuses only on the public warehouse's storage function. Variations exist for bulk storage and for storage on racks. If racks are to be used, the necessary data inputs include pallet width, pallet depth, pallet height, number of units per pallet, the weight of each unit, the height of each stack of pallets, the depth of each storage slot, the space between pallets, the aisle width, several space utilization factors (or ratios), average inventory to be held, pallets shipped each month, inventory turnovers, and several cost "markup" factors.[15] A third personal computer software program developed by the AWA is called The Inventory Clerk; it is used for maintaining inventory records for the public warehouse and for its users. Records are kept on the basis of individual users' accounts and include information about inventory status and inventory transactions. The type of information stored in the inventory status file includes account number, stock code, stock description, balance on hand, pieces per unit, lot number, lot date, method of packaging, unit weight, storage location(s), carrier freight classification, and warehouse billing codes.[16]

Private warehouses tend to have more sophisticated computer systems because they handle more standardized products and are only one segment in the firm's overall computerized system of materials management. Because they handle more standardized products than do public warehouses, private warehouses are also more likely to possess sophisticated storage and handling equipment[17] (discussed in the next section). Much of this equipment is controlled, one way or another, by computers or by programmable controllers. Figure 9-6 shows an example of computerized order picking. The worker is picking an order for a single customer from the racks on the left and placing the items into the box on the right, which moves slowly along the conveyer. On the left, just above the worker's hand, is a small device mounted on the rack under each separate SKU (stock-keeping unit); the device is called a readout unit. When the readout unit is lit, it shows the number of items at that slot that must be picked. After the worker places that number into the large box, he punches the "clear" button on the readout unit; he moves along until he reaches the next readout unit, which also is illuminated. The order picker must clear all of the readout units before he can move the large box out of the warehouse zone in which he is working.

Computers also link different locations, buyers, and sellers. Many large Ford and Lincoln-Mercury dealers are tied into Ford Motor Company's parts

---

[14] John A. Bohm, "Step by Step Through Your AWA Handling Rate Analysis Program," *Warehousing Review* (Spring 1983), pp. 13–27.

[15] "Public Warehousing Storage Rate Analysis System," (Chicago: American Warehousemen's Association, June 1983), p. 11.

[16] "Computer Information Advisory," (Chicago: American Warehousemen's Association, Aug. 1983), p. 3.

[17] Philip C. Smith and Ernest W. Harris, "Computer Applications in Private Warehouses," *Papers, NCPDM Annual Meeting, 1982,* Vol. 1, pp. 415–424; and "Computers in Manufacturing and Warehousing," *Modern Materials Handling* (Nov. 21, 1983), pp. 33–41.

Figure 9-6 Example of Computer-Assisted Order Picking

Credit: Rapistan Division, Lear Siegler, Inc.

distribution center using conventional telephone lines. Special equipment is used at the dealers' sites, involving a keyboard terminal with a cradle to hold the telephone headset. The dealer's computer terminal can then "talk" to the computer in the parts distribution center. The dealer can check on parts availability or place emergency orders. The computer in the parts distribution center has a complete list of substitute parts. If another model of auto uses the same part or if one part can be substituted for the part the dealer needs, the dealer's terminal will be told that number of the substitute part so that a check can be made to determine whether they are in stock.

Both buyers and vendors are likely to have computerized inventory control and warehousing systems. In Figure 9-7, which is a food chain purchase order, note that the vendor has an item code. The buyer also has an item code and a slot number that tells where in the buyer's warehouse the goods should be placed. Some goods even have batch numbers or serial

> *Batch* numbers indicate the time and location a product was made. Products with identical numbers came from the same batch.

numbers that can be entered into the computerized records. One frozen food processor cannot release a product until it has been frozen a given number

Figure 9-7 Computerized Purchase Order

354

SAFEWAY STORES, INCORPORATED
P. O. BOX 3093 · SAN FRANCISCO, CALIFORNIA 94119
ACCOUNTING DEPARTMENT

MAIL INVOICE TO →

SHIP TO: SAFEWAY STORES, INCORPORATED
GROCERY WAREHOUSE - WHSE #70
2900 HOFFMAN BLVD.
RICHMOND, CALIFORNIA

VENDOR: DOLE CORPORATION
HALL-ROEPKE COMPANY
1450 CHAPIN AVENUE
BURLINGAME, CALIFORNIA 94010

SHOW P. O. NUMBER ON INVOICE, BILL OF LADING AND ALL LOADING SHEETS.

NO BACK ORDERS

PURCHASE ORDER NUMBER: 005882

VENDOR'S COPY

DATE ORDERED: MO 6 / DAY 04 / YEAR

PAGE NO. 01

DATE TO ARRIVE: 6/11/

WAREHOUSE FACILITY:

SPECIAL INSTRUCTIONS

SELLER # PER BUYER: 612-01
BUYER # PER SELLER:

SHIP VIA: TRUCK
SHIPPING POINT: OAKLAND

CASH DISCOUNT: 2%-10
SWELL ALLOW (SA) ITEM X: 1/3 OF 1%
TRADE-DISCOUNT
FREIGHT ALLOWANCE (FA) ITEMS X

F.O.B.: OAKLAND

OTHER ALLOWANCE: 266.05 PCWT
FREIGHT CHARGE (FC) ITEMS X

QUANTITY ORDERED	UNIT	VENDOR ITEM CODE	VENDOR UNIT PACK & SIZE	DESCRIPTION	VENDOR LIST COST	S/A SA	FF/AC	VENDOR UNIT ALLOW	SAFEWAY ITEM CODE	SAFEWAY PALLET PATTERN	SAFEWAY SLOT #	R
96	CS	849	8/6-6 OZ.	DOLE PINEAPPLE JUICE-SLEEVE PAK	3.80	X	X	.485	36604	16X6	15631	
105	CS	824	24/12 OZ.	DOLE PINEAPPLE JUICE	2.40	X	X	.003	36605	21X5	15621	
672	CS	803	12/46 OZ.	DOLE PINEAPPLE JUICE	3.40	X	X	.484	36606	8X7	14751	
105	CS	604	24/13.25 OZ	DOLE CRUSHED PINEAPPLE	5.20	X	X	.007	37825	21X5	17711	
93	CS	143	24/20 OZ	DOLE SLICED PINEAPPLE-WASH JCE	7.75	X	X	.01	37829	14X7	17571	
84	CS	613	24/20 OZ	DOLE CRUSHED PINEAPPLE IN JCE	7.75	X	X	.01	37830	14X6	17641	
84	CS	473	24/20 OZ	DOLE CHUNK PINEAPPLE IN JUICE	7.75	X	X	.01	37831	14X6	17601	

• ORDER NUMBER MUST BE SHOWN ON INVOICE AND ALL SHIPPING PAPERS

Weight: 47,193
Cases: 1,244

TRAFFIC OAKLAND
Special P. O. Distribution

IMPORTANT NOTICE: This order is expressly conditioned upon acceptance of and compliance with the instructions, terms, and conditions on the face and reverse side hereof.

SAFEWAY STORES, INCORPORATED

BY E. P. CAMERON
BUYER

FORM NO 632 IMPC (EXPER) (REV 3-69) 11-70-112-20

PRINTED IN U.S.A.

of hours. Computers are programmed to indicate that an item is in stock but not available for delivery until a certain number of hours have passed.

Scanners can be linked to computers for warehouse record keeping, and scanners adjacent to conveyor belts recognize and tally each carton as it passes by. The scanner may be tied into a system that sorts each carton with respect to where it should be stored. Once the goods are in storage, inventories can be checked by passing a pen-sized scanner near each label.

Storage and Handling Equipment

Conventional single-story warehouses and distribution centers accommodate material at heights up to approximately 20 feet. Although it is possible to *store* most materials stacked on top of each other, this is inconsistent with the distribution center concept of fast throughput. The oldest pallet would always be on the bottom and the pallet loads above it would have to be removed in order to get at the older pallet load. Hence, steel shelving or pallet racks are used and each pallet sets on an individual shelf and can be stacked or removed without disturbing other pallet loads. City building codes regulate rack installation. California building codes discourage high storage racks in an effort to minimize earthquake damage.

Within the warehouse, the goods are moved by a variety of manual and mechanical devices. In small warehouses, a wheeled cart may have only a lifting device that must be pushed along the floor. More sophisticated devices are powered for moving along the floor, and they may or may not contain accommodations for the user to ride in it. The fork lift truck is the standard "workhorse" in many warehouses.

Some warehouses have tow lines that are set in the floor. Carts are equipped with gripping devices and pulled along. Carts can be "programmed" to follow different routes within the warehouse.

Most high-rise warehousing equipment moves up and down narrow aisles and services materials on both sides of the aisle. Aisle widths are narrower than in the case of conventional warehouses. Because equipment can move both horizontally and vertically at the same time, the most efficient layout of goods along any one aisle may be a path of upward and downward undulations. This would consume less time than a path which took the equipment along a horizontal path and stopped; then moved up or down and stopped; then continued along the horizontal path and stopped, and so on.

In addition to high-rise systems involving human order pickers, there are also completely automated warehouses. They have automated order picking devices that move along an aisle, stop in front of a bin and, with a lateral handling device, either store or remove a container.

Even though one often reads of highly automated warehouses in trade journals, the vast majority are either not automated at all, or have only one or two operations that might be considered as being automated. One consultant has warned that "most warehouses should not be automated. For example, in most cases, a warehouse shouldn't be automated if it's not a high-volume operation, if total space is under 100,000 square feet, if labor rates aren't high, if customer orders vary considerably in size and frequency, if seasonality is a factor, if flexibility is important."[18]

Warehouse Operations

There are many facets to operating a warehouse. Figure 9-8 is a cost-estimating sheet used by one public warehouse. It demonstrates the wide range of activities that take place within a warehouse operation.

Warehouse management is an exacting task. Work-force motivation is difficult because of the repetitiveness of the operation. The work is strenuous. Only five aspects of operation will be touched upon here—worker safety, hazardous materials, facility cleanliness, inventory controls, and handling of stock-outs.

Employee Safety

A 1972 survey showed that nationwide there were 19.2 injuries per 100 public warehouse workers. This compared very unfavorably with the 10.9 per hundred figure for all industries.[19] Warehouses are dangerous because of the functions they perform. Goods and workers are in constant motion. A warehouse may receive a pallet that was improperly loaded, and this will not become apparent until a worker attempts to handle it.

Even with the best of practices, a small percentage of all goods a warehouse receives, stores, and ships are damaged. Special procedures must be established for handling any broken or damaged item just from the standpoint of employee safety (in addition to assuming or assigning responsibility for the breakage). A broken bottle of household ammonia, for example, results in three hazards: noxious fumes, broken glass, and slippery floors.

Warehouses generate large volumes of waste materials such as empty cartons, steel strapping, broken pallets, or wood and nails used for crating and dunnage. This must be properly handled because it poses a threat to

> *Dunnage* is material used to block and brace products inside carrier equipment in order to prevent the shipment from shifting in transit and becoming damaged.

employee safety and may also be a fire hazard. One of the purposes of the warehouse trash conveyor belt shown in Figure 9-4 is to remove the trash promptly from the area where people are working.

OSHA. In 1970, the Federal Occupational Safety and Health Act (OSHA) became law. It resulted in increased federal and state supervision of indus-

---

[18] *Davis Database* (Englewood Cliffs, N.J.: Davis and Company, July 1984), p. 4. See also, Perry A. Trunick, "Giving Warehouse Efficiency a Lift," *Handling and Shipping Management* (April 1983), pp. 58–64.
[19] *Warehousing Review*, (Sept.–Oct. 1974), p. 12.

Figure 9-8 Warehouse Cost-Estimating Form

SERVICE SPECIFICATIONS

FOR CUSTOMER USE IN CONTACTING ALLIED MEMBER COMPANIES REGARDING WAREHOUSING SERVICES.

ALLIED DISTRIBUTION INC

6145 N. MILWAUKEE, CHICAGO, ILL. 60646

312/792-0433

FULL AND EXACT NAME OF YOUR COMPANY   DATE

COMPLETE ADDRESS – NUMBER, STREET, STATE, ZIP CODE   AREA CODE – TELEPHONE NUMBER

NAME OF PERSON MAKING INQUIRY   TITLE   ADDRESS, IF OTHER THAN ABOVE

COMMODITY, PACK, TYPE OF CONTAINER	OVERALL DIMENSIONS IN INCHES			GROSS SHIPPING WEIGHT IN LBS.	VALUE OF PACKAGE AND CONTENTS
	LENGTH	WIDTH	HEIGHT		

Estimated Average Stock: _____ Estimated Through-put _____

INBOUND: Rail _____% Truck _____% Loose _____% Palletized _____% Who Unloads Trucks? _____

CL _____% LCL _____% TL _____% LTL _____% Pallet Size: L _____ W _____ H _____ (including pallet)

OUTBOUND: CL _____% LCL _____% TL _____% LTL _____% Who Loads Trucks? _____

Loose _____% Palletzed _____% Cartage Needed? _____

Estimated Number of Outbound Orders: _____ Per _____

Outbound Order: Minimum _____ Lbs. Average _____ Lbs.

No. of Different Items or Separations in Account: _____

B/L Used: Warehouse _____ Customer's _____

Check among the following accessorial services those to be required from the warehouseman in addition to the "Handling" and "Storage" services:

_____ Handling for immediate distribution.
_____ Reporting marked weights, numbers, etc., on receipt and/or delivery.
_____ Making out-of-town shipments.
_____ Prepaying freight charges
_____ Filling orders from a credit list
_____ Invoicing customers for storer.

_____ C.O.D. collection on behalf of storer.
_____ Furnishing reports in addition to usual notification as to receipts and deliveries.
_____ Kind and frequency (attach samples)
_____ Weighing on receipt and/or delivery
_____ Storage-in-transit

Indicate other services required, and give information regarding any special storage characteristics of commodities: (Stacking Limitations, Hazardous, Breaking Cartons, Controlled Temperature, Pick by Package or Serial Number, Odorous or Susceptible to Odors, etc.)

Courtesy Allied Distribution, Inc.

trial safety practices. Standards have been set for equipment and operations, and inspectors frequently make inspections. They can issue citations and monetary fines may be levied. During the 1970s, OSHA was probably the most controversial issue in the warehousing industry. However, during the Reagan administration, enforcement has become less rigorous. Nonetheless,

OSHA standards are complex and lengthy. What follows are excerpts from an OSHA report of violations at a specific location. In several instances penalties were assessed and they are noted.

1. Failure to maintain passageway, storerooms, and service rooms in a clean and orderly condition.
2. An open-sided platform more than four feet above the adjacent floor level was not guarded by standard railings or the equivalent and was not provided with a toeboard.
3. Failure to provide railing on each side of a stairway less than 44 inches wide and having both sides open.
4. Safety shoes were not provided or required to be worn by employees exposed to foot and toe injuries when handling material, equipment, appliances, or similar items—i.e., truck drivers, helpers, and warehouse employees. Penalty: $25.
5. Fire extinguishers were obstructed or obscured from view.
6. Failure to install portable fire extinguishers on hangers or brackets or set on shelves.
7. Fork-lift trucks did not bear a label identifying marks or nameplates. Penalty: $25.
8. Failure to adjust work rest on a grinding machine to the required maximum of ⅛-inch.
9. Failure to guard pulleys located less than seven feet from floor level.
10. Failure to guard a horizontal belt located less than seven feet above the floor.
11. Failure to provide guards for gears.
12. Failure to mark legibly disconnecting means for motors and appliances.
13. Exposed noncurrent-carrying metal parts of cord and plug connected equipment that was liable to become energized not provided with ground. Penalty: $25.[20]

Employee safety is a matter of continual concern. It involves training, motivation, and never-ending supervision. In the aftermath of the severe blizzards that struck Chicago in early 1979, many warehouses had to send men up on their roofs to shovel away the accumulated snow.

> One had to be careful to prevent any congregating of men in groups on the roof. If you have a crew of twenty men working on your roof and the foreman calls them all together to give them instructions, you could precipitate a serious collapse by the sheer weight of people clearing snow off the roof. . . . Several warehousemen said that they made it a point to provide all instructions before ascending to the roof and the supervisor ordered that no more than two people could get together to prevent straining the roof.[21]

[20] *Warehousing Review* (March–April 1975), p. 19.
[21] *Warehousing Review* (Summer 1979), p. 18.

Figure 9-9 Materials Stored in Warehouses Can Damage Other Materials or the Warehouse Structure

Yes, sir, I know freezing will not hurt your product, but what will it do to my floor when it thaws?

Courtesy *Warehousing Review*, 6, no. 2: p. 7. Drawn by Art Stenholm, copyrighted 1977 by the American Warehousemen's Association.

Hazardous Materials

Chapter 6 discussed hazardous materials from the standpoint of transportation. Many of these materials also move through warehouses and must receive extra attention because of the injuries and property damage they could cause. (See Figure 9-9.) Department of Transportation regulations require that shipping documents indicate the hazardous nature of materials being transported. Warehousemen must note these warnings when they receive materials and must be certain that they are included on the outbound shipping documents when the materials leave the warehouse.

Fires are a constant threat at warehouses. Most materials used for packaging are highly flammable. Plastics, once ignited, can be very difficult to extinguish.[22] High-rise warehouses are also more vulnerable to fires, since the vertical spaces between stored materials serve as "chimney flues" and help the fires burn.[23] Grain dust is also hazardous; two major grain elevators in Gulf ports were destroyed by fires and explosions in the late 1970s.

[22] "SPI Fire Tests of Stored Plastics in Warehouses," *Fire Journal* (May 1979), pp. 30–35.

[23] William Goodall, Jr., "Preventing Distribution Center Disaster," *Handling and Shipping Management 1978–1979 Presidential Issue* (1978), pp. 64–74. See also, Stephen L. Frey, *Warehouse Operations: A Handbook* (Beaverton, Ore.; M/A Press, 1983), chaps. 4 and 7 for a further discussion of warehouse safety measures.

Sanitation

Warehouse cleanliness is another never-ending concern. The small amount of space devoted to it here does not do justice to its importance. Sanitation is related to both employee safety and to the quality of the products handled.

The U.S. Food and Drug Administration (FDA) is concerned with the sanitation of food and drugs moving in interstate commerce. Its efforts were strengthened in mid-1975, when the U.S. Supreme Court upheld the *criminal* conviction of the *president* of a large food chain (nearly nine hundred retail outlets) because of unsanitary conditions in one of the firm's warehouses.[24] This demonstrates that sanitation is a "top management" responsibility.

Stock Controls

A principal and continuing problem is keeping an accurate count of merchandise moving through the warehouse. If the count is off—either too high or too low—sophisticated handling procedures will be undermined. The initial error occurs when the worker at the receiving dock assumes that all the goods listed on the delivering carrier's bill of lading are, in fact, there. A second type of error occurs when the receiving clerk assumes responsibility for on-the-spot adjustments of overages and shortages. He may note that there is one too many cartons of brown shoe polish and one too few cartons of black shoe polish. Because the price is the same he may accept the shipment without noting the discrepancy. The receiving clerk's single error gets multiplied, because counts for both colors of polish will be off.

Accurate counts of merchandise leaving the warehouse/distribution center are important although there is a partial control in that whoever receives the goods next will, if he or she is doing their job properly, report discrepancies. Shortages will be reported. Most methods of control involve the setting up of systems where any one person's count must be verified—perhaps on a sampling basis—by another individual. Or manual counts may be compared with computerized records. In situations where perishable products are handled, stock controls are needed to move out older stocks (see Figure 9-10).

Stock-outs

Stock-outs were discussed in Chapter 7, and methods were shown for reducing or eliminating them. Nevertheless they occur. Warehouse/distribution centers must have policies to answer such questions as:

1. Will the customer permit substitutions and, if so, what types of substitution are acceptable?
2. If, because of a partial outage, it is impossible to ship a large enough load to meet minimum load quantities, what should be done?

[24] *Warehousing Review* (July–Aug. 1975), pp. 2–9.

Figure 9-10 Stock Controls Are Necessary

"SO THAT'S WHERE THE PAPAYAS ARE.
MAYBE YOU'D BETTER CALL LOGISTICON."

If papayas (a tropical fruit) are kept too long, they attract insects. The cartoon accompanied text for an advertisement for a computerized warehouse/inventory control system.

Credit: Logisticon, Flexible Material Management Systems, Santa Clara, CA.

3. Will the customer accept partial delivery? Will he or she accept back orders? If freight charges are higher because of these split shipments, how shall they be assessed?

4. If shipping dates cannot be met, what actions should be taken?[25]

Highly computerized distribution centers have answers to most of these questions programmed into their system, and the "answer" can be determined quickly. Unfortunately, not all exceptions can be thought of in advance. Therefore, it is necessary to know to whom the situation should be reported so that a decision can be made.

These examples relate to the customer service element of distribution. Usually a separate report is made to the sales person handling the account whose service is being delayed or altered. It may be preferable to have him or her contact the customer waiting for the shipment. If there are some alternative solutions to the problem from which the customer can choose, it may be wise to give the customer the choice. In this case the distribution center's exception policy would be to have the sales person contact the customer.

Summary

Warehouses and distribution centers are but one link in the distribution system. They perform the adjustment function of receiving, breaking down, reassembling and shipping. They must be located, designed, and operated in a manner that contributes to the overall performance of the firm's PD needs. In *warehousing* the emphasis is on storage. The emphasis of a *distribution center* is on fast, accurate throughput of merchandise. A distribution center assumes some of the inventory maintenance functions of the retail outlets it serves.

Public warehouses are analogous to common carriers. They can be integrated into a firm's distribution system and can perform all of the necessary functions. Their principal advantage is that the user avoids a large investment in fixed facilities and commitment to a warehouse work force.

When arranging a distribution center, the initial goal is to reduce the number of times an item is handled. However, for control purposes it is necessary to have a system of checks and rechecks to make sure accurate tallies are kept of incoming and outgoing materials. Warehouses and distribution centers are being automated and computerized.

Questions for Discussion and Review

1. Distinguish between a *warehouse* and a *distribution center*.
2. List the various functions performed by warehouses and distribution centers.
3. Discuss the liability that public warehouses have for the products stored in the warehouse.

[25] Warren Blanding and Howard E. Way, *100 Ways to Improve Warehouse Operations* (Washington, D.C.: Marketing Publications, 1972), p. 6 and James A. Cooke, "How to Motivate Your Public Warehouse," *Traffic Management* (May, 1985), pp. 49–55.

4. What is a *bonded* warehouse?
5. What is OSHA? How does it affect warehousing?
6. What are the functions of a plant warehouse?
7. Why is safety of warehouse employees a problem?
8. What is high-rise storage? What limitations, if any, are there on height?
9. Why must accurate counts be kept of merchandise (a) entering, (b) inside, and (c) leaving, a warehouse/distribution center?
10. What are the advantages of public warehouses? When would private warehouses be used?
11. Discuss the *adjustment function,* as defined by Bowersox.
12. How are "consolidation" points selected?
13. Why do warehouses offer incentives for goods loaded on pallets?
14. In a distribution center, which is the more important function—order picking or stock replenishment? Why?
15. Discuss the advantages of *fixed* and *variable* slot locations in distribution centers.
16. Discuss use of computers in warehousing.
17. How are optical scanners used in warehousing?
18. What are batch numbers? How are they used?
19. Why must distribution centers have developed procedures for handling stock-outs?
20. What special precautions must be taken when handling hazardous materials in a warehouse? Why?

Additional Chapter References

Ackerman, Kenneth B., and Norman Landes. "Warehouse Operations." *The Distribution Handbook* (New York: Free Press Division of Macmillan, 1985), pp. 563–583.

American Warehousemen's Association. *Public Warehousing Storage Rate Analysis System.* (Chicago: AW, 1983).

Baum, Samson R., Jon Shapiro, and Daniel Dunlap. "Micro-computer Based Application of Warehouse Financial Management." *Annual Proceedings of the NCPDM,* (1984), pp. 143–152.

Countryman, James A., Hardy F. Miller, and John R. Busher. "Planning and Budgeting Warehouse Operations." *Annual Proceedings of the NCPDM* (1984), pp. 109–130.

Gallitano, Henry J. "Retail Food Warehousing Productivity Improvement." *Annual Proceedings of the NCPDM* (1983), pp. 557–571.

Gardner, R. William. "Distribution Facility Design and Construction." *The Distribution Handbook* (New York: Free Press Division of Macmillan, 1985), pp. 584–599.

Kennedy, James D., James D. Kennedy, and Michael G. Lapihuska. "What Is Contract Warehousing? Is it Public or Private?" *Annual Proceedings of the NCPDM* (1983), pp. 421–433.

Prior, Robert L. "In Search of Excellence in Public Warehousing." *Annual Proceedings of the NCPDM* (1984), pp. 261–269.

Schwartz, Joseph. "The Financial Information for Warehouse Planning and Control." *Annual Proceedings of the NCPDM* (1983), pp. 253–258.

Smith, Philip C., and Ernest W. Harris. "Computer Applications in Private Warehouses," *Annual Proceedings of the NCPDM* (1982), pp. 415–422.

Sterling, Jay U., and Douglas M. Lambert. "A Methodology for Identifying Potential Cost Reductions in Transportation and Warehousing." *Journal of Business Logistics* (Sept. 1984), pp. 1–18.

White, John A., and Michael A. Mullens. "Management Support Systems for Warehousing." *Annual Proceedings of the NCPDM* (1984), pp. 557–570.

CASE 9-1

Obregon Restaurant Supply Company

The Obregon Restaurant Supply Company was a partnership owned by two brothers, Juan and Jose Obregon, and located in Bakersfield, California. It sold nonfood supplies to restaurants. Paper supplies, silverware, and dishes were its three principal lines and accounted for 80 per cent of the firm's sales. The other 20 percent were accounted for by a wide range of articles such as napkin dispensers, toothpick dispensers, kitchen pans, and utensils. The sales territory included the area bounded by Fresno, San Luis Obispo, Santa Barbara, and Barstow, all in California. (See Exhibit 9-1.) The firm did not sell in the Los Angeles area, and there was no market to speak of east of Bakersfield. Juan and Jose took turns staying in the office and selling on the road. Four other full time salespeople were also employed.

The firm's market was the relatively unsophisticated restaurants throughout the entire territory. Salespeople drove small vans in which they stocked the new items they were trying to sell and a variety of small replacement items for which there was frequent demand. Most of the restaurants were regular customers. A salesperson would call at a fairly regular time each week and take an order. At the end of the day, the order would be handed in to the Bakersfield office (or phoned in if the salesperson were staying away overnight). The next day either Juan or Jose, whoever's turn it was to be in the office, would tally all of the orders and, in turn, place Obregon's order with about six principal suppliers. These suppliers were located in Bakersfield, Fresno, and in the Los Angeles area. All these goods were bought on an FOB plant or warehouse basis and, late in the afternoon on the day after the Obregons placed the order, the goods would be picked up by an Obregon truck that had finished delivering supplies to restaurants. Obregon trucks would then take them to the small Obregon office/warehouse, where the goods would be unloaded. That night, outgoing orders would be made up and loaded aboard the Obregon trucks.

The truck routes for delivery were fairly regular, as were the pickups of supplies. During the afternoon, one of the Obregon brothers would write out the delivery documents and pickup instructions for each of tomorrow's drivers. That evening, a night crew of two would assemble the next day's outgoing orders, load them—in reverse order of delivery—aboard each truck, and clean and lock up the premises.

About 90 per cent of Obregon's business was handled in the manner described. Some kitchen utensils had to be ordered from firms in the East and would be mailed or sent via parcel service to the Obregon office and then delivered on an Obregon truck. Some of Obregon's outgoing shipments went by motor common carrier. These were

Exhibit 9-1 Obregon Restaurant Supply Company's Market Area

usually those destined toward San Luis Obispo, and since there was no backhaul for Obregon trucks from that area, it was cheaper for the Obregons to use common carriers. Common carrier truck service was relatively good despite the small size of the Obregon shipments because Obregons had a regular volume of business. Obregon's salespeople also made a few deliveries each week, mainly to restaurants in isolated locations. In these instances, the salespeople would deliver last week's order while taking the order for delivery next week.

In the past two years, the Obregons had been losing business to a Los Angeles-based competitor who gave "next-day" delivery, which meant that the supplies would be delivered to the restaurant one day after the salesperson took the order. (The comparable time for an Obregon order was three to four days after the order was given.) The Los Angeles firm's salespeople just called on larger restaurants on the principal north-south highways between Los Angeles and South San Francisco, where their firm also maintained a warehouse. One day a truck's delivery route would be Los Angeles to South San Francisco and the next day its route would be from South San Francisco to Los Angeles.

The Obregons lost some of their best accounts to this new competitor. The restaurants which switched said that the main reason for switching was improved delivery times. If trends continued, the Obregons would be left serving only two categories of restaurants—small ones in isolated areas that nobody else wanted to serve, and those owned by Americans of Mexican descent who preferred to do business with others of similar origin.

The Obregons decided that in order to remain competitive they would have to maintain an inventory of all supplies in Bakersfield. They also could provide "next-day" delivery along the north-south highways where their competitor was active.

They were somewhat surprised when they calculated that their dollar investment in inventory would not be large. This was because they would be buying in much larger volumes and would enjoy substantial quantity discounts. Some of the suppliers indicated that if the Obregons ordered in rail carload quantities, they could receive goods directly from the factory at even greater savings.

In their investigation, the Obregon brothers talked with several public warehousemen in Bakersfield. In addition, the warehouse foremen in their suppliers' warehouses were helpful, especially with suggestions with respect to handling their own types of product. It was agreed by all, that the Obregons would need about 10,000 square feet of warehouse space. The question then was whether to use a public warehouse or to buy a private warehouse. In addition to the 10,000 square feet of space, they needed: a loading/unloading dock wide enough so that three trucks could be handled simultaneously; parking space for six trucks and six autos; 200 square feet of office space; and, perhaps, a location on a rail siding so that they could receive by rail. Their products were of moderate value and could be handled with relatively unsophisticated warehouse equipment. The suggestion was made that about 1,000 square feet of the area be fenced with chicken wire and kept locked most of the time. Inside it would be kept open cases.

Jose Obregon investigated the public warehousing available in Bakersfield and found three different firms with which he would be willing to do business. In California, warehousemen's tariffs are regulated by the state public utilities commission, and Jose believed that if the decision was made to use public warehouse facilities, he would talk with users of all three to determine which offered the best service. Jose was sold on public warehouses and told Juan of their advantages. "The main advantage is flexibility," he said, "Our business may be more volatile than we think and if competition increases we may have a smaller volume of sales and inventory. Then we'll be stuck with empty space. Also, if we're making the right decision, all three public warehouses have rail sidings so we could start receiving paper products by rail. Our only big cash outlay is for inventory. We'd be stretching our credit rating to borrow for a building. Interest rates are such that we'd be paying 18 to 20 per cent."

"What would monthly charges at a public warehouse be?" asked Juan.

"That depends on what we're handling and the amount of labor. For our mix of product, renting the space would be about $1,400 per month. In addition, we'd need about 300 hours of warehouse labor per month, which is figured at $11 per hour."

"That's high," said Juan.

"You're right," said Jose, "but we use two men for eight hours every night here."

"Yeah, but they cost us only $7 per hour. If we had a private warehouse, one could work the day shift and receive and stock goods and the other could work at night, loading outgoing trucks."

"What would a private warehouse cost us?" Jose asked his brother.

Juan answered: "There are two private ones we can rent. One is 12,000 square feet, which we could have for 10 cents a square foot a month on a five year lease. The second one would be 10,000 feet in a larger structure that a consortium of local investors wants to build. We could get 10,000 square feet at 13 cents a square foot but we'd have to sign a ten year lease. That site has rail siding, the first one doesn't."

"I don't like those long leases," said Jose. "In a public warehouse we could change the amount of space rented every month. We'd also have to buy equipment, wouldn't we?"

"Yes, but let me finish talking about private warehouses," said Juan. "We could build a 10,000 square-foot structure on a site with plenty of room for expansion for about $85,000, including a lot and building. We'd have to pay 40 per cent down, and the rest would be paid over 15 years, in annual payments of $7,000 each (which includes 11 per cent of the unpaid balance)."

"What about property taxes?" asked Jose.

"They'd run $1,500 per year for the land and building. We'd also pay an inventory tax but, in this state, it makes no difference whether you're in a public or a private warehouse. As I see it, we'll need only a crew of two for forty hours a week apiece and our wages are only $7 per hour."

"Yes, but they need equipment," exclaimed Jose.

"We won't need much more than we use around here to load and unload trucks," responded Juan. "The only immediate need would be a fork lift truck so we can stack higher. We'd only be using it an hour or so a day and I think we could assume, if we bought a used one, that the cost would be about $1,000 a year."

Jose asked: "Did the sites you consider have rail sidings?"

Juan said that they were alongside rail tracks and that the Obregon firm would have to pay the cost of the siding on their land. If they generated enough traffic the railroad would not charge them for the costs of the siding that was on railroad property.

Question One: The Obregons have decided that "in order to remain competitive they would have to maintain an inventory of all supplies in Bakersfield." How will their new inventory carrying costs compare with those under the former system? What are some of the elements which will contribute to the change in costs?

Question Two: How would you go about calculating the value to the Obregon brothers of locating on a railroad siding?

Question Three: Obregon salespeople sometimes phone in their orders. Design a form to be used in the Obregon office when a salesperson calls in with an order. What information is needed, and in what order should it be arranged? (Restrict the size of your form to no more than one 8½- by 11-inch sheet of paper.)

Question Four: Obregon salespeople "drove in small vans in which they stocked the new items they were trying to sell and a variety of small replacement items for which there was frequent demand." How would you go about determining which items should be stocked in the vans for possible sale? Draft a memo for the Obregons to use indicating which items salespeople can and cannot stock in their vans.

Question Five: Based on the information given so far, which warehousing alternative would you recommend? Why?

Question Six: Before making the decision which the Obregon brothers are going to have to make, what additional information would be useful?

CASE 9-2

Saginaw Auto Parts Company

Saginaw Auto Parts Company was located in Saginaw, Michigan. It manufactured and bought automobile replacement parts that it distributed to chain auto supply houses, some service station chains and to two mail order houses. It did wholesale business only. Its principal warehouse was in Saginaw, where over 40,000 different parts were stored. One giant conveyor belt, 36 inches off the floor, moved through the entire warehouse. On either side of the conveyor belt were racks with shelves placed 3, 21, 39 and 52 inches above the floor.

The warehouse was divided into 15 order-picking zones. Empty baskets left the office with small tabs raised for zones where portions (or all) of the order were to be picked. As the basket reached the zone, the raised tab would activate a mechanism that removed the basket from the belt. There an order picker would fill the basket with whatever parts were located in that zone, release the cocked tab for that zone, and place the basket back on the belt where it would travel to the next zone for which a tab was cocked. When a particular zone was especially busy and accumulated a batch of unfilled baskets, a worker would place some of the unfilled baskets back on the belt without touching the cocking mechanism. The basket would then move to the next station for which a tab was cocked and eventually would return to the station where the temporary overload had existed.

Over 98 per cent of all items were handled by the conveyor belt system. The only exceptions were engine blocks, which were too heavy, and tail pipes, which were too long. These items were handled separately out of a room near the loading dock.

Saginaw Auto Parts Company had always been profitable and, in 1968, it had been acquired by a large conglomerate. In 1986, the conglomerate's new president, in an effort to improve the conglomerate's image as a "socially responsible" concern, announced that all subsidiaries were being instructed to increase the percentages of minorities and of women on their payrolls. In an "internal" memo, Saginaw's management was given two weeks to come up with a plan that would meet the conglomerate's pledge. It happened that Saginaw Auto Parts was already one of the largest employers of minorities in Saginaw, so little could be done in that direction. Their parts warehouse activities had always been considered "man's work" for various reasons, the main one being the size and weight of materials being handled. However, in the last decade, as autos became smaller, so did many of their component parts.

Saginaw Auto Parts' entire moving belt and storage system had been designed on the assumption that men would be doing the picking of orders. Because, in warehousing, women have different capabilities than men, some redesign would be necessary.

There are many concerns in laying out a warehouse. In the Saginaw warehouse, each of the fifteen zones contained a "family" of items such as electrical equipment, and transmission parts. A different buyer was responsible for each of the fifteen zones. Within the zones, the goods were located according to two criteria. The fastest moving items were in the shelf 39 inches from the floor because that was the quickest location from which to pick. Very heavy items, 35–50 pounds, were also at that level because it was closest to the level of the belt, and a higher percent of the work force could handle heavy loads if no vertical change was involved. Fast-moving items were also

Exhibit 9-2 Electrical system parts section of Saginaw's Warehouse—Distribution of units sold by weight.*

Weight of Unit of Merchandise, (in lb.)	Fast-Moving Items (which represent or total 80% of all units sold by this section) SKUs	Slow-Moving Items (which represent or total 20% of all units sold by this section) SKUs
less than 10	26	50
10 up to 20	5	10
20 up to 30	2	5
30 up to 50	2	5
TOTAL SKU's	35	70

*The table was made in this manner: Records were kept of the number of units sold by each different SKU. A tally sheet listed SKUs in descending order of units sold. A cumulative total was kept as each item was tallied; as it happened, when item 35 was tallied and its unit sales added to the cumulative total, the total reached 80 per cent of all unit sales. All 35 items are on the left—they account for, in total, about 80 per cent of the warehouse section's activity.

put in the 52-inch shelf since most men were tall enough to see and handle items stored at that height. The slowest moving items were in the bottom shelf.

Some items handled weighed 50 pounds or over, but additional lifting equipment was provided to workers handling them. However, stronger workers were still needed to handle the heavier items because they had to be pulled onto and off of the lifting devices.

The distribution of items, by weight, differed for each zone. In the engine block zone, nearly every item weighed over 100 pounds. In four zones, nothing weighed over 25 pounds. Exhibit 9-2 shows the distribution, by weight, of items kept in the electrical systems section, and Exhibit 9-3 shows similar data for the engine blocks section. The "20/80" analysis (see Chapter 7) was applied to both sections. On both tables, the left-hand columns are for those SKUs that account for about 80 per cent of each section's activity (or units sold). The right-hand column are for the SKUs that

Exhibit 9-3 Engine assembly parts section of Saginaw's Warehouse—Distribution of units sold by weight.*

Weight of Unit of Merchandise, (in lb.)	Fast-Moving Items (which represent or total 80% of all units sold by this section) SKUs	Slow-Moving Items (which represent or total 20% of all units sold by this section) SKUs
less than 10	11	11
10 up to 20	5	5
20 up to 30	3	5
30 up to 40	1	7
40 up to 50	6	15
50 up to 75	4	20
75 up to 100	2	30
100 and over	16	25
TOTAL SKUs	48	118

*This table was constructed using same methods as described at bottom of Exhibit 9-2.

account for only about 20 per cent of the unit sales. In each section, four order pickers are kept busy, and in these particular sections nearly every order is for a single item only.

Exhibit 9-4 was provided by an insurance company, and the portion regarding males had been used in determining shelf level locations in Saginaw's present warehouse. Items had been placed at heights so that two-thirds of "industrial men" could handle them. (Some of Saginaw's work force, especially older men, could not meet these standards. They were assigned to zones where none of the items were very heavy.) New employees were given physical examinations before they could become order pickers. During the first two weeks, they were carefully instructed and closely supervised with respect to proper lifting techniques. Workers were expected to meet order-picking standards for their zone. Continued failure to do so was a recognized reason for dismissal although, as just noted, older workers who had been with the company for some time were assigned to less demanding tasks.

The center and right columns on Exhibit 9-4 are for females. Industrial women are experienced industrial laborers. Housewives have less lifting ability, yet they are actively seeking work in the industrial area and presumably represent the individuals whom Saginaw should be attempting to hire.

Several questions following this case deal with the arrangement of slots for holding or stocking different SKUs. (For purposes of this case it is assumed that one slot is

Exhibit 9-4 Percents of Workforce That Can Perform Lift of Various Weights from Specified Heights to the Height of 36 Inches (Figures Are Hypothetical).

	Lbs.	Industrial Men	Industrial Women	Housewives
From 52″	10	100	100	85
	20	90	85	70
	30	75	70	60
	40	65	60	45
	50	55	45	30
	60	45	35	20
	70	40	25	10
From 39″	10	100	100	90
	20	90	85	75
	30	80	75	65
	40	75	65	50
	50	70	50	35
	60	60	40	25
	70	45	30	15
From 21″	10	100	95	85
	20	90	80	60
	30	75	65	50
	40	60	50	45
	50	50	40	35
	60	45	35	20
From 3″	10	95	90	80
	20	85	75	55
	30	75	60	45
	40	60	45	35
	50	45	35	30

Exhibit 9-5 Warehouse Rack, Viewed from Front

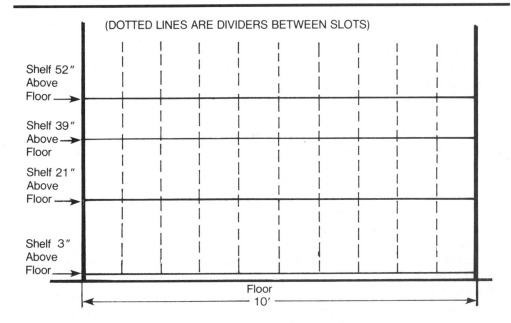

sufficient for stocking any SKU.) Exhibit 9-5 is a warehouse rack, viewed from the front. It is 10 feet long and has horizontal shelves, 3 inches, 21 inches, 39 inches, and 52 inches above the floor. Assuming each SKU requires one slot, and each slot uses one linear foot of shelf space, the warehouse rack, as shown, can be used to stock 40 SKUs.

Question One: The electrical system parts section consists of three racks, similar to the one shown on Exhibit 9-5, and offering a total of 120 slots. Assign 105 slots to the various items by weight and whether they are fast or slow moving. (You may leave 15 slots empty.) Your objective should be a warehouse section where all or nearly all the order pickers are women, especially those in the "housewife" category.

Question Two: Because the electrical system parts are small and the shelves are adjustable, you are told to change the level of some shelves and add an additional one. The shelves are now one foot apart and at 3 inches, 16 inches, 29 inches, 42 inches, and 55 inches above the floor. (The inch is for the thickness of the shelf.) Each SKU slot requires only one linear foot, so each linear foot of rack holds five SKUs. You need only 21 linear feet of rack (105/5). Now arrange your SKUs on the five-shelf racks in a manner which allows you to use the highest percentage of women—especially housewives.

Question Three: Although the proposal outlined in question two saves floor space (compared to the arrangement in question one), it may also cause congestion because the four order pickers will be grouped more closely. Describe in detail how you would determine whether the proposal in question two would cause congestion.

Question Four: The foreman in the engine assembly parts section believes that all of the fast movers should be on two racks—similar to the rack shown on Exhibit 9-5. However, items weighing 100 pounds or over have to be kept on the bottom shelf. Assign the 48 "fast movers" to individual slots. You may leave 32 slots (80–48) empty.

You want to maximize the number of females who can be employed in this section. Note that this question deals with fast movers only.

Question Five: Your boss looks at your asnwer to Question Four and says that too much congestion will be created because about 80 per cent of all activity will take place in front of the two racks. She suggests that you lay out slots for all 166 SKUs in the engine assembly parts section. This will require five racks of the kind shown in Exhibit 9-5. Indicate where you would locate all SKUs by weight and whether they were fast or slow movers. Items weighing 100 pounds or more must be on the bottom shelf. You want to maximize the number of females who can be employed in this section of the warehouse. Note that you will be leaving some slots empty.

Question Six: The questions in the case have dealt mainly with arranging a warehouse in order to meet the lifting abilities of various groups of workers. Two other factors are the time it takes the order picker to remove items from the shelves at different heights and the congestion or queuing situation that occurs because several workers have to take items from the same location at about the same time. How would you take these factors into account in laying out the warehouse?

Question Seven: What other factors do you think influence how one arranges the items inside a warehouse so that they can be picked by order pickers in an orderly and efficient manner?

Question Eight: If you have access to computers and can program or find software, attempt to develop a computer simulation of the order picking process which might be used to test varying shelf arrangements.

Bagged sugar is loaded into a vessel's hold through use of two giant rotating spiral loaders.
(*Credit:* Port of Antwerp Promotion Association. Photo by F. Coolens.)

Packaging and Materials Handling

Over the past few years, a clear picture of the niche for robots in case palletizing has emerged. First of all, they excel at handling many different palletizing patterns. You can put an unlimited number of programs on a cassette. The robot can switch from one pattern to another automatically, say on receiving a signal from a bar code reader. . . .

Modern Materials Handling
September 7, 1984

Approximately 75 per cent of all cargo losses are preventable. The prudent shipper recognizes that efforts in properly preparing, packing, and marking shipments have a great influence on successful delivery of his goods.

Insurance Company of North America
Ports of the World: A Guide to
Cargo Loss Control
1984

Introduction

This chapter deals with the physical handling of products. Each product has unique physical properties that, along with the accepted volumes or quantities in which it is traded or moved, determine how the product is packaged or how it is handled when it moves in bulk (loose) form. The first portion of this chapter deals with packaged goods; the second portion examines products shipped in bulk. The distinction is not absolute because a good may move in bulk form from the manufacturer to a wholesaler who will package it for retail distribution.

Packaging and materials handling are closely related to several topics currently considered to be on the cutting edge of logistics thinking and operations. Materials Requirements Planning (MRP) is concerned with obtaining more efficient management over the flow of all materials and products within a firm's production system. Robotics, although still used mainly in manufacturing, is being introduced to a number of functions related to the physical handling of both packaged and bulk materials.

Product Characteristics

Each product has unique physical properties. For example, density of bulk materials varies. The Great Lakes steamer Richard J. Reiss, when carrying ore, uses only two thirds of its cubic capacity, yet the 15,800 tons of ore will lower the vessel to its maximum allowable draft of 24 feet, 8 inches. When loaded with coal, the vessel, "cubes-out;" i.e., the cubic capacity is filled, and the vessel will lower to only 20 feet, six inches. Grain loads even lighter, and the Richard J. Reiss' draft then is slightly less than 20 feet.[1]

---

[1] Correspondence from The Reiss Steamship Company to the authors.

A material's *angle of repose* is the angle size that would be formed by the side of a conical stack. The greater the angle, the higher the pile of materials that can be placed on a specific area. Anthracite coal has an angle of repose of approximately 27 degrees, whereas for iron ore the figure is 35 degrees. This means more cubic yards of ore can be stockpiled on a certain site and the ore can be carried on a slightly steeper or narrower conveyer belt system.

Bulk liquids also have unique handling characteristics. Resistance to flow is measured as viscosity, which can be lowered by increasing the temperature of a liquid. Molasses, cooking oils, and many petroleum products are heated before an attempt is made to pump them.

Gases also have unique handling properties, although most of them are handled within completely enclosed pipeline systems. An exception is LNG, liquified natural gas, which is cooled and compressed into liquid form which is $\frac{1}{630}$ of its volume in gaseous state. In its liquified, highly pressurized state it is transported by ocean-going vessels in special tanks.

The handling process itself may change the characteristics (or quality) of the product. Rice grains cannot fall far without being broken. This influences the design of loading and unloading facilities so that the grains of rice never drop more than a few feet at any one time. When sugar is handled, a "dust" is formed because of abrasion between sugar crystals. This dust is also sugar but in much finer form and with different sensitivities to moisture. The dust must be separated from the rest of the sugar; otherwise the quality of the final product in which the sugar is used will be affected.

The physical characteristics of some goods change while they are moving in the distribution channel. Fresh fruits and vegetables are the best-known example. Even after they are picked, they continue to give off gases and moisture and to generate heat—a process known as respiration. Fruits and vegetables are harvested before they are ripe so that they will reach the retail stores as they ripen. Ripening processes can be delayed through the use of lower temperatures or application of gases. Products such as fresh produce, meats, fish, and bakers' yeast are referred to as perishables. They require special packaging, loading, storage, and monitoring as they are moved from source to customer.

Several years ago, an experiment was conducted to determine whether Colorado and California carnations should be picked and shipped in bud, rather than full-flower form. The buds had better transport characteristics because they were less voluminous (more could be loaded into a carton) and also they weighed less because the stem with the bud contained less water than did a stem with a full flower. An advantage at the receiving end of the shipment was that the buds had a longer shelf life because ripening could be delayed by keeping the buds at a low temperature. The disadvantages were also at the receiver's end because ripening the carnations required temperature-controlled space and some labor to trim and place the stems into buckets of ripening solutions.[2]

---

[2] *Transport and Handling of Carnations Cut in the Bud Stage—Potential Advantages.* Report No. 899. (Washington, D.C.: U.S. Department of Agriculture, Agricultural Research Service, Marketing Research, 1971).

In addition to physical characteristics, products also possess chemical characteristics that affect the manner in which they should be handled. Certain "pairs" of products are incompatible. For example, "commodities which are sensitive to ethylene such as mangoes, bananas, and brocoli should never be held for more than a few hours in the same area as those products which emit ethylene, such as apples, avocados, and cantaloupes."[3]

Hazardous Cargo

Under certain conditions, almost any material can possess hazardous qualities. Flour dust will explode, or grain in elevators will self-ignite and burn. Special care is needed to handle these and many other such substances. In the 1970s there was an increase in governmental regulations involving the movements of so-called hazardous materials, which often are classified into seven categories: explosives, compressed gases, flammable liquids, oxidizers, poisons, radioactive materials, and corrosive materials.

The specific requirements differ for each hazardous commodity, but all of them involve labeling, packaging and repackaging, warning on shipping documents and advance notification of carrier. A common requirement on transferring flammable materials is that the vehicle and the receiving or discharging device both be electrically grounded. Care must be taken to properly clean tanks, pumps, hoses, and other cleaning apparatus to avoid contamination of the next cargo that is handled.

Numerous regulations exist and are issued by all levels of government, and there are differences between domestic and international moves. At the local level, sometimes there are prohibitions on the use of certain tunnels or bridges during specified hours by trucks carrying explosives or other dangerous cargo. Shipping documents must also indicate whether the cargo is of hazardous nature.

Packages, containers, trailers, and rail cars carrying hazardous materials must carry distinct signs, or placards, identifying the hazard. These are shown on Figure 10-1 although, in reality, they are more distinctly and brightly colored.

Environmental Protection

Public concern for environmental protection has had an impact on packaging practices. Use of disposable packing materials is often viewed as wasteful. Many of the materials used in packaging can be recycled. This has happened in the case of wooden pallets that tripled in price, creating an incentive for many firms to devise methods for reusing them rather than indiscriminantly disposing of them.

Increased enforcement of water pollution controls forced some paper and container manufacturers out of business. Higher prices for logs have diverted lumber resources to other uses. There are often shortages of certain

---

[3] *A Commitment to Excellence in the Shipment of Perishable Commodities*, (Elizabeth, N.J.: Sea-Land Service, Inc., 1980), p. 4. See also, Association of American Railroads, Damage Prevention Section, *Handling and Shipping Fresh Fruits and Vegetables by Rail* (Chicago: 1976).

Figure 10-1 Examples of Hazardous Materials Labels

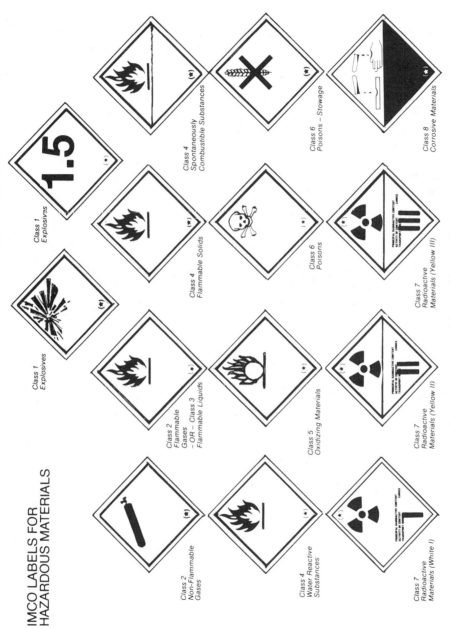

IMCO LABELS FOR
HAZARDOUS MATERIALS

Class 1
Explosives

Class 1
Explosives

Class 4
Spontaneously
Combustible Substances

Class 4
Flammable Solids

Class 6
Poisons – Stowage

Class 6
Poisons

Class 8
Corrosive Materials

Class 2
Flammable
Gases
– OR – Class 3
Flammable Liquids

Class 5
Oxidizing Materials

Class 7
Radioactive
Materials (Yellow III)

Class 2
Non-Flammable
Gases

Class 4
Water Reactive
Substances

Class 7
Radioactive
Materials (White I)

Class 7
Radioactive
Materials (Yellow II)

Courtesy: Insurance Company of North America, *Ports of the World, A Guide to Cargo Loss Control,*
1979.

379

types of packing and packaging materials. Prices have risen and this has caused some users to recycle their shipping containers. The result is not always without danger, however, since problems arose when goods in reused containers were contaminated by traces of whatever product had been carried earlier. It was necessary for the FDA to issue an order restricting the reuse of containers to avoid food contamination. Dressed poultry often carries salmonella organisms (which are killed in cooking), but the organisms survive in the wooden crates and spread to vegetables if they are transported later in the same crate.

Dust and vapors produced during bulk-cargo transfer operations are also being scrutinized more closely by public agencies. Coal dust will blow for several miles from a large coal pile. Some states require those who handle petroleum products, including retail gasoline stations, to install vapor recovery systems. For liquids with vapor-escape problems, the transfer processes are redesigned so that tanks and other receptacles are loaded from the bottom rather than the top. This change—when applied to tank truck loading—reduces vapor emissions by 80 per cent.

Metric System

More and more products will be packaged and sold on a metric measure basis. New packages will be in metric units with the nonmetric equivalents printed in smaller type. Although entire change may take several decades, many of the steps necessary to implement the adoption of the new system must be taken in the next few years.

One U.S. industry that did convert to metric containers was the wine and liquor producers, who introduced entirely new sizes of bottles. The conversion was apparently successful and in spite of the fact that the industry is subjected to more than its share of regulation because its product is heavily taxed and many of these taxes were drawn up to be applicable to other sizes of containers.

U.S. exporters are coming under increasing pressure to market their products overseas in metric units. Some importing nations even levy fines against products that are not sold in metric measurements. "For multinationals, there's no doubt the world's a metric marketplace."[4]

Packaging

Packaging can be thought of as a system of building blocks. The smallest units are the retail or consumer packages or cartons one sees on the shelves of stores. These are usually packed into boxes of one to two cubic feet and light enough in weight so they can be carried by a stock clerk. This discus-

---

[4] Statement by Lon Parsons of Honeywell, in *Modern Materials Handling* (Aug. 1979). p. 7. A more recent "industry survey of *Fortune 1,000 firms* found that 62 percent of them produce at least one metric product, 32 percent of their net sales are from metric products and 34 percent of new products use metric designs." This study was cited in a Gannett News Service article appearing in the Marin *Independent Journal* (San Rafael, CA) Feb. 26, 1985, p. A6.

sion of the building-block concept will emphasize rectangular-shaped containers, but it can be applied to other shapes as well.

> Terminology for describing all of the various containers used in packaging varies. In carrier tariffs, *boxes* are defined as being more rigidly constructed than *cartons* or *packages*.

The building-block hierarchy is important to remember because each of the different building blocks is inside another and their total effect must be to protect the product. They function in a complementary sense. If the consumer-sized package, as one sees on the shelves of stores, is very solid, such as the wooden boxes in which salt codfish are packed, the larger packaging elements require less sturdy packaging materials because the smaller package (the wooden boxes) are themselves sturdy. At the other extreme would be lightbulbs with a retail packing of single face corrugated fiberboard that may protect them from breakage but contributes nothing to the internal strength of the larger container.

Sales Functions of Boxes

Boxes are thought primarily to be protective although they may contain features with a sales orientation. Some products are sold in either a consumer-sized pack or a larger box or case. Some merchants build displays using box or case lots of goods to create the impression they have made an extra large purchase of a certain item—presumably at a lower price per unit that is being passed on to the consumer. In this instance, it would be appropriate to have some advertising on the outside of the box. Some boxes are designed so that they do not have to be unpacked by the stock clerk for stocking on shelves. Instead, the stock clerk cuts away the top two thirds of the box and places the bottom third, with its contents still in place, on the shelf. Figure 10-2 illustrates a box that is packed, as we see it, at the factory. The retailer needs only to remove the front and add the header card at the top.

The advertising and protective functions of packaging sometimes conflict. Although, from a retailing standpoint, it may be desirable to have an attractive advertising message on the outside of each box, when these boxes are in a warehouse the same message might make it easier for a thief to determine quickly which boxes contain the most valuable items. Using code numbers alone on the outside of the box would slow down the thief.

Figure 10-3 illustrates another issue involving sales and protective packaging. The razor blade container, shown at the bottom, is quite small. Because razor blades are often displayed next to chain store check-out stands, from a marketing standpoint it is useful to display them on a rack. However, to reduce the problem of shop lifting, it is necessary to mount the blades on a stiff card that is larger than most people's pockets. The net effect of these two steps is to increase the cube or the volume of each razor blade package by 700 to 800 per cent.

Figure 10-2 Shipping/Display Carton

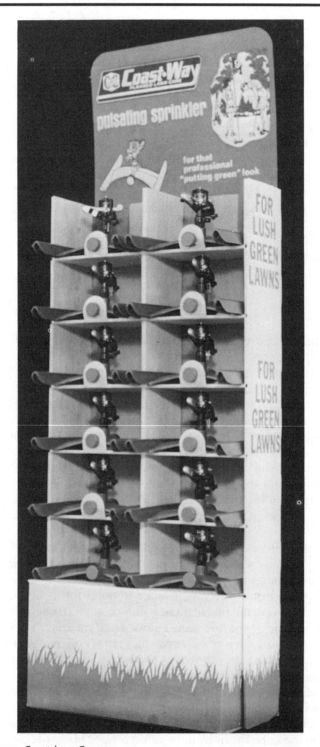

Courtesy Stone Container Corp.

Figure 10-3 Impact of Item's Cube Due to Packing It So It Can Be Hung on Rack

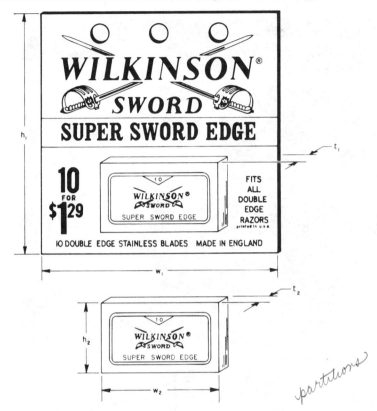

Courtesy E. Ralph Sims, Jr., and Associates.

Protective Functions of Packaging

A protective package should perform the following functions. It must

1. Enclose the materials, both to protect them and protect other items from them.
2. Restrain them from undesired movements within the container when the container is in transit.
3. Separate the contents to prevent undesired contact, such as through the use of corrugated fiberboard partitions used in the shipment of glassware. (A unique example of separating a package's contents is shown on Figure 10-4, a package used for expensive water faucets. The plumber pulls at the horizontal tab, which is between the top and bottom of the box. This removes the top, outer half, giving him access to all of the fittings necessary to install the faucets, which is the most time consuming of the plumber's tasks. The bottom part of the package holds the expensive faucets themselves, which are used last in the installation process. Because

Figure 10-4 Package Separating Plumbing Fixture Parts into Sequence When Needed

Courtesy Georgia-Pacific Corporation.

the plumber will not remove them until they are needed, they are less likely to get lost or dirtied.)
4. Cushion the contents from outside vibrations and shocks.
5. Support the weight of identical containers that will be stacked above it as part of the building block concept. This could mean, in some situations, stacks in a warehouse that are over 20 feet high.
6. Position the contents to provide maximum protection for them. If one were packaging combined sets of waste baskets and lampshades, the package would be designed so that the lampshades were protected by the wastebaskets.
7. Provide for fairly uniform weight distribution within the package, because most equipment for the automatic handling of packages is designed for packages whose weight is evenly distributed. Also, individuals handling packages manually assume that the weight inside is evenly distributed.
8. Provide sufficient exterior surfaces so that identification and shipping labels can be applied along with specific instructions such as "this side up"

The Elements of Physical Distribution/Logistics Systems

Figure 10-5 Checklist for Box Users

checklist for box users

The corrugated box contains and protects your product, but it can also serve many functions which aid in packing, storage, distribution, marketing and sales. This checklist is a guide to the information you'll want to supply to your box maker. He can then offer suggestions and recommendations to utilize every value-added advantage that corrugated can offer.

YOUR PRODUCT

	yes	no
1. Have you given your box maker a description of your product and its use, the exact dimensions, weight and physical characteristics?	□	□
2. Is the product likely to settle or shift?	□	□
3. Is it perishable, fragile, or hazardous in any way?	□	□
4. Will it need extra protection against vibration, impact, moisture, air, heat or cold?	□	□
5. Will it be shipped fully assembled?	□	□
6. Will more than one unit be packed in a box?	□	□
7. Will accessories, parts or literature be included with the product?	□	□
8. Have you provided your box maker with a complete sample of your product as it will be packed?	□	□

YOUR PACKING OPERATION

	yes	no
1. Is your box inventory adequately geared to re-order lead time?	□	□
2. Is your box inventory arranged to efficiently feed your packing lines?	□	□
3. Is your inventory of boxes properly stored (see *Recommended Practices*, p. 32)?	□	□
4. Will you be setting up the boxes on automatic equipment? (If so, what type? Size? Method of closure?)	□	□
5. Will your product be packed automatically? (If so, with what type of equipment?)	□	□
6. If more than one unit or part goes into each box, have you determined the sequence?	□	□
7. Will inner packing—shells, liners, pads, partitions—be inserted by hand?	□	□
8. Is your closure system—tape, stiches, glue—compatible with the box, packing line speed, customer needs and recycling considerations?	□	□
9. Will the box be imprinted or labeled?	□	□
10. Will a master pack be used for a multiple of boxes to maintain cleanliness or appearance?	□	□

YOUR STORAGE

	yes	no
1. Have you determined the gross weight of the filled box?	□	□
2. Does the product itself help support weight in stacking?	□	□
3. Will the bottom box have to support the full weight in warehouse stacking?	□	□
4. Will boxes be handled by lift trucks which use clamps, finger lifts or special attachments?	□	□
5. Will filled boxes be palletized? (The size of pallet and pallet pattern may justify a change in box design or dimensions, if only to reduce or eliminate overhang.)	□	□
6. Would a change in box style or size make more efficient use of warehouse space?	□	□
7. Will filled boxes be subject to unusual conditions during storage—high humidity, extreme temperatures, etc.?	□	□
8. Is the product likely to be stored outdoors at any time during its distribution?	□	□
9. Would color coding simplify identification of various packed products?	□	□

YOUR SHIPPING

	yes	no
1. Have you reviewed the appropriate rules of the transportation service you intend to use (rail, truck, air, parcel post, etc.)?	□	□
2. Is your container authorized for shipment of your product?	□	□
3. If the package is not authorized, have you requested appropriate test shipment authorization from the carrier?	□	□
4. Does your product require any special caution or warning label or legend for shipment?	□	□
5. Have you determined the actual inside dimensions of the transportation vehicle so that you can establish how your filled boxes will be stacked or braced?	□	□

YOUR CUSTOMER

	yes	no
1. Does your customer have any special receiving, storage or handling requirements that will affect box design?	□	□
2. Will the box be used as part of a mass display?	□	□
3. Is the box intended as a display-shipper?	□	□
4. Will it contain a separate product display?	□	□
5. Will it be used as a carry-home package, requiring a carrying device?	□	□
6. Does it need an easy-opening feature?	□	□
7. Can surface design, symbols or colors relate to promotional materials or to other products of the same corporate family?	□	□
8. Should instructions or opening precautions be printed on the box?	□	□
9. Can the box be made to better sell your product?	□	□

Courtesy Fibre Box Association.

or "keep refrigerated."[5] Today this would also mean providing a uniform location for the application of bar-code markings.

9. Be "safe" in the sense that the package itself (both in conjuction with the product carried and after it has been unpacked) presents no hazards to consumers or to others.

Figure 10-5 is a checklist prepared by the Fibre Box Association and indicates the range of considerations that go into package choice. Firms that sell packaging material are helpful sources of information to potential users. Often they will provide technical advice. Packaging is a science, and costs can be calculated for various solutions to any packaging problem. Package choice is a concern of physical distribution and logistics management because it is related to transportation and storage facilities. It is also related to materials-handling techniques and equipment used in factories, assembly plants, and warehouses.

Common Carriers' Packaging Requirements

Prior to common carrier deregulation, the carriers' tariffs and classifications influenced (if not controlled) the type of packaging and packing methods that had to be used. In the freight classification documents the type of packaging was specified. The commodity was listed, followed by a comma, and then by a phrase such as "in machine pressed bales," "in barrels," "in bales compressed to more than 18 lb. per square foot," "folded flat, in packages," "celluloid covered, in boxes," "SU" (set up), or "KD" (knocked down or disassembled and packed so that it occupies one third or less of the volume it would occupy in its set-up state). The carriers had established these different classifications for two main reasons. First, packaging specifications determined by product density encourage shippers to tender loads in densities that make best use of the equipment's weight and volume capabilities. Second, specifications that deal with protective packaging reduce the likelihood of damage to products while they are being carried, and this, in turn, reduces the amount of loss and damage claims placed against the carrier. Figure 10-6 shows the type of label that motor carriers and railroads required on any fiber boxes used for shipping freight. This label is the fiber box manufacturer's assurance to the motor carriers and railroads that the boxes will be sturdy enough to meet their handling specifications. Note that a number of different measures are used.

In today's "deregulated" environment, it's difficult to know exactly how much carrier tariffs and classifications control shippers' packaging. Where there has been no deregulation, such as intrastate trucking in some states, the rules still hold. On the national level, however, it is not clear that car-

---

[5] List adopted from Richard C. Colton and Edmund S. Ward, *Practical Handbook of Industrial Traffic Management,* 4th ed. (Washington, D.C.: Traffic Services Corporation, 1965), pp. 157–158.

Figure 10-6 Box-Maker's Guarantee

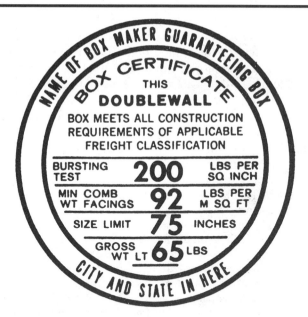

Courtesy Fibre Box Association.

riers can still meet to discuss topics such as packaging requirements without being accused of antitrust violations.[6] As specific contract rates are negotiated and drawn up between individual carriers and shippers, packaging requirements may, of course, be one element of negotiation. (However, when a group of West Coast traffic managers participating in a panel at San Francisco State University in late 1984 were asked whether packaging requirements were an element in their negotiations with carriers, their answers were "no." They said that, in the negotiations, the carriers desired to limit their—the carriers'—liability for loss and damage claims so much that the shippers subsequently were reluctant to cut back on their packaging because most of the risk for damage in transit had been passed to them.)

Airlines, express delivery companies, and the postal service also have packaging requirements although they are somewhat less detailed than those used by rail or motor common carriers. Export packing is discussed briefly in Chapter 11. The International Air Transport Association regulates packaging of air shipments; there are fewer requirements regarding ocean shipments. However, exporters nearly always buy additional insurance coverage for their export shipments, and the type of packing influences the insurance rates.

---

[6] "Is the Packaging Spec an Endangered Species?" *Traffic Management* (Sept. 1982), pp. 80–82. In late 1984 the National Freight Claim Council and the American Trucking Associations proposed sweeping changes in the National Motor Freight Classification packaging rules, the main thrust being to make the shipper assume more of the burden for adequate packaging. See *Pacific Traffic* (Sept. 1984), p. 30.

When new products or new packaging techniques are about to be introduced, it is sometimes advisable to have the packages pretested. Various packaging material manufacturers or their trade organizations provide this service free. Independent testing laboratories can also be used. The packages are subject to tests that attempt to duplicate all the expected various shipping hazards: vibration, dropping, horizontal impacts, compression (having too much weight loaded on top), over-exposure to extreme temperatures or moisture, and generalized "rough handling."

Sometimes specialized tests are devised. The following quotations describe tests conducted on a new type of pallet:

> After bearing a 2,400-pound load for 48 hours and being checked for deformation, the pallet was again loaded with a 2,400-pound load and run through a series of tests. . . .
>
> 20 times picked up and set back down on the four by fours in a rough and careless manner.
>
> 4 times picked up off the supporting beams with one fork under the center of the pallet only and lifted to a height of 4 feet; then rapidly lowered and raised. This attempt was to crack the pallet in the center.
>
> 10 times raised 6 inches by a fork that had a fast fork drop rate, and then very rapidly dropped back on its supporting beams.
>
> We then tried to mutilate the loaded pallet by
>
> 1. Twisting the forks within the pallet-fork openings; i.e. backing up at an angle before disengaging the forks from the pallet. We were able to put a slight tear near the corner of one fork opening.
>
> 2. Roughly, we pushed the pallet to different positions while flat on the floor with one fork. This was done in the attempt to split the outside corners.[7]

Computer software has also been devised that allows one to test different packaging. One program allows the user to simulate the use of various grades of lumber and the numbers and sizes of nails to be used in constructing wooden pallets. The software will then calculate the average life expectancy of pallets—and their average cost before needing repair—for each combination of lumber and nails.[8]

In addition to the testing of new products or new packages, shippers should keep detailed records on all loss and damage claims. Statistical tests can be applied to the data to determine whether the damage pattern is randomly distributed. If it is not, then efforts are made toward providing additional protection for areas in the package that are overly vulnerable. Carriers also have provisions that allow shippers to follow special rules while testing new packaging materials. UPS allows customers to ship "sample" parcels to various UPS district offices, and UPS employees at those sites then report back with comments about how well the packaging withstood the trip.[9]

[7] Source anonymous.

[8] "How the Software Designs and Analyzes Wooden Pallets," *Modern Materials Handling* (Oct. 5, 1984), pp. 60–61.

[9] *Packaging for the Small Parcel Environment* (Greenwich, Conn.: United Parcel Service, 1974), pp. 174–179.

Figure 10-7 An Impact Indicator

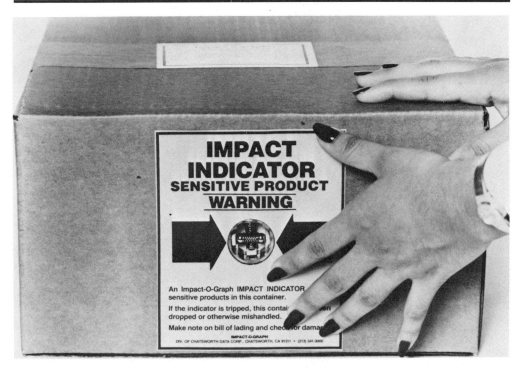

The indicator is implanted in the package's side, and the consignee is instructed to see whether the mechanism was ''tripped'' during shipment. If it was, the consignee is supposed to indicate that on the shipping documents.

Credit: Impact-O-Graph, Chatsworth, California

Related to package testing is actual monitoring of the environment the package must pass through. This is done by enclosing recording devices within cartons of the product that are shipped. The measuring devices may be very simple, such as hospital-like thermometers that record only temperature extremes or springs that are set to snap only if a specified "G" (a measure of force) is exceeded. Figure 10-7 shows one such device being inserted in the side of a package. More sophisticated devices record over time a series of variables, such as temperature, humidity, acceleration force, and duration (in several directions). Acceleration force and duration are usually recorded along three different axes, which makes it possible to calculate the precise direction from which the force originated. Kaiser Aluminum, which was troubled with problems of water-stain damage, devised a small sticker with the "happy face" expression. Above the happy face's smile are two eyes, but one of the eyes is printed with a special ink that dissolves when it comes into contact with moisture. If the receiver of the shipment notices that the eye is distorted, he can assume the shipment has been exposed to moisture and should be inspected for damage. One of these labels is shown on Figure 10-8.

Sophisticated monitors are expensive, but they may be necessary to solve

Figure 10-8 Kaiser Aluminum's "Moisture Alert" Label

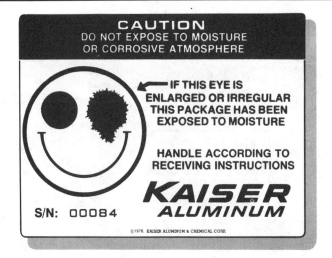

When the product is shipped, both eyes are ''normal,'' i.e. look like the one on the left. This is how the label looks if the product has been exposed to moisture. The receiver is supposed to record the condition of the label on the shipping documents accompanying the goods.

Credit: Kaiser Aluminum & Chemical Corporation. The label was copyrighted by them in 1978.

a problem of recurrent in-transit damage. Less complicated devices are used to record temperatures and may or may not be used as the basis for a damage claim against a carrier. They may be used aboard a shipper's own equipment to ensure quality control. A frozen food distributor would want to be certain that his product had not thawed and been refrozen in transit. Large shipments of apples are accompanied by a mechanical temperature recorder, which provides the receiver with a greater workable knowledge of each load, giving him valuable information on temperature variation that may effect the speed in which he should handle and merchandise its contents. Figure 10-9 contains the description of a shipping problem where the difficulties occurred while the product was in transit. Note also the steps taken to overcome the problem.

Labeling and Price Marking

Once the material being packaged is placed into the box and the cover is closed, the contents are hidden. At this point it becomes necessary to label the box. Whether words or code numbers are used depends upon the nature of the product and its vulnerability to pilferage. Retroreflective labels that can be "read" by optical scanners may also be applied. "Batch" numbers are frequently assigned to food and drug products.

Packaging is usually done at the end of the assembly line. Package labeling also occurs here, since using this location avoids accumulating an inventory of preprinted packages. This is also a key point for control because

The Elements of Physical Distribution/Logistics Systems

Figure 10-9 Problems in Transporting Bees

The following account describes methods used to determine a successful way of shipping bees. "USDA" refers to U.S. Department of Agriculture, and "OT" refers to that department's Office of Transportation.

This past April, 526 packages of bees valued at about $12,000 died during an air shipment from Phoenix, Arizona, to Canada. Each package contained 2.5 pounds of bees and a queen intended to start new colonies for crop pollination and honey production this coming summer.

The current Canadian export market for package bees exceeds $5 million annually and is increasing. It is difficult to winter bees outdoors in Canada, and many apiarists find it more economical to purchase starter bees in the spring than to build winter storage buildings.

OT researchers went to Arizona and worked with bee shippers and airline carriers to develop improved packaging and shipping procedures for bees. The researchers found that overheating during transit was a major factor in the shipment where all of the bees were lost.

They also found that most aircraft cargo compartments do not have positive air ventilation and that temperature in the compartments generally is maintained at 70° F by electric heaters in the aircraft walls. These electric heaters are not thermostatically controlled; therefore, when a large number of heat-producing animals is stowed in the compartment, there is a tremendous amount of heat buildup.

A small test shipment of 60 packages of bees was made by OT researchers with instruments to record temperature and humidity buildup. The bees in this shipment arrived in good condition, but the sugar water packed in cans to feed the bees had all leaked on the floor of the cargo compartment. This problem also had been reported in previous shipments. It was determined that pressurization changes caused this leakage, since the cans were packed at sea level and the cargo compartment was pressurized at 8,000 feet.

The shippers maintained that the bees needed some type of liquid to prevent dehydration during flight where relative humidity levels may go as low as 15 percent. OT researchers mixed "super slurper", a moisture-absorbing starch derivative developed by USDA, with the sugar water which formed a gelled substance. Small cotton muslin bags were filled with the gelled sugar water and stapled inside 125 shipping cages.

These cages were packed with bees for a second test shipment. The plane's cargo compartment was precooled with a ground air-conditioning unit prior to loading the bees. This shipment of bees arrived in Canada in excellent condition and without food spillage.

OT researchers plan to work further with the airlines and shippers on procedures for loading and maintaining cargo hold environments for bees, baby chicks, and other small animals which are shipped routinely by air.

Source: Transportation Update, issued by the Office of Transportation, U.S. Department of Agriculture, Washington, D.C. (May 1980).

this is where there is an exact measure of what has come off the assembly line. As the packaged goods are moved from the end of the assembly line they become "stocks of finished goods" and the responsibility of the firm's PD system. Near the point where product packaging occurs, it is necessary to maintain complete inventory of all the packages, packing materials, and labels that will be used.

For products that are sold off of retailers' shelves, provision must also be made for price marking. When prices are applied as the goods are placed on the shelves, no special provisions are required. If the price is to be applied at an earlier stage in the distribution process, special package designs are required. A box containing a batch of smaller packages may have a perforated strip that can be removed exposing a small area of each package to which an adhesive price label may be attached.

The discussion in the last few paragraphs, and for much of this chapter, has emphasized the outward movements of finished goods. For sophisticated materials management systems, it is also necessary to label inbound parts and components so that their locations can be continually monitored. Bar codes are commonly used, and they are read by scanners or sensors. These "sensors do more than signal the presence of a container or part. They also give the computer as much information as it needs about that part to maintain accurate production and inventory records and/or to determine the routing of that part from one work station to another."[10]

Unit Loads in Material Handling

As was mentioned earlier, packaging of materials begins with and is based on the building-block concept—putting products in containers that will provide efficient yet manageable units. This section discusses unit loading, an extension of the building-block concept to very large quantities. The basic unit in unit loading is the pallet or skid. Unit loading involves the securing of one or more boxes to a pallet or skid so that it can be handled by mechanical means, such as a fork-lift truck. The boxes or any other containers secured to a pallet are known as a unit load. The word unitization is used to describe this kind of handling.

More often than not, the unit load is placed on a wooden pallet. Although somewhat lowly in status, wooden pallets receive considerable attention both in trade journals and at trade meetings. The degree of attention is usually correlated with the price of lumber, and pallets are no longer thought of as "free." Shippers are now forcing consignees to return the same number of pallets or billing them separately for unreturned pallets. On the West Coast, some drivers receive a 25-cent bonus for every pallet they return. Firms are now repairing pallets which several years ago would have been scrapped.

One disadvantage of the conventional pallet is its height (approximately six inches). A pallet may occupy as much space as a layer of cases of canned soft drinks. When goods are loaded aboard pallets into rail cars, trailers or containers, the space occupied by the pallet is unproductive. The alternative is to strap a heavy flexible material, known as a "slip sheet," under the unit load in place of the pallet. The goods are placed on conventional wooden pallets when they are unloaded from the vehicle. The disadvantage is that handling time is increased because the fork lift operator must use the equipment much more carefully to avoid damaging the product.

Even though the wooden pallet does occupy space in a vehicle, its construction and physical properties do provide a favorable cushioning effect. However, the quality of individual pallets has varied widely, although the grocery industry once attempted to establish a pallet interchange pool that

---

[10] "Automatic Identification," *Modern Materials Handling* (March 5, 1984), pp. 98–105.

was to have minimum standards of quality. But the grocery industry lost interest in the pallet interchange pool because members believed that slip sheets would replace pallets in unit loading.[11] There is considerable disagreement concerning the relative merits of slip sheets and wooden pallets. However, both involve unit loads and unitization. The disagreement is over the best way to handle them.

The unit load offers several advantages. It gives some additional protection to the cargo because the cartons are secured to the pallet by straps, shrink wrapping, or some other bonding device. This provides a sturdier building block. Pilferage is discouraged because it is difficult to remove a single package or its contents. Also, a pallet can be stacked in such a manner that the cartons containing the more valuable or more fragile items are on the inside of the unit load. The major advantage of the unit load is that it allows mechanical devices to be substituted for hand labor. Many machines have been devised that can quickly build up or tear down a pallet load of materials. One example, a "depalletizer," is shown on Figure 10-10. A full pallet, waiting to be depalletized, is shown on the far left. On the right is a pallet-load, which has been turned a full 90 degrees, with grips pressing in on its sides. One level of cases is being shown as it is being lowered from the pallet load, which is on its side. The entire operation is tilted downward toward us, and the layer of cases will pass toward us on the roller system. Robots are used when much more sophisticated integrated movements are needed for loading or unloading pallets. Examples of robot-assisted palletizing and depalletizing exist in the printing industry, where bundles of printed pages must be stacked in a specified order; and in the auto industry, where automobile instrument panels are unloaded from a pallet, have some protective packing removed, and are fed to the assembly line in a certain sequence.[12]

The unit load does have limitations. It represents a larger quantity of an item than a single box—often thirty to fifty times as much. Therefore, it is of limited value to shippers or consignees who deal in small quantities. A pallet load of material may be nowhere near the EOQ amounts calculated through the methods developed in Chapter 7. Some shippers recognize this and have a price break at both the pallet-load quantity *and* at the pallet-layer quantity. Thus, a canner ships in pallet loads to a distributor, who sells to retailers who may only buy in pallet layers or loads. All of the distributor's items are in boxes that can be arranged on the conventional 48-inch by 40-inch pallet (although the number of boxes which would cover one layer varies). Nonetheless, the distributor's price break is at the pallet layer quantity, so that the retailer might decide to order one layer (which might be twelve boxes or cases) of canned peaches; two layers (which might be fifteen cases each) of catsup; and so on. The distributor, in loading the pal-

---

[11] "Pallets vs. Slip Sheets: The Great Controversy!" *Modern Materials Handling* (June 1979), pp. 66–71. See also, "Push-Pull's Global Progress," *Handling & Shipping Management* (Dec. 1979), pp. 36–42; "Pallet Interchange: Troubled Progress," *Traffic Management* (May 1978), pp. 71–76; and Bob Promisel, "Unit-load Technology: Current and Future State of the Art," *NCPDM 1980 Papers*, pp. 125–141.

[12] "Palletizing and Unitizing: How Robots Stack Up," *Modern Materials Handling* (Sept. 7, 1984), pp. 59–62.

Figure 10-10 A De-Palletizer at Work

Credit: Columbia Machine, Inc.

let, would load each layer separately, yet the goods would leave his ware-house as a full pallet, or unit load. He would have given an even lower price if the retailer had purchased a full pallet load of a single item because in that instance the distributor would have avoided manual handling of the product completely; he would have merely shipped out one of the full pallet loads he had received from the canner.

Before moving to the next step in the building-block concept, we should make one additional point. Our discussion to this point has emphasized the building of loads from small blocks into large blocks. The reverse is also true; i.e., the large units or blocks must be broken down into their smaller component blocks, with the very smallest unit being the single item the retail customer carries home. Figure 10-11, a high-rise warehouse four tiers high illustrates this. At the right, a lift truck places full unit loads into a gravity-flow rack system. The pallets move, as used, to the left, where order pickers break down the unit loads into single boxes.

The Elements of Physical Distribution/Logistics Systems

Figure 10-11 Warehouse Where Unit Loads Are Broken Down into Boxes

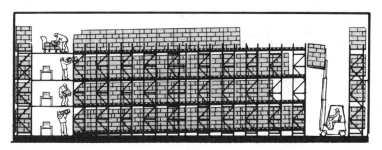

Courtesy of Interlake, Inc.

Containers

For surface cargo, the next-sized block beyond the unit load is the container, which usually is 8 feet wide, 8 or more feet high, and 20, 28, 35, 40, or 45 feet long. Containers are widely used in the U.S. foreign trade. Because they are interchangeable between rail, truck, and water carriers, they can be used in intermodal applications and reap the advantages offered by each of several modes. Both ocean carriers and railroads are developing methods of handling two or more containers at one time, thereby reducing the number of individual lifting, storage, and stowage moves that take place in container operations.

Most containers are dry-cargo boxes. Some are insulated and come with temperature-controlling devices; some contain one large tank; and some have a flat-bed configuration. There are also specially designed containers for the transport of livestock and automobiles.

Some airlines use 8- by 8- by 20-foot containers constructed of light-weight metals, which are interchanged between air and motor carriers. Only the largest of the jumbo jets carries containers of this size. Most other aircraft containers have somewhat irregular shapes, dictated by the shape of the fuselage contours into which they must be fit. Aircraft containers are discussed in more detail in Chapter 11.

Manufacturing operations often receive their components from suppliers loaded on "custom" reusable racks. The racks are then returned to the supplier to be loaded again. These racks are designed with certain palletlike characteristics because they are handled with mechanized equipment and, ideally, maximize use of the vehicle's cubic carrying capacity.

Equipment Loading

The next step in the building-block process is to stow the unit-load pallets into a waiting truck trailer, rail car, or container van. Slight clearances must be maintained between pallets to allow for the loading and unloading pro-

Figure 10-12 Inflated Inflatable Dunnage Bag

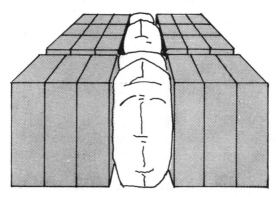

Courtesy of Sea Land Service, Inc.

cesses. Bracing or inflatable dunnage bags are used to fill narrow empty spaces. When inflated, they fill the void space and function as both a cushion and a brace. Figure 10-12 shows inflated dunnage bags.

A problem involved with any bracing or cushioning device is that the load is subjected to forces from all directions. Figure 10-13 shows five of the forces to which a surface-sea load may be subjected. Sea loads are subjected to more forces than the ones illustrated since a vessel in a rolling sea can be subjected to almost any pattern of force. Even when cargoes are properly braced, the various forces can still cause damage. Continued vibrations may

Figure 10-13 Various Forces to Which Cargo Is Subjected

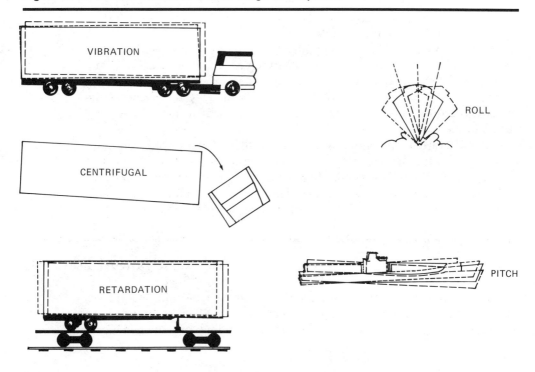

The Elements of Physical Distribution/Logistics Systems

Figure 10-14 Bracing of Heavy Machinery Inside Rail Car

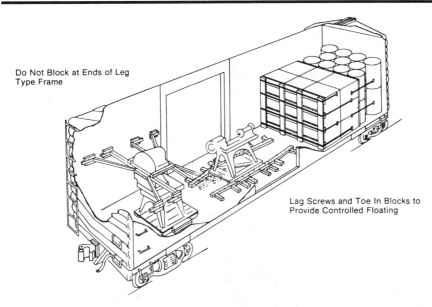

Do Not Block at Ends of Leg Type Frame

Lag Screws and Toe In Blocks to Provide Controlled Floating

Courtesy Damage Prevention Section, Operations and Maintenance Department, Association of American Railroads.

loosen screws on machinery. Vibrations can also cause contents of some bags or packages to settle, which can change the nature of support they were offering to materials packed above them. For products where this presents a problem, special preloading vibrators are used to cause the load to settle immediately.

Some goods are so heavy that they utilize the rail car or trailer or container's weight capacity without filling its cubic capacity. These loads, such as heavy machinery, must be carefully braced and the weight must be distributed as evenly as possible. In highway trailers, for example, it would be dangerous to have one side loaded more heavily than the other. In addition, the load should be distributed evenly over the axles. Figure 10-14 shows bracing and straps used to secure a load inside a rail car.

The building-block concept ends with the container or vehicle load, although carriers do offer rate incentives for multiple-container, trailer, or rail-car shipments. Indeed, most carrier/shipper contracts today involve movements in those quantities. Figure 10-15 summarizes the building-block concept, insofar as buildup a load. It does, of course, also work in reverse, going back down to the consumer-sized pack.

Bulk Materials

Bulk materials are handled in loose rather than packaged form by pumps, shovel devices, conveyer belts, or the mere force of gravity. The decision must be made as to where in the distribution system the bulk materials

Figure 10-15 The "Building Block" Concept of Packaging—Summarized

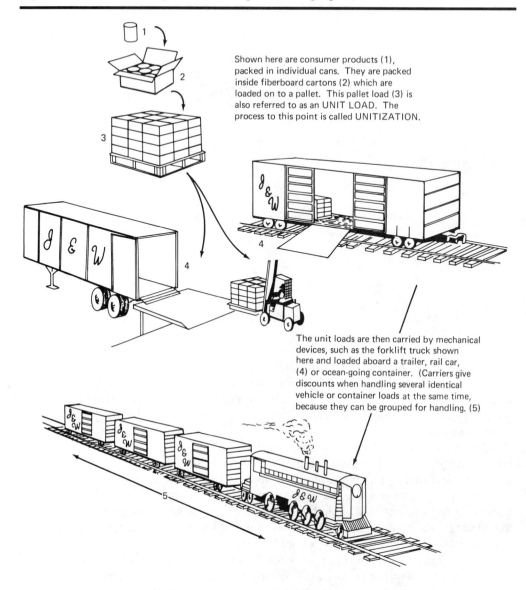

Shown here are consumer products (1), packed in individual cans. They are packed inside fiberboard cartons (2) which are loaded on to a pallet. This pallet load (3) is also referred to as an UNIT LOAD. The process to this point is called UNITIZATION.

The unit loads are then carried by mechanical devices, such as the forklift truck shown here and loaded aboard a trailer, rail car, (4) or ocean-going container. (Carriers give discounts when handling several identical vehicle or container loads at the same time, because they can be grouped for handling. (5)

should be placed into smaller containers for further sale or shipment. Sometimes bagged and bulk quantities of the same material are part of the same shipments. In vessels, bagged rice is placed on top of bulk rice to provide load stability. The photo at the beginning of the chapter shows *huge* quantities of sugar being handled in bagged form.

Bulk cargoes have various handling characteristics. An equipment configuration that is "ideal" for one bulk cargo may not be able to handle another. Another consideration is the size of particle of the cargo in question; there are costs involved in pulverizing to a uniform size so it can be handled by pneumatic or slurry devices.

Slurry Systems

Slurry systems involve grinding the solid material to a certain particle size, mixing it with water to form a fluid muddy substance, pumping that substance through a pipeline, and then decanting the water and removing it, leaving the solid material. Rail cars can also be used to carry slurry. For example, kaolin (a clay used in paper making) is mined and separated from the accompanying sand by a water process. The sand-free clay is then subjected to a number of mechanical processes that reduce its moisture content to about 35 per cent. The result is a substance that has the viscosity of heavy cream, which is about the same consistency desired by the paper-making plants, so it is shipped in this form, despite the fact that, by weight, a substantial percentage of what is shipped is water. In this instance, the economics are such that it is less costly to transport the water than it is to remove it near the quarry and add it after shipment at the paper mill.

Dry Bulk-Handling Systems

Systems for handling dry bulk materials are often large and "custom engineered" to fit specific needs. Three examples will be illustrated, mainly to give an idea as to the scale at which these facilities are designed and constructed. Figure 10-16 is a cross-section view of a coal car unloading facility. The cars carrying coal are joined in a unit train whose cars are permanently coupled. However, this coupling is unique because it allows each car to swivel and be turned upside down while still remaining coupled. The train comes to a stop with the first coal car in exact position within the rotating drum. "Grips" extend from the drum to secure the car, and it is rolled over, nearly 180 degrees, dumping the coal. It is rolled back, ungripped, and the train moves ahead until the next car is in position. It takes 90 seconds to unload each car, which holds 100 tons. The unit train consists of 110 cars.

A taconite loading facility is shown on Figure 10-17. This one is located at Two Harbors, Minnesota, on the western end of Lake Superior. Taconite is partially processed iron ore in pellet form. The site in question can store two million tons of taconite (that is about 20,000 rail carloads). The ore is received by unit train at the unloading station shown at the top of the figure (which is similar to the facility shown in Figure 10-16). The ore pellets are then moved out to the storage piles, where they are held until loaded aboard a vessel, via conveyer belts. One reason why such a large storage area is needed is the difference in receiving and shipping seasons. Taconite is received on a year-round basis but is shipped only during an eight-month season because most of the Great Lakes are closed to navigation during the winter.

Figure 10-18 illustrates another bulk cargo handling facility, a large grain elevator located at the Port of Seattle. The facility receives grain by both the rail and truck. The drawing is fairly self-explanatory, and only two additional comments will be made. First, note the references to dust collection and dust suppression systems. Second, note that incoming trucks have their grain sampled. The grain is "graded" to determine its price. (Shipments re-

Figure 10-16 Cross-Section of Coal Car-Dumping Building in St. Louis, Missouri

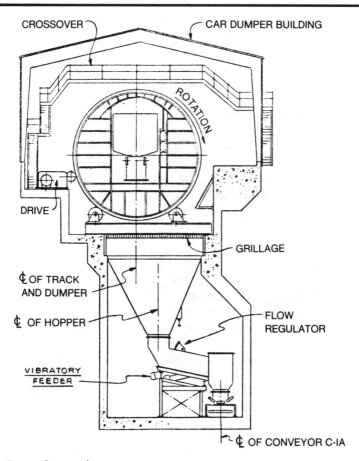

Courtesy Dravo Corporation.

ceived by rail have already been graded at the initial inland elevator where they were handled, while most truck shipments are received direct from the farm.)

Vehicle and Vessel Equipment Choice

Bulk cargo movements are unique in that they almost always utilize a vehicle's entire capacity. A bulk cargo shipper thinks in terms of truck loads, barge loads, railcar loads, or ship loads. Many different types of equipment are used to transport bulk materials.

Many handbooks and newsletters are published to serve those who are trying to match up cargoes, origins, destinations, and means of carriage. Figure 10-19 shows a page from one such handbook, *Greenwood's Guide to*

The Elements of Physical Distribution/Logistics Systems

Figure 10-17 Taconite Storage and Loading Facility at Two Harbors, Minnesota

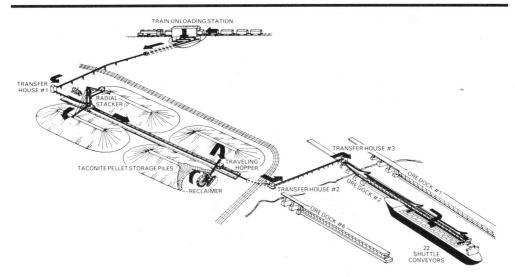

Credit: Duluth, Missabi, and Iron Range Railway Company

Great Lake Shipping. The page deals with self-unloading vessels. The vessel's exterior measurements are important because in many Great Lakes ports there are physical restrictions, such as narrow bridge openings, which limit the size of vessel that can reach certain docks. The vessels have several compartments (holds) that are important in shipping different grades of coal. The boom length and degrees of swing indicate how far inland the vessel can discharge. The farther inland the boom reaches, the more material can be stockpiled. Note that the vessel's allowable safe draft changes by season; this is significant if a dense cargo, such as iron ore, is being handled. *Greenwood's Guide* has similar data for shoreside facilities, indicating how large a vessel can be accommodated and the loading-unloading equipment available.

Choice of equipment is also influenced by the investment the shipper and consignee want to make. Great Lakes coal docks using self-unloaders described on Figure 10-19 do not have to invest in vessel unloading facilities—the vessel owner has made the investment in the conveyer and discharge system. Great Lakes vessel rates for carrying coal on self-unloaders are about 10 per cent higher than for vessels that the consignee must unload. The consignee can pay that higher rate or invest in his own shore-based unloading equipment.

Another consideration with respect to bulk cargo handling deals with ownership of equipment. The several handling facilities discussed involve massive investments in fixed facilities and specialized vehicles. From a distribution and logistics management standpoint, bulk cargoes require unique, often "custom-built," handling facilities and there is always uncertainty as to who should provide them—the buyer, the seller, or a third party.

A marketing problem may be that a specialized unloading device will pay for itself only if a specified number of customers install a new type of

Figure 10-18 Export Grain Elevator at the Port of Seattle

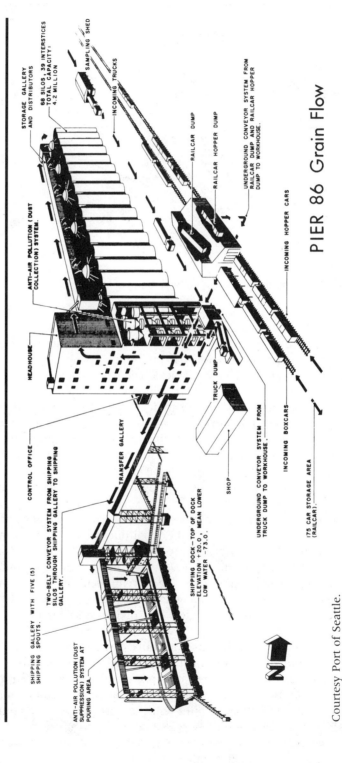

STORAGE GALLERY AND DISTRIBUTORS

68 SILOS, 39 INTERSTICES; TOTAL CAPACITY: 4.2 MILLION

SAMPLING SHED

INCOMING TRUCKS

RAILCAR DUMP

RAILCAR HOPPER DUMP

UNDERGROUND CONVEYOR SYSTEM FROM RAILCAR DUMP AND RAILCAR HOPPER DUMP TO WORKHOUSE.

INCOMING HOPPER CARS

ANTI-AIR POLLUTION (DUST COLLECTION) SYSTEM.

HEADHOUSE

CONTROL OFFICE

SHIPPING GALLERY WITH FIVE (5) SHIPPING SPOUTS.

TWO-BELT CONVEYOR SYSTEM FROM SHIPPING SILOS THROUGH SHIPPING GALLERY TO SHIPPING GALLERY.

TRANSFER GALLERY

TRUCK DUMP

SHOP

UNDERGROUND CONVEYOR SYSTEM FROM TRUCK DUMP TO WORKHOUSE.

INCOMING BOXCARS

ANTI-AIR POLLUTION (DUST SUPPRESSION) SYSTEM AT POURING AREA.

SHIPPING DOCK—TOP OF DOCK ELEVATION +20.0, MEAN LOWER LOW WATER −73.0.

175 CAR STORAGE AREA (RAILCAR).

N

PIER 86 Grain Flow

Courtesy Port of Seattle.

Figure 10-19 Page from Guide to Great Lakes Vessels

SELF-UNLOADERS ON THE GREAT LAKES, (cont'd.)

FIRST LINE: Fleet No. / Vessel
SECOND LINE: Cubic feet per Compartment with coal capacity shown in Net Tons

NOTE (Size column): Coal stowage factor 42 C.F. per Net Ton similar to slack coal

Fleet No. / Vessel	Size	Gross Reg. Tons	Net Reg. Tons	Keel	B.P.	O.A.	Beam	Depth	Compartments	Mid-Summer Draft	Summer Draft	Degrees Boom Can Swing Right/Left	Intermediate Draft	Type of Self-Unloader	Winter Draft	Chutes	Capacity at M.S.	Boom Length
6 Hutchinson, John T. B 16-½-24	38x11	9,775	6,964	595'0"	605'0"	620'0"	60'0"	35'0"	4	24'6"	23'11"	120	23'0"	Chutes	21'11"		14,650	250'
2 Jodrey, Roy A. (Can.) 18–24	#1 P & S 12 x 11 #2 2–18 49 x 11	Can. 16,154 U.S. 13,974	11,133	603'3"	619'7"	640'6"	72'0"	40'0"	4	28'6"	27'10"	100	26'10" At 26'0"–Seaway–	Conveyor	25'7"	None	23,500 20,500	250'
6 Kling, John A. 30–12	38x9	6,829	5,413	538'0"	546'6"	561'3"	56'3"	30'3"	7	21'1"	20'9"	100	19'11"	Conveyor	19'0"		10,850	205'
6 Kyes, Roger M. 20-24	49'6" x 11 5-5-5-5			664'6"	664'6"	680'0"	78'0"	42'0"	4	27'6"	27'6"	96	27'6"	Conveyor	27'6"	30'	25,650	260'
35 Lakewood B 4–uneven	1–23x12 2–23x64 3–23x84 4–23x14	3,751	2,708	370'0"	377'6"	390'0"	48'0"	28'0"	4	19'5-½"	19'5-½"	100	19'1-½"	Conveyor	18'7-½"	None	3,950	142'
60 Leadale (Can.) 27–12	36x9	7,073	4,701	504'0"	512'0"	524'0"	56'0"	30'0"	6	20'2"	19'9"	120	19'2"	Conveyor	18'5"	30'	8,950	200'

Second-line (cubic feet per compartment with coal capacity in Net Tons):

- 6 Hutchinson, John T.: 1) 94,070 C.F. - 2,320; 2) 171,170 C.F. - 3,870; 3) 168,390 C.F. - 3,820; 4) 135,095 C.F. 3,070 Total: 13,080 N. T.
- 2 Jodrey, Roy A.: B 1) 229,230 C.F. – 5,470; 2) 179,495 C.F. –4,275; 3) 179,495 C.F. –4,275; 4) 234,885 C.F. –5,580 Total: 19,600 N.T.
- 6 Kling, John A.: B 1) 58,850 C.F. – 1,400; 2) 26,950 C.F. – 670; 3) 52,800 C.F. – 1,250; 4) 64,050 C.F. – 1,500; 5) 47,200 C.F. – 1,130; 6) 58,850 C.F. – 1,400; 7) 65,500 C.F. 1,540 Total: 8,900 N.T.
- 6 Kyes, Roger M.: B 1) 234,545 C.F. -5,600; 2) 227,980 C.F. -5,425; 3) 227,980 C.F. -5,425; 4) 213,930 C.F. -5,100 Total: 21,500 N.T.
- 35 Lakewood: 1) 12,700 C.F. - 200; 2) 47,000 C.F. - 1,450; 3) 64,000 C.F. - 1,900; 4) 15,600 C.F. - 400 Total: 3,950 G. T. Sand or Stone
- 60 Leadale: 1) 63,500 C.F. - 1,600; 2) 50,100 C.F. - 1,350; 3) 49,600 C.F. - 1,400; 4) 87,000 C.F. - 2,300; 5) 49,900 C.F. - 1,300; 6) 53,000 C.F. - 1,200 Total: 9,150 N.T.

Courtesy: Greenwood's Guide to Great Lakes Shipping, 1975 edition; Freshwater Press, Inc.

403

receiving equipment. What kinds of financial incentives should the seller offer to get customers to install the new receiving equipment? What types of long-term commitments must each party make to the other to insure a necessary return from the required investment? An example of this situation comes from the food industry where "liquid egg" distributors supply the contents of shelled eggs or egg-base concentrates to food processors, commercial bakeries, and institutional food service industries. Because eggs in the shell have unfavorable transportation characteristics, a truck carrying the eggs' contents after they are shelled can carry about twice as much weight in the same space as a truck carrying eggs in conventional cartons. The supplier must invest in an egg-breaking machine located near the egg farms, and also invest in trucks with refrigerated tank trailers which can pump out their own contents. Sanitation is important and must be maintained. The customers' investments are in one or more tanks to receive the yolks, the egg whites, or a mixture of both. Even without knowing the quantities or the costs involved, it is clear that quite a few calculations would have to be made and numerous alternatives would have to be considered.

Special Moves

Regularly recurring shipments usually lend themselves to logistics analysis that results in either lower-cost shipments or a more efficient method of handling the shipment, or both. In some industries, however, each movement is so unique and so difficult that a specialized engineering/logistics study is needed to determine how the move should be accomplished. Examples are generators being delivered to dam sites, or the delivery of oil-field and pipeline materials to Prudhoe Bay in northern Alaska.

Sometimes the product has to be assembled at the factory to make sure that it functions, then disassembled for shipment because it is too large for any one type of carrier to deliver. Therefore, it is delivered in pieces, and reassembled at the site. Clearly there can be savings if the amount of disassembly and reassembly involved can be reduced. Therefore, studies have to be made of shipping routes and procedures that will accommodate shipments that have unusual dimensions.

High-weight trucks are sometimes used. Heavy dollies, which are additional axles, are placed under the load so that less weight is exerted on each axle. When passing over a bridge of limited capacity, the dollies must be spaced sufficiently far apart that no more than the allowable weight is on the bridge at any one time. Once the bridge is crossed, the load is stopped, and the dollies are placed closer together again to make it easier to negotiate curves. Special permits would be required and police might keep other traffic off the road. Highway engineers along the route determine the maximum allowable load. If bituminous pavement were involved, the move may be restricted to cooler times of the year or of the day since the cooler pavement is less likely to be permanently "marked" by the tires of the dollies. Equipment such as this can carry loads of 500 or more tons—if enough dollies are used.

Weight is only one limitation of these kinds of moves. There may be height restrictions such as electric wires (which can be moved) or tunnels (which cannot). Modular housing (prebuilt structures that are transported to home sites) is not especially heavy, but it tends to be large. A study regarding industrial sites for manufacturing the modules said:

> Because the housing modules themselves are high and wide, access from the plant to the market areas both by over-the-road and rail, becomes a critical portion of the investigation. Access to the Interstate System is of absolute necessity. And siding needs for outbound shipment from the plants are vastly different than for ordinary industrial sites. When going by rail, the modules will travel on long cars and in trainload lots. Minimum curvatures of about 400 feet and accessible siding lengths of about 250 feet are required.[13]

Curvature of the road or steepness of grade impose other limits. The move must be carefully analyzed by individuals who are both familiar with the transportation complexities as well as with the piece of equipment being moved.

Figure 10-20 is an information sheet issued by one railroad to indicate the weight of loaded rail cars that can be handled on various tracks within its system. The same carrier also issues sheets which indicates height limitations throughout its entire system.

One of the most unique "special moves" occurred during the late 1970s when two specially designed Japanese barges were used to tow two halves of a woodpulp-processing plant, built in Japan, to a site in Brazil's Amazon river basin. Two barges were built in the Japanese yard, and then the pulp plant and the accompanying power plant were built on top of each barge. Very careful attention was paid to determining how the weight of the pulp and power plants would be distributed on their respective barges. The plants were then towed by tugs the entire way to a site on the Jari River in Brazil that had been partially enclosed by a dike. At the places inside the diked area, where the pulp and power plants were destined to be placed, wooden pilings had been driven into the bottom. When the two barges with the plants arrived, they were towed inside the diked area and moored next to the pilings. The dike was then extended to completely enclose the area, and water was pumped in to raise the barges. The barges were then floated directly above the piles, the water level was lowered, and the barges holding the two plants were then resting on top of the piles. Windows were cut in the sides of the barges, and the barges became the lower floors of the pulp and power plants. It was estimated that construction costs were reduced by 20 per cent and two years were saved by having the plant built in Japan and towed to Brazil rather than having it constructed at the Brazilian site.[14]

[13] Carl J. Liba, "The Transportation Market Potential in Modular Housing," in *Proceedings of the Sixty-second Annual Meeting of the American Railway Development Association, 1971*, pp. 27–32.

[14] "Shipbuilder in Japan Delivers Completed Pulp Plant to Brazil," *Surveyor* (May 1978), pp. 14–18.

Figure 10-20 Railroad Weight Limits

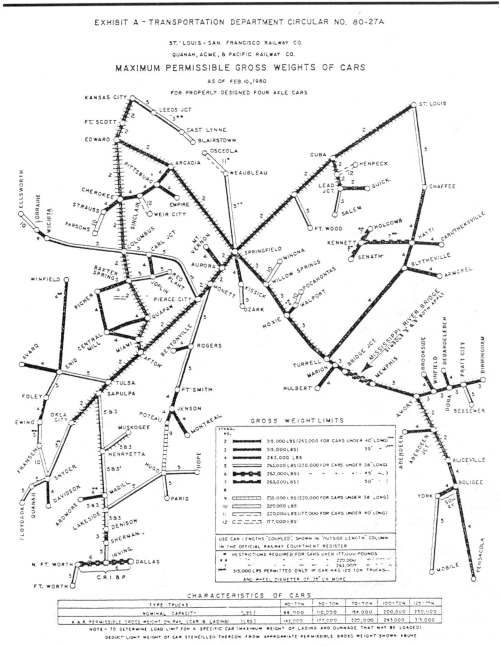

Courtesy: St. Louis-San Francisco Railway Co.

Summary

Although the physical handling of cargo is often thought of as one of the less glamorous—although critical—areas of logistics, it is also the area where computers, and even robots, can be found in many applications. The pivotal idea in handling many materials, regardless of size or characteristic, is the building-block concept. For packages with precise physical dimensions, each item is packaged, and grouped into pallet or unit loads that can be handled by mechanized equipment. Because unit loads do not necessarily match a firm's EOQ, the PD/L manager can cut the firm's cost for products by accepting a shipper's unit-sized loads that do not conform to the firm's EOQ. The largest sizes in the building-block concept are containers and transport vehicle bodies. They must be properly loaded to avoid in-transit damage to cargo.

Despite deregulation, carrier tariffs frequently control the type of packaging that must be used. Nevertheless, buyers may blame the seller—rather than the carrier—for damaged products.

Bulk cargo is usually handled by the rail carload, barge load, or the like. Bulk handling equipment is very expensive and calls for long-term financial commitments by its users. A new development in handling dry bulk materials is to add water, creating a slurry, and then apply fluid-handling methods to the mass of material.

Sometimes the product being moved is so large that special transportation routes with extra-large clearances must be laid out. Buyers of these products often buy on a "delivered" basis so the seller must determine the least expensive way to install them.

Questions for Discussion and Review

1. What is the difference between the *selling* function of packaging and the *protective* function of packaging? Are the two functions related?
2. Describe the function of conventional pallets. What are their disadvantages?
3. Discuss the specific protective functions that a protective package must accomplish. Does every package have to accomplish every function? Discuss.
4. How do slurry systems work?
5. Are there reasons why a liquor distributor should not print his cartons' contents in plain English?
6. How do self-unloading vessels function? What are their advantages and disadvantages?
7. What are the various physical forces to which a package in transit might be subjected? What other hazards might it encounter?
8. What is shrink-wrap packaging?
9. What is unit loading?
10. Why should a load's weight be distributed evenly inside a truck trailer?
11. What are the advantages of pretesting a package prior to its introduction?
12. There is great popular interest in recycling. How does or should this affect packaging? Discuss.
13. What is the building-block concept that is applied to handling of packaged goods?
14. Discuss the relationship between the level of protective packaging used

relative to the packaging requirements of common carriers. Is carrier deregulation having an impact upon shippers' packaging? Discuss.

15. Give some examples of package testing.
16. Describe some of the devices mentioned in this chapter that are used to monitor the journey a shipment makes.
17. What is *Greenwood's Guide?* What purpose does it serve?
18. Discuss the "special move" involving a shipment transported from Japan to Brazil.
19. Give some other examples of "special," or "one-time," moves.
20. What are slip sheets? How are they used?

Additional Chapter References

Cox, Ralph M. and Kenneth G. Van Tassel. "The Role of Packaging in Physical Distribution." *The Distribution Handbook* (New York: Free Press Division of Macmillan, 1985), pp. 737–773.

Fibre Box Association. *Fibre Box Handbook* (Chicago: Fibre Box Association, 1984).

Handling and Shipping Fresh Fruits and Vegetables by Rail (Chicago: Association of American Railroads, Damage Prevention Section, 1976).

Packaging for the Small Parcel Environment, (New York: United Parcel Service, 1974).

CASE 10-1

Hanvey School Furniture Company

The Hanvey School Furniture Company had one plant, located in Knoxville, Tennessee. It sold school desks and tables throughout the southern and eastern United States. It operated through distributors, with exclusive marketing areas and used rail carloads for outbound shipments. The usual method of selling was through a distributor who would bid on supplying a school district with several hundred desks of various sizes. There were few "rush" shipments involved since most bids allowed delivery anywhere from 60 to 120 days after the successful bid was selected.

The Hanvey line consisted of a chair with writing table attached on the right side (or on the left side if so specified). Eight different sizes were available, one size for each of the primary grades (1–6), a junior high size, and senior high size. Desks were manufactured, assembled, and finished in the plant. The four smaller sizes were packed two to a corrugated fiberboard box, and the larger ones were packed one to a box. Damage in shipment was not much of a problem because the desks themselves were sturdy and the carton was designed to provide additional protection to the writing surface on the desk. The average price of a desk was $47, and the average shipping cost per desk (in 10,000 pound rail carload quantities) was $9.

Rich Nelson, the logistics manager for Hanvey School Furniture, was attending a special staff meeting in the marketing manager's office. The marketing manager explained why he had called the meeting by saying, "For years we've sold only a set-up, finished desk. In part, this is because wage rates around here are relatively low, and we never thought it would be cheaper to assemble and finish them elsewhere. However, up in the Northeast, several large school districts are using some new governmental program to increase employment, and they are toying with the idea of buying desks unassembled and doing the assembling and finishing themselves. Personally, I don't think the idea will go very far, but some of our distributors are being asked to submit bids on unassembled, unfinished, desks. I've had my secretary copy the bid specifications. They differ slightly from each other, but in general they have the following points in common:

1. The orders are large, ranging from 1,000 to 2,200 desks.
2. They require the unassembled desk to consist of no more than twenty separate pieces, exclusive of hardware.
3. Solid-glue construction is required, and the supplier should, as part of the bid, indicate sale price and rental prices for various glue clamps or other types of hardware or equipment needed to assemble the desks.
4. There should be no more than twelve unassembled desks in each separate carton. They want to assemble each small batch separately and don't want thousands of parts lying around.
5. Most bids are to be on a delivered basis.

The marketing manager then asked for questions. Carlos Ramirez, from the production department, spoke up: "What about quality control? What if they use cheap glue, and the desks fall apart? Do we want our names on them?"

"I don't know," answered the marketing manager. "You check with your people and come up with recommendations."

Nelson said, "Carload rates are important to us. Can we keep the minimum order size so large that we can fill up carloads?"

"I think so," answered the marketing manager. "Will you please calculate the costs for unassembled desks in carload quantities?"

Ramirez asked, "Should we offer to have an engineer available to supervise the assembling?"

The marketing manager answered, "It would be a sales help, but we'd have to be careful regarding costs. Who will pay for it? What if the problems are lack of supervision for the untrained work force?"

David Campbell who was in the marketing department, spoke up, "Maybe the distributor should pay this cost. We could supply the engineer, and the distributor could reimburse us. The distributor would be a better judge of how much of our help would be needed."

"Any other questions?" asked the marketing manager and paused, "Hearing none, I want you three to work together. Dave can report to me every day. We will need cost estimates to quote our distributors by the week's end."

Nelson returned to his office and took out the railroad freight classification. It flopped open to the page he used most in the furniture section. The entry is Exhibit 10-1. Nelson then looked up the definitions of packages he had nearly forgotten since Hanvey furniture had been purchasing package type 3F, a double-faced corrugated fiberboard container. For each desk, the *average* cost of containers and packing material was $2, taking into account some desks were packed one to a carton; others, two to a carton.

Nelson then phoned Tom Bates who supplied Hanvey School Furniture with cor-

Exhibit 10-1 Excerpt from Railroad Freight Classification

ARTICLE	Less Carload Ratings	Carload Minimum (Pounds)	Carload Ratings
Furniture			
Desks, school			
Wooden, set up and finished in packages 3F or 6F, packed no more than two to a package	200	10,000	70
Wooden, knocked down, finished or unfinished, in packages 4F or 7F, packed no more than twenty to a package	150	20,000	60

rugated fiberboard containers. Nelson told Bates as much as he knew and told Bates to phone Ramirez directly to get details of how the unassembled desks might be packaged. Nelson hung up, and a few minutes later Ramirez phoned to say that Bates was visiting the next morning to discuss packing methods.

The next morning Nelson, Campbell, Ramirez, and Bates met in a conference room. Ramirez had several unassembled desks lying on a table. He had dimensions of all pieces of all desks. The three talked for a while, and then Bates said, "Give me all the dimensions, and I'll go back to my office to see what kind of containers you need. One thing would help: Can you tell me how many unassembled desks you want in a carton?"

Campbell responded, "Nearly all bids I know of are in multiples of 10."

Ramirez said, "That's OK for a start, Tom. Unless anyone here objects, let's figure on ten unassembled desks per carton."

There were no objections, and the meeting broke up. Later that day, Bates phoned Ramirez and said, "Package 7F will meet all your needs, so far as I can tell. The material is not as strong as the one you're using, but the packages' contents will provide more internal strength. The average cost for a carton to hold ten unassembled desks will be three dollars. You'll need some internal wrapping material, especially for the writing surfaces. For ten desks per carton, this material would be ten cents per desk. Labor costs also have to be calculated. You know those better than I." Ramirez relayed this information to Nelson.

Nelson had been figuring new densities and calculated that ten unassembled desks in a carton would occupy 0.4 times as much space per desk as when the desks were assembled. This would allow them to load carloads with shipments weighing an average of 25,000 pounds.

The last piece of information needed was cost of packing each carton. Ramirez called in the shipping room foreman, and the two of them spent some time experimenting with how long it would take to pack a carton containing parts for the ten desks. Their "guesstimate" was that the cost per unassembled desk would be 25 cents; this was less than the cost when desks were set up and finished, which was 50 cents. The main reason for the higher costs for the set-up desks was they were finished and, because of this, required more careful handling.

Question One: Based on the information given in the case, what would be the average packing and packaging costs per unassembled desk?

Question Two: What would be the average rail transportation costs for each unassembled desk?

Question Three: If the Hanvey School Furniture Company decided to enter the unassembled desk field, they will have to use a new type of packing material, in addition to the one they are already using for assembled desks. Draft a memo indicating how much of each type of packaging material the company should have on hand at any time.

Question Four: Ramirez asked, "Should we offer to have an engineer available to supervise the assembly?" This would be an element of customer service. Draft a memo, to be distributed to potential buyers, indicating the conditions under which the Hanvey School Furniture Company will provide this type of "on-site" technical assistance to those doing the assembling.

Question Five: In the memo that summarized the bid specifications for unassembled desks was the statement that most bids were to be on a "delivered" basis. What, precisely, do you think this means to Hanvey School Furniture Company? Is it sufficient for them to be concerned only with the costs by rail? If not, what else must they take into account?

Question Six: Assume that one of the potential buyers of unassembled desks telephones and says, "We may have a truck in the Knoxville area and could pick up the desks ourselves. How much will we save?" One savings is in the railroad costs. What about packaging costs? What type of packaging, if any, should be used in this instance? How do selling terms change? Does this also influence choice of packaging? Discuss.

CASE 10-2

Harry S. Truman Centennial Plate

Located in Hartford, Connecticut, the Hamilton Silverplate Company produced a series of ornamental silver plated and pewter dishes and bowls. Most were sold through small gift shops or through firms with mail order catalogs. Between 15 and 20 per cent were sold directly through the mail in response to small advertisements placed in various homemakers' magazines. The company designed and began producing a "Harry S. Truman Centennial" plate, which had a profile of Truman in the center and was surrounded by inscriptions of several of Truman's better-known sayings. The plates had been successfully test-marketed, and regular buyers had placed large orders.

Because of these large orders, Hamilton's had decided to stop production of several other patterns and devote the facilities to Truman plates. Because a large portion of the firm's output was to be standardized product, it appeared that some changes could also be made in packaging.

Walt Drummond was Hamilton's executive vice-president. He had called a meeting in his office of three subordinates, Amanda Carter, the sales manager, Jerry Stevens, the production manager, and Harry Epstein, the distribution manager. At present, at the end of the assembly line, three workers wrapped each plate in crumpled newspapers and then placed each wrapped plate in a corrugated container. A packaging consultant, Martin Bauer, had been retained to evaluate the present packaging system and make recommendations for a new system. Bauer was also present.

After the group had been seated and Stevens had finally gotten the right mixture

Exhibit 10-2 Bauer's Chart

	Cost of newspaper-wrapped dish in carton with number only on carton	Change in cost if dish placed in sealed bag	Change in cost if bubblewrap used	Change in cost if advertising on carton
Packing time	.20	+.08	−.05	
Carton cost	.20		−.10	+.10
Sealed bag cost		+.02		
Cushioning mat'l. cost	.02	−.01	+.10	
w/h space	.06		−.02	
w/h handling	.12		−.02	−.02
shipping costs				
to warehouses	.10		−.01	
shipping cost				
from warehouse	.20		−.10*	+.15**

*average figure. (For individual C.O.D. mail orders, depending on postal zone, price reductions ranged from 25 to 80 cents.)

**for individual carton shipments, wrapping in plain paper required to mask carton's contents.

of sugar in his coffee, Drummond started the meeting by saying that Bauer's report was ready and that he wanted the group to hear it. Bauer stood up and placed a large chart (Exhibit 10-2) on the wall. Bauer said, "I've costed out wrapping your Truman Centennial plates. Along the left, I listed the various work and material item costs. At the top I listed your present method on the left. The second column shows changes in costs of placing each plate in a plastic bag and sealing it."

"Why that operation?" asked Stevens. "We don't do it now."

"You're right," said Bauer, "but for what you're asking for the plates, it adds a little more class."

Carter added, "Protection from tarnish is important to the shops handling the plates because they won't have to polish the plate. Right now, they have to polish those plates that have been in stock for a while."

"Maybe they'll order in large quantities," said Drummond, "if they don't worry about tarnish."

"I hope so," said Epstein.

"Let's continue with Bauer's presentation," said Drummond.

Bauer continued, "The next column shows what happens if we substitute bubble wrap for crumpled newspaper. The main savings comes from use of smaller corrugated cartons. That's because a small thickness of bubble wrap gives much more protection than the newspaper. Note how these costs carry all the way though the handling system."

Carter said: "We and some of our mail order outlets sell plates by mail COD. This should lower the customer's price. That's good."

Bauer continued: "Because you'll have a new corrugated carton, I thought you should consider a one color printing showing a small profile of Truman and an advertising message." Bauer noted that Epstein was fretting, but he continued, "I know this will be controversial. Amanda wants the message in because she thinks it helps retail sales in small shops where only one plate is on display but the customers want one that's still in a box. If the boxed plates are displayed nearby, the customer may pick up a box and carry it to the cashier. Unfortunately, Harry thinks the advertising message

The Elements of Physical Distribution/Logistics Systems

will encourage pilferage of those cartons shipped by mail. So, we added 15 cents for wrapping each mailed carton in plain brown paper."

"Like mailing X-rated videotapes," snickered Stevens.

"I wouldn't know," retorted Drummond. "What I do want to know is this: Assume Bauer's cost calculations are correct—and I think they're pretty close—how do we allocate them between production, sales, and distribution? You represent three different divisions, and I know none of you is going to volunteer to absorb all these costs. What's a fair way for us to allocate these costs?"

Question One: Assume you are Amanda Carter. What do you think is the sales department's "fair" share? From a bargaining standpoint, Amanda will claim a minimum of benefit from the proposed changes. What is this minimum? How would she develop an argument that most of the costs should be paid by the other departments?

Question Two: Answer Question One from the standpoint of Jerry Stevens and his department. (Note that the production department will package each plate at the assembly line before they are turned over to the distribution department.) Also note that Stevens will minimize the value of the changes to his operation, and attempt to show that other departments should pay most—or even all—of the new costs.

Question Three: After reading questions one and two, assume that you are Harry Epstein. Develop his argument that most of the costs should be paid by the other departments and minimize the costs that should be paid by his department.

Question Four: You are Drummond. What would you decide? How would you allocate costs? Why?

Question Five: Evaluate Bauer's presentation.

Question Six: Bauer proposes wrapping those cartons that are mailed in order to mask the product's identity. Another alternative would be to use both printed and unprinted cartons. How would you calculate the total costs of this alternative? What are all the cost items that must be considered?

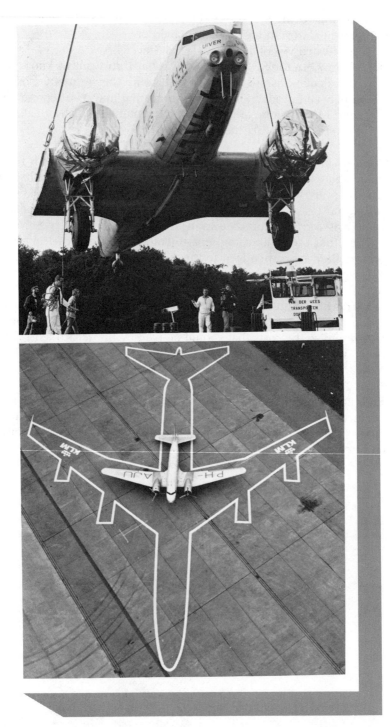

Shown here is the world's only surviving Douglas DC-2 (the short-lived predecessor of the much more famous DC-3). This DC-2 was used by KLM, Royal Dutch Airlines, in a 1984 re-enactment of KLM's participation in the 1934 London to Melbourne air race. In the 1934 air race, the KLM DC-2 made 18 intermediate stops, and its entire trip took three days, 18 hours, and 17 minutes. Today, KLM's Boeing 747's make the same trip in 22 hours and 25 minutes, with two intermediate stops. The bottom photo shows the DC-2 compared with the 747. KLM estimates that the 747 has the annual traffic capacity of 435 DC-2's.

(*Credit:* KLM Royal Dutch Airlines)

International Logistics

Another example of how things change, once you leave the United States: At new-product press conferences in the United States, the questions revolve around product features and the producer's general sales projections as well as some trivia. In Germany most of the questions are about prospects for export sales in foreign markets.

Ken Kelly
Transportation Engineer
July 1983

The buyer today, when looking for a source of supply, looks at the whole world to find where it's most economical to source it.

Bernd E. Mueller
Ford Motor Co.
American Shipper
June 1983

The ripple effect of these changes extends beyond the United States. Canadian railroads have voiced concern about the greater competitive flexibility of U.S. railroads. In Germany forwarders and port officials are noting a rerouting of international cargoes through Bene-lux ports, rather than German ports, because trucking in Benelux countries is not subject to the strict and extensive regulation of trucking within West Germany. A heated debate is underway in Europe on how to react to these new forces of price and service competition.

Peter J. Finnerty
Sea-Land Corporation
October 23, 1984

Key Terms

- International sourcing
- Letter of credit
- Customs collection
- Import quotas
- Nontariff barriers
- Flying a nation's flag
- Flags of convenience
- Ocean liners
- Cross-traders
- International freight forwarders
- NVOCCs
- Customs house brokers
- Export management companies
- Export trading companies
- Shipper associations
- Export packers
- Load center
- Land bridge
- IATA
- Shipping conferences

Learning Objectives

- To examine the importance of international trade to the United States
- To explain the concept of international sourcing
- To identify the reasons for governmental intervention in the area of international trade
- To distinguish between the unique activities of each international trade specialist
- To examine issues involved in international air transportation
- To relate activities involved in international ocean transportation

Introduction

International logistics is the movement of goods across national boundaries. It would occur under any of the following situations:

1. The firm exports a portion of the product made or grown, for example; paper-making machinery to Sweden, wheat to Russia, or coal to Japan.
2. The firm imports raw materials, such as pulpwood from Canada, or manufactured products, such as motorcycles, from Italy or Japan.
3. Goods are partially assembled in one country and then shipped to another, where they are further assembled or processed. For example, a firm stamps electronic components in the United States, ships them to a free trade zone in the Far East, where low-cost labor assembles them, and then the assembled components are returned to the United States, where they become part of the finished product.
4. Products are assembled in foreign countries for distribution in that and other foreign countries and the firm's home country. Some autos sold in the United States are assembled in Canada. (Because of a special Canadian-U.S. trade agreement, the U.S. auto manufacturer who relies on Canadian plants to supply a part of its U.S. markets can export to Canada—with few or no tariff restrictions—an equal volume of other models assembled in the United States.)

Figure 11-1 Canadian Map Showing Three Routes to Alaska

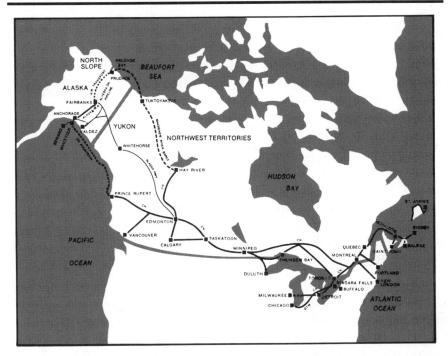

Note: Some of the more challenging specialized moves in recent years have involved oil field and pipeline equipment to Alaska where the transportation system is relatively undeveloped. This is a map from an advertisement by Canadian National Railways indicating that they offer several routes to the North Slopes. The Aquatrain is a railroad car-carrying ferry operating between Prince Rupert, British Columbia, and Whittier, Alaska, where railcars are transferred to and from the Alaska Railroad. The Mackenzie River is used as a barge route to Prudhoe Bay during the summer months only. The highway route is from Edmonton, where shipments are transferred from rail. Note that CN is a "total" transportation company and—in this instance—is advertising three different modes.

Map courtesy CN, Montreal, Quebec.

5. A very special case occurs when, because of geography, a nation's domestic commerce crosses foreign borders, often "in bond." Goods moving by truck between Detroit and Buffalo or between the lower 48 states and Alaska, through Canada, travel in bond. (See Figure 11-1.) In this case, the move and its accompanying paperwork possess both domestic and international characteristics.

> Goods moving completely through a country travel *in bond*. The carrier handling them has a special legal obligation to keep them "sealed" and to make certain that they are not released for sale or for use within the country they are traveling through. Products shipped in bond are not subject to normal duties of the country through which they are passing.

Until World War II, concepts of international trade were simple. Industrialized powers maintained political and economic colonies that were sources of raw materials and markets for manufactured products. When dealing with colonies, manufacturers in the mother country bought low and sold high. World War II brought an end to the colonial system, as such, and since then emerging nations have attempted to develop their own political and economic systems with varying degrees of success. As emerging nations attempt to flex their political and economic muscles, they cause changes in the traditional ways of conducting international business.

Developing nations insist that an increasing proportion of assembling and manufacturing be conducted within their own borders. Because the role of these governments in their own economies is substantial, they are able to exert considerable influence over outside firms desiring to do business within their borders. Local labor must be used whenever possible. Demands are also made that supervisory and managerial talent be recruited from native sources and trained to replace the managers from outside countries.

Developing nations are also becoming more insistent that much of their foreign trade be carried on vessels or planes owned by companies headquartered within their boundaries. Also, they want their local firms to have their "fair" share of revenues from the sale of freight forwarding services, marine insurance, and other transportation and distribution functions.

Traditionally the United States has been a major exporter of manufactured goods and agricultural products. Because of our wealth, we also imported many consumer goods. However, in the last decade several major changes have taken place that have upset those traditional patterns. A new equilibrium has yet to be reached. With the rise of oil-producing nations, and their freedom to charge high prices for petroleum, the United States has been running trade deficits annually because of its large purchases of imported oil. In addition, many major U.S. industries, once the backbone of our industrial might, found themselves uncompetitive in overseas and even in U.S. markets. Frequently, their lower-cost competitor was in Japan.

The most recent change has been caused by the "strength" of the U.S. dollar (compared with foreign currencies). This has allowed us to import more goods and attract foreign sources of investment funds. However, another result has been a drastic drop in many export movements because our products are now too expensive for many foreigners to buy. The direction of product flow for many international carriers has also changed. Pan American World Airways' vice-president for cargo, J. Bruce Gebhardt, said: "The event that has characterized 1983 more than anything else is the tremendous shift in the direction of cargo flow. It amazed me, and I think most of us in the industry, to see the strength of the inbound market and the relative weakness of the outbound market. That is true of Europe, Asia, and of Latin and South America."[1]

---

[1] "Pan Am's Gebhardt Talks Cargo," *Air Cargo World* (Feb. 1984), p. 28.

International Marketing

Marketing overseas is often different from marketing in the United States.[2] Therefore, generalizations are difficult to make since each country of the world possesses unique characteristics when viewed as a market. Conventional marketing analysis is applied, although it must take into account a wider range of differences. In many countries, the size or scale of firms used in the distribution operation is much smaller than would be the case in the United States. Street vendors, merchants operating out of the "holes-in-the-wall," and small shopkeepers may be the rule. In these countries customers shop on a daily basis and buy small amounts, and retailers are more likely to pull the requested good from a shelf behind the counter so there is less need for the type of packaging used in U.S. self-service markets. (There are, of course, many countries that have retail stores similar to those in the United States.)

Firms selling products under their own brand names are concerned about maintaining a reputation for quality in all markets. This can pose problems with respect to customer service. For example, how many parts depots should be located throughout the world? What kinds of guarantees can a U.S. firm make to foreign buyers? How enforceable are they? What changes must be made in a product to adapt it to export?[3]

Chapter 7 discussed push and pull inventory systems. In international distribution, push systems are rare because the international credit system is not as well developed as is the credit system within the United States or other similarly developed economic areas. In international business, if "the buyer or borrower be unwilling or unable to pay, collection of the debt can prove difficult or even impossible in foreign courts. Furthermore, even though the buyer or borrower may be willing and able to pay, he may not be permitted to do so because of foreign-exchange restrictions, expropriation, or political upheavals."[4] If the supplier is uncertain about receiving his payments, he is unlikely to "push" unwanted goods onto his overseas distributors. One of the ways a supplier can be assured of payment is to insist on payment in advance or else to operate through "irrevocable letters of credit," which means a bank guarantees payment provided the supplier meets certain conditions. (See Figure 11-2 for a sample copy. Note the terms.)

International Sourcing

The term *international sourcing* means looking anywhere in the world for sources of raw materials or components; it implies choice from a worldwide selection of sites for processing, manufacturing, or distribution. The strong

---

[2] See Lynn E. Gill, "Beware of Booby Traps in Multinational Distribution," *Handling and Shipping* (March 1976), pp. 44–46. See also, Robert L. Vidrick, "The Impact of Distribution on International Marketing," *NCPDM 1980 Papers*, pp. 415–420.

[3] *Adapting Products for Export* (New York: Conference Board, 1983) discusses many aspects of deciding whether to export a domestic product.

[4] Laurence P. Dowd, *Principles of World Business* (Boston: Allyn 1965), p. 393.

Figure 11-2 Letter of Credit

Since ◇ 1852

WELLS FARGO BANK, N.A.

FORMERLY WELLS FARGO BANK AMERICAN TRUST COMPANY
HEAD OFFICE: 464 CALIFORNIA STREET, SAN FRANCISCO, CALIFORNIA 94104

INTERNATIONAL DIVISION   COMMERCIAL L/C DEPARTMENT   CABLE ADDRESS WELLS

OUR LETTER
OF CREDIT NO. 27724   AMOUNT: US$12,288.00   DATE: April 1, 19
THIS NUMBER MUST BE MENTIONED
ON ALL DRAFTS AND CORRESPONDENCE

- The Japan Co.   • Wells Fargo Bank N.A.
- Box X 25   • Fuji Bldg., 2-3, 3-chome
- Tokyo, Japan   • Marunouchi, Chiyoda-ku
-                    S P E C I M E N   • Tokyo, Japan

GENTLEMEN:

BY ORDER OF   Wards, Oakland, California

AND FOR ACCOUNT OF   same

WE HEREBY AUTHORIZE YOU TO DRAW ON   us

UP TO AN AGGREGATE AMOUNT OF   Twelve Thousand Two Hundred Eighty Eight
                                         and No/100 U.S. Dollars
AVAILABLE BY YOUR DRAFTS AT sight
ACCOMPANIED BY
Commercial Invoice and two copies certifying merchandise is in accordance
   with Purchase Order No. 08142.
Signed Special Customs Invoice in duplicate.
Certificate of Origin in duplicate.
Packing List in duplicate.
Full set clean ocean bills of lading to order shipper, blank endorsed,
   freight collect, notify Wards, Oakland, California, dated on
   board not later than May 25, 19 .

Relating to: Transistor Radios from FOB vessel Japanese Port to
   San Francisco Bay Port.

Partial shipments permitted.   Insurance to be effected by buyers
Transhipment is not permitted.

Negotiating bank is to forward all documents attached to the
   original draft in one airmail envelope.

Courtesy Wells Fargo Bank

DRAFTS MUST BE DRAWN AND NEGOTIATED NOT LATER THAN   June 5, 19
ALL DRAFTS DRAWN UNDER THIS CREDIT MUST BEAR ITS DATE AND NUMBER AND THE AMOUNTS MUST
BE ENDORSED ON THE REVERSE SIDE OF THIS LETTER OF CREDIT BY THE NEGOTIATING BANK.
WE HEREBY AGREE WITH THE DRAWERS, ENDORSERS AND BONA FIDE HOLDERS OF ALL DRAFTS
DRAWN UNDER AND IN COMPLIANCE WITH THE TERMS OF THIS CREDIT, THAT SUCH DRAFTS WILL
BE DULY HONORED UPON PRESENTATION TO THE DRAWEE.
THIS CREDIT IS SUBJECT TO THE UNIFORM CUSTOMS AND PRACTICE FOR DOCUMENTARY CREDITS
(1962 REVISION), INTERNATIONAL CHAMBER OF COMMERCE BROCHURE NO. 222.

W/ SPECIMEN
AUTHORIZED SIGNATURE

Courtesy Wells Fargo Bank.

U.S. dollar has made it difficult for foreigners to buy U.S. products and, as a result, the U.S. share of world exports "has been sinking steadily for four years."[5] Hence, U.S.-based firms are forced to look outside this country.

[5] *Business Week* (Oct. 8, 1984), p. 168.

Transaction and Exchange Channels

Chapter 2 discussed transaction channels and exchange channels; transaction channels are the channels through which the ownership of goods passes, and exchange channels are the chain of physical moves. This distinction is useful in discussing international distribution. In domestic marketing the flows of the transactions and exchange channels are concurrent. In international distribution this is less likely to be so. The seller usually wants to be certain the payment is guaranteed before shipping the goods. Hence, for a single sale, the activities in the transaction channel must be nearly completed before the goods are placed into the exchange channel.

Documentation accompanying international shipments is excessive. One recent shipment to Santiago, Chile, reportedly "required 150 separate documents."[12] Preparing these documents, assembling them, and assuring that they arrive where and when needed, is a minor logistical operation in itself.

Governmental Controls of Flow of International Trade

National governments play a more significant role in international transactions than they do in domestic transactions for several reasons. The main reason is that governments tax the importation of many items. The taxes are called customs or duties. (At one time, customs collections represented the major source of revenue for the U.S. government.) Goods, including baggage accompanying travelers, are inspected as they cross borders. If any customs are due, they must be paid before the goods can be transported farther.

Customs or duty rates are set high on many goods to "protect" local manufacturers, producers, or growers. Initially, local interests will argue that theirs are "infant" industries and need protection for only a few years in order to prevent foreign-based competitors from "dumping" goods in the country at prices that are below cost. But once tariff barriers are built, they are not easily torn down. Rather than the infant outgrowing the crib, the walls of the crib are built higher. The results are that local consumers pay more for goods than if local industries were not protected. In addition, national resources may be allocated in a wasteful manner because they are being used for processes that are inefficient when viewed from a worldwide perspective. Sometimes the tariff the importing nation charges differs according to the nation from which the good is coming. From an international sourcing standpoint, this influences the choice of production site.

Related to tariffs are *import quotas;* they are physical limits on the amount that may be imported from any one country during a period of time. They are often used for commodities where no tariffs exist, and they serve to protect local producers in years when local prices are high but foreign prices are low.

Many nations are concerned with stopping the spread of plant and animal diseases and will inspect various commodities or products to make cer-

---

[12] *Davis Database* (Oct. 1983), p. 1.

tain that they do not contain these problems. If material is found to be infested, it cannot enter a country until it is cleaned.

Entry of other products may be prohibited because they do not meet safety standards. For example, electrical appliances have different voltage requirements throughout the world. Products that do not meet a country's voltage specifications will not be imported by that country. Another situation is the Japanese restriction on imported foods containing two preservatives—benzoic acid and sorbic acid. "The reason for this is that these two preservatives, if permitted for open use in Japan, would be used extensively on all types of fish. Because fish forms a more important part of the Japanese diet than the diets of other nations, there is a clear danger of overconsumption of these two preservatives. . . ."[13] Because of the danger of earthquakes in Japan, upright refrigerators must be built so that they will remain upright even when tilted as much as 10 degrees.[14]

Products can be modified so that they meet each nation's requirements. Conversion costs per unit are high in instances where only small numbers of units are involved. From an inventory control standpoint, slight variations in acceptable standards mean that products become less homogeneous. Parts are less likely to be interchangeable, and stocks in one country may not be substitutes for stocks of similar products in an adjoining country.

Some nations restrict the outflow of currency. This is because a nation's economy will suffer if it imports more than it exports over a long term. These regulations are not concerned with specific commodities; they are concerned with restricting the outflow of currency. All imports require advance approval, and goods that arrive without prior approval are not allowed to enter. Mexico enacted such restrictions in late 1982 and "only imports approved by the government and for which payment has been authorized by Mexico's nationalized banks" were permitted to enter.[15]

Firms with operations in several nations are subject to the taxes of each, and any intracompany move between two nations involves a sale for the one subsidiary and a purchase by the other. The transaction, therefore, determines the income, tax, and profit of both subsidiaries.[16] Tax auditors from both countries can also be expected to ask how the "price" was established for this intrafirm movement and whether one of the results of the "price" selected was a minimization of tax liability to the country in question.

Figure 11-3 is from a guidebook prepared by an international airline that outlines, in general terms, the various restrictions that apply when shipping to African nations. From the example of the two nations listed, it is easy to see that exporting involves complications. Note that their embassy locations in the United States are listed. Consular offices are current sources

---

[13] Japan External Trade Organization, *Japan's Import and Export Regulations* (Tokyo, 1974), p. 10.

[14] Japan External Trade Organization, *Japan's Import and Export Regulations*, p. 17.

[15] *Pacific Traffic* (Nov. 1982), p. 34.

[16] Paul T. Nelson and Gadi Toledano, "Challenges for International Logistics Management," *Journal of Business Logistics* (1979), p. 10. See also, David Ronen and Michael R. Czinkota, "Order Sourcing and Transfer Pricing in the Multinational Corporation," *Journal of Business Logistics* (March 1983), pp. 65–76.

Figure 11-3 Examples of Restrictions of Exporting to Other Nations

SENEGAL

GOVERNMENT REPRESENTATION

The Republic of Senegal is represented in the United States by an Embassy at 2112 Wyoming Ave., N.W., Washington, D.C. and a United Nations Mission at 51 East 42nd St., New York. Both also act for Canadian affairs.

GENERAL INFORMATION

Customs Airports: Dakar, Saint Louis and Ziguinchor.
Collect Service acceptable to Dakar and Saint Louis only.
COD Service not acceptable.
Free House Delivery not acceptable.

DOCUMENTATION

Commercial consignments—2 commercial invoices containing the following declaration: "Nous certifions que les marchandises denommees dans cette facture sont de fabrication et d'origine (country of origin) et que les prix indiques ci-dessus s'accordent avec les prix courants sur le marche d'exportation."
Sample consignments—Without commercial value: No documents. With commercial value: same as for commercial consignments.
Gift consignments—no documentary requirements.

RESTRICTIONS

Live animals: Health certificate.
Dogs and other domestic animals: Health certificates issued not later than 3 days before shipment and stating that the animals originate from an area free from contagious diseases of the species for the preceding 6 weeks, and in case of cats and dogs, that no rabies has been detected for the same period.
PROHIBITED: Hares and rabbits.
Live plants and plant material: Health certificate.
Arms and ammunition: Special import permit.

PROHIBITIONS

All goods of Portuguese or South African origin; skins of hares and rabbits; beetroot sugar; blankets; cloth of textile fibers; cotton cloth; fibres; flower pots, stoneware, pottery, clay products, matches, ornamental bricks and other clay products for building purposes; outwear, shirts, except shirts over CFA 1700. value; shoes, except fashionable shoes over CFA 400. value; trousers under CFA 1900. value; sisal carpets and rugs; sugar cane, yarn and thread; cotton, apéritifs of alcohol or wine basis; digestives.

IMPORT AND EXCHANGE REGULATIONS

Liberalized items may be imported without quantitative restrictions on the basis of an import certificate, which is made out by the importer, endorsed by the Customs on clearance of the merchandise and delivered to an authorized bank for visa by the Exchange Control Office.
Non-liberalized goods require an import license, issued by the Director General for Economic Services and visaed by the Exchange Control Office. Validity of certificate and license is 6 months.
The currency exchange is obtained through the authorized banks on strength of import certificate or import license. No tolerance in value or quantity shown on import certificate or import license is permitted.
The importation of goods competitive with locally produced items may be prohibited from time to time.
Rate of exchange: 247 C.F.A. Francs = $1.00

SIERRA LEONE

GOVERNMENT REPRESENTATION

Sierra Leone is represented in the United States by an Embassy at 1701 19th Street, N.W., Washington, D.C. and a United Nations Mission at 30 East 42nd St., New York. Both also act for Canadian affairs.

GENERAL INFORMATION

Customs Airport: Freetown.

Collect Service acceptable.

COD Service not acceptable.

Free House Delivery not acceptable.

DOCUMENTATION

Commercial consignments—4 combined certificates of value and origin in English bearing the supplier's letterhead and his seal or stamp against his signature or that of his representative. In case of occasional shipment, when overprinting of the letterhead is prohibitive, the combined certificate must be accompanied with the supplier's own invoice duly signed against his seal or stamp, and containing the certification: "We hereby declare that this commercial invoice is in support of the attached certificate invoice No. . . . and that the particulars shown on the certified invoice are true and correct in every detail."

RESTRICTIONS

Live animals: Import authorization from Veterinary Dept.

Dogs: Additional health and rabies vaccination certificate in English.

Live plants and plant material: Import authorization from Agricultural Department.

PROHIBITED: Aniseed and Indian hemp.

Medicines and narcotics: Import license from Director of Medical services.

PROHIBITIONS

Arms and ammunition from Liberia, obscene photographs, shaving brushes from Japan, traps for night hunting.

IMPORT AND EXCHANGE REGULATIONS

Most goods may be freely imported under "Open General License." Specific import license required for a short list of specified items only . . . issued by the Import Licensing Authority of the Ministry of Commerce and Industry; the validity is generally 12 months.

Exporters should avoid overshipment of goods covered by specific import licenses. No tolerances are permitted.

The currency exchange is obtained through authorized banks. No exchange permit is required. An import license, whether specific or open, automatically entitles the importer to buy the relative foreign exchange.

Rate of exchange: 1 Leone = $1.20

Courtesy Sabena Belgian World Airlines.

of information regarding their nation's import and currency exchange regulations. Most nations maintain consular offices in major U.S. port cities, and these offices—for a fee—prepare a "consular invoice," a document that contains approximately the same information as a commercial invoice. The importing nation uses it as the basis for levying applicable import duties.

International Logistics

425

Political Restrictions on Trade

For political or military reasons, nations ban certain types of shipments. The United States does not ship military equipment or certain "strategic" materials to Communist Bloc nations. Political events often lead countries to break off economic relations. For example, U.S. trade with Cuba is also restricted and in early 1981, there also were restrictions on U.S. trade with Iran and with Russia.

Israel and Arab nations, except for Egypt, do not trade with each other, and some Arab nations do not even allow vessels or planes from third nations to sail or fly directly between Israel and themselves. Arab nations also refuse, in varying degrees, to do business with firms that also do business with Israel. To complicate matters further, the United States has laws that discourage U.S. firms from complying with the Arab boycott.

Nontariff Barriers

All of the actions of various governments listed to this point tend to impede the flow of international commerce. Sometimes a government is bound by treaty to grant another nation certain "preferential" (or lower) tariff charges on imports. Later, the nation wishes it had not set such low rates but feels bound by treaty to honor the specified rates. An action it then might take is to establish what is known as a nontariff barrier, a rule that has the effect of reducing the flow of imports. A widely publicized example in late 1982 was the French decision that all video recorders being imported into France move through the small Customs post at Poitiers, in central France. The move, just before Christmas, caused bottlenecks and delays and prevented many Japanese imports from reaching retailers' shelves before Christmas.[17]

Sometimes the barriers are created by other government agencies, whose primary interests are in matters other than trade. The Canadian province of Quebec requires that the French language be used on all product labels, instructions, and brochures. The Japanese Construction Ministry and the National Police Agency both enforce limitations on the heights of highway vehicles, which effectively prohibit the use of the new 9'6" high intermodal containers. (Interestingly, containers of this same height are also manufactured in Japan and *are* allowed on the highways in their move from inland point of manufacture.)[18]

Governments' Role in International Transport

As in other aspects of international business, governments are more involved in international transportation than they are in domestic transportation. One reason for this is that ocean vessels or international airline aircraft operate as "extensions" of a nation's economy, and most revenue they re-

[17] *San Francisco Chronicle* 2 December 1982, p. 29.
[18] *American Shipper* (Jan. 1984), pp. 58–49; and *Containerization International* (Jan. 1984), pp. 43–45.

ceive flow into that nation's economy. To that nation, international carriage functions as an "export" with favorable effects on the nation's balance of payments. However, to the nation on the other end of the shipment, the effect is the opposite since it must "import" the transport service and this has an adverse impact on their balance of payments position. Some nations with very weak balance of payments positions will issue an import license or permit on the condition that the goods move on a vessel or plane flying that nation's flag, which means they are importing only the goods, *not* the transportation service required to carry them. Situations such as this dictate carrier choice.

As used here, *flying a nation's flag* is meant to be synonymous with being owned by private or public entities in that nation. *Flags of convenience* are issued by nations with relatively lax maritime safety and work standards to investors of other nations who want to avoid their home nation's control.

In the last decade, the Russian merchant fleet has grown immensely and is making inroads into most shipping routes. By Communist state accounting techniques, the merchant marine investment has proven to be profitable. The fleet is earning scarce foreign exchange while keeping purchases from foreign countries to a minimum. Russian flag vessels are fueled in the mid-ocean by Russian tankers rather than buying fuel at non-communist ports.

> By cutting prices and operating at a loss, Soviet lines are making serious inroads in commerce once dominated by non-Communist nations. And by showing the flag and providing espionage cover, Soviet vessels from tankers to fishing trawlers have become a formidable military auxiliary for use in time of conflict.[19]

In order to develop international fleets and air lines, most nations provide subsidies. Many nations train their own merchant marine officers, absorb portions of the costs of building commercial vessels, and engage in other activities to promote a "home-grown" merchant fleet. Some own—in total or in part—ocean carriers. International scheduled airlines, except those of the United States, are owned, at least partially, by governments and they receive subsidies. International air and vessel rates are frequently established by carrier cartels. Nations rely on carriers they subsidize to represent national interests as they vote on international rate and service issues.

Less developed nations also desire to carry more of their own waterborne traffic but seem unable to penetrate the existing shipping market, which is dominated by vessel lines from developed countries. In 1983 working through the United Nations' Conference on Trade and Development, an international agreement was adopted that (in theory) will allocate "liner" traffic

[19] *U.S. News & World Report* (June 4, 1984), p. 90.

> Ocean *liners* that carry cargo call on a regularly scheduled basis and carry "less-than-shipload" lots of relatively high-value general cargo.

between nations on a 40/40/20 split. The exporting and importing nations will each have 40 per cent of the business and "cross-traders" would be

> *Cross-traders* carry cargo between other nations. An example would be a ship or plane, registered in country A, carrying traffic between countries B and C.

restricted to 20 per cent. If interpreted literally, the 20 per cent limitation on cross-traders is severe because in many markets it would represent insufficient cargo to keep them in business.

International Trade Specialists

Few companies involved in international logistics rely solely on in-house personnel to manage all of the shipping operations. Specialist firms have developed and are known as international freight forwarders (who generally handle exports) and customs house or import brokers. Sometimes the same firm provides both services and has offices in many countries. Most companies involved in international trade eventually use one or more services that these specialists provide.

International Freight Forwarders

International forwarders usually specialize in handling either vessel shipments or air shipments. Yet their functions are generally the same. The following is an explanation of their functions.

Booking Space on Carriers. Space is frequently more difficult to obtain on international carriers than domestic ones for several reasons. Vessel or aircraft departures are less frequent and the capacities of planes or ships are strictly limited. Connections with other carriers are more difficult to arrange, and the relative bargaining strength of any one shipper, vis-à-vis an international carrier, is usually weaker than it is with respect to domestic carriers. Forwarders are experienced at keeping tabs on available carrier space, and, because they represent more business to the carrier than an individual shipper does, they have more success when finding space is difficult.

Preparing an Export Declaration. An export declaration is required by the U.S. government for statistical and "control" purposes and must be prepared and filed for nearly every shipment.

Preparing an Air Waybill or Bill of Lading. The international air waybill is a fairly standardized document; the ocean bill of lading is not. The latter may differ between ocean lines, coastal areas through which the shipments are moving, and for a variety of other circumstances. Ocean bills of lading are frequently negotiable, which means that whoever legally holds the document may take delivery of the shipment. Because nearly every ocean vessel line has its own bill of lading, a forwarder's experience is necessary to fill it out accurately.

Obtaining Consular Documents. Consular documents were discussed briefly in the previous section. This process involves obtaining permission from the importing country for the goods to enter. Documents are prepared that the importing country will use to determine duties to be levied on the shipment as it passes through their customs.

Arranging for Insurance. Unlike domestic shipments, international shipments must be insured. Either the individual shipment must be insured or else the shipper (or forwarder) must have a blanket policy covering all shipments. International airlines offer insurance at nominal rates. Rates on vessel shipments are higher, and the entire process is complex because of certain practices that are acceptable at sea. For example, if the vessel is in peril of sinking, the captain may have some cargo jettisoned (thrown overboard) to keep the vessel afloat. The owners of the surviving cargo and the vessel owner must then share the costs of reimbursing the shippers whose cargo was thrown overboard.

Preparing and Sending Shipping Notices and Documents. The financial transaction involving the sale of goods is carefully coordinated with their physical movement, and rather elaborate customs and procedures have evolved to assure that the seller is paid when the goods are delivered. The export forwarder handles the shipper's role in the document preparation and exchange stages. (The forwarder serves to coordinate the exchange channel and the transaction channel.) It is also necessary to have certain documents available as the shipment crosses international boundaries.

Advising the Shipper as to Selection of Terms of Sale. Chapter 2 discussed briefly some different terms of sale for domestic transactions. In international transactions, a much wider variety of selling terms is employed. Ownership can change at any point (in time or in geography) between the buyer and seller. Even while at sea, ownership of goods can change. Eight different points follow here where title to the goods, responsibility for insurance coverage, and responsibility for transportation costs can change for an export shipment from an inland point in one country to an inland point in another.

1. At the seller's loading dock.
2. Loaded aboard an inland carrier's rail car or truck next to the seller's loading dock.
3. Alongside the vessel at the port of export.

4. Loaded aboard the vessel at the port of export.
5. Loaded aboard the vessel at the port of import.
6. Unloaded from and alongside the vessel at the port of import.
7. Cleared through customs at the port of import.
8. Delivered to the consignee/importer.[20]

Today, with the widespread use of containers and through rates for container movements from an inland point in the exporting nation to an inland point in the importing nation, the point of transfer should either be where the container is loaded or unloaded. (On the list just given, it would be point 2 or point 8.)

Serving as General Consultant on Export Matters. Questions continually arise when dealing with new products, new markets, or new regulations. The forwarder knows the answers or how to find them. A conscientious forwarder will also advise a shipper as to when certain procedures, such as similar shipments to the same market, become so repetitive that the shipper can handle the procedures in his or her own export department at a lower cost than the fees charged by the forwarder.

Export forwarders' income comes from three sources. Similar to domestic forwarders, they "buy space wholesale and sell it retail"—by consolidating shipments they benefit from a lower rate per pound. Second, most carriers allow the forwarders a commission on shipping revenues they generate for the carriers. Third, forwarders charge fees for preparing documents, performing research, etc.

NVOCCs

In recent years, a modified form of forwarder operation known as the non-vessel operating common carrier (NVOCC) has developed. The NVOCCs can perform most—but not all—of the functions of a freight forwarder. However, they have much greater ability to enter into rate agreements with ocean and inland carriers, and they may issue single-rate quotations between inland points in one nation and inland points in another. NVOCCs frequently affiliate with forwarders so that they can offer their customers a more complete package of services.

Customs House Brokers

An opposite, but similar, function is performed by import or Customs house brokers. They oversee the efficient movement of an importer's goods (and accompanying paperwork) through customs and other inspection points and

---

[20] Usually, ownership of the goods and responsibility for insurance and transportation costs all change at the same point and time, but sometimes this is not the case. See Insurance Company of North America, *Marine Insurance—Notes and Comments on Ocean Cargo Insurance* (Philadelphia, 1971); and "Anatomy of An Export," *Distribution* (Oct. 1980), pp. 75–80.

In early 1984 one of this book's authors interviewed Jan Van Alsenoy, who is legal counsel for the freight forwarders and import brokers in Antwerp, and asked Alsenoy what he thought was the most common error committed by U.S. foreign traders. His response was: "Choice of the wrong terms of sale."

also stand ready to argue for a lower rate in case one of two commodity descriptions apply.

Very few firms attempt to handle this complex process by themselves. In 1974 the Japanese manufacturer of Toyota automobiles contracted with Harper Robinson & Company—a worldwide freight forwarder and Customs–house broker based in the United States—to handle the imports of all Toyota parts into the United States. Some 50,000 different part numbers were involved. "Processing this vast array of parts through customs will involve complex entry procedures to keep parts moving into Toyota's U.S. distribution channels. Harper Robinson will also coordinate pickup and delivery to nine parts depots across the country."[21] Chrysler Corporation of Detroit also relies on the same firm. They contracted with Harper Robinson to be their ocean freight forwarder for both auto components for assembly overseas and vehicles completed in the United States for shipment overseas. The contract covered all Chrysler traffic to South Africa, Australia, Greece, Peru, Lebanon, Japan, and Guam.[22]

Export Management Companies

Sometimes the manufacturer who wants to export retains the services of an export management company, a firm that specializes in handling overseas transactions. They represent U.S. manufacturers and help them find overseas firms that can be licensed to manufacture the product. They handle sales correspondence in foreign languages, ensure that foreign labeling requirements are met, and perform other specialized functions. When handling the overseas sales for a U.S. firm, the export management firm either buys and sells on its own account or else provides credit information regarding each potential buyer to the U.S. manufacturer, who can judge whether to take the risk.

Export management companies and international freight forwarders are closely related because, together, they can offer a complete overseas sales and distribution service to the domestic manufacturer who would like to export but just does not know how. Sometimes international forwarders and export management firms work out of the same office, the only apparent distinction being which phone they answer. Export management companies are also retained by very large firms that have exported for many years, because they can perform their very specialized service less expensively than can the principal firm itself.

Export Trading Companies

Export trading companies attempt to combine all facets of international business: sales, finance, communications, and logistics. They are widely used by the Japanese. On October 18, 1982, President Reagan signed into law the Export Trading Company Act of 1982. The law relaxed some of the antitrust restrictions that had prevented firms that competed in domestic

---

[21] *Pacific Traffic* (Nov. 1974), p. 26.
[22] *Distribution Worldwide* (Oct. 1973), p. 40.

markets from cooperating in overseas ventures. In addition, banks were given the right to acquire up to 100 per cent equity interest in ETCs (provided that the Federal Reserve Board approved). In 1983 announcements were made as various ETCs were formed, but—to this date—little is known about their performance.[23]

Shippers Associations

Widely used in foreign countries, shippers associations are trade groups that represent shippers of similar cargo who join together to bargain as a single entity with ocean steamship conferences (groups of ocean liner operators). They were not allowed in the United States until the Shipping Act of 1984. As of mid-1985, the Federal Maritime Commission (FMC) and the Department of Justice were attempting to agree on guidelines about what types of shippers associations and what types of shippers association activities were to be permitted under the new law.

Export Packers

As with the other export functions discussed to this point, there is a specialized service called export packing performed by firms typically located in port cities. They will custom pack shipments when the exporter lacks the equipment or the expertise. However, when exporters have "repeat" business, they usually perform their own export packing. Export packaging involves packaging for two distinct purposes (in addition to the "sales" function of some packaging).

The first is to allow goods to move through customs easily. For a country assessing duties on the weight of both the item and its container, this means selecting lightweight packing materials. For items moving through the mail, it might mean construction of an envelope with an additional small flap that a customs inspector could open and look inside without having to open the entire envelope. For crated machinery, this might involve using open slats rather than completely closed construction. (The customs inspectors could probably satisfy their curiosity by peering and probing through the openings between the slats.)

The second purpose of export packing is to protect products in what almost always is a more difficult journey than they would experience if they were destined for domestic consignees. For many firms, the traditional ocean packaging method was to take the product in its domestic pack and then enclose it in a wooden container. Ocean shipments are subject to more moisture damage than would be the case for domestic moves. Variations in temperatures are also more extreme. Canned goods moving through hot areas "sweat," causing the can to rust and the label to become unglued.

Recent transportation equipment innovations have helped overcome these climatic problems. International air freight, a post-World War II development, has made it possible to reach major cities throughout the world within 24 or 48 hours, avoiding the long sea voyage. Packaging for international

---

[23] Leslie Kanuk, "Export Trading Company Act," *World Ports* (Jan. 1983), pp. 10–12.

Figure 11-4 Metric Equivalents

weights and measures

metric equivalents

weight

one kilo =	2.2 pounds
pounds ×	0.454 = kilos
ounces ×	0.028 = kilos
cwt. ×	45.4 = kilos
tons ×	907.2 = kilos

length

one inch = 25.4 millimeters
inches × 25.4 = millimeters
inches × 2.54 = centimeters
feet × 0.305 = meters
miles × 1.609 = kilometers

capacity

one imperial gallon = 1.2 U.S. gallons
U.S. gallon × 0.833 = imperial gallon
U.S. gallon × 3.78 = liters
liters × 0.264 = U.S. gallon

Courtesy Air France Cargo.

air freight is sometimes no different than packaging for domestic markets. Containerships and LASH (lighter-aboard-ship) are discussed later in this chapter. These vessels are able to provide better care for cargo since shipments are in individual containers that come equipped with freezing, refrigerating, or air circulating equipment in case the cargo demands. Each container can be handled differently, and the ship's personnel are detailed to check temperature gauges outside containers several times daily.

Goods sold in foreign markets require additional labels. The metric system is widely used outside the United States, and most measurements of products must be expressed in metric terms. Figure 11-4 shows some simple metric equivalents.

Figure 11-5 Some Symbols Used for Packing Export Shipments

Courtesy Air France Cargo.

For goods moving in foreign trade, it is not safe to assume that handlers can read English. Hence, cautionary symbols must be used. (See Figures 11-5 and 11-6.) Cargo moving aboard ocean vessels contains a distinct mark that identifies the shipper, the consignee, the destination point, and piece number (in multipiece shipments). As with domestic cargo, care must be taken so that pilferable items are not identified. This may include changing the symbols every few months. Figure 11-7 shows a package with the various marks required for movement in foreign commerce. These marks should be applied with a stencil, using waterproof ink. The bill of lading, packing list, letter of credit, and any other documents pertaining to this shipment must contain some of the similar markings.

Exchange Channels in International Distribution

In both Chapter 2, and early in this chapter, we distinguished between transactions channels and exchange channels. To this point, the chapter has dealt with the international transactions channels. The remainder of the chapter deals with the exchange channel which handles the physical movement of the goods. The entire export process is complicated. (The following chapter contains an application of network analysis to an export shipment.)

Most of this section deals with transportation. The first part deals with

The Elements of Physical Distribution/Logistics Systems

able for east coast firms doing business with the Orient. In 1979, American President Lines, a U.S. ocean carrier, contracted with several railroads so that it could operate it own "Linertrains" carrying containers between the two coasts. They have their own fleet of container-carrying flatcars and are not dependent upon railroads for supplying them. Thus, American President Lines can offer a more dependable connecting service, linking the ocean and rail carriage of containers. Time savings are significant. "APL's ship/rail combination makes possible a transit time from Yokahama to New York of 15 days—a full week faster than most all-water services for the route."[24]

The services described in the previous paragraph, as well as the interior point pricing mentioned earlier are examples of *land-bridge* operations. Figure 11-8 illustrates three forms of land bridge service offered by railroads. Figure 11-9 is an ad for mini-bridge service, with trains departing from the West Coast. The vessels sail from Gulf and Atlantic ports to the Middle East. The West Coast shipper gives the cargo to the ocean shipping line in either Seattle/Portland, San Francisco, or Los Angeles by the specified date, and the ocean carrier moves it by rail across the United States.

International Air Freight

In relative terms, air freight has probably had a more profound effect on international distribution than on domestic distribution because the airplane has reduced worldwide distances. While transit times between the two U.S. coasts have shrunk from five days to less than one, some international transit times have shrunk from as much as thirty days down to one or two.

There are two types of international air freight operations, chartered aircraft and scheduled air carriers. Chartering an entire aircraft is, of course, expensive, but sometimes the expense can be justified. For example, chartered aircraft have been used in the international transport of livestock sold for breeding purposes. In 1969, one charter airline carried 7,000 cattle from Texas to southern Chile. Nineteen flights were involved, each lasting 15 hours. The comparable time by sea was twenty days, and past experience showed the sea journey had been hard on the cattle, causing either lung damage or else long delays before the animals could be bred. The cost of the chartered aircraft was justified by the reduction in time that the breeding stock was nonproductive. The aircraft were specially equipped with lightweight flooring, gates, and kick-panels (an animal's sharp hoof can pierce the side of the plane). Prior to being loaded aboard the plane, the livestock were kept in feedlots and given a transitional diet that combined both the food to which they were accustomed and the food they would be getting at their destination.

The schedules and routes of international air carriers are established by negotiations between the nations involved. Rates are established by the International Air Transport Association (IATA), a large cartel consisting of all the western world's scheduled airlines (with one or two exceptions). The

---

[24] American President Lines, *Panorama*, (1983) number 9, p. 15. See also Joseph T. Kane, "The New Land-Sea Intermodalism," *Handling and Shipping Management* (April 1985), pp. 54–58.

Figure 11-8 Examples of Land-Bridge Rail Traffic in the U.S.

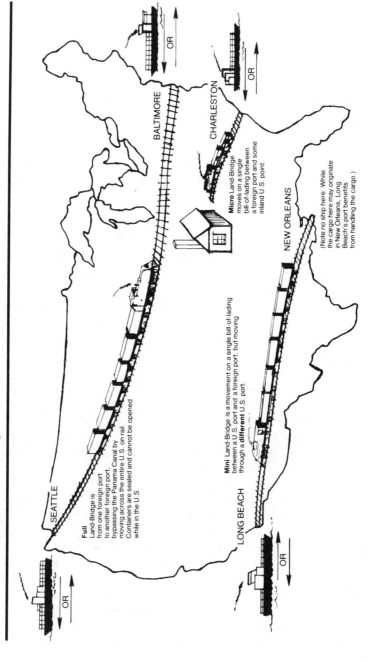

SEATTLE

Full
Land-Bridge is from one foreign port to another foreign port, bypassing the Panama Canal by moving across the entire U.S. on rail. Containers are sealed and cannot be opened while in the U.S.

BALTIMORE

CHARLESTON

Micro Land-Bridge moves on a single bill-of-lading between a foreign port and some inland U.S. point.

LONG BEACH

Mini Land-Bridge is a movement on a single bill-of-lading between a U.S. port and a foreign port, but moving through a **different** U.S. port.

NEW ORLEANS

(Note no ship here. While the cargo here may originate in New Orleans, Long Beach's port benefits from handling the cargo.)

OR

Figure 11-9 Mini-Bridge Schedule

USA/Middle East Express Container Service

MINI-BRIDGE DEPARTING	BARZAN V-36	JEBEL ALI V-36	ADDIRIYAH V-35	AL WATIYAH V-35
SEATTLE / PORTLAND	JUL 13	JUL 27	AUG 13	AUG 28
SAN FRANCISCO	JUL 17	JUL 31	AUG 16	AUG 30
LOS ANGELES	JUL 20	AUG 3	AUG 20	SP 3
SAILS				
HOUSTON	JUL 26	AUG 9	AUG 26	SEP 10
SAVANNAH	JUL 30	AUG 13	AUG 30	SEP 14
NORFOLK	AUG 3	AUG 15	SEP 1	SEP 16
BALTIMORE	AUG 4	AUG 16	SEP 2	SEP 17
NEW YORK	AUG 6	AUG 18	SEP 4	SEP 18
ARRIVES				
JEDDAH	AUG 22	SEP 3	SEP 20	OCT 4
DUBAI	AUG 28	SEP 9	SEP 26	OCT 10
BAHRAIN	SEP 4	SEP 16	OCT 3	OCT 17
DAMMAN	AUG 30	SEP 11	SEP 28	OCT 12
JUBAIL / ABU DHABI / DOHA	SEP 4	SEP 16	OCT 3	OCT 17
KUWAIT	SEP 1	SEP 12	SEP 29	OCT 13
BOMBAY	SEP 4	SEP 16	OCT 3	OCT 17
MUTTRAH	SEP 4	SEP 15	OCT 2	OCT 16

FCL to Iraq all vessels.
LCL accepted from EC/GULF to all ports except Iraq.
Cut off date for LCL cargo from EC/GULF ports is three (3) working days prior to ETD.
Reefer containers available from EC/Gulf ports.
Ras Al Mishab on inducement.
FCL accepted from Jacksonville, Miami, Tampa, Charleston, Philadelphia, Boston, Montreal and Toronto.

GENERAL AGENTS

KERR STEAMSHIP COMPANY, INC.

LONG BEACH	SAN FRANCISCO	PORTLAND/VANC., WA	SEATTLE	VANCOUVER	HOUSTON
4401 ATLANTIC AVE. (213) 422-1132	ONE MARKET PLAZA (415) 764-0200	ONE S.W. COLUMBIA ST SUITE 450 (503) 220-2500	800 FIFTH AVE. (206) 628-6700	1135 TWO BENTAL CENTRE (604) 682-5881	2727 ALLEN PARKWAY SUITE 1500 (713) 521-9600

Credit: United Arab Shipping Co. (In the notes, FCL and LCL refer to "full" and "less-than-full" container loads. "On inducement" means that the vessel will call at that port if there is sufficient cargo.)

principal function of international airlines is to carry passengers. Freight is a secondary product, although a few scheduled airlines use some all-freight aircraft in certain markets. Lufthansa, the German airline, was the first airline in the world to use an all-cargo Boeing 747. It was used in trans-Atlantic service and connected Germany with the northeastern United States. It replaced several smaller planes. Compared with earlier jets, the 747 has enormous capacity. Figure 11-10 shows the difference in capacities of several all-freight configurations and compares them with passenger/freight configurations of the 747 and the McDonnell-Douglas DC-10. Note that the 747 in a passenger/cargo configuration can carry more cargo than the all-cargo versions of the smaller planes.

In early 1980s, the most significant international air cargo development

Figure 11-10 Aircraft Freight Capacity

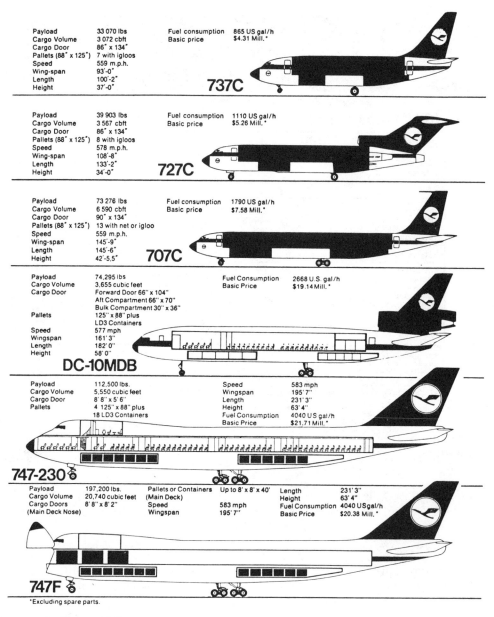

Payload	33 070 lbs	Fuel consumption	865 US gal/h
Cargo Volume	3 072 cbft	Basic price	$4.31 Mill.*
Cargo Door	86" x 134"		
Pallets (88" x 125")	7 with igloos		
Speed	559 m.p.h.		
Wing-span	93'-0"		
Length	100'-2"		
Height	37'-0"		

737C

Payload	39 903 lbs	Fuel consumption	1110 US gal/h
Cargo Volume	3 567 cbft	Basic price	$5.26 Mill.*
Cargo Door	86" x 134"		
Pallets (88" x 125")	8 with igloos		
Speed	578 m.p.h.		
Wing-span	108'-8"		
Length	133'-2"		
Height	34'-0"		

727C

Payload	73 276 lbs	Fuel consumption	1790 US gal/h
Cargo Volume	6 590 cbft	Basic price	$7.58 Mill.*
Cargo Door	90" x 134"		
Pallets (88" x 125")	13 with net or igloo		
Speed	559 m.p.h.		
Wing-span	145'-9"		
Length	145'-6"		
Height	42'-5.5"		

707C

Payload	74,295 lbs	Fuel Consumption	2668 U.S. gal/h
Cargo Volume	3,655 cubic feet	Basic Price	$19.14 Mill.*
Cargo Door	Forward Door 66" x 104"		
	Aft Compartment 66" x 70"		
	Bulk Compartment 30" x 36"		
Pallets	125" x 88" plus		
	LD3 Containers		
Speed	577 mph		
Wingspan	161'3"		
Length	182'0"		
Height	58'0"		

DC-10MDB

Payload	112,500 lbs.	Speed	583 mph
Cargo Volume	5,550 cubic feet	Wingspan	195'7"
Cargo Door	8'8" x 5'6"	Length	231'3"
Pallets	4 125" x 88" plus	Height	63'4"
	18 LD3 Containers	Fuel Consumption	4040 US gal/h
		Basic Price	$21.71 Mill.*

747-230

Payload	197,200 lbs.	Pallets or Containers	Up to 8' x 8' x 40'
Cargo Volume	20,740 cubic feet	(Main Deck)	
Cargo Doors	8'8" x 8'2"	Speed	583 mph
(Main Deck Nose)		Wingspan	195'7"
		Length	231'3"
		Height	63'4"
		Fuel Consumption	4040 US gal/h
		Basic Price	$20.38 Mill.*

747F

*Excluding spare parts.

Courtesy Lufthansa Airlines.

was the introduction into numerous foreign trade routes of Boeing 747s with main deck cargo configurations. The three different 747 models that can carry cargo on their main deck are the 747-200F, an all-freighter, and the 747-200C and the 747-200B, both of which can have their main deck in all passenger, all cargo, or various combinations of seating and cargo-carrying configurations. Some of these 747s have a movable bulkhead, which

Figure 11-11 New Boeing 747 with Stretched Upper Deck Being Constructed for KLM.

Credit: Boeing

is changed as the relative amounts of passengers and cargo vary. This allows the airline to adjust for seasonal changes in passenger travel. Also, the carrier has more flexibility in case there are changes in the relative strength of passenger and freight movements. This occurred in 1984 when the strong U.S. dollar caused an increase in the flow of tourists from the United States but a decrease in the flow of goods. Figure 11-11 shows a Boeing 747-300 being built for KLM Royal Dutch Airline. This is designed to carry both passengers and cargo on its main deck and has a large main-deck cargo door in the aft rear fuselage. What is unique is the stretched second level, or upper deck, which is 23 feet longer than on other 747s. This provides carrying space for forty-four more passengers.

Because of the differences in aircraft cargo compartment shapes, more than twenty different container types are in use, although IATA is reducing the number of different containers styles its members will accept from shippers. Figure 11-12 shows some of the large containers in use.

Many containers used by international air lines are smaller than those shown in Figure 11-12. Some hold as little as 20 cubic feet. They have several special features required by IATA such as a solid floor (to distribute the weight of the contents evenly), and an air flow device allowing air to flow into and out of the container so that air pressure will not be trapped when the plane climbs. Use of these IATA-approved containers reduces charges in three ways. First, they take the place of fiberboard boxes that otherwise would have to be used. Second, the weight of the container is *subtracted* from the weight of the shipment so that the container itself travels free. Third, a rebate—approximately the cost of the container—is given to the shipper; the rebate is subtracted the the freight charges.

For shippers of large quantities, the international airlines offer a unit-load incentive in conjunction with some FAK (freight all kinds) rates. The

Figure 11-12 Large Airfreight Containers

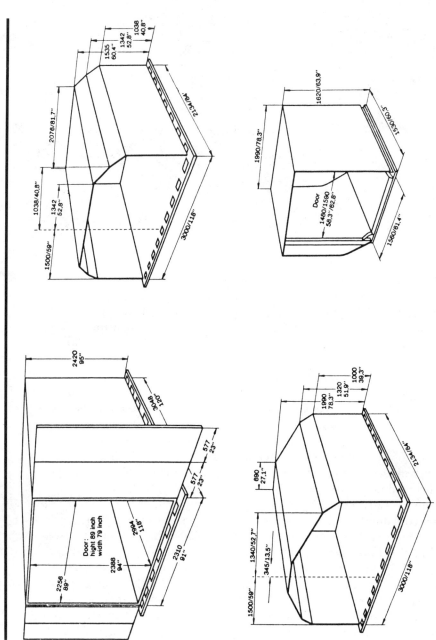

Courtesy Lufthansa German Airlines.

442

airline supplies large pallets and, if necessary, igloos (a fiberglass pallet cover placed over the load to protect it and to insure that it does not exceed the allowable dimensions). To obtain the lower rates from IATA carriers, the shipper must tender the pallet loaded to airline specifications, and at the other end of the journey, the entire pallet must be destined to one consignee. A special charge is made if it is necessary to unload or partially unload the pallet for customs inspection. Both the shipper and the consignee may have the pallet for 48 hours each before demurrage charges are assessed.

The results of the IATA incentives to use containers and unit loads has been to increase the average size of shipments handled by the airlines. This has reduced the number of individual packages each airline terminal must handle. Air freight forwarders have benefited since they are frequently in a better position than individual shippers to take advantage of incentives offered to larger shipments.

International air freight forwarders use a document entitled "shipper's letter of instructions," which is frequently the only document the shipper must execute. Shippers not using forwarders need to have their own air waybill prepared. Figure 11-13 shows the air waybill form. Twelve copies of each waybill are prepared.

International air cargo rates are published in tariffs available from the airlines. There are both general cargo rates and lower specific commodity rates. Rate breaks encourage heavier shipments.

A new development in international air freight has been the international courier services. The couriers provide land pickup and delivery services for documents and small parcels, and they connect with scheduled airline flights. These courier services are of special significance to international logistics because often they provide the fastest service between many major points. They also are often employed to carry the documentation that is generated by—and very much a part of—the international movement of materials.

Ocean Shipping

In the past decades there have been two significant advances in shipping technology. The first has been much larger vessels. Tankers are now being built that have thirty to forty times the capacity of the World War II-vintage T-2 tanker. The second change has been in cargo-handling techniques, especially of break-bulk general cargo, which for centuries has been loaded or unloaded on a piece-by-piece basis after being lifted by the ship's boom and tackle.

Types of Ocean Cargoes.   Much of the world's shipping tonnage is used for carrying petroleum. Tankers are either owned by the oil companies or else leased (chartered) by them from individuals who invest in ships. Vessels are chartered for either specific voyages or for large blocks of time. The charter market fluctuates widely, especially after events such as the Suez Canal closing or opening or the announcement of U.S. wheat sales to Russia or China. (Tankers can carry dry cargo, although the reverse is not always true; however, dry cargo and tanker charter rates tend to follow each other.)

Figure 11-13 International Airway Bill

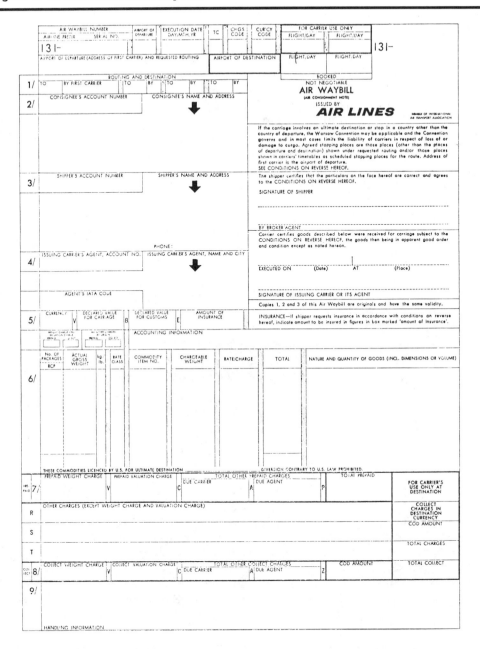

International commodity traders follow the vessel charter market very closely because they know the differences in commodity prices in different world markets. Whenever the charter rate between these two markets drops to a point where it is less than the spread in the commodity prices, a vessel will be chartered to carry the commodity.

Dry bulk cargoes, such as grain, ores, sulfur, sugar, scrap iron, coal, lumber, and logs, also usually move in complete vessel-load lots on chartered vessels. Brokers exist who match shippers of large fractional shiploads so they can pool their cargo and fill an entire ship. There are also large specialized dry cargo ships, usually owned by the shipper. Nissan Motor Company of Japan (which manufactures Datsuns) has eight auto-carrying ships, four of which carry 1,200 Datsuns apiece and four others can carry 1,900. Most of these vessels carry autos to the United States and load with soybeans or other agricultural products for their return voyage.

"Tramps," or independent dry cargo vessels, can be chartered for carrying relatively large shipments of high-value cargo in situations where the cargo can be assembled at one time. The traffic manager of General Electric International, which manufactures and ships huge generators and turbines, indicated that one advantage of chartering an entire ship to carry all equipment and materials needed for an overseas project is better scheduling because all participants do everything possible to be ready for the sailing of the ship. This procedure has worked better than the traditional approach of sending the equipment and materials on a series of liner sailings. People need to meet one specific date—there isn't "always another vessel" sailing next week.[25]

If a single shipper's needs do not fill the vessel completely, the vessel is "topped off" with compatible bulk cargo, such as grain, that can be loaded into an unused hold. This helps defray the total voyage costs for the party using the ship. There are agents who specialize in chartering fractional spaces (often individual holds) in vessels.

Shipping Conferences.   Ocean general cargo (or break-bulk liner) rates are set by conferences, which are cartels of all vessel operators operating between certain trade areas. Conferences provide stability in markets where cargo offerings fluctuate. Members agree to provide relatively regular service, and a shipper who agrees to use them exclusively pays a rate that is lower than that charged to shippers who do not agree to use the conference regularly. Over one hundred different conferences serve U.S. ports. Examples are the Gulf/UK Conference, which handles trade from U.S. Gulf Coast ports to England, Ireland, Scotland, and Wales; and the Israel/U.S. North Atlantic Westbound Conference, which handles trade from Israel's Mediterranean ports to U.S. ports from Portland, Maine, to Hampton Roads, Virginia. Some conferences are very stable and well disciplined; others are not.

Containers.   Today, operators of general cargo vessels may never handle, or even see, cargo on a piece-by-piece basis. Their ships are fully containerized, which means the only way they can load or unload cargo is to have the cargo stowed inside containers. Shippers or forwarders tender full containers, and if a shipper tenders a less-than-container lot, the vessel operator must load all the less-than container lots into containers so that the cargo can be loaded aboard the containership. Modern containership technology is less than twenty-five years old, yet use of containers has grown

[25] Comments of Jack Scally, traffic manager, GE International, at Port of Oakland's International Transportation Conference, October 26, 1978.

rapidly. In 1964, there were fewer than 90,000 containers (measured in TEUs), whereas in 1984, the number stood at four million.[26]

> *TEU* stands for 20-foot container, or its equivalent in cubic capacity. Its usual dimensions are 20 feet long, 8 feet wide, and 8½ feet high. *FEU* stands for 40-foot equivalent.

Figure 11-14 shows the side and top views of a large containership. Note that some of the containers are carried above the level of the deck; this increases the vessel's cubic carrying capacity.

Most container movements are between a relatively small number of major ports. Service between ports (and, for that matter, for the container's complete journey) is faster than the former means of handling cargo. This is because the containers can be handled much more quickly both in ports and by land and water carriers. In 1983 the world's top ten container ports, in terms of TEUs handled, were Rotterdam (2.3 million), New York (2.1 million), Hong Kong (1.8 million), Kobe (1.6 million), Kaohsiung (1.5 million), Singapore (1.3 million), Antwerp (1 million), San Juan (989,000), Seattle (950,000), and Keelung (943,000).[27] However, from a worldwide perspective, containerization is not developing evenly because many small ports are unable to afford the large investment in shoreside handling facilities, or else because the economy served by the port does not handle cargo of the volume or type suitable for containers. One example is the string of U.S. and Canadian Great Lakes ports served by the St. Lawrence Seaway. Relatively small ocean vessels call at numerous ports, discharging or taking on very small tonnages of cargo at each one. The same traffic patterns exist at port areas on the other end of the journey. The entire scale of operations is too small to benefit from containerships. Container facilities are also slow in being adopted by LDCs.

LASH vessels handle floating containers and can be used most advantageously in areas where the central port is connected to inland areas by shallow waterways. Similar conditions must exist on both ends of the voyage, and this limits somewhat the applicability of the system. LASH barges are approximately 60 feet long, 30 feet wide, and 13 feet deep, or about 20,000 cubic feet. They carry about 400 short tons. The LASH concept is relatively new, and its success is still being evaluated. The "Seabee" concept is similar, although the barges are larger. A typical Seabee barge is 100 feet long, 35 feet wide, and 13 feet deep.

RO-RO (roll on–roll off) vessels are somewhat like large, floating parking lots. They have large doors in the stern or on their sides. Ramps are stretched to the shore, and cargo is moved on or off the ship in trailers. RO-RO vessels are also used to carry vehicles that can move using their own power. A RO-RO vessel that operates between Florida and Puerto Rico is shown on Figure 11-15.

[26] *World Ports* (June 1982), pp. 49–52; *Containerisation International* (Aug. 1983), pp. 38–47.

[27] *Port of Seattle Tradelines* (Sept.–Oct. 1984), p. 5. Three other U.S. ports placed in the top 20: Oakland, with 800,000 TEUs, Long Beach (798,000), and Los Angeles (734,000).

Figure 11-14 Layout of Containership

Containership "Hongkong Express"

Service area: Trio-Service between Europe and Far East
Tonnage: 57.525 GRT
Deadweight: 48.064 to

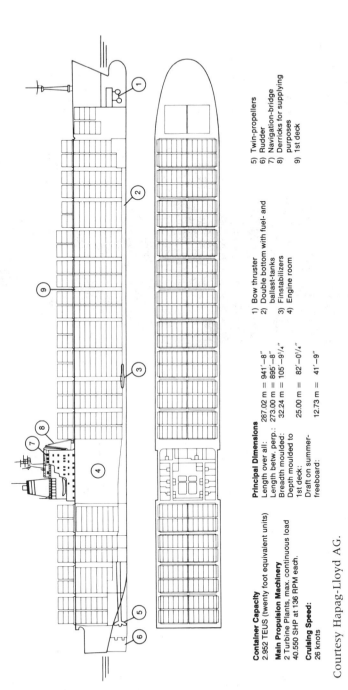

Container Capacity
2.952 TEUS (twenty foot equivalent units)

Main Propulsion Machinery
2 Turbine Plants, max. continuous load
40.550 SHP at 136 RPM each.

Cruising Speed:
26 knots

Principal Dimensions

Length over all:	287.02 m	= 941'–8"
Length betw. perp.:	273.00 m	= 895'–8"
Breadth moulded:	32.24 m	= 105'–9¼"
Depth moulded to 1st deck:	25.00 m	= 82'–0¼"
Draft on summer-freeboard:	12.73 m	= 41'–9"

1) Bow thruster
2) Double bottom with fuel- and ballast-tanks
3) Finstabilizers
4) Engine room
5) Twin-propellers
6) Rudder
7) Navigation-bridge
8) Derricks for supplying purposes
9) 1st deck

Courtesy Hapag-Lloyd AG.

447

Figure 11-15 A RO-RO Vessel in Jacksonville

Credit: Jacksonville Port Authority

For purposes of discussion, the various types of vessels have been introduced separately. In reality, many vessels carry cargo loaded by various techniques. Most LASH and RO-RO vessels, for example, also carry containers.

Specialized vessels also exist. One example is shown in Figure 11-16. That vessel, the *Starman Asia,* is designed to lift and transport exceptionally heavy pieces of cargo. The picture was taken in Antwerp and shows the *Starman Asia's* cranes lifting a 590-ton load.

Surface Transport in Other Countries

The quality of transport facilities in foreign nations varies. Some are as well developed as they are in the United States, but two rather universal differences should be pointed out. First, few foreign nations have as wide a range of modes to choose from, because in the United States an effort is made to allow all modes of transportation to exist. Second, the degree of nationalization of transportation is higher in most foreign countries than in the United States. In the Republic of South Africa, the "railroad, which is the government, will not permit anything to move by road that could be brought by

Figure 11-16 Loading a 590-ton Etylene Cracking Tower Aboard *Starman Asia*

The tower was built in Willebroek, Belgium and, using two trailers with 64 wheels each, was loaded aboard the pontoon shown on the left, which was floated to the Port of Antwerp, where this picture was taken. The tower was then carried to Yanbu, Saudia Arabia.

Credit: Port of Antwerp; G. Coolens

rail. . . . Not only does a shipper or consignee have to submit documentary proof that his freight could not be moved by rail in order to use a for-hire trucker—he has to do the same thing if he wants to operate the private carriage!''[28]

The widespread use of seaborne containers has brought about hopes of standardizing land vehicles for carrying containers on the landward legs of their journey. The European Common Market has been making progress in its attempt to standardize truck dimensions within all its member countries. Truck-borne containers are now familiar sights throughout Europe.

Rail equipment sizes and clearances vary throughout the world with most nations using equipment much smaller than is used in the United States. Frequently, containers that can be loaded ''two-to-a-railcar'' in the United States are carried on individual railcars elsewhere.

One of the difficulties in implementing international transport technological improvements is that fairly identical handling equipment must be in

[28] John T. McCullough, ''Africa,'' *Distribution Worldwide* (October 1973), pp. 69–70. France restricts the number of truck operators in order to support rail business, see *World Business Weekly* (October 6, 1980), pp. 11–12.

place at each end of the trip. In some parts of the world, grain and sugar are still stowed or unloaded by stevedores carrying individual bags on their shoulders and walking up and down gangplanks.

The incidence (or burden) of costs is also significant. RO-RO shipping involves the use of trailers rather than containers to be carried aboard ship as though it were a large ferry boat. Once loaded, there is considerable waste space—essentially the height of each trailer box above the deck floor. Thus, a vessel cannot carry as much cargo within a given amount of space. Yet the required port facilities are relatively inexpensive; there need only be a ramp for driving the trailers on or off the ship. The trailers can be hitched to tractors and hauled directly to or from their landward destination. So, although more is spent per ton of cargo on vessel operations, less is spent for port operations. Vessel lines can sometimes force a port to add cargo-handling equipment by placing a surcharge against the port for all shipments until such equipment is installed.

International Trade Inventories

Under the best of conditions, the movement of products in an international distribution channel is never as smooth as a comparable domestic movement. Because there will always be additional uncertainties, misunderstandings, and delays, safety stocks must be larger. "Unlike many U.S. and Japanese firms, which are adopting versions of Kanban, or JIT inventory planning, overseas firms elsewhere tend to overstate their needs as a hedge against delays, errors, contamination in transit . . . and just to make their firms seem bigger."[29]

Firms must modify their inventory policies, or at least give them some very careful thought. Most nations represent smaller potential marketing areas than the United States; thus, the inventory necessary to serve any one of them will be smaller. An inventory held in one nation will not necessarily serve the needs of markets in neighboring nations because there may be minor, but significant, variations in the specifications of the product sold in each country. "The thorniest conflicts between domestic and international interests [within a firm] often center around issues of market size. Plans for domestic production and inventory tend to be geared to demands of the company's primary market—usually the domestic one. So when a compromise is struck for purposes of export modification, as one executive notes: 'A lot of that compromise is based on who is going to buy the most, and what market has the greater potential.'"[30]

Also, duties may have to be paid each time a product crosses a national boundary, although frequently there is a provision for "duty-drawbacks" that provide the rebate of all (or nearly all) of a duty if the imported product is exported, usually within a specified time period of its initial entry.

"Return" items are virtually impossible to accommodate in an interna-

[29] *Davis Database* (Oct. 1983), p. 2.
[30] *Adapting Products for Export* (New York: Conference Board, 1983), p. 23.

tional distribution operation, especially if the return involves movement of the goods across a national boundary. This has some implications to a firm trying to achieve a high level of customer service standards on an international basis since it may be unreasonable to tell buyers to return a defective item to the factory where it was built. One U.S. retail chain tells its stores to deal directly with domestic producers with questions regarding product defects. However, for imported products, there is no recourse. The stores are told to either destroy them or sell them at "salvage" prices.

Import and export quotas affect values of inventories. Inventory valuation is difficult on an international scale because the relative values of various currencies continue to change. The value of wheat held in a nation's grain elevators will be the world market price unless the government places an embargo on wheat exports (or imports). The value of the wheat within the nation then becomes the domestic price. In times when a nation's (or the world's) currency is unstable, investments in inventories rise because they are believed to be less risky than holding cash or securities.

Computer programs have been developed that aid in managing international inventories. One such system, used by the Cummins Engine Company, is located at that firm's Brussels warehouse, which handles distribution to eighteen countries in Western Europe. Some of its unique features include its multilanguage capabilities and its use of current relative values of the various national currencies. The multilanguage capability allows translation into whatever languages are necessary to prepare all the shipping documents, invoices, and so on. The currency-conversion feature allows invoices to be drawn in the buyer's home currency. In addition, a feature is used to instruct the warehouse to fill the order in a way that minimizes the amount of duty to be paid. To accomplish this, the computer needs to know the applicable tariff rates between the goods' nation (or nations) of origin and the nation of sale. It must also take into account that day's relative values of world currencies because this will also have an impact on the "true" amount of duties that must be paid.[31]

Summary

International logistics is sufficiently complicated that most firms rely on outside "specialists" to assist them. The paperwork involved and the changing rules and regulations of every nation make it almost mandatory to rely on specialists such as international freight forwarders and customs-house brokers.

Many nations have physical distribution systems that are as sophisticated as found in the United States. However, transfer of goods between any two countries is difficult, and one cannot assume that an inventory in one nation can be shifted to meet the needs of a neighboring market.

Aside from trade with Canada and Mexico, U.S. foreign trade moves aboard ocean vessels or aircraft. Both types of carriers are increasing their use of containers, making it more necessary for shippers to deal in con-

[31] The system was developed by Distribution Systems Management Systems, Inc., of Lexington, Massachusetts, and is described in their brochures.

tainer-sized lots. This trend has helped the international freight forwarders since they are often in a better position to assemble larger lots of cargo.

Air freight has had a profound effect on international commerce since it has shrunk time distances around the globe. International air freight rates are established by a cartel, the IATA.

Vessel rates on general cargo are also set by cartels, known as shipping conferences. Shippers who agree to use a conference exclusively receive lower rates.

Questions for Discussion and Review

1. In what ways does international logistics differ from domestic logistics?
2. What are some documents that are required in international trade but not required for domestic transactions?
3. Why are international freight forwarders needed? What functions do they perform?
4. How are transportation rates for international shipments set?
5. Why are international air carriers and vessel operators using more containers? What impact does this have on the individual shipper?
6. What is a land bridge? A mini-land bridge?
7. How are international freight forwarders compensated?
8. Why do developing nations prefer that their own citizens rather than foreigners be employed in new industries?
9. Why should international shipments be insured? What is especially unique about the need for insuring cargo on vessels?
10. What services do export management firms perform?
11. What are the differences between managing an inventory of goods for *domestic* consumption and goods destined for *international* consumption?
12. What functions do import brokers perform?
13. How are "irrevocable letters of credit" used in international transactions?
14. Why do governments exert considerable control over international trade?
15. How does the Russian merchant fleet serve the Russian economy?
16. How does export packing differ from packing for domestic shipments?
17. What is international sourcing? Give some examples.
18. What is IATA?
19. What are the differences between using a tramp vessel versus a conference vessel?
20. Discuss briefly each of the following:
    a. RO-RO vessels
    b. "Duty-draw back"
    c. TEU
    d. Flags of convenience
    e. "Cross-trader"
    f. NVOCC

Additional Chapter References

Alexander, Cathy M., and Don H. Jones. "Potential Revenue Sources for Ocean Ports," *Annual Proceedings of the Transportation Research Forum* (1984), pp. 352–361.

Anderson, David L. "International Logistics Strategies for the Eighties," *Annual Proceedings of the NCPDM* (1984), pp. 355–376.

Bender, Paul S. "The Challenge of International Distribution." *Annual Proceedings of the NCPDM* (1984), pp. 41–52.

———— "International Distribution." *The Distribution Handbook* (New York: Free Press Division of Macmillan, 1985), pp. 777–814.

Bess, H. David. "U.S. Maritime Policy: A Time for Reassessment." *Transportation Journal* (Summer 1982), pp. 4–14.

Binkley, John A. "Closed Conferences, Rationalization, and U.S. Maritime Policy." *Annual Proceedings of the Transportation Research Forum* (1983), pp. 707–715.

Branch, Alan E. *Economics of Shipping Practice and Management* (London: Chapman, 1982).

Bronzini, Michael S. "Analytical Model of Operations at Inland River Ports and Terminals." *Annual Proceedings of the Transportation Research Forum* (1982), pp. 490–498.

Bruning, Edward R. "Code of Conduct For Liner Conferences: Its Significance For Developing Nations," *Transportation Practitioners Journal* (Spring 1985), pp. 340–348.

Button, K. J. "Regulation and Coordination of International Road Goods Movement Within the European Common Market: An Assessment." *Transportation Journal* (Summer 1983), pp. 4–16.

Calabro, Pat J. "Distribution and Marketing Implications of Foreign Trade Zones." *Annual Proceedings of the NCPDM* (1983), pp. 469–478.

———— "Foreign Trade Zones—A Sleeping Giant in Distribution." *Journal of Business Logistics* (March 1983), pp. 51–64.

Campbell, Thomas C., and Amy Dalton. "Coal Exports: A Problem in Energy and Transportation." *Transportation Journal* (Spring 1983), pp. 34–46.

Collison, Frederick M. "Market Segments for Marine Liner Service." *Transportation Journal* (Winter 1984), pp. 40–54.

Davies, J. E. "Freight Rate Stability and Resource Allocation in Liner Shipping." *Annual Proceedings of the Transportation Research Forum* (1983), pp. 74–81.

Davis, H. Craig. "Regional Port Impact Studies: A Critique and Suggested Methodology," *Transportation Journal* (Winter 1983), pp. 61–71.

Donovan, Paul M., Jean C. Godwin, and Lauren V. Kessler. "The Shipping Act of 1984." *ICC Practitioners' Journal* (July–Aug. 1984), pp. 463–475.

Duffy, T. Brogan. "Barriers, Cost Considerations, and Marketing Considerations to Selling Coal FOB Destination." *Annual Proceedings of the Transportation Research Forum* (1983), pp. 621–625.

Elliott, Andrew. "The Transportation of Canadian Potash to World Markets." *Annual Proceedings of the Transportation Research Forum* (1984), pp. 163–169.

Foster, Thomas A. "Recent Trends in International Distribution." *Annual Proceedings of the NCPDM* (1983), pp. 660–672.

Fruin, Jerry E. "Alternative Grain Export Routes from Minnesota and the Dakotas." *Annual Proceedings of the Transportation Research Forum* (1982), pp. 570–577.

Gidwitz, Betsy. *The Politics of International Air Transport* (Lexington, Mass.: Heath, 1980).

Gourdin, Kent N. "International Aviation Policy and Strategic Aircraft: A Critical Appraisal." *Transportation Journal* (Winter 1983), pp. 20–27.

Hazard, John L. "A Competitive U.S. Maritime Policy." *Transportation Journal* (Winter 1982), pp. 32–62.

Hoffer, George, and J. T. Lindley. "Registration Reciprocity, the International Registration Plan, and Effective Motor Carrier Tax Rates." *Transportation Journal* (Spring 1981), pp. 37–47.

Holmberg, Roger. "How a High Technology Manufacturing Firm Manages International Distribution." *Annual Proceedings of the NCPDM* (1982), pp. 425–454.

Jachimiak, Bernard. "Transport and Mastery of Energy in France." *Annual Proceedings of the Transportation Research Forum* (1983), pp. 208–220.

Jacobsen, Thomas R., and Thomas L. Kennedy. "A Study in Contrast U.S. Versus South African Transportation Policies." *Annual Proceedings of the Transportation Research Forum* (1983), pp. 410–417.

Johnson, James C., James P. Rakowski, and Kenneth C. Schneider. "U.S. Coal Exports: Problems and Prospects." *Colorado Business Review* (April 1982), pp. 2–4.

Kruse, William J. "The International Transportation Company as a Warehouse: Past, Present and Future." *Annual Proceedings of the NCPDM* (1984), pp. 345–354.

Kyle, Reuben, and Laurence T. Phillips. "Maritime Protectionism: A New Call for Cargo Preference." *Annual Proceedings of the Transportation Research Forum* (1983), pp. 700–706.

LeBlanc, Louis A., and Bruce C. Payne. "A Risk-Adjustment Model for Capital Budgeting Decisions in Transportation: The Capital Asset Pricing Model Approach to Port Investment Projects." *Annual Proceedings of the Transportation Research Forum* (1982), pp. 499–506.

Lee, Tenpao, Charles R. Hurburgh, and G. Phillip Baumel. "Fuel Consumption and Fuel Costs in Exporting Grain to Japan and Europe." *Annual Proceedings of the Transportation Research Forum* (1984), pp. 303–311.

Liba, C. J. "Future Canadian Competition for Midwest U.S. Imports and Exports." *Annual Proceedings of the Transportation Research Forum* (1984), pp. 54–59.

Marcus, Henry S. "Improving Port Productivity: Research Trends and Issues." *Annual Proceedings of the Transportation Research Forum* (1984), pp. 347–351.

Martin, Michael V., and David A. Clement. "An Analysis of Port Specific International Grain Rates: The Case of the Lower Columbia River Port Area." *Transportation Journal* (Fall 1982), pp. 18–26.

McLennan, Kay, and Tracey Kennedy. "A Summary Discussion of the Utility of a Transportation-Oriented Export Trading Company." *Annual Proceedings of the Transportation Research Forum* (1984), pp. 298–299.

Nersesian, Roy L. *Ships and Shipping: A Comprehensive Guide* (Tulsa, Okla.: PennWell, 1981).

Pastor, John A. "Time and Cost Efficiency of International Shipments." *Annual Proceedings of the NCPDM* (1983), pp. 673–690.

Phillips, Laurence T., and K. Michael O'Connell. "The International Commercial Aircraft Market: Challenges and Opportunities for the 1980s." *Annual Proceedings of the Transportation Research Forum* (1983), pp. 183–192.

Picard, Jacques. "The Management of Physical Distribution in Multinational Corporations." *Columbia Journal of World Business* (Winter 1982), pp. 67–73.

Pixton, Charles E., and Luella G. White. "Transportation of Export Coal from Appalachia." *Annual Proceedings of the Transportation Research Forum* (1982), pp. 233–242.

Pope, David J., Evelyn A. Thomchick. "U.S. Foreign Freight Forwarders and NVOCCs," *Transportation Journal,* (Spring 1985), pp. 26–36.

Ronen, David. "Review of Cargo Ships Routing and Scheduling." *Journal of Business Logistics* (March 1984), pp. 112–125.

Scrafton, D. "Transport Policy, Administration & Decision-Making in Australia." *Annual Proceedings of the Transportation Research Forum* (1983), pp. 273–281.

Senf, David R., and Jerry E. Fruin. "An Analysis of the Potential for Steam Coal Exports Through Great Lakes Ports." *Annual Proceedings of the Transportation Research Forum* (1983), pp. 649–658.

Sletmo, Gunnar K., and Jacques Picard, "International Distribution Policies and the Role of Air Freight," *Journal of Business Logistics* (March 1985), pp. 35–52.

Stephenson, J., and Arnold E. Balk. "Fast Track Legislation—Public/Private Sector Roles in Harbor and Channel Deepening Projects." *ICC Practitioners' Journal* (March–April 1983), pp. 310–321.

Suykens, F. "The Difficult Road Towards a Common European Seaports Policy." *Annual Proceedings of the Transportation Research Forum* (1983), pp. 100–107.

Thomchick, Evelyn A., and Lisa Rosenbaum. "The Role of U.S. Export Trading Companies in International Logistics." *Journal of Business Logistics* (Sept. 1984), pp. 85–106.

Thuong, Le T. "Government Railroading, Japanese Style." *Transportation Journal* (Winter 1982), pp. 21–31.

Tretheway, M. "An International Comparison of Airlines." *Annual Proceedings of the Transportation Research Forum* (1984), pp. 34–43.

Vidrick, Robert L. "Selecting Your International Distribution Team." *Annual Proceedings of the NCPDM* (1983), pp. 645–659.

Waters, W. G. and Dean H. Uyeno. "Logistics Management and Coal Exports: A Cross-Country Comparison." *Annual Proceedings of the Transportation Research Forum* (1983), pp. 300–311.

Wilson, Maragret A., and Peter Sandor. "Forecast of Canadian Grain Shipments Through the St. Lawrence Seaway 1985–2000." *Annual Proceedings of the Transportation Research Forum* (1982), pp. 578–588.

CASE 11-1

Belle Tzell Cell Company

Headquartered in Tucson, Arizona, the Belle Tzell Cell Company manufactured one standard-size battery for use in portable power tools and in military weapons. Nell Tzell was the company's current president. Her mother, Belle, had retired from active management ten years before, although she and several of Nell's aunts still owned a controlling interest in the company. Belle and her late husband, Del, had founded the firm in 1945, and it had prospered by selling batteries and dry cells to a number of electronics firms that sprung up in the Arizona-New Mexico area after World War II.

Toward the end of her presidency in the late 1960s, Belle had taken one action that increased the capacity of the firm. In response to a bid by the Mexican government, she had moved part of her operations "south of the border" into Nogales to take advantage of low-cost Mexican labor and Belle's fears that both the U.S. and Arizona governments would increase their controls on pollution and would require safer working conditions for employees. The Mexican government provided a low-cost loan and required Belle to enter into a partnership with a Mexican citizen who would own 51 per cent of the Belle Tzell Cell Company's Mexican operation. The operation that Belle moved to Nogales was the facility for making lead panels. This operation involved combining strong acids with lead, and was considered hazardous to employee health. Noxious vapors damaged the workers' lungs, and the acidic wastes left over from the curing processes were dumped into a nearby stream bed, killing aquatic life for at least 10 miles downstream.

Belle retired a few months after the Nogales plant went into production and told Nell that it would take "only a few more months to get the bugs out." That was over 10 years ago, and, if anything, the bugs had increased. Although actual production costs remained low and the Mexican plant was still nonunion, its production was very undependable. Because it was under Mexican ownership, the Mexican who owned 51 per cent of the stock insisted that most of plant's management be Mexican also. However, neither the Mexican who owned the 51 per cent of the stock nor most Mexicans capable of managing the operation cared to live in Nogales. They preferred the bright lights of Mexico City. The plant's work force was continually changing. Despite the fact that wages were high by Mexican standards, new workers soon suffered either burns from acid splashes or lung irritation because of the fumes. Also, because Nogales was just south of the U.S.–Mexican border, Mexican workers would often cross the border illegally and work at higher paying jobs in the United States until they were found by the U.S. immigration authorities and deported. The border-crossing situation to the Mexicans was like a revolving door. Arizona employers would encourage Mexicans to enter the United States illegally because they would work for lower wages than their U.S. counterparts. When the U.S. employers no longer needed the Mexican help, they would complain to the U.S. Immigration Service about the large number of illegal aliens in their area.

Although Nell would have preferred to close her Nogales lead panel plant, the cost of establishing such a facility in the U.S. made such a move impossible. This was because of the new worker safety requirements of the federal government, operating through OSHA, and the new controls on air and water pollution administered by the U.S. Environmental Protection Agency (EPA). Transportation costs for delivering acids to the plant would also be very high because carriers considered them to be an extremely "hazardous" material requiring specialized, expensive trailer tanks to avoid acid spills.

The final problem faced by Nell with her Nogales plant was referred to euphemistically as the "Mexican work ethic." Never before had Nell realized the number of religious holidays celebrated in Mexico. At such times, output would halt. Although the Mexicans were capable of turning out high-quality products, lax supervision resulted in wide variations in the quality of the final product. Sometimes this would not be noticed until the workers in the Tucson plant attempted to install the lead plates that had been received from Nogales.

Relatively little of the Tzell company's operations were in Tucson. Their offices were on the second floor of a building, cramped on a narrow lot with little room for expansion. Downstairs, the lead plates from Nogales were combined with printed circuits from Taiwan and placed inside plastic cases purchased from one of several suppliers in Tucson. Each day's production filled two 35-foot trailers parked at the north end of the building. At night, the two trailers would be delivered to various buyers. The Tucson plant was operating at capacity and rarely ever caught up with sales. Several times Nell had wanted to increase the number of production lines, but she was unable to expand the building at its present site. In addition, Belle and her aunts who still controlled the company were unwilling to allow her to relocate to a new site or to a larger plant because the financial resources required for the move would cut into their current incomes. Because of their ages, they were not willing to forego current income for some anticipated future gain.

The present Tucson plant was a long, narrow building, set in a north-south direction between two parallel streets. The south fronted on 17th Street and contained a receiving dock which was built to accommodate only one trailer. There was no street parking allowed on 17th, and neighbors would complain to the Tucson Police Department if a truck parked on 17th Street for even a few minutes. The building stretched north, with the east and west sides within one foot of their respective lot lines. The north end of the building was on 16th Street. Here was a large parking lot used by employees and the loading dock that could accommodate three trailers. Prior to the opening of the Nogales plant, the employee parking lot filled every day, with all 32 slots occupied. Today, only about 10 slots were used because employees were using car pools and local buses. Even Nell was in a carpool, sharing rides with David Kupferman, her operations manager, who lived in the same apartment complex as she did, but on the side without a view.

Kupferman had only worked for the Tzell Company for a few weeks, and as he and Nell were driving from work one day, she said: "Dave, you know I'm caught between two rocks and two hard places. My mother and aunts won't let me expand here in Tucson, and our Nogales plant produces more ulcers than anything else. Your predecessor left because the strain of coordinating the two plants was too great. Believe it or not, the majority of our operations take place in Nogales. You'd better visit there, soon, to see what it's like."

"I can hardly wait," responded Kupferman. "After my last argument with them over poor quality, I'm afraid they'll dunk my head in an acid vat if I ever set foot inside that plant. How come you became so dependent upon Mexico for your operations?"

Nell explained the reasons, already given here, and added: "For many years these savings gave us a competitive edge. In cost or money terms, two thirds of our operation is down in Nogales."

"Two thirds?" asked Kupferman. "That seems high. How do you figure it?"

"Look at it this way," said Nell. "We take in a little over $4 million dollars per year, or about $16,000 per working day. We spend about $15,000 per working day. Of that, about $10,000 is spent at Nogales for labor, raw materials, and overhead. We spend just over $1,000 dollars a day moving the lead plates from Nogales here, although $800 of that is import duties on the lead plates. Here in Tucson, our manufacturing operation takes only about $3,000 per day; about two thirds for labor and one third for the printed circuits and plastic battery cases. The remainder of the money goes for companywide overhead, and for profit."

"I see," said Kupferman. "How, then, do you see the problem?"

Nell answered: "First of all, our problems are caused by our success in selling. Right now we have a backlog of orders, but I am unable to expand capacity either here or in Nogales. Mother and my aunts won't allow major capital improvements, and while I might be able to build a small addition to the north of the Tucson plant the cost would be prohibitive, especially when one considers the small increase in capacity that would result."

"It's too bad your family won't let you expand more," offered Kupferman.

"Actually, I don't blame them," said Tzell. "Our business is really volatile and I've also been unable to interest serious outside investors in helping me expand. Several bankers told me that I'd have to get my production coordinated better before I should think about either expanding or borrowing much outside money. Right now, the banks will loan me any working capital I want at 12 per cent, if it's secured by inventories or equipment. However, I'm unable to assemble enough funds for any type of expansion.

"I still don't understand your coordination problem," said Kupferman. "Your Nogales plant produces one trailerload of battery plates per day, which is exactly the input you need for a day's output at Tucson. The battery plates can be trucked at night, and if you can get your quality control act together at Nogales you'd have a smooth, continuous operation."

"I hate to say this," said Nell, "but your predecessor said just about the same thing eight months ago. And like you, he thought that quality control at Nogales was the key to solving my problem."

"So what did he do wrong?" asked Kupferman.

"He was going to use a two-pronged approach, which I'll tell you about in the office," said Nell as she wheeled her Porsche from 16th Street into the parking lot at the north end of the Tucson plant. "Get me a cup of coffee and we'll continue this conversation in my office," she said as they climbed the stairs to the second floor offices.

Kupferman got two cups of coffee, walked into her office, and sat down. Nell was looking through her messages and exclaimed, "Dammit, it happened again! We just got penalized $3,000 because of a late delivery to Jedson Electronic Tools. They, then, were late on delivering a government order and decided we were responsible because our delivery was late, which it was. Their purchase order to us had a penalty clause in it and now they're going to collect. This is exactly the problem we have to lick! The Nogales plant either misses making a shipment or sends a load of such poor quality that we can't use it right away. We then assign our people here to other tasks for the day, such as inserting only the printed circuits into the plastic cases. They do this until the battery plates arrive, and then they add all the battery plates. At the end of two days we're caught up, except that yesterday we made no deliveries and yesterday's promised output is one day late. That's why we lose customers. To them, we're just another supplier of components. Right now the industry practice is to specify a delivery date, with cost penalties included for either early or late deliveries. Indeed, some of our customers are adopting JIT inventory systems and are trying to specify a sixty-minute window during which they'll accept our daily deliveries. Some of our major competitors are already dancing to this tune, and we will have have no choice but to follow."

"How often do we have this kind of problem where we can't make deliveries because of some foul-up in our quality?", asked Kupferman.

"For a long time, it was only once a month or so," responded Tzell, "but as we reached our plants' capacity and there was less slack, the problem has been happening almost weekly. One week, about two months ago, we hit the jackpot and had three days of bad production in a row. That threw us out of kilter for nearly two weeks, even after paying overtime both here and at Nogales. That's when your predecessor's ulcer started bleeding and he left. Too bad, too, because I think he was just about ready to solve our problem. Too bad his stomach lining couldn't have lasted a few months longer."

"What changes here had he intended to make?" asked Kupferman.

"Tell you what," responded Nell, "you get us both some more coffee and I'll continue." David complied, and Nell continued, "Your predecessor had studied probability in college and had computed the chances of foul-ups in Nogales occurring one right after the other. He calculated that we should close down our Tucson plant for five days or have the Nogales plant five days of overtime so that they could produce a five-day supply of lead battery plates. He said that if we kept the Nogales plant scheduled so that there were always five days worth of plates between Nogales and Tucson, we would never have to be out of usable lead battery plates here in Tucson."

"If his calculations were accurate, why haven't you implemented his plan?" asked Kupferman.

"We couldn't figure out where to store the approximately five loads of battery plates," responded Ms. Tzell. "It's more complicated than you think. Here, let me read to you your predecessor's memo, written while he was recovering from surgery, no less. It says, and I quote: 'There are four alternatives: warehousing in Nogales, warehousing here in Tucson, or leasing five truck trailers and parking them either outside the Nogales plant or in the 16th Street parking lot here in Tucson.' " Nell looked at David directly and continued, "David, what I want you to do is to figure out the costs of these four alternatives and get back to me with a recommendation."

Kupferman took his empty coffee cup and walked back to his office and started gathering the cost figures Nell had asked for. He discovered that to warehouse the five loads of lead battery plates in Nogales would cost $300 per week, plus $120 per week for local drayage in Nogales, i.e., trucking the plates from the plant to the warehouse. To truck the plates directly from the Nogales plant to a Tucson warehouse rather than to the Tzell Tucson plant was the second alternative. Few Tucson warehouses wanted to touch the business for fear that the plates would contaminate other merchandise they were storing. The best quote David could get was for $350 per week plus a requirement that Tzell provide a bond to protect the warehouseman from damages the plates might cause. Local drayage costs within Tucson from the warehouse to Tzell's 17th Street receiving dock would be $150 per week.

The trailer idea involved leasing five trailers, loading them with battery plates, and parking them at either the Nogales plant or at the 16th Street lot of Tzell's Tucson plant. Trailers could be leased and licensed for use in both Mexico and Arizona for $3,000 per year each. In addition, a used truck-tractor, costing approximately $5,000, would have to be purchased and used for shifting trailers around whichever of the two plants where they were stored.

The advantage of storing the trailers at Nogales was to delay the payment of import duties of about $800 per trailer load of battery plates. However, a problem with the current system was that Mexican border agents, sensing the urgency in the Tzell shipments, attempted to shake down the Tzell drivers to let the trailers exit from Mexico. Trailers were subject to delays and sometimes would be searched thoroughly to make certain that they were carrying no works of art or Mexican national treasures. One Mexican agent inspected trailers ever so slowly, complaining aloud that the reason he moved slowly was that he was depressed by the fact that Christmas was coming (no matter what month it happened to be) and that he lacked sufficient money to buy gifts for all of his family.

Kupferman had yet to visit the Nogales plant, but before presenting his findings to Tzell, he wanted to make certain that the parking lot at the Nogales plant was fenced. He phoned the Mexican plant manager, who said very little until he realized that Kupferman was not calling to complain about something. He answered Kupferman's query by saying that the yard was not fenced but that it would be possible to park the loaded trailers with their closed rear doors against a solid masonry wall, making entry impossible. "Besides," he added, "this plant has such a bad reputation for causing illness and injury that no local thief would come within a mile of it."

Kupferman was trying to think of a witty response and the Nogales manager continued, "but you said 'up to five trailers.' Why so many?"

Kupferman then told him of his predecessor's calculations that the Nogales plant should produce five days of output in advance of that needed by the Tucson plant.

"Why so many?" repeated the Mexican manager.

"To make sure that Tucson never has to shut down or be late with orders," answered Kupferman. "The only reason we have problems here is because of delayed or poor-quality shipments from you. When Tucson falls behind, we can't make deliveries and that costs us money."

"Nonsense!" responded the Mexican. "You blame all your problems on us. Let me tell you two things, Gringo. First, not all production delays are caused down here. It's just that we're not in the same building as the home office, and we tend to get blamed for everything. Second, because the Tucson plant makes a single standard product, it would be cheaper to have them produce a day or two's inventory in advance, ready to use in case *either* the Tucson plant or my operation fouls up. You'll have to excuse me now. We've just had another acid spill. Adios, amigo."

Kupferman heard a click and then a humming sound. He hung up. He decided to walk to Nell's office and tell her what the Mexican plant manager had said.

Nell admitted that the Mexican was correct, "just a bit," about some of the delays being at the Tucson plant. In fact, she conceded that Kupferman's predecessor had overlooked the problems at the Tucson assembly line when he made his calculations that the Nogales plant produce a five-day advance supply of battery plates as a cushion. She told Kupferman to start over and assume that delays could occur by conditions in either plant or both. She felt that Kupferman would find that sales should be cut back for a few days so that either or both plants could turn out some advance production that would serve as a continual cushion or safety stock. She wanted enough inventory in reserve so that the Tzell Cell Company could fill 99 per cent of all orders on time. Kupferman would have six months to set up the system and six months to test and "debug" it. After that, he would be expected to maintain a 99 per cent performance level of filling orders on time.

During the next few days of ride sharing, Tzell and Kupferman talked about everything except work. Nell commented that she missed seeing David at the swimming pool and that she had heard two other girls at poolside asking what had happened to "that cute young fellow with the beautiful bod." Kupferman blushed, and responded that he had been spending his time indoors, studying probability.

After several weeks, Kupferman's tan completely faded, but he felt the loss was worthwhile since he had finally calculated the probabilities that would allow Tzell Cell Company to maintain Nell's required 99 per cent level of on-time deliveries. First of all, his predecessor had been correct, insofar as he had calculated. One solution was to have the Nogales plant produce five days' worth of battery cell plates in advance of the Tucson plant. This was because the Tucson plant was responsible for only two of the delivery delays in a year of 250 working days. However, Kupferman also made calculations about the sizes of completed stocks for the Tucson plant to manufacture in advance and keep as a safety stock cushion. If the Tucson plant produced and maintained as safety stock one days' output of completed batteries, then the Nogales plant would only have to maintain a four-day lead in production of lead battery plates ahead of their use in Tucson. If the Tucson plant produced in advance and maintained as safety stock two days' output of completed batteries, then the Nogales plant would have to produce only two days' worth of battery plates in advance of their use in the Tucson plant. And, if the Tucson plant made three days' output in advance and held it as safety stock, then the Nogales plant would not have to produce a surplus of plates in advance of what was required each day at Tucson. That is, each night the truck would leave with the Nogales' output and drive to Tucson where the plates would be used the next day. Even if there were problems with the Nogales shipment, there would be a three-day safety stock of finished batteries in Tucson.

Kupferman intended to determine warehousing costs for the safety stocks of completed batteries in Tucson, but Ms. Tzell told him to plan on using the trailer idea instead. The trailers would be parked in the 16th Street lot. At night they would be parked so that none of their doors were exposed. For $3,000 the lot's fence could be made more secure and a gate would be added. Nell Tzell told Kupferman that deliveries would be made out of the trailer that had been parked the longest (usually two or three days). This would ensure orderly inventory turnover, which was important since batteries have a limited life.

Kupferman took a clipboard with a pad of paper and made four columns, one for each of the alternatives. The column headings looked like this:

I	II	III	IV
5 days' worth of plates in Nogales	4 days' worth of plates in Nogales	2 days' worth of plates in Nogales	no extra plates in Nogales
no extra batteries in Tucson	one days' worth of batteries in Tucson	2 days' worth of batteries in Tucson	3 days' worth of batteries in Tucson

Each alternative would give Nell's firm the ability to provide a 99 per cent level of on-time order filling.

Question One: What are the total inventory carrying costs of alternative I?

Question Two: What are the total inventory carrying costs of alternative II?

Question Three: What are the total inventory carrying costs of alternative III?

Question Four: What are the total inventory carrying costs of alternative IV?

Question Five: Which alternative do you think Kupferman should recommend? Why?

Question Six: Nell "wanted enough inventory in reserve so that the Tzell Cell Company could fill 99 per cent of all orders on time." This is, as you may recall, a customer service standard. How reasonable is a 99 per cent level? Why not, say, a 95 per cent level? How would Nell and Kupferman determine the relative advantages and disadvantages of both the 95 per cent and the 99 per cent service levels? What kind of cost calculations would they have to make?

Question Seven: Jedson Electronic Tools invoked a penalty clause on a purchase order that Tzell Cell Company had accepted and the Tzell Cell Company had to forfeit $3,000. Draft, for Nell's signature, a memo indicating when—and under what conditions—the Belle Tzell Cell Company should accept penalty clauses in purchase orders covering "missed" delivery times.

CASE 11-2

HDT Truck Company

HDT Truck Company is a small firm that has been located in Crown Point, Indiana since 1910. Its only product is large trucks, built to individual customer specifications. The firm once produced automobiles and light trucks as well, but dropped out of the auto business in 1924 and out of the light truck business in 1937. The firm nearly went completely out of business at that time, but by 1940 its fortunes were buoyed by receipt of several military contracts for "tank retrievers," large wheeled vehicles that could pull a disabled tank onto a low trailer and haul it to a location where it could be repaired.

Since World War II, HDT manufactured only large "off-the-road" vehicles, including airport snowplows, airport crash trucks, oil field drilling equipment and the like. HDT purchased all components from small manufacturers who were still clustered in the Milwaukee-Detroit-Toledo–Cleveland area. Essentially, all HDT does is assemble the components into a specialized vehicle containing the combination of frame, power plant, transmission, axles, and cab that were necessary to do the job.

The "assembly" line was relatively slow moving. After wheels were attached to the frame and axles, the night shift labor force would push the chassis along to its next "station" on the line so it would be in place for the next day's shift. By using one shift, two trucks could be assembled each day. If large orders for identical trucks were involved, it was possible to assemble three trucks per day. Quality declined whenever the pace became quicker. HDT officials had decided they could not grow and became satisfied with their niche in the very heavy truck market. With only two exceptions, since 1960 they had always had at least a four-month backlog of orders. In the 1960s, their best market had been airports, but since 1970 their best market had been for oil field equipment, first for the North Slope in Alaska and then for the Middle East. This case discusses a situation that faced HDT in the mid-1970s.

In late 1975, HDT received an order for fifty heavy trucks to be used in the oil fields of Iraq. The terms of sale were delivery on or before July 1, 1976, at the port of Al Basrah, Iraq. Specifically, HDT would receive $52,000 per truck in U.S. funds FAS (free along side) the discharging vessel in Al Basrah, which meant HDT was responsible for all transportation costs up until the time and point the trucks were discharged from the ship's tackle at Al Basrah. Once each truck was unloaded, HDT would be paid for it.

Chris Reynolds, production manager at HDT, estimated that production could start approximately April 1, 1976, and the order would take 18 working days to complete. Because weekends were involved, all fifty trucks would be completed by April 20–25. Reynolds thought that May 1, 1976, was a more realistic completion date because he had always found it difficult to restrict the assembly line to constructing trucks for only one account. The reason for this was that Vic Guillou, HDT's sales manager, liked to have trucks being built for as many accounts as possible on the assembly line at any one time. Prospective buyers frequently visited the plant and were always more impressed when they could see a diverse collection of models being built for a wide range of uses.

Norman Pon, HDT's treasurer, always wanted to give priority to building trucks that were being sold on an FOB plant basis because that would improve his cash flow position. At the time the $52,000 price had been set on the truck sale to Iraq, Pon had argued (unsuccessfully) that the price was too low. Guillou, on the other hand, argued that the sale was necessary since the Arab world represented a "growth market" by anyone's definition and he wanted HDT trucks there. HDT's president, Gordon Robertson, had sided with Guillou. Robertson thought that Pon was a good treasurer but too much of a "worrier" when it came to making important decisions. Pon, in turn, thought that Robertson had yet to shed the "playboy" image he had acquired in the 1960s when his late father was president of HDT. Pon had lost count of the number of times the elder Robertson had needed cash in order to buy his son's way out of some embarrassing situation. Guillou was young Robertson's fraternity roommate in college and Pon thought the two of them shared a similar love of "life in the fast lane."

At the time the order was signed in 1975, Guillou argued that the FAS destination port represented the best terms of sale because ocean charter rates were declining because of an oversupply of tanker tonnage and the reopening of the Suez Canal. Guillou predicted that by mid-1976, charter rates would be so low that the cheapest method of transport would be to load all fifty trucks on one vessel. Pon countered that HDT should try to make a profit only from the manufacture of trucks since nobody in the firm knew much about ocean shipping. Robertson, who was a gambler at heart, of course, disagreed.

It was now March 1976, and Reynolds had the fifty-truck order scheduled to be on the line from April 2–29, which represented 2½ trucks per working day. Other work was scheduled for the assembly line at the same time so the production schedule was considered to be "firm." Component parts for the oil field trucks and for the other trucks were already arriving. Right now, orders were backlogged for over seven months, the highest figure since 1967. This was due, almost in total, to Guillou's additional sales of oil field equipment to Arab producers. Three separate orders were involved and totalled 115 trucks.

Robertson and Guillou left Crown Point for an industry convention in San Diego. Robertson phoned from San Diego that he and Guillou had decided to vacation in Mexico for a while before returning to Crown Point. Robertson knew that HDT could function in his absence and knew that with Pon "watching the store," the company's assets would be safe. Several days later, a Mexican postcard postmarked "Tijuana" arrived saying that both were enjoying Mexico and might stay longer than initially planned.

Pon was relieved to learn that Guillou and Robertson would be gone for a longer time and immediately began wondering what types of bills they were accumulating in Mexico and for which ones they would want company reimbursement. Both had several credit cards belonging to the company. Based on experience, Pon also expected Robertson to phone for cash about once a week. As usual, Pon started wondering how paying for the Robertson/Guillou vacation venture would affect HDT's cash flow. Pon looked at his cash flow projections, which were always made up for six weeks in advance, in this case through the first of April when some of the bills for components of the oil-field trucks would come due. In fact, if Reynolds' schedule were adhered to, all the components would be on hand by April 10 and, if HDT were to receive the customary discounts, all of the components would have to be paid for in the period between April 8 and April 20 (HDT received a 1 per cent discount for goods paid for within ten days of actual or requested receipt, whichever came later). For a moment, Pon thought that the worst might happen, i.e., the component bills would be due the same time as Robertson's and Guillou's travel bill, so he called the Crown Point Bank and Trust Company, where HDT had a line of credit and found that the current rate was 10 per cent per annum. He then asked Bob Vanderpool, who was HDT's traffic manager, when the oil field trucks would arrive in Iraq.

"I don't know," was Vanderpool's reply. "I assumed Guillou had arranged for transportation at the time you decided to charge $52,000 per truck. But I'll check further." He did and phoned back to tell Pon that Guillou's secretary could find nothing in the files to indicate that Guillou had checked out charter rates.

"That figures," muttered Pon. "Would you mind doing some checking?"

Vanderpool said yes he would mind doing some checking. Pon then suggested to him that there were several other newer orders also destined for the Arab countries, so Vanderpool should start thinking about widening his area of expertise. Vanderpool reluctantly agreed, and Pon heard nothing from him for a few days until Vanderpool passed him in the hall and said the assignment was much more time-consuming than he had imagined.

One week later, Vanderpool said he had done as much as he could and would turn the figures over to Pon. He also said that he (Vanderpool) did not have the authority to charter a ship and suggested that Pon determine who could, in Robertson's absence. Later that day, Vanderpool came to Pon's office with a thick file. "It looks like you've been doing a lot of figuring," said Pon.

"No, not me," said Vanderpool, "but two outsiders. One is Bob Guider, an international freight forwarder in Chicago who we use for our export parts shipments. And he put me in touch with Eddie Quan, a New York ship broker who is on top of the charter market. We have two alternatives."

"What are they?" asked Pon.

"Well," answered Vanderpool, "the St. Lawrence Seaway will open in mid-April so we could use it. The problem is that the Seaway route is circuitous, especially to reach the Arab countries. Also, there aren't many scheduled Seaway sailings to that area, and because the Seaway will just be opening again, cargo space is hard to come by. Therefore, if we're not going to charter a ship, the best bet is to use Baltimore."

"What about chartering a ship?" asked Pon, "why not use Baltimore for that?"

"In theory, we could," answered Vanderpool, "but Quan says the size ship we want is rather small and not likely to be sailing into Baltimore. We could arrange to 'share' a ship with another party, but many bulk cargos are pretty dusty and might not be compatible with our vehicles. Quan says there is one foreign vessel entering into the Great Lakes in April which is still looking for an outbound charter. Seaway vessels, you know, are somewhat smaller because of the lock restrictions. If we want to charter that vessel, we'll have to move quickly, because if somebody else charters her, she's gone."

"What kind of vessel is it?" asked Pon.

"The vessel's name is the Nola Pino, the same name as a French movie actress in the 1960s. You may recall that some Greek shipping magnate named the vessel after her, but his wife made him give up both Nola Pino the actress and Nola Pino the ship. At present, she's scheduled to be in Chicago the last week in April with a load of cocoa beans and ready for outbound loading May 1. Quan thinks we could charter her for $1,200 per day for 30 days which would be enough time for her to load, transit the Seaway, reach Al Basrah, and discharge the trucks by May 29 or 30."

"Tell me about the alternative," said Pon.

"Baltimore has fairly frequent sailings to the area we want to reach," said Vanderpool. "We could load two trucks per day on rail cars here and send them to Baltimore. There are two ships a week scheduled from Baltimore to Al Basrah. It would take the trucks an average of four days to reach Baltimore where they would wait an average of three days to be loaded aboard ship. The figure should be 3½ days, but the railroad will hustle if they know we're trying to connect with an outgoing sailing. Sailing time to Al Basrah averages 15 days, a little more, a little less, depending on the amount of cargo to be handled at ports in between."

"That averages to 22 days per truck," stated Pon who had been putting the figures in his new pocket calculator. "What are the charges?"

Vanderpool answered: "It costs $60 to load and block two trucks on a flatcar, which is, of course, $30 apiece as long as they move in pairs. Sticking to pairs, the rail rate for two on a flatcar totals $896 to Baltimore. Handling at Baltimore is $100 per truck and ocean freight rate from Baltimore to Al Basrah is $720 per truck. We also have to buy insurance, which is about $75 per truck."

"That totals $1,395," said Pon, after consulting his calculator, "What are the costs if we charter the Nola Pino? You said it would be $36,000 for the vessel. What else is involved?"

"There are two ways of getting the trucks to port," said Vanderpool. "There are no 'export' rates to Chicago, but the domestic ones aren't so bad. The loading and blocking would be only $20 per truck because we'd be doing all fifty at one time. The rail rate per truck would average out to $90 each and it would take one day for them to reach Chicago and another day to be loaded. We'd be tying up a wharf for one day and the wharfage charge runs $1 per foot and the Nola Pino is 535 feet long. We'd be responsible for loading and stowing the cargo and this would cost $4,000 for all fifty trucks. The Seaway tolls are 90 cents per ton or, in our case, $27 per truck. At Al Basrah, the unloading costs will be $2,100 for the entire vessel. Marine insurance will be $105 per truck."

"Are there any other alternatives?" asked Pon.

"The only other one that came close was to drive the trucks from here to Chicago," answered Vanderpool. "We would have needed temporary licenses and a convoy permit and pay to have the fuel tank on each truck drained before it was loaded.

Exhibit 11-1 Map of Northeastern U.S.

The problem was that the convoy would cross state lines, and we would have needed temporary licenses and permits in Illinois as well."

"Do me one favor," said Pon. "Please call Frank Wood, our outside counsel, and ask him what steps we have to go through to charter a ship. Tell him I'm especially concerned about the liability. Give him Quan's phone number. I want to make sure there are no more costs involved. If Robertson's fooling around is on schedule, he'll be phoning me asking that I cable cash. I'd really appreciate it if you would summarize what you've told me in two columns, with the charter costs on the left and the overland-Baltimore cost column on the right. Then when Robertson calls, I can ask him to decide."

"One question," asked Vanderpool.

"Shoot," responded Pon.

"Why should the charter figures be on the left?"

"Because on a map (See Exhibit 11-1), Chicago is to the left of Baltimore and that's the only way I'll keep them straight when I'm talking on the phone."

Question One: Assume you are Vanderpool. Draft the comparison Pon just asked for.
Question Two: Which routing of the two would you recommend? Why?
Question Three: Assume that the buyer in Iraq has made other large purchases in the United States and is considering consolidating all of his purchases and loading them on to one large ship, which he will charter. He contacts HDT and—although acknowledging his commitment to buy FAS Al Basrah—asks how much HDT would subtract from the $52,000 per truck price if the selling terms were changed to FOB HDT's Crown Point plant. How much of a cost reduction do you think HDT should offer to him? Under what terms and conditions?
Question Four: This case was written some years ago when interest rates were lower.

Assume, instead, that the year was 1980 and that HDT's line of credit with the Crown Point Bank and Trust Company would cost about 18 per cent per annum. How, if at all, does this affect the cost calculations in the answer to question one?

Question Five: Is there an interest rate that would make HDT change from one routing to another? If so, what is it?

Question Six: Assume it is 1980 and the cost to HDT of borrowing money is 18 per cent per year. Because the buyer will pay for trucks as they are delivered, would it be advantageous for HDT to pay overtime to speed up production, ship the trucks as they were finished via the Port of Baltimore, and collect their payment earlier?

Part **III**

Analyzing, Designing, and Implementing a Physical Distribution/Logistics System

The previous chapters presented an overview of physical distribution and logistics and focused on all of the individual components of a PD/L system. Part III will examine methods of analyzing, implementing, and controlling the logistics concept as used by the firm.

Chapter 12 focuses on the techniques involved in PD/L systems analysis and design. These techniques are designed to isolate inefficiencies in a firm's PD/L operation so that corrective action can be taken.

Chapter 13 examines various control systems that must be implemented to ensure that the logistics system operates efficiently. Controls are also needed to minimize losses from pilferage and theft.

Chapter 14 is based on combining the system one might have designed in Chapter 12, along with the controls that Chapter 13 indicated were necessary. The result—for many firms—would be a more integrated logistical approach. Chapter 14 will discuss various alternative organizational strategies and their implementation.

The concluding chapter, 15, speculates on some of the changes that may well confront the logistics manager between now and the end of this century.

A thinker, aided by a computer, was pictured on a consultant's brochure entitled "Managing Complexity: Logistical/Marketing Strategies. . . ."

(*Credit:* Ernst & Whinney/Shycon Associates, Inc., Waltham, Massachusetts)

Physical Distribution and Logistics System Analysis and Design

General Motors Corp. will let a computer decide where to put its $3.5 billion Saturn Corp. manufacturing complex unless a tie-breaker is required, a top official says.

San Francisco Chronicle
May 4, 1985

In the future, ... the primary problem of business may not be the promotion and marketing of end goods, but instead the maintenance of profitability by the effective management of higher distribution costs resulting from raw material shortages, high priced energy, and other crises. As a consequence the scope of business logistics management may be extended to include the physical supply of raw materials and the maintenance of an equilibrium throughout the pre-production, production, and marketing processes. *(Emphasis added.)*

Roy Dale Voorhees and
Merrill Kim Sharp
Transportation Journal
Fall 1978

What are the initial results of our efforts to streamline distribution and warehousing at Firestone? We think the numbers help tell the story: In October of 1979, finished goods inventories were valued at $528 million, an 8.2-to-1 turnover ratio. Last October (1982) finished goods inventories were valued at $332 million, with a 9.0-to-1 turnover ratio.

Leon R. Brodeur, President
Firestone Tire & Rubber Co.
Handling & Shipping Management
Presidential Issue, 1983–1984

Once the new deregulation act was signed into law, we put into motion our plan for intercorporate hauling immediately. The new program yielded more than seven hundred truckload backhaul opportunities in the first year and provided annual savings of $1 million.

Charles F. Dransfield
North American Philips Corp,
Handling & Shipping Management
Presidential Issue, 1984–1985

Key Terms

- Systems analysis
- Industry standards
- Logistics system design
- System constraints
- System objectives
- System goals
- Product audit
- Existing facilities audit
- Vendor audit
- Customer audit
- Competition audit
- PERT
- Simulation
- Design implementation

Learning Objectives

- To examine the problems and opportunities involved in system analysis
- To relate the importance of industry standards to system analysis
- To discuss the five steps involved in designing a PD/L system
- To explain the utilization of PERT and simulation in data analysis

Introduction

Because few things in the business world are static, a system that optimized yesterday's situation may be less than optimal today. Logistics, of course, is no exception. Changes in the price of fuel have changed the relative transportation costs paid out by distribution operations. Markets are constantly shifting; even public utilities do not consider their demand patterns to be fixed. Consider, for example, all of the changes suddenly taking place in the telephone industry.

As used here, the phrase *systems analysis* means an orderly and planned observation of one or more segments in the logistics network to determine how well each segment and, ultimately, the entire system is functioning. Analysis can be a simple operation, such as a "time and motion" study of individuals who handle incoming freight at a receiving dock. Or, it can be nationwide, or even worldwide, in scope, with the idea of completely redesigning a firm's entire logistics system, including its relationships with many long-time suppliers and customers. The observations provide data that will be subjected to statistical analysis. In some situations, the next step will be to incorporate the data into programmed models of the logistics network. A model *simulates* some real-world condition to determine how well the present system, or a contemplated system, would respond to various happenings. Based on the simulation and other analytical analysis performed, the final procedure may involve redesigning the entire logistics system.

Many firms have staff personnel who conduct systems analysis projects throughout the firm. Other firms prefer to use outside consultants because they can be more objective. Although consultants vary in quality, they bring outside viewpoints and broader perspectives to bear on most problems.

Problems Involved in Systems Analysis

The focusing of a logistics system analysis (or audit) is always the first and possibly most difficult part of a systems analysis. Should the focus be the work practices at the receiving dock, or the dock's location in the building, or the building's location in the system? Are the products being handled properly? Are customer service standards adequate, or should the order-processing function be automated? What is our competition doing? The types of analyses that could be performed are limited only by the analyst's imagination and the amount of money his or her firm or client is willing to spend for the analysis.

Another problem of focus deals with the time span for the implementation of new ideas. Some improvements might deal only with specific adjustments within the network without altering the network itself. Ordering procedures or packaging may be changed, or a decision might be made to link all warehouses by computer. More basic changes, such as changes in the number and location of distribution centers and warehouses, take more time to implement. There might be a period of overlap when the old system is being phased out while the new one is being phased in. Maintaining levels of customer service in such a period would be difficult. Long-range changes (taking from two to five years to implement) result from decisions to redesign a firm's entire logistics system.

Friction is inherent in any attempt to analyze and/or redesign a distribution system. Operations managers are typically performing as well as they can. Systems analysts, whether employees of the firm or outside consultants, cannot continue in business by telling every client that all aspects of the present operation are perfect. If analysts did so, they could no longer justify their functions. Thus, their goals and the goals of operating personnel and operating managers differ. Labor may view with suspicion any suggestion that appears to be a "speed up" or that reduces the hours or numbers of workers needed, or hints that existing facilities might be closed.

Partial Systems Analyses

It is often not feasible to examine all functioning aspects of a system. What follows are examples of analysis focused on only a single aspect of logistics. Sometimes, for the purposes intended, such partial analysis is sufficient. However, its confined focus is also a limitation, because whatever findings are developed are also narrow. They cannot be used to improve an entire system. A situation of suboptimization, such as discussed in Chapter 1, may occur if improvements are made in a subsystem without understanding their impact on the total system.

Figure 12-1 illustrates a large metal basket with fold-down sides mounted on a pallet. It provides the advantages of unit-load handling while allowing

Figure 12-1 Metal Basket Container Mounted on Pallet

a wide variation in the size and shape of the individual cartons (or smaller building blocks). The use of such equipment would probably be justified after analysis of practices at *both* the distribution center where they are loaded *and* at the retail outlets where they are received and unloaded. The combined savings in *both* the warehouse and retail stores must be sufficient to justify the investment in the equipment. If the savings are not evenly divided between both the warehouse and the retail outlets, the party enjoying the greater share of savings may have to compensate the other, in order for the other party to agree to make whatever changes are needed to accommodate the new equipment. Such decisions would be the result of partial systems analysis. The only danger posed by making decisions based on partial analysis of a system is that one might inadvertently commit the entire system without having tested whether the entire system would benefit. An example would be a commitment to use only railroads for outbound shipments while the firm's marketing planners might be deciding that the best potential for sales growth was customers who did not, for some reason or other, have access to railroad service.

Partial analysis is one of the building blocks of total systems analysis because it is difficult to measure a system's overall performance without measuring and understanding the performance of the various components that make up the entire system. Partial analysis contributes toward understanding how an entire system functions. Several examples will be cited. An explanation of why the partial analysis was performed will also be offered.

Customer Profitability Analysis

The following example deals with a route-analysis system that a large dairy chain used to help its delivery personnel analyze the profitability of each stop on their routes. The accompanying forms are filled out by hand. Although both the forms and the procedures appear unsophisticated by today's standards, they force the individual involved to focus directly on the question of what makes a customer profitable or unprofitable. Figure 12-2 is a time tally sheet completed by the driver/salesman's supervisor on a day he travels along, with a stopwatch.[1]

The data collected on the form shown in Figure 12-2 and from the driver/salesman's monthly records were then transferred to several other forms so that they could be analyzed more critically. Figure 12-3 is a tally sheet showing each customer's dollar volume across the top and the number of deliveries the customer receives along the vertical axis. It uses the same data and points out which customers are "overserviced." High dollar volume combined with a low number of deliveries per month is the goal. Thus, entries toward the upper right-hand corner of the chart show more desirable stops. Entries in the lower left corner of the chart represent less desirable stops. A step downward diagonal line is drawn between the upper left and lower right-hand corners. The inference drawn is that entries below the diagonal should be shifted either upward or to the right or both.

One of the reasons these forms are relatively unsophisticated is that the driver/salesman is an independent or semi-independent operator. He both sells and delivers and decides who should and who should not receive what type of service. Because he is paid a salary plus commission, the commission portion of his pay is an incentive not to waste time. However, the dairy is interested in time utilization because it pays the salary part of his wages. Rather than tell him who he can and cannot serve, they have to use an approach such as the one just shown to demonstrate to him how his time can be reallocated in a more productive manner.

[1] The dairy supplying these forms asked to not be identified. See also, Donald F. Wood, "The Driver/Salesman and His Changing Role," *Proceedings, Transportation Research Forum,* 1973 (Oxford, Ind.: Cross Co., 1973), pp. 631–637; and Lynn G. Sleight and James W. Gruebele, "Compensating the 'Human Costs' of Increased Productivity of Fluid Milk Drivers," *American Journal of Agricultural Economics* (Aug. 1974), pp. 594–599.

```
AM Starting Time, Load a/o Unload_____ Time  4:10   Salesman _____
Starting Mileage (at plant)_____ 568      Time  4:15   Route # 9
Mileage at First Stop_____ 569            Time  4:18   Super. _____
Mileage at Last Stop_____ 590             Time 11:45
Ending Mileage (at plant)_____ 573        Time 11:54
PM Ending Time, Load a/o Unload  45 min   Time 12:41
Check In (Finish Day)_____ 12 min         Time 12:56
                   Total Time:  Hours 8        Minutes 46
```

	Front Porch	Back Porch	Inside or Ask	Solicitations
Time 1st hour: 5:18	45 35 30 / 55 30 35 / 90 110 120 / 63 55 34 / 88 35 / 50 55 / 45 51 / 45 30	85 / 75 / 85 / 103 / 50	NONE	Hour 6th Time :51 / Hour 6th Time 5:03 / Hour 6th Time 1:01 / Hour___ Time___ / Hour___ Time___ / Hour___ Time___
Miles 1st hour: 574				
Dollars Sold: 30.31 ave 1.13				
Accounts Served: 20 1 5 10				
Time 2nd hour: 6:18	20 35 42 30 / 23 87 38 30 / 35 60 28 50 / 30 30 25 70 / 182 38 48 60 / 30 108 70 / 23 64 82 / 45 44 37	75 / 120 / 60 / 61 / 60	NONE	Collections from Customers not receiving delivery: / Hour 3rd Time 3 0 / Hour 7th Time 33 / Hour___ Time___ / Hour___ Time___ / Hour___ Time___ / Hour___ Time___
Miles 2nd hour: 577				
Dollars Sold: 95 ave 111				
Accounts Served: 20 1 5 10				
Time 3rd hour: 7:18	20 30 40 / 25 38 23 / 42 41 / 55 41 / 70 28 / 92 65 / 22 45	NONE	120	Hour___ Time___ / Hour___ Time___ / Hour___ Time___ / Hour___ Time___ / TOTAL → 3 33 1/2
Miles 3rd hour: 580				
Dollars Sold: 33 ½ ave 193				
Accounts Served: 18 1 9 11	53 / 56 / 120 / 55 / 50 / 60 / 35	85 195 / 128 240 / 95 / 98 / 97 / 120 / 20	Rest/Eating Stops: / Hour 3rd Time 30 0 / Hour 4th Time 11 8 / Hour 7th Time 31 4 / Hour___ Time___ / Hour___ Time___ / TOTAL → 58 min 12 Sec
Time 4th: ___ Dollars Sold: 31½ ave 100 Accounts Served: 10 1 7 19	44 / 30 / 17 / 20 / 21			
Time 6th hour: 10:18	20 / 31 / 10 / 75 / 55 / 58 / 30	73 / 73 / 90 / 45 / 75 / 75 / 126 / 117	170 / 110 / 85 / 60 / 180 / 120 / 120 / 126	REMARKS: / MARK UP Book 1st 7.00 / " " " 2nd 5.20 / " " " 3rd 3:00 / " " " 4th 4:00 / STRAIGHTEN' TRUCK OUT 6.00 / MARK UP Book 6th 3:50 / TOTAL → 28 min 50 Sec
Miles 6th hour: 586				
Dollars Sold: 3401 ave 148				
Accounts Served: 7 1 8 18				
c 7th hour: 11:18	30 / 48 / 23 / 47 / 42	65 / 60 / 63 / 40	77 / 290 / 97 / 85 / 90	BROKE UP 2 TIMES because of DEAD END STREET TOOK = 30 SEC
Miles 7th hour: 589				DELIVERIES 170
Dollars Sold: 14.49 ave 104				Dollar Sales 191.53
Accounts Served: 5 1 4 15				COMMISSION 32.92 / SALES PER STOP 1.13

Vendor Quality Control Report

The next example was from a university bookstore caught between professors' tardiness in placing textbook orders and publishers' lack of speed in filling orders. The bookstore compiled and published their listing of publisher performance. The principal criterion was delivery time. The following scale was used:

Salesman *Don Harriel*   Route # *9*   Supervisor *Buchanan*

DELIVERIES PER MONTH	LESS THAN $5.00	$5.00 to $7.50	$7.50 to $10.00	$10.00 to $12.50	$12.50 to $15.00	$15.00 to $17.50	$17.50 to $20.00	$20.00 or MORE
4 or LESS 27	23	3	1					
5								
6								
7					141			
8								
9 154	59	32	24	12	4	3		
10								
11								
12								
13 174	11	33	30	29	27	15	7	22
14								
15			194 OVERSERVICE?					
16 or MORE								

Excellent	14 days or less
Very good	20 days or less
Good	20–25 days
Fair	25–30 days
Slow	30 days
Very slow	30–40 days
Extremely slow	40–45 days
Poor	45 days plus
Very poor	Practically no response at all.[2]

[2] This discussion is based on a memorandum from the bookstore manager at San Francisco State University, dated November 5, 1973.

Some publishers were rated on their ability to respond in case of problems delaying the order, such as sending notices that the distribution facility is out of stock or that the book is out of print. Personal contact between the publishers' representatives and both bookstore personnel and faculty was considered to be an asset for two reasons. First, problems could be worked out more quickly in person than by mail. Second, the bookstore was relieved of a portion of the burden of transmitting messages between the faculty members and the publishers.

This report served several purposes. It may have prodded some professors to speed up their own textbook ordering practices. It would have been read with interest by any publisher attempting to maintain or improve a "customer service" image, and it may have affected some professors' choice of textbooks. (This would occur in a situation where they wanted to make their choice later than usual and still wanted to make certain the books would be available at the start of school.) And also, the report may have helped reduce the number of professors' complaints regarding bookstore operations. The report may have functioned as a lightning rod and transmitted some of the professors' anger directly to the publishers.

A recent variation on the idea of vendor analysis will also be cited. Figure 12-4 is an article from *Automotive News* describing General Motors' efforts to develop closer sources of supply for one of its assembly plants. In one sense, they're letting potential and existing vendors evaluate their own prospects of future business with GM and then bid accordingly. (In 1983, Gerald E. Bodrie, the executive director of GM's logistics operations, said "Transportation is such a key issue that supplier location and sourcing decisions are becoming more critical. GM is fast approaching the point where almost 94 per cent of all parts by volume will be sourced within a 300–mile radius, or about one day's transit time from the Midwest assembly plants, and 68 per cent of these parts will come from within a 100-mile radius.")[3]

Consolidation Analysis

A form used for manual consolidation analysis was shown in Figure 9-1. Computerized records and packaged software make it possible to analyze large masses of data somewhat effortlessly. The following quote, although dealing with a make-believe firm, shows how this analysis is performed. (The individual performing the analysis is named Amos.)

> Waggles Widgets never had the time to try to consolidate. When orders came in, shipments went out right away. What Amos needed was a summary of his shipments to each state in the United States. He turned again to his computer, asking for a printout of shipments by state and by weight.
>
> In just 12 minutes, the machine came back with the printed report on each state. . . .
>
> Amos decided to zoom in on California first. What he needed for a closer look at the situation was a list of shipments to that state in ZIP code

[3] *NCPDM 1983 Annual Proceedings*, pp. 496–497.

Figure 12-4 Clipping from *Automotive News*, July 23, 1984

GM suppliers get word
on cutting freight costs

ST. LOUIS. — Some 60 current and prospective General Motors part suppliers visiting the auto maker's just-completed $500 million Wentzville Assembly Plant heard GM express its desire to slash freight costs.

The visitors to the 3.7 million-square-foot plant mostly supply plastic injection molding products, sound-deadening materials and rubber products.

"The obvious answer is for such suppliers to be l o c a t e d closer to the plants," said Gary Cowger, p l a n t m a n a g e r. "Through the fair, we sought to identify some new closer suppliers and to tell our current ones that we're serious about the need to cut freight costs."

The targeted industries are those in which f r e i g h t costs often exceed the cost of the product itself. For example, the plastic bottle to contain windshield washer fluid costs three times as much to ship as to purchase from the manufacturer.

The two-day event was patterned after GM's first trade fair last year in California. More than $750,000 in piece cost and freight savings are expected to be realized from that event.

Although the W e n t z v i l l e plant will receive most of its parts by rail, at least $150,000 annually could be t r i m m e d from freight costs for such products as foam sound-deadening pads and gaskets, air outlet seals and bumper protectors, said Robert Gallagher, car distributor and trade-fair coordinator.

The impact for all of GM's Missouri and Kansas p l a n t s could easily exceed $1 million, he said. He also said it will take at least 12 months for GM to know the results of the event, but added, "With the enthusiastic response of the attendees, we anticipate the payback will be excellent."

Reprinted with permission from *Automotive News,* Copyright, 1984.

order. Such a list would immediately separate out the potential consolidations from the necessary LTL freight. . . .

According to the report, shipments were made to 67 points defined by *five-digit* ZIP code. Right off the bat, Amos thought, he could consolidate away 14 shipments to California alone. That is, of course, providing there were no customer service constraints involved.

The news was even better when Amos looked at shipments to California by three-digit ZIP code.

If trucks could be loaded according to three-digit ZIP destination, those 81 movements to California could be cut down to 26 larger shipments.[4]

Amos made good use of his analysis. According to the story, he sent notes to the distribution staff suggesting that shipments to certain market areas in California could be consolidated. And, more

importantly, he began to set up a system for putting shipment information from customer orders and/or bills of lading into his computer. The data from freight bills already in the computer could tell Amos where he missed

[4] *Handling & Shipping Management* (July 1984), p. 16.

Physical Distribution and Logistics System Analysis and Design   **479**

consolidation opportunities. Advance information, from orders or bills of lading, could give him consolidation information in time to do something about it.[5]

Note the references to ZIP codes. They are becoming an increasingly important factor in many facets of logistical systems analysis, design, and operations.

Warehousing Productivity Analysis

In the late 1970s, the National Council of Physical Distribution Management undertook a large-scale study concerning measurements of distribution productivity. One of several activities studied was warehousing. To give an idea of the extent of detail involved:

1. Approximately ten different warehousing activities were defined, such as, storage, packing and marking, and shipping.
2. About twenty different input or output terms were defined, such as, vehicles, weight, pallets, SKUs, cartons, demurrage time, and demurrage charge.
3. Approximately forty different tables containing lists of various measures were used. These were divided into measures of productivity, utilization, and performance and were compared with inputs of labor, equipment, warehouse space, and financial investment. One could make all of these comparisons for each and every warehouse activity such as packing and marking, or one could combine all specific activities under the heading of overall output or throughput.

The analyst would take these suggested measures, ratios, and other indicators and apply them to the warehouse operation he or she was studying. Comparisons would have to be made with other facilities or with measures for other time periods in order to determine the relative performance of the activity subject to scrutiny. (The report also included numerous suggestions for improving warehouse productivity.)[6]

Industry Standards

This kind of analysis, industrywide, is performed by a trade association rather than an individual firm. Individual firms cooperate in supplying data concerning their own operations to a centralized research body. The research body then compiles data for the entire industry and reports it in a manner that guarantees (one hopes) anonymity for each individual firm. The firms that contributed data then look at the industrywide tabulation and can tell how they compare with industrywide performance.

[5] Ibid.

[6] A. T. Kearney, Inc., *Measuring Productivity in Physical Distribution.* Prepared for the NCPDM (Chicago, 1978). See also, Stephen L. Frey, *Warehouse Operations: A Handbook* (Beaverton, Ore.: M/A Press, 1983), chap. 9.

One example of such a study is a periodic tabulation regarding the operations of grocery chain distribution centers.[7] Respondents who were responsible for operating fifty different distribution centers supplied the data. The researchers who compiled and analyzed the data felt that there were six key measures. They, and their medians, are:

Tons per man-hour of direct labor	2.12
Cases per man-hour of direct labor	152.00
Tons per man-hour of total labor	1.30
Cases per man-hour of total labor	93.00
Cases unloaded per hour from RR cars	231.00
Cases selected per man-hour	161.00

Data were also given for rates of unloading trucks; picking orders by use of various types of equipment: tow trains, chain tows, hand trucks, and pallet jacks; and in loading outgoing trucks with cargo that is unitized or in baskets or cages.

Good performance by some criteria must sometimes be paid for by poorer performance by other criteria. The direction for improvement is usually apparent after examining data for all fifty distribution centers. In one instance, however, the direction for improvement was not apparent. That statistic was the one for number of employees per supervisor. Distribution centers with the largest number of employees per supervisor and distribution centers with the smallest number of employees per supervisor appeared to be more efficient by most criteria than did firms with the median, or near median, number of employees per supervisor.

Logistics System Design

Logistics encompasses a wide range of activities. Because the various functional areas of logistics interact, logistics system design is a complex undertaking that requires sophisticated analytical techniques. Two of the more commonly used procedures—PERT and simulation—will be examined, although no attempt will be made to present an exhaustive discussion of either. It is also necessary to distinguish between discussion earlier in this chapter and what follows. Examples given earlier were of partial system analysis—that is, one examined a part of the system and hoped that the part under examination fit properly into "the big picture." The big picture in this instance is the entire logistics system; and systems analysis attempts to determine how well all the components fit and function together.

Figure 12-5 illustrates a logical procedure for designing a logistics system. The discussion that follows will be based on this sequence of events.

---

[7] Wendell Earle and Willard Hunt, *Grocery Distribution Center Efficiency Report* (Ithaca, N.Y.: Cornell University, in cooperation with the National Association of Food Chains, 1973). Similar—although not exactly comparable—data for more recent years can be found in *Modern Materials Handling* (Feb. 22, 1980), p. 59.

Figure 12-5 Steps in Designing a Physical Distribution/Logistics System

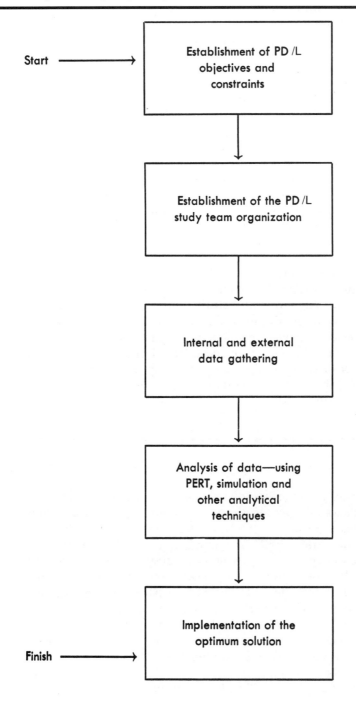

Establishing Objectives and Constraints

Before a logistics system can be designed or redesigned, it is imperative that the goals and objectives of the analysis be delineated. Is cost cutting the objective? What about profits or return-on-investment as goals? Must customer service standards be improved? By how much will improved control over flow of inbound materials influence the performance of our assembly line? Are the goals long or short term in nature? An example of a clearly stated objective would be the following:

> Eighteen months from the start of this study, the objectives stated here will be achieved at the lowest possible cost.
>
> Objectives
>
> 1. Order transmittal time for our customers will be less than 24 hours.
> 2. Orders will be processed within 16 working hours of receipt.
> 3. Eighty per cent of orders will be completely assembled within 16 working hours. All orders will be assembled within 24 working hours.
> 4. Order delivery time from our dock will be no longer than 96 hours for 85 per cent of all customers. All domestic orders must be delivered within six days of tendering to the carrier.
> 5. Stock-outs will not be accepted for greater than seven per cent of units requested. Customers experiencing a stock-out will be immediately advised by phone. The out-of-stock product will be replaced within ten days and expedited transportation will be used to reach the customer.

Notice that the preceding statement has *measurable* objectives. This is important because when the study has been completed and the new system implemented, it is then possible to determine if the objectives are being met. This is also a psychological stimulus to managers because they can determine whether their efforts are successful.

Goals tend to be somewhat broader than objectives; examples are increased market share, cost minimization, and profit maximization. Logistics consultant Harvey N. Shycon, in reviewing studies over the last several decades, has said:

> Over the past twenty years most logistics planners have been designing distribution systems to a concept of low cost. Utilizing sophisticated mathematical models with many variables and costs, even trumping their optimizing characteristics, the "scientific method" has been applied. On the basis of such studies there has been a major movement in the past two decades toward fewer distribution centers and a larger proportion of the distribution dollar spent on transportation.
>
> The criterion for these distribution evaluations have [sic] almost universally been *lowest total cost*, i.e., the mathematical and financial criteria have been low cost. But when the question is then posed whether the service provided by such a system is adequate, a qualitative examination is made, some minor adjustments frequently made in the results obtained (possibly destroying the optimality of the result identified), and the system is implemented.

But, companies are not in business primarily to reduce cost. Companies are in business to generate profit, growth, and a reasonable return on investment. Why then do we not use these criteria when we design the distribution system?[8]

Before system design, or redesign, can be initiated, there must be agreement on goals and on measurable objectives. System *constraints,* if any, must also be specified. Constraints involve factors in the system that cannot be changed for one reason or another. The following are examples:

1. The distribution center at Detroit will not be closed nor its employment decreased because the firm has publicly pledged to support the downtown area of this city.
2. Order-transmittal will continue to be based on a telephone system because this equipment was purchased just six months ago at a cost of $2½ million.
3. The Sherwood Trucking Company will be utilized whenever it has competitive trucking rates.

In one sense, each constraint simplifies the situation because it tends to reduce the number of alternatives to be analyzed. However, it is probably fair for the study teams to question some of the constraints, especially if their impact appears to run counter to the stated goals and objectives.

Organization of the Study Team

Once measurable objectives have been established and the constraints outlined, the next step is to organize the firm's personnel for the analysis. John F. Magee, a management consultant, found that it is preferable to have two separate groups working on the analysis. One group is the *working analysis team.* This group involves the managers of the functional areas involved and other staff and quantitative specialists. The customer service director, traffic manager, warehousing manager, director of purchasing, the production scheduler, and other relevant managers are members of this team. If outside management consultants are used, they work with these team members on a day-by-day basis. This team is responsible for the actual analysis performed and for the testing, designing, and implementing of the new system.

The other group is the *management supervisory committee.* This group works with the working analysis team. They represent a broader perspective, the overall viewpoint of the firm. Marketing, law, finance, production, personnel and accounting executives are represented on this committee. This group is on call to clarify and amplify system objectives. It also plays the role of the devil's advocate and occasionally probes the working analysis team on *why* they took the action they did. Magee states that meetings between the two groups should be regularly scheduled. In many cases, a monthly meeting seems appropriate.[9]

[8] Harvey N. Shycon, "The Folly of Seeking Minimum Cost Distribution," a paper distributed by Shycon Associates, Waltham, Massachusetts, 1983.

[9] John F. Magee, *Physical-Distribution Systems* (New York: McGraw-Hill, 1967), p. 95. For a description of the study-team approach in action, see Frank J. Morgan, "Interdepartmental

The third and perhaps the most important stage in designing a logistics system involves data collection. Obviously the validity of the study can be no stronger than the accuracy of the data base. Five comprehensive audits must be performed: product, existing facilities, vendors, customers, and competitors. Each will be examined.

Product Audit. The *product audit* involves a comprehensive analysis of both the existing product line and new product trends. Specific information that must be determined for each product includes: (1) annual sales volume, (2) seasonality, (3) packaging, (4) transportation and warehouse information, (5) present manufacturing or assembly facilities, (6) ease with which manufacturing of product can be scheduled, (7) warehouse stocking locations, (8) present transport modes utilized, (9) sales by regions, (10) complementary products that are often sold at the same time as the product under consideration, and (11) product profitability. This list is *not* exhaustive, it simply indicates the type of product information needed. Most of the information needed to perform this audit is available in existing company records.

Existing Facilities Audit. The *existing facilities audit* comes next. Every logistics system is unique, and the working analysis team must have a comprehensive audit of its facilities. This includes the following: (1) the location and capacity of production plants, (2) the location and capacity of storage warehouses and distribution centers, (3) the location of the order processing function, and (4) the transport modes utilized (especially when the firm is somewhat locked into their usage). When constraints are used, they typically involve aspects of existing facilities that are not to be changed. This audit tells where the firm is now utilizing facilities and it is essential data when contemplating changes in the system.

Vendor Audit. The vendor audit looks at sources of supply for raw materials and components. This would include their (1) location, (2) dependability, (3) quality of work, and (4) the costs and performance of inbound transportation.

Customer Audit. The *customer audit* focuses on characteristics of current customers. Potential new customers are also analyzed. The following information must be collected: (1) the location of present and potential customers, (2) the products that each customer orders, (3) the seasonality of their orders, (4) whether they buy FOB origin or destination, (5) the importance of customer service, (6) special services they require, and (7) the volume and profitability of sales for each customer. The customer audit provides a key input for system analysis because in the end, the system is designed to satisfy the needs and requirements of firm's customers.

Teamwork Builds Profitability," *Handling & Shipping Management Presidential Issue* (1984–1985), pp. 18–24.

Competition Audit. The *competition audit* outlines the competitive environment within which the firm is selling. The following information should be ascertained: (1) the order transmittal methods of competitors, (2) the accuracy and speed of their order processing, (3) the speed and consistency of carrier movements used by competitors, (4) the ratio of orders given to competitors that could not be filled because of a product stock-out, (5) the competitor's experience with loss and damage claims, and (6) a narrative statement regarding customers' perception of the customer service strengths and weaknesses of the firm and its competitors.

Unlike the other four audits, the information required for the competition audit is generally not available within a company, although salespeople can often provide some of it. Also, outside marketing research firms are used to survey competitors to gather the required data. Outside research firms can usually design the questionnaire in such a manner as to disguise the ultimate recipient of the information.

Analysis of the Data

When the information from the five audits has been assembled, the next step is to "massage" it—in the vernacular of the analyst. This can be accomplished using relatively unsophisticated techniques or complex methods. Earlier in this chapter there was a description of the relatively simple but effective techniques used by the dairy driver/salesmen. When systemwide analysis is desired, the quantity of data to be analyzed is usually so massive that more sophisticated techniques must be used. Two methods will be examined here—PERT and simulation. PERT (an acronym for Project Evaluation and Review Technique) is of value when the analyst is attempting to determine the relationship between all tasks that must be performed. Simulation assumes that the relationships are known; it is used to determine how well a system—actual or proposed—will perform under varying stresses.

PERT. PERT is a form of network analysis that places all component tasks in the sequence they are to be performed. It recognizes that some tasks can be performed only in a certain simultaneous order, while for others no such relationship exists. There is a period when either, neither, or both can be performed. What follows is an example of how PERT can be applied to the export process, where some twenty different steps are involved.[10] They are listed here and assigned identifying letters. Letters early in the alphabet are assigned to tasks that must be performed first. However, there is no absolute relationship between the letter assigned to a task and when—in comparison to other tasks—it must be performed. Although the word *task* is implied, the word *event* will be used. *Event* means that the task has been completed.

Event A   An order from a foreign customer is received.
Event B   Applicable governmental controls concerning the export transaction are determined.

[10] See James W. Tatterson and Donald F. Wood, "PERT, CPM and the Export Process," *OMEGA, The International Journal of Management Science,* **2**: 421–426 (1974).

Event C Transportation mode, carrier, and routing are selected.

Event D The goods needed to fill the export order are made available.

Event E The export declaration is prepared.

Event F Space is reserved on the carrier.

Event G Insurance coverage for the shipment is obtained.

Event H Packaging requirements for the export shipment are established.

Event I The delivery permit for the export shipment is obtained.

Event J The commercial invoice covering the shipment is prepared.

Event K The shipment is packed, marked and weighed.

Event L Inland transportation to point of exportation is arranged.

Event M The certificate of origin covering the goods in the shipment is obtained.

Event N The bill of lading or airwaybill for the shipment is prepared.

Event O The consular invoice is obtained from the government representative of the importing country.

Event P Any special certificates required for importation are obtained.

Event Q The shipment is onloaded aboard inland carrier for transport to point of exportation.

Event R The shipment arrives at point of exportation and receipt for the goods is issued.

Event S The shipment is loaded aboard the international carrier; the bill of lading or airwaybill is issued.

Event T The shipment arrives at the designated point of entry. (For purposes of our analysis here, this is as far as we are concerned. Beyond this point, the buyer has responsibility.)

In order to perform the analysis, it is necessary to have some real figures as input data. The example used is a 2,000-pound shipment from an exporter in the San Francisco area destined to a consignee in Manila. The shipment quotation is CIF (cost-insurance-freight) Manila; this means that the exporter is responsible for the performance of all export process events until the shipment is off-loaded in Manila. In addition to the regular documentation required, the shipper must obtain a delivery permit from the steamship company. Shipment value is $36,000. The exporter purchases the merchandise at Event A; he receives payment from the customer at Event T. No mode, route, or time limit is specified. Because of the high value and small size of this shipment, the shipper is uncertain whether to ship by sea or air or whether to expedite the shipment.

Estimates of cost and time must be made for each of the twenty tasks, or events. Instances where one event has a sequential relationship with others must be recognized. Figure 12-6 depicts all of these relationships in network form. Tasks that must be performed in sequence follow along the same line. Tasks that can be performed simultaneously are shown on parallel lines. Cost figures, in dollars, are represented by the first number, the second number represents time, in days. Four alternative types of shipment are involved. Each line between Event A and Event T is a path. The time to travel along each path is then added, giving these results:

Figure 12-6 Network for Example Export Shipment

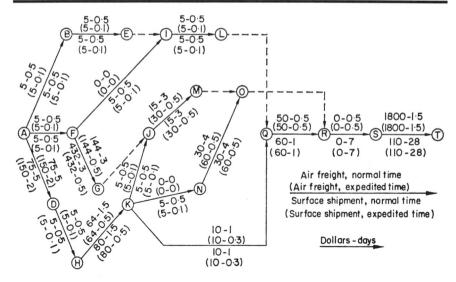

This chart first appeared in OMEGA, Vol. 2, no. 3, p. 424.

Network Path	Total Days Required to Traverse Path
ADHKQRST	44.0
ADHKNORST	46.5 (critical path)
ADHKJMORST	45.5
AFGJMORST	41.5
AFILQRST	37.5
ABEILQRST	37.5

These figures are for the normal shipment via water. Even though all paths must be traversed, one path—ADHKNORST—has been designated as the *critical path* because it takes the longest amount of time to traverse. The reason it is considered as *critical* is that if one wishes to speed up the normal surface process, the time-saving improvement *must* be made on one or more events that occur on this path. It would do no good to speed up task J because even if J is accomplished in less time than originally estimated, it won't affect the total time of the tasks on the critical path.

In fact, the shipper could allot more time to task J than it presently takes without slowing down the export process. The question is "how much?" This is where the path concept is useful. Note that event J appears on several other paths, although not on the critical one. Path ADHKJMORST contains task J and is closest in time value to the critical path. It takes 45.5 days to complete while the critical path takes 46.5 days. Thus, the shipper could add one more day on to the time to complete task J without affecting overall delivery time. Other tasks not on the critical path could be analyzed in a similar manner. If the shipper did not want to improve delivery time, he could reduce costs by allowing more time for the completion of tasks that are off of the critical path.

Figure 12-6 could also show how to improve delivery time. Using the normal surface transport figures, the shipper would concentrate on tasks that are on the critical path since overall time could be reduced only by reducing their required times. Task D (or event D) appears on the critical path. Any reduction in time to complete D will reduce the time required to traverse the critical path by the same amount. At present, D takes five days. If the event could be completed in, say, .5 days, this would reduce the critical path from 46.5 days to 42.0 days. There is a limit to improvements that can be made on the critical path, however. Saving time on events D, H, and K, for example, is useful up to a total savings of five days. At that point, path AFGJMORST becomes the controlling, or *critical* path, and D, H, and K are no longer critical.

The PERT chart suggests how the shipper should go about making adjustments in the time allocations for each task. Costs of altering the time spent on each task should also be known. For events off the critical path, time allowances could be extended if cost reductions will occur. For events on the critical path, any change in time allowance has a direct impact on system performance. This holds until the time saving becomes so great that the path itself is no longer critical.

Note the usefulness of the PERT chart in evaluating a complete distribution process. It allows the user to relate tasks and focus attention on any task without losing sight of where it fits in the "big" picture.

Simulation. The computer technique that is most widely used for logistics system planning is *simulation*. Simulation usually involves a computer model that is a series of mathematical relationships. Simulation reliability is achieved by making the model as close to the real world as possible. Such factors as transport mode availability, transportation costs, location of vendors, warehouse locations, customer locations, customer service requirements, and plant locations must all be accurately reflected in the model. Although logistics simulation models may require many programmers working together for long periods, they allow the firm to have the capability of asking "what if?" questions, such as:

- If we reduced the average order cycle time for our customers from 12 days to 7 days, what would be the additional cost involved? Would sales increase?
- If we presently use our trucks for outbound movements only, and are debating whether to use them to pick up some of our inputs on their return trips, how will this affect our current schedules of outbound deliveries?
- If we started to use railroad service instead of motor carrier, what would be the ramifications on customer service and on overall costs?
- If we reduced the number of distribution warehouses from 32 to 19, what would be the effect on customer service standards? What about costs?
- If our vendors improved the accuracy of their delivery times, by how much could we safely reduce our stocks of components?

- If the minimum order accepted were increased from $20 to $100, what would be the effect on total sales?
- If private carriage were substituted for motor common carriage, what would be the changes in total logistics costs and what effect would this have on customer service standards?
- What happens if we shift the *order penetration point* nearer to or farther from the customer? (The order penetration point is when—and where—a specific item in an inventory or production process is earmarked for a particular customer.) [11]

The primary advantage of simulation is that it allows the firm to test the feasibility of a proposed change at relatively little expense. In addition, it prevents firms from experiencing the public embarrassment of making a major change in their logistics system that might result in a deterioration of customer service levels or an increase in total operating expense.

Career logistics people should familiarize themselves with computer simulations because they are important to logistics planning and will become even more important in the future. Many consultants have also developed expertise in simulation techniques and have devised "models" that can be used by various clients. Figure 12-7, from a consultant's brochure, contains descriptions of three different computer systems that would be useful to a client attempting to make decisions involving the location of distribution facilities.

An H. J. Heinz study gave an early indication of the possibilities that simulation studies offer.[12] The H. J. Heinz Company was concerned with the configuration of its warehouse network. Specific questions involved the following issues: (1) How many warehouses should be utilized? (2) Where should they be located? and (3) Which customers should be served from each warehouse? Because of the size and complexity of the problem, consultants Harvey N. Shycon and Richard B. Maffei decided that a simulation model would be the best analysis technique.

When the study was initiated, Heinz had 68 warehouses in the United States. Over time, Heinz officials had noticed that the "Mom and Pop" retailers were becoming less important in grocery distribution. Chain stores were the dominant factor and they received their products in fewer locations and in much larger quantities. It was obvious that Heinz had too many warehouses.

Once the objective of the study had been determined and the working analysis and management supervisory groups established, the product, ex-

[11] The order penetration's point is important for several reasons. One deals with inventory carrying costs because once a product is committed to a particular buyer it is no longer available to any other buyer, yet the inventory carrying costs continue. The point is also important from a forecasting standpoint since it represents actual demand. See: Graham Sharman, "The Rediscovery of Logistics," *Harvard Business Review* (September–October 1984), p. 75.

[12] Harvey N. Shycon and Richard B. Maffei, "Simulation—Tool for Better Distribution," *Harvard Business Review* (Nov.–Dec. 1960), pp. 65–75. See also, Donald J. Bowersox, "Planning Physical Distribution Operations with Dynamic Simulation," *Journal of Marketing* (Jan. 1972), pp. 17–25; and O. Keith Helferich and Lloyd B. Mitchell, "Planning for Customer Service with Computer Simulation," *Transportation and Distribution Management* (Jan.–Feb. 1975), pp. 17–21.

Figure 12-7 Description of the System Simulation Services Offered by a Consultant

LOCATE Software Systems

LOCATE

LOCATE is an interactive static simulation model that helps managers analyze multiple facility distribution systems. LOCATE is a high-speed analytical package that evaluates alternative distribution networks proposed by the user. The program will generate (1) market to distribution center assignments; (2) total system costs; and (3) system service performance measures for any distribution system the user wishes to examine. LOCATE was constructed to evaluate distribution systems proposed by managers who want to explore a relatively limited set of alternative networks, rather than consider all possible systems.

LOCATE / FORMULATE

LOCATE/FORMULATE is a large-scale interactive static simulation model that can analyze complex, multiechelon, multiproduct distribution systems. Given a list of possible distribution sites, LOCATE/FORMULATE can formulate the best distribution system under five different customer assignment strategy scenarios: (1) least cost; (2) maximum service; (3) least cost while satisfying a specified and/or desired service level; (4) least cost with bundling (i.e., requiring a predetermined set of products and/or shipment sizes to be shipped from the same DC, selected by the model on the basis of least cost); and (5) fixed assignment. LOCATE/FORMULATE provides the user with the unique analytical capability of facility deletion. LOCATE/FORMULATE can identify, in sequence, facilities eliminations which will generate the greatest incremental cost saving. This LOCATE/FORMULATE feature is used to systematically decrease the number of facilities so the user can quickly evaluate the performance of different potential facility configurations.

LOCATE/ALLOCATE

LOCATE/ALLOCATE is an interactive, mathematical optimization model. LOCATE/ALLOCATE is the first and only optimization system for logistics planning that provides the user with interactive data entry and editing, multiple run capability and detailed user-oriented solution reports. Given a list of possible sites for distribution facilities of various capacities, LOCATE/ALLOCATE determines the optimal location of facilities and the optimal allocation of their capacities to meet customer demands at minimum cost. LOCATE/ALLOCATE generates a solution that simultaneously: minimizes the sum of all fixed and variable costs; specifies which facilities to use and the products handled by each; specifies for each customer zone which facilities should be used to fill its demand and the shipment levels by commodity to be made from each facility.

Courtesy Cleveland Consulting Associates.

491

isting facility, customer, and competition audits were completed. Shycon and Maffei determined that there were three alternative distribution methods that could be used. First, products could be shipped directly from the production plant to the customer. Second, products could be transported from the factory to other production facilities, consolidated with other products, and transported immediately to the customer. Or, third, the products could flow from the factory to a storage warehouse and then to the customer. The first two alternatives did not use warehousing facilities. Warehouses were needed for customers who do not order in large enough quantities to warrant direct shipments and for those who require relatively short order cycles.

The computer was told to try various numbers and locations of warehouses for shipments that required intermediate warehousing. For each configuration, a year's worth of sales data were simulated and the costs and customer service levels were determined for each alternative. Each alternative configuration required approximately 75 million mathematical calculations by the computer. When each alternative was tested, the results indicated that the optimum number of warehouses was about 40. With this number of warehouses, customer service standards were achieved, and total distribution costs were minimized.

There is very little business behavior that cannot be simulated. Figure 12-8 illustrates this fact.

Figure 12-8 Computers Can Simulate Many Forms of Business Behavior

*"It can't actually think, but when it makes a mistake,
it can put the blame on some other computer."*

Reproduced by permission of the artist and the Masters Agency.

Design Implementation

The final activity in system design is the implementation of the findings. It is a rare situation in which an operating logistics system is completely revised at one time. One-time across-the-board revisions are typically too traumatic for most firms to tolerate because they inevitably result in a breakdown of customer service functions. Orders are lost, incorrect quantities are shipped, stock-outs are frequent—these are the typical problems when a system is changed too radically in a short period of time. In addition, personnel may resist the changes.

Most firms prefer to use their simulation, and PERT analysis to find those areas that should be changed first, because these functions are the greatest bottlenecks to efficiency. Also, the payoffs may be greater.

Summary

This chapter dealt with various types of system analysis. The purpose of the analysis is to determine whether improvements can be made in the logistics system. Systems analysis is difficult because one must determine which aspects or functional area should be subjected to the analysis. Partial analysis deals with specific segments of the total systems. It attempts to understand how these parts can be made to perform more efficiently.

Industry standards are available in selected areas of business and these standards allow each firm to compare their own ratios or other performance measures to industry averages.

Effective system design involves five basic steps: (1) establishment of objectives and constraints, (2) establishment of the study team organization, (3) internal and external data gathering, (4) analysis of the data, and (5) implementation of the findings. Physical distribution and logistics system design is often based on complex analysis using simulation or PERT techniques.

Questions for Discussion and Review

1. Read the introductory quote by Professors Voorhees and Sharp. Based on your understanding of PD/L system analysis and design, comment on the validity of their statement. Be specific in your answer.
2. What is the purpose of systems analysis in PD/L? What are its strengths and weaknesses?
3. "Systems analysis is the most important activity supervised by senior physical distribution management." Do you agree? Why or why not?
4. Why are outside consultants frequently employed to analyze a firm's distribution practices?
5. Discuss the problems often encountered in PD/L systems analysis.
6. Why is partial systems analysis so commonly used?
7. What is your reaction to the customer profitability analysis utilized by the dairy driver/salesman? Could it be improved? Discuss.
8. What are the advantages of having a trade group collect and then dis-

tribute data concerning the relative efficiency of its various members' operations?

9. Discuss the basic procedure used in system design. Does this procedure appear logical to you? Discuss.
10. Why is it important to clearly specify the objectives of a study?
11. What are system constraints? Are they important? Why?
12. "Design objectives should *not* be measurable, because if they are they tend to make the systems analysis inflexible and difficult to implement." Do you agree? Defend your answer.
13. Discuss the duties and responsibilities of the working analysis team and the management supervisory committee. Which group is more important? Why?
14. Discuss the information that should be contained in each of the following audits: product, existing facilities, customers, vendor, and competitors.
15. Of the preceding five audits, which is the *most* and *least* important? Why?
16. What is PERT? What types of problems can be solved using this technique?
17. What is the *critical path?* Why is it important? Discuss.
18. What is simulation? What are its strengths and weaknesses?
19. Outline the problems and procedures used in the H. J. Heinz simulation. Did the analysis used appear logical to you? Discuss.
20. "Design implementation is often accomplished in stages rather than all at once." Is this logical? What are the strengths and weaknesses of the gradual approach?

Additional Chapter References

Bartley, Jack. "Department of Defense Project Management: Bar Coding." *Annual Proceedings of the NCPDM* (1984), pp. 159–164.

Beaulieu, Jeffrey, Robert J. Hauser, and C. Phillip Baumel. "Inland Waterway User Taxes: Their Impacts on Corn, Wheat and Soybean Flows and Transport Costs." *Annual Proceedings of the Transportation Research Forum* (1982), pp. 272–282.

Benton, W. C., and Bellur Srikar, "Experimental Study of Environmental Factors that Affect the Vehicle Routing Problem," *Journal of Business Logistics* (March 1985), pp. 66–78.

Biggs, Dee, and Bill Coyne. "Distribution Applications for General Purpose Software Products on Stand-Alone Micros." *Annual Proceedings of the NCPDM* (1984), pp. 535–556.

Conlon, Patrick J., and William A. Townsend. "The 'How to' of Transportation Productivity Programs." *Annual Proceedings of the NCPDM* (1984), pp. 53–74.

Copacino, William, and Donald B. Rosenfield. "Analytic Tools for Strategic Planning." *Annual Proceedings of the NCPDM* (1984), pp. 397–426.

Copacino, William C., and Lawrence Lapide. "The Impact of Uncertain Transportation Costs on Physical Distribution Planning." *Journal of Business Logistics* (Vol. 5, No. 2, 1984), pp. 40–56.

DeSapio, Mary. "Analysis of Strategic Business Opportunities and Capital Formation." *Annual Proceedings of the NCPDM* (1982), pp. 759–766.

Dube, William R. "Closed Loop Planning for Manufacturing and Distribution." *Annual Proceedings of the NCPDM* (1984), pp. 491–508.

Eastburn, Melvin P., and Lawrence R. Christensen. "A Case Study Showing Dramatic Fleet Cost Reduction Through Micro-Based Vehicle Scheduling Software Package." *Annual Proceedings of the NCPDM* (1984), pp. 333–344.

Ertell, Bruce R. "Survey of Software for the Distribution Industry." *Annual Proceedings of the NCPDM* (1982), pp. 97–208.

Foggin, James H. "Decision Assisting Maps for Distribution Management." *Journal of Business Logistics* (Vol. 3, No. 1, 1982), pp. 86–101.

————"Improving Motor Carrier Productivity with Statistical Process Control." *Transportation Journal* (Fall 1984), pp. 58–74.

Gochberg, Howard S. "Anatomy of a Transportation Productivity Project." *Annual Proceedings of the NCPDM* (1984), pp. 887–902.

Green, F. B. "Simulating a Variable Cargo Transport System." *Journal of Business Logistics* (Vol. 3, No. 1, 1982) pp. 73–85.

Gustin, Craig. "Survey of U.S. Logistics Information Systems." *Annual Proceedings of the NCPDM* (1982), pp. 681–712.

Hammesfahr, R. D. Jack, and Edward R. Clayton. "A Computer Simulation Model to Assist Intermodal Terminal Managers in Operations Analysis." *Transportation Journal* (Summer 1983), pp. 55–68.

Heijmen, Ton C. M. "Transportation Cost Analysis: Techniques and Uses." *Annual Proceedings of the NCPDM,* (1983), pp. 892–938.

Helferich, Omar Keith, and Drew G. Seguin. "Fourth Generation Software— An Overview for the Materials and Logistics Manager." *Annual Proceedings of the NCPDM* (1984), pp. 85–98.

Helferich, Omar Keith and Ray L. Rowland. "Expert Systems Software: An Overview for the Materials and Logistics Manager." *Annual Proceedings of the NCPDM* (1984), pp. 249–260.

Helms, Theodore J., "The Nitty Gritty Aspects of Developing a Distribution Costing Model." *Annual Proceedings of the NCPDM* (1983), pp. 405–420.

Hull, David P., Michael H. Sterling, and Richard A. Carpenter. "Development of Logistics Systems with Prototyping Techniques." *Annual Proceedings of the NCPDM* (1983), pp. 331–357.

Huyser, Curtis D., and C. Phillip Baumel. "Impact of Inland Waterway User Charges on Fertilizer Flows and Transport Costs." *Annual Proceedings of the Transportation Research Forum* (1982), pp. 283–293.

Hyman, William A. "Constructive Uses of Contradictory Thinking in Transportation." *Annual Proceedings of the Transportation Research Forum* (1983), pp. 498–506.

Ketchum, Peter. " 'National Dispatch' Program Improves Productivity for Both the Shipper and Carrier." *Annual Proceedings of the NCPDM* (1982), pp. 315–330.

Klingman, Darwin D., and G. Terry Ross. "Decision Support Models for Improved Integrated Logistics Network Planning." *Journal of Business Logistics* (Vol. 4, No. 2, 1983)

LaCagnina, Michael L. "Omega Improves Productivity 50%." *Annual Proceedings of the NCPDM* (1982), pp. 283–314.

Lancioni, Richard A., and Martin Christopher. "Managing and Forecasting Environmental Factors in Distribution." *Annual Proceedings of the NCPDM* (1982), pp. 777–788.

McCarren, J. Reilly. "Data Bases—Improving Transportation Analysis Productivity." *Annual Proceedings of the Transportation Research Forum* (1982), pp. 103–109.

McGinnis, Michael A., and Bernard J. LaLonde. "Strategic Planning and the Physical Distribution Manager." *Annual Proceedings of the NCPDM* (1983), pp. 790–799.

McGinnis, Michael A. "Avoiding Pitfalls in Strategic Planning." *Annual Proceedings of the NCPDM* (1984), pp. 701–706.

Morehouse, James E., William J. Best, and William J. Markham. "Improving Logistics Productivity—The Successful Companies." *Annual Proceedings of the NCPDM* (1983), pp. 193–212.

Moscevsky, Walter. "Use of Computers to Solve Distribution Problems in Small Business: Distributors Services to Small Customers." *Annual Proceedings of the NCPDM* (1983), pp. 939–942.

Read, William A., and Randall A. Elmhorst. "Logistics Software Products Designed for the Stand-Alone Microcomputers." *Annual Proceedings of the NCPDM* (1984), pp. 377–396.

Robeson, James F., and Robert G. House. *Distribution Handbook* (Oak Brook, Il.: NCPDM, 1985).

Robeson, James F. and David Kollat. "Channels of Distribution: Structure and Change." *The Distribution Handbook* (New York: Free Press Division of Macmillan, 1985), pp. 225–234.

Rosenfield, Donald B. "Interactive Modeling in Distribution and Logistics." *Annual Proceedings of the NCPDM* (1983), pp. 388–404.

Schmitt, Rolf R., and Alan E. Pisarski. "Diverging Information Needs and Resources in Transportation Research." *Annual Proceedings of the Transportation Research Forum* (1983), pp. 438–443.

Sharman, Graham, "The Rediscovery of Logistics," *Harvard Business Review*, vol. 62, no. 5, (Sept.-Oct. 1984), pp. 71–79.

Sheffield, W. H. "Canadian Transportation Research—A Shipper's Perspective." *Annual Proceedings of the Transportation Research Forum* (1984), pp. 111–115.

Shrock, David L., and Lonnie L. Ostrom. "A Survey of the Use of Quantitative Methods by Motor Carriers." *Transportation Journal* (Summer 1981), pp. 86–92.

Smith, Ronald R., and Marcia P. Helme. "A Mathematical Model for the Optimization of Purchasing and Distribution Strategies." *Annual Proceedings of the NCPDM* (1983), pp. 358–387.

Stingle, Stephen D. "Managing Demand Forecasting and Improving ROI." *Annual Proceedings of the NCPDM* (1982), pp. 767–776.

CASE 12-1

Alberta Highway Department, Region VI

Region VI of the Alberta Highway Department was responsible for highway maintenance in Alberta in an area west of Lethbridge, Calgary, and Red Deer. One of their
most important responsibilities, in the public's mind, was to keep open Canadian Route
Number 1, which went across all of Canada. At the very west of Region VI were the
Rocky Mountains, and in a six-mile stretch between Lake Louise and the British Columbia border, the highway climbed from 3,000 to 6,000 feet. The climb in this stretch
was uniform, the road's elevation increasing 500 feet each mile as it moved to the
west.

At present, a highway maintenance station was near Lake Louise, one mile to the
east of the six-mile section. At this station were based several heavy duty dump trucks
that, in the winter were mounted with snow plows in the front and sand spreading
devices in the rear.

Sanding was used after frosts or freezing rains and in the spring when melting
snows would refreeze at night. The higher elevations required more sanding because
they were subject to more freezing temperatures. For the last ten years, since the highway was opened, records were kept for the amount of maintenance required by each
mile of highway. (See Exhibit 12-1.) In terms of sanding, here is the average number
of days per year that each mile required sanding:

Mile 1	3000'–3500' elevation	40 days
Mile 2	3500'–4000' elevation	48 days
Mile 3	4000'–4500' elevation	53 days
Mile 4	4500'–5000' elevation	58 days
Mile 5	5000'–5500' elevation	65 days
Mile 6	5500'–6000' elevation	70 days

Exhibit 12-1 Canadian Route Number 1

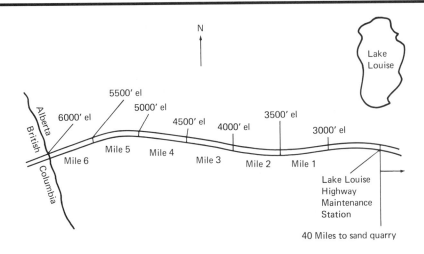

Physical Distribution and Logistics System Analysis and Design

The dump trucks could carry 10 tons of sand, which was enough to spread over one mile of highway in both the eastbound and westbound lanes. Spreading sand was a slow process because, under slippery conditions, highway traffic moved slowly. Several trucks were needed because when sanding was needed, it was needed quickly.

At the Lake Louise maintenance station were large silos for holding the salt-treated sand. At present, the silos could hold nearly 6,000 tons of sand, some of which was used for lower stretches of highway. During summer months, the silos were filled by special trailer dump trucks that carried the sand up from a quarry near Bow Valley, 40 miles to the east of the Lake Louise maintenance station. The silo was of such design that it could be split into two. Split segments of the silo could hold different capacities or they could hold equal capacities of sand. However, their total capacity would be 6,000 tons.

Through a departmental program for encouraging employee suggestions, a proposal had been received from a sander truck driver that a portion of the Lake Louise sand silos be moved west toward the higher elevation where more frequent sandings were needed.

The highway was constructed so that at one-mile distances (in this case at elevations of 3,000, 3,500, 4,000, 5,000, 5,500 and 6,000 feet), it was possible for maintenance trucks to turn around. The shoulders were also wide enough at these points so that the silos could be placed alongside. The silo relocation could be performed during summer months using regular maintenance crews and equipment.

The principal reason for splitting and relocating a portion of the silos would be to place sand closer to where it was needed and to reduce travel time of maintenance trucks to and from the silos. The work crews were paid a constant rate for a fixed number of hours, and if they were not sanding, they were performing other tasks. Hence, the only relevant costs were those of truck operation.

The facts and assumptions to be used in the analysis follow:

1. Costs of trucking sand from the quarry to the Lake Louise silos or to the relocated silos would be three cents per ton-mile for the length of the full haul in one direction. (Empty backhaul costs are taken into account with these calculations.)
2. Some sand silo capacity must be kept at the Lake Louise maintenance station.
3. Spreader dump trucks are more costly to operate to carry sand between silos and where it is needed. The cost is 10 cents per ton-mile (which also takes empty backhauls into account).
4. There are no costs assigned for spreader trucks to initially reach silos. The reason for this is that they are randomly located on the highway at the time the decision is made to spread sand. Truck crews are then dispatched by radio.
5. If a new silo is located, it must be at one of the turnaround sites between each of the miles.
6. If a new silo is located an even number of miles from the Lake Louise station, a midpoint will be established halfway between the two silos and sanders will load at the silo nearest the mile of road needing sand.
7. If a new silo is located an odd number of miles from the Lake Louise maintenance station, a determination must be made as to which silo will provide sand for the middle one. (This is because maintenance trucks cannot turn at the middle of mile sections.)
8. No costs are assigned to operating the spreaders within a mile on either side of the silo. This is because they start spreading sand immediately upon leaving the silo.

However, for sanding a stretch that was, say, between two to three miles from the silo, the cost of reaching the areas would be two dollars (10 tons $\times$ 10 cents $\times$ 2 miles.)

Question One: Should one portion of sand silos at the Lake Louise maintenance station be relocated to a point to the west, at higher elevation? If yes, where should it be relocated, how much capacity should it have and what are the projected annual savings in truck operating costs? Show your work.

Question Two: Assume that it was discovered that it would be impossible to split the silo into sections. However, it would be feasible to move the entire silo to another site, farther up the slope. The section of highway between the Lake Louise maintenance station stretching west one mile to where it reaches the 3,000 foot elevation point must be sanded for 30 days per year. All points east of the Lake Louise maintenance station can be serviced from other points. Should the entire silo be moved to another point? If so, to where? What will the savings be? Show your work.

Question Three: Ignore all statements made in question two and assume, instead, that the silo can be divided into three sections, one remaining at Lake Louise, and the other two located somewhere in the six-mile stretch. If two sections are to be located within the six-mile section, where should they be placed? What will the savings be over the present system? Show your work.

Question Four: This case was written some time ago, when fuel costs were very low. The spreader dump truck now cost 35 cents per ton-mile to operate (compared to 10 cents), and the trailer dump truck used to move sand from the quarry now costs 20 cents per ton-mile to operate (up from 3 cents). Answer question one, taking into account these new truck operating costs.

Question Five: Answer question two, taking into account the new trucking costs outlined in question four.

Question Six: Answer question three, taking into account the new trucking costs outlined in question four.

Question Seven: Do you consider the situation in the case to be an example of *partial* systems analysis or of *total* systems analysis? Why?

CASE 12-2

The Minnetonka Warehouse

(Note: Many students will find this case to be difficult. It might be best if the instructor covers—in class—the material up to the mention of Wayne Schuller.)

Queueing theory is an analysis of the probabilities associated with the length of time an individual or object must wait in a line or queue. Because of the nature of this analysis, it is also called *waiting line theory*. There are many applications of queueing theory in physical distribution. Should the firm have one, two, or three shrink wrap machines in the warehouse? How many desks should there be in the warehouse that hands out the orders to be filled by the warehouse employees? How many inspectors should check the accuracy of the assembled orders?

An unloading dock design application will be illustrated here. The manager is trying to decide if the receiving area for the plant should have an additional loading/

unloading dock. It already has one and the manager is trying to decide whether addition of a second one would have much impact upon reducing the waiting time of trucks, backed up waiting their turn to use the dock.

To analyze the above problem, a complementary procedure to queueing theory will also be used. Monte Carlo simulation involves recreating real-world elements by using probability. The name *Monte Carlo* comes from picking events at random, such as would take place if a roulette wheel were used.

To analyze the receiving dock situation, it is necessary to study the actual arrival times of trucks at the receiving dock. An employee with a stop watch notes the time between arrivals for a reasonable length of time. Assuming that the period studied was representative, Exhibit 12-2 can be generated. The vertical axis is the *cumulative* probability of the time between arrivals. Thus, 25 per cent of all delivery trucks arrive slightly less than ten minutes after a previous truck has arrived. Fifty percent arrive within about 20 minutes after the previous truck and 75 per cent come within 34 minutes after the previous vehicle.

One can simulate, via the Monte Carlo technique, a queueing problem. Because Monte Carlo requires a number of random events, a *table of random numbers* (Exhibit 12-3) will be utilized. This is a listing of numbers, typically generated by a computer, which are totally random in order. The table of random numbers will be used to generate twenty arrival times. In a real problem, a computer would be used and probably 1,000 arrivals would be tested. Using the first number in the upper left-hand corner of

Exhibit 12-2 Delivery Truck Arrival Times

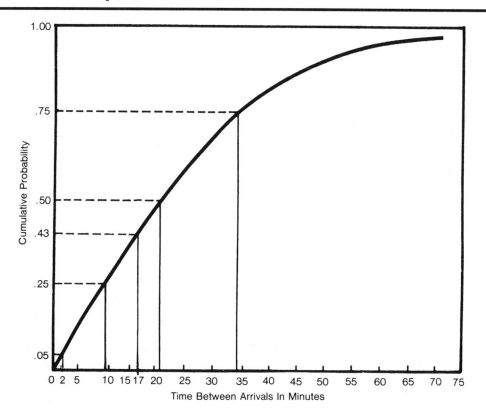

Exhibit 12-3 Table of Random Numbers

05	04	31	17	21
43	06	61	47	78
31	85	99	63	92
10	47	39	30	36
39	80	05	45	53
94	20	87	97	04
63	43	14	33	07
99	50	51	80	11
65	29	51	29	85
80	83	09	53	45
87	16	71	77	59
77	58	82	37	85
24	40	43	03	94
99	07	39	40	71
05	17	36	22	20
08	04	63	25	15
63	71	78	62	46
05	67	76	50	85
07	55	97	43	99
49	17	34	63	62
39	56	01	25	83
91	19	08	99	68
22	61	19	61	08
03	67	69	29	02
51	91	76	33	80

the table—05—the time for its arrival is 2 minutes. This figure is determined by treating the 05 as .05 probability (meaning 5 per cent probability) and reading .05 on the vertical axis of Exhibit 12-2; then the time between arrivals is approximately two minutes. In this problem, assume that once a truck is cleared to enter a delivery dock, it takes each truck an average of 20 minutes to unload the freight and drive out of the dock area.

The time of the second arrival is determined by the second number in the table of random numbers. It is 43 and we use .43 for Exhibit 12-2 to see that the second truck arrives 17 minutes later. With only one dock, the second truck must wait because the first truck is still unloading. The second truck is delayed three minutes and then it starts to unload. Exhibit 12-4 presents the waiting times for 20 arrivals, for both one dock and two docks. Continuing for the case of a single dock: Truck three arrives 13 minutes later and it must wait ten minutes before the dock is free. Notice that a significant bunch-up takes place with the arrival of the fifteenth truck. Because the trucks are arriving fairly frequently, the waiting time starts to significantly increase.

The two-dock situation is illustrated by the right-hand two columns. Because two docks are available, the waiting time is significantly lower. The first truck arrives a :02 and is unloaded at that time. The second truck arrives at :19 and it proceeds directly to the second dock for unloading. The third truck arrives at :32 and it proceeds directly to the first dock which was empty 20 minutes after the first truck arrived at :02. The fourth truck arrives at :36 and it must wait. Why? Because the second truck began to unload at :19 and it will not be finished until :39. Therefore the fourth truck must wait

Exhibit 12-4 Monte Carlo Simulation

		Arrival		1 Dock		2 Docks	
Arrival Number	Random Number	Time Between Arrivals (min.)	Time of Arrival	Time Service Starts	Waiting Time (min.)	Time Service Starts	Waiting Time (min.)
1	05	2	:02	:02	0	:02	0
2	43	17	:19	:22	3	:19	0
3	31	13	:13	:42	10	:32	0
4	31	13	:32	:42	10	:32	0
5	39	16	:52	1:22	30	:52	0
6	94	60	1:52	1:52	0	1:52	0
7	63	28	2:20	2:20	0	2:20	0
8	99	75	3:35	3:35	0	3:35	0
9	65	30	4:05	4:05	0	4:05	0
10	80	42	4:47	4:47	0	4:47	0
11	87	50	5:37	5:37	0	5:37	0
12	77	35	6:12	6:12	0	6:12	0
13	24	10	6:22	6:32	10	6:22	0
14	99	75	7:37	7:37	0	7:37	0
15	05	2	7:39	7:57	18	7:39	0
16	08	4	7:43	8:17	34	7:57	14
17	63	28	8:11	8:37	25	8:11	0
18	05	2	8:13	8:57	44	8:17	4
19	07	4	8:17	9:17	60	8:31	14
20	49	20	8:37	9:37	60	8:37	0
		Total Wait in Minutes			320		35
		Average Wait in Minutes			16		1.75

three minutes. The fifth truck arrives at :52 and it does not have to wait because the dock used by the third truck just became available. Notice that with two docks and both being used, the time for the next free dock alternates. When the sixteenth truck arrived, it had to wait 14 minutes. The dock was free, *not* after the fifteenth truck had unloaded, but when the fourteenth was finished.

The average waiting period can be calculated for one dock and two docks. They are 16 minutes and 1.75 minutes, respectively. The Monte Carlo approach to this queueing problem does not tell us whether the second dock should be added. It does, however, tell us how much truck delays will be reduced. Having seen how queueing theory can be applied to a truck dock problem, let's now see whether we can apply it to a problem confronting the Minnetonka Warehouse, and its owner, Wayne Schuller.

Wayne Schuller had been a coal miner in Lewistown, Pennsylvania, but because of an unfortunate incident, he and his family moved to Minnetonka, a western suburb of Minneapolis. Using the proceeds from an out-of-court settlement in Pennsylvania, Wayne purchased the Minnetonka Warehouse company. The operation of the warehouse was a family project. Wayne was in charge of overall warehouse operations. Norma, Wayne's wife, was in charge of sales. Terry, their daughter, was responsible for the financial aspects of the operations. One son, Rick, was a salesman and the other son, Jeff, was foreman of the warehouse labor force.

Within five years after the purchase of the warehouse, significant results had been achieved by the diligence of the family. Sales had gone from $495,000 when purchased, to over $6.1 million annually. The company initially had seventeen employees and it now had 146.

Minnetonka's newest customer was the Cornell Anderson Candy Company. "Corny Candy" was a perennial best seller in New England and the southern states. The product was manufactured in Portland, Maine, and sales in the upper midwestern region of the United States were starting to grow. Dissatisfied with their previous public warehouse the candy company had chosen to use Minnetonka.

Ron Solheim, director of distribution for Anderson Candy, was discussing their warehouse requirements with Wayne Schuller. Ron stated that the warehouse would be electronically connected to the order-processing center of the Anderson Candy Company. Each 15 minutes from 8:15 A.M. to 5:00 P.M., Monday to Friday, the company would send the orders they received for the upper mid-west region to the Minnetonka warehouse. The minimum order for a 15-minute period would be 10 cases and the largest would be about 1,400 cases. Upon receipt of each order, pickers would load the cases on pallets. Each pallet could hold a maximum of 80 cases. (To simplify discussion, assume that the number of pallets loaded in each 15 minute period is the total number of cases/80 and any fraction remaining is loaded on a separate pallet. If 250 cases were ordered, this would mean four pallets: 80 + 80 + 80 + 10. If only 20 cases were ordered in a 15-minute period, this would be one pallet.) After the cases have been placed on the pallets, a sheet of shrink-wrap plastic is wrapped over the cases and secured to the wooden pallet. The pallet and contents are then placed in a "heat tunnel" where heat at 140 degrees F. is applied for a few minutes. (This amount of heat will not damage the Corny Candy.) The loaded pallet and its contents are then removed and the plastic sheet starts to shrink. The plastic gets very taut and securely holds the cases to the pallet. In addition, the cases are protected from dirt, grime, rain, air pollution, etc. Shrink-wrapping is a common technique for products where cleanliness and sanitary conditions are important.

At present, Minnetonka Warehouse does not possess any shrink-wrap equipment. Because the Minnetonka and Anderson companies have entered into a long-term agreement, Wayne has decided to purchase the necessary shrink-wrap equipment. The question is—how many shrink-wrap tunnels should be purchased?

Wayne asked Terry—as their financial person—to solve this question. Terry studied the problem and decided it would be appropriate to use Monte Carlo simulation with queueing theory. Exhibit 12-5 is based on information supplied by the Anderson company, in response to Terry's inquiry.

The vertical axis is the cumulative probability of the number of cases that will be received in any 15-minute period. Thus, 30 per cent of all orders will be equal to 210 or fewer cases, per 15 minute period. Fifty per cent of all orders will be for 420 cases or less, and so on.

Terry determined that each shrink-wrap machine could process one pallet (of up to 80 cases) per five-minute period. Thus one machine could process in 15 minutes up to 240 cases. Because the maximum ever received per 15-minute period was 1,400, the average was 700 or less per 15-minute period. She reasoned, therefore, the maximum number of machines required would be three.

Another requirement of the Anderson Company was that all orders received during one day had to be ready for shipment by 8:00 A.M. the next day. Terry decided to simulate one day's activity and see if one, two, or three shrink-wrap machines would be optimal. She also determined the following:

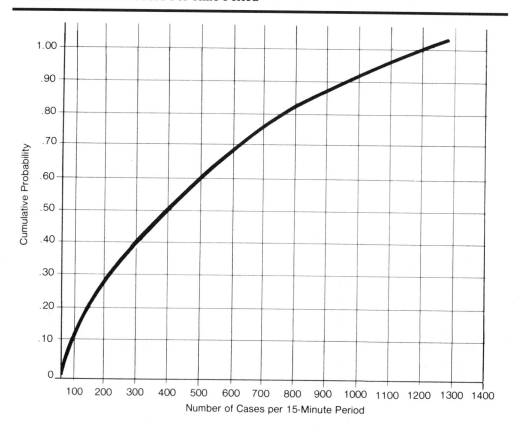

Exhibit 12-5 Ordered Cases Per Time Period

SPECIFIC READINGS FROM THE ABOVE DIAGRAM

Random Number	Number of Cases	Random Number	Number of Cases	Random Number	Number of Cases
04	— 35	31	— 220	78	— 810
05	— 40	33	— 240	80	— 870
06	— 45	36	— 270	85	— 970
07	— 55	39	— 300	87	— 1000
10	— 80	43	— 350	92	— 1110
14	— 100	45	— 360	94	— 1140
17	— 115	47	— 375	97	— 1250
20	— 130	53	— 460	99	— 1300
21	— 135	61	— 550		
30	— 210	63	— 580		

1. The daily cost of a shrink-wrap tunnel was $30—this included capital amortization and energy costs.
2. One employee can successfully operate one, two, or three of the shrink-wrap machines.
3. The average regular rate of pay—including fringe benefits—is $7 per hour.

Exhibit 12-6 Terry's First Ten Calculations of Delays

15 min. Intervals	Random Number	Number of cases Ordered	Number of Pallets to Shrink-Wrap	Time to Shrink Wrap	1 Machine		2 Machine		3 Machine	
					Time behind (Gained) this period	Total Time Behind	Time behind (Gained) this period	Total time behind	Time Behind (Gained) this period	Total Time Behind
8:15 a.m.	05	40	1	5	(10)	0	(25)	0	(40)	0
8:30	04	35	1	5	(10	0	(25)	0	(40)	0
8:45	31	220	3	15	0	0	(15)	0	(30)	0
9:00	17	115	2	10	(5)	0	(20)	0	(35)	0
9:15	21	135	2	10	(5)	0	(20)	0	(35)	0
9:30	43	350	5	25	10	10	(5)	0	(20)	0
9:45	06	45	1	5	(10)	0	(25)	0	(40)	0
10:00	61	550	7	35	20	20	5	5	(10)	0
10:15	47	375	5	25	10	30	(5)	0	(20)	0
10:30	78	810	11	55	40	70	25	25	10	10

Exhibit 12-6 is the first 10 entries of Terry's simulation. She used the table of random numbers in Exhibit 12-3 starting at the upper-left hand number and using that row, and then the next row, and so on.

For the first time period of 8:15 A.M. (36 time periods will be used in total up to 5:00 P.M.), the first random number is 05. Using Exhibit 12-5, we see that it corresponds to an order of 40 cases. Forty cases will fit on one pallet. One pallet requires 5 minutes in the shrink-wrap machine. Therefore 10 minutes of excess time is available if we had one machine. In the column "total time behind," the answer is 0.

At 8:30 A.M. the second order is received. Random number 04 tells us the order is for 35 cases, which will again fit on one pallet. Again we have excess capacity on the one machine, because we can process three pallets in 15 minutes.

At 9:30, notice the random number is 43, which corresponds to an order of 350 cases, which can be accommodated on five pallets. Five pallets, however, cannot be processed by one machine in 15 minutes, so we are 10 minutes behind this period, and because we were not behind before, our total time behind is 10 minutes. Note that with the two machine column at 9:30 A.M., there is no delay because six pallets can be serviced in each 15-minute period. However, look at the 10:00 time period. The random number is 61, yielding a total of 550 cases on seven pallets. With two machines, they are 5 minutes behind, whereas with one machine, they fall 20 minutes behind. With three machines, there still is no delay, because nine pallets (at 5 minutes each) can be serviced in each 15-minute period.

Question One: Terry's first comparisons are going to be between having one or two machines. Complete the additional 26 time periods until 5:00 P.M. Uncompleted work remaining at 5:15 P.M. must be completed at the overtime rate of pay which is double time, or $14 per hour. Which is preferable from a cost standpoint, one or two machines? Why?

Question Two: Terry's next comparisons are going to be between two and three machines. Answer this question in the same manner as question one. Which is preferable, two or three machines? Why?

Question Three: If two workers are used, the shrink-wrap tunnels can process a pallet every three minutes. Would it be advantageous to assign two workers to the task? Why or why not?

Question Four (continuation of question three): Another possibility is to split one warehouse worker's assignment so that he or she helps (i.e., becomes the second worker) at the shrink-wrap machine when work starts backing up. At what point(s) should the foreman tell the second warehouse worker to leave his or her other tasks and to help at the shrink-wrap operation?

Question Five: A salesperson for a competing shrink-wrap oven manufacturer claims that her machine will handle a pallet every two minutes and require only one worker. She indicates that the equipment is available on a lease basis only but she isn't ready to talk an exact price. In comparison to all of the other combinations discussed in answers to earlier questions, what would this competing machine be worth to Minnetonka Warehouse on a daily basis?

Question Six: Both questions one and five dealt with single machine installations. What are the disadvantages of being dependent upon a single machine? How would you assign dollar values to these disadvantages?

Insurance companies often take extra precautions to protect the inventories they have insured. The top picture, from the early 1930's shows a ''Fire Insurance Patrol'' crew riding in a Diamond-T truck. These crews were used in large cities and were privately funded by insurance companies. They would respond to major fires, and their main efforts would be to reduce smoke and water damage to property. The cartoon, from 1984, carries this idea forward. Lloyd's of London insured many of the tankers and cargo that were subject to attack in the Iran-Iraq war.

(*Credit:* Top photo: National Automotive History Collection, Detroit Public Library; bottom cartoon: © 1984 by Miami News.)

Logistics System Controls

Beware of inventory figures from accountants, who delete items valued at zero dollars—dropping them out because they have been fully depreciated—although these items are still in your warehouse.

Robert B. Footlik
Modern Materials Handling
November 19, 1984

San Jose police conducted a two-month undercover investigation with the aid of company officials who became suspicious after noting discrepancies in their inventory of Apple III computers. . . . Computers were disappearing when they reached the company's shipping and receiving department, according to San Jose Police Sergeant James Emmons. "They got them out in various ways," he said. "Employees usually would overload a truck, one to three computers at a time, and then they would actually sell them from the company truck."

San Francisco Chronicle
May 15, 1982

. . . James Burke made a decision that will probably be studied in business schools for a long time to come. Going against the advice of government agents and some of his own colleagues, the chairman of Johnson & Johnson decided to spend whatever millions it would cost to recall 31 million bottles of Tylenol capsules from store shelves across the United States.

Time
October 17, 1983

Key Terms

- Accounting controls
- Worker productivity
- Short-interval scheduling
- Warehouse work rules
- Tachograph
- Product recalls
- Batch numbers
- Pilferage
- Organized theft
- Hijacking
- Computer security
- System security

Learning Objectives

- To understand the use of accounting techniques for PD/L system control
- To examine the worker productivity issue
- To discuss problems and solutions involved in a product recall
- To note how to reduce pilferage and organized theft
- To identify techniques to decrease computer and document theft

Introduction

If logistics management were only a matter of establishing a system and putting it in operation, it would be a relatively simple matter. Unfortunately, systems do not always work the way they are "supposed to." No list of potential problems confronting the logistics manager would be complete. This chapter deals with only a few separate topics ranging from the rather mundane problem of costs getting out of control to the more exciting problem of protecting shipments from thefts.

This chapter is especially important to individuals training for entry level positions in logistics management. Much of their initial performance with their new employer will be evaluated on the basis of how well they exercise *control* responsibilities. Inability to carry out control functions is easily spotted at the beginning levels of management.

The previous chapter dealt with logistics systems design. In the process of designing a system, the need to "control" the system must not be overlooked. Indeed, the control mechanisms must be built into the system, and their effectiveness must be continually monitored. This discussion deals more with those controlling functions that are somewhat *protective* in nature. They must be employed to keep a firm's position from worsening. In a competitive world with small, and sometimes shrinking profit margins, application of tight controls may allow a firm to maintain its position while competitors fall behind.

The word *control* was chosen deliberately. The problems discussed here cannot be eliminated; they can only be controlled. A person involved in logistics management will confront the issues and problems presented in this chapter many times during the course of his or her career.

Accounting Controls

In the early 1970s, a number of firms belonging to the National Council of Physical Distribution Management (NCPDM) funded a study conducted by Professor Michael Schiff that dealt with accounting controls in physical distribution management. In his report, Schiff was critical of two industry practices, both of which dealt with what he felt was improper cost allocation. He believed that physical distribution costs should be considered as selling costs insofar as determining sales strategies and incentives. Goals were set for salesmen, but the goals ignored physical distribution costs and therefore sales personnel ignored this expense item.

Schiff also felt that decisions to increase inventory should be subjected to the same amount of management scrutiny as decisions to commit a like amount of funds to any other undertaking. He found this problem could be overcome by assigning an imputed interest charge on the additional investment in inventory to the unit or individual responsible for the decision to increase inventory size.

Schiff devoted a chapter to methods of controlling physical distribution costs and described four methods. They were: use of budgets, use of standard costs, comparing shipment costs with costs of similar movements stored in a computer's memory, and establishing costs and standards for maintaining desired levels of customer service.[1]

More recently, the NCPDM has commissioned additional studies involving the use of accounting tools as they relate to logistics. Reports resulting from these undertakings include *Transportation Accounting and Control—Guidelines for Distribution and Financial Management* (1983) and *Warehouse Accounting and Control* (1985).[2] Controls are an important segment of these reports; for example, topics covered in the transportation study include responsibility accounting, management by exception, performance accounting, and internal controls.

An example of one firm's efforts to control distribution costs came from the Crown Zellerbach Corporation.[3] They (1) identified physical distribution costs; (2) established standards, including customer service standards, by which performance could be measured; (3) took specific actions to reduce costs or improve performance; and (4) undertook long-range distribution planning that would allow for more orderly facility expansion and market development. In part of their analysis, they scrutinized private truck operating costs at one of their distribution centers. Through accurate methods of cost determination and allocation, they determined that they should not operate their

---

[1] Michael Schiff, *Accounting and Cost Control in Physical Distribution Management* (Chicago: NCPDM, 1972). See also, Howard M. Armitage and James F. Dickow, "Controlling Distribution with Standard Costs and Flexible Budgets," *NCPDM 1979 Meeting Papers*, pp. 99–122; and John L. Boros, "An Applied Distribution Cost Accounting System," *NCPDM 1980 Meeting Papers*, pp. 431–451.

[2] These reports are available from NCPDM, 2803 Butterfield Road, Oak Brook, IL 60521.

[3] This discussion is adapted from a paper by E. L. Weinthaler, Jr., of Crown Zellerbach, delivered at the NCPDM annual conference in October 1974.

own trucks for hauls beyond a radius over 150 miles. These hauls were turned over to common carriers.

Crown Zellerbach also developed "lanes" that are linked origins and destinations over which large volumes of the firm's traffic move. Each month a report is prepared for each lane, giving details on the type of product shipped, the volume in each shipment, the mode, and the cost. At the end of the month management is able to determine which loads should have been consolidated or to identify a lower cost carrier mode. The resulting information suggests what actions should be taken in the future to improve performance on any lane in question. This information is also useful when conducting rate and service negotiations with carriers. However, the principal value of the monthly lane report is that it enables management to review performance and make suggestions for improvements.

Looking at another firm, here is how John J. Mahan, director of distribution for The Gillette Company, described the distribution accounting function in his firm:

> Distribution accounting reports to Distribution on a dotted line basis and provides financial consulting services to distribution management. It prepares operating and capital budgets and interim forecasts, as well as establishes performance standards. The group also prepares management reports on freight expense, private fleet results and public warehouses, and operating expense variance analysis.
>
> In addition, they maintain and operate an internal control system for distribution and insure its adherence to corporate guidelines for the approval and payment of invoices, contracts, leases, capital expenditures, and the protection of company assets. Finally, they insure accurate reporting of all finished goods inventory.[4]

Note how many of these functions described are of a controlling nature. Recall the description of the interfaces between a firm's logistics staff and its accountants, which was also discussed in Chapter 2. In addition, it is possible to establish statistical controls over logistics systems, setting tolerance ranges within which performance is considered to be satisfactory.

Worker Productivity

Labor is expensive, and its efficient use is necessary for a profitable operation. The two most frequent uses of labor in physical distribution are in warehousing and in transport of goods. Both warehousing and trucking involve heavy investments in capital equipment (which frequently reduces the need for workers). The workers and the equipment must be used in a manner that achieves the lowest cost for a given volume of output. In most areas, warehouse workers, drivers, and helpers are unionized, and work rule

---

[4] John J. Mahan, "Management and Control of Distribution Costs," NCPDM *1983 Papers*, p. 967. "Dotted line" refers to the firm's organization chart and—as used here—implies that distribution accounting is not under the direct, complete control of the firm's distribution function manager.

provisions influence productivity.[5] In areas where warehouse workers' unions resist changes in work rules, a warehouse may become prematurely obsolete, not because of its structure or equipment, but because of high-cost work practices that the union insists on continuing. Firms faced with such a situation can improve warehouse efficiency by locating a new warehouse in an area outside the original union's jurisdiction. The new warehouse should be either nonunion or, if unionized, the union should be one that accepts the new work practices.

Efficient use of labor is usually increased by scheduling work in advance. In a warehouse the time for performing each task, such as opening a truck door, stacking a pallet, or "picking" a case of outgoing goods, is calculated. Precise time breakdowns—to the number of seconds—are used. The location of the pallet load in the warehouse or its height above the floor makes a difference. Outgoing cases being picked also require different amounts of time, again depending on their location, volume, and weight. Picking and assembling an outgoing order comprising cases of different dimensions is more time consuming than if all cases are of the same or similar size. These data are used in two ways. First, they indicate that the goods within the warehouse should be arranged so that the more popular, or faster-moving, items are located in slots where they will require less time for storage and retrieval. Second, through use of computer programs, an order picker's travel sequence can be arranged in a way that minimizes time that he or she (and whatever equipment is being used) will require.

As might be expected, work scheduling systems become involved in labor-management controversies. Safeway's northern California warehouses were subjected to a long strike in 1978, with one of the issues being a computer-based work schedule system:

> Al Fernandez, 34, has worked in the warehouse since the program was initiated. . . . He is big, well-muscled. His opinion of the work rating system is printed across his T-shirt: "Fork It."
>
> "You can't do it. Well, maybe if you're a guy out of football training camp, but that's it. I'm in good shape. I play ball, work out. And according to their system, I'm behind an average of 13 minutes each hour."[6]

Statements such as this were countered by Safeway's management, which was able to keep the distribution centers running during the strike. A management spokesman said, "We've been using many strike replacements, some who are female, and many supervisors not used to physical work. Yet they are matching or bettering the standard."[7]

Short-Interval Scheduling

One method of analysis is short-interval scheduling which means looking at each worker's activity in small time segments. An amount of time is assigned to each unit of work, and then the individual's work is scheduled in

[5] See Frank Dorsey, "Preparing the Union for Work Standards," NCPDM *1982 Papers*, pp. 581–594. See also: "Fleming's Fast Rise in Wholesale Foods," *Fortune* (January 21, 1985), p. 54.

[6] *San Francisco Sunday Examiner and Chronicle,* September 10, 1978.

[7] Ibid.

a manner that (1) utilizes as much of each worker's time as possible and (2) maximizes output for each worker. This scheduling technique is useful to supervisory personnel. Each day's work for the operation is plotted out and is, in essence, a summation of each worker's tasks. For a warehouse, the scheduling may also be tied into departure times for delivery trucks (also controlled by computerized scheduling) and arrival of trucks with incoming freight. (Large buyers frequently require suppliers' trucks to arrive within rather limited time blocks, say, 30 minutes or an hour, because this reduces congestion at the receiving dock and spreads the arrival of inbound materials throughout the working day.) Because an operation's entire work day can be prescheduled, the supervisor can tell as the day progresses how the actual progress compares to the schedule. If at the end of the first hour in an eight-hour shift, less than one eighth of the work has been completed, the supervisor must take steps to catch up within the second hour (or at least to fall no further behind). Short interval scheduling can also be used by intermediate management to assess the effectiveness of supervision. One firm has a "lost time review" report to be filled out by the immediate supervisor on a daily basis. In case the immediate supervisor fails to note or explain the lost time, the information appears on a form entitled "unexplained lost time," which intermediate management prepares to cover instances when more time was spent on a job than had been assigned *and* the immediate supervisor failed to report it.[8]

Improving Performance

Knowledge of supervisory techniques is important to college students of physical distribution and logistics because, fairly early in their career, they are likely to receive an assignment that includes supervision of others. Some workers are more obviously in need of supervision than others (see Figure 13-1); the skills of workers assigned to the same task also may vary (see Figure 13-2). The supervisor's goal should be to improve performance. Emery Air Freight Corporation uses a three-pronged approach, consisting of performance audit, feedback, and positive reinforcement. After a worker's performance is measured, it is important that this information be fed back to him, so he knows his relative performance. According to a spokesman for Emery, several clues will indicate that lack of feedback is a cause of poor performance:

1. When asked, a worker does not accurately and immediately know his level of performance.
2. When asked, a worker does not know a performance standard exists.

[8] Roland T. Fisher, "Short Interval Scheduling" (a paper presented at the NCPDM San Francisco Roundtable Workshop, April 29, 1975). Also, since the early 1970s, the American Warehousemen's Association has been developing and refining "standard" times for the handling of materials in warehouses. They also provide personal computer software to their members to allow them to implement these scheduling systems daily.

Figure 13-1 The Objective of Supervision Is to Improve Performance

"That new man may bear watching."

Reproduced by permission of the artist and the Masters' Agency.

3. Whenever a specific performance is consistently below standard.
4. When an employee says he does not know what he is supposed to do.[9]

Once performance information is made available to the worker, the next step is to continually reinforce his or her instances of good performance with some form of reward that may be anything from an approving nod to a large Christmas bonus. The Emery spokesman asked the question as to which of the following is the better use of an available reward:

a. "John, would you agree to take the day shift starting Monday?"
b. "John, your order processing performance for the past three months has been ten percent above our goal. That's an outstanding accomplishment. As a result, you may choose your shift assignment. Starting Monday, which shift would you like?"[10]

Previously it was noted that union work rules are usually inflexible and impossible to change. This is not always true. Sometimes, as part of the bargaining transaction, it is possible for management to get unions to agree to alter some work practices. Usually management must demonstrate that

---

[9] Paul F. Hammond, "Increasing Productivity Through Performance Audit, Feedback, and Positive Reinforcement," in *1974 Papers of the American Society of Traffic and Transportation,* p. 31.
[10] Ibid.

Figure 13-2 Employees Have Varying Degrees of Skills

Reproduced by permission of the artist and the Master's Agency.

neither the union as a group nor its members as individuals will be adversely affected. Thus, when performance standards are measured, some attention should be paid to those standards that are influenced or controlled by contractual work rules. As it goes into collective bargaining sessions, management must know the savings from eliminating or altering a work rule because these calculations establish a "value" of each contemplated change.

Performance standards, as such, may not be included in the contract. However, provisions have to be made giving management the right to establish them and to use them. Unions want protection from "unreasonable" standards, and mutually agreed-upon procedures are also necessary for handling new or continuing employees who consistently fall below established standards.

In order to maintain and improve productivity, it is also necessary to have in existence a set of work rules that are to be enforced. These serve many purposes, but the important one to be mentioned here is that they keep a work force (or its individual members) from backsliding into poorer performance. Figure 13-3, which appeared in *Warehousing Review,* is one public warehouseman's set of work rules.

Financial incentives may also be used. Sometimes they are given as bonuses to warehouse supervisors. They can also be used carefully to encourage teamwork on the part of all employees. Some warehouses will pay a bonus (beyond whatever provisions exist in their contract with workers)

Figure 13-3 Example of Warehouse Work Rules

Ours is a company that has been built on service to its customers. Our business has grown both in the number of customers and in the area which we serve. We are constantly striving to improve our service, because it is only through growth and progress that a company can give to its employees the good wages, increased benefits, and job security that everyone wants.

In order to meet these aims it is necessary to adhere to a set of rules. Whenever people work together they have certain rights and privileges. Along with these rights they have certain obligations and responsibilities. So that each employee will know what is expected of him we have drawn up a list of work rules which are necessary for the orderly and efficient operation of our business. By following these rules you contribute to the progress of the company and therefore to the stability of your own job. These rules therefore benefit you rather than hinder you. They are fair rules and to keep them fair to everyone they will be enforced in every required situation.

These rules are listed in two groups, by type of violation, and are as follows:

- Violations subject to discharge on the first offense.
- Violations subject to constructive discipline.

Violations Subject to Discharge on the First Offense

(1) The possession of, drinking of, or use of any alcoholic beverages or narcotic drugs on company property; or being on company premises at any time under the influence of alcohol, or drugs, or while suffering from an alcoholic hangover which materially affects work performance.

(2) The transportation of, or failure to notify the company of, unauthorized persons on company equipment or its property.

(3) Theft or misappropriation of company property or the property of any of its customers or employees.

(4) Deliberate or malicious damage to the company's equipment and warehouse facilities or to the merchandise and property of its customers.

(5) Intentional falsification of records in any form, including ringing another employee's time card, or falsifying employment application.

(6) Fighting while on duty or on company premises or provoking others to fight.

(7) Smoking in a building or van, or any restricted area, or while loading or unloading merchandise and other items.

(8) Immoral or indecent conduct which affects work performance or makes the employee unsuited for the work required.

(9) Unauthorized possession of, or carrying of, firearms or other weapons.

(10) Insubordination — refusal to perform assigned work or to obey a supervisor's order, or encouraging others to disobey such an order.

Violations Subject to Constructive Discipline

The rules printed below are subject to constructive discipline. This means that for the first offense you will be given a constructive reprimand. For a second offense you will receive a disciplinary layoff without pay, the length of which will depend upon the seriousness of the offense; subject to the terms of the collective bargaining agreement which may exist between employee and union. For a third offense you will be discharged, subject to the collective bargaining agreement.

If you have had a violation, followed by a record of no violations for a nine (9) month period, the original violation will be withdrawn from your record.

(1) Excessive tardiness regardless of cause. (Being tardy and not ready to perform work at the designated starting time may at the company's option result in the employee being sent home without pay.)

(2) Absenteeism without just cause and excessive absenteeism regardless of cause. If you must be absent for a justifiable reason notify the company in advance. Justified absence will be

(Continued)

Figure 13-3 (Continued)

excused if the company is notified as soon as possible before the beginning of the shift; however, too many justified and excused absences may be grounds for constructive discipline as well as unjustified, unexcused absence. If you are absent from work for three consecutive work days without notification followed by failure to report for work on the fourth day you will automatically be removed from the payroll with the notification "quit without notice."

(3) Failure to work reasonable overtime.

(4) Unauthorized absence from assigned work location.

(5) Failure to observe proper break periods, lunch periods, and quitting times, unless otherwise directed by your supervisor.

(6) Disregard for common rules of safety, safe practices, good housekeeping and sanitation.

(7) Unauthorized or negligent operation or use of machines, tools, vehicles, equipment and materials.

(8) Loss or damage to the property of the company or its customers which could have been reasonably avoided.

(9) Failure to complete work assignments within a reasonable length of time or loafing on such assignments.

(10) Garnishments not satisfied prior to the hearing before the court issuing same.

(11) Gambling on company premises.

(12) Use of immoral, obscene or indecent language on company premises.

(13) Trying to persuade or organize other employees to disobey any of these rules and regulations. ■

Courtesy of *Warehousing Review,* Vol. 4, no. 5, p. 9. Copyright 1975 by the American Warehousemen's Association.

if certain performance elements—such as percentage of accurately filled orders—are improved.

Another concern in setting performance standards must be safety. One runs the risk that as performance or production is increased, there is an increased risk of accidents that injure workers or damage merchandise or equipment. (See Figure 13-4.)

Driver Supervision

When discussing supervision of logistics labor, a distinction has to be made between warehousing and trucking. In warehousing, the supervisor or foreman is physically present and expected to be "on top" of any situation. However, once on the road, truck drivers are removed from immediate supervision. In addition, they are in day-to-day contact with customers. And, while on the road, they and their trucks can be seen by thousands of motorists. Because of these factors, different types of supervision, as well as different types of workers, may be needed.

When a worker in a warehouse falls behind schedule, the fact is noticed almost immediately and corrective action can be taken. A foreman can choose from a range of supervisory techniques to provide an incentive for the worker to improve performance. On the other hand, the work of a truck driver is more difficult to evaluate. If he falls behind schedule, it may be because of traffic conditions or a bottleneck at the consignee's loading dock.

Figure 13-4 There are Dangers Associated with Over-Achieving

"I said not such a heavy load, Hooper!"

Reproduced by permission of the Master's Agency.

Initially, all that a supervisor can do is to accept the driver's word. On the other hand, it is necessary to have a control mechanism so that drivers who continually encounter delays can be distinguished from those who do not. Figure 13-5 is a computer printout showing the monthly delivery performance. Shown are the number of cases and weight handled; the amount of time spent waiting, unloading, and driving; and the truck's average speed. The *P* indicates that pallets are utilized and that the receiver uses a fork-lift truck to unload the trailer. *C* means specialized wheeled carts are used instead of pallets. Various comparisons are made including the average cost per ton and the average cost per case. "Adjusted cases per hour" takes into account both waiting time and unloading time.

This arrangement of data can be used, for example, to support a driver's contention that his relatively poor performance is caused by delays at the customer's receiving dock. His contention could be verified by having a different driver make the deliveries to determine whether the delays still happen. If they did, the supplier would approach the customer with these printouts and indicate that some improvements were needed in his receiving procedures.

If it is determined that the cause of the problem is an inadequacy of the customer's receiving ability, care would have to be used in informing the customer. The supplier's marketing staff would have to be made aware of the problem, and calculations would have to be made of how profitable the account was at the present time, given the unloading handicaps. If it were determined that the unloading delays made servicing the account unprofitable, then the supplier might threaten to discontinue service or raise prices.

Figure 13-5 Delivery Performance

ASSOCIATED FOOD STORES INC.

ASSOCIATED FOOD STORES INC.   PAGE NO. 2

DELIVERY PERFORMANCE ANALYSIS
WEEK ENDING 11/01/

REPORT NO. 2 —STORE—

DRIVER		P	STORE	CASES	WEIGHT	WAIT	UNLD	CS/HR	ADJ CS/HR
B	,D.	P	BEL AIR MARKET # 7	467	30,699	.1	.3	1,556	1,167
D	,P.	P	BEL AIR MARKET # 7	1,055	6,000	.1	.5	2,110	1,758
F	,J.	P	BEL AIR MARKET # 7	242		.1	.4	605	484
M	,J.	P	BEL AIR MARKET # 7	120		.2	.3	400	240
			TOTAL	1,884	36,699	.5	1.5	1,256	942
F	,J.	C	BELL MARKET # 1	1,038	24,525	.1	1.1	943	865
F	,J.	C	BELL MARKET # 1	446	14,306	.1	.9	495	446
F	,J.	P	BELL MARKET # 1	50	2,000	.1	.2	250	166
			TOTAL	1,534	40,831	.3	2.2	697	613
F	,J.	C	BELL MARKET # 2	300	12,000	.1	.7	428	375
M		C	BELL MARKET # 2	729		1.2	1.5	486	270
M		C	BELL MARKET # 2	1,242	30,420	.1	1.8	690	653
V	,B.		BELL MARKET # 2	1		.1	.1	10	5
			TOTAL	2,272	42,420	1.5	4.1	554	405
G	A.	C	BELL MARKET # 3	913	23,049	.2	1.0	913	760
M		C	BELL MARKET # 3	1,200	30,601	.3	1.0	1,200	923
			TOTAL	2,113	53,650	.5	2.0	1,056	845
M		C	BELL MARKET # 4	408	10,392	.2	.9	453	370
M	J.	C	BELL MARKET # 4	671	15,109	.2	.9	745	610
			TOTAL	1,079	25,501	.4	1.8	599	490

Courtesy Associated Food Stores.

If it were found that servicing the account was profitable in spite of the unloading delays, a more tactful approach would be employed.

This illustrates an important interface between marketing and logistics. Care has to be used when establishing customer service standards to insure that they do not become a drain on profits. In this example, one does not know what his competitors would do; they are probably handicapped by the same inefficiencies at the customer's receiving dock. The buyer might respond that the problem is not at his dock, but that he runs a friendly and relaxed operation, and if delivery drivers want to have a cup of coffee and chat for a few minutes before unloading their trucks, he doesn't mind. What he does mind, however is having this friendly atmosphere labeled as "inefficient" by some supplier's computer. In this situation, the customer has indicated that he likes the supplier's drivers but he does not like the supplier's computer. The point of this example is that supervision of the driver could be related to a firm's selling efforts.

Another device used to aid in controlling one's truck drivers is the *tachograph*, a precision recording instrument that is installed inside the vehicle and produces a continuous written record of the operations of the truck, and presumably, the driver. Figure 13-6 shows a used tachograph chart and the data that were recorded. The nomenclature and graduation of the chart follow the figure. (Letter references are to Figure 13-6.)

An individual experienced in working with these charts can tell quickly how efficiently the truck and driver are being used. If the driver works on a regular route, it may be possible to rearrange his stops so he can avoid areas of traffic congestion. Bad driving habits such as high highway speeds, or excessive engine idling, are also obvious. In case of an accident, the chart is invaluable in reporting, and perhaps explaining, what had occurred just prior to impact.

One trucking magazine carried an article that said, in part:

> The use of tachographs in its 85-van fleet has improved gasoline use by 15 per cent, largely through improvements in driving habits, . . . reports Auto Glass Specialists.
>
> The company sends its installers from 17 service centers in Wisconsin, Michigan, and Iowa to the customers' site, where they replace windshields and windows in vehicles. The customers include commercial fleets and farmers, as well as auto and truck dealers and body shops.
>
> . . . the firm knows in advance how long each installation will take and the distance between jobs. By correlating the tachograph records with the installers' logs, . . . the company ensures that equipment and installation time is maximized.
>
> Good driving habits are readily identifiable from the tachograph charts, such as holding speeds on upgrades, reducing idling time, maintaining smooth acceleration and braking, and . . . driving no faster than 55 mph.[11]

Product Recalls

A vexing physical distribution/logistics problem, one which has cost several physical distribution or product-line managers their jobs, involves the inability to cope with a product recall crisis. A product recall occurs when a hazard or defect is discovered in a manufactured item that is already in the distribution channels. This necessitates a reversal in the usual outward flow of merchandise. One manufacturer who undertook a product recall instructed all his retailers to ship the goods in question back to his plant. To his dismay, he discovered that many of his retailers did not know how to write a bill of lading or to take any of the other necessary steps to accomplish the movement.[12]

[11] *Transport Topics* (July 14, 1980), p. 24.

[12] Information obtained in an interview during a research project that resulted in the following paper: Ronald S. Yaros and Donald F. Wood, "Recalling Products in the Drug and Cosmetic Industry," *Journal of Business Logistics*, **1:** 48–59 (1979).

Figure 13-6 Tachograph Chart

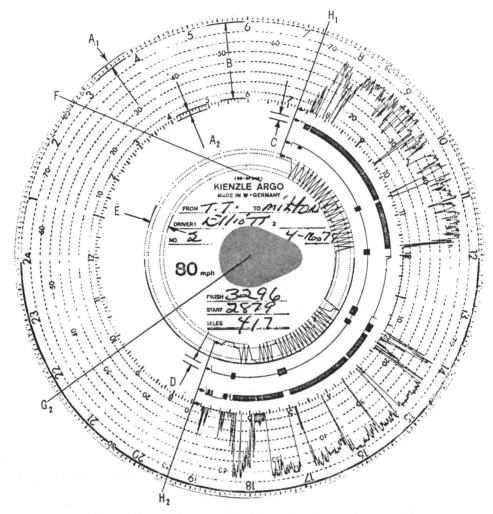

Source: Argo Instruments Corp., Long Island City, New York.

In recent years there have been well-publicized recalls involving soups, drugs, toys, and autos. From the manufacturer's standpoint, the publicity is undesirable. This is an instance where the saying "There's no such thing as bad publicity" does not hold. If the manufacturer plays down the amount of publicity, he runs the risk that a user will be harmed by the defective product after the defect has been known to exist by the manufacturer. In a subsequent lawsuit, the injured consumer might allege that the manufacturer failed to devote sufficient effort and publicity to his recall campaign.

The best-known recall in the past few years was of Tylenol. The recall, which took place in late 1982, cost Johnson & Johnson an estimated $50 million. The firm undertook the action on its own, after seven individuals in the Chicago area died after using the product. The product had been tampered with by an individual who is believed to have removed the bot-

Figure 13-6 (Continued)

A₁, Outer Time Scale	0:00 to 24:00 hrs. (Military)
GRADUATION:	Single line at 5 min. intervals, full hrs., in wider line also printed out in numbers in 70 to 80 MPH circle. PM time (12 to 24) identified by continuous wider beam.
B, Speed Range (next inner circle from A₁)	0 to 80 MPH
GRADUATION:	Every 10 miles also by dotted concentric lines at 50 min. intervals except at full hrs. 10 to 80 printed out equally spaced and staggered from bottom to top over periods (four times repeated).
A₂, Inner Time Scale (next inner circle from B)	2 times—1 to 12 hrs. (consecutive)
GRADUATION:	As A₁ Full hrs. printed in numbers between "o" line and 10 MPH field.
C, Stop and Go Range (next inner circle from A₂)	Blank space, recording for go periods is a wide beam, for stop periods a thin line.
D, Engine Idling Range	Blank, recording for engine idling is a wide beam. At other times a thin line.
E, Distance Scale (next inner circle from D)	Between two upper and two lower circles, also, concentric lines at 5 min. intervals.
GRADUATION:	One mile each between two upper and lower circles. Total of 5 miles for full band.
F, Center Field	For entries such as date, vehicle number, driver's name, destination, mileage at start and finish, total trip mileage, also manufacturer's name and order number.
G, Cut-out	For proper fastening and synchronizing on instrument.
H₁₋₂, Beginning (1) and Ending (2) of Recording Periods	Whenever the stylii are engaged, are disengaged from the chart, a comma-like marking is made.

tles' caps and added cyanide-laced capsules. The company already had a recall plan ready so it could respond to such an emergency. The product was reintroduced with more tamper-proof packaging and—within a year—the firm had regained more than 80 per cent of its one-time market share.[13]

Once a recall campaign is completed (or under way, depending on how it is conducted), the manufacturer and his distributors must take immediate steps to refill the retailer's shelves with either defect-free batches of the same product or with a substitute product. Although this step is not as important as the recall, it must be undertaken to minimize losses. Otherwise, competitors will take the opportunity to suggest that the retailer use their own product to fill his empty shelf spaces.

Sometimes products are recalled through different channels than they are distributed. The National Wholesale Druggist Association favors a policy that eliminates the wholesaler in product recalls. Goods are returned to the manufacturer even though he may simply destroy them after he receives them. In theory, it would be easier to authorize retailers or wholesalers to destroy them. However, if the goods are, in fact, hazardous, it may be desirable for the manufacturer to supervise their destruction. There is always a risk that the defective goods may not be properly disposed of and individuals will be injured. Accounting controls are necessary to ensure that individuals returning the recalled materials are reimbursed only for the goods they return.

Sometimes the problem can be overcome by merely changing the product's label or adding a warning label. A lamp manufacturer might be required to add a sticker to each lamp, saying, "Do not use light bulbs larger than 100 watts in this lamp." In this instance, the manufacturer could have the stickers attached at some intermediate point between the place of manufacture and the retail outlet.

Product recall takes many forms. The differences depend upon the type of product. The responsible government agency (including state and local, as well as foreign governments) all have their own procedures. The degree of danger posed by the defect also differs, the worst defects being those that are discovered to be life-threatening on a direct cause-and-effect basis. Less serious are the defects that are discovered to be *possible* threats to life, such as being linked to causes of cancer if exposure is over a long period of time. An even less serious problem is posed by products that are discovered to be merely mislabeled such as saying "contents 16 ounces" when, in fact, the label should read "contents 12 ounces." In this last situation there is no hazard to potential users; however, the manufacturer, and possibly the distributors, would be guilty of violating statutes dealing with consumer fraud.

Federal Agencies Involved with Recalls

The Federal Food and Drug Administration (FDA) is concerned with food, drugs, and cosmetics. In what they consider to be a "Class I Recall," i.e., the most serious of hazards, such as botulism toxin in foods, the FDA will

---

[13] *Time* (Oct. 17, 1983), p. 67; and *Security Management* (April 1983), pp. 50–51.

insist that the product be recalled at the consumer level and all intermediate levels, and that 100 per cent effectiveness checks be made of all distribution points. They will also cause a public warning to be issued.

Another involved federal agency is the Consumer Product Safety Commission (CPSC). It is less concerned with recall procedures as such, since its approach is to *ban* the sale of products they deem to be hazardous, thereby making it an offense for a retailer, wholesaler, or other distributor to sell a banned product. If the CPSC bans the sale of a specific item, it becomes "frozen" in all distribution channels because it cannot be sold. Manufacturers and distributors are required to *repurchase* the banned items. The CPSC does not concern itself with the items handled by the FDA, although it may concern itself with how the items are packaged. The CPSC is a much newer agency and has taken over product safety functions of several older federal agencies. It also administers some new programs such as those dealing with flammable fabrics. From a distribution control standpoint, note that the FDA has procedures for *recall* that result in a reverse flow of the defective products from the consumer back to the manufacturer. The CPSC merely bans sale of the product and halts it in its place in the distribution network.

A third federal agency is the National Highway Traffic Safety Administration, which is concerned with motor vehicles and their accessory parts. It does not engage in recalls; it is responsible only for causing the manufacturer to *notify* each purchaser that a defect has been discovered. In practice, the buyer is told to take his auto to the nearest dealer who will correct the defect at no cost to the buyer. The method of notification is registered mail to the first purchaser of record. Sometimes it is not necessary for the owner to take the vehicle back to the dealer. In one instance, the manufacurer had to issue a corrected sticker showing different tire pressures; the owners were instructed to place that decal over the original one (and to see a dealer if they had difficulty following the instructions).

Publicity, Liability, and "Fire Drills"

Product recall, whatever form it takes, is an extremely serious matter for the manufacturer and all parties in the distribution network. Adverse publicity and large lawsuits can be devastating. Top management must be involved in any recall activity. Other involved staff should include members of the firm's legal, controller, public relations, quality control, product engineering, and marketing staffs. Management, who may never have known how the firm's logistics system functioned, will be anxiously examining its effectiveness in handling a product recall. Usually a firm designates one individual to be responsible for handling recall activity. Some firms even have practice or "fire drill" recalls to determine their speed and degree of coverage. All actions that a firm takes to prepare for a hypothetical recall are important for two reasons. First, they will allow better performance when the real emergency arises. Second, in case the recall is not completely successful and lawsuits result, a portion of the firm's defense might be the precautionary measures it had undertaken.

The possibility of defective products and product recalls increases the need for positively identifying each product or batch as it leaves the assembly line. If a defect is detected, it is easier to zero in on the group or batch of items produced at about the same time (which should, at least, be inspected to assure that they are not also defective). Items such as office machines contain serial numbers, and their entire move through a distribution system is recorded by that number. In a recall, they are relatively easy to trace. For items that do not contain serial numbers, a ''batch'' number is commonly used. An example would be 33 C 6 B 2 5, where

33 was day of the year (February 2)
C was plant
6 was year 1986
B was production line B
2 was second shift
5 was fifth hour of that shift

A computerized inventory control system might record the batch number stenciled on each carton. (This information would also be used to insure that the inventory was being turned in proper sequence.) If the batch numbers were recorded as the goods moved through the distribution system, in a recall it would be possible to trace each carton to a warehouse or to a retailer. The problem, and the accompanying adverse publicity, could then be more regionalized than if the manufacturer had to undertake a nation-wide search campaign.

Figure 13-7 is a public warehouse's inventory activity report (prepared for one of its grocery customers). Every time they receive a shipment of an item, it is given new lot number, and at one time the warehouse may have large quantities of the same product whose only difference is their lot numbers. The warehouse's computer is programmed to pick the oldest lot for outgoing shipment, which results in a FIFO system. If a product recall does occur, the warehouse's record indicates which customers received goods from the various lots.

A FIFO (first in/first out) system insures an orderly movement of goods in stock. The alternative is LIFO (last in/first out).

Pilferage

A continual problem of nearly all business is theft and pilferage. Pilferage is, of course, one form of theft, and it is usually thought of as theft by one's own employees on a somewhat casual, although repetitive, basis. Materials stolen are usually for the employee's own use, whereas theft is more likely

Figure 13-7 Excerpt from Warehouseman's Activity Report Tracing Lot Numbers from Manufacturer to Retailer

```
IRP04                                    LEDERER TERMINAL  WAREHOUSE CO.
     ANDERSON CLAYTON FOODS       0085
     MERCHANDISE STORED AT-                INVENTORY ACTIVITY REPORT      AS OF   1/31/80        PAGE   1
     LEE ROAD
```

DATE	ITEM #		DESCRIPTION	SHP/RLS # B/L-OSD#	RCPTS	SHPPD	ADJ.	BAL
12/31/79	01058	CS	12/8-7 SEAS HERBS & SPICES			BEGINNING BALANCE		610
1/03/80	LOT# 5240		TRLR 847L40LT RIGGS	3923379 C 8611	160			
1/28/80	LOT# 6506		ACF TRK	3925754 C 8980	160			
1/30/80	LOT# 6717		G22095B COLDWAY	3930165 C 9028	320			
1/02/80	LOT# 3508		AMERICAN SEAWAY FDS INC	3923035 3923035		60		
1/02/80	LOT# 3508		SCOT LAD FDS INC	3923465 3923465		60		
1/03/80	LOT# 3508		A & P TEA CO INC	3922970 3922970		9		
1/03/80	LOT# 3897		A & P TEA CO INC	3922970 3922970		31		
1/08/80	LOT# 3897		SCOT LAD FOODS INC	3924771 3924771		100		
1/09/80	LOT# 3897		MCLAIN GROC	3925427 3925427		13		
1/11/80	LOT# 4167		HEINENS INC	3926031 3926031		23		
1/11/80	LOT# 3897		HEINENS INC	3926031 3926031		16		
1/14/80	LOT# 4167		SEAWAY FOODS INC	3926635 3926635		60		
1/15/80	LOT# 4167		SCOT LAD FOODS INC	3926610 3926610		77		
1/15/80	LOT# 5036		SCOT LAD FOODS INC	3926610 3926610		13		
1/18/80	LOT# 5036		THOROFARE MARKETS INC	3928014 3928014		80		
1/21/80	LOT# 5036		CAHRLEY BROTHERS	3928421 3928421		52		
1/22/80	LOT# 5036		SCOT LAD FOODS INC	3928492 3928492		15		
1/22/80	LOT# 5240		SCOT LAD FOODS INC	3928492 3928492		65		
1/23/80	LOT# 5240		MCALIN GROC	3929105 3929105		26		
			ITEM WEIGHT	7,700	640	700		
						ENDING BALANCE		550
12/31/79	01582	CS	12/8-7 SEAS GREEN GODDESS DRSG			BEGINNING BALANCE		1,185
1/28/80	LOT# 6621		RIGGS	3929538 C 9008	320			
1/02/80	LOT# 9579		SCOT LAD FDS INC	3923465 3923465		20		
1/03/80	LOT# 9579		TAMARKIN CO	3923569 3923569		39		
1/04/80	LOT# 1373		GOLDEN DAWN FDS	3924195 3924195		5		
1/04/80	LOT# 9579		GOLDEN DAWN FDS	3924195 3924195		5		
1/07/80	LOT# 1373		FRANK FORTUNE GROC CO	3924551 3924551		10		
1/08/80	LOT# 1373		SCOT LAD FOODS INC	3924771 3924771		60		
1/08/80	LOT# 1373		BETSY ROSS FOODS INC	3924972 3924972		20		
1/09/80	LOT# 1373		CARDINAL FDS INC	3925085 3925085		25		
1/09/80	LOT# 1373		MCLAIN GROC	3925427 3925427		26		
1/11/80	LOT# 1373		HEINENS INC	3926031 3926031		13		
1/14/80	LOT# 3565		TAMARKIN CO	3926630 3926630		38		
1/14/80	LOT# 1373		TAMARKIN CO	3926630 3926630		1		
1/15/80	LOT# 3565		SCOT LAD FOODS INC	3926610 3926610		20		
1/17/80	LOT# 3565		ASSOCIATED GROCERS INC	3927559 3927559		10		
1/18/80	LOT# 3565		THOROFARE MARKETS INC.	3928014 3928014		80		
1/21/80	LOT# 3580		CAHRLEY BROTHERS	3928421 3928421		40		
1/21/80	LOT# 3565		CAHRLEY BROTHERS	3928421 3928421		12		
1/22/80	LOT# 3767		SCOT LAD FOODS INC	3928492 3928492		38		
1/22/80	LOT# 3580		SCOT LAD FOODS INC	3928492 3928492		22		
1/22/80	LOT# 3580		THE TAMARKIN CO	3928498 3928498		78		
1/23/80	LOT# 3580		CARDINAL FOODS INC	3928736 3928736		20		

Courtesy Lederer Terminals, Cleveland, Ohio.

to be conducted by outsiders, although one's employees may be involved. Theft is conducted on an organized basis, and it is likely that the goods are stolen for resale. An East Coast importer made the distinction this way: "Theft we consider as individual packages, or the loss of the whole package; pilferage is where packages are opened and a certain portion . . . taken."[14]

Since pilferage involves a firm's own employees, controls must begin with the hiring process and must continue with supervisory practices. This is an area where double standards exist. A warehouse employee caught carrying a can of the company's gasoline out of the warehouse and placing it in his private auto would be subjected to disciplinary action or might even be fired. Yet the warehouse superintendent may use the company car, with company gasoline, to run personal errands.

[14] Statement by Edwin A. Elbert before U.S. Senate Committee on Commerce considering cargo security legislation (S. 3595 and S.J. Res. 222), September 29 and 30, 1970, p. 85.

Pilferage is widespread and cannot be completely eliminated. Employees at lower levels tend to view pilferage as their opportunity to obtain comparable disguised (and nontaxable) income. Most firms find it less expensive to tolerate a small amount of pilferage than to impose a system of "total" control. The principal cost of total control is in employee turnover; many individuals choose not to work under such close scrutiny and supervision.

A toll bridge authority installed an elaborate toll collection monitoring system that made it virtually impossible for toll collectors to cheat. Turnover among toll takers increased drastically for two reasons: The total income of most toll takers was apparently reduced. And, without a chance to attempt to "beat" the supervisory system, the tedious job of toll collection became even more tedious. Costs of increased employee turnover soon exceeded the savings from the "cheat-proof" system. The bridge authority then decided to adopt an unannounced policy of letting each collector pilfer up to $10 per week. That is, even though they knew exactly what a toll collector should have collected, they would say nothing to him until the losses for which he was responsible exceeded $10 per week.

> The toll-collection manager has an informal system to signal to the collector that he is under suspicion. A brightly painted authority police car parks right in front of the malefactor's toll booth. The toll taker gets the message. Theft drops back to a tolerable level.[15]

Organized Theft

Organized theft is more than employee pilferage. It is the organized efforts of outsiders to steal merchandise while it is in the firm's distribution channels. Sometimes thefts, or for that matter, the pilferage, occur while the merchandise is within the custody of a common carrier or a warehouseman. The common carrier or the warehouseman is then liable. However, the incident may still be disadvantageous to the shipper, and for several reasons:

1. The planned flow of the goods in the channel has been interrupted and may result in a stock-out at some later stage.
2. The carrier's or warehouseman's liability may not cover the entire value of the shipment.
3. Time, telephone, and paperwork costs are not covered.
4. Employees who had knowledge of the shipment's route and timing may come under suspicion.
5. The stolen products may reappear on the market at a low price to compete with goods that moved through legitimate channels.

[15] Lawrence R. Zeitlin, "A Little Larceny Can Do a Lot for Employee Morale," *Psychology Today* (June 1971), p. 64. See also, Joseph F. Hair, Jr., Ronald R. Bush, and Paul Bush, "Employee Theft: Views from Both Sides," *Business Horizons* (Dec. 1976), pp. 25–29; and "How Many Criminals Do You Employ?" *Industry Week* (Sept. 22, 1975), pp. 23–30.

Commodity	Frequency	Percent	Loss Value	Percent
CLOTHING	44	20.5	$2,284,816	28.7
FOODSTUFFS (Meat (26) 424,262) (Coffee (3) 245,000) (Other (19) 265,500) (Seafood (6) 148,000)	54	25.1	1,082,762	13.6
ART WORKS	3	1.4	682,000	8.6
CAMERA EQUIP. & FILM	7	3.2	670,200	8.4
METALS	3	1.4	417,000	5.2
TEXTILES, PIECE & LEATHER GDS.	6	2.8	368,000	4.6
RADIOS, STEREOS, TVS.	7	3.2	288,959	3.6
CASH	3	1.4	246,385	3.1
SHOES/FOOTWEAR	4	1.9	220,000	2.8
LIQUOR/BEER	16	7.4	203,816	2.6
MISC.	9	4.2	182,985	2.3
WATCHES	3	1.4	161,940	2.0
CIGARETTES	9	4.2	147,775	1.9
TELEPHONES	2	.9	120,250	1.5
ENGINES & PARTS	3	1.4	118,000	1.5
HOUSEHOLD GOOD/APPL.	9	4.2	115,325	1.4
FURNITURE	1	.5	100,000	1.3
SEWING MACHINES	1	.5	93,440	1.2
PLUMBING SPLYS.	2	.9	75,000	.9
BATTERIES/ELEC. SPLYS.	3	1.4	60,000	.8
COSMETICS & DRUGS	3	1.4	57,000	.7
POOL COVERS	1	.5	50,000	.6
MUSICAL EQUIP.	2	.9	45,000	.6
FUEL (GAS/OIL)	13	6.0	39,620	.5
OFFICE SPLYS.	3	1.4	33,400	.4
STROLLERS	1	.5	27,200	.3
HANDBAGS	1	.5	25,000	.3
PAINT BRUSHES	1	.5	20,000	.3
ASSTD. GUNS	1	.5	20,000	.3
TOTALS	215	100.0	7,955,873	100.0

Source: Reprinted from *Commercial Car Journal* (March 1980). Copyright 1980, Chilton Company. Note: Included in the 215 are 132 hijackings and 83 "grand larcenies" (meaning the loaded truck or trailer was stolen without threat to an individual). The figures were compiled by the New York State Motor Truck Association and appeared in *Commercial Car Journal* (March 1980).

Professional thieves have learned that thefts from carriers are much less risky and often more profitable than the traditional targets, such as banks and armored cars. Figure 13-8 shows the various commodities stolen in 1979 in the metropolitan New York City area as the result of either hijacking of

Hijacking involves a threat or injury to the vehicle's driver *and* theft of the truck; grand larceny—in this instance—is theft of a loaded, unattended truck or trailer.

trucks or theft of loaded trucks (without threat of danger to the driver). Even items without commercial value must be protected from theft. Nuclear weapons could be seized by terrorist groups and, because of this, must travel under conditions of great security.

Building Security

In recent years, there has been increased interest in providing security for warehouses and other distribution facilities. Figure 13-9 shows some of the measures that can be built into a warehouse. Electronic devices are available to perform three different security functions. First, closed-circuit TV with

Figure 13-9 How to Plan a "Thief Resistant" Warehouse

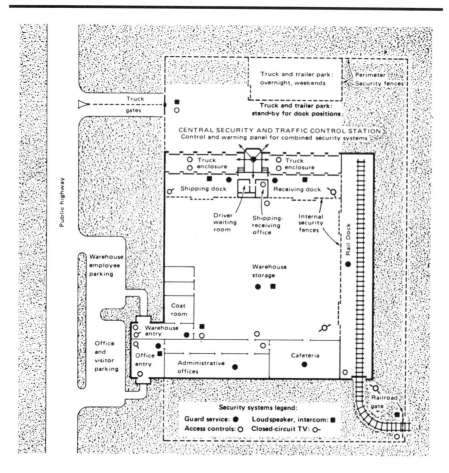

STRESS SECURITY IN LAYOUT
This layout shows good use of fences and walls for security and for access control at doors and gates. Opportunities for collusion and theft are cut by separation of receiving dock, shipping dock, storage area, and driver waiting room. Such a layout permits close direction of trucks by one guard, at a central station, with a clear view of yard and truck-enclosure areas at docks. Tightened security is provided by combined systems: guard services, access controls, loudspeakers and intercom, and closed-circuit TV, all centered at the control station.

Courtesy: *Modern Materials Handling.*

cameras can be used to view different areas. The picture is shown on a monitor screen constantly observed by a guard. For areas where there should be no movements, it is possible to have monitoring devices "remember" the image that contained no movement and convert this video information to a "binary format and store it in a digital memory and, when a change in the image occurs—such as would be caused by an intruder in a freight storage area—initiate an alarm"[16] The second form of electronic devices are used for access control. An example is an encoded tag that each employee must insert into a sensing device that both records the event and determines whether the door or gate should be unlocked. The third category and the most common are continuous wire circuits on all doors, windows, and other openings that cannot be broken without triggering an alarm. There are also invisible photoelectric beams and many types of listening devices that can record unauthorized movements. Within a warehouse, heavier security may be placed around areas where higher-value material is kept. Outside firms are sometimes retained to provide night-time security for warehouse buildings. There is no limit to the sophistication or cost of the security devices that can be employed. It is, unfortunately, another cost of doing business.

Truck Security

Methods and equipment are also being developed to discourage thefts from (or of) trucks. Numbers can be painted on top of truck trailers to make them easier to spot from the air in case they are stolen. (See Figure 13-10) An alternative is to place a transponder (a small device that will respond to radio signals from an outside source) aboard trailers that are likely to be hijacked. Improved locking devices are helpful because thieves have been

---

[16] Miklos Korodi, "Stop Thief!" *Distribution Worldwide* (Dec. 1974), p. 47. See also, "Warehouse Security," *Warehousing Review* (Summer 1979), p. 20.; and "Controlling the Risk of Mysterious Disappearance," *Warehousing and Physical Distribution Productivity Report* (Sept. 1982), pp. 1–14.

Figure 13-10 Suggested Marking for Tops of Trucks, Trailers, and Containers

TRUCK-TOP MARKINGS
FOR VISUAL IDENTIFICATION

Courtesy U.S. Department of Transportation.

Figure 13-11 Warning About Roadside Hijackings

I should've known he wouldn't stop. It's one
of those safety minded B. F. Walker drivers.

Courtesy B. F. Walker, Inc., Denver, Colorado. The cartoon appeared in the June
1947 issue of *Boll Weevil Newspaper,* a company publication.

known to climb onto the rear of a truck waiting at a traffic signal and then
force their way inside the vehicle. This is an area where continual training
of employees is necessary. Figure 13-11, which would be considered sexist
today, is from the late 1940s. It originally appeared in a trucking firm's
employee newsletter and served as a warning against roadside hijackings.
Notice the Thompson submachine gun near the suitcase.

Computer and Document Security

Computer and document security problems exist when individuals (frequently one's employees) know how a company's various computer and
paperwork systems "work" and then use the knowledge to defraud the

company. They may be able to manipulate the system so that it ships additional products, issues unauthorized refund payments, or the like. As firms rush[17] to adopt computerized systems to handle their logistics functions, they must take steps to ensure that the systems are safeguarded against unauthorized access and that sufficient controls are incorporated to prevent fraud.

International transactions and movements are especially vulnerable to documentation fraud. In these instances, the owner of the goods may be thousands of miles away from the cargo and is dependent upon the honesty of many different parties in different lands who prepare and verify the cargo's documents.[18]

Product Identification Number Security

Mention has been made of inventory control systems based on product serial or product batch numbers. These numbers also have certain advantages with respect to discouraging theft and pilferage. If items are discovered to be missing, it is possible to identify them by number. This makes it possible to reclaim the goods if they are recovered and facilitates prosecution of the people in possession of these goods. These facts are also known to pilferers, thieves, and "fences" and tend to make the "hot" merchandise somewhat less valuable. Altering or destroying the serial or batch numbers is time consuming and arouses the suspicions of legitimate buyers.

Truck leasing companies, in efforts to thwart truck theft, now etch vehicle identification numbers "in forty different locations on each vehicle— glass, frame, drive line components, various engine parts, and virtually any other part with resale value."[19] The number is cut on a special stencil, and a sand blast gun is then applied.

System Security

One of the best methods of protecting goods is to keep them moving through the system. Goods waiting in warehouses, terminals, or to clear customs are more vulnerable to theft than goods that are moving. No list of methods of improving security is complete, and a determined thief could overcome almost any hindrance or barrier placed in his way. However, a few suggestions are offered, mainly to reflect the breadth of measures that might be taken.

[17] It is believed that, initially, computers bring about tighter controls. Mike Rowan, editor of *Modern Materials Handling*, wrote (in the May, 1985 issue, page 59) about the problems "created by the lack of effective control over both the physical movement of materials and the flow of information in the plant or warehouse," and he listed a number of specific maladies. He continued: "Effective control can be achieved—with today's technology in materials handling and information handling. Computer-based identification systems, for example, virtually eliminate errors in data entry. Estimates put the error rate in bar-code scanning at one in 300,000 reads and at one in 300 key strokes with manual data entry."

[18] See "Fraud on the High Seas," *American Shipper* (Sept. 1984), pp. 46–50; and "Cargo Documentation Fraud," *Security Management* (Feb. 1983), pp. 39–40.

[19] "Vehicle Identification: How Leasing Companies' Experience Can Help Your Operation," *The Private Carrier* (Aug. 1984), pp. 46–48.

- Decals are required for autos in employee parking lots.
- Fork-lift trucks in warehouses are locked at night, making it difficult to reach high items or to move heavy items.
- Seals (small wirelike devices that once closed cannot be opened without breaking) are used more and more, with dispatchers, drivers, and receiving personnel all being made responsible for recording the seal number and inspecting its condition.
- Some companies have a "continuous" receipt system, so that an employee is considered responsible for each item until he can pass the item on and have the receiver sign a receipt. Although somewhat cumbersome, it has been helpful because it enhances the employee's sense of personal responsibility, and he views any effort to steal or tamper with the goods as an assault on his own integrity.
- One retail chain requires its retail stores to report any overages received from company warehouses. On occasion, it deliberately ships "too much" to determine whether the overage will be acknowledged.
- Sealing tape, with a pattern containing the company's logo, is used for sealing all outgoing packages and cartons. Although it does not prevent theft, it does make it more difficult to cover up evidence of pilferage or theft.
- A shoe manufacturer was plagued with thefts from trucks until he decided to ship left shoes in one truck and right shoes in a different truck. They were matched (hopefully) and boxed at their destination.
- In most (but not all) states it is permissible to fingerprint, photograph, and apply lie detector tests to potential employees. Where this is possible, it has been helpful to employers.

Energy–Saving Controls

With the sudden, and large, increases in energy costs that took place in the 1970s, logistics managers have had to pay increasing attention to keeping energy costs under control. The brief mention given to the topic here is not in proportion to its importance.

There are two areas in logistics systems where most energy costs occur, and where energy-saving measures should be focused. One is in warehouses, where both design factors (such as avoiding placing doors on the north side of a building) and operating procedures (such as having workers turn out unneeded lights) can reflect the need to lower energy consumption.[20] Solar energy can be employed to reduce purchase of other forms of energy.[21] One California walnut-processing and storage facility now uses shells—from shelled walnuts—as fuel to heat the structure.

The other area of logistics where considerable amounts of fuel can be saved is transportation. Almost any changes in shipping practices and pat-

---

[20] *Modern Materials Handling* (Nov. 19, 1984), p. 29; and *Organizing and Managing for Energy Efficiency* (New York: Conference Board, report no. 837, 1983).
[21] *Modern Materials Handling* (July 6, 1983), p. 15.

terns that reduce transportation costs probably utilize less fuel. Indeed, part of the rationale for deregulating our domestic transportation system was to do away with some of the inefficiencies (including fuel inefficiencies) of the regulated system.

Summary

Control, as the word implies, is an ongoing part of day-to-day business operations. A firm's inventory system directly or indirectly involves controls over virtually all aspects of the firm's operations. A firm's accounting controls concern many selling strategies that sometimes overlook distribution costs and may, in fact, cost more than they are worth. Employee productivity, always a concern, can be improved by using a variety of controls, such as computer printouts showing a truck driver's performance. Product recall operations, a potentially serious threat to a firm's reputation and profits, can minimize a bad situation if properly controlled. Pilferage and theft are two problems that, without proper control, can needlessly drain a company's profits. Finally, a logistics manager must be concerned with keeping the cost of energy under control.

Questions for Discussion and Review

1. What is the difference between pilferage and theft? From a management standpoint, which would you consider to be more significant? Why?
2. Describe how tachographs function. What bad driving habits can they detect?
3. What steps can be taken to discourage thefts from trucks and truck hijackings?
4. What steps can be taken against pilferage?
5. Do you think that job applicants should be subjected to lie detector tests? Why or why not?
6. What steps should a firm take to prepare for a product recall?
7. Why are serial numbers or batch numbers important?
8. What kind of accounting controls are used in PD/L?
9. What is shrinkage? How is it measured?
10. Why do you think that shippers of large quantities of product have more influence over the quality of service offered by carriers?
11. Give some examples as to how a logistics manager might reduce his or her firm's use of energy.
12. What is short-interval scheduling? How is it used?
13. What questions might you ask an employee to find out if he knows his relative level of performance?
14. How are standard costs calculated? How are they used to monitor performance?
15. List the similarities and differences in controlling outbound shipments moving on one's own vehicles and on common carriers.
16. Read the warehouse work rules in Figure 13-3. Referring to the violations in the first list that calls for immediate discharge, are there viola-

tions that (a) you would add to this list? (b) you would transfer to the second list? or (c) you would delete entirely from the first list? Why?

17. Why should a firm control access to its computer system?
18. What are product recalls? Give some examples.
19. List and discuss the various federal agencies that might be involved in product recalls.
20. Why do you think that logistics systems controls are a matter of *continual* concern to management?

Additional Chapter References

Allport, William W. "Labor Relations." in *The Distribution Handbook* (New York: Free Press Division of Macmillan, 1985), pp. 856–886.

Ballou, Ronald H., and Omar K. Helrich. "Measuring Physical Distribution Performance." *Annual Proceedings of the NCPDM* (1983), pp. 836–851.

Ballou, Ronald H. "The Weak Link in the Application of Artificial Intelligence to Physical Distribution." *Annual Proceedings of the NCPDM* (1984), pp. 509–512.

Biggs, Dee, and Bill Coyne. "Precluding Crisis Through Practical Contingency Planning." *Annual Proceedings of the NCPDM* (1983), pp. 213–231.

Collard, Thomas A. "Service Planning and Control for Railroad Operations." *Annual Proceedings of the Transportation Research Forum* (1982) pp. 168–175.

Cummings, Ron E. "Monitoring Distribution Cost Service Performance." *Annual Proceedings of the NCPDM* (1982), pp. 625–652.

Curtis, Ellen Foster. "Quality Circles in Transportation: The Milwaukee Road Experience." *Transportation Journal* (Spring 1984), pp. 63–69.

Dorsey, Frank. "Preparing the Union for Work Standards." *Annual Proceedings of the NCPDM* (1982), pp. 581–594.

Gallagher, Patrick (ed.). *Logistics: Contribution and Control* (Cleveland: Oberlin Printing, 1983).

Harari, Oren. "Motivating the New Workforce." *Annual Proceedings of the NCPDM* (1982), pp. 611–624.

Kinnunen, Raymond M., and Paul A. Jannell. "Management Control in the Railroad Industry." *Transportation Journal* (Fall 1982) pp. 4–10.

Langley, C. John, and Jack L. Hartzell. "Statistical Process Control Applications in Material Management." *Annual Proceedings of the NCPDM* (1983), pp. 986–997.

Loyden, John J. "Nabisco Brands: Budgeting for the Distribution System." *Annual Proceedings of the NCPDM* (1984), pp. 637–642.

Mahan, John J. "Management and Control of Distribution Cost." *Annual Proceedings of the NCPDM* (1983), pp. 962–985.

Martha, Joe, and Dennis McGinnis. "Microcomputers in Distribution: How to Use Them More Effectively," *Annual Proceedings of the NCPDM* (1983), pp. 943–961.

Novack, Robert A. "Transportation Standard Cost Budgeting." *Annual Proceedings of the NCPDM* (1984), pp. 607–622.

Senn, Larry. "Accountability, Teamwork, and Increased Performance in Distribution." *Annual Proceedings of the NCPDM* (1983), pp. 572–580.

Snitzler, James R., and James A. Caron. "Measuring Productivity in Distribution Operations of Regional Farm Supply Cooperatives." *Annual Proceedings of the Transportation Research Forum* (1984), pp. 300–302.

Talley, Wayne K. "Motor Carrier Platform Costing." *ICC Practitioners' Journal* (Jan.–Feb. 1983), pp 176–195.

White, John A., Jr. "Management Guide to Productivity." *The Distribution Handbook* (New York; Free Press Division of Macmillan, 1985), pp. 319–369.

CASE 13-1

The Johnson Toy Company

Located in Biloxi, Mississippi, the Johnson Toy Company was celebrating its seventy-fifth year of business. Amy Johnson, who was president, and Lori Johnson, who was vice-president, were sisters and the third generation of their family to be involved in the toy business. The firm manufactured and sold toys throughout the United States. The toy business is very seasonal, with the majority of sales occurring before Christmas. A smaller peak occurs in the late spring/early summer period when sales of outdoor items are good.

The firm relied on several basic designs of toys—which had low profit margins but were steady sellers—and on new designs of unconventional toys whose introduction was always risky but promised high profits if the item became popular. The firm advertised regularly on Saturday morning TV shows for children.

Late last year, just before Christmas, the Johnson Toy Company had introduced a "Jungle Jim the Jogger" doll, modeled after a popular TV show. Sales skyrocketed and every retailer's stock of "Jungle Jim the Jogger" dolls was sold out in mid-December; the Johnson Company could have sold several million more units, if they had been available before Christmas. Based on the sales success of this doll, Amy and Lori made commitments to manufacture ten million "Jungle Jim the Jogger" dolls this year and to introduce a wide line of accessory items that they hoped every doll owner would also want to have. Production was well under way, and many retailers were happy to accept dolls in January and February because they were still a fast-selling item, even though the toy business itself was sluggish during these months.

Unfortunately, in the aftermath of a Valentines Day party in Hollywood, the TV actor who portrayed "Jungle Jim the Jogger" became involved in a widely publicized sexual misadventure, the details of which even shocked many hard-nosed Hollywood gossip columnists. Ratings of the TV series plummeted, and within a month it had been dropped from the air. On March 1, the Johnson Company had canceled further production of the "Jungle Jim the Jogger" dolls, although it had to pay penalties to some of its suppliers because of the cancellation. The company had little choice because it was obvious that sales had stopped.

On April 1, a gloomy group assembled in the Johnson Company conference room. Besides Amy and Lori, those present included Carolyn Coggins, the firm's sales manager; Cheryl Guridi, the distribution manager; Greg Sullivan, the controller; and Kevin Vidal, the plant engineer. Coggins had just reported that she believed that there were between 1.5 and 2 million "Jungle Jim the Jogger" dolls in retailers' stores, and Sullivan had indicated that there were 2,567,112 complete units in various public warehouses in Biloxi. Vidal said that he was still trying to count all of the unassembled component parts, adding that one problem was that they were still being received from suppliers, despite the cancellation.

Amy said, "Let's wait a few weeks to get a complete count of all the dolls and all of the unassembled component parts. Lori, I'm naming you to work with Carolyn and Kevin to develop recommendations as to how we can 'recycle' the Jungle Jim item into something we can sell. Given the numbers involved, I'm willing to turn out some innocuous doll and sell it for a little more than the cost of recycling because we can't take a complete loss on all these damned Jungle Jim dolls! Greg says we have nearly 2.6 million of them to play with, so let's think of something."

"Your 2.6 million figure may be low," said Ms. Coggins. "Don't forget that there may be nearly 2 million in the hands of the dealers and they will return them."

"Return them?" questioned Amy. "They're not defective. That's the only reason we accept returns. The retailers made a poor choice. It's the same as if they ordered sleds and then have a winter with little or no snow. We are no more responsible for Jungle Jim's sex life than they are!"

Cheryl Guridi spoke up: "You may be underestimating the problem, Amy. One of our policies is to accept the dealer's word as to what is 'defective' and right now there are a lot of dealers out there claiming defects in the Jungle Jim dolls. One reason that Kevin can't get an accurate count is that returned dolls are showing up on our receiving dock and getting mixed up with our 'in stock' inventory."

"How can that happen?" asked Amy, angrily. "We're not paying the freight, also, are we?"

"So far, no," responded Ms. Guridi. "The retailers are paying the freight just to get rid of them."

"We've received several bills where the retailer has deducted the costs of the Jungle Jim dolls and of the freight for shipping them back from what he owes us," said Sullivan. "That was one item I wanted to raise while we were together."

"We can't allow that!" exclaimed Amy.

"Don't be so sure," responded Sullivan. "The account in question has paid every bill he's owed us on time for forty years. Do you want *me* to tell him we won't reimburse him?"

"This is worse than I imagined," said Amy. "Just what are our return policies, Lori?"

"Well, until today, I thought we had only two," said Lori. "One, for our small accounts, involves having our salesman inspect the merchandise when he makes a sales call. He then picks it up and gives the retailer credit off of his next order."

"Sometimes he picks up more than defective merchandise," added Ms. Coggins. "Often he'll take the 'slow-movers' out of the retailer's hands. We have to do that as a sales tool."

"That's not quite right," interjected Vidal. "Sometimes the returned items are just plain shopworn—scratched, dented, and damaged. That makes it hard for us because we have to inspect every item and decide whether it can be put back into stock. When we think a particular salesperson is accepting too many shopworn items, we tell Carolyn, although it's not clear to me that the message reaches the salespeople out in the field."

"I wish I had an easy solution," said Ms. Coggins. "We used to let our salespeople give credit for defects and then destroy everything out in the field. Unfortunately, some abused the system and resold the toys to discount stores. At least now, we can see everything we're buying back. I agree we are stuck with some shopworn items, but our salespeople are out there to sell, and nothing would ruin a big sale quicker than for our salesman to start arguing with the retailer, on an item-by-item basis, as to whether something being returned happens to be shopworn."

"Is there a limit to what a salesman is permitted to allow a retailer to return?" asked Amy.

"Well, not until now," responded Ms. Coggins. "But with this Jungle Jogger snafu, we can expect the issue to occur. In fact, I have several phone queries on my desk concerning this. I thought I'd wait until after this meeting to return them."

"Well, I think we'd better establish limits—right now," said Amy.

"Be careful," said Lori. "When I was out with salespeople last year, I gathered the impression that some were able to write bigger orders by implying that we'd take the unsold merchandise back, if need be. If we assume that risk, the retailer is willing to take more of our merchandise."

"Are there no limits to this policy?" asked Amy.

"Informal ones," was Ms. Coggins' response. "It depends on the salesperson and the account. I don't think there is much abuse, although there is some."

"How do the goods get back to us under these circumstances?" asked Amy.

"The salespeople either keep them and shuffle them about to other customers, or—if it's a real loser—they ask us what to do," replied Ms. Coggins.

"Greg," said Amy, "do our records reflect all these returns and transfers?"

"Oh, fairly well," was his response. "We lose track of individual items and quantities but if the salesman is honest—and I think ours are—we can follow the dollar amount of the return to the salesman's inventory, to another retailer, or back here to us. We do not have good controls on the actual terms that are allowed for returns. Kevin and I have difficulty in reconciling the value of returned items that wind up back here. Carolyn's records say they're OK for resale, and Kevin says they're too badly damaged."

"I insist on the reconciliation before we allow the goods back into our working inventory," said Ms. Guridi. "That way I know exactly what I have here, ready to ship."

"You know, I'm finding out more information about inventories and returns than I thought existed," said Amy.

"Too many trips to Paris, dearest," said Lori, and the others all suppressed smiles.

Amy decided to ignore Lori's remark, and she looked at Ms. Guridi, and asked, "Are you satisfied with your control over inventories, Cheryl?"

"I have no problems with the ones here in Biloxi," was Ms. Guridi's response, "but I have an awful time with the inventories of return items that salesmen carry about with them, waiting to place them with another retailer. I'm not always certain they're getting us top dollar, and each salesman knows only his own territory. When Carolyn and I are trying to monitor the sales of some new item, we never know whether it's bombing in some areas and riding around in salesmen's cars, as they try to sell it again."

"Have you now described our returns policy, such as it is?" asked Amy, looking at everybody in the room.

"No," was the response murmured by all. Sullivan spoke: "For large accounts we deduct a straight 2 per cent off of wholesale selling price to cover defectives, and then we never want to hear about defectives from these accounts at all."

"That sounds like a better policy," said Amy. "How well is it working?"

"Up until Jungle Jim jogged where he shouldn't, it worked fine. Now a number of large accounts are pleading 'special circumstances' or threatening to sue if we don't take back the dolls."

"They have no grounds for suit," declared Amy.

"You're right," said Ms. Coggins, "but several of their buyers are refusing to see our sales staff until the matter is resolved. I just heard about this yesterday and meant to bring it up in today's meeting. I consider this very serious."

"Dammit!" shouted Amy, pounding the table with her fist. "I hope that damned jogger dies of jungle rot! We're going to lose money this year, and now you're all telling me how our return policy works, or doesn't work, as the case may be! Why can't we just have a policy of all sales being final and telling retailers that if there is an honest defect they should send the goods back here to us in good old Biloxi?"

"Most of the small accounts know nothing about shipping," responded Vidal. "They don't know how to pack, they don't know how to prepare shipping documents, and they can't choose the right carriers. You ought to see the hodge-podge of shipments we receive from them. In more cases than not, they pay more in shipping charges than the products are worth to us. I'd rather see them destroyed in the field."

Sullivan spoke up. "I'd object to that. We would need some pretty tight controls to make certain the goods were actually destroyed. What if they are truly defective, but improperly disposed of, fall into the hands of children who play with them and the defect causes an injury? Our name may still be on the product, and the child's parents will no doubt claim the item was purchased from one of our retailers. Will we be liable? Why can't we have everything come back here? We have enough volume of some returned items that we could think in terms of recycling parts."

Vidal responded: "Recycling is a theoretical solution to such a problem but only in rare instances will it pay. In most instances the volume is too small and the costs of taking toys apart is usually very high. The Jogger Jim product involves such a large volume that it is reasonable to think up another product which utilizes many of the parts. It would even pay to develop special machines for disassembling the Jogger Jim doll."

"As I listen to this discussion," said Lori, "one fact becomes obvious. We never will have very good knowledge about volume or patterns of returns until it's too late. That's their very nature."

Ms. Guridi asked, "Could we have field representatives who did nothing but deal with this problem? The retailers would be told to hang onto the defectives until our claims reps arrived."

Ms. Coggins answered, "This would be expensive, because most retailers have little storage space for anything and would expect our claims rep to be there p.d.q. Besides, it might undermine our selling efforts if retailers could no longer use returns to 'deal' with as they talked about new orders."

"That may be," interjected Amy, "but we cannot continue having each salesperson tailoring a return policy for each retailer. That's why we're in such a mess with the jogger doll. We have to get our return policy established, made more uniform, and enforced. We cannot go through another fiasco like Jungle Jim the Jogger for a long time. We're going to lose money this year, no matter what, and I have already told Kevin that there will be virtually no money available for retooling for next year's new products.''

Question One: From the standpoint of an individual concerned with accounting controls, discuss and evaluate Johnson Toy Company's present policies for handling returned items.

Question Two: Answer Question One, but from the standpoint of an individual interested in marketing.

Question Three: Propose a policy for handling returns that should be adopted by the Johnson Toy Company. Be certain to list circumstances under which exceptions would be allowed.

Question Four: Should this policy, if adopted, be printed and distributed to all of the retailers who handle Johnson Toy Company products? Why or why not? If it should not be distributed to them, who should receive copies?

Question Five: Assume it is decided to prepare a statement on returns to be distributed to all retailers, and that it should be less than a single page of double-spaced typing. Prepare such a statement.

Question Six: Take the policy in your answer to Question Three, and develop instructions for the Johnson Toy Company distribution and accounting departments with respect to their roles and procedures in the handling of returns.

Question Seven: Assume you are Cheryl Guridi, the firm's distribution manager. Do you think that the returns policy favored by the distribution manager would differ from what would be best for the firm? Why or why not?

Question Eight: Until the policy you recommend in answer three takes effect, how would you handle the problem of retailers wanting to return unsold Jungle Jim the Jogger dolls?

CASE 13-2

Red Spot Markets Company

The Red Spot Markets Company operates a chain of grocery stores in New England. It has a grocery distribution center in Providence, Rhode Island, from which deliveries are made to stores as far north as Lowell, Massachusetts, as far west as Waterbury, Connecticut, and as far northwest as Springfield, Massachusetts. There are no stores beyond the two northernmost points in Massachusetts. There are stores to the west, but they are supplied by a grocery warehouse located in Newburgh, New York. The Providence grocery distribution center supplies 42 Red Spot retail stores.

Robert Easter, Red Spot's distribution manager, is responsible for operations at the Newburgh and Providence distribution centers. By industry standards, both were fairly efficient. However, of the two, the Providence center lagged in two important areas of control: worker productivity and shrinkage. Warehouse equipment and work rules were the same for both the Newburgh and Providence centers, yet the throughput per manhour was 4 per cent higher for the Newburgh facility. Shrinkage, expressed as a percentage of the wholesale value of goods handled annually, was 0.36 per cent for the

Newburgh center and 0.59 per cent for the Providence center. Jarvis Jason had been manager of the Providence distribution center for the past three years and, at great effort, managed to narrow the gap between the performance of the two Red Spot facilities. Last week, he requested an immediate reassignment, and Easter arranged for him to become the marketing manager for the Boston area, which would involve supervising the operations of eleven Red Spot markets. The transfer involved no increase in pay.

Easter needed a new manager for the Providence distribution center, and he decided to pick Fred Fosdick for the task. Fosdick graduated from a lesser Ivy League college where he majored in business with a concentration in physical distribution and logistics. He had been with Red Spot for two years and rearranged the entire delivery route structure so that two fewer trucks were needed. As part of this assignment, he also converted the entire system to one of unit loads, which meant everything loaded on or unloaded from a Red Spot truck was on a pallet. Fosdick was familiar with the operations of both the Providence and Newburgh centers. He has been in each facility at least fifty different times. In addition, he spent two weeks at the Providence center when the loading docks were redesigned to accommodate pallet loading. Fosdick was surprised that Jason requested reassignment to a slot that did not involve an upward promotion. That was his first question to Easter after Easter asked whether he was interested in the Providence assignment.

"I'm sorry you started with that question," said Easter to Fosdick. "Now we'll have to talk about the troublesome aspects of the assignment first, rather than the positive ones. To be frank, Fred, one of the union employees there made so much trouble for Jason, he couldn't stand it."

"Who's the trouble-maker?" asked Fosdick.

"Tom Bigelow," was Easter's answer.

Fosdick remembered Bigelow from the times he had been at the Providence center. Thomas D. Bigelow was nicknamed T.D. since his days as a local Providence high school football star. Fosdick recalled that during work breaks on the loading dock, Bigelow and some of the other workers would toss around melons as though they were footballs. Only once did they drop a melon. Fosdick recalled hearing the story that Bigelow had received several offers of athletic scholarships when he graduated from high school. His best offer was from a southern school and he accepted it. Despite the fact that the college provided a special tutor for each class, Bigelow flunked out at the end of his first semester and came back to Providence, where he got a job in the Red Spot warehouse.

In the warehouse Bigelow was a natural leader. He would have been a foreman except for his inability to count and his spotty attendance record on Monday mornings. On Mondays he was groggy, tired, and irritable. On Mondays he would even hide by loading a forklift truck with three pallets, backing into any empty bay, lowering the pallets in position (which hid the lift truck from view) and fall asleep. The rest of the week Bigelow was happy, enthusiastic, and hard-working. Indeed, it was he who set the pace of work in the warehouse. When he felt good, things hummed; when he was not feeling well or was absent work dragged.

"What did Bigelow do to Jason?" Fosdick asked Easter.

"Well, as I understand it," responded Easter, "about two weeks ago Jason decided that he had had it with Bigelow and so he suspended him on a Monday morning after Bigelow showed up late, still badly hung over. It was nearly noon, and he told Bigelow to stay off the premises and to file a grievance with his union shop steward. He also told Bigelow that he had been documenting Bigelow's Monday performance—or non-performance—for the past six months and that Red Spot had grounds enough to fire Bigelow if it cared to. He told Bigelow to go home, sober up, and come back on Tuesday when they would discuss the length of his suspension. Bigelow walked through the distribution center on his way out, and I'm sure Jason felt he had control of the matter.

"However," continued Easter, "by about one o'clock, Jason realized he had a work slowdown on his hands. Pallet loads of bottled goods were being dropped, two fork-lift trucks collided, and one lift truck pulled over the corner of a tubular steel rack. At 4:00 P.M. quitting time, there were still three trucks to be loaded; usually they would have departed by 3:30. Rather than pay overtime, Jason let the work force go home, and he and the foreman loaded the last three trucks.

"On Tuesday, Bigelow did not show up, and the slowdown got worse. In addition, retail stores were phoning with complaints about all the errors in their orders. To top it off, at the Roxbury store, when the trailer door was opened, the trailer contained nothing but empty pallets. Tuesday night somebody turned off the switches on the battery chargers for all the lift trucks, so on Wednesday, the lift-truck batteries were dying all day. I got involved because of all the complaints from the stores. On Wednesday, Jason got my permission to pay overtime and the last outgoing truck did not leave until 7:00 P.M. In addition, we had to pay overtime at some of our retail stores because the workers there were waiting for the trucks to arrive. While I was talking to Jason that afternoon, he indicated that he had fired Bigelow."

Easter lit his cigar and continued, "On Wednesday, I decided to go to Providence myself, mainly to talk to Jason and to determine whether we should close down the Providence center and try to serve all our stores out of Newburgh. This would have been expensive, but Providence was becoming too unreliable. In addition, we had a weekend coming up. When I showed up at Providence, Jason and I had breakfast together in my hotel room Thursday morning, and he told me pretty much the same thing I've been telling you. He said he knew Bigelow was behind all the disruption and that today (meaning Thursday) would be crucial. I'd never seen Jason looking so nervous. Then we drove to the distribution center. Even from a distance, I could tell things were moving slowly. The first echelon of outgoing trucks, which should have been on the road, were still there. Another twenty of our trucks were waiting to be loaded. On the other end of the building, you could see a long line of arriving trucks waiting to be unloaded; usually there was no line at all. I knew that our suppliers would start complaining because we had established scheduled unloading times. However, I decided not to ask Jason whether he had begun receiving phone calls from them."

"Inside the center, the slowdown was in effect. Lift truck operators who usually zipped by each other would now stop, turn off their engines, dismount, and carefully walk around each other's truck to ensure there was proper clearance. Satisfied of this, they would then mount, start their engines, and spend an inordinate amount of time motioning to each other to pass. This was only one example. When we got to Jason's office, he had a message to phone Ed Meyers, our local attorney in Providence who handles much of our labor relations work there. He called Meyers and was upset by the discussion. After he hung up he told me that Meyers had been served papers by the union's attorney, charging that Wednesday's firing of Bigelow was unjustified, mainly because there existed no provable grounds that Bigelow was behind the slowdown. Meyers was angry because, in firing Bigelow on Wednesday, he (Jason) may have also blown the suspension of Bigelow on Monday. Jason and I started talking, even arguing. I talked so much that my cigar went out," said Easter, "so I asked Jason, who was sitting behind his desk, for a match. He didn't carry matches but looked inside his center desk drawer for one. He gasped and I didn't know what was the matter. He got up, looking sick, and walked away from his desk. He said that a dead rat had been left in his desk drawer, and he wanted a transfer. He was in bad shape and the distribution center was in bad shape, so I had the opening in the Boston area and I let him have it. Actually, right now he and his family are vacationing somewhere in eastern Canada. He needs the rest."

Fosdick was beginning to feel sorry that he knew all the details, but he persisted. "Then what?" he asked Easter.

"Well, I took over running the distribution center. I phoned Meyers again, and he and I had lunch. He thought that Jason had blown the case against Bigelow and that we should take him back. So on Friday, Meyers, Bigelow, the union attorney, the shop steward, Bigelow's foreman, and I met. Jason, of course, was not there. It was a pleasant meeting. Everything got blamed on poor Jason. I did tell Bigelow that we would be documenting his performance and wanted him to know that Jason's successor, meaning you, was under my instructions to tolerate no nonsense from him (Bigelow). Bigelow was so pleasant that day that I could not imagine him in the role of a trouble maker. The amazing thing was when he went out into the center to resume work, a loud cheer went up, and all the drivers started blowing their lift-truck horns. For a moment, I was afraid all the batteries would run down again. But I was wrong. They were plain happy to see Bigelow back. You know, the slowdown was still in effect when Bigelow walked onto the floor. I'd say it was 10:00 A.M. and they were an hour behind. Well, let me tell you what happened. They went to work! By noon we were back on schedule, and by the end of the shift we were a half hour ahead of schedule. In fact, the last half hour was spent straightening up many of the bins that had been deliberately disarranged during the slowdown. I tell you, Tom Bigelow does set the work pace in that warehouse!"

"So what do you suggest I do at the center?" asked Fosdick.

"Well, the key is getting along with Bigelow. Talk to Meyers about the kind of records you should keep in case you decide to move against Bigelow. Be sure to consult with Meyers before you do anything irreversible. Frankly, I don't know whether Bigelow will be a problem. We never had trouble with him that I knew about before Jason was there. According to Bigelow and the union attorney, Jason had it in for Bigelow. If I were you, I'd take it easy with Bigelow and other labor problems. See what you can do instead about the inventory shrinkage."

On the next Monday morning, Fosdick showed up at the Providence distribution center. After gingerly looking in all his desk drawers, he had a brief meeting with his foremen and then walked out to meet the entire work force on a one-to-one basis. Many remembered Fosdick from his earlier visits to the facility. Because it was a Monday morning, he had not expected to encounter Bigelow. But Bigelow was present, clear eyed, alert, and enthusiastic. He was happy to see Fosdick and shook his hand warmly. Bigelow then excused himself saying he had to return to work. The truck dispatcher said that the work force was ahead of schedule again: it was 11:00 A.M., and they were about 15 minutes ahead. Fosdick returned to his office, and there was a phone message from Ed Meyers. Meyers asked to postpone their luncheon for that day until Tuesday noon. Then Robert Easter called to ask how things were going on Fosdick's first day. Easter was pleased things were going smoothly.

It was lunch time. Fosdick decided to walk to a small cafe where he had eaten at other times. It was two blocks from the distribution center and on the side away from the office. So he walked through the center, which was quiet since it was closed for lunch. He walked by the employee's lunch room where there were the normal sounds of fifty people eating and talking. Just outside the lunch room was one lift truck with an empty wooden pallet on it. As Fosdick watched, one of the new stock clerks came out of the lunch room with an opened case of sweet pickles from which three jars had been taken. Next came another new stock clerk with an opened carton of mustard from which two bottles had been removed. One of the clerks suddenly saw Fosdick and said weakly, "We take these opened cases to the damaged merchandise room." Fosdick went into the lunch room. There, on the center table were cases of cold meat, cheese, soft drinks, catsup, and bread. All had been opened and partially emptied to provide the workers' lunch.

Bigelow was making himself a large sandwich when he saw Fosdick approach. "Don't get uptight, man," he said to Fosdick. "You've just come across one of the noncontract fringe benefits of working at the Red Spot Providence distribution center. Can I make you a sandwich?"

Question One: How should Fosdick respond to the immediate situation?

Question Two: What controls, of the type discussed in chapter 13, might have been used by Red Spot Markets to reduce or eliminate the problems discussed in the case?

Question Three: What longer-range steps should Fosdick take to control the operations of the Providence distribution center?

Question Four: What longer-range steps should Fosdick take to improve the Providence distribution center's productivity?

Question Five: What longer-range steps can Fosdick take to reduce the distribution center's high rate of shrinkage?

Question Six: Assume that Fosdick decides that the practice of free lunches from the opened cases of goods must be stopped. Develop and present the arguments he should give in his meeting with the union shop steward.

Question Seven: (continuation of Question Six): Assume, instead, that you are the union shop steward. Develop and present your argument that the free lunches represent a long-standing employee benefit enjoyed by the distribution center's employees, and that management's attempt to stop them is a breach of an unwritten contract and will be resisted.

Question Eight: Much of the situation described in the case seems to evolve around the personality of T. D. Bigelow. How should he be treated? Why?

The pallet load, or unit load, is widely used and is the common denominator in the designs for the flow of goods through most logistics systems. Here are two disparate examples of its use. The upper picture shows bulk salt being bagged at a Port of New York facility. On the right, we can see the filled bags being built up into pallet loads. The bottom picture, taken in California's San Joaquin Valley, shows a "traveling packing shed" which takes the individual melons picked by the field workers, cleans and sorts them, and packs them into pallet loads. The rig is pulled by a tractor through the fields. On the top level, the worker takes flattened carton tops and bottoms and uses the machine to form them into their three-dimensional shape. They move by conveyor belt to the lower level where they are filled with melons. As each carton is filled, a cover is placed on it, and then it is loaded on to a pallet. At the end of each row, the rig stops, and a fork lift removes the loaded pallets (as shown on the left) and then will load them on to highway trucks for delivery to market.

(*Credit:* top photo, VIA Port of New York/New Jersey; bottom photo, U.S. Bureau of Reclamation.)

Organization for Managing Physical Distribution/Logistics

Do you know the easiest way to bomb a new product? Poor materials management—you can't get the right materials, or the quality is off, or you can't get the product through the factory, or you can't coordinate transportation and distribution to get the product into the hands of the customer.

An anonymous corporate president quoted by
Jeffrey G. Miller and Peter Gilmour
Harvard Business Review
July–August 1979

. . . U.S. manufacturers find product rejection levels of 1 per cent or 2 per cent acceptable, said Alan E. Loebel of Harris Corp. This attitude can sabotage efforts to achieve Japanese-style results. Loebel suggested looking at rejection levels in the terms of parts per million. A zero defects concept becomes more imperative when a 1 per cent rejection level is equated to 10,000 scrap parts for every one million produced.

Viewed in this manner, a 1 per cent or 2 per cent rejection level can be readily identified as a obstacle to achieving true Just-In-Time manufacturing.

Modern Materials Handling
December 10, 1984

We were talking about who owned the data. In the client's view, Sales and Marketing own both the forecast and the customer order data, and Manufacturing owns the master schedule data. Because the company has separate data processing staffs for marketing systems and manufacturing systems, the client asked, "Who owns the system?" (The answer is, THE COMPANY.)

This ridiculous question is very indicative of the massive communications problem that exists in this and many manufacturing companies between Sales, Marketing, and Manufacturing.

Richard C. Ling Report
October 1984

Key Terms

- "Status quo" organization
- Linking-pin organization
- Unified department organization
- Matrix management
- Centralized PD/L organization
- De-centralized PD/L organization

Learning Objectives

- To note why PD/L has frequently caused animosity among other functional areas
- To explain that dispersion has frequently been found for PD/L functional areas
- To examine a number of organizational alternatives
- To describe a number of techniques for achieving PD/L coordination
- To distinguish between the centralized versus decentralized PD/L organization

Introduction

PD/L is not an isolated function. It takes place within an organizational framework that influences how the principles we have described are applied. This chapter deals with the placement of the PD/L function within the framework of a firm's organizational structure. Most examples are drawn from larger firms, although the same issues exist for organizing the PD/L function within a smaller firm. Organizational decisions of the type described here are made by the firm's top management. The practitioner is affected by them and, although the practitioner cannot make the decisions, he or she can provide valuable input to the organizational (or reorganizational) decision-making process.

Logistics organizational problems are bewildering. There are two major reasons for this. The first involves the organizational location of the various PD/L functions. These activities are scattered throughout the firm's organizational structure, which leads to many communication and coordination problems.

The second complication is that there are no norms or standards regarding an "ideal" PD/L organization. A decade ago, Professor Bernard J. La-Londe made a comment that is still valid, when he said: "Other corporate functions, such as production, marketing, and accounting, have had from three decades to more than three centuries to develop appropriate organizational formats and operating procedures. The corporate PD function has been in existence for less than ten years in most firms and as a result there remains much uncertainty and 'trial and error'."[1] Figure 14-1 illustrates the

---

[1] Bernard J. LaLonde, "Strategies for Organizing Physical Distribution," *Transportation and Distribution Management* (Jan.–Feb. 1974), p. 21.

Figure 14-1 Physical Distribution/Logistics Executives May Receive Animosity from Other Corporate Officers

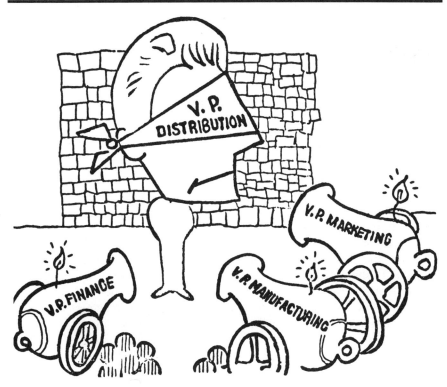

Source: Reproduced by permission of *Distribution Worldwide.*

relationship between a firm's more traditional functions and the "newcomer." (If the new function fails, then many of its activities will be transferred back to finance, manufacturing, and marketing.)

Many firms have attempted to reorganize in order to implement the PD/L concept successfully. The driving force behind this was the recognition by top management that PD/L can be and is of monumental importance to the overall welfare of the firm. Some 15 years ago, Michael Schiff noted the tendency for top management to view PD/L activities as important as manufacturing and marketing.[2] A more fundamental problem became apparent in the late 1970s. It dealt with the perplexing question as to whether the organization should be focused on the concepts of physical distribution, which emphasize the importance of outbound movements of finished goods, or whether it should focus on the concepts of overall logistics management and be concerned with both inbound and outbound movements.

While this chapter deals mainly with domestic corporations, brief mention should be made of several other forms of organization where the prin-

[2] Michael Schiff, "Accounting and Control in Physical Distribution," *Proceedings of the NCPDM* (1971), p. 6. See also, James P. Falk, "Organizing for Effective Distribution," *Proceedings of the NCPDM* (1980), pp. 181–199.

ciples mentioned here may also be applicable. The first is international corporations with operations in many countries. These firms must organize whatever structure suits their multinational interests best. The international physical distribution/logistics manager must be familiar with domestic logistics operations within many nations and the physical and legal complexities involved in transferring materials between nations. The second kind of organization is the government agency. At all levels of government—federal, state, and local—there is considerable activity involving the purchase, storage, and distribution of materials. These agencies could follow many of the practices mentioned in this book and increase their operating efficiencies.

Military logistics is a specialty in itself, and we must remember that many facets of logistics—as we practice them today—originated in the U.S. military establishment. In the Falkland Islands dispute of a few years ago, the British demonstrated their ability to manage a military operation where the logistical challenges were probably greater than the challenges of actual battle.

Organizations that are thought of as providers of services, rather than of goods, also have formidable logistics requirements. At the United Airlines (UAL) main maintenance base, near the San Francisco airport, is an inventory of over 170,000 different SKUs, all needed to keep the airline's fleet operating. This system processes over 100,000 inventory transactions each month.[3] Hospitals also maintain large inventories because they must be prepared to provide whatever might be needed to treat an illness or injury. These inventory costs are a factor in causing all health care costs to be high.

Firms also have their own internal logistics needs, and they deal with the transport, within the firm, of materials, supplies, and people. For example, a firm may have its own printing operation which produces all the forms, letterheads, brochures, etc., that the company uses; and these printed materials must then be shipped within the firm's internal communications and logistics network. Figure 14-2 shows a custom-built desert vehicle used to carry portable offices and equipment sheds needed to support an oil exploration operation in the Middle East.

Some firms provide logistical services to others. Traveling music groups retain firms to handle the transportation of performers, instruments, sound systems, and stage equipment from tour site to tour site. Specializing firms also transport, assemble, and disassemble traveling displays used by their clients' marketing managers who are, say, conducting a series of sales meetings throughout the nation.

One-time functions also may have major logistical needs. The best recent example was the 1984 Summer Olympics held in Los Angeles. In addition to providing for the athletes and guests, there was a large quantity of specialized equipment to be handled, such as each team's yachts, rowing shells, canoes, gym equipment, or judo mats. Over three hundred horses were brought into the country for use in equestrian events.[4]

---

[3] Information given on a tour of a UAL maintenance base conducted by the Northern California Chapter of the International Material Management Society, October 25, 1984.

[4] " 'Olympic Fever' Is Heating Operations for California Customhouse," *Air Cargo News*, (Feb. 1984), p. 9. At the National Football League's Super Bowl XIX, played at Palo Alto, California in early 1985, the ABC television network's broadcasting operation at the event

Figure 14-2 A Mobile Office

Credit: Arabian American Oil Company

Dispersion of PD/L Activities Is Par for the Course

The organizational difficulties of PD/L are magnified because the existing functional areas are already located within various divisions of the company. Table 14-1 illustrates this situation. It is based on 358 questionnaire responses to the question which functional areas were currently within the firm's PD/L department. Although the table shows the percentages that are *in*, it is easy to see that—for many firms—these key functions are *not* in the PD/L department's jurisdiction.

The size of a firm also has an influence on the placement of distribution and logistics functions. In small firms there are definite limitations as to how thinly managerial talent can be spread. In such situations, one consideration in organization may be to even out the work loads of supervisors. In an effort to examine how firm size influences control over the various logistical functions, a study was conducted of paint manufacturers in the San Francisco Bay area.[5] The firms vary in size, and they manufacture both household and specialized industrial paints. Figures 14-3 through 14-10 illustrate

required 24 trucks and one helicopter. (Marin *Independent Journal* January 25, 1985, page TV 1.)

[5] The study was performed in late 1979 by Peter Sownie, a graduate student in the School of Business at San Francisco State University.

Table 14-1 Functional Areas Presently
Included in PD/L Departments of 358 Firms

Functional Areas	Percentage Located in PD/L Departments
Transportation/Traffic	92.2%
Warehousing	74.9%
Inventory control	51.1%
Materials handling	49.7%
Order processing	45.0%
Protective packaging	43.6%
Customer service	42.2%
Purchasing	24.0%
Other	11.2%

Source: Adapted from James C. Johnson and Donald L. Berger, "Physical Distribution: Has It Reached Maturity?" *International Journal of Physical Distribution,* **7:**287 (1977).

the placement of the logistical functions in eight of the survey firms. The
figures are *not* organizational charts, as such, but list along the bottom line—
from left to right—eight logistical functions in the approximate order they
occur: purchasing, inbound transportation, production scheduling, inventory control (primarily for finished products), warehousing (also primarily
for finished products), outbound transportation, order processing, and customer service. Above these functions are shown—in ovals—the supervisory
framework and coordinating umbrellas under which these functions fit. Ovals
on the same horizontal level represent positions of approximately the same
level within the firm.

Figure 14-3 is for the smallest firm, owned and managed by a single
individual and employing only six. All logistical functions are supervised
directly by the owner-manager.

A slightly larger firm, also family operated, is depicted on Figure 14-4.
This firm recently created the position of shop foreman to relieve the owner

Figure 14-3 Supervision of Logistical Functions in Smallest Paint Firm

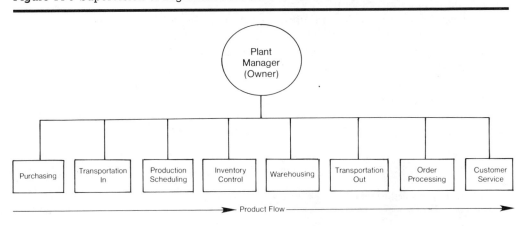

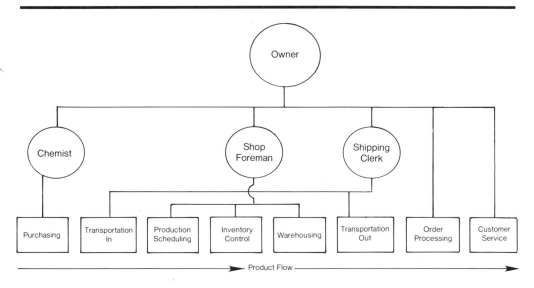

from production responsibilities and allow him to spend more time with sales.

The third firm has several owners. One owner has overall responsibility for supervision, whereas the other concentrates on supervising most of the outbound functions. (The third owner has retired and exercises a minor role in the firm's management.) Figure 14-5 shows this firm. Note that purchasing is supervised by a technical director; in the previous case it was super-

Figure 14-5 Small Firm's Division of Logistical Supervisory Functions Between Owners

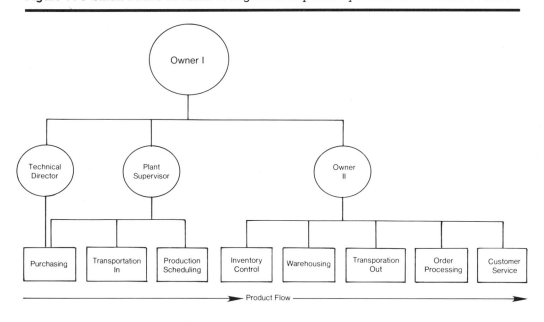

Figure 14-6 Medium-Sized Firm's Allocation of Logistical Supervision

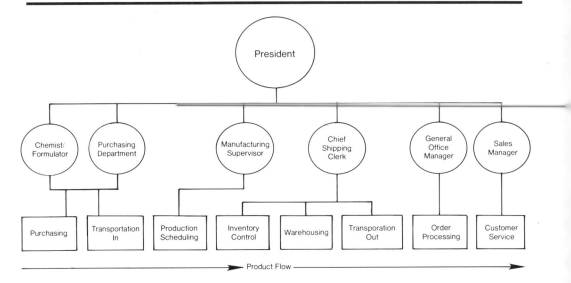

vised by a chemist because the nature of the paint-making process makes control of quality of inputs crucial.

A medium-sized paint manufacturer is depicted in Figure 14-6. The eight logistical functions are under the control of six different supervisors. These supervisors, in turn, are coordinated by the president, who is also the general manager. The purchasing department handles routine purchases and also arranges for inbound transportation. However, when nonstandard paints are being manufactured, the chemist-formulator handles the purchasing of and inbound transportation for the specialized inputs.

A medium-sized firm that specializes in industrial paints is the subject of Figure 14-7. This particular firm is required to make large batches of custom paint for special orders, which explains why more of the logistical functions are under the control of the manufacturing manager.

Another medium-size firm's arrangement of logistical supervision is shown on Figure 14-8. This paint firm's traffic manager is responsible for warehousing and for both inbound and outbound transportation. He reports to the vice-president of operations.

Much larger firms, operating several factories each, are depicted on Figures 14-9 and 14-10. Both figures show operations in a single factory only, not the firms' entire operations. In Figure 14-9, note that a materials distribution manager supervises all logistical functions, except for production scheduling. He shares responsibility for coordinating purchasing with the firm's director of purchasing who is headquartered in the firm's home office and makes many of the arrangements with major suppliers.

A single plant of another firm is shown on Figure 14-10. This particular plant apparently has no control over purchasing, order processing, or customer service. Responsibility for these functions is exercised in the firm's headquarters.

The particular aspects of information depicted on Figures 14-3 through

Figure 14-7 Medium-Sized Specialty Paint Manufacturer's Allocation of Logistical Responsibilities

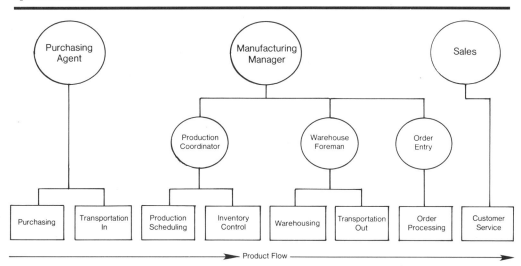

14-10 may not apply to all industries, but they are representative of the different arrangements for supervising logistical functions and how they change as a firm increases in size. Interestingly, four of the eight paint manufacturers shown here, including the three largest, combine supervision of inbound and outbound transportation.

The integration of inbound and outbound movements should not be surprising. Current professional thinking is that this coordination is needed. André J. Martin, a well-known advocate of MRP and DRP, has written:

Figure 14-8 Medium-Sized Paint Firm With Traffic Manager Also Supervising Warehousing

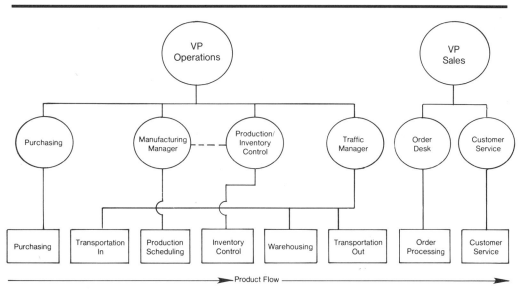

Figure 14-9 Plant of a Large Paint Firm Utilizing a Materials Manager to Supervise Many Logistical Functions

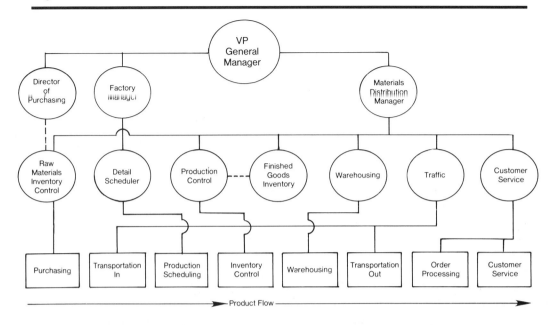

Figure 14-10 Plant of a Large Paint Firm, Where Many Logistical Functions Are Supervised from Headquarters

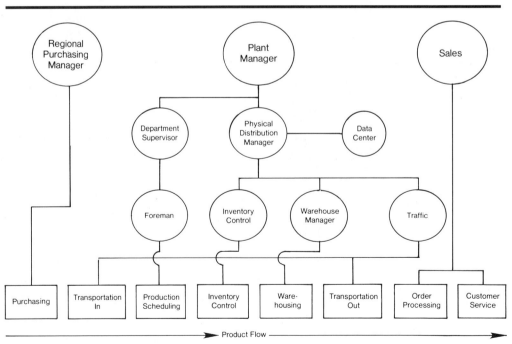

Most books on distribution inventories assume that allocating the inventory once it is available is the problem. They must believe that the inventory which the distribution centers need just appears out of nowhere! The *real* problem is planning manufacturing, be it within one's own company or with outside suppliers, to make sure that the inventory will be available when needed. Integrating the production planning for distributing inventories with the production planning for manufacturing inventories is a subject that has gotten little attention in the conventional literature on distribution inventories.[6]

TOM # Achieving Coordination

The key to effective PD/L operations is a high level of coordination between the functional areas. George A. Gecowets, executive director of the NCPDM, commented that the key to implementation is *coordination*, which may be nothing more than a continuing exchange of information among the traditional functions that combine to form the PD/L department.[7]

To achieve a high level of coordination, a firm can choose one of three organizational strategies. These include making no change in the present system, experimenting with unique ways of coordination with the existing system, or reorganizing of the functional areas of PD/L into a newly established PD/L department. There are, actually, more alternatives, but they are just variations. The actual alternative selected may depend on the firm's strategic plans, including those formulated to cover its logistical activities.[8] In any event, considerable thought must go into the organizing or reorganizing the firm—and its vendors and buyers—in order to achieve a more desirable flow of goods and services.

The Status Quo

For some companies it is feasible to obtain the required coordination between the functional areas of PD/L without any formal change in the organizational structure. This is accomplished by both formal and informal operating procedures that guarantee that the various areas will coordinate and discuss their various problems and proposals. This concept of coordination is generally most feasible when the overall size of the firm and the number of employees trying to coordinate across departmental lines, is not large. For many firms, this is a viable alternative; and it avoids the problems associated with actually transferring and reassigning functional areas.

---

[6] André J. Martin, *Distribution Resource Planning* (Englewood Cliffs, N.J.: Prentice-Hall, 1983), p. 2. Martin was an associate of the late Oliver Wight, one of the principal figures in the development of MRP.

[7] George A. Gecowets, "PDM—Pro and Con," *Distribution Worldwide* (March 1973), p. 39.

[8] See also, Michael A. McGinnis and Bernard J. LaLonde, "Strategic Planning and the Physical Distribution Process," *NCPDM 1983 Papers,* pp. 790–799; Bernard J. Hale, "Avoiding Common Pitfalls in Implementing the Strategic Planning Process," *NCPDM 1983 Papers,* pp. 800–806; and Douglas M. Lambert and James R. Stock, *Strategic Physical Distribution* (Homewood, Ill.: Irwin, 1982).

One problem of maintaining the status quo organizational structure is that the influence of PD/L thinking never gets an opportunity to express itself. Because PD/L activities are scattered throughout the firm, they always remain subservient to the objectives of the senior department (i.e., marketing, manufacturing, finance) in which they are housed.

The Linking-Pin Concept

The second organizational structure is similar to the status quo option. In this case, certain individuals would be assigned the responsibility for ensuring coordination between PD/L activities. Known as linking pins, they are assigned to work in two or three functional areas. An individual may simultaneously be assigned to the traffic department (which is a part of production) and to the warehousing department (which is a part of marketing). The advantage of this system is that the linking-pin members of each work group are able to coordinate and express the problems and concerns of each decision as it relates to the respective departments within which the linking pin operates.

There are serious problems with this concept. The most basic is that it violates the classic organizational principle of unity of command. Because the linking pin in effect belongs to two or more departments, who is his or her boss? Who evaluates job performance? Who decides about promotions? Linking pins may find themselves in the position of having no "home." It is possible for the linking pin member to alienate all the departments for whom he or she works. They may feel that the linking pin members are becoming too global in outlook and no longer a member of that department's "team." Also, under the linking-pin arrangement, PD/L is close to being considered a staff rather than a line function, with the accompanying inference that staff activities are never quite as important as line activities.

A Unified Department

Another alternative is to combine all the functional areas of PD/L into one department. This solution is intuitively the best because coordination between traffic, warehousing, inventory control, production, and the other functional areas is facilitated when they are combined into one operating department. This alternative has worked well for many companies and appears to be the preferred solution to successfully overcoming the coordination problems in a PD/L department. Under this alternative, PD/L is a line activity.

Professors Jeffrey Miller and Peter Gilmour have advocated a materials management department for some firms to be on the same level as the traditional departments of manufacturing, finance, and marketing.[9] As an example of the type of firm needing such an organizational structure, they cited an electronics manufacturer that once had grown with little competition and was now in a "mature" market, confronting many new competi-

---

[9] Jeffrey G. Miller and Peter Gilmour, "Materials Managers: Who Needs Them?" *Harvard Business Review* (July–Aug. 1979), pp. 143–153.

tors. Cost control was of increasing importance and the decision was made to have a single materials manager.

> Most important is justifying this reorganization was a plan for a new procurement program that promised to save the company millions of dollars a year by long-term contracting for groups of related materials instead of buying each material separately on a spot basis.
>
> The production planning group figured prominently in the proposed program because it controlled materials inventories and thus determined when releases needed to be placed against the new contracts. Thus the production controllers would be in contact with vendors on a more frequent basis than the purchasing department.
>
> Through their expediting and ordering decisions, the production planners could also significantly affect contract prices. Some managers felt that if production planning and purchasing reported together, their boss, the materials manager, could be sensitive to both materials costs and vendor relations along with inventory and ordering costs.[10]

Matrix Management

Another useful form of management organization is referred to as *matrix* management. With this approach the firm has a conventional management structure for handling most routine matters. However, many of the same people are also assigned—usually on a short-term basis—to teams that have been established to deal with specific, unique problems. Individuals are assigned to these short-term projects because they possess special skills:

> The term matrix . . . comes from the notion of organizing across functions at various levels . . . . A manager, or indeed, any individual with two or more roles and two or more superiors, is operating in a matrix environment. For instance, individuals working on a task force to develop a special project might also retain their functional roles as transportation specialists or lawyers or researchers.[11]

Although, at first reading, this might appear to be the same as the linking-pin concept, it is not. The linking-pin concept involves a longer-term commitment toward achieving coordination among several logistical activities. Matrix management implies a structured organization with some fluid teams going into and out of existence and serving only to attack specific—usually unanticipated—problems.

Channel Management

Another consideration in logistical organizations deals with managing channels. The channel can be thought of as the firms and people who, working together, function in a way that moves raw materials and components through

---

[10] Ibid., p. 147.
[11] Robert E. Murray, "Matrix Management and Distribution," *Handling and Shipping Management Presidential Issue,* 1980–1981 (1980), p. 82.

processing and manufacturing and on to retailers and customers. Any individual firm may choose how much of each channel it wishes to own, as well as the degree of control (usually through contract) it wishes to exercise over other segments or members of the channel. At one extreme is the *vertically integrated* firm, the best example being the Ford Motor Company of the 1920s, which owned forests and steel mills, and exercised tight control over its dealers. At the other extreme might be, say, an individual who deals in postage stamps for collectors and who buys, sells, receives, and delivers through the mail.

Most firms are somewhere in between, owning some logistical functions themselves and relying on vendors or customers to perform the others. (During the late 1970s, when unionized Teamsters wages were very high, some firms gave up their private fleets and switched to using common or contract carriers. This may have increased their transportation costs. However, when negotiating with other operating unions within their plants, management no longer had to explain why they were paying the unionized Teamsters so much.)

There are concerns in addition to efficiency: the firm may not wish to be completely dependent on one source of supply. In 1953 GM's transmission plant in Livonia, Michigan, was completely destroyed by fire. At the time, it was GM's only source of Hydra-Matic transmissions, which were used in Pontiacs, Oldsmobiles, and Cadillacs.[12] It may also be risky to have too small a number of customers because one may become overly dependent on them. Since the Reagan administration began in 1981, many of our government's domestic programs have been curtailed or eliminated; and this has hurt suppliers who were dependent on those programs as customers.

In any event, one must carefully think through the entire network of channels in which her or his firm operates, before being able to decide what form of PD/L organization will best orchestrate all of the performers in the logistics system.[13]

SHARON   # Centralization vs. Decentralization

A final issue in PD/L organization strategy is whether the PD/L department should be centralized or decentralized. A centralized PD/L department implies that the corporation will have one PD/L organization that will administer the activities for the entire company. Decentralization results in PD/L activity decisions being made separately at the divisional or product group level, or in different geographic regions.

The size of the firm, its product, and the geographic area over which sales are made and inputs purchased must be taken into account before some centralization-decentralization decisions can be made. By way of example, note Figure 14-11, which shows where the Hormel Company, a

---

[12] William B. Harris, "The Great Livonia Fire," *Fortune* (Nov. 1953), pp. 132–135, 171–178. It took about four months to resume full production of Hydra-Matic transmissions. In the interim, Chevrolet's Power-glide transmissions were placed in Pontiacs and Buick's Dynaflow transmissions were placed in Oldsmobiles and Cadillacs.

[13] Lambert and Stock, op. cit., pp. 477–480.

Figure 14-11 Location of Hormel Company Facilities

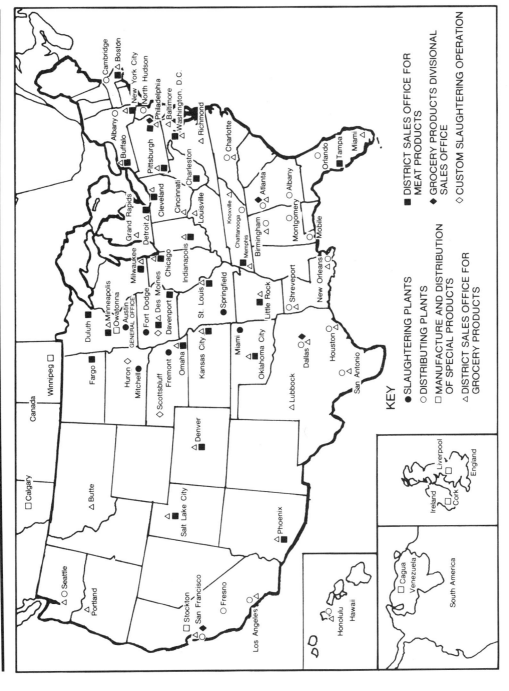

KEY

● SLAUGHTERING PLANTS

○ DISTRIBUTING PLANTS

□ MANUFACTURE AND DISTRIBUTION
OF SPECIAL PRODUCTS

△ DISTRICT SALES OFFICE FOR
GROCERY PRODUCTS

■ DISTRICT SALES OFFICE FOR
MEAT PRODUCTS

◆ GROCERY PRODUCTS DIVISIONAL
SALES OFFICE

◇ CUSTOM SLAUGHTERING OPERATION

Courtesy George A. Hormel Company.

Minnesota-based meat packer, has located its various plants and offices throughout the United States and in several other countries.

Arguments in Favor of a Centralized Department

Two factors argue for a centralized system. The first centers around the *firm's computer facility*. The PD/L department is a significant user of the company's computer system. For many firms, PD/L is second only to the accounting department in its use of computer time because the PD/L function, by its very nature, involves keeping track of thousands of details and bits of information. The PD/L department is dependent on its daily computer printouts that spell out the current logistical situation and also indicate future problem areas. Because of PD/L's dependence on computer reports, many companies have found it best to have their PD/L department in proximity to the corporation's main computer facility. Sanford Abrahams, director of corporate distribution for Carrier Corporation—part of United Technologies Corporation (UTC)—said: "You can't manage large complex transportation functions without a data base. At UTC we have an in-house system with input costs paid by the providing company. The system running costs are paid by the Corporation. Eight weeks per year we enter all freight bills to get real life snapshots of our transportation world. Data that is [sic] developed goes back to the providing company, the Action Group for project initiation, and private fleets to determine if they can save money on intercorporate hauling."[14]

This quotation leads to the second argument for a centralized management, and that is the *ability to consolidate shipments most effectively*. A firm can significantly reduce its transportation costs on a per unit basis if it can ship in large quantities and qualify for the TL, CL, or incentive rates. It may also make better use of its own truck fleet. In addition, with greater volume being tendered to the carriers, it becomes more feasible to have a companywide system of make-bulk and break-bulk distribution center warehouses, which we discussed in Chapter 6. The J. I. Case Company of Racine, Wisconsin, exemplifies a firm using a centralized physical distribution department. *Traffic Management* magazine noted the basic reason for this organizational structure: "Logistics centralization gains a new momentum these days as sharp cost increases force managements to learn afresh the basic economic law underlying freight transport: maximum point-to-point movement at regular intervals yields lowest cost."[15]

Arguments in Favor of a Decentralized PD/L Department

Two arguments are generally made for a decentralized PD/L department. The first stresses the unmanageability of a centralized system in large, multidivisional firms. In highly decentralized firms, it is often preferable that the

[14] *NCPDM Papers, 1982,* p. 338. The "Action Group" referred to is made up of logistics representatives from the various companies that make up UTC. These companies are the "providing companies" and UTC the "Corporation."
[15] "A Case for Corporate Traffic," *Traffic Management* (Dec. 1975), p. 30.

line distribution functions remain in each autonomous division. This organizational system appears to function best when the various product lines of each division have very little in common.

The second factor questions the ability of a centralized PD/L department to provide the required levels of customer service standards. If customers are willing to wait 30 to 60 days to receive their orders, then a centralized PD/L department would not prove a handicap to a multidivisional firm. If customers require 24 to 48 hour service, the centralized PD/L function may not be responsive enough to yield this high level of service. This type of customer service standard may require an in-house (i.e., within the division) PD/L department that is attuned to the specific physical distribution requirements of the division.

Examples of Successful PD/L Organization Systems

The final section of this chapter will examine the PD/L organizational structures of two major United States corporations: Litton Microwave and the North American Philips Corporation.

Litton Microwave

Litton Microwave is a division of Litton Industries.[16] The firm is a major manufacturer of microwave ovens with sales of approximately $250 million in 1979. Raymond R. Murray is director of distribution, and he and his staff coordinate the entire flow of materials—from inbound raw materials to finished products shipped to customers.

The distribution department reports directly to the vice-president of consumer operations. In addition, the directors of manufacturing and marketing also report to the same vice-president. This allows the distribution function to be relatively neutral because it is not looked at exclusively as a support function for either marketing or manufacturing.

Illustrative of this neutrality is the relationship of distribution to manufacturing. Prior to the present organizational arrangement, each plant manager could authorize air freight from vendors on an emergency basis—and air freight was heavily used. Now, air freight (which is also known as premium transportation) can only be used if it is required to prevent a plant assembly line from shutting down. Vendors who disregard instructions and send products to Litton Microwave via air freight instead of surface transportation are told that they must bear the added transportation costs. Traffic Manager David L. Swanson noted, "In addition, we assess chargebacks internally when purchasing people make undue use of premium transportation service. Our new procedure is quite effective. It reduced the premium transportation volume from 16 per cent of the total inbound freight bill to 5

[16] This discussion is based on Jack W. Farrell, "Distribution Dynamics at Work: Litton Microwave Division," *Traffic Management* (April 1980), pp. 53–59.

per cent within a year. This is against an inbound freight cost that runs typically at a $3 million annual level."[17]

Inbound transportation activities at Litton Microwave are as important as the distribution of the finished products. A number of production inputs are shipped from the Orient. These include magnetron tubes, oven ceramic shells, certain unique electrical items, and other parts. These components, in most cases, are shipped via full containers on vessels that arrive at Seattle. From there they go by rail to Litton's production plants.

Distribution of finished products involves both domestic and export shipments. Full-container shipments are made to Hong Kong, Latin America, Australia, and western Europe. These shipments are via air freight. The order-processing function is centralized at the corporate headquarters in Plymouth, Minnesota. Products are shipped from the closest distribution center. Centers are located at Plymouth, Chicago, Detroit, San Francisco, Los Angeles, Newark, Dallas, and Miami.

Protective packaging also reports to the distribution department. This function is of great importance for sophisticated products that are easily damaged—such as microwave ovens. Recently, a classic trade-off was used. Styrofoam inserts were utilized to protect the ovens, where fiberboard inserts had been previously utilized. While the foam protection was more expensive per unit, its use significantly reduced in-transit damage. Ray Murray stated that protective packaging is a key aspect of the distribution function:

> There is a service aspect to damage prevention, which is sometimes overlooked. In addition to the actual cost of damages, there is the problem of potential lost sales, either because a consignee is disappointed, or because customers at the retail level will choose competitive merchandise rather than wait for a shipment to replace defective goods. Through sound packaging, reliable delivery schedules, and efficient order processing, a distribution department makes an important hidden contribution to the bottom line by protecting against lost sales.[18]

North American Philips Corporation

North American Philips Corporation (NAPC) is a conglomerate with twenty-eight operating divisions and subsidiaries in the United States, that manufacture a variety of lighting, electrical, and electronics items.[19] Each division and subsidiary was—and is—considered to be autonomous. However, when the Motor Carrier Act of 1980 was passed, the corporate (NAPC) distribution department (which consisted of only three people—a director, a manager, and a secretary) convened a meeting of transportation managers from the eighteen divisions and subsidiaries that made the most use of transportation. The group's initial purpose was to formulate and put into motion a plan for intercorporate hauling (which became more permissible after the

---

[17] Ibid., p. 54.

[18] Ibid., p. 59.

[19] This discussion is based on Charles F. Dransfield, "Getting It All Together," *Handling & Shipping Management Presidential Issue 1984–85,* (1984) pp. 28–34.

1980 Motor Carrier Act). The group decided that the corporation would have more clout in negotiating contracts for truckload freight than would its various subsidiaries and divisions. This strategy proved to be correct, and the contracts entered into resulted in annual savings of approximately $2 million.

Because of this success, a more formalized, but smaller, permanent committee was organized, representing NAPC's eight subsidiaries with the largest freight bills. This group became involved with studying and improving methods used to handle less-than-truckload and small-parcel flows. Information gathered was also used to consolidate the freight movements and warehouse utilization of several subsidiaries. The committee also negotiated a single corporate contract with Chase Manhattan Bank to process and pay all of NAPC's freight bills. Charles F. Dransfield, of NAPC, said:

> Custom-designed reports are printed by Chase each month and sent to each NAPC company, along with consolidated accounting and traffic reports for corporate-level review. Soon this information will be available through microcomputers.
>
> The data we have captured . . . have already been instrumental in developing new programs and monitoring and improving projects previously implemented. For example, we can now check closely to see how cost-effective our selection of carriers for LTL freight is and quickly change that selection, if necessary.[20]

The corporate committee is now achieving corporatewide savings of approximately $5 million per year. NAPC has established a new corporate position, vice-president of logistics, who is responsible for domestic and international transportation, warehousing, corporate distribution information, and distribution support for all of NAPC's twenty-eight divisions and subsidiaries. The corporate logistics staff remains small and still sees much of its mission as being consultants to NAPC's operating divisions and subsidiaries.

Note that not all of what this textbook considers to be logistics functions are handled by the NAPC framework just mentioned. However, the example is illustrative of a successful attempt of organizing—or reorganizing—some logistics functions in a conglomerate type of business.

Summary

Organizing the logistics operations within a firm is a difficult task. This is because the individual functions are scattered throughout the firm, and there is no norm with which proposed logistical operations can be compared. The framework for supervising logistical functions in eight different paint manufacturers showed little similarity among firms, except—perhaps—the tendency of larger firms to combine supervision of both inbound and outbound transportation. Current professional thinking favors coordination of inbound and outbound movements.

There are several methods for achieving better coordination of logistical

[20] Ibid., p. 34.

functions. The ultimate method is to establish a new materials management or PD/L department at a level comparable to the existing departments of finance, marketing, and manufacturing. Less dramatic would be use of the linking-pin concept, wherein various individuals are assigned simultaneously to two or more logistical operating areas.

Another issue is whether the logistics operation should be centralized or decentralized. The main arguments for a centralized operation are to get maximum benefits from the firm's computer system and to be able to consolidate freight shipments. The main argument in favor of decentralization is to be nearer to customers and their needs.

The chapter closed with a description of logistics operations in two firms: Litton Microwave and North American Philips Corporation.

Questions for Discussion and Review

1. Management consultant John F. Magee once stated, "Logistical system management poses some puzzling organizational problems to the typical, functionally organized firm." Discuss this statement fully.
2. "Luckily, PD/L organization structure has been subjected to so much study and analysis that the ideal organizational setup can now be easily predetermined for all firms." Comment critically on this statement.
3. One of the sections of this chapter was entitled, "Dispersion of PD/L Activities Is Par for the Course." What is scattered, and why does this make the organizational issues more difficult?"
4. It has been said that effective PD/L can be of great assistance in accomplishing a high level of good customer service. Why is this true?
5. Why is the support of top management necessary to effectively establish a PD/L department?
6. Effective coordination is often thought to be one of the important aspects of PD/L. This chapter suggested several methods that can be used to achieve this objective. Discuss briefly each of the alternatives. Which one do you feel is the best? Defend your answer.
7. Who is a linking-pin person? What problems and opportunities does this organizational alternative present?
8. Discuss briefly the pros and cons of an independent PD/L department that is equal to marketing, manufacturing, and finance.
9. "The PD/L function logically should be a subpart of the marketing department." Discuss this statement.
10. What is the difference between a centralized and a decentralized PD/L department? Which is more desirable? Why?
11. Present carefully an argument for the centralization of PD/L departments.
12. What is matrix management? Do you believe it is a practical solution for PD/L organizations? Defend your answer.
13. Discuss the PD/L organization at Litton Microwave.
14. Discuss the logistics organization at North American Philips Corp. How many *logistics* functions are managed at the *corporate* level?

15. Eight different PD/L organizational structures for paint manufacturers were examined. What trends can you identify that took place as the firms became larger?
16. Of all the PD/L organizational issues examined in this chapter, which do you believe is the most important? Why?
17. Assume you are in charge of establishing a new PD/L department. Which functional areas would you want to initially be part of the new PD/L department? Why? How would you go about actually implementing your new department?
18. In what ways might military logistics differ from logistics as practiced by conventional business firms? List and discuss.
19. What is channel management? How might it affect a firm's choice of logistical organizational structures? Why?
20. Why should a firm avoid becoming overly dependent on a single source of supply or a single customer?

Additional Chapter References

Cafiero, William. "The Integrated Parts System." *Annual Proceedings of the NCPDM* (1984), pp. 221–234.

Delaney, Robert V. " 'Fixing What Is Broken'—A Strategy for Diversified Distribution Service Companies." *Annual Proceedings of the NCPDM* (1984), pp. 269–308.

Elam, Joyce J., Darwin D. Klingman, and Robert F. Schneider. "Experiences with an Integrated Logistics Planning System." *Annual Proceedings of the NCPDM* (1982), pp. 281–292.

Hale, Bernard J. "Avoiding Common Pitfalls in Implementing the Strategic Planning Process." *Annual Proceedings of the NCPDM* (1983), pp. 800–806.

La Howchic, Nicholas J. "Merging the Distribution Operation of Nabisco and Standard Brands and Customer Service." *Annual Proceedings of the NCPDM* (1984), pp. 179–196.

Heskett, James L. "Organizing for Effective Distribution Management." *The Distribution Handbook* (New York: Free Press Division of Macmillan, 1985), pp. 817–833.

Mallory, Lynn C. "Integrated Logistics: How to Make It Happen in Your Company." *Annual Proceedings of the NCPDM* (1983), pp. 731–750.

Pollock, Ted. "Management Support Systems for Strategic Decision Making." *Annual Proceedings of the NCPDM* (1984), pp. 235–248.

Redmond, John B. "Participatory Management: A Case History." *Annual Proceedings of the NCPDM* (1983), pp. 712–730.

Shapiro, Roy D., and James L. Heskett, *Logistics Strategy* (St. Paul: West, 1985).

Webster, Francis M. "An Executive's Primer on Project Management (or, How to Avoid Schedule and Cost Overruns)." *Annual Proceedings of the NCPDM* (1984), pp. 921–950.

CASE 14-1

Columbia Lumber Products Company

The Columbia Lumber Products Company (CLPC) was headquartered in Portland, Oregon, where it had been founded in 1899. For many years, its principal product had been only lumber; in the 1940s it began producing plywood, and in 1960, particle board. The first two products, lumber and plywood, were produced at various sites in Oregon and marketed on the West Coast and as far east as Chicago.

Particle board was produced in Duluth, Minnesota, at a plant built with a U.S. Area Redevelopment Administration Loan in 1962. Initially, the input to the plant was trimmings and other scrap from CLPC's Oregon operations. Particle board sales increased so quickly that the Duluth operation consumed not only all of the former waste from CLPC's Oregon plant but also waste purchased from various lumber and wood products operations in Minnesota and Northern Wisconsin.

CLPC's sales, in terms of product volume, doubled between 1960 and 1985. However, nearly all the growth had been in particle board; lumber and plywood sales remained relatively constant (although varying with changes in the home construction industry). In 1985, exports accounted for 9 per cent of CLPC's sales. Nearly all of this was plywood sold to Japan. Fifteen per cent of CLPC's 1985 purchases were from foreign sources, 5 per cent was mahogany from the Phillippines used for plywood veneer, and 10 per cent was wood scrap purchased from Ontario, Canada, for use in CLPC's Duluth plant. Particle board produced in Duluth was marketed in all states east of the Rocky Mountains, although sales in the southern United States were somewhat less than spectacular.

The slowdown in home production, which started in the late 1970s, and really never ended, resulted in many years of little or no growth in CLPC's sales. Common stock dividends had been cut several times. In 1985 they were 37 cents per share, down considerably from their peak—in 1976—of $2.21.

Stockholders, the outside directors, and various lending institutions were becoming increasingly unhappy. After a long, angry board of directors' meeting, agreement was reached only with respect to what some of the organizational problems were. A partial list follows:

1. The corporate headquarters was in Portland although the growth was in the Midwest. Possibly the headquarters, or at least more functions, should be shifted to an office in Duluth where the plant was, or to Chicago, where the largest sales office was. A major relocation away from Portland would be difficult. Many employees would choose to remain on the West Coast. Even for those willing to relocate, there was a split between those willing to relocate to Duluth and those willing to relocate to Chicago.

2. There were too many vice-presidents. (See Exhibit 14-1.) Because four vice-presidents (engineering, finance, personnel, and purchasing) would reach mandatory retirement age by 1987, the number of vice-presidents should be reduced from nine to no more than six (plus one executive vice-president).

3. Logistics and distribution costs were higher than industry averages. Also, the majority of customer complaints dealt with poor deliveries. In Exhibit 14-1 a T shows

Exhibit 14-1 Columbia Lumber Products' Organizational Chart

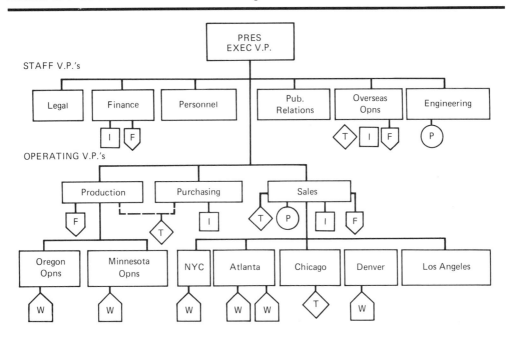

where a traffic management function was located. Geographically, the traffic manager for overseas operations was located in Seattle, which was a foreign trade center for the Pacific Northwest. The Chicago sales office had a traffic manager who handled all fiberboard distribution, and lumber and plywood distribution east of the Rockies. Production and purchasing shared a traffic manager who was headquartered in Portland and whose principal duty was overseeing shipments of waste products from Oregon to Minnesota. Another traffic manager (in Portland), who reported to the sales vice-president, was acknowledged to be the firm's senior traffic manager and more or less coordinated the efforts of the other three. He was the only one authorized to initiate action before regulatory bodies and also handled the serious negotiations with carrier rate-making bodies, and with carriers. (CLPC used contract truckers and rail for most of its shipping.)

4. The purchasing department handled the details of fleet management, which included about 100 autos on long-term lease for use by management and by the sales force. Several light trucks were leased for use around the plants.

5. CLPC also owned two small aricraft, which often were the target of questions during stockholders' meetings. One plane was based at Portland, the other, Duluth. Each was used in its respective region for trips to sites without scheduled airline service. Both planes were under control of the production department. Other departments—especially sales—complained that the planes were being used for the benefit of the production department, rather than for the benefit of the entire firm.

6. *P* on the figure shows two packaging engineering functions. The one under engineering was located in Portland and dealt with plywood products. The one under sales was located in Chicago and handled particle board products. The two packaging engineering functions saw their roles differently. The one in Portland was concerned mainly with safe packing and packaging of products moving between CLPC

plants or from CLPC plants to customers. The Chicago packaging engineers were interested in finding new markets for particle board and lumber as packaging materials to be sold to others. *W* on the figure shows where there are company-owned warehouses. Numerous public warehouses were also used, although not continually. *I* shows locations of individuals concerned with inventory levels. All four individuals were located in Portland. *F* indicates where sales forecasting took place. Only sales and production devoted much staff effort to forecasting. Each quarter, however, the financial vice-president's office coordinated all forecasts to ensure comparability. Computer operations were under control of the engineering division. CLPC's executive vice-president determined priorities for computer access and use.

7. The personnel department handled employee moves, although only a few had taken place since 1980. An outside director, who was familiar with current federal legislation, suggested that CLPC negotiate a contract with a household goods carrier to handle all CLPC employee moves. This action would be especially significant if a major reorganization resulted in numerous employee transfers.

Question One: Draw a new organization chart for Columbia Lumber Products Company that you feel overcomes best the directors' criticisms of CLPC's present (January 1, 1986) organization. Indicate the geographic location of all operations shown on the new chart. Explain why you established the organization chart the way you did.

Question Two: Assume that the firm should be reorganized in a manner that emphasizes sales and marketing. This would include a physical distribution system, which would support the marketing effort. Draw an organization chart that you think would accomplish this aim. Indicate the geographic location of all operations on the new chart and explain why you drew the chart as you did.

Question Three: In the text of Chapter 14 is a quotation from André Martin that deals with the integration of inventory and production planning. Read Martin's quote, and then draw an organization chart for CLPC that gives full weight to Martin's views. Explain your actions.

Question Four: Assume that a major reorganization appears unlikely, but you are told to draw up a plan for implementing the linking-pin concept mentioned in the text. Describe how you would accomplish this. Between which functions, or geographic sites, would you establish linking pins? Why?

Question Five: Assume the firm wants to reorganize into a highly centralized form, closely managed from a single home office. Draw a new chart that takes this desire into account. Indicate the geographic location of all operations on your new chart and explain why you organized as you did.

Question Six: Assume, instead, that the firm wants to reorganize into a highly decentralized form, where many important decisions can be made out in the field. Draw a new chart, including the geographic location of all activities. Explain why you drew it as you did.

Question Seven: When making new organizational charts, what additional types of information—not given in the case—would be useful? Why?

CASE 14-2

Easing Ira's Ire

Ira Pollack was difficult to work for. A self-made millionaire, he paid extremely high salaries but demanded much from his subordinates, including being "on call" 24 hours per day. In his Las Vegas penthouse, he would study and restudy each detail of his conglomerate's performance, and then call some unlucky underling—at any hour—to vent his anger and demand that something or other be improved. His tantrums were legendary.

One of his underlings was Tamara Wood who was driving her new red Mercedes convertible along Rodeo Drive in Beverly Hills, looking for a parking space. Her college class (Northern Illinois University at DeKalb) was holding its fifth reunion in Chicago, which Tamara planned to attend. She wanted to buy a new outfit for the event, to show her old classmates that she had "arrived." A chauffeur-driven Rolls pulled away from the curb, leaving an empty space right in front of Tamara's favorite couturier. Tamara expertly swung her Mercedes into the empty space, looked up, and was pleased to see that there was still nearly an hour left on the meter. "Daddy was right," she thought to herself, "clean living does pay off."

As she turned off the ignition, the telephone mounted below the dash started buzzing. Tamara hesitated. Would it be John, calling to thank her for that wonderful evening? Would it be Matt, seeing if she were free to spend next weekend on Catalina Island? Or, maybe it was Jason, who was always wanting her to accompany him to Waikiki. Tamara finally picked up the phone and, in her sweetest voice, said: "Hello, love."

"Dammit! Don't 'hello love' me!" shouted a man's voice at the other end.

Tamara's stomach churned, her muscles tightened, and she said, weakly, "Sorry, Mr. Pollack, I was expecting somebody else."

"That's obvious," he retorted. "At this hour of the day, you're on *my* time and *should* be thinking of business. How come you're not in the office?"

"I'm just making a customer-service follow-up," responded Tamara, hoping that Mr. Pollack would not ask for too many details.

"Well, you *should* be worried about customer service," said Pollack. "That's why I've called. I've been studying performance records for all my operations dealing with the amount of time that elapses between our receipt of an order and when our customer receives his shipment. The performance of your distribution center in West Hollywood *stinks! Drop* what you're doing, *forget* about your love life, and *get your tail back to your office* and figure out what's wrong! Then tell me what's needed to speed up your operation. Call me at any hour."

Tamara heard the phone click. She forgot about DeKalb. She forgot about Chicago and the new outfit. She forgot about her night with John, about Catalina Island, and about Waikiki. She heard a faint "beep" to her left. She saw a maroon Jaguar, with a Beverly Hills matron motioning with one of her white-gloved hands as if to say: "If you're leaving, may I have your parking spot?"

"Dammit," thought Tamara to herself as she pulled away. "If it weren't for one hundred thou a year, I'd tell Pollack what he could do with his order processing system."

Still muttering, she pulled into her reserved slot next to the West Hollywood distribution center. "Aloha!" chirped Ellen Scott, her assistant, as she walked in. "Jason has called three times about wanting you to fly to Hawaii. Also, you have two calls from John, one from Matt, one from your Mother, who asked why you never phone her, and one from some fellow who wouldn't leave his name, but said it was 'very personal.' Tell me about the outfit you bought. I'll bet it's stunning."

"Forget about them, and hold all my calls," said Tamara, crisply. "I'm not going anywhere. Pollack called me and is mad because our order-processing/delivery times are out of whack."

Two days passed. Tamara had put her social life on "hold" and had not even phoned her Mother. All her time was spent trying to figure out how to speed up her order-processing system. But she didn't know how to start. The accuracy of the system was not an issue, although additional costs could be. When Mr. Pollack paid his bonuses last year, he had told Tamara that if her operation had cost one cent more to run, she would not have received a bonus. Because her bonus had paid for her new Mercedes, Tamara was cost-conscious, to say the least.

Ellen helped her, too—at least through late Friday afternoon. Ellen explained that she couldn't work on Saturday and Sunday because she'd accepted an invitation to spend the weekend at Catalina Island with an unnamed friend. Before Ellen left, she and Tamara had decided that there were twelve distinct operations involved in processing and shipping orders. Some could be performed at the same time, whereas others had to be performed in sequence—that is, one could not be started until the other was completed. These tasks, the amount of time it takes to complete each, and the sequential relationships—if any—are shown on Exhibit 14-2.

After completing the information shown in the exhibit, Ellen left. Tamara was left with the task of trying to relate all those tasks to each other. She recalled a college textbook that she had never much cared for but that she had come across a few weeks earlier as she was searching for her Northern Illinois University yearbook. Tamara looked at a PERT chart in that book (Figure 12-6 in *this* textbook) and knew that she would have to construct something similar in order to analyze her distribution center's order-processing/shipping operations. She studied the text accompanying the chart, sighed, and thought to herself: "Where was I—or at least where was my mind—the day the professor explained all of this in class?"

Question One: Arrange all of the tasks shown in the exhibit into a network or PERT chart arrangement.

Question Two: Determine the critical path. What is the least time it takes between receipt of an order and its delivery to a customer?

Question Three: Offhand, looking at your answers to Questions One and Two, what areas of activity do you think Tamara should look at first, assuming she wants to reduce order-processing/delivery times? Why?

Question Four: Now that she's a Californian, Tamara wants to be able to impress Mr. Pollack that she's "with it" in terms of current technology. Recently, a sales representative from a warehouse equipment company called, trying to interest her in installing a "Star Wars-Robotic" order picker for the warehouse. Controlled by lasers, and powered by magnetic levitation, the device would pick orders (task *H*) in 15 minutes, rather than six hours (.75 days), the current time. How valuable would such a device be to Tamara? Why?

Exhibit 14-2 Order Processing and Shipment Tasks (listed in approximate order of completion)

Task	Description	Duration (in days)	Precedence Relationships: Tasks on right of < cannot commence until tasks on left are completed
A	Order received and entered into computer	.25	A < D
B	Determine whether to fill from warehouse, or ship direct from factory	.50	B < C
C	Print picking order	.30	C < H
D	Verify customer's credit	.35	D < G,E
E	Check and determine buyer's eligibility for discounts	.15	E < F
F	Prepare invoice, enter in accounts receivable file	1.00	F < K
G	Determine mode of transport; select carrier	1.65	G < J
H	Pick order at warehouse	.75	H < I
I	Pack and label shipment	1.20	I < L
J	Notify carrier, prepare shipping documents	2.25	J < L
K	Transmit copy of invoice to shipping dock	1.20	K < L
L	Transport order to customer	3.50	

Question Five: Another alternative is to use faster transportation. How should Tamara choose between paying more for faster transportation or paying more for other improvements? Assume her only goal is speed.

Question Six: To offset some of the costs of speeding up the system, does the PERT chart indicate where there might be some potential savings from assigning fewer people to some tasks, thereby increasing the amount of time needed to complete these tasks? If so, which tasks are likely candidates? Why?

Adaptability to changing markets is never ending. The container ship manages to utilize tremendous space above deck carrying lashed containers. As this photo shows, some changes had to be made to accommodate the developing market in the U.S. for yachts built in the Far East. The ship is the Sea-Land Innovator.

(*Credit:* Sea-Land Corporation)

Physical
Distribution/Logistics:
Future Directions

Unless freight trains can be designed and built which offer a quantum decrease in the unit costs of operation, our participation in new America will be disappointingly small. And with heavy reliance on the shrinking markets of old America, growth prospects will be limited.

Richard L. Spence
Vice-president, Seaboard System
Railway Age
May 1984

Distribution executives, although relatively new to the highest levels of management, must not bask in their new-found glory. As the effects of deregulation stabilize, distribution executives must creatively seek ways to ensure that the total distribution program is compatible with the firm's overall objectives.

**Professors Bernard J. LaLonde
and Larry E. Emmelhainz**
Annual Proceedings of the NCPDM,
1984

Early in 1985 the BN will begin testing a satellite-based train tracking system. On-train computers will be linked to a series of six military satellites which will relay to BN headquarters in St. Paul precise information as to the trains' locations and speed. Accuracy is said to be within 150 feet and one mile per hour. The BN expects the new system, developed in conjunction with a division of Rockwell International, to improve dispatching the train handling. Reduced fuel consumption and increased safety are anticipated benefits.

Walter A. Appel
Railfan & Railroad
March, 1985

Key Terms

- Multinational sales
- Balance of trade
- Metric conversion
- Satellite navigation and communication
- Solid-fuel locomotives
- Integral trains
- Lighter-than-air cargo vessels
- Sailing cargo ships

Learning Objectives

- To understand how increased international trade will affect PD/L management
- To examine the impact of metric conversion on PD/L personnel
- To analyze the impact of computers on the PD/L function
- To identify future changes in technology that will impact on PD/L
- To note the future importance of PD/L

Introduction

This book has examined the fundamentals of PD/L as they exist today. The purpose of this chapter is to speculate about the future directions of PD/L. Because of the spectrum of activities in PD/L, we have limited our discussion. Any discussion of this sort is subject to the criticism that it tends to be subjective. Nevertheless, it is important for students of PD/L to take time to contemplate future changes in their discipline.

The following pages will start with the broader, macro viewpoint and then progress to the more specific, micro issues.

Increased Growth of Multinational Sales

The United States continues to have a serious balance-of-trade deficit (imports being at a higher level than exports). In 1980 the United States imported products and services worth $250 billion, while exporting about $215 billion. By 1984 exports were $230 billion, whereas imports had advanced to $329 billion. As can be seen, the trade balance is getting worse, not better. Nevertheless, many U.S. companies are successful exporters. In terms of total sales, General Motors is the most successful, with $6.5 billion in 1983. Boeing is in second place, with Ford Motor and General Electric coming in third and fourth, respectively. As a percentage of total sales, international sales are only 9 per cent of General Motor's total sales. Number one in this category is Boeing, with 43 per cent of its sales from foreign countries. In second place is Caterpillar Tractor with 29 per cent representing foreign sales. Table 15-1 lists foreign sales of ten large U.S. companies.

American-based multinational companies contribute significantly to offsetting our balance-of-trade deficit by repatriation of dividends, royalties, technical assistance fees, and interest and repayments of loans by foreign

Table 15-1 1983 Foreign Sales by U.S. Companies

Name of Company	1983 Foreign Sales as a Percent of Total Sales
1. Boeing	43.3
2. Caterpillar Tractor	29.2
3. International Minerals and Chemical	26.9
4. McDonnell Douglas	26.0
5. Northrop	25.4
6. Hewlett-Packard	23.5
7. A. E. Staley Manufacturing	21.5
8. Archer Daniels Midland	21.0
9. Digital Equipment	19.1
10. Dresser Industries	18.5

These numbers are substantially reduced from previous years. The reason is that in 1983 the U.S. dollar was very strong, meaning that other currencies could not be exchanged for as many dollars as in previous years. The result was that foreign individuals and firms could not afford American-made products; this explains why our exports were not strong in 1983. For example, in 1979 IBM made 54 per cent of its sales to foreigners, whereas in 1983 this figure was 6 per cent. *Source:* "Leading 50 Exporters," *Fortune* (Aug. 6, 1984), p. 65.

subsidiaries. Most important, however, is the direct influx of funds as United States products are sold in foreign commerce. The astute PD/L managers of the future must adjust themselves to the cultural shock that is often inherent in dealing with foreign PD/L operations. For instance, the latter half of the 1980s will continue to be one of developing trade with Communist nations. They will be markets primarily for producers' goods because their political/economic system does not especially motivate creating and satisfying demands for consumer goods.

Why has the balance-of-trade moved against the United States?[1] One major reason is that the cost of imported oil has increased tenfold since 1970.[2] A factor of equal importance is that we are rapidly becoming a world community where production will take place wherever it is most efficient. In more and more situations, this means that the production work that formerly took place in the United States is being shifted to foreign countries. John Naisbitt in his highly acclaimed book, *Megatrends,* has noted: "U.S. manufacturers will continue to produce less and less in the world market while foreign manufacturers will make even stronger inroads with American consumers."[3] Many Americans are frustrated and angry about this trend. Workers in Milwaukee tore down a Japanese flag that had been temporarily hoisted to honor a visiting Japanese executive. Employees at one company

---

[1] The following discussion of international distribution is based on James C. Johnson, "Seven Transportation Megatrends for the Late 1980s," *Transportation Practitioners Journal* (forthcoming).

[2] James C. Johnson, James P. Rakowski, and Kenneth C. Schneider, "U.S. Coal Exports: Problems and Prospects," *Colorado Business Review* (April 1982), pp. 2–4.

[3] John Naisbitt, Megatrends: *Ten New Directions Transforming our Lives* (New York: Warner Books, 1982), p. 62.

in Virginia who drive to work in a foreign made auto must park in a remote parking lot compared to where domestically produced cars can park.[4]

Despite occasional worker resentment, the overall trend of expanding world trade will not recede. One powerful factor propelling world trade activity is the concept of production sharing. An example is baseball mitts; 95 per cent of the mitts sold in the United States are manufactured in Japan. However, the leather in the gloves is typically American cowhide that was shipped to Brazil for tanning before traveling to Japan for manufacturing. Many products today that state "Made in Japan" are actually assembled in Singapore, Indonesia, or Nigeria, where labor rates are considerably lower than in Japan.[5] This trend will not abate: it will accelerate. In 1983 Warner Communication's Atari division closed down plants producing computer and video games and moved the production from California's Silicon Valley to the Orient. The result was the loss of 1,700 U.S. manufacturing jobs.[6] National Semiconductor Corporation designs and fabricates computer chips in California's Silicon Valley. The chips are then transported to developing countries—such as Sri Lanka, Barbados, Philippines, Virgin Islands, and Panama (where in 1983 the minimum wage was 66 cents per hour)—to be assembled and tested. Finally, the finished products are transported back to the United States and other countries for distribution to customers around the world.[7] A final example of worldwide production is Caterpillar Tractor Company. It recently closed a plant in Mentor, Ohio, that produced lift trucks. Production was shifted to less costly plants in Korea and Norway.[8]

Not all examples involve the United States losing manufacturing jobs to other countries. In March 1984 Ford Motor Company announced that, after years of utilizing engines made by its foreign subsidiaries and then assembled and sold in the United States, the firm will start in 1986 to ship 250,000 engines per year to its European subsidiary. Ford noted that its Dearborn, Michigan, plant was producing four-cylinder engines so efficiently that it became advantageous to run this plant at high-level output and ship the surplus production to Europe.[9]

From an international logistics viewpoint, this trend is both challenging and fraught with opportunities for disaster. International logistics is inherently complex. Henry Wagner, a well-respected logistics executive, once aptly observed: "International distribution is truly an octopus."[10] An example of the perplexing issues involved in international shipments is export documentation. An export shipment can typically require between 75 to 100 separate documents. A single shipment to Santiago, Chile, requires almost

[4] Manuel Schiffres, "Force Four: Foreign Competition," *U.S. News and World Report* (March 19, 1984), p. 46.

[5] Nasibitt, op. cit. p. 67.

[6] Schiffres, op. cit., p. 43.

[7] Roger Holmberg, "How a High Technology Manufacturing Firm Manages International Distribution," *Annual Proceedings of the NCPDM* (1983), pp. 427–429.

[8] Ralph E. Winter, "Expecting Lean Times, Many Firms Try Hard to Increase Efficiency," *Wall Street Journal,* 23 November 1983, p. 26.

[9] "Ford Will Ship Engines to Europe From the U.S.," *Wall Street Journal,* 12 March 1984, p. 18.

[10] As quoted in James C. Johnson and Donald F. Wood, *Contemporary Physical Distribution and Logistics,* 2nd ed. (New York: Macmillan, 1982), p. 437.

150 documents to be executed.[11] Most of this paperwork is required by the receiving country. It is estimated that export documentation alone represents about 7 per cent of the market price of the products being sold.[12] Also, foreign sales typically involve larger ratios of inventory to sales because of longer lead times between when orders are received and when they arrive. Professors Donald J. Bowersox and Jay U. Sterling estimate that multinational firms require up to 50 per cent more inventory levels to support foreign sales than domestic operations.[13] For this and other reasons, international logistics is expensive. In domestic operations it is estimated that logistics costs are about 5 to 6 per cent of the total cost of each order received. For international shipments, this figure jumps to the 10 to 25 per cent range.[14]

Presently there is no optimum organizational structure for an international logistics operation.[15] However, the trend to increase worldwide production will accelerate, and this will continue to put additional pressure on the logistics department to coordinate shipping activities efficiently. Logistics personnel must become familiar with international distribution because the probability is that their employer is now—or will be in the future—contemplating an expanding role in international trade.

Metric Conversion

The United States is the only major industrialized country in the world that is not using the metric system of weights and measures. The federal government has been studying the metric issue for almost two hundred years. In 1790 President George Washington asked Congress to decide if the metric system should be adopted in the United States. Secretary of State Thomas Jefferson, noting the use of the metric system in Europe, argued strongly for metrication in the United States. Congress, however, was unable to decide and therefore took no position regarding this issue.[16]

More recently, it was generally assumed that if the United States decided to convert to the metric system, a relatively long conversion period would be beneficial in order to make the transition as smooth as possible. During the first half of the 1970s, the metrication bills before Congress called for a ten-year conversion period. A compromise metrication bill was signed into law on December 23, 1975. The Metric Conversion Act creates a seventeen-member U.S. Metric Board whose job is to plan the conversion and to educate the public regarding the benefits of the metric system. The board has no enforcement power and no time limits for complete conversion

[11] "Did You Hear the One About the Square Barrel?" *Davis Database* (Oct. 1983), p. 1.

[12] Lisa H. Harrington, "Plugging into World Markets," *Traffic Management* (Oct. 1983), p. 31.

[13] Donald J. Bowersox and Jay U. Sterling, "Multinational Logistics," *Journal of Business Logistics,* **3:**21 (1982).

[14] DAVIS DATABASE, loc. cit.

[15] Jacques Picard, "The Management of Physical Distribution in Multinational Corporations," *Columbia Journal of World Business* (Winter 1982), pp. 67–73.

[16] Ky P. Ewing, Jr., Speech before American National Metric Council (April 3, 1979).

are established. The softening of the ten-year deadline for conversion came at the insistence of organized labor. The board can recommend to Congress if any federal subsidies are required to help meet conversion costs, especially for workers required to purchase metrically dimensioned hand tools. In 1981, with federal deficits growing, Congress searched for federal programs that could be eliminated to save funding. The Metric Board was a victim of those cutbacks, and it closed on September 30, 1982.[17]

A corollary organization to the U.S. Metric Board, the American National Metric Council (ANMC), was established in 1973 under the guidance of the American National Standards Institute. ANMC was recognized by the U.S. Metric Board as a basic source of development of voluntary private sector conversion plans. This privately operated, nonprofit organization, is dedicated to the principle that "policy determination, timing, and the degree of metric usage should be determined by those affected."[18]

Most U.S. business executives now recognize the inevitability of conversion to the metric system. A survey of physical distribution practitioners asked, "Are you in favor of the United States converting to the metric system?" Fifty-five per cent of the respondents answered yes. Assuming the change to the metric system is inevitable, 68 per cent of the respondents thought the change should be mandatory by government edict.[19] (See Figure 15-1). The general public is not as enthusiastic about the metric system. In a Gallup Poll of only those people who understood the metric system, it was found that 39 per cent of the respondents favored its adoption, 53 per cent opposed it, and 8 per cent were undecided.[20]

The majority of multinational firms are already involved in metric conversion plans. One reason for this trend is that the European Common Market announced that, starting in 1978, all products exported into their member countries had to move in metric measurements. Substantial noncompliance penalties were mandated. Other foreign countries have similar laws; for example, Kenya requires all imported products to be in metric measurements.

The American Warehousemen's Association has stated that conversion to the metric standard would not have an unduly severe impact on their operational efficiency. In fact, some members stated that the change would probably produce only a minimum of problems. This is because the versatile fork lift truck now successfully handles a large variety of pallet sizes, and the addition of one or a few more metric pallet sizes would not complicate the situation.[21]

[17] C. Priestley, "Metric Board Closes; Conversion Inches Along," *The National Magazine for Purchasing Agents* (Oct. 7, 1982), p. 15.

[18] Chuck Ebeling, "Metrics Makes Sense," *Handling and Shipping Management* (Aug. 1980), p. 43.

[19] "Survey Converting to Metric," *Transportation and Distribution Management* (July–Aug. 1975), p. 47.

[20] Arlen J. Large, "The Slow March to Metric," *Wall Street Journal* 16 November 1977, p. 18. See also, "Shift to Metrics Moving by Millimeters," *U.S. News and World Report* (Oct. 30, 1982), p. 77.

[21] Fred R. Keith, Jr., "Metric Warehousing: a Minimum Impact?" *Transportation and Distribution Management* (Feb. 1973), pp. 23–25.

Figure 15-1 The Metric System Will Bring Changes

"I'm sure glad your Pa ain't alive to see this."

Reproduced by permission of the artist and *The Wall Street Journal.*

Increased Computer Utilization

In early 1984 *U.S. News & World Report* featured a special article entitled, "10 Forces Reshaping America." The computer "revolution" was one of the "forces."[22] It is estimated that in the United States from the first computer developed in the late 1940s until 1977, approximately one-half million computers were purchased. However, in 1983 alone, 6.7 million computers were sold.[23] As a further indication of the computer revolution, in 1983 an estimated one in five white-collar workers utilized a desk-top computer in their daily work.[24]

In the logistics field, daily computer interaction has long been commonplace, and the trend is accelerating. Literally hundreds of "canned" logistics software programs are available to logistics personnel.[25] These programs have

---

[22] This section is based on Johnson, op. cit.

[23] Cindy Skrzycki, "Force Three: Computer Revolution," *U.S. News and World Report* (March 19, 1984), p. 42.

[24] Mark B. Solomon, "Use of Microcomputers in Distribution Field Explored at Roundtable," *Traffic World* (Nov. 28, 1983), p. 28.

[25] For a comprehensive listing of logistics software programs, see John A. Miller, "Survey of Software for Physical Distribution," *Annual Proceedings of the NCPDM* (1983), pp. 33–170; and Richard C. Haverly, "Survey of Software for Physical Distribution," *Annual Proceedings of the NCPDM* (1984), pp. 717–886.

found ready acceptance because most logistics people do not have the ability to design sophisticated computer programs themselves. Furthermore, many logistics people do not have the time to teach in-house programmers the basics of logistics.[26]

Prior to 1970, computer utilization was primarily in these areas: order entry, invoicing, bill of lading preparation, and some aspects of inventory control.[27] Since 1970 the most profound change in computer utilization has been the introduction of on-line systems, which allow multiple users simultaneous direct access to the computer. The following are current examples of computer applications in logistics: (1) direct electronic data interchange between carriers, shippers, and their customers;[28] (2) carrier costing analysis, which is a basic ingredient in carrier rate negotiation;[29] (3) industrial site location models;[30] (4) order processing;[31] (5) inventory management;[32] (6) dispatching, routing, and shipment consolidation;[33] (7) equipment scheduling;[34] (8) domestic and foreign documentation;[35] (9) tracing;[36] (10) distribution resource planning;[37] and (11) materials resource planning.[38]

A final indication of the importance of computerization to logistics personnel was revealed in the 1983 annual survey of logistics executives conducted by the Ohio State University. For the past thirteen years, when asked in which area of business they would desire to obtain additional skills, the

[26] Joe Martha and Dennis McGinnis, "Microcomputers in Distribution: How to Use Them More Effectively," *NCPDM Annual Proceedings* (1983), p. 954.

[27] Martin Flusberg, Jai Jaikumar and Marshall Fisher, "Computers in Physical Distribution—The Revolution Continues," *Handling and Shipping Management, Presidential Issue* (1983–84), p. 52.

[28] Thomas C. Dulaney, "Now's the Time to Get On-Line," *Distribution* (Feb. 1983), pp. 23–24.

[29] Paul K. Sugrue, Manfred H. Ledford, and Nicholas A. Glaskowski, Jr., "Operating Economies of Scale in the U.S. Long-Haul Common Carrier Motor Freight Industry," *Transportation Journal* (Fall 1982), pp. 27–41; and Wallace R. Wood, "A Robust Model for Railroad Costing," *Transportation Journal* (Winter 1983), pp. 47–60.

[30] Robert M. Sutton, "Macro Issues in Site Selection: The Impact of Changing Environmental Conditions," *Annual Proceedings of the NCPDM* (1981), pp. 819–828.

[31] Roy Cummings, "Installing Order Entry Systems," in Peter M. Lynagh, ed., *Annual Proceedings of the American Society of Traffic and Transportation* (1982), pp. 127–135.

[32] Brian F. O'Neil and Gerald O. Fahling, "A Liquidation Decision Model for Excess Inventories," *Journal of Business Logistics*, 3:85–103 (1982).

[33] Martha C. Cooper, "Freight Consolidation and Warehouse Location Strategies in Physical Distribution Systems," *Journal of Business Logistics*, 4:53–74 (1983).

[34] Kevin N. Bott and Ronald H. Ballou, "Vehicle Routing and Scheduling with Intermediate Movements," *Journal of Business Logistics*, 4:75–94 (1983).

[35] Colin Barrett, "Computer Software for Transportation," *Traffic World* (May 23, 1983), pp. 118–121; and Lisa H. Harrington, "Plugging into World Markets," *Traffic Management* (Oct. 1983), pp. 31–38.

[36] "New Computerized System Allows Roadway Shippers Direct Freight Tracking," *Traffic World* (Feb. 6, 1984), pp. 27–28.

[37] James Aaron Cooke, "DRP: A Dynamic Approach to Distribution," *Traffic Management* (July 1983), pp. 55–58; and André J. Martin, *Distribution Resource Planning* (Essex Junction, Vt.: Oliver Wight, 1983).

[38] Allan F. Ayers, "Improving Productivity Through MRP," *Annual Proceedings of the NCPDM* (1982), pp. 455–472.

answer was "finance." In 1983 the first choice was "data processing, simulation, and models."[39]

Advances in Equipment Technology

In the past, PD/L management has always benefited from a steady, uninterrupted flow of new equipment technology that has allowed firms' overall PD/L operations to become more efficient. The following are just a few examples of this situation: containerization, stacker-cranes, which allow higher warehouse storage, wide-body jets, and computerized railroad classification yards.

Can PD/L management assume that equipment technology will continue to develop at the same pace as in the past? This technological development issue must be considered because without this important stimulus to efficiency, PD/L management would have to look into other areas if improvements in efficiency are to be continued.

Decreasing Rate of Technological Development

Professor James L. Heskett has argued that, for a number of reasons, the pace of technological development is waning.[40] First, there are certain physical constraints on technology. Rail cars, for example, cannot be substantially increased in height because of the restrictions imposed by the size of tunnels and highway over and underpasses. Trucks cannot become substantially wider (the industry has lobbied for a six-inch increase in width) because of the standard size of highways, and there must be some weight restrictions on trucks. (Trucks on Interstate highways of up to 80,000 pounds—from 73,280 pounds—were authorized by the federal government with state approval in December 1974, the first increase since 1956.)

A second factor involves a lack of significant economies of scale as larger transportation equipment is contemplated. In the late 1960s the 747 aircraft was predicted to revolutionize air freight transportation through greater efficiency. In fact, it has not substantially reduced air freight rates. A few ocean tankers are presently operating in the 300,000-ton to 500,000-ton category. Although marine architects are confident that ships with a one million-ton gross weight carrying capacity are technologically feasible, such tankers probably will not be built in the near future because diseconomies of scale are present in both the construction and operation of these mammoth ships. Indeed, in the late 1970s, tanker charter rates dropped, and construction of several of the behemoths was halted, and many other large tankers were laid up because of lack of business. They continue to be laid up for a reason

[39] Bernard J. LaLonde and David E. Lloyd, "Career Patterns in Distribution Profile 1983," *NCPDM Annual Proceedings* (1983), pp. 179, 189.

[40] James L. Heskett, "Sweeping Changes in Distribution," *Harvard Business Review* (March–April 1973), pp. 123–132.

that might not surprise readers: to fill the giant tankers requires too large an investment in inventory at a single time.

Another factor suggested by Heskett is that, at present, PD/L departments have been overwhelmed by the increasing sophistication of technological developments. The result has been that a significant amount of present technology has yet to be incorporated into daily operations. Most firms are still not fully utilizing existing technology. Therefore, there may be less demand for new technological advances because many firms have yet to use what is currently available.

It is interesting to note the conclusions of an international symposium that attempted to predict the future of transportation in the decade from 1980 to 1990. They forecasted that "one should not expect any introduction or rapid expansion of new transport techniques between 1980 and 1990."[41] This statement was based on three basic premises. First, because transport equipment must frequently be interchanged internationally, the probability of change is reduced because many countries do not currently or in the foreseeable future have any desire to alter their existing transportation and support equipment. Second, new transportation techniques and equipment tend to be very capital intensive, and many countries do not have the ability to fund these types of projects. The current problems that the supersonic passenger plane, the Concorde, is experiencing illustrate this situation. Developmental costs of this aircraft were many times higher than originally projected and current demand for the plane is substantially lower than the original worldwide forecasts. Third, the report noted, "The discounted future costs of new transport techniques exceed those of existing modes of transport. In other words, all existing modes of transport offer the advantage of existing. This is not a mere philosophical concept but a fact."[42]

Faster Technological Advancement

Although the preceding discussion points to slower technological development in the coming years, there are many indications that the forecast decline has not yet materialized. Alvin Toffler believes that the increasing rate of technological advancement will continue. He noted that each new machine has the effect of changing all the existing machines because the old and the new can be combined to produce even more efficient machines. The result is that while new equipment increases at an arithmetic rate, the number of potential combinations of old and new machines increases exponentially.[43] Despite the very real problems associated with technological growth, technology probably will continue to expand at an ever increasing rate. Five examples, each taken from transportation, will illustrate this trend.

[41] J. P. Baumgartner, *Summary of the Discussion: Fifth International Symposium on Theory and Practice in Transport Economics—Transport in the 1980–1990 Decade* (Paris: European Conference of Ministers of Transport, 1973), p. 25.

[42] Ibid.

[43] Alvin Toffler, *Future Shock* (New York: Bantum, 1970), pp. 28–29.

Satellite Navigation and Communication

The Norfolk Southern railroad is experimenting with train control by satellite. If successful, it will eliminate the need for trackside signals, cables, and the like. The system will utilize three satellites to pinpoint the exact location of every train anywhere on the railroad property. The system to be tested in 1985 is known as NAVSTAR Global Positioning System.[44] This concept is also being tested for ocean vessel navigation.

Another application of satellites is communication that is available anywhere in the United States or the world. A company that is advancing this idea is Geostar Corporation. It plans to launch three satellites in 1987. Each satellite will link portable transceivers to a large computer. This system has many transportation applications. A *transceiver*—a device that both sends and receives signals—located on a truck will allow the company to locate the vehicle anywhere in the United States within seven yards of its actual location. Thus, a trucking company dispatcher will always know the exact location of the trucks in the system. In addition, each truck driver could communicate with his or her home base using this system.[45]

The Rebirth of Solid-Fuel Railroading

With the rapid advances in the price of oil, the possibility of the return of coal powered locomotives has become feasible. In 1970 a million BTUs (British Thermal Units, a measurement of energy) generated by oil cost 51 cents more than the equivalent amount of energy produced by coal. By 1974 the difference was $1.21, and in March 1980 it was $4.46. Fuel cost is the second largest railroad operating expense after labor.

Because of the potential for using a significantly less costly fuel, the American Coal Enterprises (ACE) Corporation is designing a modern coal-powered locomotive. (See Figure 15-2.) Known as the ACE 3000, it is designed to produce, at 1980 fuel costs, a minimum fuel savings of at least one third, compared to a comparable locomotive using diesel fuel. If all locomotives in the United States were coal powered, the annual savings would have been $1.2 billion in 1980. The ACE 3000 weighs 650,000 pounds and produces 3,000 horsepower. It is a two-unit locomotive, comprised of a service module and the power unit. The former will carry three 11-ton coal packs that are loaded at a coal mine and transported by rail flatcar. In addition, the service module transports the water that will be converted into steam. Coal is automatically fed, via conveyor belt, into the firebox in the power unit. This system allows the ACE 3000 to travel 500 miles between fuel stops and 1,000 miles before water must be taken aboard. It has a maximum sustainable speed of 80 miles per hour.

To make the ACE 3000 environmentally compatible, it will collect almost all ash produced. The ash will be scrubbed from the exhaust gases and

[44] See Luther S. Miller, "A Throughbred on the Move," *Railway Age* (Dec. 1984), pp. 31–33.

[45] See Benn Kobb, "Geostar Is Wherever You Are," *Personal Communications* (March 1984), pp. 40–42.

Figure 15-2 The Ace 3000: A Modern Coal-Burning Locomotive

Source: John A. Armstrong, "Solid-Fuel Railroading in the '80s," *Railway Age,* (October 13, 1980), p. 36.

conveyed to a five-ton ash pack module that is removed during servicing. The ACE Corporation hopes to have two prototypes of the ACE 3000 in operation by the late-1980s. It is estimated that both prototypes will cost $25 million.[46]

In 1983 two railroads, the Burlington Northern and the Norfolk Southern (NS), entered into a joint research project with General Electric to produce a coal-powered locomotive. Robert B. Claytor, chairman of NS, commented: "It is time to try again to reestablish coal as the primary locomotive fuel on American railroads. This could help our coal industry and assist our nation by improving our balance of payments and lessening our dependence on foreign oil."[47]

Integral Trains

In April 1984 the Association of American Railroads (AAR) asked railroad suppliers to meet with them in Chicago to discuss a new type of train that the AAR had been designing. Figure 15-3 is an artist's drawing of the integral train concept. The most striking difference between this concept and traditional trains is that the power units are spread throughout the train. An advantage of this concept is that the empty weight of the train is considerably less than conventional trains, which allows substantially greater fuel efficiency. Because the cars are permanently coupled, there is greatly reduced slack action when the train starts and stops, which results in less damage to freight. A number of railroad equipment suppliers have shown an interest in the integral train, which is designed to reduce operating costs between 35 to 50 per cent on intermodal container shipments. The AAR hopes that suppliers will have their first prototypes ready for testing in 1986.[48]

[46] See "The ACE 3000," *Railfan and Railroad* (Sept. 1983), p. 24; and "In Search of a New Coal-Burner," *Railway Age* (April 1984), pp. 54–56.

[47] "NS Joins the Search for a Coal-Burning Locomotive," *Railway Age* (Dec. 1984), p. 25.

[48] "Integral Trains Could Slash Costs 35–50%," *Railway Age* (May 1984), p. 22; John C. Kneiling, "Looking at What Was Never Looked at in 150 Years," *Trains* (July 1984), p. 18A; and Stephen Kindel, "The Electronic Horse," *Forbes* (June 3, 1985), pp. 196–198.

Figure 15-3 An Integral Train

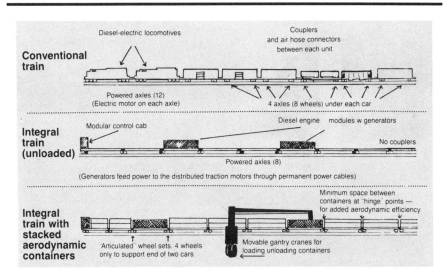

Source: "Integral Trains Could Slash Costs 35–50%," *Railway Age* (May, 1984), p. 22. Used with permission.

Lighter-Than-Air Cargo Vessels

Because of the high cost of fuel, a small British air cargo company has ordered four helium airships from Airship Industries, Ltd.[49] The four airships will be delivered to Redcoat Cargo Airlines by 1986. Each airship is 600 feet long and costs about $2.5 million and will have the carrying capacity of one and a half wide-body aircraft. Fuel savings are estimated to be about 30 per cent less per ton-mile than jet cargo planes. Each of the airships will have a maximum lift of 58 metric tons and will cruise at 85 miles per hour. Propulsion is provided by four 1,120 horsepower engines.

Why did Redcoat order these airships? Keven McPhillips, a director of Redcoat stated, "We're opting out of conventional aircraft. Redcoat decided a long time ago that fuel costs would be the main problem to be faced in the future and decided to go for alternatives."[50] Redcoat plans to use the new airships in service in West Africa, the Middle East, and in Central America. In addition, two and one half day Atlantic crossings between the United States and Europe are contemplated.

Additional lighter-than-air cargo vessels are being designed. One concept will use a helium airship that provides lift for four helicopters attached below the airship. To date, more than $25 million has been spent on the first prototype, which will have a total lift capacity of 25 tons. The U.S. Forest Service and the U.S. Navy have provided some development funds.

[49] "In the Hindenburg's Wake," *Forbes* (April 11, 1983), p. 182.
[50] "Redcoat Cargo Line Looks to Dirigibles to Cut Fuel Costs," *Wall Street Journal,* 14 July 1980, p. 16.

Figure 15-4 Modern Sailing Vessel

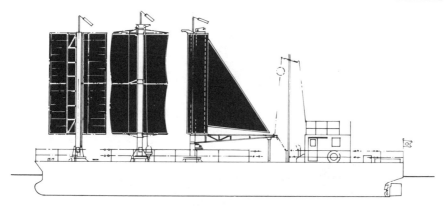

Source: Thomas Loughry, "Fresh Winds for Commercial Sail," *Surveyor,* published by the American Bureau of Shipping (May 1980):14.

The project is currently progressing slowly, but the first prototype is expected to fly in 1985.[51]

Another company, American Skyship, is seeking $35 million to develop its prototype aircraft, which is designed to lift 27.5 tons and cruise at 115 miles per hour. The aircraft will be greater than 300 feet in length and eight stories high. The first prototype is planned to be in operation in 1988.[52]

Sailing Cargo Vessels

As the prospects of a coal-powered locomotive indicates, technology can recycle. The last technological change to be examined here also represents just one situation where technology has evolved full circle. Two hundred years ago all large ocean vessels used wind as the means of propulsion. Then mechanical techniques were discovered. Today, because of energy costs, sailing vessels are making a comeback. (See Figure 15-4.) The Japanese government has been a leader in testing ships that have both engines and sails. Notice that the sails in the ship in Figure 15-4 can be furled (opened and closed by means of rolling into a compact roll) by remote control from the ship's bridge (the location from which the ship's officers control the vessel). In addition, each mast can be rotated from the bridge by means of large electric motors. This allows the sails to catch the wind most advantageously.

The test vessels operated by the Technical Research Center in Kawasaki, Japan, have been able to consistently use approximately 10 per cent less fuel, compared to a similar size ship without auxiliary sails. Under favorable wind conditions, the sails save over 20 per cent of the fuel utilized by a ship without sails,[53] although concern for safety limits use of sails to winds under

---

[51] Patricia A. Bellow, "Dream of Big Blimp for Heavy Hauling Stays Up in the Air," *Wall Street Journal,* 5 June 1984, pp. 1, 30.

[52] Raymond Klempin, "Cargo Industry Seen a Prime Target for Development of Rigid Airship," *Jet Cargo News* (Dec. 1984), p. 18.

[53] Thomas Loughry, "Fresh Winds for Commercial Sail," *Surveyor* (May 1980), pp. 14–16; and "Sail Power Comes of Age," *Port of Houston Magazine* (May 1983), pp. 12–13.

40 knots. Lloyd Bergeson, a well-known naval architect, predicted that by the 1990s, 75 per cent of all ocean vessels will be designed with auxiliary sails.[54]

The PD/L Concept: Its Future

American firms have generally accepted the logic of the PD/L concept—the total-cost concept, the usage of cost trade-offs, and the avoidance of functional suboptimization. Nevertheless, PD/L can only continue to make its appropriate contribution to the firm if it has highly capable and knowledgeable management.

It is encouraging to note the continually increasing number of PD/L courses being taught in graduate schools and four year and two-year colleges. The need for thoroughly educated physical distribution/logistics managers is apparent. The Ohio State University delved into demographic data of senior level PD/L executives. It was found that 93 per cent possessed an undergraduate degree and more than 40 per cent had earned a graduate degree.[55]

Future PD/L executives will have to be both *generalists* and *specialists*. The former is basic because, as early chapters indicated, the PD/L manager does not operate in a vacuum. He or she is continually interacting with the other functional areas of the firm—marketing, production, finance, and accounting. In addition, the PD manager must have a high degree of specialized knowledge in transportation, warehousing, inventory analysis, customer service, and order processing.[56] One study by two Ohio State University professors concluded: "With this greater emphasis on distribution has come a broadening of activities for which the distribution executive is responsible. No longer can executives in distribution be proficient in only traffic and warehousing. They must interact more and more with marketing, production, finance, and data processing. They also must spend a greater part of their time in what they consider general management or administration. Distribution executives find themselves increasingly involved in the total firm."[57]

One survey asked respondents, "Do you believe PD/L management will become more or less important to your firm in the 1980s?" Surprisingly, 96.4 per cent of the marketing executive respondents checked the "more important" box on the questionnaire. This unanimity of opinion speaks well for the future of PD/L management. Representative statements by marketing executives include the following:

---

[54] Walter Sullivan, "Cargo Ships of Future May Sail into Port," *Minneapolis Tribune,* 6 May 1979, p. 10; and Christopher Power, "A New Age of Sail?" *Forbes* (Oct. 10, 1983), pp. 188–191.

[55] Bernard J. LaLonde and Larry W. Emmelhainz, "Distribution Careers: 1984," *Annual Proceedings of the NCPDM* (1984), pp. 1–20.

[56] Kofi Q. Dadzie and Wesley J. Johnston, "Skill Requirements in Physical Distribution Management Career-Path Development," *Journal of Business Logistics,* **5**:65–84 (1984).

[57] LaLonde and Emmelhainz, op. cit., p. 7.

"Our market is becoming more competitive and our demands for sales performance are increasing; therefore, requirements for delivery and distribution performance will increase and require faster and more effective positive response."

"Customer service is an increasingly important marketing tool; increasing financial cost of carrying inventory means that it will have to be tightly controlled and balanced against deterioration in customer service availability."

The results of the survey indicate that the future for PD/L management appears excellent. PD/L will become increasingly important to the efficient operation of a firm, and so will PD/L executives.[58]

Future PD/L managers would do well to broaden their horizons as much as possible during college. Although many of the specialities of PDL can be learned on the job, it is difficult to obtain a feeling for the other functional and environmental aspects of the areas. Besides courses in PD/L, students should take as many courses as possible in marketing, accounting, economics, public speaking (both large and small group), international business, management science (with emphasis on computer applications), and governmental relations with the business community. These courses will provide the student with the ability to grasp both the micro and macro aspects of PD/L management.

Summary

Most marketing observers believe that multinational sales by United States based firms will continue to grow in importance. This trend will place additional demanding requirements on the firm's PD/L department. Imports will also increase. Consistent with this trend is the continuing increased utilization of metrics by U.S. firms. Because many of our trading partners require metric dimensioned products, metric usage is an economic necessity.

There is no trend in PD/L development that is more predictable than the increased use of computers. Computer technology has been and can be extremely beneficial in carrier operations, warehouse operations, inventory planning and control, strategic planning, and forecasting.

Technological developments in the area of transportation equipment will continue to advance. This will include satellite navigation and communication systems, solid-fuel locomotives, integral trains, lighter-than-air cargo vessels, and sailing cargo ships.

The future for PD/L executives is excellent for two reasons: PD/L represents a large cost item that must be professionally managed, and many firms' have discovered that dynamic distribution is an effective marketing technique.

[58] James C. Johnson and Donald L. Berger, "The Future of Physical Distribution Management," *Defense Transportation Journal* (June 1977), pp. 32–37.

Questions for Discussion and Review

1. Why is the U.S. government concerned about exports? Do you believe the federal government should encourage exports? Defend your answer.
2. Why were the years 1983 and 1984 difficult years for U.S. companies to export products?
3. Discuss the implications to the United States of the concept of a world economy.
4. What makes international trade more complicated than domestic trade?
5. What is the general public's attitude toward using the metric system in the United States?
6. What is the federal government's position regarding metrication? Do you believe this position is correct? Why?
7. Why have many U.S. companies voluntarily converted their products to metric dimensions?
8. Why have computers become so commonly utilized in PD/L?
9. Discuss a number of areas in which computer programs are currently available for PD/L personnel.
10. Do you believe equipment technology will increase or stay stable in the future? Defend your answer.
11. Give a number of examples that argue that equipment technology (a) will be stable or (b) will decline in the future.
12. Discuss satellite navigation and communication.
13. Do you believe coal-fired locomotives will become common in the next ten years? Why?
14. What is an integral train? Why are they being developed?
15. What do you think will be the future of lighter-than-air cargo vessels?
16. What are the advantages of sailing cargo ships?
17. Why do many people believe that PD/L will become more important in the future?
18. As you think back over the fifteen chapters in this book, which do you feel was the most interesting? The least interesting? Why?
19. Assume you could select the area of PD/L for your first job. Which area would you select? Why?
20. Now that you have almost completed this course in PD/L, which aspect of the course differed the most from what you expected? Explain.

Additional Chapter References

Elliott, Andrew. "A Transportation Regulatory Agenda for the Year 2000." *Annual Proceedings of the Transportation Research Forum* (1983), pp. 22–27.

Harrington, Ian E., and Fred L. Mannering. "Methodology for Evaluating Freight Transportation Energy Contingency Strategies." *Annual Proceedings of the Transportation Research Forum* (1982), pp. 668–676.

Jackson, Tim. "The Human Resource Challenge." *Annual Proceedings of the NCPDM* (1983), pp. 552–556.

Jaikumar, Ramchandran, and Marshall Fisher. "Computers in Transportation." *Technological Challenge: Research and Educational Applications* (Columbus: Transportation and Logistics Research Fund, Ohio State, 1984), pp. 64–89.

Kosiek, Lawrence J. "The Human Resource Challenge." *Annual Proceedings of the NCPDM* (1983), pp. 532–551.

Langley, C. John, and William D. Morice. "Strategies for Logistics Management: Reactions to a Changing Environment." *Journal of Business Logistics* (Vol. 3, No. 1, 1982), pp. 1–16.

Lukasiewicz, J. "The Future of Railway Electrification and Passenger Operations in North America." *Annual Proceedings of the Transportation Research Forum* (1982), pp. 62–79.

Mayes, R. R., J. R. Welch, and L. Peach. "Transportation Energy Requirements to the Year 2000." *Annual Proceedings of the Transportation Research Forum* (1983), pp. 82–89.

Pike, C. R. "Transportation: Learning from Our Past to Build Our Future." *Annual Proceedings of the Transportation Research Forum* (1983), pp. 17–21.

Pilnick, Saul, and Jo Ellen Gabel. "Participatory Circles—Capitalizing Human Assets." *Annual Proceedings of the NCPDM* (1983), pp. 691–703.

Sutherland, J. R., and M. U. Hassan. "Road Transportation Requirements to the Year 2000." *Annual Proceedings of the Transportation Research Forum* (1983), pp. 1–16.

CASE 15-1

The Coaltainer Case

Prior to about 1950, coal was widely used throughout the United States for heating homes, apartments, factories, and institutions. A coal-burning furnace would provide the heat that would warm air or water or create steam that would be carried by pipes or ducts. The coal furnace was often fired by a stoker. The stoker, which was placed a short distance from the furnace, consisted of a coal hopper on top into which coal would be shoveled by hand. Below the stoker hopper and leading into the furnace was an enclosed tube six inches or more in diameter. One end of the tube was below the stoker and the other end of the tube led inside the furnace to a point just above the grate where the fire was burning. An Archimedes-type screw (a continuous screw) fed through this tube and would carry coal from the bottom of the hopper to the fire burning on the grate. This is shown on Exhibit 15-1. A thermostat, elsewhere in the building, controlled the motor to the stoker. When the temperature fell, the thermostat would activate the stoker motor, which would feed more coal onto the fire. As the temperature would increase, the thermostat would switch off, stopping the flow of coal. It was necessary, however, to maintain the continual fire in the furnace. The stoker functioned only to feed more coal on a fire that was already burning. Beneath the grate on the furnace was an ash pit. Ash and clinkers remaining after the coal had burned would collect in the ash pit and would be cleaned out by hand. About 10 to 20 per cent of the coal's volume, by weight, would become ash.

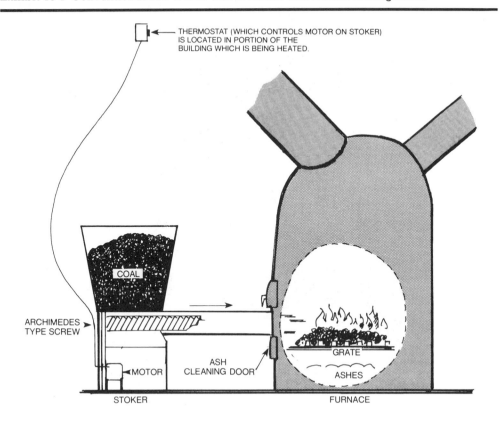

THERMOSTAT (WHICH CONTROLS MOTOR ON STOKER) IS LOCATED IN PORTION OF THE BUILDING WHICH IS BEING HEATED.

COAL

ARCHIMEDES TYPE SCREW

MOTOR

ASH CLEANING DOOR

GRATE

ASHES

STOKER

FURNACE

Deliveries to users of coal were by two means of transportation. Railroad cars carried coal directly to factories and large institutional users, often at a rail site for the sole reason of receiving coal. Trucks, such as are shown on Exhibit 15-2, were used for deliveries of smaller amounts. The conventional coal truck was unloaded by gravity, and a lifting frame was often provided to raise the level of the coal load that would increase the horizontal distance that the coal would move down chutes by gravity. Buildings that used coal for heating had the furnace located in the basement for several reasons. First, it allowed delivery of coal by a gravity method. Second, both the coal and ash were dirty and dusty, and the basement location reduced the possibility of this dirt and dust settling elsewhere in the building. Third, heating units also relied on gravity to move the hot air or water upward and cause the colder water or air to return downward for reheating.

Just before and after World War II, coal lost popularity for home and institutional heating to two other fuels: oil and natural gas, which had numerous advantages. They were cleaner burning and produced no ash. The heating units required much less space in the building. Also, it is easier to ignite an oil or gas fire, and so the unit could be used intermittently in the fall and spring. (This was not as easy to do with a stoker-fed coal furnace where the fire had to be maintained continually.) The oil and gas units had several advantages in the construction of new buildings. Less room was required, and it was less necessary to isolate the furnace unit from the rest of the building in order to reduce dust. In addition, the furnace location did not have to be near a street

In the top picture, a 1930-vintage Diamond-T with an elevated coal body dumps the coal through a window chute where it will fall into a coal bin and be shovelled by hand into a stoker. The bottom picture shows a 1935 Studebaker dumping coal which falls through the grate into a bin below.

Top photo courtesy The Heil Co.; bottom photo courtesy Fruehauf Corp.

or driveway in order to receive coal, and pumps were developed for pumping hot water or blowing hot air, which meant that the new heating units could be on the same floor as the rooms being heated. Even in older buildings where the owner did not wish to completely replace an existing furnace, it was possible to install the gas or oil burner inside the firebox of the one-time coal-burning furnace.

Oil and gas furnaces had one additional advantage: they required almost no labor on behalf of the building owner or custodian. It was no longer necessary to shovel coal into a stoker or to empty ashes from the bottom of the furnace. In factories and institutions this often meant that it was no longer necessary to have a fireman (one who tended fires) on the payroll. Thus, coal all but disappeared as a fuel used for heating homes, apartments, stores, office buildings, factories, and other institutions.

Today, however, because of the much increased prices of petroleum and occasional threats of boycotts by petroleum-producing nations, we are looking at ways of increasing our use of coal. Coal is the one fuel source of which the United States has abundant supplies. Although relative prices of energy sources differ throughout the country, in 1980, prices of fuel oil generally were nearly twice that of coal in terms of BTU content. That is, a user who had the capability of burning either oil or coal could save half of his oil cost by using coal instead. (Natural gas prices are about halfway between those of coal and fuel oil, although natural gas supplies are limited.) Lastly, within the United States the states in the Northeast are the most dependent on outside energy sources.

There are many problems involved with increasing our use of coal as an energy source. Some of these will be touched on later in this discussion. One idea, which will be developed here, deals with a method of transporting and delivering coal to users. The device to be employed will be referred to here as a coaltainer. The idea is based on the open-topped metal boxes used to collect debris from large buildings and construction sites. They sometimes have small metal wheels on the bottom, and it is possible for specially equipped trucks to deposit and collect these boxes at the sites where they are used. The coaltainer is a similar box with a few modifications.

Exhibit 15-3 shows one proposed coaltainer that is 8 feet wide, 8 feet high, and

Exhibit 15-3 Coaltainer with Archimedes-Screw Stoker

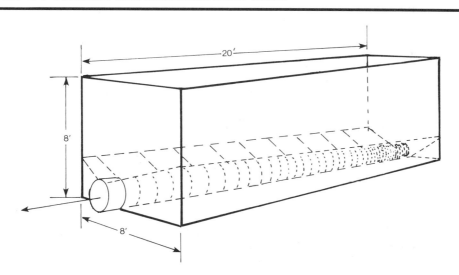

20 feet long. The bottom however is sloped on both sides down toward a center. At the bottom center, running the length of the coaltainer is an Archimedes screw. The coaltainer and Archimedes screw would be placed in position in front of the furnace and the screw would then be used as a stoker screw to feed coal into the fire as it was needed. The power unit to move this screw could either be self-contained within each coaltainer, or it could be permanently mounted near the furnace and attached to each coaltainer as it is placed in position. The electric motor would be controlled by the building's thermostat.

Exhibit 15-4 shows the modification of the proposal for the coaltainer with movable panel that covers an opening running along the bottom. This container does not contain the Archimedes screw. Instead, the screw is permanently placed in front of the furnace, and individual coaltainers are placed on top of it. This has several advantages. First, the payload of the coaltainer is increased because space does not have to be devoted to holding the screw. Second, chances of damaging the screw while the coaltainer is in transit are eliminated. Third, the cost of the entire system is much lower because the coaltainer does not include the expensive screw installation.

Another modification to the coaltainers, which is not illustrated, would be to have a small, separate compartment in each coaltainer that would be used for carrying away the ash that is a by-product of the coal's combustion. The individual tending the fire would have to shovel the ashes from the ash pit below the fire grate into the ash compartment in the coaltainer. This would be a useful feature in situations where only one coaltainer was used at a time. In instances where numerous coaltainers were located at the user's site, any empty coaltainer could be used for loading ash.

Exhibit 15-4 Coaltainer with Movable Panel

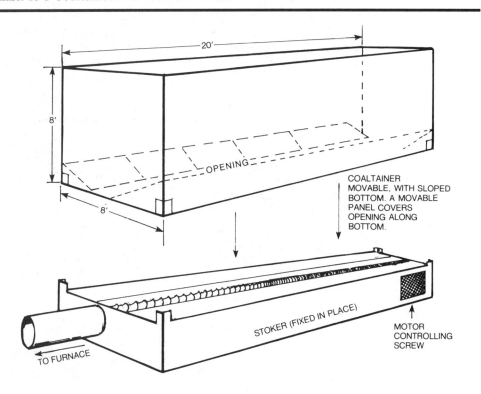

Exhibit 15-5 Moving Coaltainers Between Truck and Furnace Installation

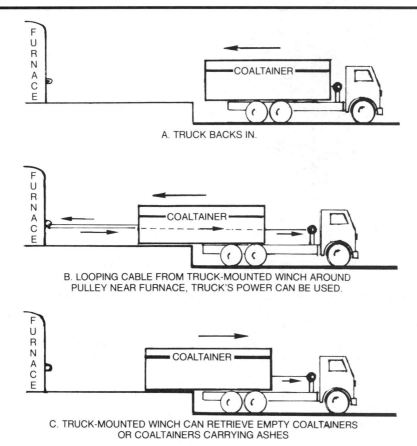

A. TRUCK BACKS IN.

B. LOOPING CABLE FROM TRUCK-MOUNTED WINCH AROUND
PULLEY NEAR FURNACE, TRUCK'S POWER CAN BE USED.

C. TRUCK-MOUNTED WINCH CAN RETRIEVE EMPTY COALTAINERS
OR COALTAINERS CARRYING ASHES

Exhibit 15-5 shows a method of unloading a single full coaltainer and later reloading it aboard the truck when it is empty. Users of single coaltainers would probably have to maintain a small reserve of coal elsewhere to be used in instances where the coaltainer's supply was exhausted.

Exhibit 15-6 shows a much larger installation where coaltainers are delivered to the left of the picture and then moved toward the right, where they are connected with the furnace. Coaltainers farther to the right are either empty or are being used for holding ashes. The coaltainer farthest to the right is being reloaded aboard a truck, where it will be hauled back to the coal dealer for refilling.

There are many problems associated with determining whether coaltainers are a feasible alternative for delivering coal. The remainder of this case will mention and discuss some of the issues that should be of concern to an individual attempting to determine whether the coaltainer idea is feasible.

In the last quarter century all levels of government have enacted stricter requirements regarding air pollution. The use of coal for heating buildings creates two sources of air pollution. The first would be the smoke from the combustion process, and the second would be dust from the coal being carried to where it was being used and from the ash being removed and taken to a disposal site.

Exhibit 15-6 Large Coaltainer Installation

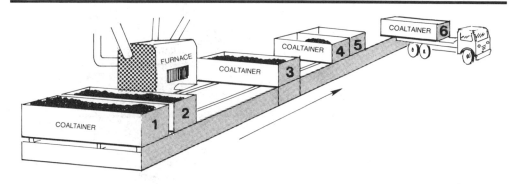

Someone studying the feasibility of coaltainers might be eligible for grants from various federal agencies that are trying to study ways of decreasing our dependence on the use of petroleum. Several new types of coal-burning furnace systems are being developed, and one related question might be whether the coaltainers are compatible with them.

The exact dimensions of coaltainers are another issue. The eight-foot width and height are fairly universal in terms of dimensional requirements on motor trucks. However, the length can vary. Although longer containers carry more, they require additional internal bracing to reduce the possibility of sagging in the middle. This is of particular concern because they must fit into a system that feeds the coal into the furnace. There are some advantages to handling a multiple number of containers on one truck or truck-trailer; however, additional space is required then to maneuver the rig. (In the late 1930s, many coal delivery bodies were very short; this was to allow them to maneuver into small areas in order to make deliveries.)

In some cities there still are requirements in safety codes that particular licensed individuals are needed to tend coal fires in buildings above certain sizes. Union jurisdictional disputes might also limit the amount of work the driver of a truck carrying a coaltainer could perform when removing the device from his truck and coupling with the furnace. In addition, strikes by coal miners are always a national threat. To date, deliveries of fuel oil and natural gas have been fairly immune from labor strikes. Coal deliveries have been and could be more vulnerable. One would also have to explore whether the idea has been patented or whether it would infringe on patents held by others.

Should the coaltainer idea be used, questions arise as to who should own the coaltainers and who should own the stoker installations. In addition, schedules of charges would have to be established which cover the cost of the coaltainer, the coal, and pickup and delivery services.

An operational problem with respect to demand for coal is that it is seasonal. Very little coal is used during the summer months for heating purposes. In the winter, coal use is related to cold temperatures, and, within a given area, coal use by all users would run in similar patterns. That is, if the winter were mild, there would be low usage by all customers. If there was a hard winter, all users would demand more coal, and all would want additional deliveries at about the same time.

Building codes exist in many communities that govern the specifications of structures. Whether they are up to date with respect to installation of coal-burning furnaces

Exhibit 15-7 An Alternative to the Coaltainer System

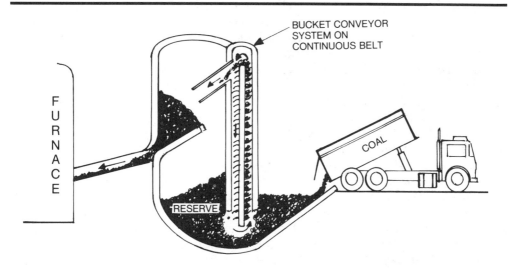

is unknown. In addition, within each community the building codes (often influenced by local conditions and pressures of various building trades, contractors, and unions) vary so that code requirements in no two communities are the same. This makes difficult the idea of developing a product that would meet a wide number of building codes.

There are many operational problems with respect to handling the coaltainers, particularly because it is necessary that they not be damaged to the extent that they make it difficult or impossible to connect with the furnace. In addition, if one malfunctions while it is in place, connected to a furnace, it must be removed quickly because it is difficult to feed the fire with coal except by hand.

It would be difficult to convert buildings built since 1950 back to burning coal. In many instances the furnace installation would be nowhere near the street or driveway where coal deliveries could be made. Within urban areas distribution sites would have to be found where coal, received by rail or barge, could be sorted, stored, and loaded aboard coaltainers for local distribution. This particular site would also create dust, and many communities would not encourage such sites near residential areas.

As was mentioned earlier, coal, when burned, creates ash. Ash disposal is a minor problem in itself. In earlier times, ash was used for surfacing driveways and roads and as an aggregate in concrete. An attempt would have to be made to find uses for ash.

Other methods are proposed for handling local deliveries of coal. One such alternative is shown on Exhibit 15-7. Rather than using the unique coaltainers, this system could rely on conventional dump trucks. Note, in this instance, that there is much less risk involved since the dump truck bodies are relatively inexpensive and could be easily resold.

Question One: Assume you work for a large coal company. You have been asked to outline a feasibility study of the coaltainer. The study's budget may be as high as several million dollars. Outline such a study with all its elements.

Question Two: Assume you want to "test market" the idea in one U.S. city. What characteristics should that city have?

Question Three: The coaltainer equipment consists of the coaltainer; an Archimedes screw that may be part of the coaltainer or might be part of the stoker below the coaltainer and not part of the coaltainer; a truck with equipment to carry the coaltainer and load it and reload it; and a furnace connection that can handle one or more coaltainers. How would you go about deciding whether the Archimedes screw device should be mounted in every coaltainer, or should it be part of the stoker, i.e. permanently attached to the furnace?

Question Four: The case stated that the coaltainer should be 8 feet high and 8 feet wide but was less definite as to its length. Assume you are on a study team to determine the length or lengths of the coaltainer. What factors should you consider?

Question Five: Assume you were on the group that was attempting to determine how the firm that employed the coaltainers should go about charging for their use. In this case the users would be the customers who bought the coal that was delivered by coaltainers. Items you should consider are the price of coal, which varies by BTU content; the cost of buying, delivering, and maintaining the coaltainers; the labor cost involved in handling the coaltainers; the trucking costs; whether ash removal is involved; and whether your driver or the user is responsible for connecting and disconnecting the coaltainers. In addition, you want to achieve certain levels of equipment utilization. Outline a pricing schedule for coal deliveries made to users who receive their deliveries in coaltainers.

Question Six: Exhibit 15-7 shows an alternative to the coaltainer system. What are the similarities and what are the differences between the system shown in Exhibit 15-7 and the coaltainer idea?

Question Seven: Is it feasible to have a coaltainer installation where the user has but one coaltainer on hand at any time—that is the one in place and feeding the furnace? Discuss.

CASE 15-2

Just-in-Time in Kalamazoo

Jim Ballenger was president of a medium-sized firm that manufactured mini-motor homes in Kalamazoo, Michigan. The firm had expanded from a local Midwest market to a national one, including Southern California and New England. As markets had expanded, so too had sources of supply for the company, with major suppliers located in Southern California, the Pacific Northwest, and Michigan. The decision to found the company in Michigan had been made for two reasons: Jim's former associates in the auto industry were there, and the largest single component of the mini was purchased from one of the "Big Three" U.S. auto makers—that is, the truck or van chassis upon which the rest of the vehicle is built.

Like others in the field, Jim's company actually manufactured very few of its components. Virtually the entire product was assembled from components purchased from outside vendors. There was, however, a very well-defined order in which each component could most efficiently be installed in the vehicle. Recently it had become clear to Jim that transportation and inventory costs were a relatively large portion of his component parts expenses, and that they might be ripe for a substantial reduction. He had been hearing about the "Just-in-Time" systems. According to some notes he had taken at a professional meeting: "The JIT production system was developed by the Toyota Motor Company over thirty-five years ago. It involves an approach to inventory that, in turn, forces a complementary approach to production, quality control, supplier relations, and distributor relationships. The major tenets of JIT can be summarized as follows:

1. Inventory in itself is wasteful and should be minimized.
2. Minimum replenishment quantity is maintained for both manufactured and purchased parts.
3. Minimum inventory is maintained of semifinished goods, in this case—partially completed motor homes.
4. Deliveries should be frequent and small.
5. Reduce the time needed to set up production lines to the absolute minimum.
6. Treat suppliers as a part of the production team. This means that the vendor makes every effort to provide outstanding service and quality; and there is usually a much longer term relationship with a smaller number of suppliers than is common in the United States.
7. The objective of the production system is zero defects.
8. Deliver your finished product on a very short lead time.

To the American inventory planner, vice-president of physical distribution, or production planner, an operation run on the preceding principles raised a number of disturbing prospects. Jim Ballenger was very aware of the costs that might arise if a JIT production system were to be established. From the materials management/PD standpoint, the idea of deliberately planning many small shipments rather than a few large ones appeared to assure higher freight bills, particularly from more distant suppliers, for which LTL rates would make the most difference.

With regard to competition among suppliers, Jim often had the opportunity, in the volatile mini-motor-home market, to buy out parts and component supplies from manufacturers that were going out of business. Those components could be obtained at a substantial savings, with the requirement that inventory in the particular parts be temporarily increased, and/or purchases from existing vendors be temporarily curtailed. Perhaps the greatest question raised by JIT, however, had to do with the probability of much more erratic production as a result of tight supplies of components. Both with suppliers' products and with his own, Jim operated with the (generally tacit) assumption that there would be some defective components purchased and that there would probably be something wrong with his product when it first came off the assembly line. For this reason, the Kalamazoo minis were extensively tested (their advertising said: "We hope you'll never do what *we* do to your Kalamazoo mini"), as were its components prior to installation. To the extent that only a few of a particular type of component were on hand, the interruption in the production schedule would be that much greater. It might entail expensive rush orders for replacement components, or equally expensive downtime for the entire plant.

Jim was also concerned about his relationship to his suppliers, as compared, say, to a large auto manufacturer. In the mini-motor-home business, generally the manufacturers are small, and the component makers are large. In this situation, it was somewhat more difficult to see the idea of the supplier as a part of the production team—in the sense that the supplier would be expected to make a special effort in terms of either quality control or delivery flexibility on behalf of one of its almost miniscule accounts.

Despite these concerns, Jim was painfully aware that he was using a public warehouse near his plant that usually contained between $500,000 to $1,000,000 in inventory, on which he paid an average of 1.5 per cent per month for the borrowed funds used to buy it, as well as expenses relating to the use of the warehouse itself. In addition, his firm was now producing so many different models (one with a bath, one with a shower only) and using so many different appliances (various types of radios, three varieties of refrigerator, and so forth) that the costs of a "safety stock" for each component were going up every day.

As an aid to making his decision on whether to try a JIT orientation at his plant, Jim had his executive assistant, Kathy Williams, draw up a table that was an overview of the anticipated impacts of a JIT system. These sheets are reproduced as Exhibit 15-8. They are based on random samples of inventory items. The major component of any mini-motor home, the chassis, would in all events be purchased on a one-at-a-time basis from Ford, Chevrolet, Dodge, or International. With rare exceptions, it was always available on demand. It would be delivered through the local dealer who—if he did not have one in stock—could easily obtain one from another area dealership.

Exhibit 15-8 is an accurate and representative 10 per cent sample of Ballenger's components inventory, and it covers weekly use of each item, the current lot size purchased, and so on. Before figuring out the total costs under the present and JIT systems, several additional facts must be noted. First, Ballenger's interest charges on money borrowed to cover inventory carrying—and other—expenses are 18 per cent per year. Second, under the current system, here is how to calculate the number of units of each type of component kept in stock. For those items purchased from vendors more than 500 miles away, a safety stock representing four weeks' use is maintained. For items

Exhibit 15-8 Random Sample of Component Inventory.

Item	Current System					Using JIT		
	Distance from Vendor (in miles)	Average Number of Units Used Each Week	Current Lot Size Purchased	Unit Cost	Average Freight Cost per Unit	JIT Lot Size	Unit Cost	Average Freight Cost per Unit (Surface)
Gas range	1,145	10	200	$100	$20	10	$105	$22
Toilet	606	10	240	$ 80	$18	10	$100	$18
Pump	26	56	125	$16	$ 3	7	$ 15	$ 4
Refrigerator (large)	22	6	120	$110	$20	6	$113	$25
Refrigerator (small)	22	7	15	$ 95	$15	1	$ 85	$15
Foam cushion	490	675	1,500	$ 8	$ 2	75	$ 7	$ 3
CB radio (type D)	1,800	9	24	$136	$11	3	$130	$26
Dome lights	3	824	1,720	$ 2	none	36	$ 4	none
Awning brackets	48	540	1,200	$ 4	$ 1	60	$ 5	$ 1
Insect screens	159	570	1,240	$ 7	$ 1	50	$ 7	$ 2

Note: The plant operates 52 weeks per year and produces ten mini-motor homes per week.

from vendors between 100 and 500 miles away, a safety stock representing two weeks' use is maintained. For items from closer sources, a safety stock representing one week's use is maintained. *In addition to* safety stocks, the average inventory of any item is the current lot size purchased, divided by 2. Third, for gas ranges, toilets, and large refrigerators, it is necessary to use a public warehouse to hold the safety stock, plus any stock in excess of one week's needs. The warehousing costs for gas ranges are $20 per year per unit, based on the average number of units stored per year; plus $2 per unit for each range that is moved into the warehouse, and $2 per unit for each range that is moved out. For toilets, the unit costs are the same. For large refrigerators, the costs are $30 per year per unit stored, based on the average number of units stored per year, plus $3 per unit for each large refrigerator moved into the warehouse, and $3 per unit for each large refrigerator moved out of the warehouse.

Question One: What is the total annual cost of maintaining the components inventory under the present system?

Question Two: What would be the total annual cost of maintaining the components inventory under the JIT system (assuming no safety stocks and no public warehousing)?

Question Three: Is there a rate of interest at which the costs to Ballenger of either his present or the JIT system would be the same? If so, what is it?

Question Four: Are there other costs, or benefits, from the JIT system that Ballenger should take into account? If so, what are they?

Question Five: If the JIT system is adopted, are there safety stocks of any item that should be maintained? If so, which ones, and how much?

Question Six: If the JIT system were to be adopted, what changes—if any—should occur in the relationship(s) between Ballenger and his suppliers of components? Discuss.

Question Seven: Assume that Ballenger has switched to the JIT system. He receives a surprise phone call from a competitor, who is going out of business. The competitor wants to sell Ballenger 7,000 dome lights of the type listed on Exhibit 15-8. Should Ballenger buy them? If so, at what price?

Appendix

The Transportation Linear Program

A linear program assumes that all the fundamental aspects of a problem have a linear, or straight-line, relationship. Thus it is assumed that transportation rates increase at a constant rate as distance increases. Because this assumption is frequently not true (transportation rates taper as distance increases), the solutions from a linear program should be viewed as "ball park" answers that will require additional refinement.

The transportation linear program is one of the most common analytical techniques used by physical distribution managers because it helps to solve a common problem: *allocation* of resources to where they are needed at the least cost. Assume a traffic manager has to decide how to utilize the firm's fleet of private trucks. In other words, at what plant should each vehicle pick up the product and to what customer should it be delivered? Assume that the Jenkins Corporation only produces one product and has four production plants. The plant locations and maximum monthly output are: Minneapolis, 500 units; Chicago, 300 units; Dallas, 600 units; and Los Angeles, 400 units. Because the product is very specialized, there are only four customers. Their locations and monthly purchases are as follows: San Diego, 200 units; Houston, 400 units; Cleveland, 900 units; and Boston, 200 units. Figure A-1 presents a summary of above information with production plants along the top and customer locations down the left-hand margin.

THE TRANSPORTATION MATRIX
Plant Locations

Consumer Locations	Minneapolis	Chicago	Dallas	Los Angeles	
San Diego	40	48	49	44	200
Houston	46	41	49	50	400
Cleveland	43	47	45	46	900
Boston	48	42	45	47	200
Dummy	100	100	100	100	100
	500	300	600	400	1800

The transportation problem requires that the quantity available to be allocated (production capacity) equal the quantity desired (customer demand). Because total customer demand is 100 units less than total productive capacity, a *dummy* customer is added. Of course, nothing will be actually shipped to the dummy customer after the optimum allocation has been determined. It could represent goods going into the producer's inventory.

The number in the upper left-hand box represents a summation of three factors in this example. One of the factors represents the production cost of each unit, which often varies among plants based on the age of the production equipment. Also, because of labor union jurisdictional disputes, a second factor represents a penalty payment that must be paid to the union in some cases if products are shipped from certain plants to certain destinations. Finally, a third factor represents the transportation costs of shipping a unit from each plant to each customer. Usually, when all plants have the same production costs and when there are no labor jurisdictional problems, the number in the box just represents the transportation cost between each plant and customer. Note that for the "dummy" row an arbitrarily high production and transportation cost is utilized. This figure (100 in the example) is set very high so that it will have a minimal effect on the allocation procedure. The problem involves deciding the quantities and plants that should be utilized to satisfy customer requirements.

Northwest Corner Initial Allocation

One procedure to establish the initial allocation is the Northwest Corner technique. Figure A-2 illustrates an initial allocation using this procedure. The idea is to start in the Northwest corner of the chart and place as large a quantity of product in it as possible. Either completely fill the customer's demand or exhaust the productive capacity available. In the example, the San Diego customer required 200 units and the Minneapolis plant had 500 units available. Therefore, the customer's total demand of 200 was filled. Notice that the Minneapolis plant still had 300 available for allocation. These units are assigned to the next customer, in this case located in Houston. Houston required 400 units, but only 300 were available from the Minneapolis plant.

Figure A-2 Northwest Corner Initial Allocation

	Minneapolis	Chicago	Dallas	Los Angeles	
San Diego	40 / 200	48	49	44	~~200~~ 0
Houston	46 / 300	41 / 100	49	50	~~400~~ 0
Cleveland	43	47 / 200	45 / 600	46 / 100	~~900~~ ~~700~~ ~~100~~ 0
Boston	48	42	45	47 / 200	~~700~~ 0
Dummy	100	100	100	100 / 100	~~100~~ 0
	~~500~~ ~~300~~ 0	~~300~~ ~~200~~ 0	~~600~~ 0	~~400~~ ~~200~~ ~~100~~ 0	1800

NORTHWEST CORNER INITIAL ALLOCATION — Plant Locations (columns) / Consumer Locations (rows)

Therefore, 100 additional had to be supplied from the Chicago plant. Chicago still has 200 units available and they are allocated to the next customer located in Cleveland. The same procedure is continued, moving from the Northwest corner to the Southeast corner.

The Northwest Corner method, although yielding an initial allocation, is not commonly used because it completely ignores the production and other costs in the upper left-hand corner box. To correct this deficiency, another initial allocation procedure can be utilized.

Vogel's Approximation

A technique designed to yield a better initial allocation is Vogel's Approximation. Professor Vogel argued that the initial allocation should not necessarily be where the costs (upper left-hand corner box) are the lowest, but where the *penalty* is the greatest for not achieving an allocation at the lowest cost.

To get an idea of what this means, assume that a customer can be supplied by an allocation from either of two plants, one having costs of $41 and the other having costs of $44. Now assume that some customers can be supplied by an alternative allocation from two other plants, one having costs of $44 and the other having costs of $50. In the first allocation, if the lowest cost, $41 could not be used, the next lowest cost, $44, would have to be used. The penalty for not using the lowest cost in this allocation would be $3, ($44 − $41). In the second allocation, the penalty for not using the lowest cost would be $6, ($50 − $44). Vogel would make initial allocations, not where the cost was the lowest, but where the penalty was the highest for not using the lowest cost.[1] Therefore, in this simple example, Vogel would use the second allocation, not the first.

Figure A-3 illustrates an initial allocation using Vogel's Approximation. The procedure is laborious yet worthwhile because it yields an initial allocation that is commonly very close to the optimum solution. To start, calculate the penalty for not taking the lowest cost for *each row* and *each column*. In the Minneapolis column it is $3, ($43 − $40); for Dallas, $0 ($45 − $45); for Chicago $1, ($42 − $41); for Houston $5, ($46 − $41); and so on. The penalty costs should be written in small numbers near the row or column involved. When all the penalty costs have been written down, find the *highest one*. In this example, it is Houston with a penalty cost of $5. This tells us that the first allocation will be in the Houston row. Next, check the costs from each plant in the Houston row and find the *lowest* plant cost. It is Chicago with a $41 cost. When the lowest is determined, make as large an allocation as possible to that square. Because Houston requires 400 units, but Chicago can only supply 300 units, then 300 units is the maximum that can be allocated from Chicago. Next, *update* the plant output and customer needs. The Chicago plant goes from 300 units to 0 units because all of its production capacity will be shipped to Houston. For simplicity's sake, draw a line completely through the Chicago column, because we can now forget about it. Why? Because all of its output has been allocated. Now update Houston's needs. They were 400 units, but it now has 300 from Chicago, so it only needs 100 additional units.

(What if there would have been a *tie* after checking all the penalties? Assume there were two rows or columns with a $5 value. Then each row or column is checked to find the lowest cost and that's where the initial allocation is made. If two or more locations tie for the lowest cost, select at random one of these and make the initial allocation.)

---

[1] For further details, see Nyles V. Reinfield and William R. Vogel, *Mathematical Programming* (Englewood Cliffs, N.J.: Prentice-Hall, 1958); and Thomas M. Cook and Robert A. Russell, *Introduction to Management Science* (Englewood Cliffs, N.J.: Prentice-Hall, 1977), chap. 7.

Figure A-3 Vogel's Approximation Initial Allocation

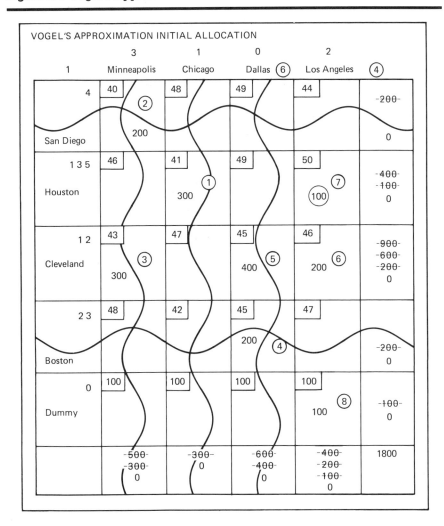

After the first allocation (300 units) and the updates, the procedure is repeated. But, any row or column that has been satisfied is completely disregarded when calculating the penalties. In this example the Chicago plant has been completely allocated and a line has been drawn through it to remind us to ignore this column. The penalties are updated and again written in small numbers next to the row or column involved. The second allocation goes to San Diego because its penalty value of $4 is now the highest. This row is checked; the lowest cost is $40, and therefore an allocation is made in this square. The allocation is always as much as possible. San Diego requires 200 units and Minneapolis can supply 500 units. Hence, all of San Diego's 200 units are allocated from Minneapolis. The update results in Minneapolis still having 300 units to allocate, and a line is drawn through San Diego because its requirements have been satisfied. The same procedure is again followed, now ignoring both Chicago and San Diego. The circled numbers in the allocated squares indicate the order in which the allocations were made.

Vogel's Approximation yields a significantly improved first allocation relative to

Figure A-4 Comparison of Northwest Corner to Vogel's Approximation

Northwest Corner Initial Allocation Cost

$40	×	200 units	=	$ 8,000
46	×	300 units	=	13,800
41	×	100 units	=	4,100
47	×	200 units	=	9,400
45	×	600 units	=	27,000
46	×	100 units	=	4,600
47	×	200 units	=	9,400
(Dummy row is ignored)				$76,300

Vogel's Approximation Initial Allocation Cost

$40	×	200 units	=	$ 8,000
41	×	300 units	=	12,300
50	×	100 units	=	5,000
43	×	300 units	=	12,900
45	×	400 units	=	18,000
46	×	200 units	=	9,200
45	×	200 units	=	9,000
(Dummy row is ignored)				$74,400

the Northwest Corner method. Figure A-4 compares the total costs of each allocation.

Optimization Check

When the initial allocation is completed, the next step in the transportation linear program is to check the solution to see if it is the best answer. To simplify the procedure, transfer the initial allocation to a clean matrix which has all the cost information, such as Figure A-5.

On this clean matrix, we will begin the optimization check by assigning check figures to the rows and columns that have squares with allocations in them. The idea behind a check figure will become clear as the discussion progresses. The first step is to assign a value of 0 to the first row, which in the example is San Diego and has a square with an allocation in its row. This value of 0 is the check figure for the first row. Now how do we assign check figures to the other rows and columns? Consider the following statement, and then we will be able to assign check figures to the other rows and columns.

For each allocated square, the sum of the check figures for the row and the column it occupies, must equal the cost in that square. Thus, if the San Diego row has a check figure of 0 and the Minneapolis column has an allocation, then the Minneapolis column has a check figure of 40. Why? Because the cost in the Minneapolis-San Diego square is 40, the San Diego row check figure is 0, therefore, the Minneapolis column check figure must be 40. [Expressed algebraically, $0 + X = 40$; therefore, $X = 40$.)

Figure A-5 Optimization Check

OPTIMAZATION CHECK

1	Minneapolis 40	Chicago 34	Dallas 42	Los Angeles 43	
0 San Diego	40 — 200	48 — +	49 — +	48 — +	200
7 Houston	46 — −1 (100)	41 — 300	49 — 0	50 — (100) 100	400
3 Cleveland	43 — (100) 300	47 — +	45 — 400	46 — (100) 200	900
3 Boston	48 — +	42 — +	45 — 200	47 — +	200
57 Dummy	100 — +	100 — +	100 — +	100 — 100	100
	500	300	600	400	1800

Let's take this a step further. Notice that the Minneapolis-Cleveland square has an allocation. We now know the check figure for the Minneapolis column. Therefore, we can find the check figure for the Cleveland row. The cost in the Minneapolis-Cleveland square is 43, and the Minneapolis column check figure is 40; thus, the Cleveland row check figure is 3 (40 + X = 43, therefore X = 3).

Moving along a bit faster now: The Cleveland-Dallas square has an allocation and the cost associated with it is 45; the Cleveland row has a check figure of 3, therefore the Dallas column has a check figure of 42. This procedure is followed until all the rows and columns have check figures.

Occasionally a problem presents itself when it comes to assigning check figures. There will be no problem if the total number of allocated squares equals the sum of number of rows plus the number of columns, minus one. In our example, there are 8 allocated squares; and also, there are 5 rows plus 4 columns, minus 1, which equals 8. Therefore, no problem and check figures can be assigned to all rows and columns. When the number of allocated squares is less than the sum of the number of rows and of columns minus one, this is called a *degeneracy,* and there will be a deficiency of one check figure.

Appendix

Degeneracy results when simultaneously a row and a column are satisfied. For example, if Cleveland needed 300 units and Chicago had 300 units, then both the Cleveland row and the Chicago column would be satisfied through a single allocation. The result would be that the initial allocations as represented on the matrix would have one less allocated square.

Degeneracy can be solved by finding a square that does not have an allocation and assigning it an allocation of 0 units. The specific square you should use can be found when assigning the row and column check figures. As you proceed in assigning check figures, you will notice a number of unallocated squares, which, if they had allocations, would allow you to assign check figures to all rows and columns. Among all the squares that will allow completion of the check figures, choose the one that has the lowest cost figure and allocate to that square a quantity of 0 units. Treat this square with 0 units as you would with any other allocated square, and the degeneracy will be solved.

The next step is to examine all squares that do not have allocations in them. In Figure A-5, notice that the San Diego-Chicago square is unallocated. Add the row value (0) to the column value (34) and subtract this figure from the cost figure of the square (48). The answer is 14. Notice that the square is marked with a plus sign (+), meaning that the answer was positive. The same procedure is repeated for *all unallocated squares*. One of three answers is possible for each unallocated square: First, a positive answer is possible, which indicates that the square in question will *not* have an allocation when the optimum solution is found. Second, a zero is possible, which means that the square may or may not be used in obtaining the optimum answer. A zero indicates that more than one optimum solution exists for the problem. In other words, an allocation can be made in the square, but it will only yield another answer of *equal value*—it will not be any less expensive than the previous solution. Third, a negative number is possible. When it is found, it indicates that the optimum solution has not been found. In our example, a negative number was found in the Minneapolis-Houston square. If two or more negative numbers are found, the square that is the most negative is used. In our example, the only negative square is Minneapolis-Houston. When a negative square is found, the optimum solution requires allocating as much as possible into the square with the negative number.

Reallocation

The reallocation procedure involves using only the allocated squares. To determine which allocated squares to use, remember that if an allocation is made in the Minneapolis-Houston square, it must also be subtracted from somewhere else because the row and column total unit quantities must remain the same after the reallocation. Minneapolis still must produce 500 units and must allocate them somewhere, and Houston still requires 400 units which must be supplied somewhere. Notice the box drawn in Figure A-5. This indicates where the additions and subtractions will be made. For every addition there must be a subtraction, but to keep the matrix in balance, notice that two additions are necessary and two subtractions. The goal is to place as large an allocation as possible in the square with a negative check value. What if we decide to do this by taking 300 units from the Cleveland-Minneapolis square? We would add it to the Houston-Minneapolis square, but that means we would have to subtract 300 units from the Houston-Los Angeles square. This cannot be accomplished because it only has 100 units in it, and no square can logically have a negative allocation. Therefore, the largest quantity to be transferred is limited by the *smallest* number of units in an allocated square from which a quantity will be subtracted. In the example, the limiting square is Los Angeles-Houston. Notice that 100 units is added to the Houston-Minneapolis square; 100 is subtracted from Houston-Los Angeles; 100 is added to Cleveland-Los Angeles; and 100 is subtracted from Cleveland-Minneapolis.

It is important that after a new allocated square has been added (Houston-Minneapolis) a former allocated square be completely eliminated (Houston-Los Angeles). Why? Because the check figures only work if the allocated squares follow the formula—rows plus columns minus one. Also, after the allocation, all the plant outputs must be the same as well as the customer total requirements.

Figure A-6 illustrates the new allocation. New check numbers were assigned for this new allocation and this time there were no negative numbers in the unallocated squares. This indicates that the allocation in Figure A-6 is the optimum allocation. Figure A-7 shows that the optimum allocation is $100 cheaper than the initial allocation using Vogel's Approximation. If the reallocation had a negative number in an unallocated square, another plus and minus type change would be accomplished and the new allocation checked. The procedure is continued until no negative numbers are found.

Figure A-6 Second Optimization Check

SECOND OPTIMIZATION CHECK

1	Minneapolis 40	Chicago 35	Dallas 42	Los Angeles 43	
0 San Diego	[40] 200	[48] +	[49] +	[44] +	200
6 Houston	[46] 100	[41] 300	[49] +	[50] +	400
3 Cleveland	[43] 200	[47] +	[45] 400	[46] 300	900
3 Boston	[48] +	[42] +	[45] 200	[47] +	200
57 Dummy	[100] +	[100] +	[100] +	[100] 100	100
	500	300	600	400	1800

Figure A-7 Cost of the Reallocation

$40	×	200 units	=	$ 8,000
46	×	100 units	=	4,600
41	×	300 units	=	12,300
43	×	200 units	=	8,600
45	×	400 units	=	18,000
46	×	300 units	=	13,800
45	×	200 units	=	9,000
(Dummy row is ignored)				$74,300

Constraints

The transportation linear programs can be easily adjusted for constraints imposed by management, labor unions, etc. Assume, for example, that a labor union provision states that the Dallas plant cannot supply the Houston market. This can be accomplished by placing an artificially high cost in the Dallas-Houston square. The problem is then solved using the above procedure and the Dallas-Houston square will not be allocated because of the high cost involved. Alternatively, assume that the Cleveland customer *must* be supplied by the Minneapolis plant. This is achieved by placing an artificially low cost figure in this square.

Computer Application

While the preceding allocation problem was solved manually, the typical procedure involves programming a computer to follow the same logic and procedures. As a rule of thumb, matrices larger than ten rows by ten columns become sufficiently complex to warrant the introduction of a computer to do the time-consuming procedures involved.

Problems

1. Using the transportation linear program method, solve the following matrix (Figure A-8).
2. Solve the following problem using the transportation linear program (Figure A-9).
3. Solve the matrix in problem two subject to the following three constraints:
   (a) Plant C must ship to Customer 3.
   (b) Plant A must supply Customer 5.
   (c) Plant E cannot supply Customer 4.

Figure A-8

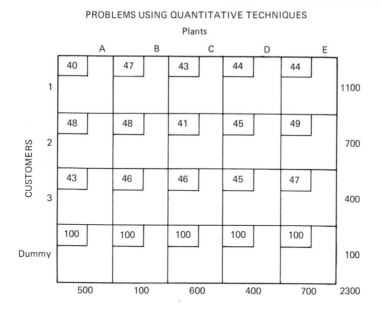

PROBLEMS USING QUANTITATIVE TECHNIQUES

Figure A-9

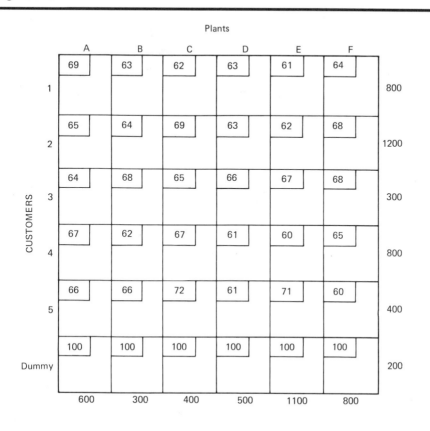

Glossary

ABC analysis. When applied to inventory management, the term means placing the items into three categories, A, B, and C, with respect to monitoring stock levels.

Accounting controls. The use of accounting records to determine the efficiency of the logistics system, especially with respect to controlling losses.

Adjustment function. Selecting a point in the exchange channel to concentrate goods, make a new selection from that concentration, and form a new selection of goods to move forward in the channel.

Auxiliary carriers. Carriers that typically specialize in shipping small shipments; included would be the federal postal system, United Parcel Service, and Federal Express.

Backhaul. A return trip or a movement in a direction of or for a purpose of secondary importance.

Back order. Materials a customer has requested but that are unavailable for shipment at the same time as the remainder of the order. They are usually shipped later.

Balance of trade. An accounting concept that monitors the value of products imported and exported during a period of time. If imports are greater than exports, the country involved is said to have an unfavorable balance of trade.

Bank payment plan. A service provided by banks for shippers. Carriers send their freight bills to the bank to be paid. The bank pays the carrier and subtracts the payment from the shipper's account.

Bar code scanners. Electronic devices that can "read" bar codes and use the number read to keep track of inventory, to order inventory, and to analyze inventory patterns.

Batch numbers. Numbers put on products when they are manufactured to identify when they were made and at what factory. These numbers are important during product recalls.

Belly freight. Cargo that is transported in the lower freight compartments of passenger airplanes.

Bill of lading. A contract stating that a carrier has received certain freight and will be responsible for its delivery.

Bonded storage. There are various types of bonded storage, the most common of which involve the Internal Revenue Service and the collection of excise taxes, such as those on cigarettes. Excise taxes do not have to be paid until the product leaves the bonded warehouse.

Break-bulk cargo. In ocean shipping, cargo handled piece-by-piece by stevedores rather than in bulk or in intermodal containers.

Break-bulk distribution center. A warehouse where large shipments are sent by the shipper. Then the shipment is broken down by specific customers and each consignee receives what was ordered. This concept is used to save freight rates.

Brokers. Companies that help both shipper and carrier achieve low freight rates and efficient utilization of carrier equipment.

Building-block concept. Trying to combine smaller packages into larger units that can more efficiently be handled at one time.

Bulk cargo. In shipping, cargo stowed loose, without specific packing, and generally handled with a pump, scoop, or shovel.

Carrier. An individual or firm in the business of carrying cargo and/or passengers.

Carrying costs. See Inventory carrying costs.

Cartage. Local hauling of freight. Similar to drayage.

Center-of-gravity approach. A location technique designed to minimize transportation costs.

Centralized PD/L organization. An organizational alternative where most of the logistical decisions are made at one location, typically at the corporate headquarters.

Charter. In international transportation, to lease or rent a vessel or aircraft for a specific trip or specific amount of time.

CIF (named point). The seller quotes a price including cost of goods, transportation, and insurance to the specified point.

Class rate. The most expensive general type of freight rate charged by common carriers. It involves using tariffs to determine a class, or rating, for each shipment, plus the utilization of the mileage the shipment is being transported.

COFC (Container-on flatcar). Piggyback traffic, or where containers are shipped on rail flatcars.

Commodity flows. An analysis of where products are made and sold, and the routes over which they travel.

Commodity rate. The least expensive of the general types of freight rates. It is typically used by common carriers as a reward for shippers who ship in large quantities or at frequent times. These rates are specific, often naming a specific origin and destination.

Common carrier obligations. Over time, common carriers assumed four legal obligations to their customers: service obligation, delivery obligation, reasonable rates, and avoidance of discrimination.

Common law. A body of law that developed over time and incorporates past decisions of judges. It is utilized to provide consistency in law.

Compensated intercorporate hauling. A concept legalized by the 1980 Motor Carrier Act. It allows one division of a company that has private transportation to provide transport service to another division of the same company. The division using the other's private fleet must pay for the service.

Competition audit. An analysis of a firm's competition, both present and projected. This would include the products they sell, the quality they provide, plant locations, and shipping points. This is part of the data-collection phase of logistics analysis.

Computer security. Steps that are taken to ensure that unauthorized people do not have access to a firm's computer records.

Concealed damage. Damage not initially apparent, but discovered after a package is opened.

Conrail. A federal government sponsored railroad that took over the Penn-Central and other bankrupt railroads in the East and upper Midwest. In 1985 the federal government was in the process of selling Conrail to private enterprise.

Consignee. The receiver of a shipment.

Consignor. The shipper of goods.

Consistency of service. The dependability of the carrier's service. It includes the consistency of pickup and delivery taking place when the carrier said each would prefer consistency of service over speed.

Containers. Large boxes, often 8 feet high, 8 feet wide, and from 20 to 45 feet long. These containers can be transported by rail, truck, air, or water carrier, although air containers are often smaller.

Contract carrier. Found in the trucking industry; recently, railroads have been offering contracts to their customers also. A contract carrier offers a specialized service to each customer based on a contractual arrangement.

Cost trade-offs. Adding more of one cost item, while subtracting some of another cost item, to achieve more desirable results without increasing expenditures.

"Critical" path. In network analysis, the necessary path that takes the longest to complete; it therefore is critical in the sense that attempts to speed up the total process must focus on it.

Cross-traders. Ships that transport cargo between two countries, neither of which is the nationality of the vessel. A U.S.-registered ship carrying products from Mexico to Spain would be cross-trading.

"Cube out." Occurs when a bulky cargo utilizes a vehicle or a container's cubic capacity but not its weight capacity.

Customer audit. An analysis of a firm's customers, both present and projected. This would include their location, products typically ordered, customer service standards required, etc. This is part of the data-collection phase of logistics analysis.

Customer service. Assisting an existing customer.

Customer service standards. A service level a selling firm wants to achieve, an example being the ability to fill 95 per cent of all orders completely within 48 hrs.

Customs collection. Tax payments collected by governments when foreign products enter their country.

Customs house brokers. Companies that help buyers bring imports into a country. They prepare the customs reports, arrange transportation, etc.

CWT. 100 pounds.

Decentralized PD/L organization. An organizational alternative where most of the logistics decisions are made in the field at the company's various regional offices.

Dedicated equipment. In railroading, cars assigned for use by a specific customer.

Delivered pricing. Price includes delivery to buyer.

Demurrage. A charge assessed by carriers to users who fail to unload and return vehicles or containers promptly.

Design implementation. The final step in logistics analysis. The changes recommended are put into use. This can be done all at once; typically the changes are implemented slowly so as not to cause the system to break down from excessive unfamiliarity with the new system.

Detention. A payment from a shipper or consignee to a carrier for having kept the carrier's equipment too long.

Distribution center. A warehouse with an emphasis on quick "throughput," such as is needed in supporting marketing efforts.

Distribution Requirements Planning (DRP). Inventory management of finished products linked to sophisticated sales forecasting.

Door-to-door. Through carriage of a container from shipper to customer.

Dovetailing. Where vendors [suppliers] locate their plants in close proximity to their customers. This idea is growing rapidly because of JIT inventory systems.

Draft. The depth to which a vessel can be loaded.

Drayage. Local trucking.

Dunnage. Wood and other packing materials used to wedge and otherwise keep cargo in place.

Economic order quantity. See EOQ.

Embargo. A carrier's temporary refusal to accept certain shipments, usually because it is unable to deliver them. An example might be during a strike or a flood.

EOQ (Economic order quantity). A size of order that minimizes the combined storage and processing costs.

Exception rate. Less expensive than a class rate, this is more costly than a commodity rate. It is determined by the same general principles as when finding a class rate, but there are exceptions to the class rules, which results in lower freight rates.

Exchange channel. A collection of firms that exists to deliver the product at the time and place needed.

Exchange function. The interactions between or among intermediaries involved in the physical movement of products from the point of production to the customer.

Exempt carrier. A carrier—from any mode—that is not regulated by a government agency in terms of rates.

Existing facilities audit. An analysis of a firm's physical facilities, including warehouses, plants, transport facilities, etc. Part of the data-collection phase of logistics analysis.

Expedited shipment. Carrier attempts to have a shipment move more quickly than normally.

Export declaration. A form filled out by a U.S. exporter for governmental statistical and export-control purposes.

Export management companies. Firms that help a domestic company become involved in foreign sales. They often locate foreigners who will be licensed to manufacture the product in the foreign country. They also take care of many details involved in exporting.

Export packers. Companies that prepare the protective packing for shipments transported by ocean vessels.

Export trading companies. Companies that provide total help to exporters. They often involve a number of firms that may be domestic competitors that are allowed to combine forces to be more effective in foreign sales.

Facility relocation. Involves the movement of a plant or warehouse from one location to another.

FAK (Freight all kind) rate. A rate applicable to a mixture of products.

FAS. The price of the goods after they have been discharged from the ship.

FIFO. An inventory management procedure whereby the oldest item in stock gets shipped first.

Fixed-order-interval inventory system. Inventory is replenished on a constant, set schedule and always ordered at a specific time; the quantity ordered varies, depending on forecasted sales before the next order date.

Fixed warehouse slot location. Each product is assigned a specific location and is always stored there.

Flags of convenience. Nations that have lax maritime registration rules. Many ships are registered in these countries because of their lenient safety and crew requirements.

Flying a nation's flag. A ship that is registered in a particular country: a ship registered in France flys the French flag.

Full-cost pricing. The carrier prices the transportation service to each customer so that the full cost of providing the service is charged to each customer in every situation.

Gathering pipeline. Pipelines that collect oil from individual wells and transport it to collection points where trunks lines then carry the crude oil.

Goods in transit. Goods moving between two points.

Grid systems. A location technique utilizing a map or grid, with specific locations marked on the north-south and east-west axes. Its purpose is to find a location that minimizes transportation costs.

Hazardous cargo. Poses hazards to handlers or to other cargos and, because of this, requires special attention. Its carriage is subject to additional regulations.

"Hazmat." Hazardous materials, or hazardous cargo.

Hierarchy of rates. Involves which rates to utilize when more than one type of rate is available. Because the least expensive rate should be used first, the carrier should first charge the customer a commodity rate if one is available. If not, then an exception rate can be used. If this is not available, a class rate can always be determined.

Hijacking. Theft that typically involves stealing both the transport vehicle and the cargo inside it.

IATA (International Air Transport Association). A cartel, or group, that sets rates for international air transport.

Import quotas. Absolute limits to the quantity of a product that can be imported into a country in a particular time period.

In bond. Cargo on which taxes or duties have yet to be paid. The owner must post a bond or use a bonded carrier or warehouse to guarantee that the materials will not be sold until taxes or duties are paid.

Incentive rates. Charging less per unit of weight for heavier shipments.

Industry standards. Average worker-output information that is available for many industries. Also, average output per warehouse, plant, truck, route, etc., is additional information that is generally available for each industry. This information helps each company compare itself to others in the same industry.

Integral trains. Similar to unit trains in that they are designed for one specific purpose. These trains are permanently coupled and will be utilized to transport highway trailers and containers. Because of their relatively light weight, they are fuel efficient.

Intermodal transportation. A shipment utilizing more than one mode—for example, a shipment moving by truck and then air.

International freight forwarders. Companies that perform the same functions as domestic freight forwarders. They buy space in large quantities and sell it to shippers requiring less vessel space. They also perform many other services for shippers, such as preparation of export documentation, arranging for cargo insurance, etc.

International sourcing. The buyer of production inputs will consider buying them from anyone in the world who offers the best service/price/quality package.

Interstate system. Limited access roads that are the premier highways in the United States. There are about 42,500 miles of Interstates.

Inventories in motion. The concept that a firm must remember that substantial quantities of inventory, at any given time, are in the transportation system enroute to warehouses, customers, etc.

Inventory. Stock of goods. As a verb, it means to count the goods in stock.

Inventory carrying costs. The cost of holding inventory, such as storage costs, insurance, interest on the money tied up in inventory, depreciation, etc.

Inventory flows. Changes in inventory levels that take place as inventory is drawn down by customers and replenished when new shipments of inventory arrive.

JIT. See just-in-time.

Just-in-Time inventory system. An inventory system that keeps production inventory to an absolute minimum.

Kanban. A Japanese inventory system using cards that allows production inventory to be kept to a minimum. Similar to the Just-in-Time inventory system.

KD (Knocked down). When an item, such as a table, is extensively disassembled so that it can be packaged in a much denser form.

L & D (loss and damage). Usually applies to loss of or damage to goods while being carried or while stored in a warehouse.

Land bridge. Trains carrying trailers and or containers to or from a coastal port, or from coast to coast.

Landed price. The buyer's calculation of the total costs of buying and receiving a product, somewhat irrespective of selling terms.

LASH (lighter aboard ship). An ocean-going vessel designed to carry barges.

Law of loss and damage. A common carrier oligation resulting from the carrier's duty to deliver freight in the same condition as it was received.

LCL. Less-than-carload, or less-than-container load.

Lead time. Time ellapsed between ordering a needed good and its anticipated arrival.

Letter of credit. A technique to ensure that the seller will be paid when the buyer is located in a foreign country. A bank in the seller's country guarantees payment if all the specific contract terms are met by the seller.

Lighterage. Using a small vessel or barge to transfer cargo between a large ship and shore, or between ships.

Lighter-than-air cargo vessels. Vessels that typically use helium to provide lift capability. Small engines then propel the vessel at relatively slow speeds, compared to airplanes.

Line item. A type of product individually listed in inventory records. See SKU.

Liners. See ocean liners.

Linking-pin organization. A logistics organization that involves individuals known as linking-pin people. These persons are assigned to two or three functional areas of logistics. Each functional area has a number of people who link that department to the other functional areas that combine to form the logistics function.

Load center. A major port where thousands of containers arrive and depart per week. These ports specialize in the efficient handling of containers.

Load factor. Percent of capacity utilized.

Loading dock. A warehouse or factory facility where trucks are loaded or unloaded.

Logistics. The flow of materials through an organization and the necessary communications needed to manage the flow.

Logistics system design. Analysis designed to improve the efficiency of existing logistics systems or to implement a new logistics operation.

Long ton. 2,240 pounds.

Make-bulk distribution centers. Frequently utilized for the shipment of production inputs. Here vendors each ship their relatively small shipments to a warehouse that is located near each vendor. At the make-bulk distribution center, a number of small shipments are combined to take advantage of the lower freight rates available when large shipments are given to the carrier.

Market dominance. Introduced by the 1980 Staggers Rail Act. The ICC does *not* have rate regulation over rail rates unless the railroad in question has market dominance over the shipment involved. Market dominance is usually defined as having 60 per cent or more of the freight in a specified market.

Marketing channel. Intermediaries—wholesalers, retailers, brokers, etc.—that a manufacturer uses to get its products to customers.

Materials handling. The efficient movement of products into and out of warehouses and transportation vehicles. Often uses pallets or skids as part of the building-block method. It also applies to large movements of bulk materials.

Materials management. Movement of raw materials, parts, and components to the production plant.

Materials requirements planning (MRP). A computer-assisted method of managing production inventory.

Matrix management. A logistics alternative that utilizes task forces established to solve specific problems. Members are drawn from various functional areas that impact on the problem. Once the problem is solved, the task force is disbanded and all members return to their other assignments.

Measurement ton. In ocean shipping, the use of 40 cubic feet (or some similar measure) as the equivalent of one ton for calculating transportation charges.

Metric conversion. The idea that the United States is slowly converting to the metric system of measures. This conversion is not required by law, although the federal government is encouraging it.

Metric ton. 2,204.6 pounds.

MRP. See materials requirements planning.

Multinational sales. A company that sells its products in foreign countries and domestically.

Nautical mile. 6,080 feet.

Nesting. Packing tapered articles inside each other to reduce cubic volume of the entire shipment.

Nontariff trade barriers. Governmental barriers that restrict trade but that do not involve tariffs or quotas. An example is a government requiring all imports of a specific product to enter the country through one small undermanned port.

NVOCC (Non-vessel-owning common carrier). In international trade, a firm that provides ''common carrier'' services to shippers but owns no vessels itself.

Occupational Safety and Health Act (OSHA). A 1970 federal law regulating workplaces to ensure the safety of workers.

Ocean liners. Ships in regularly scheduled operations that specialize in ''less-than-shipload'' quantity shipments.

Order assembly. See order picking.

Order cycle. Elapsed time between when a customer places an order and when it is received.

Order-dedicated inventory. Inventory pledged to a customer that will soon be shipped to the customer involved.

Order delivery. The time from when a carrier picks up a shipment until it is delivered to the customer.

Order picking. In a warehouse, the selection of specific items to fill a complete order.

Order processing. The activities from receipt of an order until the warehouse is notified to pick the order.

Order transmittal. The time from when the customer places or sends the order to when the seller receives it.

OSHA. See Occupational Safety and Health Act.

Overnight delivery. Goods shipped late in day one being delivered during the morning of day two.

Package testing. Simulation of the types of problems that the package will be exposed to in warehouses and in transit. The idea is to determine if either too many or too few packaging materials have been used.

Packaging. Materials used to protect a shipment physically when it is in a warehouse or in transit. Protective packaging materials are often inside a carton or individual box.

Pallet. The small platform, usually 40×48 inches, on which goods are placed for handling in a warehouse.

Palletization. See unitization.

"Paper" rate. A published rate that—for some reason or another—is not used; that is, no traffic moves at that rate.

Parcel. In transportation, a small quantity or small package.

Perishables. Cargo that spoils quickly and requires special attention.

PERT. (Program Evaluation and Review Technique). A form of network analysis that places all component parts in the sequence in which they must be performed.

Phantom freight. Occurs in "delivered" pricing when a buyer pays an excessive freight charge calculated into the price of the goods.

Physical distribution. The flow of materials from the end of the assembly line to the customer.

Pilferage. A form of cargo theft usually performed by one's employees.

Private carrier. Carrying one's own goods in one's own vehicles.

Private warehousing. Owning or leasing storage space for one's exclusive use.

Product audit. An analysis of a firm's present and future product line. Part of the data-collection phase of logistics analysis.

Product pipeline. Petroleum pipelines that transport refined products from refineries to major market cities.

Product recalls. When a company asks wholesalers/retailers/customers to return the firm's products because defects have been found.

Program Evaluation and Review Technique. See PERT.

Public warehouse. A warehouse whose owner leases space and provides services to a variety of customers.

"Pull" inventory system. Goods moving so slowly through an inventory system that the buyer must take action to speed the flow of goods in his direction.

"Push" inventory system. To the buyer it appears that the product is being pushed toward him, and he must act to stop or slow the flow.

Rail siding. A short rail track leading from a main line to a customer's plant or warehouse.

Rate bureau.   An organization of carriers that sets rates.

Rate conference.   See rate bureau.

Rate determination.   Involves the shipper trying to locate the least expensive rate charged by a carrier for a specific shipment.

Rate negotiation.   Involves the shipper and carrier negotiating the rate to be charged by the carrier.

Recycling.   Reuse of materials.

Released value.   The limits to a carrier's liability for a certain shipment, in the sense that the carrier may agree to charge a lower overall rate if the shipment's "released value" is less.

Reorder point.   As stock is consumed, the balance remaining drops to this point, at which time a replenishment order is placed.

Reparations.   Payment from a carrier to a shipper for having charged the shipper excessive rates in the past.

Right-to-work laws.   State laws that specify that a worker at a unionized plant does not have to join the union to work permanently at the facility.

RoRo (Roll on–roll off).   Ships, similar to "floating parking lots." They are loaded by driving tractors and trailers on ramps.

Run-through train.   Trains that avoid most classification yards, hence they are faster than most rail service.

Safety stock.   A reserve inventory, in addition to that needed to meet anticipated requirements.

Sailing cargo ships.   Regular ocean ships that have the ability to use auxiliary sails when wind conditions permit.

Satellite navigation and communication.   Use of satellites to navigate many types of transport vehicles. Satellites are being used for efficient communication everywhere in the world.

Scanners.   See bar code scanners.

Shipment consolidation.   Freight rates are less expensive per pound shipped when large shipments are given to the carrier at one time. Therefore, shippers try to consolidate shipments bound for the same general area.

Shippers' associations.   Shippers who join together to negotiate as a group to receive favorable ocean shipping rates.

Shippers' agents.   Firms that purchase rail TOFC/COFC service and then sell this capacity to shippers.

Shippers' cooperatives.   Nonprofit firms that provide the same service as freight forwarders. They purchase transportation space in large quantities and sell it to customers in smaller quantities.

Shipper's load and count.   On a transport document, the term means that the carrier did not independently count the items said to be shipped.

Shipping conference.   A group of ocean carriers that set identical rates for each member of the conference. Each conference operates in one direction only between specified origin and destination ports.

Short-interval scheduling.   An analysis of worker's productivity over short periods of time. Each worker is assigned specific duties that should be able to be completed during the time period provided. If the work is consistently not completed, additional analysis is required to find out why.

Short ton.   2,000 pounds.

Shrinkage.   Losses in inventory that are difficult to account for.

Simulation.   A technique to model the systems to be studied, typically using mathematical equations to represent relationships between the components of a logistics system. It allows an analyst to ask "What if?" questions about the firm's logistics system.

Single-source leasing. A firm leases both its private truck fleet and its drivers from the same source. Prior to 1980 this was not allowed by the ICC.

Skid. See pallet.

SKU (stock-keeping unit). Each separate kind of type of item accounted for in an inventory.

Slip sheet. A sturdy sheet placed under a stack of goods and serving a function similar to that of a pallet.

Slurry pipeline. Transports products that are ground into a powder, mixed with water, and then shipped in slurry form through a pipeline. This concept has been successfully used for transporting coal.

Slurry systems. Various techniques to transport solid products by grinding them into a powder and then mixing them with water or other fluids and shipping them in a pipeline or in the hold of ship after the liquid has been removed.

Solid-fuel locomotives. Locomotives that burn coal instead of oil products.

S/R. Stacker/retriever system used in automated warehouses to stow goods and remove them when needed.

Status quo organization. A logistics organizational alternative involving each functional area of logistics staying where it traditionally was located.

Steamship conferences. An organization of liner operators that set rates.

Stock-out. . Being out of an item at the same time there is a willing buyer for it.

Stuffing. Loading a container.

Suboptimization. An individual's "overachieving" to the extent that the team's efforts are harmed.

System constraints. Restrictions that cannot be violated in the logistics operation being planned. An example would be that all shipments to Tulsa must be shipped from the Chicago plant.

System goals. Goals are broader than objectives and more general. An example would be to increase market share slowly over time.

System objectives. Measurable factors that will allow management to know if it is meeting its goals. An example would be that 98 per cent of orders will be shipped within six hours of receipt.

Systems approach. Analysis where the importance of each aspect of a situation is recognized, along with the relationship of each part to all other aspects of the situation.

System security. Methods used to ensure that products are safely moved from the production point to the customer. In many cases it also involves guarding production inputs.

Tachograph. An electronic device that measures the engine RPMs [revolutions per minute] on a truck. It produces a tape or card that can be read; it tells a lot about the driver of the vehicle.

Tare weight. Weight of the empty container or vehicle.

Tariff. A book containing a carrier's charges for transportation services, *or* the charges assessed on items imported into a country.

Tax-free bonds. Issued by local and state governments. They are exempt from federal and often state income taxes. The bonds carry lower interest rates than corporate bonds because the interest on corporate securities is fully taxable.

Terminal. A carrier or public facility where freight (or passengers) is shifted between vehicles, or modes.

Throughput. A term of output used in warehousing and in pipelines; it is expressed as number of units moving through a specified system in a given period of time.

TOFC (trailer-on-flatcar). Piggyback traffic, or loading truck trailers onto rail flatcars.

Total-cost approach. All aspects of a logistics system must be considered as a whole and a manager should not be too concerned about individual cost elements.

"Toto" authority. A private carrier with authority to act as a common or contract carrier in backhaul situations.

Towboat. A high horsepower boat with a square prow that pushes barges that are lashed together.

Tracing. A carrier's attempt to find a misplaced or delayed shipment.

Transaction function. Transactions involving money and documents by which title to goods passes from the manufacturer to the ultimate buyer.

Transit privileges. Allowing goods to stop once between their initial origin and ultimate destination without having to pay additional charges.

Transportation companies. Companies that offer a multimodal transportation service to their customers.

Trunk pipeline. The largest pipelines; they transport crude oil from gathering pipelines to refineries.

Unified department organization. A logistics organizational alternative that is generally the best solution for larger firms. Here the various functional areas are combined into one department. This alternative generally results in the best coordination of the functional areas that combine to form the logistics function.

Uniform order bill of lading. This form is considered to be negotiable, and whoever holds it may claim the goods.

Uniform straight bill of lading. The most widely used bill of lading. The carrier may deliver the goods without requiring the original copy.

Union work rules. See work rules.

Unitization. The placing of goods on pallets, and designing a materials handling system to accommodate pallet loads of goods.

Unit load. A pallet load.

Unit trains. Trains with cars permanently linked, used for repetitive hauls, usually of coal.

Value-of-service pricing. Taking into account the shipper's ability to pay—somewhat irrespective of the costs of providing the service.

Variable warehouse slot location. A warehouse where incoming products are stored wherever there is empty space available.

Vendor audit. An analysis of the firm's vendors [suppliers] in terms of their locations, dependability, quality of work, etc. Part of the data-collection phase of logistics analysis.

Warehouse work rules. A set of rules that specify correct procedure at a specific warehouse. Each worker should be required to know them thoroughly.

Weight-losing product. A product that loses weight during the production process. Therefore, it should be processed as near its origin as possible. The finished product is transported, which will weigh less.

"Wind, shipping." Declaring that a shipment weighs more than it actually does in order to qualify for a lower per pound rate, which results in a lower total shipping cost.

Work rules. Often established by contracts with unions, these rules specify exactly the duties of each worker. They often restrict workers from doing more than one type of function.

Worker productivity. A measure of labor input to the output produced by that labor.

Subject Index

Motor carriers, private, 175, 230–233, 624
Multinational sales, 623

Name and Corporation Index

Association of American Railroads, 309
Atlas Traffic Consultants Corp., 224
Attwood, Peter R., 44n
Augello, William J., 220n
Avon Products, Inc., 78, 80, 229n
Ayers, Allan F., 58n, 582n

Babcock, Michael W., 141n
Bagby, John W., 236n
Bagge, Carl E., 103n
Baker, Miriam Alexander, 194n
Baker, Gwendolyn H., 236n
Baker, Robert W., 168
Baldwin, Peter L., 141n
Balk, Arnold E., 455n
Ballou, Ronald H., 536n, 582n
Banks, Gary, 27n
Baritz, Steven G., 93n
Barks, Joseph V., 16n, 17n, 130n, 172n
Barrett, Colin, 9n, 170n, 190n, 211n, 233n, 582n
Barta, Thomas J., 125
Bartley, Jack, 494n
Batts, Lana, 119
Baum, Samsone R., 363n
Baumel, C. Phillip, 194n, 454n, 494n, 495n
Baumgartner, J. P., 584n
Bean, L. L., 78
Beard, Larry H., 250n
Beaulieu, Jeffrey, 494n
Bechtel Civil & Minerals, Inc., 311n
Becker, Boris W., 254n
Beier, Frederick J., 134n, 141n, 194n, 312n
Beilock, Richard, 141n, 170, 190n
Beimborn, Edward A., 58n
Bellow, Patricia A., 588n
Bender, Paul S., 453n
Benjamin, Julian M., 28n
Benton, W. C., 494n
Berger, Donald L., 522n, 590n
Bergeson, Lloyd, 589
Berglund, Mary, 318n
Berman, Benjamin A., 193n
Berry, Demaris A., 111n, 263n, 264n
Berry, Thomas D., 141n
Bess, H. David, 453n
Best, William J., 496n
Bigelow, John, 77n
Biggs, Dee, 494n, 536n
Bi-Modal Corporation, 135
Binkley, John A., 453n
Blackwell, Richard B., 236n

Blanding, Warren, 8n, 82n, 83n, 88, 91n, 93, 338n, 362n
Blumenfeld, Dennis E., 286n
Bobera, Kevin B., 141n
Bodrie, Gerald E., 17n, 59n, 478
Boeing Company, 441, 576, 577
Bohm, John A., 352n
Boisjoly, Russell P., 190n, 191n
Bonner, Lou, 172
Boone, Louis E., 41
Borden Company, 43
Borg-Warner Corporation, 185
Borger, Donald L., 36
Borghesani, William H., 190n
Boros, John L., 511n
Bosscher, Howard J., 227n
Bosworth, Janet, 44n
Bott, Kevin N., 582n
Bowersox, Donald J., 5n, 7n, 27n, 39, 336, 490n, 579
Boyd, Don A., 226
Boyd Company, 303n
Boyer, Paul, 27n
Bradley, John C., 236n
Branch, Alan E., 453n
Brand, Richard, 28n
Brimelow, Peter, 135n
Brodeur, Leon R., 15n, 471
Bronzini, Michael S., 141n, 453n
Brown, Terence A., 130n, 141n
Bruce, Harry J., 18n
Bruning, Edward R., 141n, 190n, 209n, 236n, 453n
Bryan, Morgan F., 79n
Buffalo Equipment and Chemical Company, 227
Bukal, Miro, 193n
Bunce, Elliott, 190n
Bunting, P. M., 141n
Burck, Charles G., 17n
Burdg, Henry B., 141n, 142n
Burke, James, 509
Burlington Northern Air Freight, 128, 264
Burlington Northern Railroad, 103n, 110, 111n, 172, 174, 211, 265, 575, 586
Burns, John J., 142n
Burnworth, Essie, 238n
Burt, David N., 48n
Bush, Paul, 528n
Bush, Ronald R., 528n
Busher, John R., 363n
Butler, Robert M., 174n
Button, Kenneth, 191n, 453n

Fisher, Marshall, 582n, 592n
Fisher, Roland T., 514n
Fites, Donald V., 421
Fitzsimmons, E. L., 142n
Fleming Foods, 109
Fletcher, George, 190n
Flexner, Donald L., 234n, 237n
Flood, Kenneth U., 142n
Flusberg, Martin, 582n
Flying Tiger Line, 126
Foggin, James H., 495n
Foley, Timothy P., 19
Folk, J. F., 142n
Footlik, Robert B., 509n
Ford Motor Company, 13, 172, 208, 352, 415, 560, 576, 578
Foster, Thomas A., 3, 12, 13n, 205n, 453n
Franco, John J., 67n, 69n
Freed, Charles L., 237n
Freeman, James, 170, 170n, 190n, 192n
Frey, Stephen L., 192n, 359n, 480n
Fruin, Jerry E., 453n, 455n
Fuerst, Judith A., 130n, 133n
Fuller, Stephen, 192n

Gabbard, Michael C., 347n
Gable, Jo Ellen, 59n, 592n
Gallagher, Matthew J., 421
Gallagher, Patrick, 59n, 536n
Gallitano, Henry J., 363n
Gardner, Leland L., 191n, 236n
Gardner, R. William, 363n
Gaskins, Darius M., Jr., 111, 142n
Gebhardt, J. Bruce, 418
Gecowets, George A., 18, 557
General Electric, 445, 576, 586
General Foods Corporation, 208, 316
General Mills, 109
General Motors Corporation, 17, 18, 26, 59n, 249n, 262n, 263, 264, 265, 266, 301, 422, 471, 478, 479, 560, 576
General Tire and Rubber Company, 185
Geoffrion, Arthur M., 307n
Georgia Pacific Corporation, 384n
German National Railroads, 110
Germane, Gayton E., 142n
Ghoshal, Animesh, 142n
Gidwitz, Betsy, 454n
Gill, Lynn E., 286n, 419n
Gillette Company, 12, 512
Gilmour, Peter, 547, 558
Glaskowski, Nicholas A., Jr., 135n, 145n, 582n

Glawson, Jerry A., 144n
Glorfeld, Louis W., 192n
Gochberg, Howard S., 495n
Goddard, Walter E., 261n
Godwin, Jean C., 453n
Goicoechea, Ambrose, 142n
Goldschmidt, Neil, 142n
Goldstein, Gary I., 130n
Goodall, William, Jr., 359n
Goodman, Sam R., 83, 84n
Gourdin, Kent N., 454n
Grande, Margaret, 264n, 265n
Green, F. B., 495n
Greene, Paul, 264
Greenwood, Dione H., 210
Grimm, Curtis M., 27n, 192n
Gritta, Richard D., 142n
Gruebele, James W., 475n
Guandolo, John, 192n
Gundrum, Lawrence J., 286n
Gustin, Craig, 59n, 495n

Haessler, Robert W., 260n, 262n, 286n
Hair, Joseph H., Jr., 528n
Hale, Bernard J., 75, 557n, 567n
Hale, Lord, Chief Justice, 160
Hall, Randolph W., 286n
Hall, Robert W., 261n
Hallowell, W. Elmer, 28n
Hall's Motor Transit, 134
Hamlett, Cathy A., 194n
Hammes, Patrick J., 237n
Hammesfahr, R. D. Jack, 495n
Hammond, Paul F., 515
Hanna, Randall L., 67n, 68n, 93, 93n
Hapaq-Lloyd AG, 447n
Harari, Oren, 536n
Harbour, James, 263
Harmatuck, Donald J., 192n
Harper, Donald V., 40n, 169, 170, 192n
Harper Robinson & Company, 431
Harper Truck Service, 227
Harrington, Lisa H., 18n, 130n, 209n, 210n, 232n, 579n, 582n, 591n
Harris, Ernest W., 352n, 364n
Harris, Robert G., 192n
Harris, William B., 560
Harris Corporation, 547
Hartgraves, Al L., 250n
Hartzell, Jack L., 536n
Hassan, M. U., 592n
Haupt, Richard, 172

Kinnunen, Raymond M., 536n
Klass, Bertrand, 84, 84n
Klempin, Raymond, 588n
Kletke, Marilyn G., 194n
Klingman, Darwin D., 495n, 567n
KLM Royal Dutch Airlines, 414n, 441n
Kobb, Benn, 585n
Koenig, Richard, 109n
Kohon, Jorge C., 143n
Kolbe, A. Lawrence, 144n, 194n
Kollat, David, 496n
Korodi, Miklos, 531n
Kosiek, Lawrence J., 592n
Krapfel, Robert E., 237n
Krenn, John M., 93n
Krishnan, R., 286n
Krollck, Reuben H., 192n
Kromberg, P. N., 237n
Kruse, William J., 454n
Kuah, Geok-Koon, 93n
Kullman, Brian C., 260n, 262n, 286n
Kursar, Robert J., 111n
Kyle, Reuben, 454n

La Howchic, Nicholas J., 567n
Labick, Kenneth, 167n
LaCagnina, Michael L., 496n
LaForge, Raymond W., 237n
LaLonde, Bernard J., 3, 5n, 20, 28n, 69n, 260n, 496n, 548, 557, 575, 583n, 589n
Lambert, Douglas M., 68n, 93n, 269n, 286n, 364n, 557n, 560n
Lamkin, Jack T., 192n
Lancioni, Richard A., 6n, 53n, 143n, 144n, 496n
Lande, Richard, 192n, 193n
Landes, Norman, 363n
Lane, Lee, 141n
Langley, C. John, 18n, 28n, 536n, 592n
Lapide, Lawrence, 494n
Lapihuska, Michael G., 363n
Large, Arlen J., 580n
Larson, Thomas D., 144n
Lazar, Lee A., 193n
Leach, Jim, 16
Lear Siegler, Inc., 249n, 353n
Leaseway Transportation Corporation, 343n
Leatham, Jerry, 335
Le Blanc, Louis A., 454n
Lederer Terminals, 527n
Ledford, Manfred H., 145n, 582n
Lee, Alfred M., 59n

Lee, Lamar, 48n
Lee, Tenpao, 454n
LeFebvre, S., 192n
Lehr, Lewis, 293
Levin, Marvin J., 110n
Levine, Joseph E., 227n
Liba, Carl J., 143n, 405n, 454n
Lieb, Robert C., 143n, 193n
Lindley, J. T., 454n
Lindquist, R. E., 142n
Linehan, Ronald, 304n
Ling, Richard C., 547
Linzer, Joel, 237n
Litton Industries, 68, 563, 564
Lloyd, David E., 28n, 583n
Loebel, Alan E., 547
Loughry, Thomas, 588n
Lounsbury, Charles B., 28n
Low, Christopher R., 237n
Loyden, John J., 536n
Ludwick, E. M., 193n
Lufthansa German Airlines, 127n, 200, 200n, 440n, 442n
Lukasiewicz, J., 592n
Lynagh, Peter M., 28n, 36, 36n, 59n, 209n, 236n
Lystad's Inc., 227

MacAllister, Sean, 74, 93n
McBride, Michael F., 193n
McCabe, Douglas M., 144n
McCarren, J. Reilly, 496n
McCarthy, Coleman, 115n, 117n
McConville, Daniel J., 117n
McCrary, Isaac, 318n
McCullough, John T., 449n
McDonnell Douglas, 186, 577
McElhiney, Paul T., 11n, 176n
McGee, Michael P., 144n, 237n
McGinnis, Dennis, 536n, 582n
McGinnis, Michael A., 496n, 557n
Machalaba, Daniel, 109n
McKesson Corporation, 74
McLaughlin, M. S., 51n
McLennan, Kay, 454n
McLeod, A. D., 144n
McMillan, T. E., 315n
McNamara, Thomas M., 141n
McPhillips, Keven, 587
Maffei, Richard B., 490n
Magee, John F., 11n, 82, 484

Oberdick, Larry E., 141n
O'Connell, K. Michael, 455n
Oliver, David C., 144n
O'Neil, Brian F., 252n, 582n
O'Neill, William J., 28n, 59n
Ongman, John Will, 238n
Oster, Clinton V., 193n
Ostrom, Lonnie L., 496n
Outboard Marine Corporation, 421
Overnite Transportation, 117, 169

Pacific Southwest, 167
Pan American World Airways, 142n, 418
Parsons, Kathleen J., 59n, 274n
Parsons, Lon, 280n
Pastor, John A., 454n
Paul, Bill, 135n
Pautsch, Gregory R., 194n
Payne, Bruce C., 454n
Peach, L., 592n
Penney Company, J. C., 16, 26, 159n
People Express, 165, 167
Perl, Jossef, 318n
Perreault, William D., 84, 84n
Perrine, Lowell E., 45n
Peterson, Roger A., 169, 170n, 195n
Petri, David L., 144n
Phillip, Craig E., 93n, 141n
Phillips, Don, 111n, 171n, 172n
Phillips, Karen Borlaug, 194n
Phillips, Laurence T., 454n, 455n
Picard, Jacques, 455n, 579n
Pickett, Gregory M., 194n
Piedmont Aviation, 167
Pike, C. R., 592n
Pilnick, Saul, 59n, 592n
Pinnekamp, Dale J., 238n
Pisarski, Alan E., 496n
Pixton, Charles E., 455n
Poist, Richard F., 28n, 36, 36n, 59n, 144n
Pollock, Ted, 59n, 567n
Polzello, Richard, 94n
Pope, David J., 455n
Posey, Emmitt J., 93n
Potter, Ronald S., 144n
Powder River Basin, 172
Powers, Richard F., 307n
Pratt & Whitney, 282
Preston Trucking Company, 115
Price, Marshall, 267n
Priestley, C., 580n
Prior, Robert L., 363n

Promisel, Bob, 393n
Purdy, H. L., 134n
Purolator, 128
Pustay, Michael W., 194n

Quaker Oats, 109, 276
Quebec Cartier Railway, 110–111
Quinn, Francis J., 55n, 175n, 206n, 264n

Rader, Charles, 20
Rakowski, James P., 166n, 454n, 577n
Rao, Kent, 141n, 144n
Read, William A., 496n
Redcoat Cargo Airlines, 587
Reinholdt, Ernst F., 347n
Reiss Steamship Company, 376n
Republic Airlines, 167
Restaino, Thomas J., 94n
Reuter, Vincent G., 52n
Revlon, 8
Rice, William C., 28n
Richards, Bill, 115n, 122n, 168n, 172n
Riley, Cathleen P., 28n
Riley, Daniel W., 250n, 286n
Ritz, Christopher J., 94n
Roadway Express, 114, 186, 223, 264
Roberts, Merrill J., 144n, 191n
Robeson, James F., 496n
Robinson, Raymond M., 318n
Ronen, David, 94n, 424n, 455n
Rose, Warren, 11n, 194n
Rosen, Stanley B., 238n
Rosenbaum, Lisa, 455n
Rosenberger, Roger L., 251n
Rosenfield, Donald B., 494n, 496n
Ross, G. Terry, 495n
Ross, Richard K., Jr., 144n
Rowan, Mike, 533n
Rowe, John W., 144n
Rowland, Ray L., 495n
Reutten, James E., 59n
Ruppenthal, Karl M., 134n
Russ, Frederick A., 84, 84n
Ryder/PIE Nationwide, 186

Sabena Belgian World Airlines, 425n
Safeway Stores, 42, 354n, 513
Salzano, Carlo J., 217n
Sampson, Roy J., 44, 44n, 144n
Sanders, Malcolm S., 194n

Name and Corporation Index

Weber Marking Systems, 267n
Weinfuss, Jerome J., 59n
Weinthaler, E. L., Jr., 511n
Weiss, James R., 238n
Weiss, Martin A., 94n
Weitman, Julie P., 58n
Welch, J. R., 592n
Wells Fargo Bank, 420
Welty, Gus, 110n
Western Pacific Railroad, 206, 208
Western Union, 77
Westmeyer, Russell E., 175, 175n
White, John A., 335, 364n, 537n
White, Luella G., 455n
Whiting, R. Scott, 260n, 262n, 263n, 286n, 343n
Whitman, Edmund S., 316n
Whitten, Herbert O., 176n
Whybark, D. Clay, 286n
Wienfuss, Jerome J., 40n
Wight, Oliver W., 248n, 284n, 286n, 557n
Willett, Ronald P., 87
William Underwood Company, 77
Williams, Ernest W., Jr., 170n, 195n
Williams, Joseph D., 35, 249n
Williamson, Kenneth C., 169, 170n, 195n

Wilson, Hal, 79n, 94n
Wilson, M. A., 455n
Wilson, Walter K., 120n
Winter, Ralph E., 578n
Wolfe, K. Eric, 226n, 238n
Wood, Donald F., 135n, 165n, 475n, 486n, 521n, 578n
Wood, Doreen, 145n
Wood, Wallace R., 142n, 145n, 236n, 582n
Wren, E. A. C., 204n
Wright, Donald A., 144n
Wyckoff, D. Daryl, 135n, 238n

Yaros, Ronald S., 521n
Yarusavage, George A., 145n, 209n
Yellow Freight System, 114, 169

Zeis, Paul M., 177n
Zeitlin, Lawrence R., 528n
Zellerbach Paper Company, 217, 219n
Zemke, Douglas E., 68n, 93n, 269n, 286n
Zink, Daniel, 193n
Zinszer, Paul H., 69n, 287n
Zissman, Lorin, 93n

$\frac{part}{week} = 6/8$